The Tarikh-i Ḥamidi

THE *TARIKH-I ḤAMIDI*

A Late-Qing Uyghur History

MUSA SAYRAMI

TRANSLATED BY ERIC SCHLUESSEL

COLUMBIA UNIVERSITY PRESS *NEW YORK*

Columbia University Press wishes to express its appreciation for assistance given by the Chiang Ching-kuo Foundation for International Scholarly Exchange and Council for Cultural Affairs and the Wm. Theodore de Bary Fund in the publication of this book.

Columbia University Press
Publishers Since 1893
New York   Chichester, West Sussex
cup.columbia.edu

Library of Congress Cataloging-in-Publication Data
Names: Sairami, Musa, 1836–1917, author. | Schluessel, Eric, translator.
Title: The tarikh-i ḥamidi : a late-Qing Uyghur history / Musa Sayrami ; translated by Eric Schluessel.
Other titles: Tarikhi ḥamidi. English.
Description: New York : Columbia University Press, [2023] | Includes bibliographical references and index.
Identifiers: LCCN 2022058472 (print) | LCCN 2022058473 (ebook) | ISBN 9780231210027 (hardback) | ISBN 9780231210034 (trade paperback) | ISBN 9780231558235 (ebook)
Subjects: LCSH: Uighur (Turkic people)—History—19th century. | Muslims—China—History—19th century. | Xinjiang Uygur Zizhiqu (China)—History—19th century. | Xinjiang Uygur Zizhiqu (China)—Ethnic relations. | Xinjiang Uygur Zizhiqu (China)—Politics and government. | Asia, Central—History—19th century.
Classification: LCC DS793.S62 S39 2023 (print) | LCC DS793.S62 (ebook) | DDC 951/.6035—dc23/eng/20221215
LC record available at https://lccn.loc.gov/2022058472
LC ebook record available at https://lccn.loc.gov/2022058473

Cover design: Julia Kushnirsky
Cover image: Lund University Library, Jarring Prov. 561, "Genealogical table from Adam to Hazrat Khan Khwaja Muhammad and Yaqub Beg"

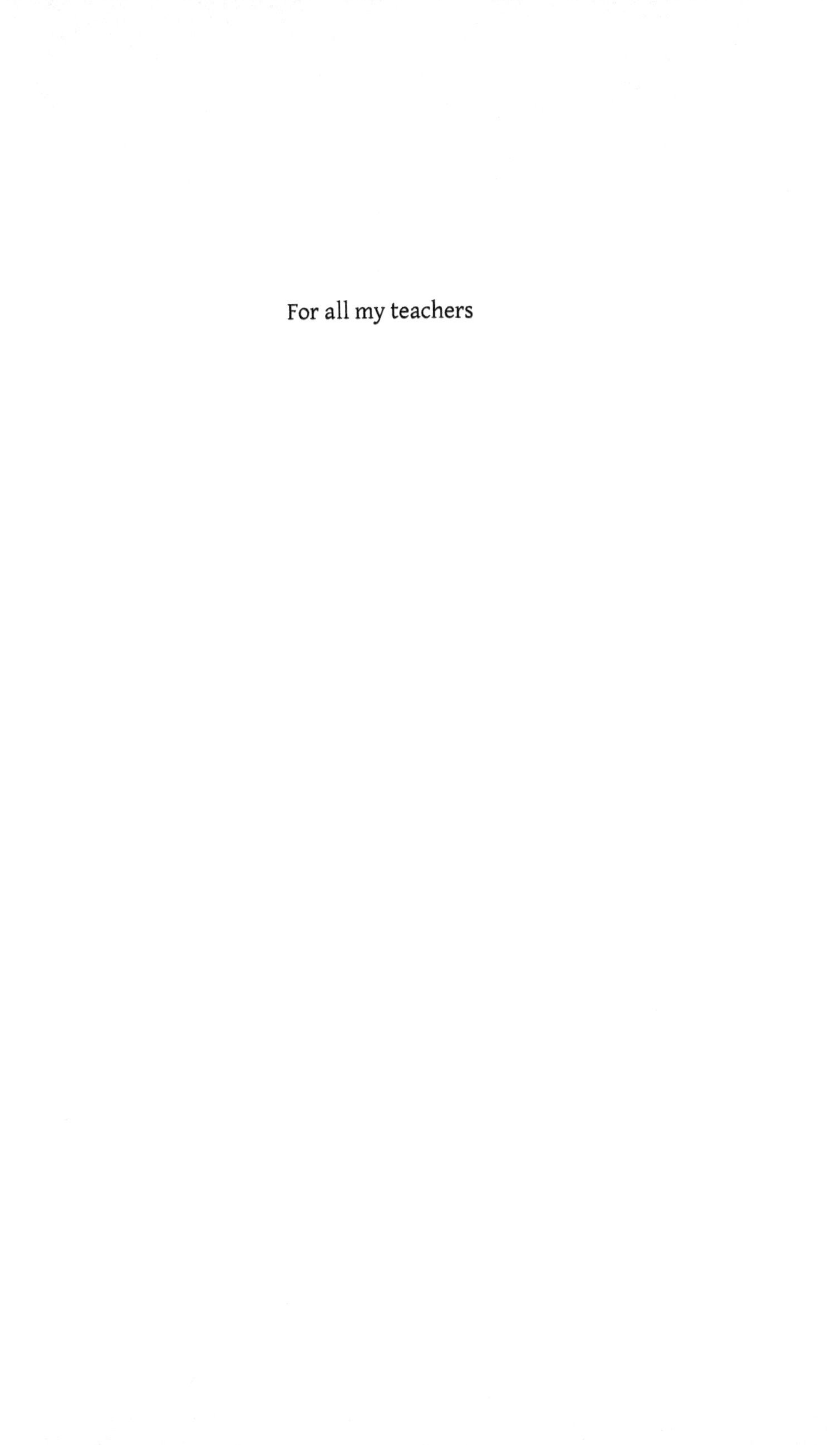

For all my teachers

Contents

Prolegomenon

The First Epic

The Second Epic

CONTENTS

CONTENTS

Description of Moghulistan

Acknowledgments

SOMETIME IN 2011, I opened up the *Tarikh-i Ḥamidi* because I wanted to answer the question, "What did Muslims in East Turkestan think about being ruled by the Qing?" The question seems obvious—it's the sort of thing we historians are meant to ask, particularly when our aim is purportedly to bring marginalized voices to the center of our practice and discourse and thereby interrogate the nature of power. At the time, however, to attempt an answer meant wading through a mound of obscure and rather haphazardly documented manuscript sources, plus a handful of printed works, in hopes of retrieving some scrap of information, which one could only hope to contextualize properly. Reading was a bit like holding a séance, or playing with a spirit board: on a good day, you would get five or six people around a table, all ask questions into the ether, and interpret the words that came achingly slowly out, and in the end, you might wonder whether someone had been pushing the planchette all along.

The *Tarikh-i Ḥamidi* and its author, Musa Sayrami, emerged in murky outline: disparate notes, a transliteration, a comparison of one paragraph across two manuscripts, Sayrami's perceptive comment about tax. Early on, I brought many passages to read with Wheeler Thackston, without whose guidance I would have no idea how to interpret this text, and to whom I remain eternally grateful. As we looked at greater length, I began to perceive a text that was much stranger, more critical, more dissonant than most people realized.

In 2015 and 2016, Noriko Unno, Joshua Freeman, Koh Choon Hwee, and I—then a collection of graduate students—convened fortnightly in the Harvard-Yenching Institute to see what we could make of Sayrami's text. The Fairbank Center and Asia Center at Harvard University jointly awarded us a small grant to buy lunch (usually burritos) as we puzzled through the differences between the manuscripts. (This was, incidentally, an excellent demonstration of what young scholars can do when provided with money and food.) We learned a great deal about the manuscripts and their variations, determined what might be the most interesting passages to examine going forward, and got a grasp of Sayrami's peculiar language and style. We quickly found out that if we annotated every single difference between five versions, it could yield over 1,400 footnotes for a single chapter. Consequently, we established some ground rules for compiling a critical edition. Things began to snowball.

In May 2017, the Henry Luce Foundation/American Council of Learned Societies Program in China Studies generously funded a reading workshop, "Towards a Scholarly Edition of the *Tarikh-i Ḥamidi*, a Chaghatay Chronicle of Modern Xinjiang." Alexandre Papas, Jun Sugawara, Nicholas Walmsley, Elise Anderson, and Rian Thum very kindly agreed to spend a few days in Missoula, Montana, where we read several chapters collaboratively around a pile of dictionaries and grammars. The workshop challenged all of us to read Sayrami closely, not just as a source but as a text. We established some key principles for translating the whole work. One major conclusion was that the *Tarikh-i Ḥamidi* would need to be understood not only as a historical text but also as a drama of justice and tyranny, and one that drew on a panoply of sources in often obscure ways.

Later that summer, a meeting with some colleagues from Xinjiang confirmed the importance of such a project. Musa Sayrami, we agreed, was not simply a good historian—he was a complex thinker, whose peculiar viewpoint did not fit into contemporary political narratives. In the *Tarikh-i Ḥamidi*, he does not unambiguously favor any ruler or state but rather points a critical eye at power and emphasizes the needs of ordinary people. Voices such as his, we thought, could offer nuance to the contemporary discourse around the Uyghur region and point toward different sorts of research questions about the lived experience of empire. Of course, the Chinese state itself had long since supported the publication of modern translations of the *Tarikh-i Ḥamidi* into Uyghur, and there had been a recent Chinese translation as well. This suggested that Sayrami's writing might actually serve as a vehicle for dialogue outside of established paradigms. Instead, several of those colleagues were imprisoned later that year. Sayrami's works have since been stricken from the shelves of libraries and bookstores in the Uyghur homeland, along with any other alternative to official historical narratives. I resolved to finish the project in honor of the plans we had made and the reasoning that we shared.

I had naïvely conceived of the translation as a collaborative effort, but wiser minds convinced me that it would ultimately need one authorial voice. Fortunately, the National Endowment for the Humanities agreed and very generously awarded a fellowship to create the critical edition and translation in 2019–2020 (FEL-262358-19, "An Edition and Translation of the *Tarikh-i Ḥamidi*, a Nineteenth-Century Uyghur History of Eurasia"). Most of the work was accomplished during that time, along with a complete transliteration of the base text with extensive annotations, which I hope to publish in the near future. The COVID-19 pandemic, however, slowed progress almost to a complete halt. The translation has since been completed with the help of a research grant from the Humanities Center at the George Washington University.

Along the way, many other scholars have offered aid, advice, and observations that greatly improved the final product. They include Ablet Kamalov, Zulfiya Karimova, Nicholas Kontovas, Aysima Mirsultan, Mutallip Anwar, Ahmet Hojam, Mohammad al-Sudairi, Kevin Kind, Alexander Morrison, Christopher Atwood, Ali Asgar Alibhai, Guangtian Ha, Kristian Petersen, Michael Gibbs-Hill, John Chen, Sakura Christmas, David Stroup, and Gwendolyn Collaço. David Brophy's comments have been particularly illuminating. Christine Dunbar and Christian Winting at Columbia University Press shepherded the book through the production process and located three very thoughtful external reviewers, whose notes were invaluable. All remaining errors are my own.

Today I am pleased to say that this volume joins a number of new translations of important writing by people from the Uyghur region. At last, the voices of people from that place, as best as translators can construe them, are taking a more central role in the international dialogue about it. I hope that this translation will encourage more people to think not only about Sayrami but also with him, as they approach the land and times that he wrote about.

Introduction

THE *TARIKH-I ḤAMIDI* is a chronicle of the Muslim uprisings against the Qing empire (1636–1912) in the nineteenth century. It focuses on events that took place in the land that the Qing named Xinjiang, and which its own people called "the Seven Cities," in the years 1864–1877. The people of that region first rose up in search of justice and cast off their Qing rulers, but then fell into factional conflict, submitted to foreign Islamic rule, and ultimately witnessed the return of Qing power in a new form. Those experiences, coupled with the global shifts that took place in the same era, led many people to question why and how their land's brief but hopeful independence had fallen apart so quickly and caused so much suffering.

The author of the *Tarikh-i Ḥamidi*, the local Muslim scholar Mullah Mūsá b. Mullah ʿĪsá Khoja Sayrāmī (1836–1917), was an eyewitness to those tumultuous thirteen years. In the first decade of the twentieth century, he assembled primary sources, both oral and written, and complemented them with his own recollections in order to create a rational account of the events. Sayrami revised his text several times from 1903 to 1908, during which period he expanded and edited the work significantly in response to new information and his own evolving perspective on Qing and Islamic power.

The *Tarikh-i Ḥamidi* is also a work of scholarship that locates the uprisings and their aftermath within the history of Eurasia and the world from the dawn of humankind to the dawn of the twentieth century. Sayrami seeks not only to illuminate and memorialize a past that by his time was fading from memory but also to explain it. His framework for doing so came from his education as a traditional Central Asian Muslim scholar of the nineteenth century, but he was coming to grips with the grand geopolitical changes of his time, which pushed him to critique and think beyond many received narratives. Sayrami, from his seat in the middle of Eurasia, perceived a world order in flux, and though he wrote before the fall of the Qing, Russian, and Ottoman empires, the end of the imperial order is imminent in his text. Consequently, the *Tarikh-i Ḥamidi* reflects not only an attempt at a faithful account of events but also a mentality that Sayrami shared with other Central Asian scholars of his time, yet was also specific to Xinjiang. It is a key source for the cultural history of that country, particularly where its author ruminates at length on the nature of Qing power and of Muslims' relationship with it.

This translation is the product of many years of deep engagement with this text. Over the course of nearly a decade, as I have read and reread the *Tarikh-i Ḥamidi*, I have come to understand it to be a particularly rich, polyvocal text of the kind that emerges on the peripheries of empires such as the Qing.[1] Its blending of genres, frequent tonal shifts, and internal dissonance point to its history of compilation and revision. The *Tarikh-i Ḥamidi* is very much an example of Muslim history writing in post-Mongol Eurasia, and it belongs to the tradition of official court histories produced for the Timurids and their successors.[2] Yet its author, Sayrami, had no patron, so, like many scholars of his time, he was free to write not only as a historian but as a social and political critic. His work is a history of grand sweep, written nevertheless from the perspective of a weary scholar seeking truth in a world of ignorance and corruption.

From another perspective, the *Tarikh-i Ḥamidi* reflects the experiences of subjects across the Qing, as the Muslim uprisings in Xinjiang were intimately connected to those that occurred across the broader region of Northwest China, including the provinces of Shaanxi and Gansu. Farther afield, we can see those uprisings as the product of the same historical forces that catalyzed other contemporary mass conflicts in the Qing, while the *Tarikh-i Ḥamidi* itself resonates interestingly with memoir literature in China proper whose authors also struggled with the aftermath of traumatic violence and destruction.

This is to say that Sayrami's text is both a valuable source for the eventful history of the past and a work of literature that rewards comparison and rereading. The *Tarikh-i Ḥamidi* is also considered a monument of Uyghur writing, as Sayrami after all wrote in Chaghatay, or "Turki," the Turkic literary language of Central Asia that is a near ancestor to modern Uyghur. Modern articulations of a specifically Uyghur history, and of grievances against colonization by Qing and Chinese states, have often drawn on Sayrami's account, which is one of the very few to detail the uprising, reconquest, and subsequent reconstruction from an autochthonous perspective. To read the *Tarikh-i Ḥamidi* is therefore to engage with an Uyghur classic. At the same time, because Sayrami himself predates the modern discourse of Uyghur nationalism, his work presents an alternative perspective that in many ways cuts against nationalism and disrupts the simple political binaries of our present world.[3]

The book you hold in your hands is a translation of Sayrami's final known revision of the text, recorded in a manuscript dating to 1911. It is the first translation of Sayrami's chronicle into English. I hope that it will tear down some of the walls around the study of the Uyghur homeland's history by presenting Sayrami's complex, critical analysis of his times to a global audience. I therefore offer the following notes on the work, its author, and its afterlives as an aid to the reader's explorations.

Contextualizing the *Tarikh-i Ḥamidi*

The *Tarikh-i Ḥamidi* is rooted in the Perso-Islamic historiographical tradition, but it was written in response to changes in the Qing empire that then ruled the Seven Cities.

The Qing was a vast multiethnic empire. Its rulers came from the Manchu people of Northeast Asia, where in 1636 they founded a state that drew on Mongol and Chinese traditions as well as their own. In 1644, the young Qing state began its conquest of the Chinese-majority Ming (1368–1644) and its territories. By the mid-eighteenth century, the Qing had encompassed Tibet and Mongolia. A decades-long conflict with the steppe-based Junghar Khanate resulted in 1759 in the conquest of a land that the Qing now referred to as "Xinjiang," or "new(est) territory."

The people of Xinjiang, then as now, were in the majority Turkic speaking and Muslim. They were culturally intimately tied to the other Turkic- and Persian-speaking Muslim peoples of Central Asia, as well as South Asia and West Asia, particularly the Ottoman and Mughal empires. The Qing ruled Xinjiang—like Tibet, Mongolia, Manchuria, and China—as one of a set of distinct and separate territories, with its own rules and laws and its own local Turco-Mongol aristocracy, which was intertwined with a bureaucracy staffed by Turkic-speaking Muslims called *begs*. Above them reigned a military governor, the Ili General, who commanded garrison soldiers meant to repel invasions, which occurred several times. Overall, although the boundary between Xinjiang and China proper was not impenetrable and the administrative system associated with China and Chinese people did exist in part of this region, the period before 1864 is remembered as a time when Muslims lived under indirect rule and in accordance with Islamic law.[4]

In the mid-nineteenth century, the Qing underwent a transformation. A century of social, political, and economic change, as well as the violent encroachment of European empires, brought about tensions that the Qing was not fully prepared to withstand. A rising tide of mass violence came to a head in the 1850s and 1860s, as religious movements, organized crime, and rural militarization combined with the mass displacement of impoverished people to produce inchoate states such as the Taiping (1850–1864), Nian (1851–1868), and others that presented existential threats to the empire.[5] Meanwhile, the gradual devolution of power from the court to regional officials to other local power holders both catalyzed mass mobilization for violence and allowed the Qing to combat these threats flexibly. For example, the famed Xiang Army emerged from Hunan's local militia mobilization networks to form a modern army capable of combating the Taiping more effectively than the Qing's traditional forces. That army later reconquered Xinjiang.

The Muslim regions of the empire's Northwest were no exception to this transformation. In 1862, the Muslims of Shaanxi and Gansu provinces rose up in response to a range of threats and pressures, including increased corruption in the Qing administration, spurred in part by an empire-wide fiscal crisis.[6] Those rebels included both primarily Chinese-speaking Muslims, called Hui or Dungans, and those who spoke Turkic, Mongolic, or Tibetan languages. The rebellion in Xinjiang in June 1864 followed a similar pattern: typically, Hui officers in the Qing army began the violence in response to a perceived threat from the Qing itself, and then Turkic-speaking Muslims, chafing against increasing corruption by local officials, followed them in pursuit of justice. As Sayrami shows us, a chaotic competition between subregional interests ensued.

The uprisings in Xinjiang remain poorly understood. It is known that several states emerged, each based around a different oasis. Perhaps the most significant one was led by a powerful Sufi family, the Khojas of the oasis of Kucha. Soon, however, agents of the neighboring Khanate of Khoqand took advantage of the chaos to establish their own rule, specifically under the military officer Yaʿqub Beg (1820–1877), who then created an independent Emirate of Kashgar. Yaʿqub Beg swiftly conquered the region, but his emirate was unstable and collapsed following his death, at which point the Xiang Army swiftly reconquered the region.

One important reason this period remains somewhat mysterious is that the chief historical sources reflecting the events are written not in Chinese but in Chaghatay. While the texts are in this non-Sinitic language, they are not fully intelligible without reference to the Qing and Chinese context. Hodong Kim's book *Holy War in China* is the only scholarly manuscript in English to present a detailed history on the basis of those sources. Since Kim wrote his doctoral dissertation in 1986, few scholars have approached these widely dispersed and often challenging materials.

Modern scholars praise Sayrami's eventful history because it is based on his own original research in a variety of written and oral primary sources, as well as his own eyewitness experiences as a participant in the governments of two of the competing states: that of the Khojas of Kucha and that of Yaʿqub Beg. Between the years 1864 and 1877, Sayrami was, by turns, a young scholar and teacher, a captive, a wanderer, chief advisor to a Sufi ruler, an emissary to a rival faction, a captive again, a servant, and a tax collector. He looked at these events from their midst, never quite in the center of power but often holding some role in the administrations that allowed the ambitious to vie for control. Sayrami writes not only of the strategies of great armies and leaders but also of the price of grain, and the gallows humor of starving farmers. Rulers rise and fall; ordinary people suffer. Consequently, scholars have come to think of Sayrami's chronicle as the premiere source for the history of the Uyghur homeland in the nineteenth century, written by someone from the region.

Sayrami was not simply a chronicler of events but a skilled polemicist. I have written at length on this matter elsewhere, but some remarks may help clarify the outlines of his perspective.[7] Sayrami worked from the great tradition of post-Mongol Central Asian history writing, which was overwhelmingly directed at praising and legitimizing rulers. He wrote, however, in a strange time in which no ruler seemed truly just, and the very foundations of the world seemed to be slipping away. His chronicle casts doubt upon long-held beliefs and traditions while introducing some stories that otherwise seem to defy reason. It places the Emperor of China and Yaʿqub Beg alike under the microscope and shows how power corrupts even the purest intentions. Sayrami's perspective will be familiar to any student of Perso-Islamic political thought, and the general idea of the "Circle of Justice" familiar from across the Islamic world seems to underlie his criticisms and his praise: the ruler's chief role, Sayrami reminds us, is to provide justice and stability for the common people within the strictures of Shariah.

The composition and revision of the chronicle itself reflect Sayrami's perspective. When he began writing it in 1903, he called it the *Tarikh-i Amniyya*, in honor of his patron, Amin Beg, but also in recognition of the peace (*amīn*) that his land now reluctantly enjoyed under restored Qing rule. He subsequently lost his patron and began writing, evidently, for himself, for others like him, and for occasional foreign travelers. By 1908, as Sayrami continued to revise and expand the work, he had evidently grown even more skeptical of the Qing. He changed the title to *Tarikh-i Ḥamidi*, in honor instead of the Ottoman Sultan ʿAbdulḥamid II (r. 1876–1909). ʿAbdulḥamid II was of course the caliph, and the Ottomans, particularly through their material support of Yaʿqub Beg's state, seemed to have reasserted Muslim power and leadership. Consequently, that ruler presented the greatest hope in Sayrami's eyes for a peaceful future.

Sayrami's drama takes place against the backdrop of a temperamental and unpredictable cosmos. He periodically reminds us of the "inconstant world" and invokes the action of the stars and planets in their connection with human fate. Astrology was no mere literary device but rather a key component in a broadly accepted theory of power that chroniclers applied across Muslim Eurasia.[8] It is most evident in Sayrami's account of the fall and return of Qing power, which he depicts as a consequence of astrological change: the Qing emperor's star was unlucky, so he could not provide justice. As a consequence, the Qing empire fell into disarray, including of course the corruption of tyrannical officials in the Seven Cities, where good Muslims sought justice from their emperor but could not achieve it, so were obliged to rise up and create it for themselves.

In this corner of the cosmic stage, the *Tarikh-i Ḥamidi* makes use of dramatic tropes and character arcs to communicate its story about power. The most explicit references are to the heroes and villains of the *Shahnama*, the great Persian *Book of Kings* that for centuries stood as the most beloved epic of the Persianate cultural sphere in which the Seven Cities participated. Yet Sayrami's own characters are more subtly constructed. For a time, Sayrami shows us, the Khojas of Kucha established a state, and a clan of Sufi mystics formed the ascendant regional power. However, he emphasizes, a pious recluse makes for a poor king and perhaps an even worse general. The Khojas and people like them, in his story, can summon the raw power of popular devotion as they gather masses from the hills, ready to march to war with nothing but cudgels and country grit. His account of the Khojas is told as the chronicle's first great tragedy, as these imperfect people competed with others who sought the same power they could not handle, and ultimately defeated themselves.

The Khojas could not rule, but there was someone who could: a charismatic military officer from the Khanate of Khoqand named Yaʿqub Beg. Khoqand's ruler originally sent him to Kashgar to extend his country's power. The khan's preferred puppet was to be Buzurg Khan, a Sufi whose ancestors had ruled the Seven Cities before the Qing conquest and had since tried to retake them several times. Buzurg was to be proclaimed the new, legitimate ruler, with Yaʿqub holding de facto power. They arrived in Kashgar in 1865, in time to take advantage of the chaos, but also shortly before Khoqand was conquered by the Russian empire. This left Yaʿqub Beg isolated, but free to act—he displaced Buzurg and eliminated his competition with the help of experienced officers who fled the Russian invasion. From a certain perspective, Yaʿqub Beg betrayed the legitimate power that Buzurg Khan represented—the royal right to rule this country, Sufi leadership, and descent from the Prophet—and chose to base his state instead on his own charismatic power as demonstrated through victory in battle and bolstered by his ability to distribute booty. This kind of leader, the *ghazi*, was historically successful in gathering armies around Central Asian rulers, but Sayrami shows how it could not sustain a stable state.

In Sayrami's telling, the tragedy of Yaʿqub Beg becomes evident only gradually, as we learn that there is a fault both in his stars and in his self. Sayrami relates his origins as a roguish adventurer capable of slipping out of any scrape. He comes across as a ruthless yet heroic figure whose military aptitude and intelligence are also reflected in a cynical craftiness. The more power Yaʿqub Beg gains, and the more his charisma grows, the more frequently the rage that Sayrami locates in his nature "flares up," and he murders enemies, innocents, and even old friends and allies while committing a series of horrific crimes against other Muslims, particularly Hui. Even his distribution of justice is arbitrary and cruel, as we see a belly sliced open for a stolen meal and a man maimed with his own tools. At the climax of Yaʿqub Beg's story, as the Qing armies approach and the pressure builds, he finally commits an act revealing that he is the true villain of the story, and at that point, his fate is sealed.

This depiction of Yaʿqub Beg is dissonant with modern notions of him as an "Uyghur hero," and with the idea that the *Tarikh-i Ḥamidi* was written to honor and praise him. Yet there is something mournful in Sayrami's depiction of the Khoja and Yaʿqub Beg eras as a lost opportunity, a "Time of Islam" in which even God's revelation and sacred acts of piety were bent to the cynical acquisition of power. The *Tarikh-i Ḥamidi* is in places reminiscent of the literature that emerged from China during its decades of internal conflict. There certain writers reflected almost obsessively on a sense of loss, and how experiences of violence shaped the recounting of history and memory.[9] Sayrami seems to mourn for the world before 1864, when he was just a scholar and the Qing kept the peace by maintaining the separateness of its peoples.

We can also understand Sayrami's work as part of a wave of Central Asian Islamic writing in the nineteenth century, in which scholars sought to explain the present world using the tools of Islamic historiography and a rational approach to evidence gathered from a wide range of sources. Sayrami drew on several examples of such writing. One was Muḥammad Ḥakim Khan's (b. 1802/3) 1843 *Muntakhab at-Tawarikh*, which relates both the history of Central Asia and an account of the author's ḥajj. He also cites the 1871/2 *Tarikh-i Shahrukhi* of Niyaz Muḥammad b. Mullah ʿAshur Muḥammad Khoqandi (fl. 19 c.), which similarly recounts the history of Khoqand from the perspective of a scholar without a patron. We know that Sayrami was in dialogue with Qurban ʿAli Khalidi (1846–1913), the jurist of Tarbaghatai, whose 1889 *Tarikh-i jarida-i jadida* was likewise both an account of a pilgrimage and a collection of historical materials, and whose 1910 *Tawarikh-i khamsa-i sharqi* rivals Sayrami's chronicle as a history of the lands of Asia.

Nevertheless, Sayrami's work stands apart from other accounts of this period in the Seven Cities.[10] Other histories of Yaʿqub Beg's regime are much more clearly partisan, and they star heroic holy warriors ordained by God to vanquish evil men. Sayrami appears to have been committed to his intellectual independence, even to subverting the expectations of such chronicles. There are no winners in this story, and no true heroes—only people responding to their circumstances according to their motives and abilities. This may leave us wondering how much of his chronicle is empirically verified fact; how much is his subtle writing of distinct characters into a sociopolitical drama meant to communicate a polemic; and how much is a reflection of Sayrami's understanding of power, justice, and the cosmos. Of course, we might wonder the same thing about most history books.

The Text

The work consists of four sections: a prolegomenon (*muqaddima*), two epics (*dastan*), and an epilogue (*khatima*).

The prolegomenon introduces the work and the circumstances of its composition. It then narrates the history of the world and of "Moghulistan"—the region roughly corresponding to Xinjiang—from the time of Noah to the outbreak of the uprisings against the Qing. The purpose of the prolegomenon is to contextualize the main narrative within deeper political and sacred histories. It also serves to establish the work's main problematic, the rise and fall of rulers, and to introduce some of the major players in the uprisings of 1864 and after. Its last chapter locates the deeper roots of discontent in a history of revelation, migration, and descent. This is where the Dungans are introduced and Sayrami recounts the origins of what then seemed like an odd liminal people, simultaneously Chinese and Muslim. The prolegomenon thus sets up the intertwined themes of power, genealogy, loyalty, and justice and encourages the reader to meditate with the text on the relationship between the divine and the political.

Those themes drive the narratives in the first and second epics. Although Sayrami presents his work as a chronicle (*ta'rikh*), we should read it also as a dramatic tale, and the two epics present the mixture of prose and verse typical of the *dastan*. They are episodic, skip around in time, and include a number of anecdotes and asides meant to elucidate the narrative and its characters.

The first epic illustrates Sayrami's point well. Sayrami was an insider to the first uprising and was familiar with its leaders, the Kataki Khojas of Kucha. This Sufi order claimed descent from Jalaluddin Kataki and his son,

ʿArshuddin Khoja, who were responsible for converting the Chagataid ruler Tughluq Timur Khan (r. 1347–1363) to Islam. Sayrami depicts the lead Khojas as becoming corrupted by their success, as this group of reclusive mystics was ill suited to lead a successful and just state. Meanwhile, other factions and leaders rise and fall around the Khojas, such as Ḥabibullah Ḥajji, the sometime ruler of Khotan; the Sultan of Ili and his successors; the Dungans of Ürümchi; various minor players in Kashgar; a network of Mujaddidi Sufis called the Ḥażrats; and several others. Sayrami seems committed to showing the folly inherent in the pursuit of power, as he presents one tragic or ridiculous figure after another. The Khojas reach their apogee in the middle of the first epic, with a magnificent display of military might that marks the height of their power but also their loss of faith in God.

The second epic tells the story of the uprising from a different perspective, that of the Khoqandi officer Yaʿqub Beg. Sayrami presents him as an inherently flawed character who attempts to pursue high-minded goals yet is plagued by a deceitful, wrathful nature. Yaʿqub Beg, called by the titles "Ataliq Ghazi" ("fatherly warrior"), "Badawlat" (the "fortunate one"), and "Qushbegi" ("head of the army"), succeeds in building a state atop the bones of his fellow Muslims, and for all his success, his tendency to murder and torture portends his fall. The second epic is also where Sayrami employs astrological reasoning to explain the fall and return of Qing rule, then describes the fates of those who participated in the uprisings in the years after the reconquest. He evaluates Yaʿqub Beg, the Emperor of China, the Ottoman sultan, and others.

In the epilogue, Sayrami writes about each of the lands of the "Seven Cities," another name for his homeland. The Seven—or sometimes Six—Cities included Kashgar, Yarkand, Khotan, Ushturfan, Kucha, Aqsu, and Turfan, each of which was geographically distinct yet shared a common language and political and religious practices.[11] The epilogue is useful as a description of each oasis's economic and social characteristics at the dawn of the twentieth century, as well as a guide to their shrines.

I have elected not to include in this translation one extremely long passage of the epilogue in which Sayrami translates a proof by Saʿid Muḥammad al-ʿAsali al-Ṭarabulsi al-Shami (1870–1932?) that the Shrine of the Companions of the Cave (*Aṣḥab al-kahf*) in Turfan is not genuine.[12] This passage takes up more than 10 percent of the total length of the manuscript in which it appears, is tedious and highly technical, and clearly stands apart from the rest of the work. I have also chosen not to include the selections of poetry at the end of the manuscript.[13] These are thematically connected to the rest of the work, but I leave them for future and better translators.

The Manuscript

The *Tarikh-i Amniyya/Tarikh-i Ḥamidi* exists in at least eight known manuscripts as well as a widely circulated typeset edition, all of which I describe briefly below. It is possible to discern the relationships between the different versions by observing how Sayrami revised and expanded the text. Ultimately, I chose to base this translation on a 1911 manuscript held in Beijing because it reflects the latest stage in Sayrami's own revisions.

The Beijing manuscript of the *Tarikh-i Ḥamidi*, or "TH/Beijing," is not, however, the latest manuscript. The Lund University Library in Sweden holds three more manuscripts that postdate it. However, all of those are based on earlier versions of the text. They were evidently copied from other intermediate manuscripts that have been lost. I hypothesize that the *Tarikh-i Amniyya* and *Tarikh-i Ḥamidi* were copied much more than scholars have suspected, particularly given the wide geographical distribution of the known manuscripts. Here I present the known versions of the text in the order of the age of their contents, not the age of their ink.

My method of comparison is based on internal textual evidence, external accounts, and other paratextual information such as handwriting. Most manuscripts specify both their date of composition—which may remain the same, even if the content of the text changes—and their date of copying. Some do not offer the date of copying, but references to time within the text may change, such as the "current year" in which the text was written. European travelers sometimes left records of how they acquired or commissioned copies, as well.

The single most crucial piece of evidence for comparison comes from the additions made to the text over time. Certain sections demonstrate a clear, progressive editing process. 0:2, "Chinggis Khan," in particular shows extensive reworking over the years, such that the text from the 1905 print is almost completely different from that of the 1911 Beijing manuscript—indeed, only one sentence of 0:2 is identical across all of the examined versions. The prolegomenon saw significant additions to the text, and consequently three chapter divisions were added. The first epic is by far the most stable section, in that it has seen the least expansion or editing. In contrast, the second epic grew significantly through the addition of anecdotes. The expansion culminated in the addition of two chapters to the 1911 Beijing manuscript: 2:8 on "The Ottoman Empire" and 2:20 on "The Virtues of the Chinese Emperor." These changes allow me to establish a clear order of development:

"TA/Kazan": The earliest version of the text available to scholars is a typeset print based on an early manuscript of the *Tarikh-i Amniyya*. Sayrami gave that manuscript, completed in 1903, to the Russian orientalist Nikolai Pantusov (1849–1909), who published it in Kazan in 1905.[14] This text is a useful point of reference, although the typesetting process introduced errors of its own.

"TA/Lund": This *Tarikh-i Amniyya*, Jarring Prov. 478 of the Lund University Library, was copied in 1331/1912–13, probably for the Swedish missionary Gustav Raquette.[15] This very conservative, neatly written text hews closely to TA/Kazan.

"TA/Pelliot": This copy of the *Tarikh-i Amniyya* was made for the French orientalist Paul Pelliot on March 26, 1907.[16] It is held in the Bibliothèque Nationale de France under the shelfmark Pelliot B 1740. It displays the first major departure from the text of TA/Kazan and TA/Lund as Sayrami began to add anecdotes and make corrections. It is a complete manuscript, including the prolegomenon, both epics, and the epilogue. However, it displays an occasional error where the copyist skips an entire line, and the language has occasional morphological differences from that in the other manuscripts.

"TA/StP": Another *Tarikh-i Amniyya*, manuscript C 335 of the Institute for Oriental Manuscripts of the Russian Academy of Sciences, was completed in January 1910, evidently for the orientalist Sergei Oldenburg, who visited Sayrami around that time.[17] It is very close to TA/Pelliot but is missing some sections. I was able to consult TA/StP in the summer of 2014, and a colleague has graciously furnished me with a partial copy, but a full comparison has not been possible.

The next-oldest example of the text is the partial copy of the *Tarikh-i Amniyya* in Lund University Library's Jarring Prov. 197, which was copied on June 15, 1914. This manuscript is a fascinating artifact, which circulated among readers through at least 1926, but it requires a separate study. It only includes the second epic, and marginal notes suggest that it was produced as a celebration of Yaʿqub Beg. It was copied by Ṭalib Akhund b. Mullah Niʿmat Akhund Mingbegi, who was also the author and copyist of the 1317 [1899] *Ṣaḥibnama* chronicle of the Yaʿqub Beg period, which can be found in the Lund University Library manuscripts Jarring Prov. 115, 116, and 117. I believe that it had a similar source text to TA/Pelliot.

The Mukhlisov catalogue lists two other manuscripts of the *Tarikh-i Amniyya* held in the Xinjiang Museum, which are evidently almost identical despite being collected in Kashgar and in Aqsu, respectively.[18] These are currently inaccessible to scholars.

Sayrami renamed his work the *Tarikh-i Ḥamidi* sometime in 1907 or 1908. Both known manuscripts of the *Tarikh-i Ḥamidi* claim a date of composition of 1908, but they differ significantly. The copy from 1911 actually represents the newer text in a very reliable form, while the copy from 1927 or later presents an earlier text in a less reliable form.

"TH/Jarring": Jarring Prov. 163 of the Lund University Library was copied by ʿAbdulqadir Akhund, probably for the Swedish missionary Gunnar Hermansson, sometime after July 1927.[19] Scholars have often assumed that it must represent the latest version of the narrative. This is incorrect. Instead, TH/Jarring's text closely resembles that of TA/Pelliot. Moreover, it is replete with errors, ranging from odd changes in numbers to missing sections to passages rearranged through copyist's errors. I have noted some of the most significant changes in the notes here. At the same time, TH/Jarring includes additional text that often clarifies confusing or obscure points in our base text. This may indicate that TH/Jarring represents an expansion of the text that took place independently from Sayrami's revisions, or possibly a blend of the *Amniyya* and *Ḥamidi*. TH/Jarring is also missing part of the prolegom enon and the entire epilogue, but it does include a fascinating later text that continues Sayrami's work up to the year 1927.[20]

"TH/Beijing": The latest text is in the manuscript held at the Chinese Academy of Social Sciences in Beijing. Its composition is dated to 1908 and its copying to 1911. TH/Beijing, overall, is very cleanly and consistently written, with minimal errors and omissions. It is by far the longest and most inclusive version of the text. Uyghur scholars have suggested that this manuscript may be a holograph, written in the author's own hand, and the care evident in its production makes that a tempting hypothesis. Nevertheless, a large section later in the manuscript is clearly written not only in a very different hand but also using more modern grammar and orthography.

Regrettably, this manuscript is only available as a very coarse photoreproduction in the collection *Texts in Northwestern Minority Scripts* (Ch. *Xibei shaoshu minzu wenzi wenxian*).[21] This version is missing several pages, most of which can be found in a partial photoreproduction in the dissertation of the renowned Uyghur scholar Abduraop Polat Täklimakani.[22] A thorough examination of the Beijing manuscript would be necessary in order to make any further determinations about its origins.

In summary, there appear to have been four stages in the revision of the *Tarikh-i Amniyya* and *Tarikh-i Ḥamidi*. First, Sayrami composed the early manuscript that informed TA/Kazan in 1903, and a similar manuscript informed TA/Lund. Second, Sayrami expanded the text, perhaps because of the interest and patronage of Western travelers, producing the source text for TA/Pelliot, Jarring Prov. 197, and TA/StP around 1907. Then a minor revision, consisting mainly of a name change, created the source text for TH/Jarring in 1908. Finally, a more thoroughgoing revision and expansion led to TH/Beijing later that year.

Notes on the Translation

This translation is based on the photoreproduction of TH/Beijing. The original manuscript was foliated, but the foliation does not appear in the reproduction, so the page numbers of the published version must be used. TH/Beijing was chosen as the base text because it is the most complete and reliable realization of Sayrami's writing and revision. However, given the reproduction's lack of clarity, I have taken several measures in order to ensure the translation's fidelity.

First, I have referred to Abduraop Polat Täklimakani's dissertation, in which the final third of the manuscript is reproduced, including four of the five lacunae in the published TH/Beijing text.[23]

Second, where there are lacunae or unclear passages in TH/Beijing, I have made close reference to the other available manuscripts as well as Pantusov's printed edition. TA/Pelliot and TH/Jarring were the most useful in this regard, and the close comparison involved in creating the scholarly edition made it possible to understand the systematic differences between the versions. In my notes I have pointed out several instances where these manuscripts deviate from the sense of the core text or misplace lines, phrases, words, or entire passages.

Third, I have referred at length to two translations into modern Uyghur, Änwär Baytur's published in 1986 and Täklimakani's published in 2019.[24] Both are based on a complete reproduction of TH/Beijing, and they reflect the voices and intuitions of experienced scholars. I indicate in the notes where their interpretations differ from each other and from mine. I also consulted the Chinese translation by Aili Wufuer but found it to have distorted the text to such a degree as to be largely unusable.[25]

The tremendous amount of lexicographical and geographical scholarship produced over the past two centuries in many languages—from Uyghur to Russian to Japanese and beyond—has proven indispensable. I have endeavored to locate every place name precisely and to relate any obscure terminology to previous textual and anthropological scholarship or to occurrences of the term in other manuscripts from Sayrami's time. Local archival sources from the Uyghur homeland also informed the translation by providing examples of vernacular usage.

Conventions

The translation's apparatus has been kept to a minimum to improve readability, but I hope that the notes and accompanying maps will be useful. I have tried to match the conventions of this translation to those of David Brophy's translation of the *Tadhkira-i ʿAzizan*, entitled *In Remembrance of the Saints*.[26]

The translation reflects the multilingual nature of premodern Central Asian writing. All Turkic (i.e., Chaghatay) text is represented in standard font. Persian is given in *italics*, while Arabic is in SMALL CAPITALS. Translations of Quranic quotations follow *The Study Quran*, with chapter and verse references given in the text in square brackets.[27] Transliterations broadly follow the system of the *International Journal of Middle East Studies*, although I have omitted macrons in order to reduce visual clutter.

Because the narrative can be hard to place into historical context, I have included reign dates or birth and death dates in square brackets wherever possible. Original language is presented in square brackets where it is relevant to understanding the text, particularly when Sayrami makes a pun, or may be of scholarly interest.

The translation also reflects the differences between certain key manuscripts. If text only appears in TA/Pelliot, it is in square brackets, for example [Then he went to Yarkand]. If it only appears in TH/Jarring, it is in parentheses, for example (the soldier).

Occasional notes of clarification are in square brackets and italics, with the translator's initials: [*Note—ES*].

References to pages in TH/Beijing are given in curly brackets and superscript, for example{42}. Occasionally, where it is necessary to do so, I note foliation from TA/Pelliot in superscript and square brackets, for example[27r]. Foliation for text from TH/Jarring is noted in superscript and parentheses, for example(132v). Manuscript pages from Abduraop Polat Täklimakani's dissertation are indicated with P, i.e., P304.

Chapter titles are adapted from Hodong Kim, *Holy War in China*, appendix C.

Terminology

SAYRAMI WROTE FOR his own people and his own time. Consequently, his use of terminology, particularly for kinds of people, can be confusing to a modern reader. Rarely do Sayrami's terms match the meanings we would expect today. However, names of groups and titles of ranks do indicate membership in certain factions that are relevant to this story.

Peoples

"Muslim" (*Musulmān*) is a deceptively simple word. Sayrami uses it to indicate members of the Islamic faith in general, but he usually refers specifically to Turkic-speaking Muslims belonging to settled agrarian communities. "Muslim" in this sense is close to what modern people would call Uyghur and Uzbek. Sayrami usually means "Muslims" to exclude Dungans and Kyrgyz.

"Dungan" was the normal term for someone thought of as a Muslim who primarily spoke Chinese. In Chinese and in today's English, such a person would be called a Hui, although "Dungan" is still used in Central Asia. The idea of being Muslim and Chinese, then as now, was complex and contested, and in Sayrami's time, the boundaries between "Dungan" and "Muslim" could be fairly porous.

The term "Kyrgyz" rarely appears in the *Tarikh-i Ḥamidi* without some pejorative attached to it. It refers to nomadic Turkic-speaking Muslims from the mountains.

"Kazakh" in the *Tarikh-i Ḥamidi* describes not an ethnic group but a way of life focused on brigandage that Sayrami associated closely with the Kyrgyz.[1] He rarely calls someone a Kazakh without describing them also as Kyrgyz, although someone could become a Kazakh, or wandering brigand. He otherwise uses the term to describe certain kinds of horses or sheep.

"Qipchaq" indicates the nomadic Turkic-speaking peoples of Central Asia, particularly those tribes from the Qipchaq Steppe. Sayrami mainly indicates the Qipchaq soldiers from Khoqand who fled to Kashgar and into Yaʿqub Beg's service, but he also applies the term to certain mountain nomads from the Tarim Basin who might elsewhere be labeled "Kyrgyz."

"Chinese" in this narrative refers to all sorts of non-Muslim, non-Turkic-speaking people whom Sayrami associated with the Qing regime and its inner territories. It includes Chinese speakers, but also Manchu speakers, such as Manchus, Sibe, and Solons. The original term, *Khiṭāy*, indicates North China—it is etymologically related to English "Cathay"—and historically derives from the name of the medieval Khitan state.

"Qalmaq" usually refers to the Oirat or Junghar Mongols, including those members of the Junghar Khanate whose long war with the Qing led to the Seven Cities' conquest and those who later returned and submitted to Qing rule. The latter included the Torghuts, whom the Qing settled in Xinjiang and who play an important role in this story. Sayrami usually distinguishes the Qalmaqs from other Mongols but sometimes refers to both using the same term.

Titles

A *beg* is a minor ruler, something like a lord. Hence Yaʿqub Beg was named Yaʿqub, and *beg* was a title he received during his service to the Khanate of Khoqand. In the *Tarikh-i Ḥamidi*, it usually indicates any of the aristocratic Muslims whom the Qing assigned to positions of authority over the Seven Cities. The loftiest among them held hereditary Qing ranks such as *wáng* "king" or *gōng* "duke." Members of the aristocratic families could be assigned on a rotating basis to different regions of Xinjiang, where they might serve as the *ḥakim beg* "governor," *eshikagha beg* "deputy governor," or *ghazinachi beg* "treasurer." Lower-ranking *begs* might come from the localities where they held their positions, such as *qażi beg* "judge" or *mirab beg* "irrigation manager." There were other *beg* titles, but these are the ones mentioned in the *Tarikh-i Ḥamidi.*

An *akhund* refers to an Islamic scholar; in the Seven Cities, typically a local literate man responsible for leading ceremonies and resolving disputes. An *aʿlam akhund* was a "chief *akhund.*"

Khoja is a generic term for a Sufi master. Sufis—Islamic mystics—held significant political authority in Central Asia, and certain Sufi lineages became extremely powerful. Sayrami refers mainly to two groups as "Khojas." First are the Makhdumzada Khojas, historical masters of the great Naqshbandiyya order, who ruled the Seven Cities up to the 1760s; some of their descendants came to Kashgar with Yaʿqub Beg. Second are the Khojas of Kucha, also known as the Kataki Khojas.

Ḥażrat refers to members of a network of Mujaddidi Sufis that spanned much of Eurasia, was particularly influential in Afghanistan, and had an important outpost in Yarkand, as well as branches in Aqsu and Ushturfan.[2]

Törä originally referred to Mongol law, but it came to indicate the Junghar sovereign.[3] It was later applied to members of elite Muslim families. We might translate it as "prince." From 1:12 onward, Sayrami regularly refers to *khojas* of all kinds as *törä.*

Military officers in the Turco-Mongol system are referred to by the number of soldiers they notionally command. A *mingbashi* leads 1,000 (*ming*); a *pansad*, 500[4]; a *yüzbashi*, 100 (*yüz*); and an *onbashi*, ten (*on*).

Other ranks and titles are explained in notes.

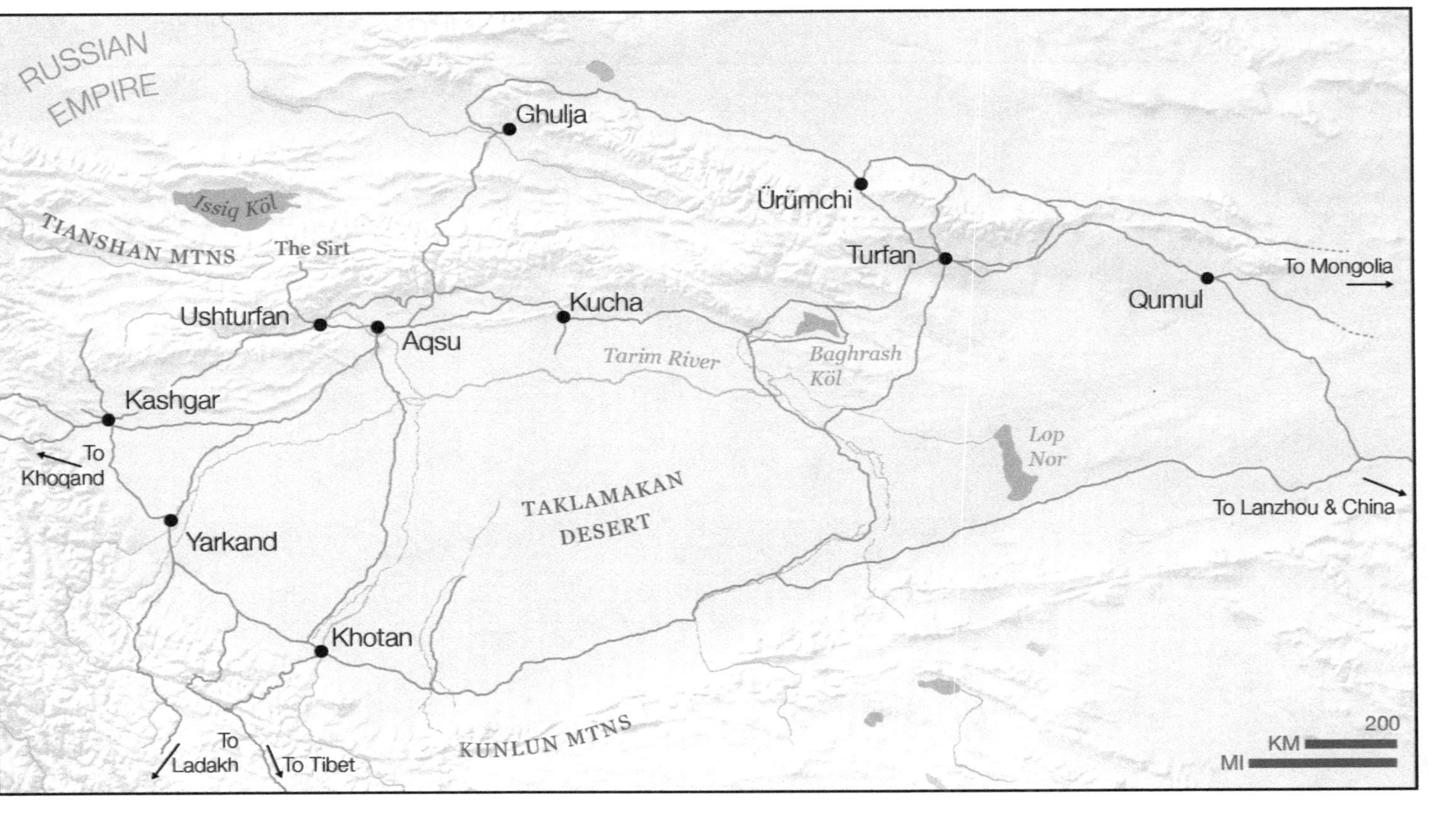

Major cities and areas of the Seven Cities in the 1860s and 1870s. Map by Evangeline McGlynn.

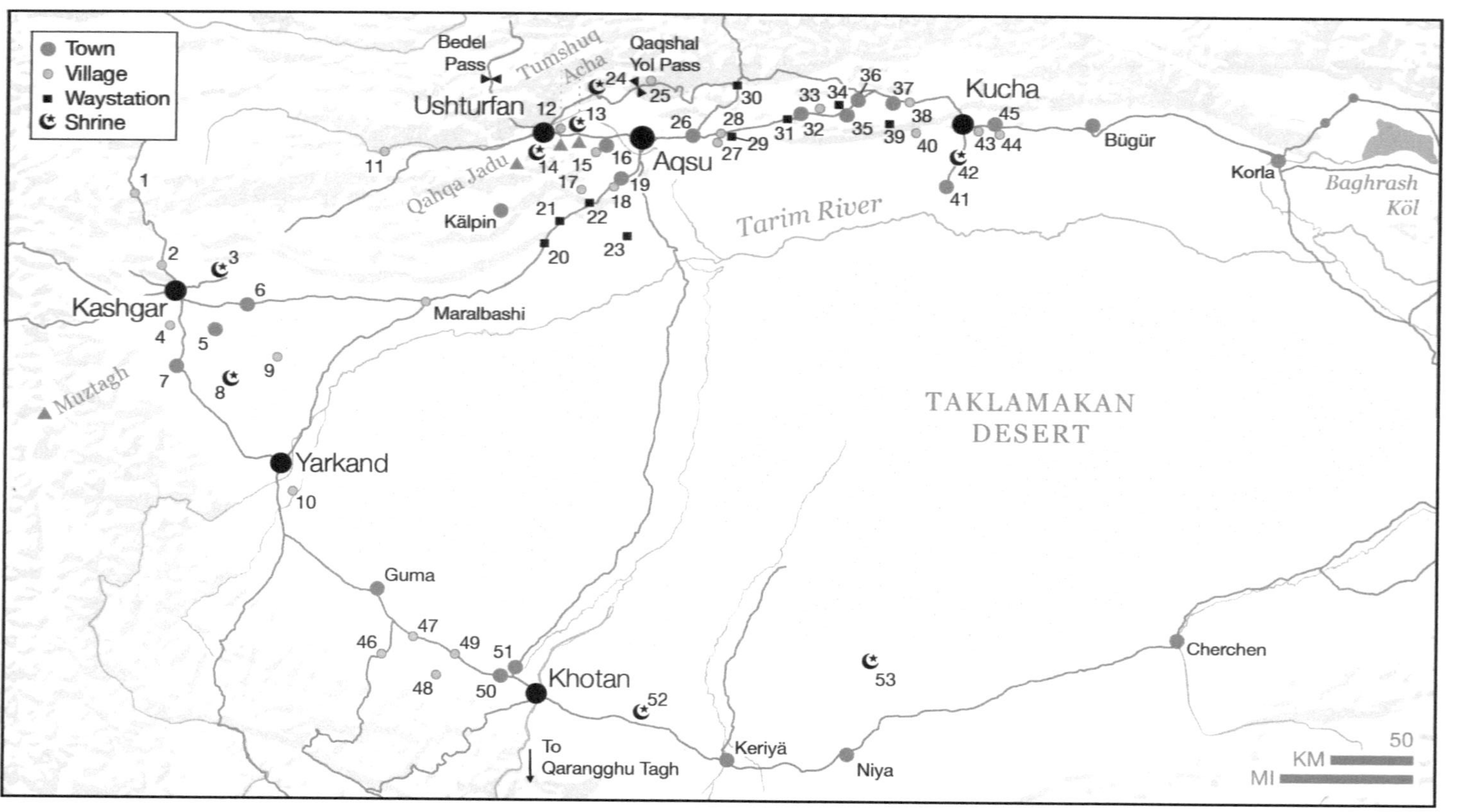

The Tarim Basin in the 1860s and 1870s. Map by Evangeline McGlynn.

1 Chaqmaq
2 Üstün Artush
3 Shrine of Sultan Sutuq Bughra Khan
4 Parash
5 Khan Eriq
6 Fayzabad
7 Yengi Hissar
8 Shrine of Ordam Padishah
9 Mughal Terim
10 Arashor
11 Qara Bulaq
12 Otbashi
13 Shrine of Imam Muḥammad Ghazali
14 Shrine of the Valley
15 Aqyar
16 Aral
17 Quruq Uzum
18 Say Eriq
19 Ay Kōl
20 Yaydi
21 Chilan
22 Chöl Quduq
23 Qaraqchin
24 Shrine of the Poplar
25 Qaqshal
26 Jam
27 Östäng Boyi
28 Qara Yulghun
29 Kohna Örtäng
30 Qizil Bulaq
31 Jogha
32 Yaqa Eriq
33 Qushtami
34 Say Langar
35 Onbash
36 Bay
37 Sayram
38 Qizil
39 Tajik
40 Yulduz Bagh
41 Shahyar
42 Shrine of Baba Qambar
43 Öchqara
44 Toqnay
45 Mazar Baghi
46 Sanju
47 Zanguya
48 Duwa
49 Piyalma
50 Ziba
51 Qaraqash
52 Shrine of Imam Jaʿfar Ṭayaran
53 Shrine of Imam Jaʿfar al-Ṣadiq

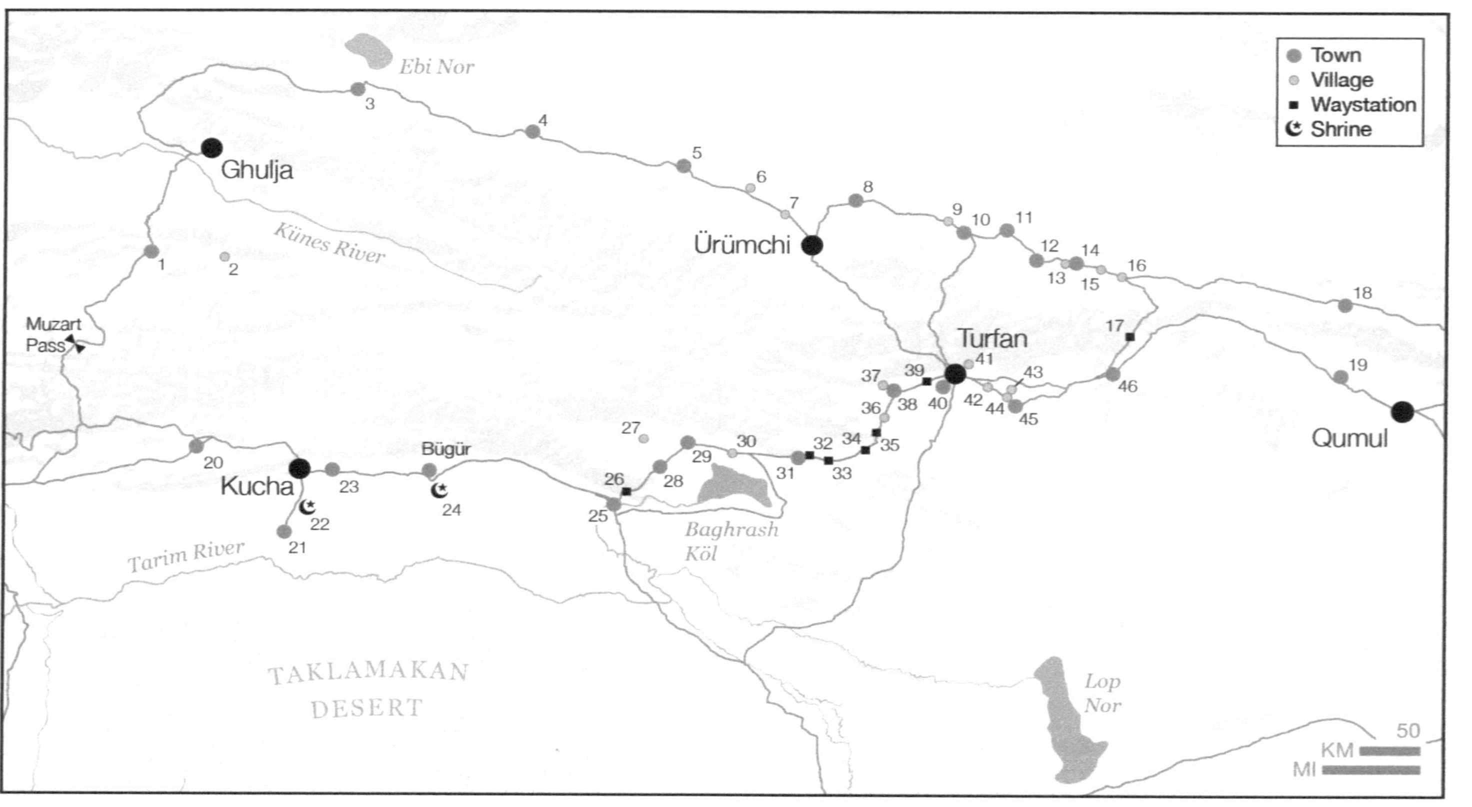

The Ili Valley, Turfan Depression, and surrounds in the 1860s and 1870s. Map by Evangeline McGlynn.

1 Kürä
2 Tekes
3 Jinghe
4 Xihu
5 Manas
6 Qutubi
7 Changji
8 Fukang
9 Santai
10 Jimsar
11 Guchengzi
12 Qitai
13 Dongchin
14 Murkhu
15 Yiban Chanza
16 Sangah Chanza
17 Taz Bulaq
18 Barköl
19 Dabanchi
20 Bay
21 Shahyar
22 Shrine of Baba Qambar
23 Mazar Baghi
24 Shrine of ʿUkkasha
25 Korla
26 Teräklik
27 Qara Modun
28 Qarashahr
29 Tapilghu
30 Ushaq Tal
31 Qara Qizil
32 Döng Dangza
33 Kömush Örtäng
34 Üjmä Döng
35 Arghai Bulaq
36 Subashi
37 Yilanliq
38 Toqsun
39 Dadong
40 Yamshi
41 Bulayiq
42 Abad
43 Tuyuq
44 Yangkhay
45 Lukchin
46 Chiqtim

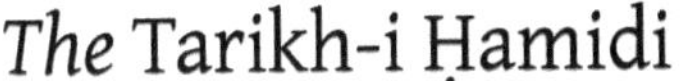

The Tarikh-i Ḥamidi

0:0 Preface

{3} In the Name of God, the Merciful, the Compassionate.

Oh, Creator of Creation, limitless praise, gratitude, and laudations are due to You, for You are the source of beneficence for all of Your creations, Your holy self is singular and without equal, and all of Your aspects are pure and immaculate. Your station is lofty, Your kingship grandiose. All beings between Heaven and Earth are within Your control, and Your rule and judgment above them. And eternal rulership is due to You, whereby You are the true king, for all of Your creations are transient.

He places the crown of rule upon the head of whomsoever He pleases, and takes it from whomsoever He pleases. He elevates whom He pleases and strikes down whom He pleases. He grants His guidance to whom He pleases and casts into error whom He pleases. He makes the high low, and the low high. He is capable of all things.

Whatever command You give to Your creations, it is done—this is Your power. It is impossible to belay or remand Your orders. You have sent Your Messenger and the prophets (Peace be upon them!) over us. And in Your book, You recounted stories and knowledge of times past—of peoples and of kings both just and tyrannical. And it is attested that You wish that Your creations should learn from these stories and take lessons therefrom, and observe and remember these past events. When people pass from this world, all of them, whether good or{4} bad, leave clear and lasting traces. We reinscribe the deeds of those who have passed in books of history, and these tell the stories of their lives.

May prayers be scattered without end upon the Seal of the Prophets, the best of the two worlds, who gave proofs and witness of events in times long past and in the days that will come. His holy name is Muḥammad (PEACE BE UPON HIM!), God's servant, Prophet, and dear friend. His stately genealogy traces back to the Prophet Abraham [Ibrahim] (THE FRIEND OF GOD), to whom You granted in full the lofty and praiseworthy offices of kingship and prophethood. And You collected all of the respective virtues that You granted to the prophets of old and gave them to him, along with his name and station. For this reason, if one remembers You, one likewise remembers Muḥammad, the Messenger of God. He put the Shariah into place, as when he was alive, likewise when he had gone. There is nothing that can abrogate, change, or delay his Shariah. He possesses AN EXALTED CHARACTER [68:4] and A NOBLE STATION [26:58].

And salutations without limit to his brothers, who were among the prophets and apostles (SALUTATIONS BE UPON THEM!); and upon all his family and progeny, his immaculate wives, and all of his holy companions. Among the most pious and worthy of imitation were the Ten, and the people of Badr, of Uḥud, of ʿAqaba, and of the Ṣuffa, all his companions and relations, and the earliest Muslims, and likewise the generation after (MAY GOD BE CONTENT WITH THEM!), and the caliphs, kings, amirs, and sultans of times past, and the scholars who treasured the Shariah, and the pious judges, and the imams who gave the law in days of yore. Salutations likewise to them, to those who have succeeded them up until the present day, and to those who will come after. Until the Day of Judgment, the Lord on High's mercy will fall upon those who travel upon the straight and correct path. Upon them great mercy, everlasting and ever increasing.

May it be clearly demonstrated in the sound and unbesmirched vision of the wise and learned of the world, and in the supremely enlightened minds of the fine scholars of our age, that one who has been condemned to obscurity on a traceless path within an unknown corner, who is wretched and poor, yet rich in shortcomings, Mullah Musa{5} b. Mullah ʿIsa Khoja Sayrami, humbly submits the following.

* * *

These lands of Moghulistan anciently passed from the hands of Muslim khans and became the possessions of the Emperor of China. However, after 122 years had passed, by divine foreordination and His hidden will, the sun of Islam rose over these Seven Cities—Moghulistan—and their people, while the cloud of tyranny dispersed.

The first were Rashuddin Khoja from the country of Kucha, Mullah Ḥabibullah Ḥajji of Khotan, and the independent khans and kings of each of the Dungan factions. All of them overwhelmed the nonbelievers and established their governments, but while they were occupied with the intractable struggles of battles, holy wars, and mass slaughter, a man named Muḥammad Yaʿqub Beg Qushbegi from the land of Ferghana, a wise hero, secured their total subjugation and enacted his own rule.[1] Six years later, in the year 1286 [1870], his intelligence and cunning prevailed over his inborn nature, and he pledged his own fealty and that of all the people of the Seven Cities to that magnificent caliph who rules the lands of the great Ottoman state,{6} and they came to enjoy his protection and grace. When Yaʿqub Beg sent Qażi Yaʿqub Khan Törä as an emissary with his pledge of allegiance, he was bound to the most noble and royal service and celestial presence of that great khan, begotten of great khans, servant of the holy apostles, the inhabitant of Paradise, ʿAbdulʿaziz Khan b. Abdulmajid Khan [r. 1861–1876]. As the common people of this land of Moghulistan fell accordingly under the enlightened judgment of that noble dweller in Paradise and the higher spheres, he took them under his personal protection and dominion. Muḥammad Yaʿqub Beg, the Ataliq Ghazi, was granted the esteemed title of Master of the Royal Stables, and by kingly grace and favor, the order of obedience, the crown of kingship, and the standard of the Ottoman state were sent to him.

During the time that we, the people of these Seven Cities, all of us the humblest of servants and subjects, spent seven years under the eternal fortune and protection of the Ottoman state in comfort and ease of mind, in prayer and refuge of God the Exalted, the All-Powerful (BLESSED BE HE!), Sultan Muḥammad Murad Khan (MAY GOD AID HIM!) ascended to the throne of the caliphate. After that magnificent leader, the shadow of God upon the nations, king of the Arabs and the Persians, Protector of the Two Holy Cities, pearl of the crown of the People of Osman, ʿAbdulḥamid Khan (MAY GOD PRESERVE HIS STATE AND GUARD HIS LIFE, AND GRANT VICTORY TO HIS COMPANIONS AND FORTUNE TO HIS FRIENDS!) became sovereign upon the thrones of caliphate and sultanate, and he endeavored greatly to secure peace for us, his humble servants and subjects. And yet, before he could establish the order of government according to his designs, Muḥammad Yaʿqub Khan Ghazi left this transient world for the gardens of eternity. At that time, the Emperor of China's officials came again to rule over us, we weak and helpless people with no leader of our own.

As far as we are aware, none of the wise or learned of our age have ventured to compose any sketch or memoir of these stories of tribulation and anarchy. Now thirty-two years have passed since his enthronement. Indeed, none of the wise men in the intervening four hundred and some years since Mirza Ḥaydar Kuragan [1499/50–1551], the compiler of the *Tarikh-i Rashidi*, up to the present day has ventured to tell the stories of those kings who have ruled over the lands of Moghulistan, and they wrote no histories.

Therefore some dear friends importuned me, "What if you were to write down these stories from beginning to end and gather them into the pages of a history—from the holy war of the Khojas of Kucha, which was the reason Islamic government was established in this land, to the fall and ruin of the Ataliq Ghazi's state? Perhaps the conquests of those *sayyids* who died in holy war and the Ataliq Ghazi's good government and prowess on the battlefield will not disappear from the people's memory. If they read it, rather, they may pray for us. As the hadith says, ONE WHO LEADS SOMEONE TO DO A GOOD DEED IS LIKE THE ONE WHO DOES IT[2]—should the Merciful receive the prayers of those who come after us and, by their grace, forgive us wretched sinners,[{7}] by God it would be no strange thing."

At this request, your humble author of no repute thought, How dare I compile a history of the grandeur of those lordly warriors and their campaigns, of the famous deeds and reign of that splendid king, the Ataliq Ghazi? And what business do I have opening my mouth and waggling my tongue on the topic of that fortunate one? What connection does a nameless unfortunate such as I have with the tales of that exalted king and denizen of the higher spheres, that I should compile them, and that I should shift my pen with regard to this great amir?

Moreover, since the beginning of the Time of Islam to the present, over forty years have passed. Most of those who witnessed those happenings have passed on to the eternal realm, and past events fallen out of the people's memory. Perhaps their stories were forgotten. I thought of how one might go about rectifying scattered tales, difficult to compare, and varying stories, difficult to correct. I followed the hadith: THE NOBLEST OF PEOPLE ACCEPT THE DIFFICULTY.

Just as I was opening my mouth to explain these difficulties, some of my dear old friends and brilliant comrades said, "Let us seize the moment. If we render with eloquence the tales of those martyrs who sacrificed their lives as they pitilessly put the infidels to Islam's sword, earning their stations as holy warriors as well as God's satisfaction, then those who come after will raise their prayers, just as it is said: GOD IS GREAT, AND LIKEWISE HIS PEOPLE.

"Moreover, it is certain that history belongs to the class of necessary knowledge and to the authoritative sciences. It is both fine and necessary to gain knowledge of history, and thus understanding. Those who possess this sort of knowledge are honored in the eyes of ordinary people and esteemed at gatherings. Those ignorant people who do not know history, regardless of whatever fine characteristics they may possess, fall far short of the esteem and credibility given to the wise. The uses and benefits of history are many. This is because the classes and kinds of peoples, their births and deaths and the courses of their lives, their morals and customs, places they have settled and cities they have cultivated, may be known from books of history.

"If not for knowledge of history,{8} we would not know of those peoples who existed in bygone ages, from Adam (GOD BLESS HIM!) to Muḥammad (PEACE BE UPON HIM!); nor indeed of the prophets and apostles (PEACE BE UPON THEM!), nor the great saints and shaykhs; nor the powerful *qaghans*,[3] khans, and kings; caesars and chosroëses, emperors of China and pharaohs of Egypt, rulers such as Nimrod and peoples such as the Amalekites; nor even of the great Muslim kings of Arabia and Persia, nor of tyrannical infidel rulers, all of whom have determined the order of the world and the state of its peoples. There is no way to learn of their existences and their lives, and so gain understanding, other than from books of history.

"Out of all of the peoples, it is the Arabs and Persians who have in every age delved into the stories of the great kings of their times and compiled them. Some of them have opted for comprehensiveness, while others when relating tales of their country's past rulers leave more abbreviated accounts. This being the case—as you have read many of the older and more recent histories, and those concerning the Turks and Mongols in particular; you have witnessed the trials and tribulations of this age, the good and the bad, and derived experience therefrom; and you have held conversation with generals and ministers, and so learned the sorts of people they were, their manners and characteristics—then you should make it your goal to gather the events and remarkable happenings that took place in these times and collect them into a history as a monument to the past. You are now over seventy years old. May a trace of you remain."

Although I thought it inappropriate to debase such resplendent jewels of eloquence by tossing them upon this lowly, dusty ground, I was nevertheless obliged to grapple with this great task, and so made myself a target for the arrow of rebuke.

Dear friends, I hope that, whatever errors or slips of the pen may lie herein, when you emend them, you may sweep them away with the hem of exemption and trim them with the penknife of generosity. As it is said, WHEN THE REWARD IS TO GOD, AND THE GRATITUDE TO THE PEOPLE. I have taken the first part of it from the contents of previous books of history and the later part from what I have seen, learned, and asked others about,{9} and settled both upon the line of composition and page of reportage.[4]

I have named this work the *Tarikh-i Ḥamidi*. It is composed of a prolegomenon, two epics, and an epilogue. There are several reasons for naming it the *Tarikh-i Ḥamidi*. One is so that the memory of receiving the grace and protection of that great khan, begotten of great khans, the ruler of the Ottoman state and the caliph upon the Earth, Protector of the Two Holy Cities, ʿAbdulḥamid Khan b. Abdulmajid Khan (GOD GRANT HIM FORTUNE AND VICTORY TO THE DAY OF RESURRECTION!) may not fly from the hearts and memories of the people but instead be published clearly on the page of the world. With this intention I named it the *Tarikh-i Ḥamidi*.

Another is that, a long time ago in the year 952 [1545], the commander-in-chief Mirza Ḥaydar Kuragan b. Mirza Muḥammad Ḥusayn Kuragan (MAY GOD ILLUMINATE HIS GRAVE!) compiled a history of the events and remarkable happenings of that age. He named his history the *Tarikh-i Rashidi*, after the ruler of his time, Sultan ʿAbdurrashid Khan b. Sultan Saʿid Khan (MAY GOD OPEN FOR HIM THE DOOR TO PARADISE!). In our times, the one who stands in protection over the Muslims is that ruler of the great Ottoman state and caliph, the servant of the apostles, Sultan ʿAbdulḥamid Khan b. Abdulmajid Khan (GOD GRANT HIM FORTUNE UNTIL THE DAY OF RESURRECTION!). Consequently I named it the *Tarikh-i Ḥamidi*.

Another is this, that there is a hadith concerning an inexperienced man who seeks explanations from experienced men, and so keeps gaining knowledge, but conceals it: HE WHO IS ASKED SOMETHING HE KNOWS AND CONCEALS IT WILL HAVE A BRIDLE OF FIRE PUT ON HIM [ON THE DAY OF RESURRECTION].[5] In hopes of freeing myself from fear of this threat, my goal in penning a few words about the kings of old, and in repeating their names and genealogies anew, is this: The lands of Moghulistan's reception of the grace and protection of the country of the Khaqan ʿAbdulḥamid Khan b. Abdulmajid Khan (GOD GRANT HIM VICTORY UNTIL THE DAY OF RESURRECTION!), and its people's finding a place in its order, that is to say being a part of the great Ottoman state, were worthy of pride in this world and the next. A hadith is attested on this matter: IF A MAN DIES WITHOUT KNOWING THE IMAM OF HIS TIME, HE WILL DIE A DEATH OF IGNORANCE.[6]{10} It is a necessity for all peoples to know the rulers of their times, indeed a means for salvation from torment in the next life. In relation thereto and in the hope that it is correct, I have for these dubious reasons named it the *Tarikh-i Ḥamidi.*

Friends of faith and reason, when your gaze falls upon this compilation, when you read it, pray do not forget your humble author in your prayers. With this I begin to write. BY HIS GRACE AND GENEROSITY, WELCOMING FROM HIM, THE ALMIGHTY, HIS GUIDANCE.

Prolegomenon

0:1 History After Noah

Beginning of the Prolegomenon

This Land of Moghulistan, or the "Seven Cities," from Adam and Noah to the Present Day; What Occurred There; Rule by Various Peoples; and the Reasons It Is Called Moghulia; the Genealogy of the Muslim Khans; and How the Emperor of China Subjugated the Seven Cities

IN ANTIQUITY, AND in books of history, this land of the Seven Cities was called Moghulistan. Moreover, in the old documents found in these cities, the phrase "in the reckoning of Moghulia" is written. What is the meaning of "Moghulia"? When did these cities first become a Muslim country? To what religions and sects did their kings belong? How many years has the Emperor of China controlled them?

No prior history contains even a brief discussion of these matters. I find the reasons for this unclear and unconvincing. One might say that everyone who writes about it fails to begin from the beginning and instead rushes to the conclusion, so the result is far from credible. Therefore, I have excerpted here some passages from the *Garden of Purity*, the *Selection of Chronicles*, and the *Tarikh-i Rashidi*, as well as other histories.[1]

May it not be hidden from you wise and insightful people that one reason for compiling this history is to relate the circumstances of the tribes of Turks; how their kings and generals achieved their rule; their genealogies, the glories of their ancestors, and their original homeland and country; and what is known about them from the sources. For this reason, I have begun with the stories of Adam, and of Noah's miracles,{11} and the events that took place among Noah's people when for fifty years short of a thousand they failed to recognize him as a prophet. On account of their great villainy, they did not accept God's guidance. The true story of how God the All-Powerful laid them to waste and sent them to Hell is well known among the Arabs and Persians. For this reason, I have not been so audacious as to write their story myself. Nor did I dare to write the stories of Noah's two sons, Sam and Ḥam, and their descendants.

His third son was Japheth. I will strive to narrate the genealogies of his descendants, the tribes of Chin, Turk, and Mongol, and then of the others who settled in the east and north, whose stories I also hope to relate in detail. For fear that someone may accuse me of being unfaithful, I have presented the descendants of Turk, son of Japheth, in abbreviated form. When a man's life draws nearer to the age of eighty, just as his steps shorten, so do his errors multiply. Pray spare me your mockery.

* * *

At the time of the Flood, by God's command, Noah built an ark, and within it he placed a pair of every kind of animal. Eventually he landed his boat upon Mount Judi. Eighty people of the line of Adam disembarked alive. However, the divine retribution enacted by the waters had laid everything to waste. In Noah's family, only three of his sons and three of his daughters survived, seven people in total. All human beings upon the Earth and all the children of Adam are descendants of these three sons of Noah. This is why he is called "the Second Adam," because on the face of the Earth there were no others left.

The names of Noah's sons were Sam, Ḥam, and Japheth. It is said that they were prophets. Sam was far smarter and wiser than the other sons. He was granted the secrets of prophethood. The other brothers were put under Sam's authority. Noah made the more temperate parts of the inhabited quarter of the Earth, and those that became its more populous places, the domain of Sam's children. He prayed that prophets and saints, sultans and generals would come from the line of Sam. Sam lived for 500 years. He bore nine sons: Arpachshad, Kayumars, Aswad, Yaqin, Lawaj, Walad, Elam, Aram, and Yur. Arpachshad is the father of prophets; Kayumars is the father of kings. Sam sent each of his sons off in one direction or another. Their descendants spoke in nineteen different languages. They settled in the lands of Babel, Yemen, Hadramaut, Oman, the Two Iraqs, and Persia. Some of them went off to the south and east and mixed with the descendants of Ḥam and Japheth. They multiplied. They built buildings and cities and settled.

Ḥam went off to the south, and he settled on the shores of the ocean. God granted him nine sons{12} named Sind, Nuba, Canaan, Zanj, Cush, Copt, Barbah, and Jash. The people of Sudan and of Zanzibar, Jash, and Hindustan are the descendants of Ḥam. His children spoke in eighteen languages. They built many cities.

When Noah landed the ark upon Mount Judi and said farewell to his son Japheth, Japheth asked his father to teach him to pray, so that whenever he wished, rain would fall. His father, Noah, made a request to God. In response, Gabriel brought him the name of God inscribed on a stone. In Arabic, that stone is called the *hajarulmaṭar*. The Turks call it by the names *yada tash* and *jada tash*.[2]

Japheth settled in the east and north around the Volga and Irtysh Rivers. He invented fine traditions, and he founded a city in the country of Beijing.[3] God granted him eleven children. Their names were Chin, Slav, Kamari, Turk, Khalaj, Khazar, Rus, Sadsan, Ghurr, Baruj, and Munshij. Each of them was given one of Japheth's own daughters as a wife. They settled their countries. God advised them, "Raise up your peoples well, that they may multiply."

Among Japheth's sons, Turk was the greatest. He was exceptionally zealous, manly, skillful, and wise. He traveled the world until he came to a place with a small river. He called that land Silük. It possessed sweet waters and magnificent meadows. Turk found that it suited him, and he settled there. He built a house of straw and leaves to live in, and so invented tent making. He and his children made themselves clothes and hats to wear from the skins of livestock. He was just and merciful. He took God's people under his protection, and he never wavered in caring for them. God blessed him with worthy children.

One of those children, whom he named Fudak, was very fond of hunting. One day in the wilderness, he made a kebab of antelope meat. As he was eating it, a bit of meat fell from his hands onto the ground. The soil was salty. He took the kebab from the ground and put it in his mouth. He found it very tasty. From that point on, he made it a custom to add salt to food. It was unknown before.

Khazar, son of Japheth, went to the countries to the north, to the banks of the Emil River. He found that it suited him and settled there. Together with his sons, he hunted foxes and lynxes and made trousers out of their skins. During Khazar's lifetime, one of his sons drowned in a river. Another time, Japheth and his retinue also drowned in a river. Reasoning that the opposite of water is fire, Khazar gathered a great deal of firewood. He summoned all of his people together and{13} had them play their drums, tanburs, and other instruments. Amid this great fanfare, they recovered the corpses from the river and burned them in the fire. Even today, this incorrect innovation is practiced among those people. It is written that their descendants gathered honey from mountain hollows and invented halva.

Then there was Rus, son of Japheth. He approached Khazar's land and sent a messenger to ask him for a place to live nearby. Khazar gladly showed him to virgin lands with good air. His descendants settled there.

Another of them was Ghurr, son of Japheth. He came to dwell in the land called Bulghar, and there he constructed fine buildings, but he was very tricky. A bloody war broke out between him and his brother Turk. The reason was that, when Japheth had drowned in the river, his rainmaking stone fell into the hands of Ghurr. All of his brothers laid claim to the rainmaking stone. Ghurr hatched a scheme: he found a stone that resembled the rainmaking stone and carved the name of God onto it, as well. The brothers decided that they would cast lots, and whoever's name came out on top would receive the stone. The lots chose Turk. Mean Ghurr gave Turk the false stone that he had prepared. Thereafter, no matter how Turk asked for rain, it was no use. He realized that Ghurr had tricked him, so he raised his forces and readied for war. Turk had not tested the stone but took it away and kept it, and Ghurr demanded the original rainmaking stone. Ghurr even sent his eldest son, Beghur, to lead soldiers into battle. It was a great and hard-fought battle, and Beghur died in it. Turk returned victorious. To this day, conflicts have continued between the peoples descended from these two brothers.

Slav, son of Japheth, settled in the west and built houses there. His children multiplied. Then his wife died while giving birth to a son. At the same time, one of his dogs also gave birth. Slav gave his son to that dog to suck. It nourished the child and raised him. The boy grew up to be like a dog, biting at people's faces and eyes. Slav gave him a wife, and they had a son, whom they also named Slav. Sometime later, this younger Slav and all of his family came to the land of Rus and asked for some land that might suit him. Rus refused and said, "This land is in short supply, and it seems like you need a great deal of it." Despondent, Slav went to Kamari and Khazar, from whom he heard the same answer.{14} Fighting broke out between them. Slav fled to a country that was at sixty-four degrees latitude, beyond the seventh clime. Because it was so exceptionally cold, they dug houses under the ground to live in.

Kamari, son of Japheth, was gregarious and fond of hunting. One time when he was hunting, he happened upon a pristine place with good air near the land of Bulghar, so he settled down there. God granted him children. One was named Bulghar and the other Bartas. Each of them went and settled in a different direction. They hunted foxes, squirrels, martens, and stoats, and they invented the custom of wearing trousers made of their skins. This custom is practiced among that people to this day.

Chin, son of Japheth, was very intelligent, clever, clear minded, and possessed of great foresight. His father, Japheth, built a city in his country and named it Chin, after him, his son. Chin was a gifted craftsman. He invented painting, drawing, and making clothes of patterned cloth. These skills he taught to his children. He also invented raising silkworms. All of those crafts that are known in Beijing come from Chin's sheer ingenuity. Then Chin was blessed with a smiling and handsome son. Chin named him Machin and gave him a wife. Their children multiplied.

Machin said to his father, "My children have multiplied. They no longer fit into this land. I am out of room. If you will permit it, might I build a city somewhere nearby?" Chin accepted, so they built a city and named it Machin. His children multiplied. He made his children trousers of wool and taught them to wear them. He had them sew trousers and wear them. He also taught them to hunt. Machin took feathers from the anqa, which is one of the loveliest of flying creatures, and pinned them as an ornament onto his sons' heads. He commanded them to wear these plumes in battle, in order to display their bravery. Their officials follow this custom to this day.[4]

Another time, Machin went out to the hunting grounds and killed an antelope. Fragrant blood flowed from its navel. Cautiously, he collected the blood. When he dried it, its fragrance became even stronger. He ordered, "Whenever anyone hunts an antelope in this manner, they should attend to the navel." So, whenever they hunted an antelope in this manner,{15} they would take its navel out. This is how people came to possess musk.

Year by year, God granted him more and more children. During the lifetimes of Chin and Machin, their progeny came to speak in thirty-six languages. As a result, the children and grandchildren of the three brothers Ḥam, Sam, and Japheth in total spoke seventy-two languages. Each of them became one people and one tribe, and when they needed to speak with each other, they spoke through interpreters and translators.[5] Each people went its own way, built cities, and settled down.

It is said that Gog, Magog, and all of their peoples and tribes are descended from Munshij, son of Japheth. If we related all eleven of the sons of Japheth, however, this story would go on too long, and it would no longer be a summary.

* * *

For our purposes, we will focus on one of the eleven sons of Japheth, Turk, and enumerate his descendants. Some histories refer to Turk as a son of Japheth and explain that he was a contemporary of Kayumars. In all, there are thousands of tribes and peoples: Turk, Mongol, Tatar, Kyrgyz, Qipchaq, Uyghur, Manchu, Nayman, Cherkez, Great Qing [*Daching*],[6] Dagestan, Torghut, Noghay, Barlas, Churas, Jalayir, Daylam, Jurjut, Gog, Magog, etc. All of them trace their lineages to Turk, son of Japheth.

Noah's third son was Japheth. His son was Turk. His son was Abulgha Khan. His son was Zib Batui Khan. His son was Güyük Khan. His son was Alinja Khan. Alinja Khan had twin sons. He named one of them Mongol [*Moghul*] and the other Tatar. He was a great and splendid ruler, possessed of prosperity and long-lasting fortune. However, at the height of his fortune, he turned against it, rejected the religion of his ancestors, and traveled instead down the path of narrowness and tyranny toward unbelief and hypocrisy.

Alinja Khan was the first of the khans. At the end of his life, he divided his country between his two sons and fixed their borders. The land he gave to Moghul Khan was called Moghulistan. The land he gave to Tatar Khan was called Tatarstan. Each of them{16} managed his own land. From that time until the present day, these lands have been known as Moghulistan and Tatarstan. (We must discuss the boundaries of Moghulistan.)

By the Grace of God, the Lofty, the Blessed, Alinja Khan's son was Moghul Khan. His son was Qara Khan. His son was Oghuz Khan. Qara Khan was by his nature very evil and hypocritical, and he held firmly to his infidel sect.

No Muslim he encountered was permitted to live. Such was the extent of his enmity.

To such an infidel as Qara Khan was born a brilliant son. For three days after he was born, he would suck neither from his mother's breast nor from any other woman's. His mother was very distressed. In a dream, her son spoke to her and said, "Oh, Mother! If you become a Muslim, I will drink your milk. If you do not, I will not. Never tell anyone these secrets!" She awoke and accepted Islam. He suckled her milk. Her husband remained in the dark, and she never revealed her faith but kept it secret.

The Mongols had a custom, according to which, after a year had passed, they would sacrifice horses, cows, and sheep and gather the whole country together for a celebration. This is when they would give a prince his name. They wondered what sort of name they might give this handsome son of theirs.

As husband and wife were discussing this matter, their one-year-old child spoke and said, "My name shall be Oghuz." His father was startled but pleased, and he named his son Oghuz. By the time Oghuz grew up, the khan's younger brother had a daughter, to whom Oghuz was wed. However, Oghuz refused to be intimate with her or even look at her, but instead went out to hunt.

When he was returning from the hunt, he stayed at the home of another uncle, who also had a daughter. "I am at your service," she told him.

Oghuz said, "If you become a Muslim, I will take you in the bonds of marriage." She became a Muslim, and they promised themselves to each other. Oghuz shared this secret with his mother. When his father, Qara Khan, found out, he accepted the girl and allowed Oghuz to marry her. They became very intimate indeed and fell in love.

When Oghuz went out to hunt again, his father asked Oghuz's previous wife why his son had not loved her. She told him that his son had accepted Islam, and that his second wife had also become a Muslim. "As for me," she informed him, "I have not strayed from the religion of my forefathers. This is why he wanted nothing to do with me."

Qara Khan{17} flew into a rage, and he sent soldiers to attack his son. Oghuz's Muslim wife found out, and she informed Oghuz, who also readied an army. Fighting broke out between the two sides. Oghuz was winning, and he gave chase. He closed in on his father, who gathered some of his own soldiers and came out to meet him in battle. Oghuz's father and many others perished in the fray.

After Oghuz's overwhelming victory, he took his place in his father's capital. He revealed his Islam, showed his people justice and concern for their well-being, and established good practices of government. He ruled for 170 years. The lands to the west, perhaps indeed most of the inhabited world, came under his rule, and he settled and cultivated it. God granted him six sons. He granted each of them four sons, making twenty-four in total. They were divided into twenty-four branches. Each branch became one people and one tribe and was known by its own name: Uyghur, Qanqli, Qay, Khalaj, Uch Oq, Bozoq, etc.

It is written that when Uyghur Khan marched toward Arabia, one of his warriors perished in battle. That warrior's wife was pregnant. She came to term, but, unable to find an isolated place, she sought refuge in the hollow of a tree, where she bore a son. The just khan heard of this, and he took that woman and her son into his harem and took care of them. Because the child was born in a tree, he was named Qibcha. (They used to call a new tree branch a *qibcha*.) Through common error as the language changed, the word *qibcha* became "Qipchaq." When Qibcha grew up, he was made a general and sent to march on the land of the Khazars. He conquered those lands and came to rule over them. It is said that all of the Qipchaq tribes are descended from this son.

Oghuz Khan made his son Kün Khan his successor. After that, his son Ay Khan ruled, then Yulduz Khan, whose son was Tengiz Khan. His son was Mangli Khan. His son was Ilkhan. It is said that there were sometimes conflicts between this Ilkhan and King Faridun's son Tur. Other times they got along and had intercourse. What we can learn from this is that Ilkhan was a contemporary of Tur.

Eight generations of Moghul Khan's descendants ruled with splendor and magnificence. When it came to the ninth, the Tatars gained the upper hand, massacred the Mongols,{18} and obliterated their families from the face of the Earth. Ilkhan's son, Qaynan Khan, and his uncle's son, Takuz, seized an opportunity to escape the rule of the Tatars. Their took their wives and children and fled with some livestock up into a hidden mountain, and there they lived. Apart from one crack in the mountain, there was no way in, and they sealed that place off. They lived within those mountains for many generations and thousands of years. Their descendants and livestock multiplied. (The descendants of Qaynan are called Qiyat and those of Takuz, Okush. They evidently comprise several peoples.) In the end, they could not fit within the mountains. They had simply accepted that this was all the land under Heaven and that there was no other place for them. They called this place Ergenekon. One day, however, they happened upon the place where they had been before. They unsealed it and walked out.

From Moghul Khan were born eight khans, fortunate and honorable, who reigned righteously and mercifully. Their line died out with the ninth. The era of these eight khans was one of joy. In the presence of these glorious khans, or among other chiefs, when one honored another with a gift, one did so "by the nines." Yet what they called a "nine" was actually eight. Wherever one went about among khans and kings, as well as among the common people, one would carry at least eight loaves of bread. They considered this to be a "nine." This custom is still practiced here in Moghulistan today.

In those days, there was a khan descended from Ilkhan named Yulduz Khan. He had two sons. Both of them predeceased their father, but one of them had a son and the other a daughter. He married those grandchildren to each other. They had a son. Around that time, Yulduz Khan died, and his grandson also died, but the grandson's wife lived. This woman became the leader of her people. Her name was Alanqoa.

Alanqoa was widowed and now unmarried. One night, a light as bright as the sun shone through the smoke hole in her yurt. It took on the form of a young man and joined with Alanqoa. She took him into her bed and became pregnant.

When the high officials learned she was pregnant, they began to murmur. Alanqoa said to them, "I am known for my chastity and honesty. I am no harlot, no mean woman. A light entered the yurt through the smoke hole, took on the form of a young man, and lay with me. I got pregnant."

{19} Thinking that the light might be ʿAli, or perhaps Gabriel, they said, "This is the perfection of God's power, just as it happened to Mary, when Jesus was born! Such a remarkable act is a mere trifle to the Lord. It is just as the noble verses say, GOD DOES WHATSOEVER HE WILL [3:40] and DECREES WHATSOEVER HE DESIRES [5:1]! When sun and moon are joined in the house of Aries and are conjoined in the sixth degree, it is possible for such things to happen." They brought these proofs of the sages and philosophers to bear, so as to lend the cast of truth to Alanqoa's story and prove it by analogy. That is, they explained it away through flimsy implications and rude contortions. This is how the story is told in the *Garden of Purity* and other works.

Nevertheless, in response to the story of Alanqoa, your humble scribbler, despite his many shortcomings, has drawn back a curtain of meaning and illuminated it. I have revealed the meanings hidden in this house of secrecy and written them upon the page. The explanation is this: those khans and kings who traced their lineage back to Alanqoa and who entered the community of Islam, such as Tughluq Timur Khan, Amir Timur Kuragan, and their descendants, all said with pride, "We are among the progeny of the chaste Alanqoa, whom no son of Adam took into his possession! As has been narrated, she became pregnant by the light, and several months later, Bodonchar [*Buzanjir*] Khan was born. We are his descendants." They believed the light to have been ʿAli, or perhaps Gabriel. Such nonsensical beliefs and stories are all far from credible—they are sacrilegious nonsense. ʿAli died in the fortieth year of the Hijra. It is known from histories that Alanqoa lived after ʿAli. Moreover, Alanqoa's country was Qarashahr,[7] and she held a high status among her people, the Qalmaqs, and their religion. They had not come to know God, the Prophet, and the Companions or been brought to the faith. They might not even have heard His blessed name. The religion of this people was simply the worship of the sun and moon.{20} If they followed jinns and demons and drowned themselves in ignorance, then why would this light be given to such fools? The Mongol tribes first accepted Islam after the year 600 of the Hijra, as all of the peoples of the world know from history. They were not people of the Book. This polytheist woman's marriage was not permissible by the Shariah.

If we did suppose that ʿAli miraculously made this polytheist woman a Muslim, and then copulation took place, it would still be mere speculation. It would not be proven either way, nor would it be a convincing argument according to the Shariah. Moreover, ʿAli never went anywhere but Iraq. People who suggest that this sacred personage miraculously left his tomb, transformed into light, and then took on the shape of a human being and became the bedmate of this infidel woman are nothing but believers in reincarnation. (The Mongols believe that the spirit casts off its own corporeal existence and then is transferred into another body, and so goes about from body to body. Some of the people of China and all Hindus believe in this too. Some Shiites and mystics are inclined to this school of thought as well, even though holding this sort of belief is nothing but blasphemy. The great master and scholarly imam, Ibn Ḥazm al-Ẓahiri, the master of heresiography, and others have written in their books that this sort of belief is absolutely prohibited.)

Moreover, a woman bearing a child without the contribution of a man is an absurdity and utterly irrational. Apart from Mary bt. Imran, this has never happened to any woman. Jesus had no father, but was born by Mary, and this is a miracle. It is specific to Jesus. It is not permitted to anyone else. Some scholarly imams also refer to Mary as a "prophet." They explain that, if she were not a prophet, then God would not have addressed her and spoken to her with his own speech. Adam had no father or mother. He was created by God's perfect power. Jesus had no father. He was born from his mother. Apart from these two, it is forbidden for any human being or living creature to be born without a mother and father.{21} God in His ancient wisdom made His perfect power manifest and brought the order of the world into being according to a single plan. It is impossible for there to be any deviation from God's plan, any event or act beyond God's plan. As the Quran says, YOU WILL FIND NO ALTERATION IN THE WONT OF GOD. [48:23]

That being the case, there is no doubt whatsoever of this story's falseness and unlawfulness. Those who tell this story and who hold such beliefs are apostates, cursed in their deviance from the path of belief and the method of deductive reasoning. That they draw their knowledge from anyone other than Gabriel and the prophets is forbidden. After the Seal of the Prophets, no person can be a prophet. With these proofs, it is demonstrated that Alanqoa never said, "A light appeared in the smoke hole of the yurt, and I found him attractive. I became pregnant. This is how Bodonchar Khan was born." That is nonsense.

The women of the Mongols know what is licit and what is permitted. Indeed, the Mongols believe, regarding marriage, that when a woman about to marry a man is a virgin or a widow, first the lama (their mullah who performs the wedding) will make her his wife for a night and take possession of her, and then hand her over to her husband. This is their wedding. For this reason, it is written, their lamas never marry.

It is stated in histories that the Mongols marry their own fathers' wives. So one of Chinggis Khan's wives, after Chinggis Khan's death, was married to his son, Tolui Khan, and they had two children. When this Alanqoa also became pregnant through adultery, the Mongols objected and complained, "This child is born out of adultery. Why should we make him our leader and follow him?" In order to combat these objections, such tales about that woman were passed around—and there is an *ayah* about women in the Holy Word. They reassured themselves with such lies and tricks.

Historians, at that time, also honored and respected their leaders, so they would write that their great king was among the descendants of khans and kings born from a woman who became pregnant from light. For this reason, whatever king happened to come to power, they would flatter them with such stories.{22} Thereby those kings gave themselves genealogies going back to such unworthy deeds and even took pride in them. GOD KNOWS THE TRUTH.

* * *

Let us return to our story. Alanqoa bore three sons. The youngest was named Bodonchar. He was an enlightened and wise king, just and prosperous. He did good deeds and established fine institutions. It is said that he was acquainted with Amir Abu Muslim Marwazi. We know from this that he was a contemporary of Amir Abu Muslim Marwazi. Bodonchar Khan's son was Buqa Khan. His son was Dumnay Khan. Dumnay Khan begat two daughters and two sons. One was named Qabil. Another was named Qajuli. Chinggis Khan's genealogy traces back to Qajuli, son of Dumnay Khan.

One night, Qajuli had a dream. He told his father about what he had dreamt. His dream was that a sun rose from under his older brother, Qabil Khan's, robes and hung in the sky. It illuminated all the world and then set. A series of other suns followed it. Each of these shone in turn, and then set in turn. Finally, when the last bright star had risen, another world-illuminating sun rose from beneath his own robes, and it shone its light upon all the world. Then this too set. But then a number of suns appeared, one after another, and each shone in its own direction. So it remained for a long time. When Qajuli woke up, he realized it was a dream, but it turned out that his father, Dumnay, had had the same one.

After some reflection, Dumnay Khan gathered the high officials and dream interpreters and told them all about his son's dream. They put their minds to it, and then presented their interpretation: "From the line of Qabil Khan will come one splendid king, and the whole world will submit to him and take shelter in his rule. Those that follow will be his children. After these are born, each of them will rule in some direction. Next, from the line of Qajuli, who had this dream, there will come a grand king indeed. His descendants will follow in his footsteps and bring order to the entire world." They raised their voices in praise.

The khan replied,{23} "Write this interpretation down in a letter. Let it say, 'After me, let Qabil Khan and his descendants reign. Qajuli and his progeny shall be their ministers, so let them learn the art of statecraft.' " They composed such a letter, placed upon it the seals of the khan and the high officials, and put it in the treasury. This letter remained in the royal treasury up until the days of Sultan Abu Saʿid Mirza, and these orders remained in place. (In the languages of the Qalmaqs and Mongols, they call such a royal letter a *faramin* or *yar.*)

Qabil Khan's son was Bartan Khan. His son was Suhu Bahadur. His son was the hero Temujin, called Chinggis Khan.

0:2 Chinggis Khan and His Descendants

That World-Conquering King Chinggis Khan, Who Was the Khan of Khans and Leader of the Mongol Khans in Arabia, Persia, and the Entire East; His Conquest and Domination; His Days of Fortune and Era of Rule; an Enumeration of His Descendants; and How His Generals and Commanders Gained Their Independence

THE MOST ELOQUENT writers of histories have related that, as a general rule, the true Lord (GREAT IS HE!) by His power and will sometimes grants victory to the pious faithful over the infidel, and sometimes to the impious infidel over the faithful.

Let us consider an example. In the year 549 [1154], the hero Temujin was born. When he was twelve years old, his father passed away. He was raised by his mother. Eventually he came to subjugate the leaders of the Jurjut and Nayman to the east and north, as well as those of Turkestan, who were called the Ong Khan, Dayang Khan, Gur Khan, Toqa Beg, and Merkit. He became ruler and master of their people. At this time, Temujin turned forty-nine years old, and his fortune increased. In the year 598 [1201/2] (597 [1200/1]), he united the Mongols and had a nine-footed throne made. They raised him up upon it, elevated him as their ruler, and titled him *chinggis qa'an*. (The title *chinggis qa'an* in Mongolian apparently means "khan of khans," which is to say, "king of kings.") Thereafter no one called him Temujin, and he became known instead as Chinggis *Qa'an*. The word *qa'an* by common error turned into *qaghan*. His capital was at a place called Karakorum Kelüren. Today this city has disappeared. In all likelihood, it is somewhere in Qalmaq territory.

{24} In those days, the khan of Cathay was called the Altan Khan. His capital was at Khanbaligh. (In Chinese, Khanbaligh is called Zhongdu. Whichever fortunate khan put his capital at Khanbaligh was called the Altan Khan.) Chinggis Khan ordered his armies to attack the Altan Khan, and they captured many cities and put them to ruin, as the khans of the Mongols and of Cathay held an ancient vendetta. Ultimately the Altan Khan could not match him, but instead secured a peace through marriage. By Chinggis's command, he submitted, and he married his daughter to Chinggis Khan. This satisfied Chinggis, and he took the Altan Khan's daughter as one of his wives. He left Cathay in peace and returned to his own country.

The eastern boundary of Chinggis Khan's territory was Khanbaligh, and to the north, the city of Kazan. (The reason people know Kazan as Tatar is simply that, when Chinggis Khan conquered Kazan, he levied Tatar men as soldiers and garrisoned them there, where they settled and ruled. This is almost certainly the reason it came to be known by the name Tatar. Later, it is said, when Amir Timur Kuragan conquered it, he forced those Tatars to migrate to his own lands.) The western boundary extended to Egypt, Syria, Baghdad, Mosul, and Rum;[1] and the southern to Azerbaijan, the River Sind, Kabul, Badakhshan, Tatarstan, Tibet, and the country of the Uyghurs.

Chinggis Khan lived for seventy-three years. For twenty-five of those, he was the sovereign ruler of most of the inhabited world. He visited such absolute destruction upon it that the most eloquent of pens is insufficient to record it. A hadith has been transmitted on this matter: AND THE HOUR WILL NOT BE ESTABLISHED TILL YOU FIGHT WITH PEOPLE WHOSE FACES LOOK LIKE SHIELDS COATED WITH LEATHER—that is, "The Day of Judgment will not be established until battle has been done with a people, and that people's faces will be broad, as though something has been fastened to their faces, and their faces will be like shields."[2] Surely this indicates Chinggis Khan and Hulegu of the Mongols and Tatars, who in the year 654 [1256], during the reign of Caliph al-Mustaʿsim, subjugated the whole of the lands of Islam. Chinggis's raids and Hulegu's attacks are said to rank among the afflictions and tribulations visited by Gog and Magog.

There is another hadith: AT THE END OF TIME THE DESCENDANTS OF QANTURA WILL COME.[3] This means that, when the End Times come, some of the descendants of Qantura will come. "The descendants of Qantura" certainly indicates the Turks. Qantura is the name of a woman who was the great mother of all Turks (and Mongols).

{25} In the revered *Mishkat*, another hadith is transmitted:[4] THE HOUR WILL NOT BE ESTABLISHED TILL A FIRE WILL COME OUT OF THE LAND OF HIJAZ, AND IT WILL THROW LIGHT ON THE NECKS OF THE CAMELS AT BUSRA. And it is said that this fire "will be visible on the steps in SIX HUNDRED FIFTY-FOUR." The 654 it refers to is a sign of Hulegu's subjugation of the lands of Islam. It is said that there is a mountain in Busra, and they call it the Camel's Neck. When it says that the Day of Judgment will not come until the Camel's Neck can be seen clearly by a fire lit in the Hejaz, this is a proof of the fires of Chinggis's and Hulegu's massacres.

It is written in historians' books that the pandemonium of Chinggis Khan is considered a greater disaster than the Flood in the age of Noah. The reason given is that there were fewer people back then, whereas in the present age people have cultivated much of the world, and their numbers have reached their zenith. Another is that, at that time, most people were ignorant of monotheism, while later on Muslim believers, scholars, and shaykhs were many. In the holy city of Bukhara, there lived Imam Abu Ḥafiẓ Kabir and hundreds of other clerics. In Khwarazm, Shaykh Najmuddin Kubra led more than 60,000 followers, all of whom were Sufi guides in their own right, so they called him "the creator of saints." He told some of his followers, "Flee to some other land. A fire is blazing to the east, and it wishes to burn everything to the west. This is a great tribulation, a disaster such as never will befall this community again." Some of them implored him, "If you pray, surely it will turn this disaster back." But the great shaykh replied, "This is one of those disasters that cannot be repelled with prayer."

There were many shaykhs and great scholars like these in every city, who were *ṣaḥib duʿas*[5] beyond praise or description, and all of them were martyred in Chinggis Khan's unspeakable massacres.

* * *

Jamshid was the king who established the laws and customs that governed rulership in days of yore. After the reign of the Seal of the Prophets, it was Chinggis Khan who set the laws, customs, and punishments, and the precepts of his descendants' *yasa* and *yosun*, their *yarghu* and *qanun*,[6] have since been arranged as examples in history books, regarded as instructions for administration, and made models for statecraft. By Chinggis's order,{26}

Qarachar Noyan was appointed his minister, and so was the Muslim Muḥammad Beg Yalavach.

Chinggis had four sons—Jochi Khan, Chagatai Khan, Ogedei Khan, and Tolui Khan—among whom he divided his realm. Jochi Khan predeceased Chinggis by six months. He left behind eighteen sons. All of Turkestan and the Dasht-i Qipchaq had been his domain. His eldest son, Berke Khan, was made his successor. When Chinggis Khan returned home from Arab Iraq, Jochi Khan gave him, among other things, 100,000 horses as a present, 10,000 horses each of a single color and kind.

Chinggis made his third son, Ogedei, his successor. The rest of his sons were made vassals to Ogedei Qa'an. He gave all of the decrees and instructions for administration that his ancestors had left behind to Chagatai Khan, along with Qarachar Noyan, and assigned him the special responsibility of compiling the rules of the *yasa*.

Tolui Khan also left four sons: Mongke Khan, Khubilai Khan, Hulegu Khan, and Ariq Boke. After Ogedei Khan departed this world for the next, Chinggis's capital was Mongke's lot. He raised levies from two tribes, readying 120,000 soldiers under Khubilai Khan's command, and sent them east to attack the Altan Khan. Khubilai Khan led his great army against the Altan Khan, and while he was sometimes triumphant and sometimes defeated, in the end, he won the war.

* * *

The Emperor of China has a history book called the *Gangjang*,[7] which apparently means "History of Khans." The Chinese reckon their history from a man named Taihaofus[8] of the lineage of Fung, who ruled 2,700 years after the time of Adam and 3,400 before the Hijra. The one they call Fung is surely the Fudak of our histories. This was Fudak, son of Turk, son of Japheth. Fung فونک and Fudak فودک are surely the name of a single person, though it may have come to be spelled erroneously.

The beginning of the history of the khans of China started with Taihaofus of the lineage of Fung, after which the kingship passed from one clan to another, twenty-five in total. As of today, in the year 1325 [1907–8], 254 people have been khan over the course of more than 4,800 years.

In their history books, they call the prophet Noah "Lu Wang."[9] Even today, the people of China are firm in their belief in the "Shariah and religion" of Lu Wang and will not deviate to any other religion.{27} "Taihaofus" might also refer to Japheth, son of Noah. But they also call Taihaofus "Fu Wang," and they begin their history from his day, divided into twenty-five dynasties. In each dynasty—which is to say, each family—twenty or thirty people ruled, or sometimes only five or six. Some ruled for seven or eight centuries, others for only two or three, and some for just twenty or thirty years. For example, in the twenty-second dynasty, the third Song dynasty, Taizu Shingdi Huangdi ruled for seventeen years. This made him a contemporary of the Abbasid Caliph al-Qadir.[10] Eighteen generations of this family ruled for 321 years. In the end, after Zhao Di Shingdi Huangdi had ruled for just two years, Khubilai Khan, son of Tolui Khan, son of Chinggis Khan, of the Mongol khans, led his great army into the land of Beijing, won the war, and subjugated it entirely. The Song khan could not match him, so went into hiding. Perhaps he killed himself.

The people of Beijing called Khubilai "Aiwang." Aiwang, or Khubilai, son of Tolui, of the twenty-third dynasty, established his capital at Peking, or Beijing, and ruled for fifteen years, during which he demonstrated his justice and wisdom. His authority extended across the country of China, and he brought it to submission. In the end, he passed away, and his son succeeded him on the throne. His descendants were called the sons of Aiwang. So did nine generations of the sons of Aiwang rule for eighty-eight years. After that, Taizu of the Ming, the twenty-fourth dynasty, led a rebellion and became khan himself.[11] When he first sat on the throne, Amir Timur was in the middle of his reign. Seventeen generations of this family ruled for 270 years. However, they remained in service to Mongol khans, gave them tribute, and welcomed them.

Eventually the Mongols and Tatars formed an alliance and conquered Beijing. Shunzhi [r. 1643–1661], son of Taizong, of the Manchu lineage of the Mongols, was crowned and placed on the throne in Beijing. To this day, the khanship remains within this family. They named this clan the Great Qing. From Shunzhi Khan of the twenty-fifth dynasty, the Great Qing, to Guangxu Khan in the present day, nine of its members have ruled over the course of 262 years.[12]

This is as it is written in the Chinese history *Gangjang*, the "History of Khans." Its translator is Mullah Qurban ʿAli Ḥajji of Tarbaghatai, who inquired with a mullah well versed in Chinese history about khans past and the religions and sects to which they belonged,[{28}] and made the translation on that basis. In it are written the names of all of the khans from Lu Wang—that is,

Noah—with their dates of rule, and how many ruled in each dynasty, and in which years they ended. It also says which prophets were contemporaries of which khans, from thousands of years after Adam to thousands of years before or after Muḥammad, and in the age of kings, which kings were around during which khans' reigns. His compilation makes the history of Beijing commensurable with the history of Islam, matching times up correctly. Your humble author has merely reproduced some of his words on this page.

* * *

Let us return to our story: When Mongke Khan sent Khubilai eastward, he also placed his younger brother at the head of 120,000 fully armed and equipped soldiers and ordered him to march westward against the Abbasid Caliphs. Hulegu conquered Mawarannahr and Khorasan, and separately subjugated Rukn al-Din Khorshah [r. 1255–1256] of Kohistan, the country of the Ismailis, before marching toward Arab Iraq. Mawlana Naṣiruddin Ṭusi [1201–1274] was alive in that time. Hulegu took him into his service. He collected astronomical observations into the *Ilkhanid Ephemeris* [*Zij-i Ilkhani*]. He made many other contributions.

Wherever there were wise mullahs or scholars, Hulegu brought them to his court, gave them favor, and kept them near. He also brought Christian scholars as well as wise men from the imperial court of China. He had the Quran translated into Mongolian, and the Bible, and also the book called the *Shanguya*, from the one called Sakyamuni whom the people of China believe to be a prophet.[13] They were strangers to the religion of Islam. They created many things.

There are many stories about the exploits of Hulegu and Khubilai, but here we are concerned with recalling the khans of Moghulistan, so we will not discuss them in detail.

Hulegu Khan made his capital in Iran and then conquered Baghdad. At that time, the thirty-sixth Abbasid caliph was al-Mustaʿṣim [r. 1242–1258]. Hulegu had molten gold and silver poured into his mouth and those of his two sons. The Abbasid caliphs who had ruled for 522 years in fortune, Hulegu destroyed in a moment's fury. The destruction was so extreme that it could never come to pass again. They took control of the treasuries, hidden and otherwise, and of the government.{29} It was the year 656 [1258]. Wherever members of the Abbasid family were, they found them, and wiped them out totally. They were concerned that thousands of Abbasids were legitimate contenders for the throne and imprisoned them, so that some were even born into and grew up in captivity. They killed them all [by drowning them in a deep river]. (Per the customs of the Abbasid caliphate, if someone needed to act as caliph, they would remove him from prison, crown him, and place him on the throne. If he were dismissed from the caliphate, then they would blind him with a needle, place a wooden bowl in his hands, and leave him sitting at the city gate or along the road. He would then live out his life begging from passersby.)

Hulegu conquered many lands of Arabia—Egypt, Syria, Aleppo, Mosul, etc.—and turned his attention to Azerbaijan. He established his capital in Iran. He ruled for nine years and was buried in Iran.

Then his son Abagha Khan [r. 1265–1282] sat upon the throne, and then his son Arghun Khan [r. 1284–1291]. Next was Aḥmad Khan [r. 1282–1284], son of Hulegu, who was a pious Muslim. Three years later, he passed on to the eternal world. Next was Geikhatu [r. 1291–1295], son of Hulegu, who brought glory to Islam once again. Then Baidu [r. 1295], son of Taraqai, son of Hulegu, ascended the throne. He was ignorant of Islam.

At that time, the ruler of Herat, Amir Nawruz [d. 1297], son of Arghun, wrote to Ghazan Khan [r. 1295–1304], son of Arghun, "If you accept the religion of Islam, then we shall attack Baidu." Ghazan Khan accepted the offer and became a Muslim. He overthrew Baidu and seized his lands. Among the Mongols, Islam was revealed, and the rays of Islam's light shone clearly upon his own countenance.

Then his son (younger brother) Öljeitü became known as Sultan Muḥammad Khudabanda [r. 1304–1316]. Islam prospered more each day. Then his son, Sultan Saʿid Ghazi Bahadur Khan [r. 1317–1335], sat upon the throne and ruled for eighteen years before passing from this world to the next at the age of thirty-two. It was the year 736 [1335]. He had no sons. The officials he had appointed to rule each territory all became independent, and none of them would submit to another. They became petty kings.

In summary, the territory of Chinggis Khan had stretched from China and Khanbaligh in the east to Egypt and Syria in the west, and from Kazan in the north to the River Sind, Tibet, and Uyghur in the south. His descendants up to Jahan Timur Khan [Jalayirid, r. 1339–1340], twenty in all, ruled this territory for 148 years. From Chinggis Khan onward, nine of the khans of his lineage ruled those great lands for ninety-five years in ignorance of Islam and instead by the law [*yasaq*] of the Mongols and Qalmaqs.

Later on, as the hadith says, YOU ARE THE COMPANY YOU KEEP: they came to accept Islam and issued their proclamations in accordance with the strictures of the Shariah. And the petty kings and their generals and ministers established their rule in various places: Shaykh Abu Isḥaq [r. 1343–1354] in Persia; the clan of Muẓaffar in Khorasan; Amir Choban b. Amir Tüläk [r. 1316–1327] in Turan, Solduz, and Syria and Damascus within Rum; and Amir Ḥasan Buzurg b. Ariq Boke b. Amir Ilgan Bahadur [d. 1356] in Arab Iraq and Baghdad.[14] The line of Ilganid kings traces back to him.{30} These generals and scholars were also of Mongol descent and the Qalmaq tribes, but they are known in history as pious Muslims and just defenders of the Shariah. The Mongol sultans thus ruled as sovereigns over these great countries for 200 years, until the rule of the Chinggisids came to a close, and kingship passed instead to the Timurids.

Yet the number of people who died in the unspeakable massacres perpetrated by Chinggis Khan and Hulegu Khan cannot be conceived of by even the most intelligent minds, save in that world in which the martyrs dwell. If anyone should wish to know more, I direct them to the *Garden of Purity.*

However, in the land of Moghulistan, Chinggisids ruled in the line of Tughluq Timur Khan [r. 1347–1363] all the way to Ismail Khan [r. 1666–1669, 1670–1680] and Muḥammad Amin Khan [of Turfan, r. 1682–1694], who governed there until the year 1120 [1708]. Meanwhile, in the Dasht-i Qipchaq and Turkestan, it is written that high-ranking princes and generals, including among the Torghuts and Qalmaqs who submitted to Russia, and many imperial consorts and princes under the emperors of China, were also Chinggisids.

* * *

In the year 736 [1335/36], when Sultan Saʿid Bahadur Ghazi Khan passed away, the great Amir Timur Kuragan came into being. In the year 771 [1369/70], he was enthroned at Balkh. He conquered much of the inhabited world, from Mawarannahr to Iran, Turan, Persia, Baghdad, Rum, Egypt, Syria, and Damascus, even to Homs, Baalbek, Anatolia, and Isfahan, south to Hindustan and north to Turkestan and Kazan. He united all of those petty kings under one rule.

Amir Timur Kuragan's genealogy traces back to Chinggis Khan's own ancestors, which is to say, to the Qalmaq peoples: Amir Timur b. Amir Taraghai b. Amir Tökäl b. Ilingiz Noyan Bahadur b. Amir Ichil b. Amir Qarachar Noyan

Bahadur b. Amir Sawganjin Bahadur b. Amir Damjin Barlas Bahadur b. Qajuli Bahadur b. Dumnai Khan, who was Amir Timur's eighth grandfather as well as the brother of Chinggis Khan's fourth grandfather. Qajuli was appointed minister to Qabil Khan [r. ca. 1120], so no matter what a great king Timur became, he remained in the servile rank of a minister. Indeed, several generations{31} passed in this status, in which they were unable to issue proclamations or to call themselves khan or king.

Timur's capital was at Samarqand. He was originally born in Shahrisabz, and when Tughluq Timur Khan conquered Mawarannahr, he entered the khan's service. He achieved the rank of his forefathers as general and minister and was appointed then to serve the khan's son Ilyas Khoja Khan, who took him to Kunduz. Amir Timur sent 90,000 soldiers in battle against Toqtamish Khan [fl. 1375–1405] of the Qipchaq khans. They set him to flight but captured him. They took him to a place where in midsummer, from sunset to the twilight's last gleaming, to the break of dawn, there was no way to perform the nighttime prayer. When he subjugated the people of Damascus, Syria, and Isfahan, he visited unspeakable massacres and plunder upon them. Then he conquered the lands of Hindustan. He ruled those aforementioned lands for thirty-six years and brought all of their haughty kings to heel. To the east, his rule extended to Moghulistan. Historians cipher the years of his life with the word "pain" [*alam*].[15] He died in the year 807 [1404/5] and was buried in Samarqand. From the time of the Prophet to the present, no other great king of the line of Mongol khans has been such a pious Muslim. His bravery and quarrelsomeness were excessive and his rage hard and quick, yet he was not totally unenlightened. After he died, Saint Bahauddin Naqshband [1318–1389] declared, *Timur died, carrying faith*—that is, "Timur died, and he took his faith with him." The words of the saints are the words of the Lord.

It is said that there were many great scholars and shaykhs in those blessed days, among them Amir Sayyid ʿAli b. Muḥammad al-Hamadānī [1314–1384], Bahauddin Naqshband, Khoja Ḥafiẓ Shirazi [ca. 1315–1390], the Erudite Taftazani [1322–1390], Amir Sayyid Sharif, and the Erudite Jurjani [b. 1339]. MAY GOD SANCTIFY THEIR HEARTS. Nevertheless, all of the people of Damascus, Syria, and Rum, and all of the scholars and historians of Arabia, including Baghdad and Aleppo, who wrote Arabic-language histories such as the *History* of Imam Kardari, the *History* of the scholar Ibn Khaldun [1332–1382], and the *History* of ibn ʿArabshah Bukhari [1389–1450], do not count Amir

Timur among the people of Islam, but rather criticize him for his Shiism and infidelity. Given that all of Amir Timur's wars were within the Islamic lands and that they resulted in such atrocities as the massacre of scholars, he is demonstrated to have been one of most tyrannical of tyrants and most sinful of sinners. When Timur conquered the people of Syria and laid siege to Damascus, he visited such unspeakable massacres upon them: after the slaughter he ordered each of his soldiers to cut the heads off of two Muslims and bring them hither into his sight. Such destruction and ruin did he bring! From the heads of those Muslims they made 124{32} towers of skulls. Each tower of skulls was made from the heads of 9,000 people. Later, when Timur attacked Anatolia in the land of Rum, he deposed Bayezid Yildirim [r. 1389–1402], had coins struck in his own name, and had sermons read in his honor. Then in Isfahan he ordered the murder of every man and woman, old and young alike. Countless men, women, and children were put to the sword.

At that time, a general at Amir Timur's court, who was one of the wise men of that age, delivered a petition to him: "Your highness, your lowly servant is ignorant. Yet he hopes that you might display your kingly grace and show a little compassion and mercy." With these gentle words, the general made a great effort to prevent the shedding of children's blood, and yet Amir Timur showed no mercy. Rather, some thousands of boys and girls were attending the king, and Timur ordered his soldiers standing by to attack the children. All of these innocent youths died under their horses' hooves. Amir Timur's mercilessness and bloodthirstiness may be known from this.

In the Six Books [*Kutub al-sittah*], where it is recorded: "The Turks—with eyes small, noses low, and faces wide and flat like platters, but high, as though two things were squeezing them together"—it surely conforms to the appearance of the Mongol kings and their peoples.[16] Moreover, one of the miracles of the Prophet is the verse in which it states, NOR DOES HE SPEAK OUT OF CAPRICE; IT IS NAUGHT BUT A REVELATION REVEALED. [53:3–4] That is, no king made war in the lands of Islam and brought destruction and ruin upon them, save for Chinggis Khan, Hulegu Khan, and Amir Timur. (Since the time of the Prophet, there have been three tyrants in Muslim form. The first was the tyrant Ḥajjaj b. Yusuf [r. 661–714]. The second was Abu Muslim Marwazi. The third was Amir Timur Kuragan. Countless wise men and pious Muslims were put to death because of these tyrants, more than can be conceived of. Accounts of them are recorded in the history books.)

When Amir Timur was besieging Syria and Damascus and was preparing to massacre their people, the author of *The Protected Fortress* [*Ḥiṣn al-Ḥaṣin*], Imam Jazari [1260–1338], fled from there, took refuge in some place, and composed his book while busying himself with the prayers handed down from the Prophet.[17] Meanwhile, the Muslims of Damascus had piled stones against the city gates, shutting them tightly, and fled in terror to their refuges.

At that time, Imam Jazari saw the Prophet in a dream, and he importuned him, "Oh, Prophet of God! These enemies have achieved victory over us. Would you pray for us, your community?" The Prophet raised his two hands in prayer, so high that the paleness of his armpits showed. In less than three days,{33} their enemies had abandoned the siege of Syria and left. This meant the Muslims' liberation, or so it is recorded in *The Protected Fortress*. This is a proof of Amir Timur's enmity toward Islam. Otherwise, the Prophet would not have raised his hands in prayers on behalf of these people. This is because, according to the Shariah, praying for harm to the Muslims is not permissible. THE ERUDITE AL-SUYUTI SAID: "IN THE YEAR 808, TIMUR THE LAME DIED. HE WENT TO HELL AND A TERRIBLE FATE." That is, in the Erudite al-Suyuti's [1445–1505] own words, "In the year 808 [1405], Timur the Lame died. He went to Hell and a terrible fate." He also records that 400 great scholars from Mawarannahr were in agreement. Yet the true Creator, in His ancient wisdom, knows the truth.

The *Selection of Chronicles* [*Muntakhab at-Tawarikh*] states that Amir Timur was enthroned in 771 [1369]. Eighteen of his descendants ruled the lands that he conquered for 160 years. Then rule over that country passed to the Uzbeks under Muḥammad Shibani Khan [1451–1501] of the line of Jochi. The reason for their being called Uzbeks and Shibani is this: Chinggis Khan's first son, Jochi Khan, had eighteen sons. His sixth son's name was Shiban. His fourth grandson was named Uzbek. When he came of age and grew up, his fortunes rose, and he took control of Ferghana and Mawarannahr and established his rule there. He was both a pious Muslim and a just ruler concerned for the people. He reigned for fifty-four years and gave great relief to the common people. For this reason, the people came to use the name Uzbek. Thereafter the descendants of Jochi too called themselves by the name Uzbek. Uzbek Khan's grandson Muḥammad Khan Shibani became king of Khorasan. Because he was of the line of Shiban, he called himself Shibani. Similarly, the descendants of Chagatai Khan were called the Chagataids.

Amir Timur Kuragan had four royal sons. The first was Jahangir Mirza [1356–1376]. He died the year that Amir Timur took the throne. The second was ʿUmar Shaykh Bahadur [r. 1393–1394]. He was entrusted with Persia. An arrow took his life while Timur was still alive. The third was Miran Shah Mirza [1366–1408]. This son was entrusted with Persian and Arab Iraq and the lands all the way to Syria. The fourth son was Shahrukh Mirza [r. 1405–1447].{34} He ruled the land of Khorasan. Those lands that his father had conquered and ruled for six years, Shahrukh ruled for forty-two, and justly at that. He held a lifelong respect for scholars. His capital was in Herat.

Then his son, Mirza Ulughbeg [r. 1447–1449], succeeded him and established his capital at Samarqand, because in his father's time he had been the governor of Samarqand. No king has been a greater scholar than Ulughbeg. According to the *Collection of Secrets* [*Jamiʿ al-Rumuz*], he was a classmate of Mawlana Shamsuddin Muḥammad. He was extensively versed in every field of the sciences. He gathered together all of the worthy wise men and astronomers of Hindustan, investigated the configuration of the stars, the planets, and the heavenly spheres; the hours of their ascensions and declensions; their timing and positions; and their configurations both fortunate and inauspicious, and compiled them with absolute earnestness and care. He collected all of these observations into a book he called the *Ephemeris of the Kuragani* [*Zij-i Kuragani*]. He gave a great gift to the world.

At this time, Ulughbeg rode west with a great retinue to Iraq. He appointed his son, ʿAbdullaṭif Mirza [r. 1449–1450], as his successor while he was away for two years on the march. In the meantime, power had corrupted his son's mind, and he seized the throne from his father and dared to proclaim himself king in his own right. ʿAbdullaṭif readied his soldiers, rode out to head his father's army off, and engaged him in battle. Ultimately, he was victorious over his father and ordered his imprisonment. He took possession of the treasuries and issued a proclamation saying, "I will do nothing whatsoever that transgresses the Shariah. Although according to the law we are father and son, I owe him no kindness."

At this time, a man named ʿAbbas appeared, and he said to ʿAbdullaṭif, "Mirza Ulughbeg killed my father without reason or guilt." ʿAbdullaṭif sent this matter to the legal scholars and obtained from them a fatwa. He informed his father of the contents of the fatwa, which stated that the situation merited retaliation, and told ʿAbbas to take his revenge. One night, he took

Ulughbeg to some secret place and killed him. Historians mark this event with the chronogram *ʿAbbas Killed.*[18] Less than six months later, ʿAbdullaṭif Mirza himself was killed by his own men.

[During the reign of Ulughbeg], Uways Khan's [r. of Moghulistan, 1418–1421, 1425–1429] son Yunus Khan [ca. 1416–1487, r. 1462–1487] fell into his hands. They took him to Shiraz and forced him into exile. After he attained his majority, he worked as an ordinary laborer and was known as Master Yusuf.{35} Thirty years passed before, in the time of Sultan Abu Saʿid Mirza b. Sultan Muḥammad Mirza b. Miran Shah Mirza b. Amir Timur Kuragan [r. 1451–1469], someone was sent to Shiraz to bring him back. In a place in Samarqand called Bagh-i Zaghan, they placed him on the throne.

Sultan Abu Saʿid Mirza said a number of notable things. He said, "May you henceforth see me as a friend, and see yourselves not as servants. In the hope that you will act as good subjects should, I send you as khans to your native lands. Do not send soldiers against me." Then he gathered 12,000 Mongols as his companions, armed them, and set out for Moghulistan.

He also said, "I am a different sort of ruler. During the reign of my ancestor Amir Timur Kuragan, he would imprison a khan, give him food to eat and clothes to wear and whatever other essentials, and issue decrees both in the name of whatever khan and of Amir Timur. If he had not done that, the nobles would never have submitted." This remained the mode of rule up until the reign of Sultan Abu Saʿid Mirza. Thenceforth they wrote instead "Sultan Abu Saʿid Mirza Khan" on the decrees. To the present day, his descendants have used the title khan, including Khudayar Khan and Malla Khan [r. 1858–1872]. He also came to be related to Yunus Khan. Yunus Khan, in a spirit of generosity, married one of his daughters to Sultan Abu Saʿid Mirza's son Umar Shaykh Mirza. Their son was Ẓahiruddin Muḥammad Babur [1483–1530]. I will need to relate some of Babur's story later on.

Sultan Abu Saʿid Mirza was an honorable and brave king, generous, thoughtful, and clement. It is said that his ideals led him to act as a competent father to this world, and thus as a competent king upon the Earth. This is not something that any other king has done, or so they say. So he sat on the Timurid throne for sixteen years, and then his son, Umar Shaykh Mirza [r. 1469–1494], succeeded him in Ferghana and Mawarannahr and ruled for twenty-seven years. Next was his younger brother, Maḥmud Mirza [1494–1495]. Two years later the Uzbeks subjugated him and became the masters of Ferghana and Mawarannahr.

During the reign of Sultan Abu Saʿid Mirza, Sultan Ḥusayn Mirza b. Mirza Bayqara b. Umar Shaykh Bahadur b. Amir Timur Kuragan [r. 1469–1506] was the governor of Khorasan. Later, Sultan Ḥusayn Mirza came to the Timurid throne. He established his capital in Herat. He ruled for eight years over 444 territories in Persian Iraq, Isfahan, Persia, and Azerbaijan,{36} and then, upon succession from Sultan Abu Saʿid Mirza, as an independent king for thirty-eight years. During this era, many worthy scholars were gathered there, and their learning was exceptional. These included Mawlana Ḥusayn, Waiz Kashifi, Mawlana Muinuddin, Mavlavi Jami(, and Mavlavi ʿAbdurraḥman Ḥajji).

He lived for seventy-two years and passed away in the year 912 [1506/7]. Historians mark it with the chronogram *Khorasan*.[19] He begat eleven sons. His sons Badiʿuzzaman Mirza and Mirza Ḥusayn ruled jointly, but, as they say, OPPOSITES WILL NEVER BE JOINED, and companionship and government cannot be joined. Their generals divided into two parties, and factions emerged in the government.

At this time, the scion of the line of Jochi and of Uzbek Khan was known by many names, including Muḥammad Shah, Bakht Khan, Shah Beg Khan, and Muḥammad Khan Shibani. However, he is best known as Muḥammad Khan Shibani b. Shah Budagh b. Abulkhayr Khan b. Toqtamish Khan [1451–1510]. He subjugated all of Khorasan. He became master of its treasuries, its armies, even of its chaste women, its pious widows, its virgins of rare beauty, and the mothers and wives of the Timurid princes, who were the finest in the world in their age. They tore from them the curtain of chastity and lifted the veils from their beautiful faces. These Uzbek-ids and Dasht-i Qipchaq-ids set about doing all manner of lawful and unlawful things, such that the most eloquent of pens is insufficient to describe them.

So Sultan Ḥusayn Mirza's sons ran for their lives, and each fled to a different land. Most of their wives, children, and relations fell into the hands of the Uzbeks, who visited such hardships upon them. Twelve years later, Muḥammad Khan Shibani was killed by the Qizilbash, Ismail Safavi [r. 1501–1524]. The Qizilbashes then controlled Khorasan. Then Kuchum Khan b. Muḥammad Khan b. Abulkhayr Khan[20] contented himself with ruling Mawarannahr. Then his sons ʿAbdullah Khan, ʿAbdulʿaziz Khan, ʿAbdulaḥad Khayr Khan, Ḥaydar Muḥammad Khan, Imam Quli Khan, and Muḥammad Khan by turns came to rule in such lands as Bukhara, Samarqand, and Urgench.

Meanwhile, Ẓahiruddin Muḥammad Babur Padishah b. Umar Shaykh b. Sultan Abu Saᶜid Mirza b. Sultan Muḥammad Mirza b. Miran Shah Mirza b. Amir Timur Kuragan could no longer remain in Mawarannahr and Ferghana,{37} and so he fled to the lands of Ismail Safavi. With Safavi's aid, he became king of Ferghana and Mawarannahr. However, he could not maintain his position but instead went to Kabul and Ghazna, conquering them, and then Delhi, where he ruled for thirty-two years. In the year 905 [1499/50] he sat upon the throne. In 937 [1530/31] he passed away. Then his son, Humayun Padishah [r. 1530–1540], ascended the throne and added many of the lands of Hindustan to his domain. His descendants Akbar Shah, Alamgir, Aurangzeb, and Shah Jahan, all the way to Aḥmad Shah seventeen generations later, ruled that country for 360 years. In 1262 [1845], the lamp of their rule burned out. Yet many fine things remain as a testament to these great kings. May their good names be preserved until this world itself is extinct. Amen.

Now that our pen has reached the edge of the page, we note that our intention was to discuss the rulers of Moghulistan, and so we will refrain from continuing this story. Interested readers may consult the *Garden of Purity.*

Some of Babur's descendants, Chamash Bi and Narbuta Khan, came to rule over Ferghana and reclaim their father's bequest from the Uzbeks. They developed the country of Khoqand and made it their capital. Their descendants to Malla Khan and Khudayar Khan ruled in Ferghana until the year 1286 [1869]. Then Ferghana fell to the Russians. Khudayar Khan had been in the Holy Land, and on his return, they imprisoned him in Kabul. Another of Babur's descendants, Muẓaffar Khan b. Muḥammad ᶜAli Khan, was murdered in Korla on the orders of Yaᶜqub Beg.[21] We are not aware of any more Timurids living today. GOD KNOWS.

* * *

It was deemed necessary in this prolegomenon to the book for this disciplined, albeit stupid, hand to provide a brief conspectus of the stories of the famous kings who ruled in those great lands that for so long fell under the rule of the Mongol peoples and their descendants: Iran and Turan; Iraq, both Arab and Persian; Hindustan, Arabia, and Turkestan. If any reader should desire a more detailed account, then I direct them to the *Garden of Purity* and the *Tarikh-i Rashidi.* Our hope is to record those kings and amirs who ruled in the lands of Moghulistan. Therefore, we have inclined our pen to the stories of the rulers of Moghulistan and nudged it toward our original goal.

We mentioned earlier how Chinggis Khan divided his territory among his four sons.{38} The story is that Chinggis's second son, Chagatai, received the land east of the Amu River, including Mawarannahr and Ferghana, the lands of the Mongols and Tatars, and the ancient Uyghur and Nayman peoples. Chagatai Khan in turn divided these lands among his generals. (For this reason, the people living there became known as Chagatais.)

At that time, Bab Daghan Dughlat of the Dughlat tribe received Manglai Suya, and he was rewarded with three honors.[22] (In Mongolian, "Manglai Suya" apparently means "Facing the Sun.") They included the lands from Baghrash and Korla in the east; to Muztagh in the north; to Alay and Katta Daban in the west; and La'l Kan, Badakhshan, and Qarangghu Tagh in the south. These lands were his reward. The descendants of Bab Daghan ruled for many years within those borders. (The name Dughlat in Mongolian apparently means "twisted silver birch." Chinggis Khan's third grandfather, Qabul Khan, had eight sons. The sixth's name was Buljar. But he was lame, so they called him Dughlat or Lame Dughlat. All of the Dughlats are his descendants.)

0:3 The Dughlat Tribe and Its Amirs

The Exploits of the Commander-in-Chief Khudaydad b. Amir Bolaji Dughlat, and of His Children, and of the Princes and Begs of His Line Who Ruled the Seven Cities, and Their Fates

ONE OF BAB Daghan's grandsons, Amir Tüläk Dughlat, reigned in Kashgar, and another grandson, Amir Bolaji Dughlat, in Aqsu. Meanwhile, Chinggis Khan's sixth-generation grandson, Esan-Buqa Khan [r. 1310–ca. 1318], was on the throne, and he had two wives. Esan-Buqa Khan's senior wife was barren, while his junior wife became pregnant with the khan's child.

One day, the khan rode out to hunt (or battle) and did not return for a long time. While he was gone, an officer named Shiravul from the Dokhtoi tribe came bearing ninety gifts and hoping for an audience with the khan. He stayed for several days, but the khan did not return. Now, the senior wife knew that the junior wife was pregnant, so, out of envy, she gave the junior wife to Shiravul as a gift and gave him leave to go. According to Mongol custom, if a senior wife liked a junior wife, she would keep her; if not, she would give her to another man.

Eventually the khan returned from the hunt (or battle). His junior wife's name was Menglig. When he asked, "Where did she go?" his senior wife responded, "Shiravul of the Dokhtoi came bearing gifts. I gave him Menglig and sent him on his way."

"Menglig was carrying my child," he said. "This is no good." But he made no further complaint. Nevertheless, the khan had no sons, and soon after, he bid farewell to this world, which meant that the Mongol people were without a khan. The descendants of Chagatai and of Tolui{39} had fallen into fierce conflict, and now on this account they were divided.

Meanwhile, in Aqsu, Amir Bolaji Dughlat gathered his generals. "Let us find some descendant of the khans," he said, "and pledge ourselves to him. Without someone of khanal descent, it will be very difficult to bring peace to our people."

When this course of action had been agreed upon, someone mentioned that Esan-Buqa Khan's wife Menglig had been carrying his child, but that she had been gifted to Shiravul. "What if the child were a boy?" he suggested. "We could bring him here and elevate him as the khan."

Another objected, "Shiravul lives far away, and the road is treacherous. There is no way to reach him."

Yet one of the commanders, a man named Tash Timur Mirza, said, "Yes, it is very far, and the road is treacherous. But give me 300 mother goats, and I will live off their milk. And I will bring you back your khan." Everyone agreed, so they found him 300 mother goats, and he drank their milk. When only one goat was left, he came to Shiravul's land.

Tash Timur found an excuse to get close to Menglig, and he explained the whole situation to her. As it turned out, she had indeed borne the khan a son, and he was named Tughluq Timur. (She had also borne Shiravul a son, whom they named Ongchi Malik.)[1] Tash Timur stayed for a few days, and then stole away with Tughluq Timur.

Sometime later, they came to the Muzart Pass. The young khan was playing and running about when suddenly he fell into a crevice. Tash Timur did not realize this, however, and when he looked for the khan, he was utterly bewildered. Just then, seven merchants approached. Their leader's name was Begchik. Begchik and his merchants searched for the khan and eventually pulled him from the crevice. For their service to the crown, Begchik was made a *beg* in his entourage, while the others were likewise granted offices according to their station. Tash Timur brought the great khan to Aqsu and presented him to Amir Bolaji.

At that time, the khan was fourteen or fifteen years old.[2] Amir Bolaji summoned the lords of the realm and, at an auspicious hour, he enthroned the khan. In return for Amir Bolaji's service, the khan named him *beglär begi* ("lord of lords"). Along with the three titles afforded to his forefathers, Amir Bolaji received three more, and enjoyed them all by khanal decree. Some days later, however, Amir Bolaji passed on to the eternal realm. His son, Amir Khudaydad, received his father's offices, making him a *zaisang*—that is, the commander in chief. (In the Uzbek language, it is called a *beglär begi*. In Kyrgyz, it is an *el begi* or *ulus begi*. In Arabic, they made him an *amir al-jaysh*.)

Amir Bolaji was one of four brothers from one father. They were named Amir Tüläk, Amir Bolaji, Amir Qamaruddin, and Amir Shamsuddin. Amir Qamaruddin said to the khan, "My brother Bolaji's{40} son is only seven years old, a mere child. I was more suited to this office. I ask that you grant it to me in his stead, so that everything would be in its rightful place."

The khan kindly replied, "What a father does is for his son." He reminded Qamaruddin of Bolaji's record of service. "While Amir Khudaydad may be young, nevertheless I granted him his forefathers' office."

Amir Qamaruddin was at a loss. Yet in his heart a desire for vengeance grew, and his humors shifted toward anger.

Not long after, the khan went to the mercy of the Almighty. Amir Qamaruddin seized the moment. He beat the breast of rebellion and murdered eighteen princes along with several officers. He seized the khan's treasuries and armaments. Qamaruddin ruled for twelve whole years, and he was a contemporary of Amir Timur Kuragan. Seven times there were bitter battles between them, and the blood of many men was spilled. Eventually Amir Qamaruddin could not match Timur, so he fled and disappeared into some wilderness, where he died. His body was never found. If the reader should be curious about this story, I direct them to the *Garden of Purity*.

* * *

When that khan passed away, he had no son but Khiżr Khoja Khan [r. 1390–1399]. Yet Khiżr Khoja Khan was two years old. Amir Khudaydad's mother, Mir Agha, was a very wise woman, and she told him, "The khan's lineage must not come to an end." So he sent Khiżr Khoja Khan away with ten men.[3] Those men took Khiżr Khoja Khan away for a time to live in Alay, and also to Badakhshan, to the wilderness of Sarikol, and to the wastes of Lop and Cherchen. Qamaruddin kept an eye on him but ultimately lost track of him. When Qamaruddin died, Amir Khudaydad located Khiżr Khoja Khan, brought him to his court, and established him in his ancestors' capital. In return,

Khiżr Khoja Khan also granted him three more titles, so that at this point Amir Khudaydad enjoyed nine titles. Later he also did a worthy service for Sher ʿAli Khan. He was granted three more honors. He now enjoyed twelve different titles and honors.

These were his twelve titles and honors: 1. Zaisang, meaning "commander-in-chief." 2. The rulership of Manglai Suya. 3. After the khan had stamped his seal upon a proclamation, it would not be valid until Amir Khudaydad affixed his seal, as well. 4. He was permitted to sit one bow length away from the khan. 5. The khan was attended by two servants who poured his tea and *koumiss*. One of them attended Amir Khudaydad. 6. He could not be questioned, save if he were accused of one of nine crimes.{41} 7. If he should be accused of nine crimes, then when he came to the place for his interrogation, he would be interrogated while he sat upon a red felt. 8. If he should be sentenced to be beaten with the rod, then a red felt would be placed upon a chair, and then him laid upon that before he would be beaten. 9. He could not be sentenced to death, save for conviction for nine crimes. 10. Should he be sentenced to death, no human being would be permitted to strike him with rod or blade, nor hang him. 11. Should he be sentenced to death, he would instead be taken to some lonesome place, and wild horses found, and they would be made to pull him apart, and so kill him. 12. After the Grim Reaper thus collected him, the khan and all of the nobles would gather in mourning and weep. They would carry the body away and bury it. Perhaps no such accusation was ever made. Such is the magnificence of the khanship.

This is all to say that that the respect accorded to this esteemed commander's progeny in the eyes of the khan was as we have described. Amir Khudaydad lived to be ninety-seven. He ruled for ninety years. "I elevated seven khans with my own hands," he would say, "and put them on the throne."

At the end of Amir Khudaydad's life, in his heart he desired more than anything to go to Mecca and Medina. He requested permission from the khan, but no clear answer was forthcoming. The amir, feeling determined, decided, "The khan did not grant me permission. Perhaps by some design I will get my wish."

At that time, Mawarannahr, Khorasan, Persia, the Two Iraqs, and Azerbaijan were all under the rule of Mirza Ulughbeg Kuragan. His intention to conquer Moghulistan as well was AS THOUGH WRITTEN IN STONE. However, he had never found the opportunity.

Amir Khudaydad sent a secret message to Mirza Ulughbeg: "If we could trouble the Mirza to travel four or five stages from Tashkent in the direction of Moghulistan, I would bring those lands of Moghulistan into Mirza Ulughbeg's realm." As soon as Ulughbeg heard this joyous news, he rode from Samarqand to Tashkent, where he rallied his soldiers and went on the march. Meanwhile, Amir Khudaydad and the khan led soldiers from Moghulia on a march to Tashkent. Eventually barely a stage's distance remained between these two columns of battle-hungry soldiers.

Amir Khudaydad said to the khan, "Let me go in person to Mirza Ulughbeg and determine his intentions, so that we can avoid unnecessary bloodshed." The khan agreed and sent Khudaydad to him.

When they met, Khudaydad said, "Oh, mirza! I have achieved my goals.{42} Return, your highness, to your throne room. My scheme brought you here. If you had not come, then all of my plans would have come to naught." He explained the whole thing to him, and the plan was revealed. Mirza Ulughbeg smiled, grudgingly congratulated him, and set out again for his throne in paradisiacal Samarqand. Amir Khudaydad had by this scheme removed himself from the khan's power and domain.

When Mirza Ulughbeg Kuragan had gone out to greet Amir Khudaydad, they walked up in front of him, lifted him by the armpits, took him from his horse, and made him demonstrate his great respect. Thereafter Ulughbeg always allowed Khudaydad to sit higher than he did, and never walked ahead of him. When Khudaydad had been in the mirza's service for a few days, Ulughbeg started to ask him many questions about government. One was about Chinggis Khan's rules and laws, the *yasaq*, *yosun*, *yarghu*, and *törä*. Amir Khudaydad replied, "BY THE GRACE OF GOD, since I was blessed with the fortune of Islam, I have had nothing to do with the khans' law." Ulughbeg then felt so guilty and ashamed about asking such a question that he felt the embarrassment of it for as long as he lived. He learned many such lessons from Khudaydad, so that Mirza Ulughbeg was a learned master in every branch of knowledge. Once they had exchanged gifts and carried out the ceremonies required for hospitality, Mirza Ulughbeg provided Khudaydad with some of his own servants and sent him on his way to the Two Holy Cities.

In the *Tarikh-i Rashidi*, it is written that Amir Khudaydad had gone to Mecca and carried out the duties of the Ḥajj in full. Thereafter he proceeded to Medina to make a pilgrimage to the Tomb of the Prophet. As he was in the midst of repentance, fatigue showed upon his face, and he departed this transient world. That night, the Prophet entered the dreams of the Sharif of Medina. He said to him, "A beloved of mine has come from Turkestan for my sake. He died here. Bury him at the feet of ʿAbbas." And he drew a line in the ground with his staff. When he awoke, he went to the tomb of ʿAbbas, where he found the line he had drawn.

"How wondrous!" he said. "What a fortunate man!" He inspected the rest of the Hijaz and found that no ḥajji but Khudaydad had died. So he had the body washed according to tradition and buried him in the indicated place.

That year, Khoja Abu Naṣr Muḥammad Parsa also made a pilgrimage to the Two Holy Cities. One of his disciples reported, "I saw with my own eyes that they had laid a stone on which was inscribed 'Here Lies the Grave of Amir Khudaydad Turkestani.' "{43} It is said that Khoja Muḥammad Parsa's [d. 1420] pilgrimage to the Two Holy Cities and his death were in the year 822 [1419], and his death on the ninth of Dhu 'l-Hijja [December 27, 1419].[4] The year of Amir Khudaydad's death ought to have been that very year.

After Amir Khudaydad, his grandson Sayyid ʿAli b. Sayyid Aḥmad Mirza became the commander in chief, and he received the office of his ancestors as ruler over the Seven Cities. Then his eldest son, Sansiz Mirza,[5] ruled for eight years. Next his younger son Ḥaydar Muḥammad Mirza ruled. Dost Muḥammad Khan's daughter Jamak Agha was married to Sansiz Mirza. She bore him two sons named Aba Bakr Mirza and ʿUmar Mirza. When Sansiz passed away, his younger brother Ḥaydar Muḥammad Mirza took her as his wife in levirate marriage.[6] She bore Ḥaydar Muḥammad two sons, as well, whom they named Muḥammad Ḥusayn Mirza and Muḥammad Saʿid Mirza. Muḥammad Ḥusayn Mirza did not care for ruling the Seven Cities, so he went to Tashkent into the service of Yunus Khan and then Maḥmud Khan. By order of Maḥmud Khan, he was governor of Uratepe for nine years. Maḥmud Khan married one of his sisters to Muḥammad Ḥusayn Mirza and granted him the status of a *kuragan*. When they were in Uratepe, Mirza Ḥaydar was born to them.

Due to a series of unfortunate events, Muḥammad Ḥusayn Mirza could not stay in Uratepe, but instead took his son Mirza Ḥaydar and entered into the service of Sultan Ḥusayn b. Mirza Bayqara of Herat. At that time, there was a reliable old commander in Herat named Baranduq. He was sent out to greet Muḥammad Ḥusayn Kuragan and dismounted his horse at an appropriate distance. There they discussed the meeting with Sultan Ḥusayn.

Amir Baranduq said, "No matter what else, when you see him, it would be good for you to bow to him." However, Muḥammad Ḥusayn Mirza refused, because he was of the Dughlat clan, while Sultan Ḥusayn belonged to the Barlas tribe, and the rank of the Dughlat was several grades higher than that of the Barlas.

Eventually they managed to meet. Sultan Ḥusayn said, "I do not wish for our ancestors' customs to disappear. If Muḥammad Ḥusayn Mirza will not bow to me when we meet, then I will bow to him," and so he did. Each of them bowed to the other and so displayed their great respect and esteem.

However, when the sun of Sultan Ḥusayn's life set into the west, it revealed his sons' factiousness, and a time of great tribulation and contention began. Muḥammad Ḥusayn realized that he could not remain in Herat, so he traveled to the Two Holy Cities. His son Mirza Ḥaydar was eight years old, and he placed him into the service{44} of Mawlana Muḥammad Qażi. Mawlana Muḥammad Qażi's disciple was the master of Makhdum-i Aʿẓam [1461/62–1542/43].

Later on, Mirza Ḥaydar Kuragan was the commander in chief of Yarkand for twenty-two years during the reign of Sultan Saʿid Khan b. Aḥmad Khan [r. 1514–1533]. He led his forces against Tibet and Bolor,[7] conquered many cities, and brought them into the Islamic lands, making their people into Muslim believers. However, during the interregnum he went to Kabul and entered the service of Babur Padishah. Babur's mother was Yunus Khan's daughter and thus a relative of Mirza Ḥaydar's mother. Mirza Ḥaydar governed Kashmir for four years on Babur's behalf, and he accomplished a number of good things. He conquered many cities in Hindustan but eventually gave up rulership and devoted his life to the faith. He wrote, "I compiled the *Tarikh-i Rashidi* in Kashmir."

The daughters of the khans were married to the descendants of Amir Khudaydad, and so they were made sons-in-law and honored with the status of *kuragans*. The word *kuragan* in Mongolian means "son-in-law to the khan," that is, *son-in-law of the king*. These mirzas' daughters were married in turn to the sons of the khans.

Sansiz Mirza's son was Mirza Aba Bakr. There are still members of this line of mirzas in the Seven Cities today, and all of them can trace their descent back to Amir Khudaydad. To whit: Mirza Aḥmad Wang Beg and his line can be traced reliably back to Mirza Aba Bakr. The point of noting this is to show that, for over 300 years from the time of Chagatai Khan b. Chinggis Khan to that of Sultan Saʿid Khan, the descendants of Bab Daghan, including Amir Khudaydad b. Amir Bolaji, for generation upon generation, one after another, ruled these Seven Cities independently. Until the reign of Mirza Aba Bakr, and after him, when Sultan Saʿid Khan took possession of them through the efforts of his nephew, Mirza Ḥaydar Kuragan, members of the Dughlat dynasty were commanders and ministers, up until Ismail Khan and Muḥammad Amin Khan, governing for more than 200 years. Indeed, their rule remained in place until the Emperor of China's people came to rule the Seven Cities.

It is written that Mirza Aḥmad Wang Beg's line also goes back to Mirza Aba Bakr.[8] It is unclear to your humble author precisely how that descent could be traced.{45} According to the one who wrote that, as of now, in the year 1326 [1908],[9] they are still ruling in the Seven Cities. To wit: Mirza Huda Beise Beg governed Yarkand.[10] Then his son, Mirza ʿUs̱man Beise Beg, governed Kashgar. Mawlana Muḥammad Ṣadiq Kashgari wrote the *Compilation of Examples* [*Zubdat al-Masail*] in the name of Mirza ʿUs̱man Beise Beg.[11] Then his son, Mirza Isḥaq Beg, received the title of wang and governed Kashgar. Next his son, Mirza Aḥmad Wang Beg, governed Aqsu for twenty-eight years, and Yarkand for eight. ʿAbdulkarim Damulla of Bukhara's book, the *ʿAqaid*, was translated into Turki in Mirza Aḥmad Wang Beg's name, and it contains a great many definitions and clarifications of words.[12] (Moreover, Muḥammad Ḥusayn Mutawalli Akhund translated the *Wonders of Creation* [*ʿAjayib al-Makhluqat*][13] into Turki in the name of the wang beg, and it contains many descriptions.)

Mirza Aḥmad Wang Beg was a fortunate man, clever and clear minded, who in his administration held firmly to the laws of government and to the way of care for the common people in word and in deed. His actions and his nature resembled those of kings in bygone days. Outwardly he served the Emperor of China, but in reality, he was a sovereign king and independent ruler. He remanded the resolution of every dispute to the Shariah courts and secured fatwas, according to the verse, IT IS A GUIDANCE FOR THOSE WHO BELIEVE. [41:44] He would then enact his own judgments in accordance with the fatwas.

Mirza Aḥmad Wang Beg deeply respected and maintained the Shariah, and he was observant of God's law and acted properly according to its rules. At the same time, he was mindful of the emperor's officials under the imperial agent's command, and he showed them the appropriate respect.[14] He himself abstained from such prohibited acts as drinking wine, smoking hashish [*bang*], and drinking grain wine [*buza*]. For this reason, among the common people and the nobles alike, even among the *begs* and their children, there were no such intoxicating beverages or other forbidden things at all, neither openly nor in secret. And after midnight, his eyes would not close in sleep. Rather, he would immediately awaken, perform ablutions, enter his chamber of worship, and perform his vigil of prayers. Afterward he would busy himself with the prayers he had learned from his Sufi master. In the chapel, there was no rug but a prayer rug. A great rope hung from the ceiling, and when he set to his duty, he would place that rope about his neck before beginning.

When it was time for prayers, he would go to the mosque, and at the beginning of prayer, gather at least fifty or sixty men around him to pray together. Never in his life did he shirk his prayers or the community. On the first and fifteenth of every month,{46} when he went to the yamens of the assistant agent and lieutenant colonel,[15] he would go dressed in the Chinese style, with a rank button[16] and peacock feather on his hat, and dressed in robes of office. The rest of the time, he was always dressed in clothing that accorded with the Shariah, the turban and the belted robe. He had great faith in scholars and masters and felt great devotion to them. For this reason, masters from surrounding countries such as Kashmir, Badakhshan, Hindustan, Bukhara, and Turkestan heard of the Wang Beg's reputation for grace and generosity, and they would come to stay. They would profit therefrom, pay their respects to him, and return to their own accustomed countries. The Wang Beg and some of his own faithful and sincere disciples likewise benefited from their companionship. He entered into both the Qadiriyya and Naqshbandiyya orders. [When he gave offerings to the masters of the Naqshbandiyya order, he would never give anything less than seven *yambu*,[17] which is 700 *tangga*. And to the masters of the Qadiriyya, he gave no less than eleven *yambu*, which is 1,100 *tangga*.] He had pious, wise, and sober mullahs trained, and had them recite the Quran, section by section, every Monday and Thursday. He provided those Quran reciters with all of their needs.

Apart from that, he also established many way stations, forts, madrasas, ponds, and mosques, and performed many other charitable acts. The money for every donation came from the land and livestock he had inherited from his ancestors. By the end of his life, none of the other descendants of Amir

Khudaydad had been such a friend to scholars and the common people as the Wang Beg was. The results of the good deeds he did for God's creations can still be seen among the common people today. For all his piety and blessings, when his life came to an end, he must have taken his place as a martyr. The scholars of his day judged him to be a great martyr, as he spilled no blood without reason, and so they recited his funeral prayers and buried him.

Then his son Mirza Ḥamid Beg gained the rank of wang. He governed Aqsu and Khotan. Next his son Mirza Muḥammad Beg inherited his father's rank, and on account of his great fortune became known as Wang Khoja.

* * *

These Seven Cities were conquered by the Mongol khan, Chinggis Khan, in the year 616 [1219] [614 (1217)]. From then up to the present day, they have not fallen under the control of anyone else.

However, when the great Amir Timur Kuragan rode with his soldiers for Iraq, he placed his grandson, Sultan Muḥammad [1375–1403], in Samarqand, the seat of the sultanate, and made another grandson, Iskandar Sultan b. ʿUmar Shaykh Bahadur [1384–1415], the governor of Andijan. Iskandar Sultan was young, only thirteen [fifteen] years old. His commanders told him they were taking him hunting, but instead ran off with him and took Kashgar. Next they moved on to conquer Yarkand. Then they took some places called Sarigh Qomush and Kelin Zali Köl. Next they besieged Aqsu for forty days and pillaged it.{47} Then they moved on to Bay, and to Kucha, which they conquered. They visited disaster upon the people of Kucha. Next they took control of a place called Tadam, and then they took Khotan. There they stayed for a few days before seizing several nines of girls, whom they took to Andijan. There they presented Amir Timur Kuragan with two nines of girls, and Sultan Muḥammad Mirza with another nine. However, because they had gone out without their uncle's permission, Timur now held them in suspicion, and he had twenty-eight commanders put to the sword. Iskandar Sultan he imprisoned. This is all narrated in the *Garden of Purity*.

The names and locations of these places called Sarigh Qomush, Kelin Zali Köl, and Tadam are unknown.[18] The time that Iskandar Sultan spent going there must have lasted more than a year. Then control of the Seven Cities returned to Amir Khudaydad's grandsons. Also, great Amir Timur Kuragan's grandson Mirza Ulughbeg Kuragan became enraged at one of Amir Khudaydad's grandsons, Qaraqul Aḥmad Mirza. He sent soldiers to conquer Kashgar and appended it to his realm for four years. Apart from that, one will not find it written in any history book that any leader came from Mawarannahr, Ferghana, or Arabia and ruled here for six months or a year, and no one is aware of that having happened—apart, of course, from Muḥammad Yaʿqub Beg. However, the Mongol people did several times conquer the cities of Arabia, and they ruled them for centuries. Their rule is recorded in every history. GOD KNOWS THE TRUTH.

0:4 Tughluq Timur Khan

The Genealogy of the King of Moghulistan, Tughluq Timur Khan (May God illuminate his resting place in Paradise!), and a Brief Enumeration of His Descendants

Tughluq Timur Khan b. Esan-Buqa Khan b. Duwa Tsetsen Khan b. Baraq Khan (who was known as Sultan Ghiyas̱uddin and was a pious Muslim) b. Yesünto'a b. Mutukan [*Mamukay—ES*] b. Chagatai Khan b. Chinggis Khan

WHEN TUGHLUQ TIMUR Khan was fifteen years old, through the efforts of Amir Bolaji Dughlat, he ascended the khanal throne in Aqsu. This story was told earlier. When he was twenty-four, he was honored with the fortune of Islam by the hand of ʿArshuddin (May God sanctify his secret!). These events will come later, God willing—He is the Patient.

When the cities of Mawarannahr had all risen in rebellion, twice Tughluq Timur Khan sent his soldiers, and he spread his dominion as far as Kunduz. At that time, Amir Timur Kuragan was the governor of Shahrisabz, and he welcomed him with many gifts. Tughluq commanded that Timur receive his ancestors' office of vizier and favored him by putting his eldest son, Ilyas Khoja, into his service in Samarqand. He himself{48} returned to his capital at Ili. A short while later, Ilyas Khoja Khan rebelled, while Tughluq Timur Khan likewise made passage from this world of trouble to the palace of Paradise. He was thirty-four years old. He was buried in Ili. It was the year 766

[1364/65] when these world-destroying events came to pass. From that time forward, among the common people, and specifically in the city of Ili, holy Islam came to be revealed and established.

As for the Seven Cities, specifically Kashgar: following a vision from the Prophet himself, Abu Naṣr Samani had come to Kashgar in the year 332 [943/4]. At the time, Harun Bughra Khan of the Bughrakhanids was reigning in Kashgar. His son, Sultan Sutuq, was thirteen years old. Through the efforts of Abu Naṣr Samani, with the right guidance of God as his companion, Sutuq entered the community of Islam. Thanks to the guidance of Sultan Sutuq, the Seven Cities too became Muslim, and among them Islam was revealed, and he came to rule them as well. (The holy hadith that says THE FIRST AMONG THE TURKS IS SUTUQ refers to him.) The leaders of Khotan would not submit, but in the year 372 [982/3] they converted to Islam. The Bughrakhanids ruled the Seven Cities from that day forward—or perhaps earlier—until the reign of Chinggis Khan. Their tombs and shrines are in Artush.

* * *

Now to return to the story we were telling: after Tughluq Timur Khan, his son Khiżr Khoja Khan [r. 1390–1399] was installed on the throne he inherited from his father. He was Shariah-loving and pious, unparalleled in courage and combat, and matchless in providing relief to his subjects and showing concern for commoners. He became friends with Amir Timur Kuragan. Indeed he betrothed his daughter, Tawakkul Begim, to Amir Timur, and so was himself honored with the status of a Kuragan. He placed his own lands in order and then rode for holy war toward Beijing. At the time, none of the people of Turfan, Qarakhoja, or Qumul knew Islam. By Khiżr Khoja Khan's hand, they were blessed with Islam. He subdued many cities of China but ultimately drank the wine of martyrdom. They brought his body back and buried it in Yamshi.

After that, his son, Shams-i Jahan Khan [r. 1399–1408], sat upon the throne. After him, (his son) Muḥammad Khan [r. 1408–1415] ascended the throne. During that period, they heard about Mirza Ulughbeg's astronomical observations at Baghlan and constructed the Stone Fort above Artush. He was a faithful Muslim and pious man. He passed away when young. He was buried at his grandfather's feet.

After that, Sher ʿAli Khan [r. 1421–1425] ascended the throne.[1] He carried out many holy wars against the Qalmaqs, and in the end said farewell to this world. After that, his son, Uways Khan [r. 1418–1421, 1425–1429], sat astride the throne. His son, Yunus Khan, was young, thirteen years old. His generals, Erazan Bairin and Mirak Turkman, at the head of 30,000 men, took him away to Samarqand to attack Mirza Ulughbeg,{49} and there many great and bitter battles took place. Eventually they were defeated. Erazan Bairin, Mirak Turkman, and the 30,000 men were put into tents and taken prisoner, and some were executed. Yunus Khan was sent to his grandfather Shahrukh Mirza in Herat. Then he was sent from Herat to Shiraz, into the care of Mawlana Sharfuddin ʿAli Yazdi. (That story was told earlier.) He was a pious king and a scholar. "Among the kings and khans, apart from Mirza Ulughbeg, there was never another more scholarly king than Yunus Khan," they would say. His capital was at Tashkent. He was a loyal disciple of Khoja Aḥrar. During that reign, ruffians would steal people from Moghulia away and sell them in their own countries. The Honored Khoja Aḥrar proclaimed a judgment of the Shariah that "Such a pious Muslim and Islamic king should neither buy nor sell his common people." And he sent a letter declaring this to the leaders of the every domain, strictly prohibiting it. Thereafter they bought people no more, nor sold them.

Yunus Khan was buried in Tashkent. Then his eldest son, Maḥmud Khan [r. 1487–1508], sat upon the throne. He reigned as khan for twelve years. He made war with Shah Beg Khan, known as Muḥammad Khan Shibani, of the descendants of Uzbek. He was victorious and made martyrs of him and his five sons. He was buried at the feet of Shaykh Muṣliḥuddin Shirazi in Khojand. Then his youngest son, Aḥmad Khan [r. 1487–1503], sat upon the throne. The Qalmaqs call him Alacha Khan. He could not stay in Tashkent [or in Andijan], but came to attack Mirza Aba Bakr [r. 1465–1514] in Kashgar. They fought, but he could not take Kashgar so went to Aqsu. Although he thought to gather his troops, ride in the spring, and take Kashgar then, the opportunity did not arise, so he was buried in Aqsu. (Aḥmad Khan's person was referred to as "golden." When the Mongols speak of the khan's person, they call it "golden," so that khans and ḥakims call his commands and proclamations "golden commands" and "golden orders." Aḥmad Khan's uncle Esan-Buqa's "golden" body is also there, so the two khans' bodies are in one place. When Khoja Shahbaz Khoja b. Khoja Isḥaq died, it was commanded that he be buried "at the khan's feet." When his loyal disciples asked to bury him in a place higher than the khan, out of reverence for Khoja Isḥaq, they responded, "The head of Khoja Shahbaz shall be level with the khan's breast. The khan is entitled to greater respect." Their tombs are still in this arrangement.)

Aḥmad Khan fathered eighteen sons. The eldest was Manṣur Khan [r. 1503–1543]. The land from Qumul to Korla was under Manṣur Khan's rule.{50} His youngest son, Sultan Saʿid Khan, was with King Babur Khan in Kabul. He came with some men to Andijan, conquered it, and ruled it for three years. Then they decided that it might be good to go to the Seven Cities. So they went and camped at Kashgar with 4,700 brave warriors from nine clans, including the Dughlat, Dokhtoi, Barlas, and Churas. At that time, King Mirza Aba Bakr, who was one of the grandsons of Amir Khudaydad, had ruled Kashgar and the Seven Cities for forty-eight years. Battles were fought. Mirza Aba Bakr could not match him but fled, and died in the mountains of Badakhshan. The throne of the Seven Cities passed to Sultan Saʿid Khan.

Mirza Aba Bakr's treasures, armaments, livestock, and gardens were beyond reckoning—and his tyranny too was in the extreme. Should any man commit the slightest of crimes, he would have that man killed and take his property for the treasury. He would even have that man's relatives brought in, and on the pretext that that member of their family had done a bad thing, would slaughter all of them. When Mirza Aba Bakr came to Aqsu, because the people there had been friendly to Aḥmad Khan, he massacred them and did unspeakable things. The rest he forced to move all over the Six Cities. For this reason, for sixteen years Aqsu was set to ruin—nests for owls, homes for divs and paris.[2] In none of the chronicles can there be seen any tyrant king like Mirza Aba Bakr. If anyone should wish to know about Mirza Aba Bakr, let them turn their gaze to the *Tarikh-i Rashidi*.

So the Seven Cities came into the possession of Sultan Saʿid Khan. And whatever man wished it, whether they be from Aqsu or from some other city, was moved to Aqsu and settled there, and cultivated it. For this reason the men of Aqsu are not unified, because those were fractious and disunified people. Sultan Saʿid Khan distributed Mirza Aba Bakr's treasures among his soldiers. None of them had any more need or care for property. The author of the *Tarikh-i Rashidi*, Mirza Ḥaydar Kuragan (MAY GOD ILLUMINATE HIS GRAVE!), wrote in his book, "At that time, I was sixteen or seventeen years old, and I had little desire for money or property. Nevertheless, in the division,

I received 17,000 sheep, apart from the cash and goods. Those who had the desire, how much did they receive! From this you can guess how much booty there was."[3]

When Sultan Saʿid Khan learned how the Muslims were weak and devastated, and of how little need the soldiers had, he issued a sublime command that ten years' worth of tax revenue from the Seven Cities should be distributed to the common people, and that for ten years nothing should be taken from them, nor imposed upon them; nor should they give anything. For five years the soldiers did very well. Eventually, however, the devastation turned to ruin, and [the generals joined together and] they took out loans as well. They barely made it through the sixth year. They had no way to say anything to the people, and the khan did not rescind his command. The high officials consulted with one another,{51} and they said to the khan, "Oh, shelter of the world! We came to the Seven Cities in the Year of the Cow; now the Year of the Horse is come. We ask you to decree that it has now been ten years, and that we may once again collect taxes from the commoners." And so they wished to disregard four years, and to consider those six years to be "ten years." The khan agreed and issued the decree. They collected taxes in accordance with the Shariah. They also wrote that it was "such-and-such year" on the declarations. And the common people took this reckoning up as their own reckoning. This is the reason the Seven Cities reckon years to be four years earlier than other cities do, although the dates are the same.[4]

He ruled as khan for twenty-two years. He passed away at forty-nine. In the year 939 [1532/33], he was buried in Yarkand.

Next, his son, ʿAbdurrashid Khan [r. 1533–ca. 1560], ascended the throne. He was unparalleled in bravery and unequaled in generosity and religiosity. He was an accomplished scholar and poet who recited his Persian and Turki *nazms* well. In the reliability of his knowledge, he was like a second Pythagoras. He created a *muqam* called "Sociable" [*ushrat-angez*].[5] During his reign, Khoja Muḥammad Sharif Pir-i Buzurgwar (MAY GOD SANCTIFY HIS HONORED SECRET!) came from Ferghana. Through his devotion and penitence, many good things came to pass. Mirza Ḥaydar Kuragan b. Mirza Muḥammad Ḥusayn Kuragan wrote a chronicle in the name of His Loftiness ʿAbdurrashid Khan and called it the *Tarikh-i Rashidi*. He lived for forty-nine years. He ruled as khan for twenty years. He passed away in the year 969 [1561/2]. He was buried in Yarkand.[6]

Next, his son, ʿAbdulkarim Khan [r. 1560–1591], sat upon the throne. Through justice he caused the country to thrive, and he overthrew the unjust and the innovators. He came to be known as ʿAbdulkarim the Just. He ruled as khan for thirty-three years. He passed away in the year 1000 [1591/92]. He was buried in Yarkand. One of his younger brothers, Sufi Sultan, was governor of Kashgar.

Another of his younger brothers, Muḥammad Sultan [r. 1592–1610], was governor of Aqsu. They brought him from Aqsu to Yarkand, where they elevated him as khan. He was both a king and a dervish. Eight years after he became khan, from Ferghana came the MASTER BY BIRTH AND BY RIGHT, Khoja Isḥaq b. Makhdum-i Aʿẓam (MAY GOD BLESS HIS HONORED GRAVE!). He showed devotion and penitence, and many good things came to pass, but if we were to relate them in detail, then our words would drift far from their course. Muḥammad Sultan lived for seventy years and was khan for eighteen. (He was buried in Yarkand.) Next, his son, Żiyauddin Aḥmad [Shujauddin Aḥmad], sat upon the khanal throne. Three years later, he himself was martyred in Barchuq. He came to be known as the "Martyred Khan." Next, his son, ʿAbdullaṭif Sultan [r. 1618–1630], was made khan. He ruled as khan for twelve years. He passed away at the age of twenty-six. [It was the year 1037 (1627).] Then Polad Khan and Maḥmud Khan each became independent khans, and the country was divided.

Next ʿAbdurrashid Khan's ninth son, ʿAbdurraḥim Khan [r. 1591–1594, 1605–1636], ruled from Qumul to Korla as khan, in the domain of Manṣur Khan. The khanship then passed to ʿAbdurraḥim Khan's first son, ʿAbdullah Khan [r. 1636–1638],{52} who was installed upon the sultanic throne. From that time, which was the year 1048 [1638/39], he sat in his forefathers' capital for thirty-two years. He was unparalleled in bravery and unequaled in grace and generosity. And yet he was merciless, tyrannical, ill-tempered, ignorant, vindictive, and mistrustful. He was suspicious of those reliable sons of the begs and faithful princes left over from the days of the former khans, and he expelled them from the country. Most of them he killed. He even expelled two of his younger brothers, Ismail Sultan and Ibrahim Sultan, and killed another of them. He trusted no one and was suspicious even of his own children. Nor could his children trust their father. Instead, he appointed Kyrgyz to govern each region. Qoy Sari Bi was made governor of Kashgar. Uljatai Bi was made governor of Aqsu. Khoja Yar Bi was made governor of Kucha, Alta Qurutqa Bi that of Ushturfan, Chiriki Bi that of Bügür, and Allahyar Bi

b. Satim Bi that of Khotan. He gave most offices to Kyrgyz. Ultimately he became suspicious of the Kyrgyz and of his governors. He senselessly spilled much blood and, unable to relax, was left with no choice but to travel to Mecca. So he said farewell and went on his way. He entrusted the country to his son, Yolbars Khan. In the year 1080 [1669/70], the capital of Moghulia passed into the possession of Yolbars Khan. A few years later, a civil war broke out.

Next, his father's brother, Ismail Khan b. ʿAbdurraḥim Khan, was installed on the throne. He scattered justice upon the people. All the common people were at ease and peace. During the khan's reign, both Makhdum-i Aʿẓam's grandson Khoja Yusuf and his son Khoja Hidayatullah, who is known as Afaq Khoja [d. 1694], came from Ferghana and arrived in Kashgar. And Ismail Khan Khoja devoted himself to Yusuf Khoja. On this account did factiousness and confusion emerge among the sayyids, within the ranks of the disciples, and across the country.

* * *

The story in detail: That pillar of the lineage, Sayyid Makhdum-i Aʿẓam, whose blessed name was Khoja Muḥammad Khojagi (MAY GOD ILLUMINATE HIS HONORED TOMB!), begat four sons, named Khoja Kalan, Khoja Muḥammad Amin, Khoja Dawlat, and Khoja Isḥaq [d. 1599]. Khoja Isḥaq's mother was a descendant of that exalted man from Kashgar, Sultan Sutuq Bughra Khan. He was the youngest of all the sons but exceeded the rest in his positive qualities. When Khoja Isḥaq first brought forth his holy steps unto the Seven Cities, Muḥammad Khan [r. 1591–1610] reigned as khan. He became Khoja Isḥaq's faithful disciple, and as Muḥammad Khan gradually attained perfection, the common people too became Khoja Isḥaq's faithful disciples. Later they became disciples to his sons, and then disciples to his grandsons, Khoja Shuʿayb and Khoja Danyal, and that is when they seized the khanship, which Ismail Khan then held.

Around that time,{53} Muḥammad Amin Khoja's son, Khoja Yusuf, and two of his grandsons, one being Afaq Khoja, came from Ferghana to Kashgar. Ismail Khan said, "The two young masters are young, while Khoja Yusuf is older, and all of them are branches and fruits of the same tree." And so he devoted himself to Khoja Yusuf.

Those two young khojas [*Khoja Shuʿayb and Khoja Danyal—ES*] said to the khan dejectedly, "Oh, Khan! Your forefathers were faithful disciples to our forefathers. Now you have cast us off and devoted yourself to our uncle, Khoja Yusuf."

"I had wondered," said the khan, putting them off, "whether the two young masters' hearts would be saddened. So guide us now, and let us importune the great spirits, and whatsoever they give us leave to do, let us proceed accordingly."

That night, Ismail Khan dreamed that a great bull camel was chasing two young camels. Suddenly the two young camels turned around to confront the bull, and in the end, the big camel turned tail and fled. Just when the khan awoke, Khoja Yusuf had been leading the young *khojas* in meditation, and they had received precisely such a vision. Khoja Yusuf found that he could no longer remain, so he took his son with him and traveled to Kashgar. Shortly thereafter, the birds of his spirit flew away to the world above. He was buried in Kashgar.[7] Afaq Khoja could not remain either, but decided to travel away to Ili.

At that time, a treacherous Qalmaq in Ili named Khung-Taiji,[8] of the line of Churas, had spread his rule beyond the Qalmaq lands, even into the country of China, and to Turkestan, and reigned independently as a *törä*, as khan and king. He whetted his appetite to rule over the Seven Cities. Now, all of a sudden, Afaq Khoja threw himself before Khung-Taiji with a request: "If you would give me soldiers, I would make you ruler and master over the Six Cities." Khung-Taiji was pleased and sent him with some soldiers. So with the aid of the Qalmaq infidel Khung-Taiji, Afaq Khoja conquered the Seven Cities, and he carried Ismail Khan and his entire family away to Ili. In the year 1022 [1613], Afaq Khoja achieved his aim, and he ruled the Seven Cities. And a Qalmaq named Galdan was made lord over him, with several Qalmaqs to aid him, and these kept watch on the Seven Cities.

The remaining Qalmaqs wished to return to Ili. However, as the rulers found it unfitting for the Qalmaqs to return empty-handed, they gathered rough-spun cloth from every place and gifted it to the Qalmaqs in proportion. This was because at that time, there was no coinage in the cities, and they had to use rough-spun cloth in place of coins. Now they demanded rough-spun cloth every year. The rulers had no choice but to provide it. The amount grew year on year. In that year this{54} awful innovation was imposed upon the Muslims.

Oh, dear friends. In that era, in order to rule, not only did the foremost among sayyids find it necessary to serve the irreligious infidels and place nonbelievers above a Muslim king and Muslim people, but also they committed tyrannical and innovative acts, giving Muslims' money and property to nonbelievers, and lived in attachment to this fleeting world. So wherefore do the common folk of today open their mouths to reproach and malign the begs, interpreters, translators, and officials? Oh Lord, please make your justice and guidance abundant. Amen.

This awful innovation remained in place until the year 1281 [1864/65]—until the reign of Rashuddin Khan.

* * *

Afaq Khoja ruled for a few years and then passed away. Next, his son, Khoja Aḥmad, ruled in his stead. During his reign, Ismail Khan's younger brother, Muḥammad Amin Khan, rose up, and he joined forces with Khoja Aḥmad. They rebelled against Khung-Taiji and established their rule. Now Khung-Taiji sent an army and again appended the Seven Cities to his domain, and they carried Khoja Aḥmad away to Ili. Neither could Muḥammad Amin Khan remain there, but he fled to Alash. The Kyrgyz in that area martyred him.

Then the government of the Seven Cities passed on to Khoja Isḥaq's grandson, Khoja Danyal. He ruled the land in collaboration with the Qalmaqs. After Khoja Danyal passed away, his son, Khoja ʿAbdullah, sat upon the throne. But during this khoja's reign, many very fine things took place. In this era, *The Noble Biography* was translated into Turki in Khoja ʿAbdullah's name.[9] Next, his son, Khoja Yaʿqub, sat upon the throne [in Yarkand, the seat of the sultanate]. He was nicknamed Khoja Jahan. One of his younger brothers, Khoja Yusuf, was governor of Kashgar. Another, Khoja Khamush, was governor of Aqsu. [His half-brother] Khoja ʿAbdullah was in Khotan. [Together they ruled the country well. Now in Ili the Qalmaq leader, Törä Khung-Taiji, was king and khan. He ruled over lands from Qumul to all the Qalmaq, Kyrgyz, and Qipchaq land, and to Turkestan, Chimkent, Sayram, and Moghulistan.] All of the khojas would send one of their sons as a hostage [*barimtai*] to Ili, to be kept captive. [The khojas submitted to Khung-Taiji's command, and every year, once or twice, they would go to Ili with presents, to pay their respects.] Then they would return and remain in their own lands.

Khoja Yusuf was a perspicacious man, who kept good counsel and was skilled in strategy. He went up to Ili with many great presents, and, having had an audience with Khung-Taiji, by trickery and strategy he freed the young khojas and swiftly carried them back to their country. When they came to Muzart Pass,{55} the *törä* sent men with orders to "retrieve the khojas, who will regret disobeying their orders." The khojas made no reply to the men who came. Instead, they fortified the pass, went to Aqsu, and sent a letter to every city explaining the situation: "All of you, drive the filthy Qalmaqs in each of your cities far from this pure land. Draw the sword of Islam across their necks without hesitation!"

As soon as the letter arrived, they killed all of the Black Khans and their families. (In those days, they would call the Qalmaqs "Black Khans" and the Muslims, "White Khans.")[10] They killed the nonbelievers in the Cities, and rebelled, and holy Islam was to be seen once more. Khung-Taiji readied his armies, but before he could take his revenge, he took his place in the chamber of annihilation. His son Dawachi [r. 1755–1759] became *törä*. Yet Khung-Taiji had another son from his younger wife. Her tribe and nation were numerous, and they wished to make this younger son the *törä*, so a war broke out. The leaders of the country split into two parties, and the Qalmaqs were divided.

There was a famed warrior among the Qalmaqs named Amursana [from the younger son's side]. He seized the opportunity to seek an audience with the Emperor of China, to whom he said, "[The *törä*ship of Moghulistan fell to my line, but others took it from us.] I would bring the land of Moghulistan into the Great Khan's rule, if he would only grant me an army." The emperor was pleased and sent him with an army, which came to the borders of Ili.

Dawachi could not match them, so he gathered as much of his treasure as he could and fled with a few of his liegemen. He knew not where he was going. There was a trustworthy man in Ushturfan by the name of Khojasi Beg, who was the governor of Ushturfan by Khung-Taiji's command. He trusted Khojasi Beg, so he came to Ushturfan. Khojasi Beg greeted him with great honor and quartered him in his palace, with 300 men. Every spot was appointed, and they were feasted well. Yet he was a man of many tricks and strategies. He had the *törä* tied up in his palace, and each of his men tied up in their quarters and he seized their treasures.

Now it became known that Chinese armies had arrived at Ili. Khojasi Beg decided, "What could be better than if we gave this filthy nonbeliever as a gift to the impure nonbelievers who are now coming?" So he took him on the road with him. When he arrived at Tekes, he met with the leader of the Chinese army and explained the situation to him in detail.

"Oh, Khojasi Beg!" he wrote to him happily in a special communique. "This *törä* is a major enemy of the Great Khan! You have done well, and come at a good time. Now go, go into the Great Khan's presence, introduce yourself to him, and then come back here."{56} He put him under guard and sent him to Beijing. His offer of service was accepted, and by decree he was rewarded with the rank of wang.

He seized him, Dawachi—made a gift of him, did Khojasi;
For doing this deed, a reward, who would need?

After that, his son, Qadir Beg, inherited the wangship. He lived out his life at the court of the Emperor of China with honors equal to those of the grand secretaries,[11] as one of the royal ministers. Next, his son, ʿAbdulmumin, known by the name of Kuchi Beg, inherited the wangship. But he and the khan's son were addicted to opium, and when their bad deeds came to light, the Great Khan was angry with him and revoked his wangship, and returned it to his treasury. Kuchi Beg was handed over to the Lifanyuan,[12] where they inspected the ancient *lu* ordinances,[13] and in accordance with ancient custom, they divided Khojasi's wangship into four parts. Three parts of it were retained in the treasury, while one part was given by decree to his half-brother's son, ʿAbdurraḥman Beg. He now received the wangship and governed Yarkand, during which many fine things came to pass. His faith was pure, and his beneficence great. He once donated 111 *yambu* to a master of the Ghawṡiyya order.

An anecdote: When ʿAbdurraḥman Beg was the governor of Yarkand, there was a great inquiry, and by the order of the imperial agent, all of the Chinese officials, begs, and *akhund*s were gathered in the yamen. At the time, it was a season when the cold weather had reached an extreme, the sun rose in the House of Aquarius, and the afflicting blizzards of the first month of winter [*day*] and the whirling winds of the second month [*bahman*] were kicking up. The imperial agent did not appear on time at the site of inquiry, but was delayed. In the meantime, the wang beg noticed that one Muḥammad Niyaz Akhund happened to have come out to the interrogation to take in the show. (At the time, Muḥammad Niyaz was still devoting his efforts to study at madrasa, experimenting with the art of poetry, and coming into his own.) The wang called him over and asked, as if to punish him, "As you are a student staying at the madrasa, what reason do you have for coming out to such a place?" Then, more temperately, he said, "I have heard that you compose fine poetry. Well, then, would you recite something for your lowly disciple?"

Immediately he improvised a reply:

They froze in the palm of Kashmir, the dumbfounded Chinese;
Shivers fell upon the beg, the *akhund* icing up and freezing . . .

He went on in this manner for ten stiches, one after the next. The wang was delighted and thanked him, and gifted him his own horse and camel to ride, with a fine saddle and mantle fit for a wang. These he rode until he entered the madrasa. Realizing the value of the saddle, he sold it, and continued his efforts at study. He had many such laudable qualities and wise words.

Next,{57} ʿAbdulʿaziz Beg ascended to the wangship. He governed Khotan. The aforementioned Mullah Muḥammad Niyaz Akhund translated the *Tarikh-i Rashidi* into Turki in the name of this Wang Beg and enumerated his many fine qualities and sayings. He fathered two sons, Muḥammad Amin Beg and ʿAbdulwahhab Khan. The wangship passed to Muḥammad Amin Beg. However, because he had no sons, it then passed to ʿAbdulwahhab Khan's son, ʿAbdulqadir Beg. He is still known today as the "Wang Khoja."

* * *

Amursana, with the aid of the Emperor of China, brought the lands of Ili to heel. When the emperor's officials granted the lands of Qalmaqistan to Amursana, he was absolutely faithful to his orders and set about governing the Seven Cities.

In Ili there was a sayyid, one of the descendants of Afaq Khoja, by the name of Khoja Burhanuddin. He was the leader and master of the White Mountaineers.[14] The White Mountaineers recalled how they had suffered at the hands of the Black Mountaineers when the sons of Khoja Isḥaq were in power. They sent him thence with a great host, both for this reason and because they concluded that, if they sent an army to the Seven Cities with Sayyid Burhanuddin at its head, the Cities would fall into their hands easily.

As soon as the army reached Aqsu, the city's leaders came out to receive the White Mountaineers and surrendered Aqsu to them. Next, they seized Ushturfan. When Khoja Yusuf heard of this, he sent an army from Kashgar under his son, Khoja Ṣiddiq. When they came to Ushturfan, many battles were fought. Ultimately, the army of Islam fell into disarray in the ranks, and they marched back toward Kashgar. Khoja Yusuf fell ill, and by the time the soldiers returned, the bird of his soul had flown from this human world to the exalted one. The infidels followed behind them, and they took Kashgar. Next, they marched on Yarkand. They were many times victorious, and many times suffered defeat. In the end, Khoja Jahan withdrew. Yet others were sent after him, and seized him, and martyred him along with his family and entourage. The things that this changeable world did visit upon the sons of Khoja Isḥaq, the forked-tongued pen is too weak to repeat, and the mind too bereft of thought.

And then they conquered Khotan as well. In the year 1162 [1749],[15] the rule of the Six Cities was remanded to the aforementioned Burhanuddin Khoja. The Chinese and Qalmaq armies withdrew to their own places. Some remained. The Chinese armies in Ili too returned to their own place, while some remained garrisoned there, as peace reigned over the lands.

Meanwhile, lust for glory and conquest corrupted the mind of Amursana. He was ungrateful for his good fortune, and he killed all the people of Beijing in Ili.{58} Now he was the *törä* in his own right, and he enacted his own rule. When Burhanuddin in the Six Cities heard of this, he placed the belt of fealty in the niche of forgetting and became an independent king. He broke the bonds of fealty, became his own master, and gave himself the title Khan Khoja Padishah, which he wrote in this manner upon his proclamations as well. When the Emperor of China learned of this, he sent his armies forth once more to Ili, where a great battle with Amursana took place. Amursana could not match him but fled, and stole away to a place called Siberia. There he met his end.

Since the old days, there had continuously been wars, disputes, and enmities between the Emperor of China and the Mongol Qalmaqs. The emperor (ordered) the people of Ili to be put to the sword, (and countless people died).[16] Some escaped with their lives and fled to live among the Qipchaqs and Kyrgyz. Once Ili was pacified, he ordered 2,000 soldiers to march on Kucha.

By this time, the Khan Khoja Padishah had rallied 12,000 soldiers from Kashgar, Yarkand, and Khotan, and they had arrived in Aqsu. Now they marched to Kucha to head the people of Beijing off, and there they barricaded the road. Now the 2,000 soldiers arrived from Ili. Bitter battles were fought. Because the people of Beijing were fewer in number, they could not match them (but met their end). Then 10,000 imperial soldiers marched on

Kucha via the Turfan road. There were many battles. Ultimately, they were victorious. The soldiers of Islam were the weaker. Burhanuddin Khan Khoja Padishah could not match them, and so fled toward Yarkand along the Muqur road, through the wilderness. The people of Beijing took Kucha, and they put many people to death. Next, they took Aqsu, and quickly marched on Yarkand. The Khan Khoja Padishah fought many battles but could not match them, and fled with his life to Khotan. The nonbelievers followed him to Khotan. There too he failed to withstand them, and turned to go to Badakhshan. The commander of the Chinese forces found out and wrote a letter to the leader of Badakhshan. There some lowlife bastards cut off the head of the Khan Khoja Padishah and sent it to the [Chinese] officers. And these officers locked it in an iron cage and sent it to the khan in Beijing. They sent it from city to city, making a spectacle of it, so that all would know.

After they pacified the Seven Cities, they garrisoned them with 40,000 soldiers.

When they took Ili, over a million people were put to death, and many others fled. Because there were hardly any human beings left in Ili, they forced people to move from the Six Cities and settled them in Ili. Because these people were brought from every city and every town,{59} they came to be known by the name Taranchi.[17] But they were not satisfied with just these people, so they moved many from Beijing and made them settlers in Ili.

When they rebelled against the Emperor of China this time [*in 1864—ES*], and Russia had taken possession of Ili, then when the people of Beijing came, the people of Ili were afraid. They sought Russia's protection, and all of them migrated into Russia. Now the land of Ili lay empty again. But the people of the Six Cities, particularly those of Kashgar, moved there by their own will, farmed, and cultivated it once more.

* * *

Oh, people of our age! Look with penetrating sight upon the actions of the people of our age, and see how, though all Muslims are of one religion and one sect, they divided into two sides, indeed into many factions. One disputed with another, and each party followed one sayyid and saw another sayyid as their enemy. Some called themselves by the name "White Mountaineers" and others "Black Mountaineers," and they brought themselves to destruction—indeed, to wickedness! And this disunity brought their land, and also their people, into the possession of the Qalmaqs, and that of the

Chinese. They found these unworthy ways right and fitting, and paid no heed to their evils. These ignorant, perfidious Sufis had no shame. Yet there was no hatred, hypocrisy, or enmity in the inborn character of these sayyids, these sons of the Makhdum. This was surely the ill fortune of immature and half-educated students. When sayyids see each other as equals, as is correct according to tradition, they certainly bear no enmity. But if they should happen to fail to see each other as such, and to open their mouths to give voice to their enmities, then that is cause for them to be painfully afflicted. A hadith has been transmitted on this matter: I SEEK REFUGE WITH GOD FROM EVIL.

After Burhanuddin Khoja of the sons of Afaq Khoja was martyred, his son Ṣaliḥ Khoja (whom some call by the name Samsaq Khoja) fled to the country of Ferghana. Several times he came to Kashgar, revenge for his father's blood in mind, but he departed, unable to achieve his goal. His son, Khoja Jahangir Khan Törä, to some degree achieved that goal for him. His story will be told later on.

For this reason, when the Khojas later came from Andijan, the White Mountaineers' world-illuminating sun rose in joy. The Black Mountaineers sent gifts to the Khojas in Beijing, while from those Khojas came treasured parcels of green tea as gifts. This "blessed tea," as it was called, was highly honored and achieved great fame. Its story will be related later, in the discussion of Ushturfan.[18] GOD WILLING, HE IS THE PATIENT.

The White Mountaineers and Black Mountaineers are still enemies today. And many members of their factions are among the people of Kashgar. The beliefs of both are false and unfounded.

{60} THANKS BE TO GOD, for I am free of Mountaineers both Black and White!
For I have eaten of the fruit of the garden of Shariah.

* * *

When the light of the khans' lamp of fortune was extinguished, thanks to the Qalmaqs' help, the Khojas' lamp of fortune burned. Sometimes the Khojas busied themselves with their recitations and duties. Other times they busied themselves with feasting and carnal delights, with entertainments and forbidden pleasures. They grew ignorant of the common people's plight and became total sycophants, associating with those men whose words are like those of the jinn, and whose aspects are like those of *shaytans*. They displayed their faith too much and became like wolves—like wolves setting upon sheep, tyrannizing the wealth of the common people, and likewise the khan's faith. And these people they called "the lovers."[19]

Generations of their forefathers, of khojas who had led their orders, had been ignorant of the affairs of state and the techniques of government. Consequently, these Khojas brought the common people to ruin, so that the people could find no rest or stability in their own houses and lands, but fled into the wilderness to make their livings. At night, when they snuck something secretly for their families to eat, they would make a meal of it. They could keep no cooking pot or dishes with them, but would toss them into wells and deep places to hide them. They had to flee to keep themselves alive. The Khojas had no patience for rule, but found it an intolerable burden.

Now some of the perspicacious former begs, who had themselves fallen into ruin and joined the ranks of the common folk, said, "The khans who ruled in olden times chose to retire into seclusion, and so 'those who live in seclusion' became khans. The common people are afflicted and destitute. The best course of action is for some of us to go to the Emperor of China, make our plea, and request an army. And if he should give us an army, then we will join his country, and be liberated of our enemies both far and near, for if we do not submit to some country, then our land will never prosper, nor will our children be at peace." This they decided, and six or seven people went on the road in a rush. Sometime later, they came upon the emperor's sentries, who took them from sentry post to sentry post until they had an audience with the Emperor of China. His favor alighted upon their plea, and he granted them a vast army. And when they came to the Seven Cities they fell to the emperor without a fight.

Each of these six men was awarded some lofty title—*wang*, *gong*, *beise*, or *beile*—and assigned several households of men to serve them, and fixed an annual stipend from the treasury, and each was made the governor of a city.[20] In that bygone era of the emperor's rule, hardly any governorship in the Seven Cities was allotted to anyone who was not one of those begs' descendants.{61} One of those six who met with such fortune was Mirza Hadi Beg. His story was earlier told in brief. Another was Cherikchi Beg. This man was also granted the rank of *beise*. This beg had two sons called Setibaldi Beg and Aq Beg. Setibaldi Beg inherited the rank of *beise* and governed Yarkand. Then the rank of *beise* passed to his son Muḥammad ʿAbdullah Beg, and he governed Aqsu and Yarkand. His grandson, Muḥammad Musa Beise Beg, is in Aqyar in Aqsu.[21] Yet he cannot attain his forefathers' rank.

Aq Beg became the governor of Ili, and later of Aqsu and Yarkand. Then his son, Muḥammad Yusuf Beg, was governor of Ili, then of Yarkand, and finally of Sayram before he passed away. His son, Muḥammad ʿAbdullah Beg, served in the rank of deputy governor. He has many descendants.

Another was Gaday Muḥammad Gong of Bay. He governed Kashgar, and then Ushturfan. [Then his son ʿAbdurraḥman Beg became *gong*. And then] his son, Ibrahim Beg, was likewise a *gong* and governed Ushturfan. Then, [because he lost the *gong*ship on account of some infraction,] the *gong*ship passed to his younger brother, Muḥammad Musa Beg. Then his son, Muḥammad Ṭalib Beg, attained the rank of *gong*, and he governed Shahyar. Then his son, Aḥmad Beg, became *gong*. Then his son, Muḥammad Ṣiddiq Beg, was honored with the rank of *gong* (in the country of Bay). [He is known by the epithet Gong Khoja.] Because the descendants of the others, and their names and genealogies, are unknown, they have not been related here.

Those six begs' likenesses were carved and a great idol temple built in Ushaq Tal, where those likenesses were installed. And it was ordered—May their mouths be filled with gravel and earth!—"I have made these begs the masters, tutors, and guardians of the Seven Cities, and granted them offices. Henceforth, should any official (or trader) in the Seven Cities pass by, they are to visit these begs." Those idols were there until the time of Islam. All manner of officials and merchants who came from Beijing, when they arrived at the place where that temple was, would dismount from their horses, and indeed prostrate themselves. According to their own customs, they burned papers, knocked their heads several times, bowed, and prayed to those likenesses for help. Then they would move along. If they had not done so, they would have been liable for punishment. The house where that idol temple was, was called the "great house." Those begs' descendants would pride themselves on being able to say, "We are the descendants of the men of the great house." So, when Islam came, that idol temple was destroyed, and those begs came to live among the common people.[22]

Fourteen years later, the imperials regained their forefathers' lands. A proclamation came from the Emperor of China, which said, "There were such-and-such men who served my forefathers. Are they alive? Or might their sons be?{62} Make inquiries and inform me." They made themselves known, and they reclaimed their forefathers' ranks. Today several generations and some years have passed. Whether they have done any service for the Great Khan is unknown. Yet from year to year, they evidently continue to collect the stipends that the khan granted them long ago. Once every three years, they go to the khan for an audience, where they display their reverence. And so, in ease and repose, each generation takes their place and lives by the fortune of their *tarkhan*.[23] Hence the Emperor of China's greatness may be seen: for one audience, they have earned an office.

Oh, King of Kings! You possess true kingship, and You are the true king. Please, accept in Your great kingdom Your servants who serve You for but fifty or sixty years, grant them a place in perfumed Paradise, give to them their fortune, and strike out their sins from first to last with the pen of forgiveness. Nothing is too strange or wondrous for Your perfect power. OH, LORD OF LORDS, OH, MOST NOBLE OF NOBLES! AMEN.

0:5 The Holy War of Jahangir

How Khoja Jahangir Khan Törä Achieved Possession of the Seven Cities; Muḥammad ʿAli Khan Came to Kashgar, and Kashgar Was Conquered; and Many Soldiers Came, and It Was Conquered Again; and How They Seized Jahangir Khan Törä and Took Him Away to Beijing; and Many Muslims Were Taken Prisoner and Taken to the Country of China; and Muḥammad ʿAli Khan Sent an Emissary and Requested the Return of Those Muslims from the Emperor of China

IN THE HIJRI year 1230 [1815], Muḥammad ʿAli Khan b. Umran Khan b. Sher ʿAli Khan ascended to rule the country of Khoqand and the people of Ferghana.

In 1244 [1828/29], Khoja Jahangir Khan Törä gathered some men from among the believers of Khoqand and Kashgar. He fled Ferghana and arrived in the Moghulistani city of Kashgar, and that country came into his possession. He prepared to conquer the Chinese city.[1]

Meanwhile, Muḥammad ʿAli Khan's anger began to boil over, and he gathered an army. He summoned the high officials and said, "The Lord of the Worlds bestowed this kingship upon Us. Should We permit Ourselves{63} to become careless or negligent, then We will appear to be distant from the chamber of government and the abode of kingship. Some undignified khoja has assembled a mob of brainless ruffians, laid siege to Kashgar, and pressed his claim on that country. He has beaten the drum of khanship and fancies himself a conqueror. Of course, such a thing is impossible. Moreover, if he should conquer the city, then the treasures that the Chinese have stored up these long years will fall into those ruffians' hands and go to waste. Now, as for the Emperor of China, he is a mighty king. When the nonbelievers rally again from Beijing and regain their mastery, there is no doubt that they will overpower that khoja, even without the use of their treasure. Then, should they set those undisciplined soldiers into even greater disorder, it is surely possible that all the treasure of the Muslim country will disappear. Moreover, when Jahangir Törä has proven unable to keep order in that country, and the Chinese troops have taken control, then he will have no choice but to flee hither. We must secure communications with the Chinese. The best course of action is for Us to go to Kashgar. If Kashgar should come into Our possession, then it will be all the better. And even if not, We will have reaped the reward of holy war." So he arrived in Kashgar with 3,000 soldiers.

Jahangir Khan Törä and some of his men came out to greet him, and they met while seated atop their horses, paying the respects due to kings. Muḥammad ʿAli Khan was quartered in a large house.

At that time, Kashgar's Chinese City was inside the Muslim City.[2] The next morning, Jahangir Törä, as a show of submission, transferred command over the siege to the sublime khan and sent his own men away. By the khan's command, the soldiers of Khoqand carried out the siege. They set gunpowder beneath the Chinese city, dug holes, and lit them on fire. One side of the city was blown into the air, spreading dust across the face of the Earth, and the bright sun became like the blackest night, in the midst of which these victorious soldiers hurled themselves upon the wall like moths to the flame. The nonbelievers realized that the Muslims were rallying to the breached side, so they blocked the hole and kept up the fight. From within the city they fired their cannons, falconets, and jezails. Muslims and nonbelievers went hand to hand as they entered the melee, and such a battle it was, as the Muslims clambered up the ladders from every side and mounted the wall like acrobats.

Yet the nonbelievers rallied and three times drove the Muslims{64} from atop the wall. By the fourth day, all paths to the top had been blocked by all the bodies of the martyrs and the wounded. Now the Khan Ghazi saw this, and sorrow filled his heart, and he wept. He had the bodies taken away and buried at the Afaq Khoja shrine. He ordered the wounded to be tended to. Now he had no choice but to break the siege and take a week of rest. Then he gave Jahangir Khan Törä his blessing and returned to Khoqand, the seat of the sultanate. A month later, by the grace of the Opener of Doors, the Chinese city was conquered. They reported the joyous news of their victory and sent the message with gifts in the hands of trusted men to the presence of the noble khan. Now by turns they took control of Kashgar, Yengi Ḥissar, Maralbashi, and Yarkand, and they were pressing the siege in Khotan.

Yet some of their soldiers had gone to Aqsu, and when they reached the banks of a river two *tash* from the city, a few crossed over it. And as they lay in repose, thinking, "Tomorrow we conquer Aqsu!" the Chinese armies arrived. Those armies came out of the city and expended all effort to give chase to those soldiers as they fled. That grim army [*qara cherik*] followed them until they took Kashgar, and likewise seized Yengi Ḥissar and Yarkand.[3]

Some estimate the size of the Chinese army at 20,000, others at 10,000. In those days, the Daoguang Khan [r. 1820–1850] was on the throne of the Emperor of China, and his power was mighty, and on none of his borders was there any trace of an enemy. Apart from such weapons of war as guns, bullets, and gunpowder, the soldiers had dried the dung of sheep and camels in oil and brought it on 200 carts. It had been decreed, "When my soldiers find themselves in the rain and snow, or are without food, or cannot find firewood to cook, let them burn that manure in place of firewood to cook their meals." When the front end of the manure train had reached Qarashahr and its rear was in Turfan, the news came that the country had fallen into their hands, and they were ordered to withdraw. From this one may infer the numerousness of the troops, and the great power of the khan.

It is written that, when describing Jahangir Khan Törä's greatness, the Chinese said, "*Jahangir dong tan, di dong tan*," which means, "When Jahangir moves, the Earth moves."[4]

To elaborate: the commander of the Chinese army was named General Ai.[5] Mirza Isḥaq Beg, who was the second son of Mirza ʿUs̱man Beise Beg of Kucha, led soldiers to the city (Kashgar). Now he pursued Jahangir Khan Törä all the way to Alay.

The *törä* had no other choice,{65} but said to him, "Oh, Isḥaq Beg! Don't despair. Tie me and take me to the Chinese leaders."

"I have no right."

But the *törä* confessed his crimes, and said, "Please," as he took his blessed handkerchief and bound his own hands with it. "Now pull this handkerchief by its end and take me away." So Isḥaq Beg submitted to his command and took him to the Chinese leaders.

"Isḥaq Beg has captured the Great Khan's enemy," he reported.

"Oh, Isḥaq Beg!" General Ai said. "Now take this Khoja to Beijing yourself, and report to the Great Khan the service you have done. Then return." He gave him an escort and sent him to Beijing. And in great honor he took the Khoja to Beijing.

Some say that the khan met with him, interrogated him, and had him killed; others, that the khan never saw him, but put him in some secret place, and he died of natural causes. THE RESPONSIBILITY IS UPON THE NARRATOR.

* * *

The imperial officers sought out those people of the Seven Cities who had been the *törä*'s friends, or held office under him, or served him. They killed them, seized their livestock and land, and took more than 12,000 of their wives, daughters, sons, and little children prisoner, some of whom they took to Lanzhou and others to Ili and Tarbaghatai, where they were given to the Chinese as servants. When Muḥammad ʿAli Khan the Triumphant learned of this, he said, "We were the cause of this." So he assigned Chief Secretary ʿAlimbay Pacha to lead several men from the capital at Khoqand to the Emperor of China with generous gifts and presents he had prepared, along with a letter to the emperor laying out a number of requests.

The first was: "None of them has raised arms against the Great Khan or rebelled. The little children and weak among them could have done no evil thing. I ask the Great Khan to forgive their infractions." Another was: "I ask to station an *aqsaqal* in the Seven Cities, to take charge of the Andijanis, so that if some evil man should enter that country, they will inform me of it, and I may punish them. May no matter trouble the Great Khan's heart." He composed his letters with such articulate demands and pleasing words as these and sent the emissaries on their way. They arrived at the capital in great honor. The emperor read the letter, and in his consummate wisdom he accepted its proposals. He sent all those prisoners back to their own country and provided them with horses and donkeys, fodder and food, at every sentry post.

In the meantime, four years had passed. Some of those prisoners had been seized by the Chinese, and now they had had children.{66} But when they were sent home with their children, they were liberated from their exile and returned to their own land, and they were joyful. All of them, young and old, raised their weary voices and recited *ghazal*s and *muqam*s: "Nazugum, oh, oh, Nazugum!"[6] As they came up along the highway, the people came from far around to see them and hear them, and they could not help but weep and lament. To this day, people still know the *ghazal* called "Nazugum." There was the commandment that an *aqsaqal* be stationed to take charge of the Andijanis in the Seven Cities. This too is still in effect today.

* * *

Eventually Muḥammad ʿAli Khan passed from this world of troubles to the palace of joy. Khudayar Khan [r. 1844–1858, 1862–1863, 1865–1875] ascended the throne. Sometime later, an armed rebellion broke out against Khudayar Khan, and they elevated his elder brother, Malla Khan [r. 1858–1862], as khan, while Khudayar Khan stole away to Bukhara. Then, thanks to the deception of Mullah ʿAlimqul, Malla Khan was martyred. His reign had lasted four years. Now, through the efforts of the governor of Tashkent, Qanaʿat Shah Ghazi Tajik, Khudayar Khan was brought back from Bukhara to be made khan again. Yet Mullah ʿAlimqul had won the loyalty of some treacherous Kyrgyz, some Qipchaq and Kyrgyz, and he gathered some ignorant ruffians. He got a desire for power into his head and beat the drum of rebellion. Day by day, Ferghana's fortune descended. In the year 1278 [1861/2], Khudayar Khan sat upon the throne a second time.

Meanwhile, Wali Khan Törä had conquered Kashgar and taken possession of its towns and pastures.[7] He had many adulterers and oppressors put to death and their bodies thrown to the birds. He had the heads of those infidels, fornicators, and filthy Muslims both male and female gathered up, mixed together, and made into four towers. The height of those towers was estimated at twelve *gaz*.[8] He had no scruples about such madness and shedding of blood.

Around that time, an old farmer woman took bread, rolls, yogurt, and cream to the *törä*'s palace. The head of his personal guards said to her, "Oh, mother! What is your request?"

"I have come to ask the khoja for a blessing," she said. "I have no other request."

"Oh, mother!" the head guard replied, with the peculiar wit of that era. "We have given out all the blessings we brought from Andijan. Now there are no blessings left—the khoja does not have any, and neither do we. But we sent horses to bring blessings from Andijan. When the blessings come, I will let you know. When they arrive, you can come get your blessing."[9]

Later on, when the grim army came,{67} the *törä* could not match them, so he fled. Much blood had been spilled unrighteously, and many men met their deaths.

It has also been recorded that a master swordsmith forged a scimitar as a gift for the *törä*, in hopes that he would be able to have an audience with him and receive his blessing. He brought with him his young son of seventeen or eighteen when he went into the *törä*'s court to present the sword.

"Oh, Master!" the *törä* said. "How does this scimitar of yours cut?"

"It cuts very well," he replied.

"Oh, boy!" the *törä* said. "Come near to me, come." And the moment the boy drew near, he struck that sword upon his neck. His head fell to the ground. "Indeed it does," the *törä* said. "Give the master robes and send him away." They sent him off with a cheap cloth robe.

He wept and wept as he carried his son's body home.

* * *

Later on, Katta Khan Törä and Kichik Khan Törä came. They were besieged for three months in Kashgar and returned to their homeland without attaining their goal. But, were I to tell their story in detail, it would drive our readers and listeners to weariness, and my words might likewise stray far from their course. In light of such considerations, I have refrained from doing so and pulled the reins of the graceful pen toward the road of their purpose, and away from their stories.

0:6 Muslims Under Chinese Rule

How, Once Upon a Time, the Emperor of China Became a Muslim; How the Dungan People Settled in the Country of Beijing; the Origins of the Conflict Between the Chinese and Dungans; and How the Government of the Emperor of China Declined and Fell

IN THE YEAR of the Snake 1281, on the first day of Muḥarram, which was a Saturday night, in the month of Gemini [June 6, 1864], Mashur Akhund, Malong Akhund, and Shamsuddin Khalifa, who had settled in Kucha, led a rebellion against the emperor. They set fire to Kucha's suburban markets[1] and killed the officials and soldiers.

Everyone tells the story differently; one person's account differs from another's. According to tradition, one would seem obliged simply to repeat what they have written here on this page. However, I decided it would be better to make use of those stories that are more appealing to the intellects of the intelligent, and then to relate them both in detail and in a manner that accords with tradition.

* * *

{68} Once upon a time, in the country of the Emperor of China, there was a just and benevolent khan named Tang Wang Khan.[2] One evening, he dreamed that a dragon appeared in his palace and wrapped itself around a pillar. When it began to strangle him, an imposing man wearing a green robe, and with something white wrapped around his head, came in and struck the dragon with the staff in his hand. The dragon split into two and died.

The khan startled awake. The next morning, he called his generals, ministers, and dream interpreters into his chambers. He related the dream and asked for its interpretation.

The wise dream interpreters said, "Recently, in the direction of the *qiblah*, there has appeared a man who fits this description. It is said that he claims to be a prophet. It would seem that this is your man."

The khan ordered, "Send that man an invitation and bring him here!"

The officials said, "Then let us prepare gifts for him." They packed up tea, porcelain, and satin as presents and selected from their servants some stout and trusty fellows to lead the mission. They traveled from city to city until they happened upon a man who fit the description—that is, they met the Prophet of the End Times. They delivered the messages to him and presented him with the tea, porcelain, and satin, one by one.

Some days later, the Prophet wrote a letter in reply and gave it to the messenger. He said, "I give you leave to depart."

"I was sent here to invite you to come in person," the messenger said, and stood politely, awaiting a reply.

"Take this letter with you," the Prophet said. "Your king must open it with his own hand. No one else may open it. At that time, I too will be there."

He went on his way and after some time came to a stopping point. Satan inspired the messenger with a desire to open the letter, and when he did, it seemed as though someone had emerged from it and then disappeared. The messenger was disappointed that nothing had happened. He closed the letter up as it had been before and went to the khan's court. He explained all that had happened.

The khan opened the letter and looked at it. The letter was written in the language of Beijing! Surprised, the khan asked, "Who wrote this?"

"I don't know," the messenger replied. In fact, he had not known about it, nor seen it happen.

"And who opened it?" the khan asked. "If you tell the truth, I will forgive your crime. If you lie, I will not permit you to live." This was the khan's judgment, and when he declared such an ultimatum, there was nothing for it but to tell the truth. The messenger told him what he had done.

The just khan forgave his crimes. But then he said, "For the crime you have committed, you must go a second time. Bring back the man himself or his letter."[69] Some time and a thousand troubles later, they came to the homeland of that exalted man.

"You followed Satan," the Prophet told him, when he saw him, "and wronged your king as well as yourself. Didn't I tell you not to open the letter?"

The Prophet selected three men from his companions—Waqqas, ʿAs, and ʿUkkasha—and sent them, along with seven other people, ten in total, to travel with the messenger. They traveled from place to place until, somewhere near Jiayuguan, one of them passed away. They buried him there. In Bügür, there is a lofty shrine called ʿUkkasha. They say it is his tomb. After they crossed through Jiayuguan, another passed away. His resting place is revered.

When the messenger brought Waqqas Babam and eight others near the khan's city, men were sent out to greet them. They entered the capital with great honor.

The khan said, "The man I saw in my dream has not come," and he was rather disappointed.

His ministers discussed whether or not he should embrace the faith. Some of them agreed, while others did not. He had twelve chief ministers. They say that the khan secretly accepted the faith without letting his ministers know.

These eight men did not know the speech of the people of Beijing, while those of Beijing did not know theirs. This caused great difficulty, as those few men were strangers in this land. The khan ordered people to be found who could communicate with the men. One of his trusted men took eighty households of Chinese subjects and brought them to Samarqand. They brought forty Muslims from Samarqand in exchange. In total, there were forty-eight Muslims. When the Dungan people claim to be from Samarqand, this is probably what they mean. The ruler of Samarqand granted spacious pastures to these eighty households. They settled there, and their progeny multiplied. It is written that those called the "Chinese Qipchaqs" come from this group.

* * *

It is related in trustworthy histories that in the time of the Prophet of the End Times, Muḥammad Muṣṭafa, Samarqand was not Muslim. Moreover, in none of the chronicles can it be read that "Beijing wrote a letter" or "An emissary came." Rather, this must refer to some miraculous master and guide who had achieved perfection in the splendid Shariah and lived in an earlier age, or a later age, or that of the prophets of old. The Dungans, being ignorant of this, thus say that their people's lineage goes back to the time of the final prophet. They say that all of them are the descendants of these forty-eight Muslims.

In every city,{70} when the Chinese people find the right guidance of God and choose the religion of the Dungans, they become (secret) Muslims. Yet the Dungans do not become Chinese, turn apostate, or deviate from their religion. They say that this is why there are so many Dungans.

* * *

So this happy and just king converted to Islam, and proclaimed that all Muslims would be exempt from the taxes levied for the state, and if they should choose not to stray from the practices of their ancestors, then this would be their decision. From days of yore, the Emperor of China according to his law has always held that, regardless of what religion his people may belong to, he does not discriminate. If people do not convert others to one faith or another, but everyone stays true to their own, he is pleased.

The emperor took in the Muslims who had come as travelers to China. In order to convince them to stay in Beijing, per the customs of that land, he put on a great *changshila*,[3] which is to say an entertainment. He ordered, "Men and women, young and old, shall all gather. But whichever members of the weaker sex attend, be they young or old, should the Muslims find them pleasing, I will grant these women to the Muslims. Even if they have husbands or children, I will pay no mind." And so the Muslims took possession of those they desired. The khan permitted it. By the Shariah of the Prophet they married them. They seized their children too. And so they took the name Dungan.

There was no consideration for women who had husbands and children. Their seizure of these women displeased the people, who said, "They are *su hui hui*!" This evidently means in Chinese, "They have no shame." When the Chinese come into conflict with the Dungans, they call them *su hui hui*. Fifty Chinese were made the equal of one Dungan, and until they had committed fifty offenses to a Chinese person's one, a Dungan Muslim would not be brought before a judge. Many Dungans were pleased by this privilege, so they were very happy. This is the reason they looked down on the Chinese.

It is written that, some years later, the Shariah-loving khan passed on to the eternal world. His son succeeded him. Over a few generations, they came to transgress the Shariah and returned to the religion of their own people. Waqqas Baba too made his journey out of this material world and into the shelter of the eternal. His shrine is renowned. Eventually many centuries passed, during which the Dungan people were carefree.

* * *

Later on, in the city of Xining,{71} the Dungans built a madrasa and a Sufi lodge. For this purpose, they asked the khan for some unused land, which they irrigated and farmed. The produce supported a pious endowment for their lodge and the students who studied at the madrasa.

One day, the Chinese people's pigs began to get into the endowment's stores of grain. They drove the pigs out several times, and it turned into a major point of contention. Eventually, when it came time to harvest the wheat, the pigs got into the unthreshed wheat and ate it up again. The Dungans got into a dispute with the pigs' Chinese owner, and they came to blows. The Chinese gave refuge to the Chinese; the madrasa students gave refuge to the Dungans.

The conflict escalated, and when the city's high officials heard about it, they wanted to calm it down. So they wrote to their superiors, "The Dungans have been working this land from the pious endowment for years and collecting its produce. Now let us seize this land for the state, sell it, and collect the proceeds." Their superiors agreed, so they set to selling the land. First they sent people to seize it, but the mullahs at the madrasa and the Dungan people resisted. They fought off the officials sent to seize and sell the land and pushed them back into the city. As soon as these officials entered the city, they bolted the gates and closed it up tightly, taking refuge from the fight.

The Dungans too increased in their numbers. In their community there was a scholar named Ma Hualong Mullah.[4] They elevated this scholar as their khan. They built a new city called Jinjipu, where they enthroned Ma Hualong as sultan, and whence he issued his commands to all quarters.

Around this same time, the English Christians had their victory in the lands of the Emperor of China.[5] They seized the country called Burma and seventy-two cities. So too did they put many cities to ruin. Elsewhere, the people called Wu Sangui or the Long-Hairs [*Changmoza*] contested for the kingship. And then, in yet another place, the Dungans rebelled.[6]

Eventually the Dungans could not stay in Jinjipu, and they decided to steal away to another land. When the Great Khan heard that the Dungans were moving westward, he sent an order to the high officials in this region: "Some Dungans have rebelled against my rule. Even though we have tried to appease them, they fear the consequences of their own crimes, so they have fled to the west. If they go that way, the Dungans in that region will sympathize with them, and the common people will lose order. When you read this command, kill all of the Dungans. Keep me informed."

He sent this letter to the Ili General.[7]{72} When the Ili General received it, he was shocked. He said, "The Dungans are a plentiful people. And their ways and attitudes have grown different from ours. If they get even a whiff of this, then 'what we eat for dinner, they'll be having for breakfast.' The Dungans coming from the interior have a long way to travel. Before they get here, let us bring in the Muslim leaders, appease them with kind words, and secure their loyalty. That way, they will keep going about their business in peace." So they brought in some Dungans, tried to appease them, and sent them on their way.

But the Dungans were not appeased. They did not sleep that night but instead spent it holding vigils in mosques and shrines. The sorts of Muslims who only do their ablutions once a month started doing them several times each day. Their anxiety grew greater each day.

The Ili General was familiar with the Dungans' ways, and he grew worried. He decided to enact the khan's command. To every city he sent this order: "On such-and-such day, at such-and-such time, carry out a massacre of the Dungans."

One Dungan in Ürümchi named Suo Dalaoye had been an officer for the Chinese.[8] His son was the manager of a postal station. When this manager learned about the command to massacre Dungans, he informed his father. His father in turn wrote letters to Dungan leaders in every city to make them aware of the situation and enclosed a copy of the Ili General's orders. The moment that Suo Dalaoye's letter arrived in Kucha, the Dungans there rose up in one night. They set fire to the suburban markets, murdered whatever Chinese they encountered, and rebelled against the emperor's rule.

In no sect is it permitted to rebuke someone for a wrong that they have not yet committed. Yet they did what they did, and they received their punishment.

* * *

One more reason the Dungans and the Muslims rebelled was this: originally, when the Emperor of China had sent soldiers and first conquered the Seven Cities, he had issued an order saying, "Inquire with wise people, old and young, as to the rules and laws that my new Muslim subjects have followed, and what deeds they have done, and report them to me." So they summoned all the good and wise men in the land, read the khan's order out, and asked them.

"We are Muslims," they replied, "and God charged us with five obligations, the pillars of Islam.{73} We have followed them ever since." This they reported to the khan.

The Great Khan commanded: "If that be the case, then I too will charge my little subjects with five tasks. They must give one-tenth of what they grow. They must serve at the way stations, and they must pass correspondence from sentry post to sentry post. They must pass on news from the sentries. They must continue to provide the rough-spun cloth in tribute according to the old rules. I have ordered them to follow these five kinds of levy. Let them not give, or take, any more or any less. Let them not give too much or too little, but live in peace as my subjects." He likewise granted each of his officials men, land, and money according to their stations, assigned them salaries and provisions,[9] and in every place established the regulations, which is to say, the customs and rules.

The officials long followed their orders closely, doing neither more nor less. Yet, over time, they came to excess, inventing all sorts of innovations and new rules, and they committed such tyrannies that the people could no longer endure it. So they wrote a petition reporting their situation to the imperial agent and the governors. ʿIsa Gunbaẕ and Muḥammad ʿAli Bughra from Bay in Aqsu led the people of Bay in writing, "We pay the five levies that the Great Khan has commanded in his customs and rules. It was commanded that we 'must not give any more, nor any less.' Likewise were the Chinese and local officials assigned their duties. It was commanded that 'My officials must live on the provisions assigned to them and monitor my little subjects in peace.' The Great Khan does not know about the extra duties that we have paid. Nor do those duties enter the Great Khan's treasury. We have not violated the Great Khan's commands—but we are unable to give more than the five duties." So they submitted this petition, and a few days passed as normal—the five duties did not stop, nor were they late in paying them. The Chinese and local officials were bothered but said nothing at all in reply.

Eventually the begs and their interpreters consulted with each other, and they sent this petition to the imperial agent: "A few men have risen up against the Great Khan and rebelled, taking up arms." Because those higher officials were unaware of the situation, they accepted the begs' petition and sent troops to capture those men. They hanged ʿIsa Gunbaẕ and sixteen others.{74} Some they imprisoned. A few they killed by nailing them alive to the wall. And some they starved of food and water, and then they mixed lime in water and gave it to them. They drank it. They stiffened. They collapsed. The begs reported that they had "died of sickness," and then burned the bodies.

The people of Kucha could not endure these excessive exactions either, and many people gathered under the leadership of Muḥammad ʿAli Shaykh and Mullah Musa Imam to present their petition. They would not hear their petition, although it was made according to the rules. So when it reached their offices, they made excuses to mollify them. And the people, when they considered the character of those officials, were not reassured. They stayed awake all night at shrines, holding vigils, reciting the Quran, and performing the remembrance of God, and they called themselves Sufis.

The begs wrote to the imperial agent, "Some people have made themselves enemies of the Great Khan and risen against him in rebellion." With this excuse, they sent soldiers to capture them. A dozen or so people, including Muḥammad ʿAli Shaykh and Ibrahim Arbab Beg, were torn limb from limb and decapitated. Others had their feet cut off to cripple them. Forty or more, among them ʿAlim Kökbashi, Taliʿ Kökbashi, and Tokhta Kökbashi, were put in chains and locked up in prison.[10]

Now people in every city went to the imperial agent in Yarkand or the general in Ili to present their petitions. However, they only remanded those petitions to those people's own local officials, who pretended to be horribly upset and said to them, "Did you take a petition to an official in another city without bringing it to me first?" The local officials in every place would receive their people's petitions, whether good or bad, and they had a responsibility—if not an obligation—to respond with compassion. They abandoned that, even executing people without hearing them.

If the Great Khan had only heard their petitions and known what was happening, not only would these Chinese and local officials have lost their positions, their money and their lives would hardly have escaped either. Because these officials turned a true petition false and a false petition true—all for the sake of saving their positions and their money—and because they reported to the Great Khan and spilled Muslim blood, they had themselves violated the Great Khan's ancient *daoli*[11] customs and rules and rent their commitment to the people asunder. They were not satisfied with that which was granted to them, and they acted against their orders,{75} laying their hands instead on the people's money and property and committing extreme acts of tyranny. Then they blamed their own ill intentions on the people, casting suspicion on them. Indeed, because it was they who rebelled, and they who deserved the Great Khan's knife, so did he put the officials who ruled these destitute people to the sword. MAY GOD PROTECT US!

If things had not gone this way, what reason would anyone have to call these men who carried out holy war "warriors" or "martyrs"? In no school or sect is it permitted to take up arms and rebel against those great kings whom the Lord of the Worlds by His ancient knowledge has raised up, nor their liege men. But the Knower of Secrets in His ancient wisdom is aware of all His creations' unworthy thoughts, wicked deeds, and evil desires. GOD KNOWS THE TRUTH.

Those officials did not hear the people's petitions but were negligent, and all the unscrupulousness they displayed in their faithlessness to this great state was why they lost power, as well as the reason the Great Khan's government diminished. The common people could not lift such tyranny and injustice from their own backs, so they turned their faces to the court of the True King, and they wept and cried out. And as they wondered what happenings might come from the holy court of the Exalted and Powerful, the Wise in All Things, the blood of those who had died unjustly overflowed and began to boil, and now came the reward for the tyranny visited upon the people.

Sudden as a storm, one night in Kucha, the Dungans rebelled and put the nonbelievers to the sword. Taliᶜ Kökbashi and his forty men had been sitting in jail as "criminals" for more than two years. The Dungans broke it open and let the prisoners out. Dungans and Muslims together attacked the hypocritical Chinese.

But I will tell this story later on. GOD WILLING! HE IS THE PATIENT.

* * *

Then fourteen years passed, and then the Great Khan was truthfully informed about his subjects and his officials. That is why he scratched out his subjects' transgressions with the pen of forgiveness and sent soldiers to collect them. Yet he did not ask his officers, "Where have my officials gone? My soldiers? What happened?"{76} What would have happened if he had asked about those transgressions? There were seven assistant agents and one imperial agent stationed in the Seven Cities. He would have held the life of one assistant agent to be worth those of a whole city of people, and he would have ordered a massacre. And something would have had to be done for the lives of all those wangs and governors, for the Great Khan would have known about everything.

* * *

Another cause for the appearance of defects in the Emperor of China's state was that Xianfeng Khan [r. 1850–1861] had inherited the throne. The emperor's fortunes had reached their zenith. Now the Westerners seized and plundered many of his cities and ruled over them. Meanwhile, the people called Long-Hairs contested for the kingship. Their battles came to an end, but then the Dungans elevated a khan from among their own and rebelled. Now each of the rulers who had raised their banners of kingship all around the empire's edges fabricated some pretext, and none would leave the Great Khan in peace. Peace and tranquility were lifted from the Great Khan and his people.

The Great Khan calls the cities out our way *kouwai*—"Beyond the Pass."[12] "We have no way to get news from Beyond the Pass," he proclaimed, "nor can I send funds or supplies to our officials stationed there. For many years now, I have taken care of the officials and soldiers Beyond the Pass by sending silver from my treasury, and I spent a great deal of treasure. Nothing at all came into the treasury from Beyond the Pass. Now abandon Beyond the Pass and return home."

However, the Chinese leaders, the general and the agent, and the Muslim leader, Mirza Aḥmad Wang, together with all the governors, decided to write to the emperor: "Even if salaries and funds are not forthcoming from the treasury, we would nevertheless like to locate mines in the Seven Cities and by our own power extract gold, silver, copper, lead, iron, and sulfur. We will provide for the Great Khan's soldiers. As for ourselves, our families have served the Great Khan for generations and benefited from his fortune. If we followed this command and abandoned Beyond the Pass, would that not perhaps be an act unbefitting the Great Khan's honor?"

The Great Khan agreed. "If that is the case," he wrote, "then locate these mines and provide for the soldiers. Do nothing that would endanger my subjects."

{77} As soon as they received this order, the officials in every city went to seek out deposits in every mountain, desert, and dune, and they drove the common people into corvée service, until they made the foot of every mountain look like a mouse's nest. They could find no deposits to mine. Even when they did find something, they still visited great injustices upon the people. The officials gave out none of their own money, while the ore that was extracted simply disappeared. Then they invented several new taxes, one of which they called "salt money," which they took from the common people. They levied another tax every month, which they called a "head tax."

In sum, the people suffered from many taxes, levies, and troubles. Relief was as rare as a phoenix egg, and peace like the Simurgh made its roost on the Mountain of Qaf.[13] Wealthy men gave money to the Chinese and the powerful begs for protection, and so all of the burdens of the state fell on the moneyless poor, the vagabonds, and the orphans. They could not lift this burden, so instead, all of their property, animals, and even the tools they used to make their living went to the Chinese, and to waste. They offered up their tears to God, weeping and crying out.

Every few days, the soldiers in each city would beat their drums and go to the officials' doors and threaten them, saying, "Give us our salaries[14] and provisions! Otherwise we will leave and go home, or else divide your possessions among ourselves!" They gave them no rest.

The officials worried for themselves, so they pasted up notices[15] in every marketplace that read, "We will grant an official position to whoever 'donates'[16] silver for the soldiers."

Some mean scoundrels saw these notices, and because they coveted offices, they gave their money and purchased positions. They continually visited great injustices upon the common people. No matter what no-account thief, gambler, or tramp paid up, they gave him an office somewhere. Never did they mind the troubles that had come to their people. If someone presented a petition to one of the Chinese officials, he would say, "The governors handle petitions from the Chantous,"[17] and send it back. This was precisely what the local governors wanted, and they got to be openly tyrannical just as they pleased. Now that people saw how the officials feared no one, people could submit no petitions. Now the interpreters acted as middlemen, and they openly sold offices for money.{78} This humiliated the begs, whose families had served the Great Khan hereditarily for generations and governed this country: Afridun Wang Beg of Turfan was the governor of Khotan, and Muḥammad Amin Wang Beg his deputy governor. Afridun Wang Beg was removed from office on account of some infraction, but then they accepted 2,000 *yambu* of silver from a Khotanese man named Rustam Beg and made him governor of Yarkand. Rustam Beg had served in Muḥammad Amin Wang Beg's office and gained his reputation as a functionary, but because he gave money, they made him governor above him, while they appointed this wang as his deputy, demeaning him in a position of servitude. It is written that he said, "It would be a thousand times better for me to die than to live like this," and killed himself.

Then Qutlugh Beg of Kucha, who had been a functionary under both Mirza Isḥaq Wang Beg of Kucha and Mirza Aḥmad Wang Beg, was made governor of Kashgar. His younger brother, Saʿid Beg, paid 1,500 *yambu* of silver and became governor of Aqsu. The old governors lost their positions, while their idle subjects became begs. Now they looked down upon the nobles of this country and paid no heed to the common people's tears. Never did they allow those troubles to cross their minds. Nothing bothered them—save for their lust for office and the pain of the silver they had paid.

Outwardly, they proclaimed, "We have served the Great Khan by providing for his soldiers and protecting his lands." But essentially they had cut the roots of the state and caused it to wither. Now the nobles and the begs wished only to retire into seclusion, while they drove poor people into corvée labor, separating fathers from their sons. The people could take it no longer, and from the afflictions of their hearts and souls, their tears fell from their eyes to the Court of the Creator, now in droplets, and now in rivers. Their bitter tears too affected the roots of the tree of state and caused it to wither. It would not be long now before all of those officials, Chinese and local alike, would perish and be united with the soil.

The words of the great Mawlana Jalaluddin Rumi seem apt. From the *Mathnavi*:

> Until the heart of the man of God was grieved,
> Never did God put any generation to shame.[18]

Finally, the cries of the awakened must have received a response from the Holy Court of the Peerless, as the countries of Moghulistan had passed into the hands of men of no name or account.{79} The Lord of the Worlds with His perfect power did as it says in the Quran: THOU EXALTEST WHOMSOEVER THOU WILT, AND ABASEST WHOMSOEVER THOU WILT [3:26]. As the indigo sphere and the inconstant, deceitful world tremor, at every moment they lay one people low and exalt another.

May it be known to the wise that you may draw experience from these strange affairs, and concentrating thereupon take a lesson from them: if you attend to the tears that the victims of oppression shed, and when those who suffer from tyranny cry out, you open the doors of justice in gratitude for your great fortune, then it will be as the hadith says: GOD GIVES GREAT REWARDS TO HIS PEOPLE.[19] As the blessed hadith AN HOUR OF JUSTICE IS BETTER THAN THE WORSHIP OF TWO RACES says, one hour of justice is greater than the worship of all the humans and jinn. This kind of faith and fortune is impossible for anyone but governors, *dadkhwahs*,[20] generals, and judges to enjoy.

God, by Your perfect power, grant right guidance to all governors, *dadkhwahs*, and officials who seek refuge in the Shariah. Open the door of justice to them and close the gates of tyranny. Amen.

* * *

In conclusion: This graceful pen dove into the stories and genealogies of exalted khans and honored kings—which are like unto a boundless ocean—and with a few plunges brought these kingly pearls into the palm of our intent and strung them upon the line of narration.

So now we bring our brief prolegomenon to a close, and we turn the reins of our tractable pen toward the historical tales that were our original purpose, where upon that vast and lofty hippodrome we shall gallop our horses. Those stories that came from the mirrors of the hearts of ordinary people of that time but were forgotten, and that escaped the memories of our contemporaries and ran wild—those stories that burned our livers, brightened our hearts, set the world aflame—these I have gathered up within these pages and shepherded firmly inside their stockade. These I have turned into a story to raise a memorial, and now I begin to scratch my pen.

By His grace and His munificence, He from whom we seek help.

The First Epic

1:1 The Holy War of Rashuddin Khoja

{80} How by the Grace of THAT MASTER OF SOVEREIGNTY, THE BENEFICENT, THE ABLE, WHO IS THE POSSESSOR OF GRACE AND VIRTUE, the World-Illuminating Sun of Islam Rose Over the City of Kucha; How Rashuddin Khoja Ascended the Throne of Khanship and Marched His Armies to the East and West; and What Happened in the Meantime

LISTEN TO THOSE tales of the strange and wondrous, those enchanting stories of adventure, of how the inconstant, topsy-turvy spheres have made it their ageless custom to lead every caper of who is above, and who below, and to conduct each time the astonishing dance that brings disquiet to great kings' states and discord to the commoners' refuge.

By the Grace and Wisdom of the Creator of the Eighteen Thousand Worlds and that magnificent and merciful Judge and True King, and by the aid of the pure souls, these Seven Cities passed from the rule of the old Muslim khans into that of the Emperor of China. They remained for one hundred eighteen years in the emperor's domain,[1] being debased by the exactions of the state and ransacked by the tyrannical Chinese and the *begs*' injustices. And so the common people cried out from the bottoms of their hearts and piteously importuned the Court of the Creator. As they prayed for the salvation of the Muslims and the ruin of the tyrannical infidels, one night the Dungans rose up, as sudden as the wrath of God. They set fire to the suburban markets of Kucha and killed every infidel in their sight.

Then the son of the governor of Yengi Ḥissar, Allahyar Beg, fell in with some disgruntled Muslims. They joined forces and set fire to the offices of the two-faced officials and imperial agent, and by the break of dawn, they had killed many infidels. As soon as the sun rose, the officials gathered their soldiers and went out to fight the rebels. Yet they could not gain the advantage but instead found defeat, and were utterly decimated. The Muslims (and Dungans) were victorious. It was Saturday, the evening of the first of Muḥarram in the year 1281, in the month of Gemini and the Year of the Snake [June 6, 1864].

At that time, Aḥmad Wang Beg had been dismissed from the governorship of Yarkand for some infraction. By imperial command, he had been sent back to his homeland of Kucha to await orders. The Dungans and Muslims approached Aḥmad Wang Beg and importuned him, saying, "Your honored family has governed for generations. You know well the ways of rule and methods of government. If you would agree to care for us and enact your rule, we would serve at your command{81} with all our hearts. We would recognize you as the foremost among all amirs and regard you as the khan."

"You are few," he replied, "and the Chinese numerous beyond reckoning. You cannot match them. As for me, my forefathers served the emperor and gained high office, and they were rewarded with property and many households of men, and we have received honors one after another. Besides, how could I, who have seen the emperor with my own eyes on several occasions, wish to do him ill? Although he is a faithless infidel, nevertheless, for generations my family has eaten his food and benefited from his grace. Whatever happens, we do not turn away from the one who gives us salt—and to keep the rule of salt is the duty of people everywhere.[2] I will not jump at your offer to rise to power and so condemn myself to ruin. Choose whomever you wish to follow. I have reached the age of seventy. I have seen all the good fortune that I will ever see. There is nothing more that I desire."

When he spoke, all of them turned on him. "You still hope for your Chinese?" they asked him, as in their frenzy, they removed him from his palace and made a martyr of him.

One of the Khojas of Kucha named Rashuddin Khoja was just then occupied with prayer at the shrine of Mawlana ʿArshuddin. He lived the life of a dervish in seclusion from humanity. He was one of those among the Muslims and Dungans who had chosen the way of obedience within the ranks of the disciples of purity. They carried this khoja against his will out of his chamber of worship. "Before you were our leader in prayer and our guide," they told him. "Now we ask that you both act as our leader in prayer and occupy the khan's seat, and that you lead us and issue your commands." Regardless of whether he was willing, they sat him atop a white felt and per the custom of bygone kings placed him upon the khanal throne. Tokhta Eshikagha Beg was made his minister. Then they killed all eight of the old begs, including the old governor Qurban Beg, and plundered their possessions. Thereupon fear and terror fell upon all. They submitted to the rule of the new khan and bowed their heads to him.

If these officials had not broken the rules of the ancient law of *lu*[3] and by their actions set themselves to ruin, God help us, would the people have ever{82} resorted to violence and holy war? GOD KNOWS THE TRUTH.

* * *

Two days later, Rashuddin Khoja appointed Burhanuddin Khoja, who was known as the Khaṭib Khoja ["Preacher Khoja"], as general, and he sent his young son, Maḥmudin Khoja, to accompany him, along with Mullah ʿUs̱man Akhund as military judge. He sent him westward with 150 soldiers, eighteen (eight) Dungans, and ten cannons.

"For some generations," Rashuddin Khoja said, "the Muslims have suffered in abasement, serving at the thresholds of infidels and tyrants. Our men have been separated from their wives and children, and children from their mothers and fathers. In our abasement, with no taste in our food, no comfort in our clothing, we have lived in suffering from their exactions. But the Lord in His mercy is on our side, and He has given us His powerful hand. We have pitilessly put the infidels to the sword of Islam and sent those in Kucha on their way to Hell. As it says, WHOSOEVER AIDS AGAINST THE INFIDEL—and so we have sent some tyrants to join them. Now, in gratitude, the most important thing of all is to use every last spark of life that remains within us on the path of holy war. The great holy war is an obligation, and one of the Prophet's occupations—indeed, it was his practice, worthy of imitation. By the Lord's command, He put the Muslims under the infidels' thumb, but with His perfect power He raised the Muslims up and cast the infidels low. Thus is made manifest the meaning of THOU EXALTEST WHOMSOEVER THOU WILT, AND THOU ABASEST WHOMSOEVER THOU WILT." [3:26]

Rashuddin Khoja commanded, "Seize the cities of Bay and Sayram, and then take some soldiers to Aqsu. There the Muslims are many and the infidels few. By the time you get there, the Dungans and Muslims may already have exterminated the infidels ahead of you. If the infidels should attack you, and you find them ready for battle, then as the Quran says, SLAY THE IDOLATERS WHERESOEVER YOU FIND THEM [9:5]—put them to the sword without hesitation or delay. Mind the meaning of the hadith, PARADISE IS UNDER THE SHADES OF SWORDS.[4] Once affairs in Aqsu, Kashgar, Yarkand, and Khotan are settled, then the leaders of Bukhara and Khoqand may see fit to establish friendly relations and to profess their obedience and submission to you, but if not—that is, should they refuse—then I will send you assistance and aid once more. Conquer the lands to the west to the greatest extent you can. I declare you to be my deputy in affairs of state both general and particular and grant you free rein." He raised his radiant command and sent them off to war.

Next, he placed Ṣiddiq Dadkhwah, Mamur Bahadur, and Tokhta Muḥammad Yüzbashi under the command of Isḥaq Khoja, along with 180 Muslims, fifty Dungans, and twelve cannons.{83} He sent them eastward, repeating the command he had issued to the Khaṭib Khoja. He recited the *Fatiha*, prayed, and sent them on their way. PEACE AND GLORY.

[From this point onward, Rashuddin Khoja is referred to mainly as "the Khan Khoja," as he now combined the roles of khoja, or Sufi spiritual leader, and khan, or temporal political leader.—ES]

1:2 The Genealogy of Rashuddin Khoja

May It Be Not Concealed That It Is Deemed Necessary to Provide a Brief Account of the Ancestry of Rashuddin Khan Ghazi Khoja

RASHUDDIN KHOJA WAS the third son of Shaykh Niẓamuddin Khoja. Niẓamuddin Khoja was one of the descendants of Mawlana ʿArshuddin. Mawlana ʿArshuddin was the son of Mawlana Jalaluddin Kataki. Mawlana Jalaluddin Khoja was a descendant of Abu Ḥafiẓ Kabir Bukhari. In the year 617 [1220] [616 (1219)], when the world-conquering king, Chinggis Khan, attacked the holy city of Bukhara and massacred its people, Khoja Abu Ḥafiẓ Kabir Bukhari was martyred. The Mongols put his family into felt tents and took them back to their own land, which was Karakorum Kelüren. Six or seven [seven or eight] generations later, Mawlana Jalaluddin was in the city of Katak when all at once the wrath of God struck the city, though instead of a storm it rained sand. Jalaluddin and some of his disciples, inspired by God, did not sleep that night but fled. After one day and one night, their steps led them to Ay Köl in Aqsu.

At that time, Tughluq Timur Khan had just ascended to the khanship in Aqsu. At the age of fifteen or sixteen, he met Mawlana Jalaluddin, from whom he received some instruction. A tenderness grew in Tughluq's heart, and he said, "This Tajik's words please me. After I have gone to Ili and am established in my capital there, let him come to me. I will join this man's faith. Were I to do so here, none of my great generals or commanders would be with me. Most of my people are in Ili—it would bode ill to do it here." So he gave Jalaluddin his promise and returned to Ili. Tughluq Timur Khan was the seventh-generation descendant of Chinggis Khan. His story was told above.

Yet Mawlana Jalaluddin got no opportunity to go to Ili, and before he could, he was buried in Aqsu at Ay Köl. His shrine there is well known. At the end of his life, he said to his son, Mawlana ʿArshuddin, "I have put oil in a lamp and prepared the wick therein. Yet there was no chance to light the flame. Now it appears that you must light it for me. The light of this lamp shall be seen across the east." And with these words he passed away.

Some time later, Mawlana ʿArshuddin Waliullah followed his father's command and went to Ili, where he met the khan.

{84} "Where is your father?" the khan asked.

"He has passed away," ʿArshuddin replied. "He bequeathed his duty to me. I came here bearing that hope."

Thereupon the blessed khan agreed to embrace the faith of Islam. Next Jalaluddin brought each of the great commanders arrayed before him in turn—the *el begi*s and *zaisang*s—and convinced them by sermons and the draught of admonishment. "There is no better act in this world," he said, and he made them Muslims. That day, so it is said, more than 70,000 faithless Mongols became pious Muslims. The khan was twenty-four years old. It was the year 756 (1355) [656/1258]. From that day forth, the faith of Islam openly took hold among the Mongols.

"Oh, great mullah!" said the khan. "Now it is up to you. Whichever city you would like to live in, it is your choice."

ʿArshuddin made his choice: "I would like to live in Kucha." So he was granted leave to go to Kucha, where he married and settled down. The khan bestowed a place in Kucha called Ich Eriq upon him as his prize, and the khan's bequest survives today as part of a pious endowment under the control of the great mullah's descendants. Eventually this weary man passed on from the world of illusion to the threshold of the palace of eternity. His great shrine and place of pilgrimage is known as the Great Mullah.

* * *

Niẓamuddin Shaykh Khoja's first son was Shaykh Naẓiruddin Khoja. His second was Jamaluddin Khoja. His third was Rashuddin Khan Khoja. His fourth [fifth] was Fakhruddin Khoja. His fifth [fourth] was Jalaluddin Khoja. [They killed Jamaluddin Khoja in Yarkand. The Khan Khoja and the other four khojas died in Kucha by the victorious Ataliq Ghazi's command.]

The Khaṭib Khoja and Isḥaq Khoja were Shaykh Niẓamuddin Khoja's nephew and cousin [*ʿammakzada*], branches and fruits of the same tree.

1:3 The Failure of the Aqsu Campaign

How the Sayyid Khaṭib Khoja and His Beloved Son, Maḥmudin Khoja, Determined to Go on a Holy War to Conquer Aqsu; How They Returned to Their Homeland Without Achieving Their Goal; How the Muslims Drank Deeply of the Nectar of Martyrdom; and Other Events That Came to Pass

THE KHAN KHOJA (Rashuddin Khoja) bid farewell to the Khaṭib Khoja and sent him westward. The Khaṭib Khoja left Kucha and made camp at a place called Qizil. Next he took Sayram, where he executed four men by the noose and the blade. Thereafter he came to Bay, where he stayed for two days to rest and also hanged six more men. These were men who had walked the evil path of sin. They received their punishment. The Khaṭib Khoja made Akram Shah Aʿlam Akhund the governor of Sayram and Mullah Afaq Aʿlam Akhund that of Bay.

Next he passed through Yaqa Eriq, whence he sent a man named Rozi Törä with 150 people to the Muzart Pass. "Break open Muzart," he said,{85} "and kill the Chinese garrison at the fort.[1] On Wednesday you must arrive at Jam. We will come from this side, and you from the other, trapping between us the Chinese at Jam in the barracks they have made.[2] We will eliminate them."

Now all of the men of Bay, Sayram, and the mountainsides joined together and formed a militia. They raised their voices in praising God—"Allah! Allah!"—and followed the Khojas. "We will go to Aqsu and take vengeance on the tyrannical infidels," they hoped. "And we will earn ourselves esteem as holy warriors. If we fulfill this promise and drink the nectar of martyrdom, then IN THE HEIGHTS OF HEAVEN we will take our place in eternal Paradise." They abandoned life and fortune for the nectar of death. Fathers did not look to their sons, nor sons to their fathers, but followed behind the Khojas on foot and mount.

In several places the Khojas stopped and told them, "Go back. Let us carry out holy war on your behalf."

Still they replied, "We have lost our patience with tyranny, and no other way is open to us. Let us leave this life behind, giving a life or taking one." They wept and wept from the bottoms of their hearts as they resolutely abandoned their precious lives. Each marched carrying his own rough bulgur gruel and crude cudgel. One could estimate that there were about 7,000 of them.

Oh, dear friends! Whatever king or governor visits tyranny upon the people, when he passes from his sweet life, he will appear in the court of the Divine, offering up the tears from his eyes as he weeps bitterly. Then the Lord's sea of mercy will begin to boil, and He will make his lowly and wretched servants victorious without weapons over this grandiose king. HE AND NO OTHER in an hour's time will bring the tyrants defeat and SCATTER THEM AS ASHES [20:105]. And He will grant the throne of kingship to the wretched and lowly, His creations without anything to their names, and grant them stations higher even than those of great kings at the court of the Eternal. The Lord of the Worlds is the Able, the Creator: HE SAYS, "BE!" AND IT IS [36:82]. Whatever He does, He has the power to do. As the Quran says: GOD DOES WHATSOEVER HE WILL [14:27], DECREES WHATSOEVER HE DESIRES [5:1], and GOD IS POWERFUL OVER ALL THINGS [2:20]. [AND UNTO HIM IS THE JOURNEY'S END (5:18).]

To make a beggar into a king is easy for Him;
It is just as easy for Him to make a king into a beggar.

The Khojas rode from Yaqa Eriq and alighted at Qara Yulghun at the time of the dawn prayer. There they caught and killed some Chinese scouts. That day they waited, for the next day was the appointed day. As they were preparing to march on the soldiers in Jam, suddenly the weather turned, and it rained. Soon after, a blizzard began to kick up. The Khaṭib Khoja and his officers all went into their tents{86} and fell asleep. The soldiers took shelter under branches, walls, and such things. They took the saddles from their horses' backs, put them under their heads, and went to sleep.

Suddenly the Chinese from Jam were upon them, with a mass of grim soldiers led by Saʿid Beg, the governor of Aqsu. The Muslims awoke to the sound of cannons and found themselves surrounded. Some of them managed to reach a saddled horse, while others rode off bareback. Those on foot and mount alike were defeated by fear. They turned tail and fled. The Chinese soldiers killed many men in melee. Those who had hoped to drink the nectar of martyrdom by God's command got their wish. Some others fled into the desert, where they died of thirst. The dead were reckoned at over 2,800. The soldiers of Islam were scattered, while the Khojas took the road back toward Kucha.

The governor of Aqsu, Saʿid Beg, wished to capture the Khojas, and he pursued them for a distance of six *paotai*,[3] at which point he received an order from the Chinese: "Hunting those who have disappeared is not *li*.[4] They might have captured Jam. Return immediately." As soon as Saʿid Beg heard this dreadful news, he turned around and came to Jam. There he found that Rozi Törä had come to Jam and killed all of the remaining Chinese wranglers, storemen, and stablehands there, just as planned. Then he heard the news: when the soldiers led by Rozi Törä learned that the Muslims had been chased from Qara Yulghun, with many killed and others taken prisoner, they realized they could not stay in Jam so went instead to a town called Östäng Boyi. There they were captured and turned over to the Chinese, who killed them.

* * *

At this point something occurs to your humble author that I cannot help but relate: the greatness and power of the Emperor of China is as clear as the sun to every human nation, while Kucha is but a small town that has no repute among great cities. A handful of Muslims from such a place as this rose up and matched a vast continent. The Khaṭib Khoja entered one howdah, and the military judge Mullah ʿUs̱man Akhund was placed in another. Yet each grew proud and complacent, and, having seized Bay and Sayram for themselves, they lost all care and worry. They had traveled not five stages when they took off their boots and trousers and lay down carefree to sleep—what soldier should trouble them, what enemy frighten them? They slept naked and so brought about the spilling of Muslim blood.

Oh, you writer, Mullah Musa, be kind—
Withdraw your tongue from rebuke.

A VERSE:

When a thorn pricks or a downy hair falls,
{87} Know this: It is by God's will.

Nothing, no matter how great or small, happens beyond His will. By the verse THEY SAID, "YEA, WE BEAR WITNESS" [7:172], one cannot help but bear witness to this world that God wrote with His own mighty pen.

* * *

Then the military judge, ᶜUs̱man Akhund, was taken prisoner at Qara Yulghun. Saᶜid Beg had been his student. Saᶜid Beg appeased the Chinese officers under his command and wrote to the imperial agent in Aqsu something like, "This man was one of the rebels' leaders. He must be interrogated as to the reasons for his actions. We might want to keep him alive." The agent agreed to his proposal, so they did not kill ᶜUs̱man Akhund but kept him prisoner with several Chinese guards.

The Khaṭib Khoja went to Kucha, but he returned with more soldiers and conquered Aqsu a month later. By then, the Khaṭib Khoja suspected that Mullah ᶜUs̱man Akhund had gone over to Saᶜid Beg's side, and he cursed him. Yet when Aqsu fell, some of the soldiers killed those Chinese, and when they entered a chamber, there they found Mullah ᶜUs̱man Akhund, firmly bound and shackled hand and foot. They brought him before the khoja in this condition, and there they struck his shackles off. The khoja's suspicions were lifted and his spirits raised. When the Chinese garrison soldiers heard that the city was taken, they hanged themselves, while some died in other ways. Yet they had not made that demand of Mullah ᶜUs̱man Akhund. The reason was that Chinese officers take their orders very seriously. No matter what, they never thought, "Let us kill a Muslim enemy before we die." The True Protector Himself had protected him. While the Khaṭib Khoja was a very simple man, and compassionate, who lacked experience of the world, he was nevertheless a pious Muslim endowed with a sense of justice. Now, in his utter shame, he could not raise his head.

1:4 The Success of the Aqsu Campaign

How on the Second Occasion Sayyid Jamaluddin Khoja Was Sent to March on Aqsu; How the Conquest of Aqsu Succeeded, and the Flowers Bloomed in the Garden of Their Intent; How Those Flowers Were Gathered Along With Their Hearts' Desire; and Other Events

IN THOSE DAYS of glory, His Highness, Sayyid Rashuddin the Khan Khoja, was installed upon the throne. The robes of rulership suited his stature, and the crown of kingship his head, and he issued commands to all his subjects great and small. All of his orders were signed with "Foremost Among the Descendants of the Prophet of God, the Triumphant, the Victorious Sayyid Ghazi Rashuddin the Khan Khoja." The preachers' pulpits{88} were beautified with the Khan Khoja's holy name, and they struck copper coins in the manner of the Emperor of China. On one side was written "Rashuddin Ghazi Khan" and on the other, "Struck in the Sultanic Capital of Kucha." These coins are still in circulation today.

When the Khan Khoja heard the dismal news that the Khaṭib Khoja had been defeated at Qara Yulghun and fled, the fire of his rage flared up, and he sentenced several innocents to death by hanging, scattering the chaff of their lives to the wind. Now all of his subjects in their terror—obsequiously, and with superficial affection—bound the rings of penitence anew to the ears of understanding, and they renewed their obedience to him as they made their apologies.

Then a khanal decree was issued, saying that the Khan Khoja, having witnessed his elder brother Jamaluddin Khoja's discipline in military matters and competence in caring for the people, would send him to Aqsu with 800 soldiers, cannons, and falconets. Jamaluddin Khoja was truly a man of great foresight, fortunate, stalwart, and skilled in the medical sciences, yet courageous, hardhearted, and passionate. For Kucha's sake he conquered Bay and Sayram. He found some brave and capable men who would be suited to the job, then had some 2,000 men trained and set scouts and sentries. Having made such cautious preparations, he abandoned the highway and chose instead the road toward Ili, stopping at a place called Arashor. There he took stock of his soldiers, had their horses and weaponry tallied up, and assessed the situation of the Chinese troops. Then he observed the heavens as he waited patiently for twenty days.

At that time, several thousand *khaniya shang* from Kashgar, Yarkand, and Khotan were bound for Ili. They had arrived at Muzart Pass when the rebellion broke out across the land, and they were stranded on the road. Now the Khojas *shang*'ed these *shang*s to their soldiers. *Shang* means "rough-spun cotton cloth."[1]

To explain: in the old days, in the time of the Muslim khan Ismail Khan, the grandson of Makhdum-i Aʿẓam, Khoja Yusuf, came from his country to Yarkand, along with his son, Afaq Khoja. Yet he fell into conflict with Ismail Khan and went to Ili, to the company of Khung-Taiji Törä.

"He drove me out!" Khoja Yusuf Khoja said, and he importuned the khan, "Would you help me?"

Khung-Taiji gave him several Qalmaq *zaisang*s to accompany him. With their aid, Khoja Yusuf Khoja became ruler of the country. He captured Ismail Khan and his family and sent them to Ili. When his Qalmaq companions were about to return home, they said they could not leave empty-handed,{89} so they took some rough-spun cloth with them from the Seven Cities. The Qalmaqs bestowed their favor in proportion. Now every year they wanted rough-spun cloth, and one could not help but provide it. This is where we get the phrase, "Rough-spun for the Qalmaqs, words for the Chinese." Because in this country there was nothing but rough-spun cloth, whenever someone bought or sold something, they had to use rough-spun instead of cash. Later, when these lands were conquered by the Emperor of China, the practice continued, though it was called by the Chinese word *shang*. From the time of Ismail Khan (and ʿAbdurraḥim Khan) to that of Rashuddin Khan, over 200 years passed, during which the governors and their clerks kept sending that rough-spun to Ili every year, although the amount swiftly increased.

Now the soldiers fashioned that rough-spun into shrouds and cloaks and even wound it around their heads like hats or turbans. "These will be our burial shrouds!" they declared, and they cried out from the bottoms of their hearts and offered their little strength to the Court of the Divine. With the Khojas leading them, and all of them wrapped in cotton cloth, they looked just like white sheep. They bound the belt of courage tightly about their waists, and in one night they rode from Arashor by the Muzart Pass road and like a sudden storm threw themselves upon the soldiers fortified at Jam. The Chinese were caught unawares. The Chinese soldiers and their Muslim reinforcements alike died by the sword or by the fury of their wrath. Only a handful saved themselves and fled to Aqsu.

Meanwhile, 500 Sibe and Solon Qalmaq soldiers had been traveling from Ili on the way to their garrison in Kashgar when they arrived in Aqsu, equipped with their bows, arrows, and quivers, as well as gunpowder weapons. Just as they were about to leave for Kashgar, they heard the news of the rebellion in Kucha, so the Aqsu authorities halted their journey and took them on the march to Jam instead. They also dressed 1,000 useless wastrels, gamblers, and tramps in Chinese array, enlisted them as reserves, and brought them to Jam. All of them without exception were ultimately put to the sword. All told, over 4,000 of the Chinese, Qalmaqs, and two-faced Muslims in Jam and Aqsu were killed.

The governor of Aqsu, Saʿid Beg, fled to Kashgar, while the governor of Bay, Timur Ghazinachi Beg, went to Khotan. In their pursuit of the Chinese, the Khojas took up positions surrounding the royal city of Aqsu. On 12 Ṣafar of that year [July 17, 1864], the assistant imperial agent in Aqsu and all his officers took stock of their situation. They gathered all their children and their wives and women,[2] and placed parcels of gunpowder around them.{90} They faced Beijing and shouted something as they wept in anxious fear. Then one man took a pull of his tobacco. He cast an ember from his pipe, and the moment it touched the gunpowder, it sent them all to Hell. Joy befell the Muslims, and misery the hypocrites, and cries of celebration rang out across the heavens.

Victorious Jamaluddin took his place upon his sultanic throne in Aqsu. He gifted the Chinese prisoners to his soldiers, and each received booty and captives in accordance with his efforts. Jamaluddin appointed ʿAbdurraḥman

Doba Beg of Kucha as *dadkhwah* and Qasim Qażi of Aqsu as a general. He retained the old chief mufti, mufti, and judge in their positions, granting them their old offices. Jamaluddin neither favored nor disfavored anyone, but each retained their former stations.

At the time that Jamaluddin Khoja had ridden from Aqsu, the Khaṭib Khoja's eldest son, Ḥamuddin Khoja, had been sent to reconnoiter at Muzart Pass with 100 soldiers. When he had stayed at Muzart Pass for a few days and Aqsu had been conquered, he left someone at Muzart Pass in his stead while he went to Aqsu to see his father. Meanwhile, the general in Ili had sent 7,000 Chinese and 3,000 Qalmaq soldiers with armaments to the Aqsu agent as reinforcements. However, they knew that someone was garrisoned at Muzart Pass, so they could not pass but instead waited fifty days before turning back.

In sum, the Khojas concluded their affairs in Aqsu, although they remained concerned about Kashgar, Yarkand, and Ushturfan. The city of Ushturfan was well fortified, and its soldiers many. The Khaṭib Khoja determined to carry out holy war in Ushturfan, and he began preparations.

1:5 Expedition to Ushturfan

How That Sayyid Ghazi, the Khaṭib Khoja, and His Beloved Son, Ḥamuddin Khoja, Set Out to Subjugate Ushturfan; How They Pursued Victory; How the Flower of Their Intent Bloomed, and They Achieved Their Desire; and Other Events

ON THE FOURTEENTH day of Ṣafar [July 19, 1864], that ghazi, the Khaṭib Khoja, and his eldest son, Ḥamuddin Khoja, along with Taliᶜ Khalifa and Tokhta Khalifa of Kucha, and with Ṭahir Daban Beg, Mullah Qasim Mirab, and Muḥammad Amin Beg of Aqsu, gathered 600 soldiers and sixteen cannons. They brought some experienced and soldierly begs with them, making Mullah ᶜAbdullah Qażi Akhund of Aqsu the chief military judge. They marched swiftly to expel the Chinese from Ushturfan, and selected some brave warriors and archers from the villages of Aral and Aqyar in Aqsu and pressed them into service. In four days, they arrived at Acha Mountain in Ushturfan.

The Chinese in Ushturfan had stationed the governor, Tokhta Beg, with a large group of soldiers at Acha Mountain as sentries.{91} As soon as the Khojas arrived, however, they immediately pledged themselves enthusiastically to the Khojas' service, proclaiming themselves to be under their command. Now all of the people of Ushturfan, one group after another, came proudly to pay their respects to the Khojas and discussed how they might conquer the Chinese city. The Khojas then directed all of their leaders in prosecuting the siege of the Chinese city, and they prepared for battle. In the meantime, the Chinese fired guns from the walls and killed many men.

The soldiers of Islam were busy binding tall ladders together, while also digging tunnels into the back of Mölchär Mountain, when suddenly the Chinese lit their arsenal on fire.[1] As soon as the gunpowder caught fire, not only the Chinese but also the walls, weapons, idol temples, and Mölchär Mountain itself were blown into dust, which mingled with the air, so that no one could distinguish or even see each other. The bright day was made dark as the blackest night. The force of the gunpowder had blown the infidels' arms and legs a distance of one or two *tash*. Some of their heads and torsos could be found hanging in trees. (Gunpowder for the Six Cities was distributed from Ushturfan. That is why the arsenal was in Ushturfan.)

In short, Ushturfan was conquered as they desired. The victorious Khaṭib Khoja took it into his own demesne. He applied the pen of forgiveness to the crimes of good, bad, and shiftless people alike and so displayed his kingly grace and royal kindness. However, there were some whores and filthy women, some profligates who had taken up the infidels' customs and gone about like infidels themselves, and he put them to death by the sword as an example to the common people. He reinstated the old chief mufti, Mullah Ataullah Akhund, as chief mufti once more. Tokhta Beg he made governor and *dadkhwah* as he had been before, and Pay Muḥammad Qażi Beg was made the judge again, and so he restored everyone to their proper places. Friends rejoiced in happiness while enemies sighed with grief, and cries of joy rang out across that glorious dome.

* * *

It has been heard, through many reports from reliable informants, that long ago, when the Emperor of China first took control of these lands, there lived in Ushturfan a beauty of sixteen, a one-of-a-kind pearl who shone as brightly as the sun.[2] She caught the officers' eyes, and they said, "Nothing could make a finer nor comelier gift for the Great Khan." So they took her into the Emperor of China's presence with other gifts. He was very pleased indeed, and all of his people approved greatly of their union.

Yet one day, when the khan went into her chamber,{92} he found that she was crying. He paused, thought a moment, and asked, "May I venture to ask—why should you cry, save that perhaps there is another khan in this world even greater than I?"

"There is a fruiting tree in my homeland," she said. "Its fruits are of gold, its leaves of silver, and its resin is of perfume. When I remember this tree, I weep."

So the khan decreed that such a tree was to be found in Ushturfan, and he ordered that it be brought thence with great speed, as it was needed for his gardens. As soon as the imperial officials received that order, they informed the governor of Ushturfan, Raḥmatullah Beg, and ordered him to secure a sapling of such a tree, take it to Beijing himself to present it to the khan, and then return home. He could not deny such an order, and so he located oleaster saplings. He pressed some men into labor to carry them. One night, when he had forced them to carry them a distance of four *paotai*, the men grew discontent.

"For us to carry these saplings to Beijing," they complained, "many men would surely die. Let us make this case to Raḥmatullah Beg. If he agrees with us, then great. If, however, he should disagree, then who knows . . .?"

So they expressed this to Raḥmatullah Beg, and he sided with them. They wielded those saplings as shillelaghs and killed the Chinese who were traveling with them. Next they took hold of the city and killed the imperial agent and all his officers and soldiers. They made Raḥmatullah Beg their governor in his own right, and he ruled for nine months.

When Beijing heard about this, however, an innumerable mass of soldiers came forth from Lanzhou. There were a great many battles, and Ushturfan was conquered for a second time, while Ushturfan's people were slaughtered. Those who were spared the sword were divided into groups of four households each and assigned to stations from Qumul to Ili, and likewise to Kashgar and Khotan, and sent there to carry letters or serve the Chinese at the stations. To this day, they call the descendants of these people Turfanis. However, those sent to Ili after a few generations adopted the ways of the Qalmaqs, and they became Qalmaqish themselves. Apparently they still call themselves Muslim-Qalmaqs. This event took place seventeen years after the people of Beijing conquered the Cities.[3]

* * *

When the powder house caught fire during the conquest of Ushturfan, your humble author saw with his own eyes how there were so many pages from old books, weaponry, saddles and blankets, harness saddles, plows, all sorts of things.{93} I asked why that was. And people told me stories like, "In the days of Raḥmatullah Beg, when the Chinese killed the owners of these objects, they kept the things as evidence. When the powder house caught fire, it blew them all into the sky. There were lots of things like these—this is just some of them." It suffices for your author to write only this much.

Earlier, when the Emperor of China conquered the Seven Cities, he had made Ushturfan their capital and stationed the imperial agent there, so that the officials in each of the other six cities answered to him. After this incident, when the emperor's forces came to Ushturfan and slaughtered its people, totally eliminating them, they moved people from the other six cities and settled them there. For this reason, its earlier name was Uch.[4] [When it rebelled another time on account of a different incident, and Manṣur Khan had its people slaughtered, they brought people from Old Turfan and settled them there. And so the name Turfan was added to the name Uch, and they called it Ushturfan or Uchturfan.] It was made the least of the Seven Cities and the officials there demoted, while the imperial agent was ordered to be stationed in Yarkand. Ushturfan is still known by the name "migrant." So for some 200 years, with the exception of the "migrants," the True King has kept the Seven Cities under His own protection, and the Muslims of Ushturfan, despite the disasters that befell them, kept their faith. Oh, Lord! In Your refuge, protect the people of all lands and cities from the wrath and tyranny of false kings! Amen.

* * *

When Sayyid Ghazi Khaṭib Khoja conquered Ushturfan, he closed the gate of tyranny and opened the door of justice. He strove to enact the Shariah of the Prophet and made serious efforts to ensure the peace and safety of the common people. He stood out among all of the khojas and sayyids for his competence in government and enactment of justice. And as his glory and reputation began to exceed those of all of the other Khojas, now the sphere began to show its tilt, and omens of ill fortune began to appear, and soon they would be exchanged for his Jovian fortune.

The prophets and apostles (PRAYERS AND SALUTATIONS TO THEM!), the great saints and shaykhs (UPON THEM BLESSINGS AND MERCY!), and the exalted kings—if God should fate them to be granted partnership and prestige, then by the Lord's command, they will first be vexed by separation, pain, and deprivation of friendship.{94} Then they will witness trials and tribulations and taste the leaven of hardship, but when this is kneaded with the dust of their sighs of contrition and baked in the oven of regret, then He will turn their path of suffering around and raise them by steps to the heights of glory. Some of them He will ennoble with supreme truth and make His beloveds and trusted intimates. Some He will place upon the throne of rulership, so that the height of their esteem exceeds that of the celestial sphere. He fills them up with magnificence and elevates them as a Shadow of God upon the Earth, so that the rays of light from the sun of his fortune may remove the victims of tyranny condemned to the abode of injustice and nourish them instead in the shade of their fortune.

Thus is it said of all kings in this hadith: EVERY ONE OF YOU IS A GUARDIAN, AND RESPONSIBLE FOR WHAT IS IN HIS CUSTODY.[5] That is, a king is like unto a shepherd. Whatever shepherd tends well to his flock and minds it, his sheep will grow fat and multiply, and he will be exalted. If, however, he should fail to mind them, and lose attention, then the owner of those sheep will remand them to a better shepherd and drive the former shepherd from his sight. So whatever king minds his subjects, he will be made prosperous and exalted, while his lands will grow populous and flourish. If, however, he should not mind them and lose attention, then that Master of Sovereignty, the Lord, will entrust them to one of His creations who cares for the common people—for one tyrant is worse than a thousand wolves. A country flourishes by justice and by tyranny falls to ruin.

* * *

That sayyid and ghazi, the Khaṭib Khoja, remained in Ushturfan for three months. News was arriving from Kashgar that a man named Ṣiddiq Beg the Qipchaq had risen up and taken power there. Now the Khaṭib Khoja determined to go to Kashgar.

1:6 Kashgar Campaign

How the Sayyid Ghazi Khaṭib Khoja and His Rightly Guided Son, Ḥamuddin Khoja, in Their Desire to Conquer the City of Kashgar Sent Forth Soldiers; What Happened Along the Way; How in Their Naïveté They Came to Suffer at the Hands of Ṣiddiq Beg the Qipchaq; and How They Were Liberated and Returned to Their Thrones

SAYYID GHAZI KHAṬIB Khoja rode out to conquer Kashgar on the twelfth day of Jumada al-Akhira [November 12, 1864].[1] He pitched his tents and established his headquarters at Otbashi, and then sent his son, Ḥamuddin Khoja, scouting ahead with 2,500 soldiers.{95} Two days later, the Khaṭib Khoja and his retinue of 1,500[2] set their boots into the stirrups of victory. They marched until they came to Qara Bulaq, where several filthy Kyrgyz soldiers attempted to betray them. The Kyrgyz were imprisoned and punished.

Meanwhile, the governor of Aqsu, Saʿid Beg, had run for his life from the Battle of Jam. He fled to Kashgar and the company of his elder brother, Qutlugh Beg, who was the governor of Kashgar. Following his brother's advice and the counsel of the Chinese officials, Saʿid Beg took the Qaqshal road to Ili with a letter for the Ili General. He traveled under the protection of a number of soldiers with the intention to return. However, some of the Kyrgyz soldiers seized him and brought him to Ḥamuddin. Just as Ḥamuddin was resolving to winnow the harvest of Saʿid Beg's life and scatter its chaff to the wind, the high officials arrayed before him were calling for his blood.

But instead, he forgave the sins of Saʿid Beg's past, granted him a place among the ranks of his commanders, and forced his interpreter, Ismail Kotwal,[3] to swear his loyalty. Ḥamuddin continued toward his destination.

When they reached Üstün Artush, Ḥamuddin said, "Tomorrow we will take Kashgar. Qutlugh Beg is a Muslim and comes from our homeland. He will come from that side, and we from this side, and we will overthrow Ṣiddiq Beg the Qipchaq in the middle!" They took this raw plan and baked it without lighting the flame, chewed it over in their thoughtless, toothless imaginations, and walked forth as though intoxicated by its sweetness.

Just then, a great dust cloud appeared on the road from Kashgar. When they reconnoitered, many soldiers came into view. Inevitably, the Khojas on this side and the Qipchaqs on the other met in the middle in battle. Men were dying on either side.

In the midst of it, a messenger came from Ṣiddiq Beg. "We wish to cease fighting with the Khojas," he requested, "and invite them instead into the city in the spirit of peace and benevolence. After all, they are the sayyids and ghazis who restored Islam, and they are guests in our country." Ṣiddiq Beg sent men to bring them with honor and esteem into the city to make camp. There he entertained his guests with gentleness and grace and made apologies to them as if he were in their service. Yet he had their soldiers stripped of their horses and weapons, and the Khojas separated from their tents and beasts of burden and installed instead in a pleasant garden on the city's outskirts. Servants were given to them, and whatever they desired, it was prepared for them with all solicitousness. But they were not allowed to ride away, nor to meet with anyone. Nine days passed in this manner. On none of those days did they see Ṣiddiq Beg, who did not visit them.

{96} Eventually, some of the good men of Kashgar acted as intermediaries. They convinced both sides to be kind to one another and make peace, so that the Khojas would no longer trouble Kashgar, nor Ṣiddiq Beg trouble Aqsu and Ushturfan. They bound their agreement with oaths, renewed their vows of unity, and embraced one another. Negotiations followed, the terms of which both sides found acceptable, and a treaty of friendship was drawn up. Ṣiddiq Beg returned the Khojas' weapons, tents, and horses, along with his profuse apologies, and gifted them robes in proportion. They returned their soldiers' weapons and horses, as well, and saw them along the road to Aqsu, but they did not pass Maralbashi. The Khojas likewise gave prayers of thanks for their safe liberation, and on the twenty-eighth of Rajab [December 27, 1864], they arrived in their home country at Ushturfan. It was the month of Scorpio.

They passed the winter in Ushturfan. The Khaṭib Khoja entrusted the affairs of state to his younger son, Maḥmudin Khoja, and did not engage in them, but instead spent his days in worship. Winter passed into spring.

1:7 Yarkand Campaign

How the Sayyid Ghazi Khaṭib Khoja, His Beloved Son Ḥamuddin Khoja, and Shaykh Naẓiruddin Khoja Determined to Conquer Yarkand in a Holy War and Mounted Their Horses; and How the Flower of Their Desire Blossomed in Its Beauty; but the Vicissitudes of the Age Proved an Obstacle; and They Could Pluck No Blossom, but Returned to Their Home Country Without Achieving Their Wish

THE STORY GOES that Shaykh Naẓiruddin Khoja and 4,500[1] soldiers marched from Kucha to carry out a holy war in Yarkand. They came to Aqsu. Meanwhile, Khaṭib Khoja and his beloved son, Ḥamuddin Khoja, marched on Yarkand from Ushturfan with 1,500 men. In total, 7,000[2] men with cannons, falconets, and guns rode from place to place until they reached Maralbashi. There were about 2,000 Chinese and Dungan settlers at Maralbashi.[3] All of them turned over their weapons, submitted to the khoja, and expressed their willingness to convert to the faith. The Khojas' armies taught them the Shahada and converted them. They divided the weapons and the food in their stores among the soldiers, placed Ma Dalaoye in command of these "new Muslims," and left them in peace and repose. Next, on they went to the district of Yarkand.{97} But in Yarkand, ʿAbdurraḥman Ḥażrat ruled, while the imam of the Dungans gave the orders. The Chinese were locked up tightly in their own city. Some days later, they did battle with ʿAbdurraḥman Ḥażrat.

Ultimately, the Ḥażrat dedicated himself to holy war. However, he sometimes sided with the Dungans and sometimes not.

As this was going on, the Yarkandi Niyaz Eshikagha Beg and some of Yarkand's leaders signed their names upon a secret letter. Niyaz sent this letter to Yaʿqub Qushbegi in Kashgar and invited him to come to Yarkand. On that account, Yaʿqub Beg saw some prospects in Yarkand and came there with a number of cavalrymen. Now the Khojas and the Dungans joined forces in combat. Sometimes they were victorious and sometimes defeated. But in the midst of battle, a two-faced Qipchaq thrust a knife into the Khaṭib Khoja's back, wounding him. He lost consciousness. Yaʿqub Beg won the day and took Yarkand.

When Ḥamuddin Khoja observed the situation, he lost his patience and instead made a show of bravery. He had the city's gates shut tightly, and (inside the city) he did battle and slew many men. Then Yaʿqub Beg's soldiers lost their patience, as they feared for their lives, and jumped their horses from atop the city walls. Some gave up hope and fled. Some others were injured as their arms or legs snapped.

But one gate remained open. The Qushbegi fled through that gate with his life and dove into a dark trench, though he was separated from his horse. Just then he encountered Muḥammad Baba Onbashi, mounted that man's horse, and with great effort carried himself far away. He reached Kashgar. Yaʿqub Beg could not match Ḥamuddin Khoja, and as he was fleeing, he thought out of admiration for his bravery, "If a father should beget a son, may he beget one like Ḥamuddin Törä." Yaʿqub Beg took the great black thoroughbred on which he rode as booty, along with its fine saddle and tack. He rode for Ushturfan.

Eventually the Khojas and the Dungans, having joined forces, made plans to take the city of Yarkand. Yet none of the Chinese inside the city even stuck their heads out—as soon as they caught sight of someone, they killed them. They never wasted their bullets. When a Muslim fired, however, they would hide behind the battlements[4] where no bullet could strike them. The Muslims were utterly vexed.

Consequently, they were forced to cut down all the trees around the city, fruiting or otherwise, and tie tall branches together to build mantlets on several sides.[5] They dug holes in a number of places, went underground, set gunpowder along the walls and gun towers, and lit it on fire. The force of the gunpowder blew the walls ten or twenty fathoms into the air.{98} Before the soldiers got there, however, the Chinese had prepared by stuffing sand and dirt into bags. Where the wall had fallen, they laid them side by side and remade it as it was before. Thus they killed many Muslims, and the city was not taken. Eight months passed in this manner. The Chinese, as it turned out, had plenty of arrows, bullets, and supplies, and they showed no sign of running out. Instead they came out to fight with greater strength every day.

Some wise, intelligent, perceptive, and reliable men commented, "Long ago, when the Emperor of China conquered the Seven Cities, they counted up the men in each city and took down their numbers. They found that in Yarkand, there were 32,000 strong men able to work.[6] In Aqsu there were 6,000, in Kucha 3,000, in Kashgar 16,000, and in Khotan 22,000 young men, which they recorded in their accounts. So the Chinese in Yarkand must have killed some 32,000 Muslims or more before they themselves perished." This is probably true.

Eventually—and inevitably—the city was conquered. There were grain, weapons, and ammunition in the stores, which fell into Muslim hands. Their cries of joy and the sound of drums and trumpets rang out across the sky.

At that moment, however, the Dungans chose to withdraw their support. ʿAbdurraḥman Ḥażrat, Jamaluddin Khoja in Qarghaliq, and all of the Ḥażrats and lordlings [*begzāda*] of Yarkand struggled over the government of Yarkand. None of them managed to ally with another, and so none could pacify Yarkand, nor gain control of it. Because Ishan Mir Ghiyas̱uddin's grandson, Mirza Jan Ḥażrat, was a descendant of the Khaṭib Khoja's Sufi master, he had him sent away in secret from the Ḥażrats in Yarkand to Ushturfan.[7] If he had not done so, much blood would have been spilt in vain.

Muḥammad ʿAli Khan's son, Muẓaffar Khan, also came to Yarkand from Kashmir. He had been living in Kohistan. When he heard about the factional struggles there, he seized the opportunity to travel to Yarkand via Tibet's mountain passes. He revealed who he was and what his name and genealogy were. The Khojas showed their respect to him, gave him an appropriate place to camp, and granted him a fitting office. However, they understood that Muẓaffar Khan's actions had a different aim, so they said to him, "Our leader is in Kucha. You shall proceed to Kucha and follow his commands." They placed him under guard and sent him on his way. The Khan Khoja{99} likewise paid his respects and granted him an office, as well as a wife from a suitable place. He lived in repose and entertained himself where he liked, staying for a while. Eventually he requested permission to go to Korla and did so. When Yaʿqub Beg took Kucha, he traveled to Turfan. His story will be told in the second epic, GOD WILLING—HE IS THE PATIENT![8] Jamaluddin Khoja was also sent to Kucha.

Ultimately the Dungans and Khojas could not sustain their alliance, nor secure control over Yarkand, and they returned to their own lands. Another reason for their retreat was that the Dungans numbered over 25,000, and they had with them many weapons. Nevertheless the Dungans thought, "It seems we brought too few people, and this has turned out to be an operation requiring heavy equipment." They left. Another reason was that Shaykh Naẓiruddin Khoja's humors were unstable. Moreover, he had come to consider himself to be like a second Amir Timur Kuragan, and he did not recognize the humanity of the great Ḥażrats and Ishans in Yarkand, or of the Dungan imams and the other nobles of Yarkand. This is why he was not a suitable leader.

The Sayyid Khaṭib Khoja's humors, however, were delicate and kind, friendly and gracious. He met well with Yaʿqub Beg Qushbegi and bound the ties of friendship. In the end, he got his reward.

If the king has gentle speech,
Then that protector makes the difficult easy.

1:8 Campaign to Kashgar and Yarkand

Sayyid Jamaluddin Padishah's Desire for Yarkand and Kashgar and His Hope to Conquer Both in One Expedition; and How, in Hunting Two Gazelles at Once, He Rode Only One Horse to the Beat of the Drum of Pride, and in Capturing One Gazelle and Pursuing the Other, He Ultimately Lost Both; How Another High-Flying Eagle All in a Moment Found Himself Stranded in the Wilderness; How He Was Deprived of Either Gazelle That He Desired; and How in His Weariness and Error He Gladly Returned to His Country

IT IS WRITTEN that, after Shaykh Naẓiruddin Khoja failed to maintain control of Yarkand and returned home, the ambition of the governor of Aqsu, Jamaluddin Khoja Padishah, began to rise. His ardor aroused, he swore a grandiose oath: "I will ride personally to conquer Yarkand and Kashgar, capture the so-called Qushbegi alive,{100} and make him my prisoner. I will torture him in ways that humanity has never seen, humiliate him, and make him walk before me as I ride. If I don't, then I am no son of Shaykh Niẓamuddin Khoja, and may I never be called a sayyid again."

All of the high officials and sycophants praised him effusively, saying, "Ah, indeed, so shall it be! Of what consequence could he be, that lowly man who fled his own country?"

Winter passed into spring with the forging of weapons and the labors of beasts. When the sprouts poked their heads above the soil and spring began,

Naẓiruddin Khoja made his younger brother, Jalaluddin Khoja, his deputy and entrusted him with Aqsu for a while. Preparations were complete.

One of the Khojas, an important sayyid who was the foremost of the old scholars and sayyids of Kucha, Akhund Khoja [Ṣiddiq Khoja] Aʿlam Akhund,[1] was called the Aʿlam Akhund Khoja. For fifty years he had worked to advance the Shariah in his position as chief mufti, and he was an experienced and authoritative scholar. That khoja was placed in command of the soldiers of Kucha and Shahyar, while Sayyid Khaṭib Khoja and Ḥamuddin Khoja brought those from Ushturfan.

At an auspicious hour, they set their feet into the stirrups of victory. They took as their companions many begs and lordlings, all of whom were capable and brave: from Aqsu, Mullah ʿAbdulbaqi Mufti Akhund, Qasim Qażi Beg, Baqish Mirab Beg, and Muḥammad Sharif Beg; from the begs of Kucha, Ḥajji Ghazinachi Beg, Yaʿqub Divan Beg, Mullash Mirab, and Aqmullah Mirab; and from the begs of Ushturfan, Aq Beg, Musa Beg, Qurban Mirab, and Ibrahim Mingbegi. And they rode for Yarkand. The number of their soldiers was tallied at 26,000, not including the sutlers, cannoneers, and storemen.

So these high officers rode with great pomp and traveled the roads to Yarkand. When they were three stages from it, Yarkand's nobles and commoners, its Ḥażrats and Ishans and Dungan imams, its low and high officials, all came out in groups to receive them with gifts. They rubbed their faces upon those stirrups of victory, raised their hands up, and offered their meager strength to the Court of the Eternal, reciting the *Fatiha* and praying for the Khojas' long lives and rule. They laid their heads low to drown in the water of their shame.{101} The Khaṭib Khoja saw that they were drowning in making excuses for their past wrongs, so he bestowed his royal favor upon them and showed them compassion for their sinful ways, which pleased them. With a great display of pomp and ceremony, he was established upon the throne in Yarkand.

Neither Dungan nor Sufi, nor any living thing, could summon the strength to object. All of the nobles bound the belt of loyalty tightly about their waists and celebrated. The sound of royal pipes and trumpets, and of drums beating out the *shadiyana* rhythm, and the voices of the peoples who had come all around to celebrate rang out across the indigo dome.[2] So they opened the gate of generosity and rolled out the carpet of justice. The sheep drank with the wolf from the same pond, and the falcon and the pigeon laid eggs in the same niche. Any conflict or quarrel between groups of people, or indeed between any of God's creations, was hidden deep within the mine of impossibility. The rule of love and brotherhood rose like the sun. Thus the Khojas reposed, and they overflowed with magnanimity as they governed in peace.

Yet they thought constantly of their hopes of pursuing their intention, which was to conquer Kashgar, and to prepare supplies for the journey, as well as soldiers and armaments. They gathered a great many soldiers from the area of Yarkand and determined an auspicious date and time. The Khaṭib Khoja entrusted the government of Yarkand to the aforementioned chief mufti and made him his plenipotentiary in all matters of state. They tallied up the soldiers, and apart from the sutlers, cannoneers, store men, and stable masters, recorded their number at 72,000 Muslims and Dungans.

The numerousness of the soldiers and their cries of "Make way!"; the crowding of onlookers in the streets and bazaars; the cries of the soldiers' kinfolk as they sent them off with "Safe travels!" and the *Fatiha*; the sound of pipes and ruckus of trumpets; the singers' pretty songs in the heart-rending *segah* mode,[3] and the heartbreaking *ghazal*s and fiery *muqam*s; and, on one side, the dirt kicked up by the hooves of the soldiers' horses—all rose from this dusty ground to the celestial spheres. The eyes of those who saw it went blind, and the ears of the listeners deaf. Their minds were bereft of their senses,{102} as though a taste of the Day of Resurrection, of cries from the doomsday plain, was manifest before them. It was the second day of Jumada al-Awwal in the year 1283 [September 12, 1866].

Upon 200 carts, besides the weapons, they brought with them chains, shackles, and fetters. "We will go to Kashgar and take it," they said, "and we will take the Qipchaqs and Andijanis prisoner and bind them fast with fetters and chains to take them home with us." They took this raw plan, baked it in a pot without lighting the flame, chewed it over in their thoughtless, toothless mouths, and walked forth as though intoxicated by its sweetness. There had never been such a gathering of soldiers during the Khojas' reign, nor such a campaign, and there never would be again.

By the grace of the Peerless Creator, Sayyid Jamaluddin Khoja donned his colorful robes of honor and placed the crown of kingship upon his fortunate head. With an Isfahani sword strapped about his waist, and riding upon an Arabian horse, decorated with complete ornament and indisputable grandeur, he entered his tent. He rested there for two days, distributing robes to his soldiers according to their stations. On the third day, he turned his attention to his goal and began slowly to move toward it. They erected his kingly tent palace at Khan Eriq. He tried to array his soldiers' forward and rear guards, considered them, and said, "If the Qushbegi determines that so many soldiers have come, then sooner or later he won't be able to stay in Kashgar. Instead, he'll run off, back to the other side of the mountains. Perhaps the people of Kashgar will wind up 'trampled beneath horses' hooves.'" And so he relied upon the numerousness of his soldiers—yet he forgot to rely on the beneficence of the Master of Kings. These cloudy fantasies obstructed his mind, and he was unaware that his ascent to the apogee had begun its declination.

At this point, a cloud of dust appeared from the direction of Yengi Ḥissar, and within that dust, flags and banners could be seen. They went to reconnoiter, and the Qushbegi's army came clearly into view. All of the scouts and sentries they had set came and informed Jamaluddin of what they had seen.

"The Qushbegi's men are few," he said. "And we are many." He directed his soldiers to the left and right and ordered them to withdraw on either side in a dragon formation, wait patiently until they had the Qushbegi's army in the middle, and then surround them like a stone wall. They were to hold fast in place, and whoever should fall into their hands was to be brought to him{103} alive. Having issued his orders, he waited calmly. Sure enough, when one regarded these soldiers, one could see that the Qushbegi's men were like unto the Pleiades, while the Khojas' men could be reckoned by all the stars in the seven spheres.

At that time, the governor of Kulab, Hamrah Khan, had come to the Khojas' aid with 250 swift and mighty men. However, they told him, "We do not need men from any foreign country," and they denied him passage. And so Hamrah Khan joined the Qushbegi instead, and they went on to witness many battles.

Meanwhile, the Qushbegi had ruminated over the preponderance of the Khojas' forces and the inferiority of his own. So he placed his trust firmly in God and divided his cavalry into groups, which galloped about in each direction. One of his cavalrymen, a bold *pansad* named ʿAbdullah, threw himself and his cavalry upon the Khojas' soldiers like a sudden storm. Meanwhile, the Dungans had been making haste, crowded around their falconets and cannons, but as soon as they arrived, they turned back. At the same time, Ghazi Beg Pansad and ʿAziz Beg the Executioner galloped in from the left and brought the fight to a fever pitch. Two or three times ʿAbdullah Pansad sallied forth: having retreated, he would suddenly launch a surprise attack on the Khojas' soldiers, then retreat again. When some of the men began to fall back, a voice called out, "Retreat!" There was no way to face them any longer, and as the hadith says, FLIGHT FROM AN IMPOSSIBLE FIGHT IS WITHIN THE TRADITION OF THE BELIEVERS—they realized that they were obligated to retreat. Forgetting their stores and animals, the tent palace, their weapons, and the food and cloth and such things in their treasury, they struck their horses with the whips of defeat and set themselves upon the road to Aqsu.

Undisciplined soldiers can do nothing;
Two hundred bold warriors are better than 100,000.

The verse of the Quran that says, HOW MANY A SMALL COMPANY HAVE OVERCOME A LARGE COMPANY BY GOD'S LEAVE! [2:249] surely suits this event. Even with the armaments paid for with taxes collected from the lands of Aqsu, Kucha, Yarkand, Ushturfan, and Korla, and prepared with hand and heart by Muslim people over the course of two years, they could not withstand two hours of combat, and so were destroyed, SCATTERED AS ASHES. [20:105]

A fragment [*qiṭʿa*]:

The Lord who is the MASTER OF SOVEREIGNTY,
Who to each GIVETH SOVEREIGNTY—
What limit might there be, for men to seize sovereignty?
A king of kings who WRESTETH SOVEREIGNTY. [3:26]

Everything that Jamaluddin Khoja said about{104} the Qushbegi, happened instead to him. It was as the hadith says: HE WHO DIGS A PIT FOR HIS BROTHER, DIGS IT FOR HIMSELF.

Many men died for nothing. Many others fell prisoner and were stripped of their horses and possessions. Naked, with neither food nor water, they disappeared in the hungry desert. Some of them reached their homes half-dead. It was as though on that day the Reckoning were revealed to them. The Khoja who had shouted, "HIM AND NO OTHER!" now became fed up with life. Now he was sometimes sane, and sometimes insane and deranged. "Was I dreaming?" he would ask as he smoked hashish, "Or was this something my imagination showed me? What has happened to me? Now what was I? And what have I become?" Like the hashish smokers whose minds have gone or the opium smokers who have eaten the stone and lost their senses, his heart was all befuddled and his tongue loose, while he would be plagued with weariness until, spent, half-dead, he retired to his chambers. So it seems did the indigo sphere and this inverted world display their skills at sleight of hand.

Meanwhile, the Aʿlam Akhund Khoja was in Yarkand, that sultanic seat. When some who had fled from Khan Eriq told him what had taken place there, he realized he could not stay, and he grew impatient. "I am going to Kashgar after all!" he pretended, while he took his leave of Yarkand and rushed off toward Aqsu. With one roll of the dice [*du*], he lost [*bay*] two great cities [for nothing][4]—for wanting to take Kashgar, he lost Yarkand as well. Now all of the contestants came to their senses, and they said, "Let us unburden ourselves of this desire for Yarkand and Kashgar, and hope no longer for these parts." And indeed, they did not go there. All that their words had set into motion now amounted to this.

> Never reject what the Lord has given you;
> The Lord himself granted it to you!

The Dungans numbered over 2,000. Now they gathered like the Pleiades themselves, and they fired their cannons until the evening prayer. Many men were killed, and no one could get near. Then a bullet struck the Qushbegi in the thigh, and he fell unconscious. In the end, they concluded a truce with the Dungans and took them with their guns and cannons to Kashgar, granting each of them gifts in proportion and swearing common cause. They took the guns and falconets out of their hands and gave them instead robes of honor and offices to win them over to their side.

1:9 The Rise of Maḥmudin

The Exploits and Rule of That Bud of Early Spring in the Vineyard of the Khaṭib Khoja's Life, and the Rare Pearl from His Nacreous Mold, Maḥmudin Khoja Padishah; and the Adventures of Your Humble Author;{105} and the Beliefs of the Sectarians

SAYYID BURHANUDDIN KHAṬIB Khoja made his youngest son, Maḥmudin Khoja, his deputy in his stead in Ushturfan. In his service he placed the governor of Ushturfan, Tokhta Beg, and Taliᶜ Dadkhwah of Kucha while he himself rode off to holy war. When the Padishah Khoja was installed as the ruler of Ushturfan, it was as the hadith says: ISLAM DESTROYS WHAT CAME BEFORE IT.[1] He did away with the practices of the tyrannical infidel officials and instead enacted the sultanic institutions. In governing, he always gave orders in accordance with the Shariah. He demolished the city's great idol temple and built in its place a great Friday mosque, which he endowed. The reign of the Khojas lasted three years and one month exactly. During it, no one could do anything sinful.

Maḥmudin was younger than all of the other Khojas, but in intelligence, wisdom, and good qualities, he was their superior. Generally speaking, he was better versed in the sciences than all the other Khojas. For a long time, the rules of the nonbelievers, their laws and tyrannies, had reigned in these cities, and the ways and innovations of the old begs had spread among the people. Just as the miraculous hadith says—COMPANIONSHIP

INFLUENCES—these had taken root. And so, although they were unable to distinguish the beauteous from the hideous, the people set their minds on their true home in Heaven, and with the tips of their knives and spears, they uprooted the unacceptable innovations that had grown there and in their place planted the great and holy traditions of the Shariah. They nourished the sword of justice with its first water, and as it sprouted, they made vegetables and herbs of it. It was as described in the holy hadith: PARADISE IS UNDER THE SHADES OF SWORDS.[2]

He appointed imams and muezzins to all of the mosques and lodges in town and country, and he had them recite the five daily prayers with their congregations. The Shariah—the boundaries set by God—he enacted in accordance with the Book and the traditions of the Messenger of God, and he issued commands in conformity with the guidance of the imams. He sought to keep the Shariah and so implemented his orders without favoring or disfavoring anyone. He even eliminated the gamblers, pigeon racers, partridge racers, and egg players by means of eloquent rebuke. Although he was himself a chess player. Maḥmudin's every action was in accordance with the Shariah, and as he managed the affairs of his common people well, so he pleased everyone, great and small alike.

* * *

Your humble author Mullah Musa was the Khoja's confidante and friend. Whether it concerned the affairs of scholars or of governors and judges,{106} he would do nothing without your humble author's advice. This is because we had spent seven years together in Kucha at the madrasa, rooming together in the same chamber. We were classmates and became close friends, as we were the same age.

One day, Pay Muḥammad Qażi Beg of Ushturfan invited your humble author to break the Ramadan fast.[3] "Come for Iftar and stay the night," he said. "Then go back in in the morning. You could get permission for that from the Padishah Khoja," he assured me. The reason was that his home was outside the city, while I could not go somewhere of an evening without answering for it. That is because I was the imam of the five prayers, as well as the preacher at the Friday mosque. Moreover, I was entrusted with secret messages and letters. I knew of everyone who entered or exited through the nine guard posts. I issued the passes, and no one could pass the guard posts without answering to me.

Moreover, when Maḥmudin ascended the throne, he was in need of a seal of office. Everyone recited something as a rhyme, and I among them rhymed:

He's gathered more glory than nobles adored,
The Son of Burhanuddin, Khoja Maḥmud'!

This pleased him, so he tasked me with having his seal carved for him. I stood before the seal carver and supervised the seal's preparation. He was so happy that he made me his seal bearer and entrusted the seal to me. Every one of his proclamations was entrusted to me, and I would press the seal upon it for him.[4]

We had also seized a granary of wheat flour, one of wheat, and one of barley, which were left over from the Chinese.[5] These three granaries were also entrusted to me. Their contents were consumed by the palace's kitchen, guards, and stables. I assigned my younger brother, Muḥammad Khalifa, to handle it in my place. We distributed the grain according to orders. We would obtain meat, oil, rice, carrots, or onions that the kitchens needed each day by selling some of the grain for cash, then buying them at the market. The flour and grain were so boundlessly plentiful that, when I went in to inspect them two years later, not even one-quarter of them had been used.

Yet, of the portion of the flour and fodder assigned to me, not one *jin*, not one *sar*, extra had been taken.[6] It was just my younger brother and me in one room. Sometimes when we needed lamp oil or candles, I would take some out, calculate its market price, and pay with cash. This was not a matter of temperance on my part, but rather one of equity and prudence. This was how nine more granaries remained full to the brim with grain, all of which later fell into the hands of the Ataliq Ghazi. We did not use them too generously, nor did we sell them off for money for ourselves.

* * *

To return to our story: I secured the permission that Pay Muḥammad Qażi Beg had suggested and went to the Iftar meal. After we said the Ramadan prayer, they took me into another room{107} and entertained me with songs and poems. They outdid themselves as hosts. At midnight, the master of the house took me from the gathering into another guest room, which was even more private. About fifteen of Ushturfan's old begs were there, including

Qurban Ghazinachi, Ismail Bajgir, [Ṭahir Mingbegi,] Mullah Amin Shaykh, and Mullah Nurlan, and this room also had a proper feast laid.

After we ate, they addressed me and said, "The Khaṭib Khoja is old, and his heart is soft and gentle; Ḥamuddin Khoja is too zealous, and too wrathful. Maḥmudin, the Padishah Khoja, however, has ruled very well. All of us, of high and low station alike, are satisfied with him. If the Khaṭib Khoja and Ḥamuddin Khoja were to insert themselves into our country's affairs, that would be no good—no, it would be a bad thing indeed. If you were to get him to favor our proposal, that would be great. Otherwise, things might go badly."

The next day, I returned to the city and explained their reasoning to the Padishah Khoja.

"No one can tell my father, nor my older brother, what they have said!" he replied. "I do agree, but I must do this my way."

After that, three days passed. On the evening of the fourth day, the people of Ushturfan took up arms. As soon as the Khaṭib Khoja heard the news, he appointed an elderly Kuchanese man named Mullah Tokhta Muḥtasib as his emissary, while the Padishah Khoja likewise appointed your humble author. The two of us exited the city. At dawn, we arrived at a place called the Shrine of the Poplar, where the rebels had gathered.[7] All of them had turned their backs on the Khojas and made the man called Mirza Jan Ḥażrat their leader, whose commands they followed. Those were very cold days.

They took us inside. We addressed them in our capacity as emissaries, saying, "We have been sent to propose that you, our countrymen, now recant your words and deeds. If our government is in any respect disordered, then let us correct it and make amends. If anyone has been offended, then let us dress them in robes, pour tea for them, and raise their spirits."

The Ḥażrat and all his followers lowered their heads in surprise. As they did so, Amin Shaykh spoke up then and said, "Even the Kyrgyz Kazakhs govern their own affairs. We are no lesser men than the Kyzgyz Kazakhs! No matter how many hardships the Khojas have suffered, they have always managed to get theirs. Now take whatever you brought with you, except your weapons, and go, and we will outfit you{108} with horses and tack and send you on your way. Now let the tea we drink be the nectar of death, and the robes we wear be our shrouds." They put a man on Mullah Tokhta Muḥtasib and sent him to the city as an emissary, but they kept me as a hostage in place of the emissary they sent.

That day was a Friday. There was a mosque at the Shrine of the Poplar. When everyone had gathered and said their Friday prayers, they placed the Ḥażrat upon a white felt and elevated him, making him their ruler. And with a rebellious outcry they marched toward the city. But the Ḥażrat fell off of the felt. This was an ill omen. When the rebels arrived at the city, they opened one gate and entered through it, but before they could open another, Ḥamuddin Khoja brought out the guns and fired on them, killing the men. They shut the gates fast. Ḥamuddin ordered his soldiers to the city walls, where they opened fire and kept the rebels from approaching. For six days and nights, the rebels gave their all in their efforts, but it was no use, and many men died.

Meanwhile, I was locked up in a cell, with several men watching me. On the seventh evening, the Ḥażrat had me removed from the cell. [In the presence of the great begs of Ushturfan, the Dungan headmen,[8] and the Kyrgyz,] he said a few words to me: "You came to us as an emissary. Now you will enter the city as our emissary and make things right between the Khojas and us, and the commoners. I have admonished the commoners—it will be as it was before, with the people as the subjects and the Khojas as rulers." He sent me on my way.

My horse had been taken as booty by a man named S̱abit Yüzbegi, and he returned it to me. Four begs were put on me with orders to take me back over Tumshuq Mountain, and to keep all of the soldiers from harming me. There was a reliable and respected merchant [and mullah] from Samarqand named Qalandar Akhund, who apparently had also been sent as an emissary after me. We were in the same cell. I requested that he accompany me into the city.

The night was dark, so that I could not even make out the soldiers. When we came to Tumshuq Mountain, one of the begs, Nawruz Mingbegi, revealed his worries in hushed tones: "It's bad luck that I fell in with this lot . . . Won't they kill me as soon as I enter the city with you?"

I considered his situation and reassured him, "Oh, my brother, Nawruz Mingbegi! Come into the city with me. No matter what happens, I will find a way to save us. I guarantee it." Everyone heard this and said, "Let's go too!" Having given them this guarantee, I took them into the city.

{109} The three Khojas were each at one of three gates. They brought me into the city through the gate where Ḥamuddin Khoja was, and we had an audience. I informed him of all that had happened.

He was very pleased, and having granted me a turban and robes of honor, he asked me, “Where are Mullah Qalandar Akhund and the begs?”

“They stopped outside the gates,” I said.

“Let them in,” he ordered.

By then dawn was breaking. A man came from the Khaṭib Khoja and took me to him. I informed the Khaṭib Khoja of everything. He expressed exceptional happiness and gratitude, and drops of tears flowed from his eyes like pearls of spring rain as he wept and prayed. For six days the khoja had been besieged in the city, and his patience had run out, as he could find no way to escape the city and could not assess the rebels’ situation, but only sat with his head bowed, accepting this calamity and God’s command.

That day, a little before Iftar, Ḥamuddin Khoja gathered the cannons and falconets and went to the Shrine of the Poplar with his personal guard. They surrounded the Ḥażrat’s home from both sides and opened fire. Everyone within was distracted with the Iftar meal, and they slaughtered them, but they took the Ḥażrat alive, bound him, and took him to the city. Many others were captured alive, including the governor of Ushturfan, Tokhta Beg; his younger brother Aq Beg; and Pay Muḥammad Qażi Beg.

All night until the dawn, they killed everyone they encountered, good or bad. Some of them, led by Kyrgyz, fled to Kashgar. The filthy Kyrgyz robbed and killed some of those, or they died in the desert and the cold, where they drank the nectar of death. Some people fled with Amin Shaykh to Ili, but they perished in the wilderness of the place called Sirt. They could get no shrouds, so the birds and the beasts devoured their bodies. Fathers knew nothing of their sons, nor children of their parents. Just as on the morning of the Day of Judgment, everyone was in shock and disarray. The dead were numbered at over 2,000, but how many perished in the desert wastes? Those were cold days.

In the days when the city was conquered, they had seized as booty a great pot that was used in the kitchen[9] to heat alcohol. This pot was gifted to the endowment of the Shrine of the Valley.[10] The rebels then brought that pot to the Ḥażrat’s chambers{110} and used it to make the porridge for Iftar. When Ḥamuddin’s forces opened fire, two rebels who had been ladling porridge out fell into the pot and were stewed alive.

Ḥamuddin Khoja interrogated those who were captured alive, and each evening he would kill some of them and have their bodies thrown into a well, so that seven wells were filled up with human corpses. They covered the wells up.

* * *

However, there was a reason such calamities happened to these "migrants." Things surely would not have happened this way without some reason.

The reason is that, while the people of Ushturfan were outwardly pious Muslims and lived according to the Shariah, they had bizarre beliefs and would claim to follow the path of the Kubraviyya, Isḥaqiyya, Niʿmatullahi, Rabudiyya, or Davaniyya orders.[11] Some of them would say, "NOBLE OF NOBLES, ALLAH KHOJA, ALLAH KHOJA!" and express excessive faith in khojas, placing them in an extravagantly exalted position. They would not place any human being or living creature between God and khojas. So when the Khojas had just arrived, they said, "Finally, we have found the khojas we have hoped and longed for!" And in their outpouring of belief, they brought their horses in their herds, the cows with their paddocks, the sheep with their folds, and their daughters—virgin and formerly married alike—to give to the Khojas as gifts. "Finally," they said, receiving their blessings, "we need nothing more!" And they kept reciting, "ALLAH KHOJA!"

However, the Khojas treated all of their Muslim people the same way, as commoners, and regarded them all as equal. For this reason, these sectarians thought, "These are not the Khojas we meant!" And ineluctably they turned their backs on them.

Also, these sectarians would gather in a big room with men and women mixed, put a great deal of green tea into a large pot, and bring cream in on saucers, which they then added to the pot, and boiled it. A trusted man would be put in charge of the tea. He would hold the handle of the ladle for ablutions, and, calling it "blessed tea," would give a little bit out to each of the assembled people as a blessing until it ran out.[12] They would take the tea with grandiose reverence, indeed in the manner of bowing in worship, and fall silent.

Then the sound of song, and the ruckus of men and women, even strangers, as together they entered into movement [*raqṣ*] and audition [*samāʿ*], now falling, now rising, drowning in intoxication, beside themselves, spittle flying from their mouths, out of their minds.{111} They have invented a *muqam* called "The Presence" [*ḥużūrum*], which these sectarians use often in their practices. Their singers perform "The Presence" at some festive parties as well. Anyway, things pass in this manner for a few hours, at which point they come to, open their eyes with an "Oh!" and sit down. They believed that this exchange was called the "way of the Kubraviyya." It is thoroughly contrary to the Shariah.

The leader of this sect came into the presence of their leader and teacher, the Khoja, and asked him for blessed tea. He said to the Khoja, "We ask for someone to lead prayers for us." The Khoja agreed and appointed your humble author to the task. I went up and observed the situation with my own eyes. First of all, they invited me to do movement and audition with the women and "lead the blessing."

"I am still young," I said and appointed an older man as my stand-in.

Once it was over, he said to me, "I can tell that you haven't done much practice along this path [*ṭarīqat*]."

"I am still young," I replied. "I still haven't completed the path of the Shariah. I am planning to practice it once I complete the path of the Shariah."

These people did not know the Khojas, and yet called them "our Khojas." Nor did they know me, but brought me to their blessed tea and called me "one of us," though they later came to regret it. It brought them no benefit.

The Padishah Khoja, who took refuge in the Shariah, knew how these lost sectarians could not separate the path of error from the road of right, nor distinguish innovation from tradition. In accordance with the Shariah of the Prophet and the equitable commands of the jurists, and in conformance with the guidance of the imams, he would secure a legal opinion from the leading scholars. He would proclaim the content of the opinion, operating according to the hadith that GUIDANCE COMES FROM REVELATION, and by means of sweet words and gentle rhetoric—and tried-and-tested admonishments sweet as candy—would show them means to resolve their contrary ways. But it was no use. When he learned that once again strange men and women had gathered to meet without a curtain between them, he had them brought before him, and with the whip of Shariah dealt them a harsh reckoning. As that did not sit well with their vile humors, they planted the seed of enmity and nurtured the thorny bush of contention. They openly beat the drum of rebellion. These hopeless people's actions found violent ends. They hurled themselves like moths{112} upon a candle's burning flame and took their places in the domicile of annihilation.

They set aside the lamp that God had lit—
The man who went "puff"—his beard is burning.

What this means is, those who went astray got their just deserts.

"But when you say 'ALLAH KHOJA,' whom do you mean? What is their name?" When one asked them, even their shaykhs and *khalifas*[13] would reply, "We cannot speak our khojas' holy names. [Nor do we know them.] Our forefathers called them 'ALLAH KHOJA.' When we too say 'ALLAH KHOJA,' they get it. Indeed, we have not heard their holy names."[14] The great Allahyar in his book *The Persistence of the Weak* relates in a *mathnavi*:[15]

There once was a God-fearing sect;
Their name was "Believers," but they loved themselves.
They would gather all the great and little,
And offer up their daughters and young wives.
If one brings forth his wife and children,
He raises up the unchivalrous and calamitous.
When someone has forbearance for forbidden acts,
Then their beliefs will be un-Muslim.
This sect, who go and lead astray—
The people of the Shariah are ashamed of them.

What this says perfectly describes these sectarians.

The Isḥaqiyya, Niʿmatiyya, and the others are of the same sort, maybe even more so. Every sect holds fast to their own beliefs. They are cautious about holding intercourse with one other at parties and public gatherings. They keep their own ways very secret and clandestine. They do not attend each other's blessed tea parties, nor speak of them. And if they happen to associate, then one will hurry to leave, or drive the other out.

Some groups at their vigils make a big loaf of bread, which they say is "for the Khoja"; and another, smaller loaf, "for the Lord"; and another, even smaller loaf, "for the Prophet." They bake these well and smear them with butter, and atop them place some incense sticks like candles. At the time of the evening prayer, they place these between them and recite the *durud*[16] and *Fatiha*, and then recite the Quran. After they are done offering their prayers, they break that loaf into tiny pieces and give a piece as a "blessing" to everyone gathered there. Or so it is written. These sectarians described here are not peculiar to the migrants, but are found throughout the Seven Cities.

When one asks them, "When you say 'Kubraviyya,' which order do you mean?" they say, "We do not know this, either." According to what they say, the shaykh from whom the Kubraviyya descend is Shaykh Najmuddin Kubra. The head of the Kubraviyya order was Shaykh Najmuddin Kubra. This individual also supported movement and audition. Of course, of course,{113} his order is not like this order. These have followed their own set of religious precepts, creating their own way, with their women unveiled, sitting among strange men, even engaging in movement and audition with them. They commit sins openly and obviously, and even say that they have taken these sins and "made a path" from them, that they have "brought about the Kubraviyya order." But this genealogy they give is nothing but unadulterated ignorance, error, and deviance. Shaykh Najmuddin Kubra was the leader and shaykh of the Kubraviyya order, and he boasted perfect attainment both in knowledge of learning and in knowledge of ecstatic states. The requirement for a woman to veil is proven by a definitive Quranic passage. If there is no evidence that this holy personage made some trivial infraction against that which is approved by the Shariah, how could he have abandoned that which was his religious duty?

Oh, God, lead those who have fallen into ignorance and deviancy, and all Your creations, to the right road, and grant them your guidance. OH, GUIDE OF THE MISGUIDED! Amen.

1:10 Khotan and Ili

What Happened to the Soldiers and Emissaries Sent to Khotan and Ili, and the Correspondence with Those Emissaries

IT IS WRITTEN that, when the joyous news of the rebellion in Kucha and the Khan Khoja's enthronement, and of how the sword of Islam was drawn across the heads of the unbelievers, came to be known to the rulers and commoners of the Seven Cities, as well as in adjacent regions, and when Muslims and Dungans in every city possessed the common goal of opening Islam and putting the tyrannical nonbelievers to the sword, then the Dungans and Taranchis of Ili likewise revolted against infidel rule and made their chief mufti, Mullah Shawkat Akhund, their independent ruler. He was a greatly learned and pious man.

The people of Khotan too rebelled against the Chinese. Yarkand and Kashgar likewise severed the thread of obedience. This is because Kucha was like a gateway to the Six Cities—when soldiers came from Beijing, they could go nowhere else without passing through Kucha. Knowing this, the Seven Cities rebelled, and the people of each city made one man their commander and another his subordinate, and all of them became petty kings.

In one case, in Khotan there was a pious, abstinent, and faithful man called Mullah Ḥabibullah Mufti Ḥajji. All the people of Khotan recognized him as deserving to be in command over them, and so they{114} elevated him, and then put the nonbelievers of Khotan to the sword. They counted the

Dungans among the infidels as well, and killed them all. He made their land as pure as the hearts of the pious and was installed upon the throne.

At that time, as Shaykh Naẓiruddin Khoja rode to Yarkand with the intent to conquer it, Ḥajji Ghazinachi Beg went with him. When they arrived at Yarkand, he sent Ḥajji Ghazinachi Beg with 1,700 Muslim and 300 Dungan soldiers to Khotan. "If Mullah Ḥabibullah Ḥajji Padishah takes pride in your arrival," he said, "binds the belt of obedience tightly about his waist, and receives you with his head bowed and displays of honor and respect, before placing you on the throne and serving you, then that will be a fine thing. Otherwise, should he be disagreeable and disobedient, and refuse you, rebelling with heart and soul, then seize Khotan and bring the Ḥajji Padishah and his sons to me." And with these vindictive and boastful words, bitter and distasteful, he sent him on his way.

Ḥajji Ghazinachi Beg marched until he came to Sanju, where he sent an arrogant letter to the Ḥajji Padishah. The Ḥajji Padishah regarded this letter. "This letter does not bear the perfume of friendship," he said. "Its enmity is evident. The appropriate thing to do is this: I will send a man to them, and we will see what pokes its head from behind the curtain of concealment." So he dispatched his eldest son, Ibrahim Khan Ṣudur,[1] with 3,000 soldiers. A battle took place at the city of Ziba, and many men perished. An arrow stuck in Ibrahim Khan Ṣudur, and he passed on to the eternal realm. Ultimately, however, Ḥajji Ghazinachi Beg could not match them. In grief and defeat, he went to Yarkand, while the Ḥajji Padishah's victorious retinue pillaged and then returned to Khotan in mourning.

The reason the Ḥajji Padishah would not submit was that Ḥajji Ghazinachi Beg was a lordling of Kucha, related to the Khojas on his mother's side, and was one of those old lordlings who had served [as interpreters for] the Chinese. One year earlier, he had gone to Yarkand to serve the imperial agent as an interpreter. His speech had come to be peppered with Chinese, just as his clothing was embellished with Chinese clothing.

The Ḥajji Padishah said, "Whoever sent Ḥajji Ghazinachi Beg to attack me must have been one of the Khojas.{115} Even if he were not—could he not find a faithful Muslim who had lived his life within the Shariah, in the clothing of the Shariah, that instead he sent a ward of the Chinese?" He held fast to his own land and people, and staunchly to his actions.

* * *

Meanwhile, the Taranchis of Ili had likewise turned against the nonbelievers. They exerted themselves to the utmost in battle, becoming ghazis. Because they made such exceptional efforts, they came to be known as the "fanatics," and many men sacrificed their own lives out of sincere intention. Yet the leader of the nonbelievers, the general in Kürä city, was not yet defeated.

At this auspicious hour, the Muslims' leader, Muḥammad Shawkat Akhund, proposed, "In our fight with the infidels, many men have perished, and many infidels have also died. Yet we need a *ṣaḥib duʿa*, of the line of the Messenger of God, to bless us. Already in Kucha they have opened Islam. We strengthened ourselves with their help and put the infidels in Ili to the sword. Let us congratulate the Khan Khoja and place ourselves under his command, as we are all of one sect and community, and we have put the head of unity through one collar. When one of us faces a problem, then in friendship we will make common cause for the peace of Muslims and the prosperity of the country." The distinguished personages then present agreed, and together they sent a letter of commitment asking for a *ṣaḥib duʿa*. Mullah Qurban Akhund and forty or so men were sent as emissaries with gifts. These emissaries left Ili and ascended through the passes of the Sirt to go to Ushturfan. This was because no one could get over the Muzart Pass.

The Khojas in Ushturfan had them camp in a place appropriate for their reception, where they explained the situation and the letter of commitment, which was passed on to the Khan Khoja. A few days later, they received the reply—"Understood."—along with another: "Let them come." The Khojas sent them with fine and trusted guards to Kucha. They stayed two months in Kucha, where the Khojas gave them a favorable response. Bahauddin Khoja's son, Saʿid Khoja, was sent to Ili with 350 soldiers, banners, drums, weapons, quivers, and arrows.

{116} They repaired the road through Muzart Pass and crossed it, despite a thousand difficulties, giving thanks to God. Through fear of assault by Qalmaqs they made it to Tekes, but then a group of filthy Qalmaqs came straight at them.

"What kind of people are you?" the Qalmaqs' leader asked. "And where did you come from? Where are you going?" They sized the Khojas up and said, "There are bad and rebellious men around these parts. Allow me to send some men with you to see you over to Ili in safety. You would be doing me a favor." He had three of four Qalmaqs join them and, in his duplicity, emphasized to them, "Take these Khojas to such-and-such a place, and then return. No one is to be allowed to harm them—or else it would be bad for us."

The Khojas were pleased, and they said, "The Lord has made light work of our worries!" When they had traveled two or three stages, they put their horses and pack animals to pasture, and in repose they busied themselves with eating. After taking their meal, they went to sleep.

Those Qalmaqs seized the opportunity to go and inform the rest of the Qalmaqs. As sudden as the wrath of God, many Qalmaqs came and looted the Khojas, slaying some of them. Some others fell captive. Some stole away to Issiq Köl and other places.

Saʿid Khoja wandered in confusion, naked, starving, on the verge of death, until he came to a town in Ili. The leader of that town gave him clothing and brought him to the Sultan of Ili. After that, it turned out that Mullah Allahyar had also been sent to Ili and arrived in safety with one of his pupils. Once Saʿid Khoja had told the Sultan of Ili what had happened to him, the sultan gave him robes of honor and assigned him duties and a salary, giving him a good position. Yet he never pledged his allegiance. (Indeed, Saʿid Khoja came to be known as "the Naked Khoja.") The reason was that, by the time the Khoja arrived, the rebels and the fanatics had deposed Mullah Shawkat Akhund on account of some crime, locked him in a box, and thrown him alive into the river. They had made another man their leader, but this leader{117} did not work out, either. These Khojas remained in Ili until the reign of the Ataliq Ghazi, and they returned to their own land.

* * *

Meanwhile, after Ḥabibullah Ḥajji had returned from putting Ḥajji Ghazinachi Beg down, he felt that, regardless of anything else, it had not been a worthy act, so he felt bittersweet. One day he advanced an opinion: "We are Muslims—of one faith and one sect. Regardless of what else has happened, it is incumbent upon us to make compromise." And so they prepared fine gifts from Khotan—its coveted silk carpets, commodities, weapons, and coins—and forged the bonds of friendship, entering indeed into the circle of submission.

Ḥabibullah Ḥajji made apologies for the battle at Ziba and, arriving now at a position of equitability, wrote, "If only someone other than Ḥajji Beg had come, I would have submitted and performed the rituals of service. For another thing, you killed the Emperor of China's finest loyal men, but then made common cause with bad men when you declared your kingship—by which I mean, you killed the Chinese but allied with the Dungans. If only you had likewise killed the Dungans, naturally I would have submitted. Nevertheless, it is the case that you, sirs, occupied the royal seat before we did. It is incumbent upon us to submit." He had some delicate words such as these written down and sent them with Aḥmad Mirab Beg as his emissary to Kucha with fifty or so men. Those emissaries arrived in Aqsu and stayed for a few days before setting out for Kucha.

When they were one stage away from Kucha, men were sent out to greet them, and they took the gifts to Kucha. Aḥmad Mirab Beg and all of his companions were separated from their horses, pack animals, and goods. Each man was given to one person in Sayram to provide him board, under stern orders to monitor him. They lived a year in the towns around Sayram and settled in the places assigned to them. When later the Ataliq Ghazi blessed that place with his approach, all of them returned to their homelands and were blessed to be unified with their families. OH, COLLECTOR OF THE SCATTERED!

1:11 The Conquest of Qarashahr

How by the Favor of the Guardian of Creation Sayyid Khoja Isḥaq{118} Marched Eastward; Many Grim Soldiers Died at Ushaq Tal; and the Conquest of Qarashahr Succeeded; and Other Events

WHEN SAYYID RASHUDDIN Khan Ghazi Khoja the Victorious ascended the throne, he was concerned about the lands to the east, which were Qarashahr and Turfan, and the nonbelievers who lived there. And so he issued a challenge: "Is there any brave man who will sacrifice his life on the path of God and His Prophet? Who will carry out holy war against the nonbelieving infidels and tyrannical polytheists? Who desires the ghazi's station and seeks the martyr's rank? Who?"

At that moment, a man called Tokhta Muḥammad Yüzbashi came forth and said, "It is I. I wish to carry out this task and attain such a rank." The Khan Khoja acquiesced and granted him 100 men under the command of Bahauddin Khoja and Ayuddin Khoja with glorious orders to march to war with the infidel. When they came to Bügür, they found nearly 100 nonbelievers there and killed all of them. Afterward they gathered some more men and marched for Korla. The was a Dungan in Bügür called Su Mullah. He became the leader of the Dungans. Behind them came Khoja Isḥaq, Khoja Ṣiddiq Dadkhwah, and Mamur Khalifa leading some 150 men. And Duʿai Khalifa of Bügür raised 100 men there. They all marched together to Korla and subjugated it. They raised men again in Korla, and having formed this host, began their march to Qarashahr.

Then their martial grandiosity and kingly pomp were displayed with banners and weapons—bows and arrows, cannons and guns—and the sound of trumpets and drums. All bound their waists tightly with eagerness and marched toward their goal in pursuit of holy war. At the riverbank, however, the nonbelievers withdrew the ferryboat and opened fire with guns, preventing them from crossing.

As they stood there nonplussed, one of the warriors from Korla named Islam Khalifa indicated a plan that gave them the hope of God: "It looks like there is no way into Qarashahr by this road. But what if we were to go around Lake Baghrash, to Ushaq Tal, and then double back and take Qarashahr?"{119} Everyone agreed, and so they turned back to Korla and went around Lake Baghrash. Nine days later, when they arrived at Ushaq Tal, they found 18,000 Chinese soldiers there sent from Ürümchi. That day it had rained, and all of those soldiers' equipment had gotten soaked. So that their guns would not get wet as well, they buried them in the sand. Now they lay there inattentively until the Kuchanese arrived, and then they set to fighting, and many battles broke out.

Back when Khoja Jahangir Törä had taken the cities, the soldiers sent against him from Beijing were led by one General Ai. In exchange for his service in wresting the cities from Jahangir, they built a great shrine for this General Ai, naming him "the Instructor and Protector of the Cities."[1] There is a great idol temple there, and it was ordered that his image be created and installed therein in accordance with their ignorant beliefs. (May his mouth be filled with stones, clay, and black earth!) Now the infidels holed up in that temple and continued the fight. Ultimately, however, they were defeated, and all of them came to their ends, put to the sword of justice. Some of the infidels tried and failed to flee toward Beijing. Others took flight to Qarashahr.

Just then, two Chinese came carelessly on horseback from Turfan. The Qalmaqs captured them and brought them to the Khoja, who verified their identities, and they produced a letter. It was evidently a letter written to the imperial agent at Qarashahr. A number of high officials had signed their names upon it, and they wrote, "By the order of the Great Khan, we are coming to your aid with 20,000 soldiers, 470 cannons, and 200 cartloads of weapons and ammunition. We will arrive in Ushaq Tal in three days. Have ready sufficient fodder, etc." When this had been read out to everyone present—and all were busy shouting “Look alive!” and “To arms!”—a cloud of dust appeared, and among the dust, grim soldiers could be seen. But the army of Islam held to the mouth of the desert and the riverbank. Those soldiers, unaware, believed that the men they saw before them were merely sent to gather supplies, so they advanced.

Suddenly, like a divine calamity, from one side, Isḥaq Khoja and Tokhta Muḥammad Khalifa approached; from another, Bahauddin Khoja and Mamur Khalifa; and from yet another, Ayuddin Khoja, Duʿai Khalifa, and Su Mullah, all of them shouting, “GOD IS GREAT!” They spurred their horses and entered the fray. Suddenly, Ayuddin Khoja and his unit were ordered to turn back, and matters took a turn for the worse. Then Isḥaq Khoja{120} raised his hands in prayer, begged God to protect him, and set himself to holy war with vigor. All as one shouted as they redoubled their efforts, “TRUST IN GOD!” And they did such battle with heart and soul that they drew left to right, and right to left, and from morning to evening, and dusk to dawn—even to noon!—the clatter of battle, the cries of “To arms!” and “Look alive!” and the roar of the guns passed beyond the sphere of the Pleiades.

In the end, the door of victory was opened by Isḥaq Khoja. For one night and two days, they fought the infidels and did away with them. Yet for every five they killed, ten of them brought death upon themselves, and for every ten they killed, thirty did so, because the way they thought of it, it was a matter of shame to die by the enemy’s hand. If they had not helpfully killed themselves, the Muslims would not have been able to kill them all in five days and nights, because the soldiers of Islam numbered fewer than 2,000, while the infidels were 24,000 or more. At most 1,000 survived. The rest perished.

In the interim, the soldiers of Islam had no time to drink any water, nor to eat any food. When they found a moment’s rest and had busied themselves with a meal, the news came that 7,000 Chinese soldiers had marched from Qarashahr with 3,000 Qalmaqs, 56 cartloads of guns and ammunition, and equipment loaded on 250 camels, and that they had now encamped at a place called Tapilghu. No food passed their gullets, nor any other thought across their minds—all set out for Qarashahr with one goal, to prosecute holy war and do battle with the infidels and the Qalmaqs.

They encountered the Chinese thirty stages away at a place called Choqur. Battle broke out.

In the end, Isḥaq Khoja took a mulberry-wood shillelagh in his hand, and with his famed warriors, he galloped toward the infidel soldiers. The infidels had made their camels sit, formed their wagons into a line, and taken shelter as they shot from behind them. Suddenly they saw the horses approaching and realized things had taken a turn for the worse. No one can say if they set fire to the gunpowder on their camels' backs or if it caught fire by the Lord's grace. Whatever the case, camels and guns alike were blown sky-high. The smoke from the gunpowder and the dust kicked up by the horses' hooves{121} blackened the surface of the dusty earth and clouded the face of the sun, so that human eyes were bereft of light and unable to distinguish night from day and day from night, as though a vision of the Day of Judgment were manifest. The infidels fled. The Khojas followed.

So they came to Tapilghu and rested. The next morning, they had the Qalmaqs lead them close to Qarashahr, where they captured two Chinese scouts. When they were interrogated, they said, "They have installed wall guns along the main road."[2] Per the Qalmaqs' advice, they abandoned the main road and instead turned leftward, passing to the south of Qarashahr, and then made camp in a place west of the city called Teräklik. On one side was the river, on another the mountains, and then on a third lay a deep stream. That day, they killed all of the nonbelievers at the suburban markets outside the city, set fire to them, and burned them down. They did much battle. One could find nowhere to walk for all the infidel corpses. Where they did battle there were two great streams where they fought, two spear lengths deep. They were blocked up with the corpses of infidels, and their water flooded out and ran in every direction. And the water of those streams ran blood red.

In the end, no infidel remained, save for those within the walls. And those fired bullets from atop the walls and threw grenades,[3] allowing no one to approach.

So then they brought some wagons and arranged them in a row, and they soaked their camels' saddles in water, moistening them, and loaded the wagons with them. Some warriors got under the wagons to shift them and carried them to the gates, which they lit on fire. When the infidels saw that the gates were burning, they went out of their minds and lost their senses, so that the bright world looked dark to them. Their weapons fell from their hands. Their feet froze in place. Knowing not whether they were alive or dead, they stood dumbfounded but upright.

A man named Khojak Qażi, who was an interpreter, said to the Qalmaqs, "Stop firing at the Khojas! One prayer, and everything will go up in flames!"

The Qalmaqs agreed, and they said to the Chinese, "For generations, ever since the time of Khoja Jahangir, when by the Khan's order we went to Kashgar and fought with the Khojas, things have gone poorly for us.{122} Sickness emerged among us, and many of our people died, and our livestock developed pox and died off. We will not fire on the Khojas." And they ran off without firing a shot. The soldiers of Islam made it to the city, and as they set fires, they massacred the people, making it a place for the *paris* and *divs* and sending the infidels' souls off to Hell.

If a king is fortunate,
That king will meet with victory.

Within a week, over 200,000 infidels and apostates had been wiped out—all of the dead officials, merchants, and settlers, the great and the petty alike. Yet not even 200 of the Muslims had achieved martyrdom. Nearly 300 were wounded. By the favor of the Creator, Sayyid Ghazi Khoja Isḥaq and every single one of his soldiers were victorious, and that guardian of liberation offered prayers of gratitude in thanks to God. Their joy rang out across the blue sky, and even beyond the seven spheres of the heavens, where they made a tumult among the holiest angels.

Truly, in no book of history, nor in any holy war, has it been seen or heard that so many unbelieving soldiers were wiped out in one short moment by so few Muslims with hardly any weapons, not in this land or anywhere else on the face of the Earth, not from the time of Adam to today. Although in the *Garden of Purity*, the *Fire Temple*,[4] and other books apart from these [such as the *Tarikh-i Rashidi* and the *Shahrukhiya*], there are cases in which more Muslims than this died or were martyred at one time and the infidels and apostates were victorious over them, in this case it was the Muslims who were victorious, while the infidels and apostates were defeated. On this account have the eyes of the era never heard, nor the ears of the age ever seen, such a joyous holy war as this occur among the suffering and downtrodden Muslims, in which they found victory over the infidel.

Now the *khalifas* and warriors, and the Muslims and Dungans, and the loyal and honest Qalmaqs in unison, with the sound of drums and trumpets, elevated that worthy son of the Prophet, Sayyid Ghazi Khoja Isḥaq the Victorious, the Master of Arms and the Shillelagh, as their leader and general.

All were proud to serve under him and at his command. They bent their heads and placed the hands of honor upon their breasts of loyalty.

> When he sat in the royal seat, in those happy days,
> He ascended the throne—{123}it was as though the garden's buds bloomed.

Those inhabitants of the deserts and wildernesses who for seven generations had saddled corpse-like horses with saddles fit to give them sores, and placed wooden stirrups and hempen cruppers upon them, now rode upon Qalmaq horses and stout Kazakh horses fixed with Beijing saddles worth a hundred *sar* of silver, and placed upon them stirrups and cruppers inlaid with silver and gold. Those who had never worn a proper cap in summer and in winter had no warm fur hat, and who had made the formal robes and tunics they wore out of two and a half bundles of rough-spun cloth, and never been able to put away five *tangga* for the tax, now wore embroidered fur hats, cloaks of fox and lynx, and trousers of silk and satin, and possessed hempen shoulder bags filled to the brim with silver and gold, and gunny sacks[5] full of silk, satin, and suchlike things. One can guess from this what kind of booty and captives fell into the hands of the *pansad*s and *yüzbashi*s, the *khalifa*s and the warriors.

* * *

When Qarashahr was conquered, they pacified that country and collected all of the captured riches, as well as the cannons and falconets that had escaped the fire. When they traveled up to Ushaq Tal to reconnoiter, and to retrieve those exhausted, half-dead men together with those who had gone,[6] they found that the stony "Black Plateau"[7] to the east of Ushaq Tal was now a "Red Plateau," like a rug stained with infidels' blood and spread out. It was redder even than the garden of tulips in the desert of Mount Behistun above the tomb of Farhad.[8] Indeed, the tulip garden at Mount Behistun would be just a sample of the redness of Ushaq Tal. So they celebrated, and offered prayers of thanks for all of the Lord's assistance. They collected the weapons, saddles, horses, and silver and gold there and returned to Qarashahr.

Once they had written up the record of this joyous and historic victory, it was a matter of course that they send it to Kucha, the seat of the sultanate. So they prepared all of those things as gifts—the weapons, the guns, the silver and gold, the tea with its clean and pleasant flavor, the desirable porcelains and satins—and sent them to Kucha with Tokhta Muḥammad Yüzbashi.

* * *

Back when Kucha had been under siege, Aḥmad Wang Beg was in Kucha. He recorded the events that had come to pass there in a report for the Great Khan. This he had entrusted to his son, Ḥamid Taji Ḥakim Beg,[9] whom he sent with three [four] trusted men through the mountains and the Qalmaq lands [Yulduz] to Qarashahr, and then to Ürümchi. When Ḥamid Taji reached Qarashahr [and met with the imperial agent there], they sent the report by the postal stations to the Khan, while he stayed behind in Qarashahr [awaiting orders]. Once the city was conquered, however,{124} he saved his own life by turning himself over to the soldiers of Islam. He met with Isḥaq Khoja and begged forgiveness. Isḥaq Khoja, being his fellow countryman, showed some respect for the memory of Ḥamid Taji's former greatness and struck his trespasses out with the pen of forgiveness. When he reported the conquest of Qarashahr and prepared those gifts to be dispatched with Tokhta Muḥammad Khalifa to the Khan Khoja, he sent Ḥamid Taji along. There he begged the Khan Khoja to forgive his trespasses, which he confessed to His Highness in a report. Once the Khan Khoja had read the account of the conquest and was enjoying his gifts, in the exhilaration of the victory he forgave Ḥamid Taji, although he ordered his men, Allahyar Kah and ʿIsa the Interpreter, to be hanged.[10] Ḥamid Taji received his kingly grace.[11]

For the forbearance that Isḥaq Khoja had shown in this punishment, Ḥamid Taji out of humanity decided, "I must return the good deed with an alliance." He had a daughter of sixteen, who had lived in seclusion within the veil of chastity, upon whom no eye but the eye of the sun had fallen, and no brightness but that of the moon, a chaste beauty and a pious woman for the age, a Venus-like rarity. He married her to Isḥaq Khoja's son Farrukhshah Khoja. The Khojas, being sayyids, had long been preachers to the common people, while the Wang Begs for generations had ruled the land, holding the ranks of kings. Had the Lord not made it so, they would not have been able to wag their tongues and speak to the members of this great house.

This is one proof of the truth of these words: when the emperor's people came and conquered the Seven Cities [*again, in 1877—ES*], Ḥamid Taji Beg had been made the governor of Kashgar. During the Time of Islam, by the order of the Ataliq Ghazi, Isḥaq Khoja and all of his family had been in Yarkand.

However, when the soldiers came, they grew frightened and worried, so they took all of their children out to the country of Ferghana, where they settled in the city called Osh.

At the time, Ḥamid Taji Beg was the governor of Kashgar. He had a letter taken to Isḥaq Khoja in Osh. "I miss my daughter," he said and asked him, "Please send her to me." They prepared to send her to him. Isḥaq Khoja sent his son Farrukhshah along with another son, telling them, "Take her as far as the garrison posts, and when you have seen her safely past them, return here. Do not enter Kashgar," he emphasized, as he sent them on their way.

The sentries along the road had received orders: "If a Khoja arrives, seize them immediately and send them to Kashgar."{125} So as soon as these sons of the Khojas arrived at the garrison post, they were taken to Kashgar. After they had spent three or four days walking through the streets and markets, Lushi Daren[12] announced, "The Kucha Khojas who threw these lands into chaos have come again from Andijan!" and locked them up in prison.[13] Now he wanted to have the daughter as a wife for himself. For a few days the daughter told him in despair, "But I have several children!"

In the meantime, Lushi Daren paid a visit to these Khojas and interrogated them. Lushi Daren gave 200 *sar* of silver to one of his officers and an interpreter. He said to them, "The sons of the Kucha Khojas knew we were coming, so they feared for their lives and fled to Andijan. Then they wanted to return to their own land, as they had come to miss the Great Khan's magnanimity. The local governor heard of their return, confiscated their possessions, and filed a report. This is why I ordered them to be detained. Now take this silver and provide the chamber where the Khojas are imprisoned with rugs and carpets, cookpots, and crockery, whatever they need. Use whatever silver remains to pay for the Khojas' expenses." Per his orders, they prepared everything that they might need and reported back on their situation. So the Khojas remained imprisoned for sixteen months.

Eventually, Lushi Daren said to Ḥamid Taji Ḥakim Beg, "It has been quite a long time since these Khojas were detained on your orders. It is becoming a problem. Now you need to ask for their freedom."

Ḥamid Taji Ḥakim Beg formally requested their release. They brought these sons of the Khojas out again, and Lushi Daren said to them, "The Great Lord was angry with the Great Khan, and so in punishment He granted these lands to your fathers. Now the Great Lord's fury has lessened, and he gave their lands to the Great Khan. The Great Khan has pardoned the infractions of all people. But now *we* have come. If you break the law again, we will punish[14] you according to the law. Your past offenses are no matter of concern.[15] Now go about your lives in peace as imperial subjects." He released them.

Another command came from the Great Khan around that time that read, "My subjects take women as wives. They do not give them up. If one should give his wife up, or separate a wife from her husband, not only are they to be punished harshly,{126} I will not pardon their former infractions, either." This was proclaimed in every city, and they pasted it up as a proclamation in the streets of every market.[16] Now Ḥamid Taji Beg saw this proclamation and understood its meaning, and he knew that, regardless of what his purpose had been, he could never make it known.[17]

* * *

Sayyid Ghazi Isḥaq Khoja was gentle and good-natured, kind-hearted, guileless, candid, a good conversationalist, brave, concerned with the people's livelihood, and unmatched in battle. It was as it says, THE PEOPLE FOLLOW THE RELIGION OF THEIR KINGS: in his time, the hearts of the victorious soldiers and their intentions were pure. The Hadith says, DEEDS ARE JUDGED BY THEIR INTENTIONS[18]: because his intentions were right and correct, all attained the ranks of ghazis. Whether or not it is a duty or a tradition, or if it is desired or licit, if one's intention is not correct, then there will be no reward forthcoming for it. The great holy war is a duty—naturally it is necessary to have a correct intention. Because that was a time when those wicked and worthless thoughts of "Let's take prisoners" or "I'll use this chance to become the governor of a city" or "I'll make my name as a hero" found no purchase in their hearts, none of them had any intent, save for working as one to put the nonbelievers and the Qalmaqs to the sword of Islam and, when the awaited opportunity came, to sacrifice their lives. The Omnipotent Judge and True King in His wisdom granted them the fortune and office of ghazihood and brought them to the exalted rank of the martyrs. These were the people who undertook holy war in accordance with the Quran, the traditions of the Messenger of God, and the sayings of the Rightly Guided Caliphs. AND GOD KNOWS THE TRUTH.

Oh God, in Your wisdom and power, grant to all Your right guidance, that they may have good intentions and pure belief. Amen. By His wisdom and generosity.

1:12 The Conquest of Turfan

How, by the Grace of the Able and Peerless, Sayyid Ghazi Isḥaq Khoja Rode to Holy War in Turfan, and His Victory Was Facilitated; the Conquest of Several Bazaars; How the Evil Chinese Were Exterminated Like Ants and Locusts; and Other Events

WHEN SAYYID GHAZI Isḥaq Khoja—that virtuous and rightful heir—was no longer occupied with the battle against the nonbelievers, apostates, and Qalmaqs of Qarashahr, he set his intention upon conquering Old Turfan. He gathered together his *dadkhwahs*, *khalifas*, and warriors{127} and opened the matter for discussion.

They responded with prudence and unanimity: "The difficulty of the road to Turfan is famous throughout the world. In illustration of its roughness, someone has used gypsum to write on the mountainside at Aghir Bulaq clear writing that says,[1]

> Those who pass along this road the first time do so out of sheer ignorance.
> Those who pass a second time do so in order to make pilgrimage to the shrines [(of the Companions of the Cave)], or out of necessity, to trade and support their families.
> Those who pass a third time are infidels and scoundrels.

No one knows when this was written, or in which age. When we set out on this journey, we will need to have prepared enough provisions, beasts, and weapons for it." Everyone was in agreement, and so they loaded arrows and ammunition, guns, provisions, and fodder onto camels, horses, and donkeys, and at the appointed and auspicious hour, they placed their boots into the spurs of victory.

Those soldiers had killed many Chinese, and now they stilled their hearts, and their eyes flushed red, as the weak became strong, and the strong became bold, until each of them seemed an Isfandiar in form and countenance and enjoyed a potency exceeding that of Rustam, when Rustam knew victory over Barzu.[2] They put their faith in the Favor of the Noble Lord, and all of them in concert and with pure and sincere intent brought to their lips the lovely words, PLACE YOUR TRUST IN GOD. And they perpetually recited, OH GOD, GRANT VICTORY TO THOSE VICTORIOUS FOR THE FAITH, AND FAILURE TO THOSE WHO FAIL THE FAITH, and all of them in unison raised their voices in GOD IS GREAT as they marched off to their object: Turfan. The sound of the trumpets and bugles, the firing of the guns and cannons, the sorrowful sound of the song "The Presence,"[3] the tumult of bows and arrows, swords and spears, all in the display that the soldiers of Islam made of their great endurance, and the crowd calling out, "Make way, make way!" rang out across the indigo sky.

Later they made camp for the night at Tapilghu. The next morning, when they reached Ushaq Tal, they found that the bodies of infidels were piled up in heaps, so high and deep that, for all the corpses, there was no way to walk along the road. On one side was the foot of the mountains and on the other the bank of a river. So they did some manly work and dragged the infidels' bodies off in all directions to clear the road. Like unthreshed wheat in a farmer's fields or the rocks of the Black Plateau, the dead desiccated and decomposed in the desert. Their bones lay drying along the road until the Chinese came again.

Yet on account of the heat of the air, some of them came to look as though their heads had been bashed in,{128} while others seemed to have been chewed on or took on the appearance of having sat before an interrogator. Later on, when any believing Muslim or noble merchant traveled that road, their horse's hooves stepped upon the bones of infidels like so many stones. As they passed, they would say a prayer and a *Fatiha* in praise of the bravery and high-mindedness of those khojas and holy warriors. When the emperor's soldiers stepped foot there again, they built a great tomb, collected the bones, cremated them, and shut them up tightly within it.

* * *

[From this point, khojas are referred to more frequently as "törä."*—ES]*

When Muḥammad Yaʿqub Beg the Ataliq Ghazi removed Isḥaq Khoja from Kucha and sent him to Yarkand, he was placed into the care of Muḥammad Yunus Jan Shighavul.[4] For his daily allowance he was granted one gold coin; every Friday, new clothes; and every year, 2,000 *charak*[5] of grain, by special royal decree. Because the leaders of every city had made great efforts to render aid to his conquering armies when they marched to Turfan to punish the Dungans of Turfan and Ürümchi, the Shighavul later made this request: "I have continued to supply Isḥaq Törä with the allowance that Your Highness had granted him. Now, as I grant him his share of salary, and as I inspect this share, I ask to direct it instead to your conquering armies. In Yarkand, even a less expensive share of salary will suffice."

The Ataliq Ghazi, however, understood the Shighavul's intent, and His Grace responded in his great wisdom and compassion, "Rude fellow that I am, I stingily granted Isḥaq Törä but a small allowance. Whatever allowance I granted him, I shall look at that command and grant twice the amount, as a favor for you. If you saw with your own eyes the holy war that Isḥaq Törä carried out at Ushaq Tal, and the skeletons of the infidels—if you had been where I was to witness them—you too would have granted Yarkand and its surrounds to Isḥaq Törä as a matter of course." And with grace and equity he sent his compliments along with this letter of appreciation. The pious and equitable Ataliq Ghazi's words are a testament to Isḥaq Törä's courage.

* * *

The victorious soldiers returned with the wranglers, storemen, and horses{129} from Ushaq Tal and prepared grass and fodder, as well as bread, rolls, and fried millet, and headed out toward their destination. That day they passed through Döng Dangza and then marched to Qara Qizil, where they made camp. After that, they spent the night at Kömüsh Örtäng. In none of these places were grass, hay, or water to be found, nor even wood to pick their teeth. But there was a little bit of water at Kömüsh Örtäng. Perhaps twenty or thirty people (households) and their children could eke out a living there.

Next they made their camp at Üjmä Döng, and then stopped at Aghir Bulaq. There was a little bit of water there too, sufficient to water their horses in turns. Thereafter they went to Subashi and Toqsun. Toqsun is quite a large city with suburban markets. After that they arrived at Turfan. This is the path by which they came into the territory of Turfan.

By the time the victorious soldiers arrived in Turfan, however: a khoja from Sayram, a sayyid named Maʿṣum Khan Khoja, had been living there. A group of Turfanese men named Qasim Jangga,[6] Wayid Khalifa, Zayid Khalifa Ḥajji, and Baqi Khalifa joined together to kill all of the Chinese soldiers, merchants, and farmers in Turfan's villages. When they came to face the Chinese in Turfan's city, those Chinese could not match them but entered the city and shut the gates up tightly, and now they remained imprisoned within. There were many Chinese merchants and settlers—that is, farmers—in the nineteen settlements within Turfan. They had been exterminating all of them, down to their young children; setting fire to their homes; and putting all to ruin. In some markets there were 7,000 or 8,000 Chinese, and in others, 2,000 or 3,000. When they had wiped out all of these, and as they now stood facing the Chinese in the city, Isḥaq Khoja came with his conquering army and established his royal camp beside it. He set sentries and lookouts all about to keep watch.

The city was shut fast, the Chinese many. Every other day, the Chinese took their guns out to fight but, being unable to match their opponents, retreated into the city. Many infidels died, while some Muslims drank the nectar of martyrdom. But they did not achieve victory. In the end, they built tall ladders in a few places, and brave warriors climbed them, but the infidels in the city would not stick their heads out. So the infidels' bullets struck the wall, while the Muslims' bullets never went to waste but struck the infidels.

At this time, a messenger came from Suo Dalaoye and Daud Khalifa in Ürümchi.[7] Their message read, "We have taken the suburban markets around Ürümchi and shut the Chinese up in the city.{130} We ask that you send soldiers under one of you Khojas to assist us."

So they put Bahauddin Khoja in command of 1,000 soldiers, and Maʿṣum Khoja of another 1,000, while Wayid Khalifa, Zayid Khalifa, and the Dungans Nur Akhund and ʿAli Khalifa were each placed in charge of 700 or 800. All at once they were sent to Ürümchi. Raḥmat Bahadur Ḥajji and Baqi Khalifa were sent after them with 1,000 men. They went to Ürümchi and did battle there, and some days later achieved victory. Over 30,000 infidels died. Next they took Jimsar. Some 6,000 died.[8] Then they went to Guchengzi. (It is written that Guchengzi was a very large city. Everyone there was a Chinese, without a single Muslim. Apparently the name Guchengzi in Chinese means "dog worms," which means "innumerable."[9] It had suburban markets and three or four bazaars, and it was quite large and imposing. There were markets belonging to Guchengzi in several other places.) The number of households was estimated at over 200.[10] They set fire to all of them, burned them to the ground, and killed the people, massacring them all. Yet some of them must have fled with their lives into the mountains. After this, they went to Santai.[11] Some 15,000 more died there. Then they marched to Fukang, where nearly 10,000 were killed. Then they moved on to Jirma Depot.[12] Some 8,000 perished. Next they moved on to Qara Basun.[13] More than 10,000 died. Then they went to Manas. They waged many battles. Some 50,000 died. After that they showed up in Jinghe. More than 20,000 died. There were such terrible battles there. The Lord in His grace granted them victory. Some *khalifas* and warriors came into possession of a great abundance of booty and captives. Yet the harshness of the cold and the driving snow became so extreme that they had no choice but to return to Turfan. Within a month (two months), they had pacified all those markets and towns, setting them all to ruin—nests for owls, homes for *divs* and *paris*.

At this time, they also placed Ayuddin Khoja in command of an army, with 700 or 800 soldiers, or at least 400 or 500, assigned to each of Ḥasan Qasim Bahadur, the Dungan He Khalifa, Hidayat Khalifa, Musa Mingbegi, Musa Khalifa of Kashgar, Qurban Khalifa, Tokhta Muḥammad Khalifa of Kucha, Mullah ʿUs̱man Shaykh Bahadur of Shahyar, Yoldash Mirza, Idris Khalifa, and ʿAshur Khalifa of Aqsu. With their bullets and their guns, 12,000 soldiers[{131}] were sent marching to Murkhu.[14] They traveled along the highway to a station with a market called Chiqtim. Next they abandoned the highway and turned instead to their left, crossing the mountains through a pass to arrive at a place called Taz Bulaq. Moving on, they came to Sangah Chanza. (Nearly 12,000 people and two great markets were there.) They fought with the Chinese and killed 10,000 (12,000). Next they marched to Yiban Chanza.[15] Nearly 2,000 died there. Then they passed through the scrubby steppe and arrived at Murkhu. Much fighting took place. It was a town with no walls but a large market, and many Chinese, all of them brave and bold. Most of them died, while a few joined the community of Muslims and were blessed to know peace. Next they passed on to Dongchin. Its walls were firm, its Chinese many. A terrible battle took place. Nearly 40,000 apostates and nonbelievers died. Yet they were not victorious, on account of the infidels' great number. In the end, the infidels won. What's more, in a frigid blizzard, the soldiers could not endure, so they returned to Turfan.

* * *

A long time ago, when the Emperor of China conquered the Seven Cities and became ruler and master of the country of Moghulistan, they took from the hands of the Muslims all those things that remained from the times of the old Muslim khans—the Mongol khans, but also the descendants of Chinggis Khan, and even the Bughrakhanids: armor and leather hats, helmets and cloth hats, spears and swords, bows and arrows with quivers, coats with steel woven in, armored chain mail, and sleeveless robes, and rifles, maces, and axes. All of these things they locked up in Dongchin, and then they brought even more weapons from the Emperor of China's own treasury and stored them in Dongchin, kept with the soldiers. Later, when Dongchin was captured, it would have taken more than seven years for all of the teamsters of the Seven Cities to haul away and sell all of those multifarious weapons and pieces of iron. By then, the emperor's people had come and taken control once again. But for now, Turfan had yet to be conquered.

A great many things had happened. One was that a Dungan named Su Mullah had stayed behind in Bügür. When he heard that Turfan had still not been taken, he swore a boastful oath: "I will eat nothing until Turfan is conquered." He and his men rushed to the city. Once they got there, they chased some Chinese into the city. In a great display of courage, they slew many infidels and{132} threw their hands and their feet—indeed, all of their organs—out of the city, over the wall. But just then, he was struck by a deadly arrow that remanded his soul to the Harvester of Spirits. The infidels stripped him of his clothing. A seal fell from one of his pockets. "He's one of their leaders!" they said, and they lit a fire, made kebabs of him, and ate him up.

All the grain in the infidels' granaries had been lent out to the people in the spring. When their grain ran out, they killed all the dogs, donkeys, and even cats—and even the elderly and the young[16]—and ate them. Now they had reached their limit. More than eight [four] (six) months had passed, and still the city had not been taken. At the time, the road through Bulayiq was closed. So they withdrew their soldiers and declared, "Now the Chinese are to depart for Beijing. They are to vacate the city. We will allow them passage." When the infidels heard this, all of them exited the city walls, but when they came to Bulayiq, the Muslim forces massacred them all. Those who had escaped the sword were made servants of the soldiers of Islam. Now all of the weapons and guns in the city, all of the implements of kingship, were handed over to the khojas, and as the Muslims laughed with joy, the infidels cowered in fear.

The Chinese officials, merchants, and farmers within the city and in its nineteen suburbs, over 150,000 infidels, must have died, while of the Muslims (and Dungans), some 400 were martyred. In the space of these seven or eight [five] (six) months, from Ürümchi to Murkhu and Dongchin, excepting Turfan, over 550,000 infidels and apostates were wiped out, perhaps even more. The imagination of no living being could encompass or comprehend the number of the dead, save that of the knower of the invisible and the visible. AND GOD KNOWS THE TRUTH.

But were we to tug the reins of the graceful pen somewhat nearer to diligence and dare to relate these words in detail, it would drive our readers and listeners to boredom; so, of 1,000 things, we have selected 100; and of 100, ten; and of ten, one; and recorded them only in summary upon the page. In sum, the *malign infidels* had infested Moghulistan and turned it to darkness and tyranny, but swords with brilliance like the sun bestowed brightness upon it once again.

God, bring repose in victory to the Muslims and humiliation and suffering to the infidels, and grant us peace of mind. Amen.[17]

1:13 The Campaign to Murkhu

{133} How the Incorruptible Sayyid Ghazi Khoja Isḥaq Sent Soldiers to March on Murkhu Again; How They Were Defeated; How They Exchanged Gifts with an Emissary from the Khanate of the Qumul Wang; and the Second Conquest of Lukchin

AYUDDIN KHOJA HAD been sent marching on Dongchin with the soldiers of Islam, but because of the freezing cold, they had returned to Turfan. They readied the soldiers once again, and now under the command of Bahauddin Khoja, and with the Dungan He Dalaoye and Tokhta Khalifa to lead them, over 15,000 armed brave warriors were sent again to prosecute holy war in Murkhu. They traveled until they came to Murkhu. Those infidels on the outskirts and in the villages who had escaped the sword the last time now regrouped and set themselves to preparations for battle. Many Muslims and infidels alike perished in a great and terrible battle. In the end, they could not match the infidels, so turned back to Turfan.

At that time, the Qumul Wang's court had run out of grain, so they sent a man named Supurga Beg with fifty carts and a hundred camels to bring more from Gucheng. These were captured on the road. Isḥaq Khoja questioned them and sent them instead to Kucha. There the Khan Khoja treated Supurga Beg kindly. Supurga Beg then made a pledge to take Qumul for the Khojas, so the Khan Khoja sent him back to Isḥaq Beg. Meanwhile, however, the chief mufti of Qumul had come bearing gifts as an emissary to the Khojas.

Among those gifts were all sort of desirable things. When Jahangir Khoja had fallen into the hands of the Chinese, the armored cuirass he was wearing had been granted as a gift to the Qumul Wang. On its shoulders, hands, and bosom, and on the tips of its knee joints, were little golden domes with the Surah "Victory" written in gold ink, each of them as brilliant as the sun itself, and its quiver likewise, and its four plates were also inlaid with gold. And the chariot in which he had traveled and all of its tack, its saddle and saddle skirt just like new, were also emblazoned with gold inlay. "Keep these as gifts of honor," they said, and presented them to the Qumul Wang, who kept it in his collection of gifts of honor.{134} Now they had sent all of this to the Khan Khoja in Kucha, the seat of the sultanate, with a message saying that these armaments and chariot belonged to the Khojas.

The emissaries arrived. After three or four days of rest, they were sent on their way to Kucha with all of their gifts and some men to accompany them. When those emissaries came to Kucha and His Highness's royal gaze took in all of the gifts, they were granted an audience. After they had rested for a few days, the Khan Khoja responded by gifting the Qumul Wang a golden turban cloth, brocade robes, and a scimitar, as well as a declaration of friendship, and to the chief mufti and his men he gave turbans, robes, and coin in proportion.

Meanwhile, just as Supurga Beg had received his reply, Isḥaq Khoja had sent ten Muslims and six Dungans under Mullah Timur Khalifa and Tokhtam Bahadur as emissaries to Qumul. These went to Qumul and had an audience with the Wang Khan, fulfilling their role as emissaries.

None of the officials in Qumul had made any threat against the Chinese, either inside or outside the city. Mullah Timur Khalifa suggested that the Khojas could prevail over the infidels in Qumul. The Wang, who was an ignorant man, produced enough weapons, armor, helmets, guns, and ammunition, as well as banners, all the things one would wear or need in war, for 500 men. Those men gathered, fought, and were victorious.

However, after the second time the soldiers came back from Dongchin, a group of Lukchin's prominent khojas and begs—including Ibrahim Khan, Ḥafiẓullah Khan, Yolbars Khan, and Shah Muḥarram—secretly brought 4,000 or 5,000 Chinese from Murkhu and encamped them there. They elevated Ibrahim Khan and beat the drum of contestation. They brought Zayid Khalifa and Wayid Khalifa to their side.

The Wang Beg had a grandson who took presents to Zayid Khalifa. In his joy he made a pledge: "What matter are these Dolans?[1] I will bring them to you." And he prepared for battle.

At that time, Khoja Isḥaq placed Naṣruddin Khoja in command of 8,000 soldiers, with Tokhta Muḥammad Mullah, ʿU̱sman Shaykh Bahadur, Bakhtmat Khalifa, Muḥammad ʿAli Khalifa of Sayram, Musa Khalifa of Kashgar, Qurban Khalifa, Hidayat Khalifa of Aqsu, and Niyaz Khalifa as their officers. As they walked, they encountered fights{135} on both sides, and they fought hard battles. Many men were lost.

Ultimately, the Khojas met with defeat and came to Turfan. Because the Lukchinese had gotten a half-baked plan into their heads—"If we capture these Khojas of Kucha and govern this land ourselves, then if the Chinese come from the interior, we will make these Khojas a present to them and gain ourselves offices"—they had caused much pain in vain, at the cost of Muslim blood.

There were over 400 households of Dungans in Lukchin. They set fire to their houses and exterminated them, down to the little children. Suo Dalaoye in Ürümchi heard of this, and with his zeal inflamed, he sent 3,000 Dungans to aid them. In this hour of successive fortunes, that great monarch of the horizons, Sayyid Ghazi Khoja Isḥaq, personally led a group of brave warriors for a second attempt. He rode for Lukchin with 15,000 battle-hungry soldiers. At a place called Abad, he made his abode [*ābād*].

The people of Turfan aided neither side but stood between them undisturbed. The men of Lukchin had readied many men, and now they came face to face. Defeat and success emerged in turn, but in the end, victory presented itself to the victorious soldiers of Turfan, and the winds of fortune scattered their adversaries like so much dust, erasing them, stuffing them into the cave of nonexistence.

Wayid Khalifa understood that the tables had turned, so he captured and bound a few of his superiors, whom he brought to the Khojas. They pardoned his offenses, eliminating them with a stroke of the pen of forgiveness. They opened the city gates and went inside, where they killed many men. They looted the city and its villages, and they sentenced several of the leaders to death and hanged them. Others fled to Qumul or Barköl to save their own lives.

* * *

The Khojas pacified the domain of Lukchin and made a Lukchinese man named Hashir Taji Beg its governor. They made Qasim Jangga the governor of Turfan. Then they paid visits to the shaykhs of the shrines. As they were showering those worthies with recitations of the holy Quran and donations of alms, offering thanks and prayers, men came from Qumul with an invitation. They determined to ride for Qumul.

1:14 The Submission of Qumul

How That Great King of the Horizons, Sayyid Ghazi Khoja Isḥaq, Went to Qumul, and Even to the Edge of Beijing; How He Was Received by the Jun Wang Khan, and Qumul Was Subjugated; and How He Returned Home on Account of an Untimely and Inauspicious Command

{136} IN THE year 1282, on the eighteenth day of the month of Muḥarram [June 13, 1865],[1] at the appointed and auspicious hour, that unimpeachable ruler, Sayyid Khoja Isḥaq, with soldiers, banners, and weapons, and accompanied by the joyful and carefree sounds of trumpets and drums, led 16,000 victorious soldiers toward his intended destination. Qumul had been cleansed of the Chinese there, and the Khojas' arrival was expected.

It is twelve stages from Turfan to Qumul. The road is hard, and in most places there is neither fodder nor food to be found. They traveled from one to the next, and when they were five stages away, several carts and camels approached, laden with a great many sheep, as well as fodder, hay, bread, rolls, and dried fruits. And after them came the Wang Khan himself, to hold a personal audience with them. Bread and tea were distributed to all of the soldiers, and they ate their fill. Next they presented them with a great many gifts, notably with 400 *yambu* and 8,000 geldings, and innumerable sheep. One can imagine from this what other things there were. After the presentation of gifts, His Lordship the Wang Khan went ahead to enter the city, and men were assigned to guide the Khoja thither. The Khoja and his victorious soldiers traveled until they approached the city for their audience with His Lordship the Wang Khan, and they were guided within and housed in a great palace. The other *khalifas* and warriors were also put up in their own quarters in proportion. Once everyone was settled in, they came with further gifts. They prepared 800 *yambu*, 8,000 geldings, weapons, equipment, and other such desirable things, and the *khalifas* and warriors likewise received more than their lot. Your humble author says that his lowly self and the soldiers also received more than their station demanded. Every four days, four men together received no less than one sheep, two *jin* of green tea, bread, rolls, straw, and fodder. The leaders received more. For three months, maybe more, we stayed in Qumul, and they continued to give us this much. His Lordship the Qumul Wang's office is lofty, and his wealth is great.

As for those horses that they gifted to the khojas and the soldiers—when we went to inspect them, we found that all were old, not a one younger than twenty years.{137} Nor were there any teeth in the sheep's mouths. We asked why this was.

"The Khan's herds of horses are vast," they told us, "and we cannot know their number. But as for sheep, he has 260 folds of them. Each fold numbers no fewer than 700, and no more than 1,200. In early spring, a *beg* and three secretaries go to record the number of horses, and another beg and three secretaries go to record the number of sheep. In five or six months, they record them, total them up, and take their numbers to report to the Wang Khan. It takes a month to reach the end of his summer and winter pastures—and we cannot know how many they are."

* * *

The Xiao Yuanshuai and Da Yuanshuai went to Qumul with 30,000 Dungans, intending to pillage it.[2] His Lordship the Qumul Wang sent forth an emissary who said to them, "What if we agreed to give one gelding and *yambu* to each of your 30,000 Dungans, and more to your leaders, and call that your 'plunder'?" The Dungans did not accept this offer but pillaged instead, and they martyred His Lordship the Wang Khan. They divided up among themselves all those things that he had seen and held, killed his men, and took prisoners, whom they drove off to Ürümchi.

Your humble author attests that a necklace strung with jewels owned by His Lordship's wife, which was set with such pure and luxurious jewels as emeralds, rubies, corundums, topaz, and diamonds, fell into the hands of

Aqmullah Bay of Kucha. He brought it to Aqsu, where in the presence of the tax collector he sold it to Mir Muḥammad Bay of Marghinan for seventeen *yambu*. Because it came cheaply as plunder, he sold it cheaply. From this you can get a sense of what else the Wang possessed.

* * *

"Qumul is home to over fifteen thousand households," they explained to us, among other things. "We all work for the Qumul Wang. Not in summer, nor in winter, do we give anything to the Chinese. If the Chinese take even a spadeful of soil from the land that belongs to Qumul, they must pay silver into the Wang Khan's treasury first. He humbles himself before no official, apart from the Great Khan. Even the Chinese officials, the assistant agent and lieutenant colonel, come to His Lordship's palace to hold their yamen, instead of going to other officials' yamens. For fifteen generations or more, we have been granted to the Great Khan, along with the land of Qumul, as *jüldü* and *jasaq*. Accordingly, we work as slaves. This is what *jüldü* means."[3]

{138} They also explained to us, "Every year, his Lordship the Wang Khan sends 360 melons and nine-times-nine *bīlāw*[4] stones to the Khan as gifts. For this he also collects many rewards. Every year, His Lordship receives seventy-four *yambu* from the treasury, and his wife Fujin Khanim[5] thirty-five *yambu*, as well as some bundles of silks and satins. He goes to Beijing once every three years. And as he travels there, all of his expenses are paid from the Khan's treasury. Each time he goes, it costs at least 350 *yambu*." Really, there is more to say than what he said. Among the Muslims ruled by the Emperor of China, there is no one greater than the Qumul Wang.

It has long been the case that, in accordance with law, custom, and his own grandiosity, he does not speak to anyone, or listen to them—whether it be another high official such as another *wang* or *gong*, or a mullah, scholar, or other great cleric. Nor, should he happen to hear them, do their words make any impression. For this reason, he has one or two begs called "the announcers." Whatever commands His Lordship the Wang Khan has, he states to the announcers, and then the announcers proclaim what he has said as "His Lordship's command." And if anyone else should have something to say, they inform him, "They respectfully say such-and-such." Regardless of what room or place he might be in, these are the rules.

In his own estimation, His Lordship the Wang Khan is a very powerful man, and likewise are the commands that he issues very important. No petty person can resist his great commands. Through the mediation of the announcers, they are humbled one degree before his commands reach them, while others' words are made very humble.[6] According to the absurd belief that His Lordship has no responsibility to listen to the words of others, they speak to his announcers, who render it according to rank, summarize what they say in a manner befitting the Wang Khan's audition, and then report it to him. Although that may be the job of yet another official.

What is even stranger is what has been written about Isḥaq Khoja. When he had killed tens of thousands, or even millions, of infidels, as well as officials and soldiers, in such cities as Turfan and Ürümchi, and conquered them, he then desired to conquer Qumul, so he rode there with several thousand battle-hungry soldiers. "If they submit," he said, "then I will grant them their property and their lives and leave them in peace. Should they choose instead to resist, then I will massacre them all, starting with the Wang, and pillage them in indescribable ways."{139} As he was marching to put the Wang to the sword, the Wang Khan went to hold an audience with him, and he and the Khoja sat on two chairs with one bow's length between them.

Then His Lordship the Wang Khan said, "We celebrate the Khojas for opening Islam and honoring us with their arrival." The announcer announced to Isḥaq Khoja that "His Lordship the Wang Khan has declared such-and-such." And they reported Isḥaq Khoja's words to him by saying, "The Khoja begs to report that such-and-such."

As they were speaking, Isḥaq Khoja spoke for himself: "Oh, announcer beg! Leave us alone. I can hear what His Lordship the Wang Khan is saying, and His Lordship can understand what I am saying." And thus it is known how the Wang grew arrogant thanks to the greatness of the Emperor of China's generosity, and to his great wealth and lack of care.

The Qumul Wangs' lineage can be traced back to the Tarkhan Begs. In the *Ẓafarnama*, it explains, "At the time when Chinggis Khan led his revolt, he did battle with the son of Nayman and fell into his clutches. But he forgave Chinggis and sought to educate him as his own, and he gave his daughter to Chinggis, making him his son-in-law. However, he worried and could not feel at ease, so attempted to assassinate him. The vizier told his wife this, saying, 'The Khan wishes to kill Temujin.' Outside the yurt were two guards. When they heard this news, they reported it to Temujin. When Temujin heard this, he luckily removed himself from danger. Chinggis Khan's original name was Temujin. When he became a great king, he made those two boys hereditary *tarkhans*, granting them orders, and placed them above his intimates. In the time of the sons of Chinggis Khan and the era of Amir Timur Kuragan, the descendants of the Tarkhan Begs belonged to the most honored and renowned of warriors. All of the Tarkhan Begs trace their ancestry straight back to those two boys."

They are pure and zealous in their belief, and their efforts on behalf of the security and flourishing of the Shariah, the splendor of scholars, the efforts of teachers and students at schools and colleges, and skill in the medical arts are beyond praise. It is on this account that the people of Qumul are all mindful of their religious duties, and its jurisprudents, mullahs, and scholars are skilled in their knowledge of jurisprudence and wise in the medical sciences. There are hardly any Turks.[7]

* * *

When Isḥaq Khoja was staying in Qumul,{140} an emissary came from the Dungans of Suzhou bearing a letter that read, "We fought with the Chinese, killed them, and pursued them into the city. We took the city, but all of those Chinese left by the various gates, and now they have us trapped inside. We are under siege. We ask that you help us: send soldiers to free us."

However, the Chinese who had fled from Ürümchi and Turfan to Barköl had joined with the Chinese of that city, making over 100,000 Chinese. They did not allow the refugee Chinese into the city, but in one place set up a barracks[8] and provided them with food, leaving them there as lookouts. So Isḥaq Khoja commanded some of his *khalifas* and warriors to lead 10,000 soldiers to Barköl. When they arrived, they found defeat and success by turns, and ultimately were victorious over the Chinese in the barracks. Now they went to the city. To one side of the city, mounted warriors [Qalmaqs] had built a fortress where they were garrisoned.

The Chinese of Barköl turned out to be incredibly bold. When some thousand Chinese came out to fight, they were all equipped with saddles and tack in Andijani style, and their numnahs were in Andijani style, as well. When we asked why, they told us, "These are the Chinese who have gone several times to fight in Kashgar, and they have seen many battles."

The marketplace of battle was busy in trade, with souls bought and sold. Those were the days of capturing and the season of conquest, and as the time arrived to pluck the flowers in the gardens of intent, fortunes increased day by day, and the light of the torch of fortune shone brightly as they made such strides in conquest.

Then an order came from the Khan Khoja. "The Kyrgyz and Qipchaqs have taken Kashgar," it read, "and Yarkand as well. All of the Khojas over there have fled hither. We have suffered great losses of weapons, equipment, and treasure. Bring your soldiers here immediately to wrest these cities from the Andijanis and the Qipchaqs. If our enemies grow in strength, it will go badly for us, because there are many enemies on our borders indeed."

This news spread among the soldiers. All of them thought of their fathers and mothers, their relatives, their children, their wives and brothers, and missed them. Their spirit for holy war evaporated all at once and went cold. They wanted to return to their homelands. "Let us return home, and then later we can go and conquer the remaining cities," they said, and all of the soldiers bowed as one at the Khojas' feet,{141} weeping. The discipline of the army crumbled all at once. The Khojas were at a loss to say anything.

In sum, the fall of every rise and the descent of every ascent from days of old came to fruition in this chaotic and unfortunate age. Just as those victorious soldiers displayed such total exertions in fortune, discipline, and honor, such an untimely command and unfortunate news threw the community into disorder. It turned the lantern of prosperity dark as a windstorm and blackened the sun of fortune with clouds of tyranny, as when an owl hoots in a desolate place, or when a rooster crows in the severe light of dusk.

In the end, they left their work in Qumul incomplete and remanded it to His Lordship the Qumul Wang. Isḥaq Khoja granted the Dungan towns of Ürümchi to Daud Khalifa and Suo Dalaoye, Turfan to Ayuddin Khoja and the Xiao Yuanshuai,[9] and Korla to his son Farrukhshah Khoja, and made Ṭahir Qażi the fiefholder of Bügür.[10] By the Lord's grace, with great fortune and dignity, the march of hooves and soldiers' boots, and the sound of trumpets and festive cheers, they arrived in Kucha, the seat of the sultanate. The noise of the crowd of people who came to greet them, of reunions between fathers and children, of the mourning of the mothers and fathers, wives and children of those who had drunk the nectar of martyrdom, and of the cheering spectators rang out across the heavens to the ninth sphere and the hosts of holy angels.

So in this manner they arrived in Kucha, coming to that high and pleasant land, that broad and fertile place, in great fortune and dignity. They saw family and strangers, wives and children, and stayed for a few days in peace and repose, providing alms to mendicants and the deserving, and clothing and money to family members.

Praise be to God in all things.

1:15 Isḥaq Khoja's Western Campaign

How That Unimpeachable Ruler, Sayyid Ghazi Isḥaq Khoja, Resolved to Undertake Holy War in Yarkand and Kashgar; How He Established a Treaty of Friendship with the Qushbegi, Muḥammad Yaʿqub Beg the Ataliq Ghazi; and How He Returned to His Homeland

IN KUCHA, THE seat of the sultanate, like the conjunction of Jupiter and Venus, the Khan Khoja{142} and Isḥaq Khoja met, and spoke, and told one another of their adventures. They exchanged gifts and fulfilled all of the obligations of hospitality, summoned their soldiers and brought them to order, and placed their boots into the stirrups of victory and set out towardtheir goal. It was the year 1282, on the second day of the month of Barat [December 21, 1865]. They traveled until they came to Aqsu, where they made their camp in the khanal gardens.

However, most of the soldiers who had followed Isḥaq Khoja's banner from Qumul had remained in Kucha. He traveled with his personal guards, aides, *dadkhwahs*, and attendants, who made more than 3,000 men, as his companions. This was because a command had been issued to the effect that Ḥamuddin Khoja was to bring soldiers from Aqsu and Ushturfan. They came to Aqsu and spent ten days there, making pilgrimage to the shrines, paying alms to the mendicants and the deserving, and giving out charity and receiving blessings. Then Tokhta Muḥammad Bahadur and Ibrahim Bahadur were sent out a day ahead of them with 2,000 soldiers. They followed with their personal guards, *dadkhwahs*, and personal bodyguards.

Surely no king in Moghulistan had ever been worthy of such pomp and ceremony, of such a display of weaponry, valor, and ferocity. At the fore were two riders, each holding a Qalmaq bugle encrusted with rubies, diamonds, and other precious stones to dazzle the eye, and two mounted trumpeters, and six mounted drummers. Behind them followed two more buglers, and each trumpet and bugle was more resplendent than the last. Twelve men on foot changed the twelve mounted drummers, trumpeters, and buglers' horses at each stop. The low rumble of the pair of buglers at the fore; the sound of the pair at the rear; the trumpets' soulful *ghazal* and *muqam*; the poignant tones both high and low; and the heartrending sound of the song "The Presence" rang out across that cerulean dome up to the sphere of the Pleiades.

However, 3,000 or 4,000 young men had disobeyed their fathers' commands and stiffened their necks at their mothers' orders, as they were imagining a walk in the garden, enjoying the roses. Without regard for father or mother, nor even for wife and children, they lost their senses and followed the army. When they had traveled two or three stages, some of them{143} stopped themselves and went home; others could not, but instead found the march agreeable and proceeded to Yarkand. Still others were retrieved by their parents, while others took the horses their parents rode and caught up with the army.

Thus they came to the domain of Yarkand. Isḥaq Khoja, by the favor of the Creator, arrived at Yarkand and made his headquarters at a great house. Yet of Ḥamuddin Khoja there was no news, and of his soldiers not a trace. Earlier, when Jamaluddin Khoja had fled from Khan Eriq, the Qushbegi appended Yarkand to his domain and appointed Kichik Khan Törä as its governor. Because Isḥaq Khoja had gone to Yarkand, the Dungans brought Kichik Khan Törä into Yarkand's New City as their own "companion" and would not allow him outside.[1] So in Yarkand, the Khojas now ruled on one side and the Dungans on the other.

When the Qushbegi heard that Isḥaq Khoja had established himself in Yarkand, he displayed his own prowess in gamesmanship by taking a host of soldiers to Maralbashi, where he did battle with the Dungans and subjugated them. One may observe his skill at chess by how he jumped his knight just once and achieved a checkmate, trapping the king—Isḥaq Khoja was now sealed up in Yarkand.

So the Qushbegi went to Yarkand and established his royal tents at the Shrine of the Seven Muḥammads. With the Qushbegi outside the city, the Khojas in the Old City, and the Dungans in the New City with Kichik Khan Törä, they passed a few days without battle, quietly observing and spying on each other. In the end, the Dungans and Isḥaq Khoja conferred, and they prepared for war. Niyaz Eshikagha Beg became aware of this development, and he informed the Qushbegi, writing that "On such-and-such an evening, nine [seven] thousand Dungans and two thousand locals are planning to emerge and carry out a nighttime sneak attack. Factor this into your plans, sir, as you will. I can do no more than this."

Now that the Qushbegi was aware, that night, he sent his soldiers away in every direction, so that they vacated their tents but stayed on guard. As they waited, the Dungans took up their weapons and came out to strike the Qushbegi's forces at night, setting upon them like moths. But now they saw that there was not a trace of any man there. All of the tents were in place.{144} Suddenly the Qushbegi's forces came upon the Dungans like a storm from every side, in a great commotion, and surrounded them. A fierce skirmish ensued in which they wiped the Dungans out. Around 600 Dungans and 800 Muslims saved themselves and escaped to safety, while the rest were undone by wrath and the punishing sword.

Isḥaq Khoja and the Dungans' warlike hearts lost their patience. Because they could find no solution to their problem other than making a truce, they resigned themselves to truce, which was the source of their salvation. Most of their soldiers had been lost. Those who had followed them because of their displays had likewise been wiped out. The rest fell prisoner. With a plea to the Qushbegi, Isḥaq Khoja went to his camp and concluded a truce. The Qushbegi showed him great hospitality and made some speeches. He assigned Isḥaq Khoja to Mirza Aḥmad Qushbegi's tent, where he spent three days and nights separated from his soldiers.

Then they brought Isḥaq Khoja in again before the Qushbegi, who was kind to him and, understanding that he was upset, inquired kindly of him, "If we had fallen into your hands, what would you have done?"

"If you had fallen into my hands," Isḥaq Khoja replied, "I would have tied you to a horse and sent you to Kucha under guard. You would have long since been on the other side of Maralbashi."

These words pleased the Qushbegi, who replied, "Oh, Törä! Your words are true. Verily you are a sayyid, I do declare!" And so he praised him greatly. "Let the Khan Khoja keep Aqsu for himself," he continued, "and stay in Aqsu, ruling the land on that side of Maralbashi, while we rule the land on this side. You have carried out many holy wars against the Chinese and attained the ranks of ghazis. Now it is necessary that we join forces, and that we maintain written communications. If one of us should happen to be attacked by an enemy, we will come to one another's aid. If the Khan Khoja does not content himself with Aqsu, however, then eventually I will need to bring armies against him. In that event, may the Lord of the Worlds and True King open the door of victory to which of us He will, and then we shall see our stars of fortune." With this, the Qushbegi had him outfitted with clothing and a turban appropriate to his station, and a fine steed with saddle and tack. They pulled him up by his armpits and placed him on the horse, and to the captives they showed kindness as well, giving them money for the road,{145} horses, and beasts of burden. In such finery they sent them on their way to Kucha.

* * *

Now no one could pass from Yarkand over to Aqsu and Kucha, nor from Aqsu and Kucha come over to Yarkand, and no one knew what happened on either side. The Khan Khoja, however, had commanded that Ḥamuddin Khoja should lead soldiers from Aqsu and Ushturfan and go to Maralbashi. Their goal was to take Maralbashi and then go to Yarkand, so as to lend aid to Isḥaq Khoja. He rode with 1,000 soldiers in total. They captured Ḥakim Khan Törä's garrison at Charbagh Örtäng and took them prisoner. Some of them they killed. Others fled and informed the Törä, who as soon as he received the news gathered his soldiers and came to fight. They fought hard for three days and nights. In the end, Ḥamuddin Khoja was defeated and turned back. Others met their preordained deaths. The rest wandered on foot, naked and hungry, and prayed that each might save his life and find his way home.

Once Isḥaq Khoja was released safely from the Qushbegi's clutches, he wandered in anguish until he came to Aqsu. The Khojas in Aqsu reproached him for having "sold Yarkand for a horse." Nevertheless, the soldiers who were meant to come with Isḥaq Khoja had ended up held back in Kucha, and so he had marched with few men. Nor had the soldiers from Aqsu joined him, for although Ḥamuddin had been ordered to go, they had not been sent. Now the Khan Khoja's favor began to slip. Instead, Isḥaq Khoja's name was on every person's lips and in every city, and all the soldiers and commoners favored Isḥaq Khoja. In whatever city he arrived, the doors of victory were opened, and he achieved his conquests—but now, on account of what had happened with Yarkand and Kashgar, the Khan Khoja intended to bring him and strip him of his weapons and his glory. Ultimately, things went as he wished.

Also, he had ordered Isḥaq Khoja to attack a multitude of enemies with few men. Once Maralbashi had been taken and the roads were blocked, his reinforcements could not get to him. The Khan Khoja forgot about his own actions and placed the blame instead on Isḥaq Khoja. Then he sent 1,500 soldiers after him. These soldiers were sent at the wrong time, so they could not get to Yarkand{146} and ended up staying in Aqsu. Those soldiers had served under Isḥaq Khoja in Qumul and Turfan. For this reason, Isḥaq Khoja was angry as he set out on the road for Kucha. All of those soldiers, as well as the older soldiers who had stayed in Aqsu, now followed Isḥaq Khoja on that road, and they did so of their own will.

Soon Jamaluddin Khoja came in person to Aqsu to speak with Isḥaq Khoja. He made apologies and took upon himself the responsibility for all these offenses, as he presented Isḥaq Khoja with singular gifts and hospitality. Then he revealed that some soldiers still remained in Aqsu, and he renewed their alliance. Isḥaq Khoja gladly acquiesced to his proposal. On the advice of those soldiers, he placed Ṭahiruddin Khoja, Mullash Ghazinachi, ʿAbdulwaḥid Beg, and ʿIsa Beg in command of 1,000 soldiers under Jamaluddin Khoja's leadership. He was very happy and grateful, so he appeased those soldiers by granting them robes. Yet their soldiers' discipline was slapdash and weak, while their fortune and leadership came up empty.

Sayyid Ghazi Isḥaq Khoja rode in fortune, and when he arrived at the city of Kucha, he stopped and wondered, "What by the Will of the Able and Exalted could possibly happen now?" He prayed and put himself at ease, and he humbled himself before the perfect grace of that majestic, incomparable Creator. After completing his five prayers, he offered an oath for the occasion, and then reunited with his family and friends and offered them clothing and coin, and reposed in happiness.

1:16 Dissension and Demise of the Kucha Khojas

The Dissension of the Kucha Khojas, and Their Former State; and Their Ingratitude for Their Great Fortune; the End of Their Rule and Other Unfortunate Events; and the Rise to Dominion of Muḥammad Yaʿqub Beg the Ataliq Ghazi

BY THE FAVOR of the Singular Creator, Sayyid Ghazi Khoja Isḥaq signed a treaty of friendship with the Ataliq Ghazi in Yarkand. They bound it with sacred oaths and sure promises in consideration of the people's well-being and in search of peace for the commoners of this country. Now that affairs were settled there, he returned to Kucha, and there he remained.

Meanwhile, however, the Khan Khoja and Jamaluddin Khoja, who were brothers,{147} as well as Jamaluddin's son Yaḥya Khoja, and all of the other Khojas, were openly doing whatever their hearts desired, proper or improper, though it were not in accordance either with the faith or with the customs of kingship.

Ḥamuddin Khoja wrote to Jamaluddin Khoja with a request: "Over the past few years, I have defeated several enemies at Yarkand and Kashgar. Other times I have been defeated, and fled, and suffered many hardships. So I ask that Aqyar be appended to my domain." Jamaluddin did not agree. Ultimately, he asserted his own power to proclaim most of Aqyar to be under his control. The overseers[1] could no longer travel from Aqsu to Aqyar. If they tried, they would be punished severely and turned back. There was no way for any of these overseers to go to Aqyar.

In the end, that crafty, two-faced Jamaluddin Khoja formed a treacherous plan and laid a deceptive trap, planting a seed of falsehood. He wrote a letter to the Khojas in Ushturfan. "My younger brother Ḥamuddin Khoja," it read, "has truly caused a great deal of trouble. He had wished to seize control of Aqyar, and this did not sit well with me. But, now that I consider the matter further, I realize that my actions were not nicely done. Should my younger brother visit you, please keep him there a few days and entertain him, so that I might present Aqyar to him in person, and he may rule it as he wishes. There is a risk that our internal conflicts might become apparent to our enemies—and that might not be good for us." He wrote down these deceptive words and sent the letter.

In his naïveté and gullibility, Ḥamuddin thought this letter of hypocrisy to be a letter of love, and he was deceived, and the craving for Aqyar whetted his appetite and sharpened his teeth, and with his guards and ministers, in grandiose commotion, he set out for Aqsu. Jamaluddin Khoja happily sent men to meet him, and having showed him honor and respect, had him establish an army camp and granted quarters to all of his men according to their needs. After the ceremonies were completed, he gave the guards leave to go, saying, "Get some rest. We two brothers haven't been able to be in one place to see each other for a long time, so let us talk and catch up before we retire." His guards too thought that it was "just like the conjunction of Jupiter and Venus," and their minds were put at ease. They went off to sleep.

Meanwhile, Jamaluddin Khoja{148} had placed a few men in hiding. Just as Ḥamuddin Khoja began to drift off, those men emerged from their hiding places and tied him up, and likewise did they seize his men where they stayed in their rooms as guests. They bound the Khoja and three of his men tightly upon some horses, and in a day and a night, brought them to Kucha to be imprisoned. They killed a man from Aqsu named Musa Beg by burying him in sand. It was as though Jamaluddin Khoja's hands had hacked wolfishly at his own feet. This was a sign that his fortune was fading.

* * *

When the Kyrgyz heard that this astounding thing had happened, they went to Kashgar and informed the Qushbegi. When he heard this happy news, he gladly granted robes, horses, and weapons to the Kyrgyz. "By God," he said happily, "it would appear at last that Aqsu and Kucha have fallen into my hands without a fight."

We should note that, before this happened, when the people of Ushturfan rose up in a vain attempt to rule their country for themselves, many people had cast their souls to the wind of death and fled to Kashgar. This was narrated in detail earlier. Some of those who had fled to Kashgar entered the Qushbegi's protection, and now they importuned him in the hope that he would let them lead him on the road thither. Meanwhile, ʿAbdurraḥman Dadkhwah of Kucha and Magistrate [*divanbegi*] ʿAbdullah of Aqsu were in the service of Jamaluddin Khoja Padishah in Aqsu. All of the commanders in the country were under their command. They pondered the khojas' situation, and with an eye to protecting their own lives, they observed the Qushbegi's rise to power and wrote him a secret message inviting him to Aqsu. The Chief Minister Tokhta Eshikagha in Kucha also wrote a letter promising to offer up that country to him. When the Qushbegi read those letters, his pulse began to race for battle, and his desire for conquest roared.

These Khojas had enjoyed their status as shaykhs of the Shrine of Mawlana ʿArshuddin. Now, for these Khojas who could fit into Mazar Baghi,[2] there was not enough room in all the Seven Cities. Their unity turned to hypocrisy. Their hypocrisy in turn became enmity. And they did not appreciate their great fortune. Ungrateful, they took their fortune for granted, and carelessly they let it slip from their hands. What a pity—what misfortune, what a pity! Once upon a time they had satisfied themselves with the produce of the holy shrine's pious endowment,{149} lived on the tithing of its farmers, and made their homes in the shrine, laying out their rugs in its chambers and passing their days in prayer. They had contented themselves with two loaves of dry bread and a dry flatbread. By the grace of the Creator and Giver of Sustenance had they been installed for a while upon the throne of kingship. Never in their lives, nor those of their ancestors, nor even in all of Moghulistan's cities, had any living being ever received such earthly fortune as the Khojas did.

Lean ye not, oh friends, on fortune's swiftness—
Fortune will sometime be taken be taken from you.
Your precious bodies will be planted in this dirt—
Fortune's wellspring will be destroyed, sighs laid low.

Every one of the Khojas now ate for his breakfast all sorts of halva, raisins, sweetmeats, several kinds of jam, *maʿjun*,[3] sherbets, cordials, and salty lamb kebabs, pasties, sugar dumplings, and fried dough,[4] all sorts of tasty Chinese foods, while enjoying all sorts of luxuries and the company of women like *houris* and *paris*, as they forgot their former lives. "We established Islam on our own," they said to themselves, "gained kingship, and came into possession of unending fortune." And so they failed to show benevolence to those around them who had also raised the banners of kingship, but looked down upon them instead. They failed to attend to Khoja Ḥafiẓ Shirazi's "voice from the hidden world":[5]

The ease of two worlds is the explanation of these two words:
With friends, kindness; with enemies, courtesy.

That is the general rule, but they ignored it, for they did not even hold together with their brothers, nor even visit one another. "We have no need of worldly things," they believed, so, in their sheer arrogance, the wickedness in their natures came to the surface as they beat the drum of I AND NO OTHER. As the Quran says, NAY, TRULY MAN IS REBELLIOUS, IN THAT HE DEEMS HIMSELF BEYOND NEED! [96:6–7]—the rebelliousness concealed within the nature of all human beings became manifest.

He is worthy of haughtiness and presumption,
He whose rule is ancient, who is endowed with riches.

Then, like the wrath of God, or a cat catching a mouse, or a raven snatching a sparrow,

a noble king like a high-flying goshawk,
Muḥammad Yaʿqub Beg the Ataliq Ghazi,

arrived on the scene, and he made the Khojas' fortunes and the Khojas themselves SCATTERED AS ASHES [20:105]. The deceptive orb and inconstant sphere returned to their ageless custom.

{150} Upon one's head placing the crown;
Throwing another from the throne to the ground.

What the wise must know is that they must disregard this world's fortunes, its rises and falls, and understand that pain and joy are all one.

Where is the Hall of Chosroes, the Tomb at Khavarnaq?
They have disappeared from this world, perishing.
Although there is no faith in goodness,
There is a word in the pages: "Faith."

* * *

To return to our story: Tokhta Khalifa was in command of 250 soldiers garrisoned in Chilan, Yaydi, and some other places. Late one night, near the break of dawn, the Qushbegi's cavalry overtook them. One of the cavalrymen from the garrison, however, had gone out to water his horse. He saw what happened and fled to inform Jamaluddin Khoja. The rest were all taken prisoner and marched off to Kashgar.

Next the Qushbegi's forces came to Say Eriq, whence they passed over to Aqsu. From Chilan, they sent a man named Khoja Naẓar Beg to Ushturfan with thirty-nine cavalrymen under the command of Mumin Yüzbashi. They took the road through Quruq Üzüm until they made camp at Acha Mountain, where they passed the news to travelers along the road, who brought it to the Khojas in the city. Once the Khojas were informed, they initially sent bedding and shelter to Khoja Naẓar Beg. But when people heard of the Ataliq Ghazi's coming, they rejoiced, and gifts were sent to him along with a letter of submission written by Yaʿqub Khoja Ishan and Muḥammad ʿAli Dadkhwah.

The next morning, Khoja Naẓar Beg came to a place north of the city called Tegürmän Bashi, and he sent two of his men in to meet with the Khaṭib Khoja [Burhanuddin]. They demanded that he hand over the keys to the granaries, armory, and treasury, and that he and all his retinue go and pay their respects to the Ataliq Ghazi, the Badawlat [*"the fortunate one"—ES*], and enter into his service. This, they said, was a royal command. So all of us left the city. Eventually, at the time of the noonday prayer, when we came to the gate, they allowed the two Khojas to leave, as well as Mullah Tokhta Muḥtasib and your humble author, along with a stablemaster. The rest had to remain.

The Reign of the Ataliq, the Badawlat, was then declared, and they fired the cannons, and they played the *shadiyana* on the drums. The five of us were brought before Khoja Naẓar Beg. They sent us to Aqsu under guard of twenty-five mounted men. We spent the night in a village called Yangkhay, and when we went back on the road the next morning and came to the Tawushqan River, we met with Muḥammad Baba Yüzbashi. At that point, Yaʿqub Beg had arrived at Aqsu and made that *yüzbashi*{151} the *toqsaba*[6] of Ushturfan, sending him with a kind command for the Khaṭib Khoja. He delivered that command. When we read it, we realized what it meant, and we looked all around us—and we prayed. The Toqsaba rode for Ushturfan; they sent us to Aqsu. I am blessed to have copied the command out exactly and written it upon this page.

A Royal Command
To His Lordship Burhanuddin Khoja, the Sufi Lord,
Salutations.

May it be apparent to you that at this time when the seeds of joy have been planted that by the grace of God, and with the intention to establish holy Islam, and to strike with the sword of the Shariah of the Prophet—just as the hadith says: PARADISE IS UNDER THE SHADES OF SWORDS[7]—indeed, by divine decree, this country has fallen to our lot.

On the twenty-fifth day of Muḥarram [May 29, 1867], when we were residing in Aqsu, we received from the hands of Yaʿqub Khoja Ishan and Muḥammad ʿAli Dadkhwah a letter written in a spirit of pure sincerity and kindness that made their submission clear, per the holy words OBEY . . . THOSE OF YOU WHO ARE IN AUTHORITY.[8] It came at a fine hour, and as we comprehended its meaning, happiness dawned upon us. By the words GIVE PRESENTS TO EACH OTHER AND LOVE EACH OTHER, they sent us gifts of four horses and some clothing, as well as a Quran. At this time Jamaluddin Khoja had grown afraid on account of certain affairs and fled. The cavalry retrieved him, and he made apologies for certain acts. We too forgave some of his old sins, drawing the pen of forgiveness across them, per the words THOSE WHO CURB THEIR RAGE AND PARDON OTHERS [3:134]. We pitied him and gave him robes appropriate to his station. He is the cream of the sayyids in this place, and his intentions were pure, and so we forgave the transgressions of him and all his people. On this account let nothing trouble him. As for us, may you no more suffer the total terror that you knew before.

AS GOD IS MY WITNESS. Dated 1284 [1867/8].

That day we arrived in Aqsu and made camp at Kohna Örtäng. Not an hour later, Hamdam Baturbashi[9] arrived with platters of sweetmeats, nuts, and candies and laid a spread for us. They thought nothing of bringing a great cookpot full of pilaf, and together with the Khojas, they took part in it. We spent no less than three whole days feasting like this. On the fourth day, they brought robes, some candies, and turban scarves from their serai,{152} loaded up the horses we had ridden upon, and took us to a royal audience where we exchanged gifts. They took the two Khojas into the royal tent for a feast. They sat the rest of us down in the hall for a meal, and they gifted us robes and turbans in proportion. By their leave we walked about the city of Aqsu. We went to the places to pray for the dead and recited the *Fatiha* before heading to our own familiar homes and seeing our friends.

At the time, Kucha had not yet been conquered, and 4,000 men had been sent from Kucha to fight the Qushbegi under the command of Ibrahim Bahadur, Yusuf Bahadur, Taliʿ Bahadur, and Yaʿqub Bahadur. They arrived in Yaqa Eriq and made their camp in Jogha. There they blocked the road, cut their opponents off from water, and after many battles fought them to a draw. They had killed many of the Qushbegi's cavalry in Qushtami, Yaqa Eriq, and Jogha, displaying exceptional heroism, and achieved victory. Yet their heroism was ill timed and ill placed, and ultimately, the Qushbegi's cavalry won and put them to the sword.

Earlier on, the Lukchinese had rekindled their previous enmity and, bringing several Dungans onto their side, drove Ayuddin Khoja and his soldiers from Turfan. They ruled Turfan for themselves and then marched westward toward Kucha. By now they had reached Bügür.

Meanwhile, Isḥaq Khoja had been dispatched specially to govern Korla. As Isḥaq Khoja went there, and while he was securing victory, Ḥamuddin Khoja was sent after to reinforce him. They met, exchanged honors and apologies, and now were sent to fight the Dungans with 4,000 soldiers, along with artillery, guns, and banners. Isḥaq Khoja and Ḥamuddin Khoja had battled the Dungans and pursued them to a place beyond Qarashahr when they received the terrible news that the Qushbegi had arrived in Aqsu. They withdrew Ḥamuddin from Qarashahr, and with further apologies gifted him with a great many robes and money before sending him and his soldiers to fight the Qushbegi. They left Kucha and came to Bay, where they concealed themselves in a grassy pasture. There Ḥamuddin Khoja quit his soldiers. He wrote instead a response to the Qushbegi with an account of the situation, telling him that the choice was his to make.

His Highness the Ataliq Ghazi was camped in Yaqa Eriq. As soon as he heard the news, he sent one of his guards with a command: "Have Ḥamuddin Törä come immediately. We are awaiting him." Ḥamuddin Törä then arrived. They had had an audience{153} and congratulated each other, and the Qushbegi asked him, "Oh, Törä! Is there anyone else fighting against me?"

Ḥamuddin Törä replied, "I was one who fought against Your Highness. Now I have entered your service. Now there is no one who fights against you. Kucha has likewise entered your domain. My congratulations!"

So the Qushbegi was boundlessly happy, and he said, "Let us get a loaf of bread and share it equally." He granted him robes and told him, "Go and pay a visit to Kashgar, and wait for us to return from Kucha to Kashgar." The Qushbegi sent him to Kashgar. For some time during the Ataliq Ghazi's reign, he was foremost among the ranks of the *töräs*, the leaders, and the honored men.

The Qushbegi rode from Yaqa Eriq until he came to Kucha. Several of his cavalry went in, and they brought the Khan Khoja out. After some reprovals, the Qushbegi gifted him robes and brought him into his palace. But the Khan Khoja grabbed a knife and stabbed one of the Ataliq Ghazi's guards. He got hold of more weapons and climbed atop the wall, where he ran about and shouted aloud, "Where have my warriors gone? Can't you beat these Qipchaq Andijanis and drive them from the city?" Some of the Ataliq Ghazi's men came and tied him up, and they brought him into the court.

The Khan Khoja, without any training or license, had taken up a salaried station just as he pleased, and as a result, a certain measure of abnormality had crept into his mind. This is why his humors did not fit the circumstances. In matters of government, he had at times sought a fatwa from the legal scholars concerning something that was disagreeable or contrary to the Shariah, and in so doing angered those scholars. He was someone who had never read the laws or regulations of former kings, but lived in the great shrine, busying himself with his students and his school; who had contented himself with prayer, knowing nothing of the rules of warfare, and ignorant of practical knowledge. His way of thinking was neither in accord with the Shariah of the Prophet nor in agreement with the *li* of the emperor. He did what his heart desired. Sometimes he would babble nonsensically. And the Khan Khoja had adopted some idiosyncratic, heretical ideas and spread them among his soldiers. One was that, in order to preserve the safety of himself and of his city, the best course of action was to permit his personal guards, cavalrymen, and infantry not to sleep at night, but to stay up gambling as they stood guard over the city. He permitted them such a heretical innovation. He even tried to encourage the gamblers by giving them money from the treasury to play their games.

His Highness, the Shariah-loving Ataliq Ghazi, said, "What rule did the beautiful Shariah provide, that although the illicitness of gambling was demonstrated by an indisputable proof, those who attained such power over this country nevertheless failed to forbid this violation of the Shariah, and even encouraged it?" So he obtained a fatwa from the scholars of Shariah, the contents of which were proclaimed. He convicted the Khan Khoja of his crimes according to the pure Shariah and had him executed. No one ever saw or heard what happened (how he was killed), or where he was buried. It was the year 1284, on the fourteenth day of the month of Ṣafar [June 17, 1867], when this event came to pass. His age was nearing sixty. He was a man of sallow complexion,{154} the color of wheat, of medium height, with large eyes and widely spaced teeth, and a large head that protruded behind.[10]

Fakhruddin Khoja would not bow to the judgment of the Shariah but mocked the judges and jurists, and even the Shariah itself. Another of his younger brothers, Jalaluddin Khoja, had taken a woman in marriage who was in her waiting period after divorce, or perhaps even still married to another man. Per *the commands of the* mujtahidin[11] (MAY GOD BE PLEASED WITH THEM ALL!), the Qushbegi secured a fatwa from the leading scholars, and he proclaimed the contents of that fatwa to the aforementioned Khojas. He had them executed as an example to the people. (The governor of Aqsu) Jamaluddin Khoja was killed in Yarkand. The Shaykh Khoja,[12] Bahauddin Khoja, and Ibrahim Törä were also executed. They took the Khaṭib Khoja and his son Maḥmudin Khoja to Kashgar, where they remanded them to Maḥmud Khoja Ḥażrat. There they lived for eleven years, eating from his table and wearing robes of honor. When the people of Beijing came once again to rule, they too returned to their homeland, where they reunited with their families and friends and lived out their lives. Today, Isḥaq Khoja, Ḥamuddin Khoja, and Maḥmudin Khoja are still among the living.

The Khan Khoja had ruled for precisely three years and one month, which is to say thirty-seven months. The boundary to the east was at Qumul and Barköl, to the north at Qalmuqistan (the place called Yulduz in the Qalmaq lands), to the west at Yarkand and Maralbashi, and to the south at Lop and

Cherchen. He laid the infidels of Beijing to waste in numbers beyond reckoning. The treasuries and weapons of the Cities came into his possession, and he collected many treasures. On account of his inexperience, they passed into the domain of Muḥammad Yaʿqub Beg the Ataliq Ghazi. In this manner, when one has amassed power, one ought to be magnanimous in one's relations with family; or give generous gifts to the preachers and the craftspeople, disdaining wealth; or have a bridge built over a river, and so provide charity; or prepare for oneself a guesthouse to live in with only one or two rooms; or renovate one's parents' tombs, and leave a legacy behind. The Khan Khoja passed without making any such name for himself. Not a single legacy or good deed remained after him.

Before, all of those governors and begs who had ruled the land, and indeed those merchants who had grown rich, all chose in their own way to leave a legacy in this transient world, and in order to do so paid in copper and silver from their own pockets,{155} building mosques, colleges (, inns, wells, and ponds). Indeed, even Chinese, Russian, and Frankish apostates have paid money in hopes that "Those mosques, colleges, and bridges that the Muslims cannot make, I will have them built, and repair their shrines, so that some trace will remain of me."

It is fitting and necessary that we somehow determine where the responsibility lies for how the Khan Khoja thus rose to power without leaving a legacy. While it is not good to speak ill of Muslims, nevertheless we could not be blamed for cursing this thing he did, though the blame may lie as well with those kin and clan led by Isḥaq Khoja b. Sarimsaq Khoja. To be specific, he could not master the ways of kingship or sciences of management, and he could not enact them. Everything that he did was of his own invention. One ought to follow the Shariah, or else enact the institutions of bygone kings. On this account he passed away without making a name. He neither found repose for himself nor brought rest to the people. During his days of rule, he had brought uncertainty and poverty to the people. Once he had gone, no one at all wished for his return or said that he had been a good ruler. His relatives and the people of his country were unhappy.

Oh, Lord! By your grace, protect us and keep us from those who thus come to power, do such unworthy things, and make the common people unhappy. Amen. In reverence for the Master of the Messengers.

*   *   *

In conclusion, the Kucha Khojas did not bring their ideas into accord with this unpredictable and inconstant world, but instead brought old and faithless ways about. They entrusted the rule and kingship of the Seven Cities to the person of His Highness Muḥammad Yaʿqub Beg the Ataliq Ghazi. And so we turn the reins of the graceful pen away from the story of the Kucha Khojas, and attempt instead to spur this horse toward those of that great ruler, the Ataliq Ghazi, which make for a broad and lofty battleground. It has taken its first step.

GOD'S BLESSINGS UPON HIM, AND UPON THE MESSENGERS.

The Second Epic

2:1 The Arrival of Yaʿqub Beg and Buzurg Khan

{156} The Story of How, by the Grace of That Lord of the Worlds and Beneficent Sovereign, Muḥammad Yaʿqub Beg the Ataliq Ghazi Gained Dominion Over the Seven Cities—the Country of Moghulistan—and How Buzurg Khan Törä Ascended to the Throne

MUḤAMMAD YAʿQUB QUSHBEGI was born and raised in his home country, a place called Piskent in Tashkent. He had dedicated himself from boyhood to the ways of the cavalryman and the study of mounted warfare.

When Nar Muḥammad Qushbegi[1] became the governor of Tashkent, Yaʿqub Beg married his sister and on this account came to serve in his personal guard, where he gradually climbed the ranks. Then, when Qanaʿat Shah Ghazi (the Tajik) became ruler of Tashkent, he once again served in the royal guard, and then became its *yüzbashi*. Next he was elevated to the governorship of Aq Masjid, one of the well-known cities of the Dasht-i Qipchaq, which is twelve stages from Tashkent. That must have been sometime during the years 1260 to 1270 [1844 to 1853/4]. (At that time, the Ataliq Ghazi was twenty-two years old. During the years when he was tending to the people of Aq Masjid,) some Russian men came and bound themselves in friendship with Yaʿqub Beg. "How about you sell us the fish in this river," they said, "and we will catch them and dry them, and take them to the cities in the interior of our country." He agreed and sold the fish in that river for 40,000 *som*, and they signed contracts. These fish were the pretext that the Russians used to come to Ferghana and conquer it. Now Yaʿqub Beg heard that the Kazakh Kyrgyz around Aq Masjid were no longer paying the taxes that they had been paying for generations, and even beating those who went to collect the taxes and taking them prisoner. He attacked them with several contingents, killed them, looted a great deal of booty and livestock, and returned whence he had come. His prosperity increased day by day, and his happiness was unblemished.

At that time, he wrote a report to the capital at Khoqand. "Your lowly servant," he wrote, "greets His Highness the Khan, and reports this to your royal audition in the hope that he might bedeck his eyes with the collyrium of your exalted threshold and make his service known. It is hoped that this may meet with your approval."{157} When the khan's royal reply arrived—"All right, come."—he had gifts prepared: they ornamented nine by nine Kyrgyz Kazakh girls in precious robes of every color with meticulous formality; outfitted nine by nine beardless dancing boys with fine robes and scimitars; and prepared nine by nine Kazakh and Qalmaq horses with fine saddles. Moreover, they prepared their gifts with every kind of treasures, exquisite objects, and weapons, and at the appointed, auspicious hour, they arrived in honor at the capital at Khoqand and displayed all of those presents in the presence of His Highness the Khan. The khan was delighted at this service, and he exalted Yaʿqub Beg with kingly grace and favor, distinguishing him from all of his ministers and generals, before granting him leave to return home. Such an array of gifts had never arrived from the Dasht-i Qipchaq, nor from any other officer.

After Muḥammad Yaʿqub Beg returned to Aq Masjid, the ministers' and generals' envy stirred, and they strove to subvert and defeat him. In Yaʿqub Beg's mind, he had hoped as a consequence of presenting these gifts to become the governor of a great land such as Tashkent. Once Piskent had come into his possession, the idea "It would be no surprise if the Unseen Judge now granted me the capital of Khoqand" was engraved in stone in his mind, because in his first robing, he had been endowed with high aspirations and a worthy nature.

But those generals whispered into the royal ears and said, one after another, "Muḥammad Yaʿqub Beg presented only one-tenth, or one-one-hundredth of the prisoners and booty that he seized, which were well beyond his description. He wanted to be the governor of Tashkent. If you should grant him Tashkent or some other great city, then he would want to make a move to upset this steady state. So much is evident from the signs upon his countenance." And these whispers influenced His Highness the Khan, who ordered his forty-man retinue, "Seize Yaʿqub Beg, and whatever he possesses, confiscate it, and remand it to your World-Turning King and the palace of this esteemed house."

But Yaʿqub Beg, like CHARITY MAKES A SLAVE OF MEN, had swayed many of His Highness the Khan's guards by means of gifts and favors, and said to them, "Whatever you hear, good or ill,{158} inform me of it." He had made ʿAbdullah Yüzbashi and some of the guards into his own private guard, and they had joined his cause. These un-confidant confidants, like FULFILL YOUR PACTS [5:1], passed that disturbing information on to Muḥammad Yaʿqub Beg.

When he heard, he sent men to meet the guards. "Some guests are coming from the capital at Khoqand," he told them. "Go out to meet them, and where you encounter them, entertain them with feasts, and report back to me. I will come to meet them and bring them to the city." He ordered them to a place three stages' distance from the city and sent them on their way.

Those attendants encountered the guards, and once they had reported back, Yaʿqub Beg told the rest of his commanders and cavalrymen, "Go and tend to those guards. I will ride at midnight and arrive after you." Thus he emptied the city. Together with his old servant, Alash Bi, he packed traveling cash into his trunk, and they rode under cover of night for Bukhara.

Those guards asked, "Yaʿqub Beg hasn't come. What's happened?" When they entered the city, there was no trace of Yaʿqub Beg. But the guards feared the wrath of His Highness the Khan, so they pursued him until they came to the Syr River. Yaʿqub Beg had slaughtered some goats in advance, making their skins into bags. He blew into the bags, filling them with his breath, held the openings tightly closed, and got up on top of them, fording his horses as he traveled safely across the treacherous river. Those guards could not cross but stood there watching. (Their arrows would not reach him.) They had no choice but to turn back.

Yaʿqub Beg arrived safe and sound in Bukhara. At the time, Malla Khan had also gone to Bukhara and entered the service of the amir. Yaʿqub Beg stayed for a few days with Malla Khan in safety from the vicissitudes of their time, but then they traveled together to the capital at Khoqand.

In that just hour, Khudayar Khan's sun of prosperity strode westward, while Malla Khan's [r. 1858–1862] bright moon rose from the east and illuminated the world.[2] It was in those days that Yaʿqub Beg was granted the governorship of Khujand. As he passed his days governing in peace, his enemies swayed Malla Khan with their nasty words. And so His Highness ordered some of his servants to go and take him away, to put him on trial. Yaʿqub Beg, that fortunate one, got news of this, and as soon as those servants entered the city, he fled out the back gate. He entered the river and crossed it in safety, and he went off to Bukhara. Yaʿqub Beg, that skillful one,{159} had kept his long experience in mind, on the banks and the shallows of the rivers around Khujand, and the Arg River. He had stationed horses on the roads toward Bukhara with men to mind them, and he mounted ready and rested horses as he traveled toward his destination. Those servants who had come now committed themselves to hopelessness and despair, and without fulfilling their mission, they returned to Khoqand, the seat of the sultanate, where, when they related the whole affair in detail, the fire of the great khan's rage flared up. As his anger overflowed, he sent a letter to the amir of Bukhara, which said, "A cavalryman named Yaʿqub Beg, fitting such-and-such description, has committed crimes and fled toward sainted Bukhara. His wickedness and ill will are known throughout the lands. You must certainly order his imprisonment. This is a matter of the good of the state." When the amir learned of the letter, he ordered the imprisonment.

Now Alash Bi and Muḥammad Baba, who were Yaʿqub Beg's companions, provided him with food and supplies and several times collected information for him. They gave gold and silver coins to the jailers and gained their confidence. It was on this account that, seven or eight months later, the amir of Bukhara sent his armies to Shahrisabz to grant amnesty to the condemned men in the prison and recruit them into his battalions. Alash Bi and Muḥammad Baba had allied themselves with some of the amir of Bukhara's courtiers, whom they informed of Yaʿqub Beg's fine qualities and how he might be useful. They took their advice and summoned him before the nobles at court, who discerned his capability from his countenance and aspect and honored him with the rank of *pansad*, giving him weapons, armor, and horse. He displayed manliness and heroism in battle. All gave him praise, and his power and rank increased, and he found peace.

Now, however, Malla Khan was pacified, and the second reign of Khudayar Khan began in Khoqand. Yet Mullah ʿAlimqul, who ran the government, was among the Kyrgyz. Yaʿqub Beg seized the opportunity. He went to Samarqand, where he made pilgrimage to the holy shrines, recited the whole of the Holy Word, and gave charity to the deserving in proportion. Then he secured permission to go and pay his respects to the great khan (amir) and came to Samarqand. There he stayed for two or three days, resting his horse, and then, one evening, he fled. He came to the country of Ferghana, where he met with Mullah ʿAlimqul.

* * *

At that time, the city of Kucha had rebelled, and the news that Rashuddin Khoja had sat upon the throne of khanship{160} had become common knowledge. In Kashgar, a Qipchaq named Ṣiddiq Beg led an uprising, gathered a host, and killed the Chinese. He locked the city up and, making Kashgar his object, sent a letter to Khoqand, the seat of the sultanate, saying, "I request one of the *töräs*, that he should come and bless us, and your humble servant would append Kashgar to the kingdom of Khoqand." When that letter arrived and Mullah ʿAlimqul learned of it, he ordered Buzurg Khan Törä to Kashgar, along with some hundred men led by Hamdam Baturbashi, Tarab Khoja Yasavulbashi, ʿAbdullah Yüzbashi, and Ghazi Yüzbashi. When they came to Osh, another hundred or so men under ʿAziz Beg the Executioner and Yaʿqub Karnay joined them.

In the meantime, a command came to Mullah ʿAlimqul from Bukhara. It read, "The one called 'Yaʿqub Beg Piskenti' was impudent to Malla Khan and fled hither. For a time I imprisoned him. Then I welcomed him again as a guest and made him a courtier. Yet he lied to me too and fled. As soon as he arrives, execute him without a moment's delay! And should you delay, then may you see the amir of Bukhara's glorious armies in the country of Ferghana! Your wretched widows will fall under my horses' hooves, and it will be on your own account!"

When this threatening message came, Mullah ʿAlimqul was shocked, and that evening he had Yaʿqub Beg brought before him. He showed him the command from the amir of Bukhara and said, "It no longer seems pertinent for you to remain in Ferghana. The best course of action would be this: at the request of Ṣiddiq Beg, I have sent Buzurg Khan to Kashgar. Nevertheless, khojas are ignorant of matters of state and ways of warfare. Follow Buzurg Khan Törä swiftly and with all haste. I grant you the rank of '*qushbegi*.' " And he sent him on his way, sending a letter of good news to inform Buzurg Khan Törä of this as well.

He met Buzurg Khan Törä when he had come to the top of a mountain pass. Buzurg was pleased at Yaʿqub Beg's arrival, and he placed all of his cavalry under the Qushbegi's command. Buzurg Khan Törä held the station of *törä*, and the Qushbegi the place of his servant, and having taken their stations, they traveled until they came to the domain of Kashgar. It was the month of Gemini in the year 1281 [June 1864].

* * *

Now Ṣiddiq Beg regretted what he had done, and reluctantly he sent men out to welcome the *törä*. Then he inevitably needed to go and greet the *törä* himself. The people of Kashgar,{161} great and small, group by group, all came out to welcome the *törä*. Having paid their respects, and full of joy, they led him into the city, where they installed him in Ṣiddiq Beg's place.

At that time, one of the people of Kashgar, a man who had faith in the *törä*, in his total devotion whispered in a low voice, "The Khoja has come. It is time to attack the Qipchaqs and drive them out!" As his voice came to be heard, armed militiamen began to beat the Kyrgyz Qipchaqs with sticks and cudgels. Because the beating was so violent, the Kyrgyz Qipchaqs tried to flee. Nor could Ṣiddiq Beg remain there, but spirited himself far away, to his own home in Parash. There he gathered 6,000 or 7,000 men, prepared them for war, and then laid siege to the city. Buzurg Khan Törä and the Qushbegi likewise took their soldiers and armed them, gathering many men for battle. Then an arrow struck Ṣiddiq Beg, and he tumbled to the ground. The Qipchaq soldiers were confounded. The *törä* and the Qushbegi seized their booty, and, victorious, they were installed upon their thrones, now free of worry even in the midst of conflict.

So the Qushbegi never did anything without the approval of the *törä*. The great palace was made the *törä*'s throne room and resting place, and day and night, he was full of joy and free of worry, with the sound of music and with sport, acting according to his whims, while his heart was never concerned with any affair of state, nor judges' inquiries, nor plans for conquest or their outcomes.

Yet the Qushbegi took up residence in the madrasa of ʿUmar Ḥakim Beg of Kucha, and restlessly, tirelessly, he readied his cavalrymen. In his preparation of arms he took no rest and had neither thought for food nor concern for sleep. He directed Ṣiddiq Beg's coffers and the produce of the land to the maintenance of these cavalrymen. He was forced to take interest-free loans of silver coin from rich men, local and outsider alike. No intent could enter his thoughts, save for the readying of the cavalry.

At that time, Niyaz Eshikagha Beg of Yarkand had secretly attached the names of several of Yarkand's leaders to a letter inviting the Qushbegi to Yarkand. The letter with its half-baked plan read, "Between the Khojas, the Dungans, and the Ḥażrats, it would appear that Yarkand has fallen unclaimed in the contest. Should you come to Yarkand with four or five hundred men, it would be possible to conquer the city." The Qushbegi pondered this possibility, but when he went to Yarkand, Ḥamuddin Khoja and the Dungans had joined forces in battle. The Qushbegi could not rally but abandoned his camp,{162} and, saving his own life, found an unsaddled horse and fled to Kashgar. All of their equipment fell into the hands of Ḥamuddin Törä. This story was told in the first epic.

Ḥamuddin Törä had comprehended Niyaz Eshikagha Beg's scheming and treachery, and when Niyaz came to pay his respects, he had him tied up and hung from a poplar tree, stripped naked. When his father the Khaṭib Khoja heard news of this, however, he had Niyaz freed. This was why Niyaz had written the letter, because of his anger. When the Qushbegi fled, Niyaz Beg in his disgrace followed after him. He made many apologies, then fled in secret back to Yarkand. The Khojas remained unaware of this.

Now ʿAziz Beg the Executioner had been appointed to lead the siege of Yengi Ḥissar. A report came from him, which read, "The conquest of the city draws near. Should you come to conquer with the *törä* in the lead, his coming would support that of your honorable self." At this moment when joy was arranged like a string of pearls, Buzurg Khan Törä and the Qushbegi rode for Yengi Ḥissar. ʿAziz Beg's forces had prepared by digging tunnels and putting gunpowder in them. Suddenly the gunpowder caught on fire! Just when the walls and their towers were blown into the air, the conquering armies rushed forth as one, but as they entered the city, the dust and the dirt that the force of the gunpowder had raised came falling back down, and near a thousand Muslims, Dungans, and Chinese perished. They pulled some of them out of the dust. So the city was conquered. Most of the Chinese met their ends. A few of them came into the fold of Islam. Friends laughed in joy while enemies trembled in pain, and they seized booty and prisoners.

It was necessary to report the happy news of this victorious conquest to the sublime audition of Mullah ʿAlimqul. So they prepared gifts of nine by nine Chinese falconets; a nine of desirous virgins, beautiful and delicate; a nine of handsome, beardless Chinese boys[3]; a nine of Kazakh and Qalmaq horses; a few nines of *yambu* and Chinese silver; nine by nine particularly darling Chinese porcelains, and new-looking silks and satins, rare and precious; and fragrant tea, delicate and much sought after. They sent these with trusted servants to Khoqand, the seat of the sultanate.

When they arrived, at that happy hour, Mullah ʿAlimqul granted them an audience. He was delighted, and he gifted the servants who brought them robes of honor, money for their expenses, and weapons. He elevated Buzurg Khan Törä as khan, and in congratulations he sent him a golden crown[4] decorated with jewels; a fine horse equipped with all its tack, decorated with little golden domes emblazoned with silver; two running footmen, quick and brave;[5] two robes of excellent cloth; a nine of horses equipped with saddles;{163} and a nine of rifles, all of them inlaid with gold. He favored him with a generosity without limit and favor without end. The servants bearing gifts arrived at a blessed and happy hour, and they held an audience. Buzurg Khan Törä placed the crown of kingship upon his blessed head. He mounted the fine horse. He took the weapons into his hands. All the people great and small cast their joyful voices across that cerulean dome, and they installed him firmly upon the throne in the manner of bygone kings. Muḥammad Khan of Artush was made his *shighavul.*[6] They filled the posts of *hudaychi*, *parvanachi*, and gatekeeper [*eshikaghasi*] in turn.[7]

God, may You raise the sun of prosperity high over the heads of Muslims. Amen.

2:2 Refugees from Khoqand

The Government of His Felicitous Majesty, the Father of Victory, Buzurg Khan Törä; How He Subjugated the Khojas of Kucha; Those High Officials Who Fled from the Country of Ferghana; the Words of Muḥammad Yaʿqub Beg Qushbegi; and Incidents Involving the Qipchaqs and Kazakhs

SO THE STORY is told, that that sayyid, that son of the Messenger, Buzurg Khan Törä b. Jahangir Khan Törä b. Ṣaliḥ Khan Törä b. Burhanuddin Khan Törä Padishah b. Aḥmad Khan Törä b. Sayyid Afaq Khoja, was installed on the throne of kingship. He appointed men as appropriate to his territories in Kashgar and Yengi Ḥissar, distributed robes of honor to them according to their stations, and showed them kingly grace and favor, placing them at ease. So the ill fortune and unhappiness of those days was turned to certainty and order.

Meanwhile, Yaʿqub Beg Qushbegi set himself to readying an army. He addressed his Majesty the Khan Törä and said, "I request that I may collect something from the people of this land, so as to supply the cavalry."

His Majesty the Khan Törä found this disagreeable and said, "To do so might bring tyranny upon the common people."

The Qushbegi was upset by this, and he ceased coming to the daily audiences, and indeed he thought to take his leave. When he left for Sarman,[1] his Majesty the Törä sent men to entreat him to return.

At that time, Muqarrab Shah Beg of Mughal Terim in Kashgar, Ghazi Pansad, ʿAziz Beg the Executioner, and Mullah Ibrahim addressed him, saying, "The Qushbegi's actions are peculiar. He has fixed his wicked mind upon laying your rule to ruin and becoming a ruler in his own right. If you would issue the royal command to your humble servants, we would bring you the Qushbegi's head, and we would cast it at the threshold of your exalted court."

Buzurg Khan Törä kindly said, "Be patient. There are binding oaths and solemn vows between us." And he refused them.

However, a servant{164} learned this secret, and he informed the fortunate Qushbegi. The Qushbegi seized the opportunity and apprehended those seditious seducers. When he brought them to be tried, the great Khan Törä and the other grandees mediated between them, and they asked what their crimes were. And as the Khan Törä said, "Whatever is done to them, may it be done instead to me," he was forced to forgive them, and he sentenced them to imprisonment. They regretted their crimes, and once they had made sincere contrition, he honored them once again. Yet an enmity had emerged between them.

Muqarrab Beg got word of what was happening and returned to his homeland, where he gathered over 1,000 men, preparing them for war. Buzurg Khan Törä and the Qushbegi marched on him and raided him. Muqarrab Beg could not match them but fled to the protection of the Kucha Khojas. The Khojas made Muqarrab their own intimate [*muqarrab*], and they took this as a good omen. They renewed their intent to make war against the Qushbegi. So the Kucha Khojas came to Khan Eriq with a great but disorganized army. The story was told in the first epic. To repeat it would cause the reader fatigue.[2]

The Qushbegi had learned of their coming and fathomed their numbers, so he beseeched the Court of the Eternal and prayed to the Judge of Life, saying, "Oh, Knower of Mysteries! The secrets in your humble servant's heart are clear and evident in your sight. If the truth is on the Khojas' side, may You grant them victory. And if the truth is on Your servant's side, then may You send to my aid all the poles of the world, and the cherubim and angels—indeed all humans and jinn, and *divs* and *paris*!" So, holding hope in victory from the Lord, he readied his soldiers, and with Buzurg Khan Törä in the lead, they made for the battlefield. Yet their soldiers did not even number 2,000. At this fortunate hour, the governor of Kulab, Hamrah Khan, came to join them with 250 ready men, and their arrival was taken as a blessing and good omen. The Khojas' soldiers were numerous beyond limit.

All at once, the two armies began to fight. A few brave warriors charged their horses into the fray and joined the battle, and many men perished. The soldiers of Kucha gained the upper hand and several times forced them to flee. Eventually ʿAbdullah Pansad and Ghazi Pansad broke their lines on one side.

At that moment, a bullet struck the Qushbegi in the thigh and lodged there. He passed out. He said to ʿAbdullah Pansad, "I've been struck by a bullet. It's bad enough that I can't sit on a horse."

As soon as he opened his mouth, the *pansad* said, "Oh, you disappointment! How could you say that at a time like this? Who are we giving and taking lives for? And which king is the greater? You have come onto the battlefield.{165} Whatever else you may be, never say that you will get off your horse!" Because of these heart-hardening words he spoke, the burning within him, and his desire for fortune, the Qushbegi cursed and rallied to the fight. At that moment, victory turned its face upon the Qushbegi's side, and the armies of Kucha turned and fled. They pursued them to a place two or three *tash* away and took them back as prisoners.

Should it come to king or pauper, fate, there is no escaping it;
You cannot but take the remedy at once, there is no escaping it.
Fortune was bestowed upon the world's people—
When it comes to them suddenly, impatiently, there is no escaping it.

Naught will come of disorganized soldiers;
Two hundred brave men are better than a hundred thousand of them.

Yet there were some 10,000 (12,000) Dungans. They all lit their cannons and falconets as they gathered close together and did not let up until the evening prayer. Then messages were exchanged, and the two armies made pledges to each other and signed treaties that suited both sides. The Qushbegi's forces took the treaties back to Kashgar with them. They gained cannons and guns, weapons, gold and silver, bullets and gunpowder as booty. It was on the twenty-second day of Jumada al-Akhira, 1282 [November 12, 1865], that these events took place.

Then they summoned an experienced surgeon, who cut the Qushbegi's thigh open with a razor and removed the bullet. It has been written that the surgeon cut the Badawlat's [*Yaʿqub Beg's, the Qushbegi's—ES*] thigh open with a sword, and so removed the bullet. The Qushbegi had brought a secretary, and during the operation he was dictating a letter of appreciation, which this secretary was writing out. His color did not change, nor did he fear, nor did he make any error in his speech. One may judge the Qushbegi's bravery therefrom.

Buzurg Khan and the Qushbegi were victorious, and they arrived in honor at Kashgar, the seat of the sultanate. With kind words, sweet talk, and many gifts, they gained the loyalty of all the Dungans, and they took the weapons from their hands without a fight and granted them robes of honor, turbans, money, and presents in proportion, assuaging them with promises, relieving them of fear.

Yet the Chinese city had not been conquered. The Chinese people's food and supplies had run out, and in the agony of hunger they killed the old and weak, and the young and innocent children, as well as the dogs and cats, and ate them all up. They were now satisfied with their lives, and as though every one of them were a lantern bearer, they opened the gates and walked out;{166} and as though they were reciting the *shahada*, they were bringing some phrase to their lips. From the beginning of the encirclement to this moment, all of thirteen months had passed. That fortunate and felicitous king showed compassion to all of the Chinese and proved the blessed faith to them. All of them recited the *shahada* and became Muslims. Each one was granted favors and gifts according to their station. One of their leaders, He Dalaoye,[3] was made their leader, and those who remained were handed over to this He Dalaoye. There was a girl of sixteen, a one-of-a-kind pearl and precious jewel who had lived in seclusion. The Qushbegi drew up a contract marrying her to himself and brought her into his harem. He showed them boundless kindness and made them happy.

> (When a king is merciful, he will gain kingship;
> When he gives one, he gives one hundred thousand.)

* * *

Less than a week after Kashgar was conquered, in Tashkent, in a place called Ming Örük, as Mullah ʿAlimqul was fighting with Russia, he was struck by a bullet and drank the nectar of martyrdom. All of his soldiers dispersed in haste, and each group went in a different direction. They found no way back to Khudayar Khan. Because they had benefited from Mullah ʿAlimqul's favors and gifts, they had followed him(—they were not obedient to Khudayar Khan). Some of their leaders had no alternative, and in fear for their lives, they headed for Kashgar. These events took place seven months after Buzurg Khan Törä had arrived in Kashgar.

So the news came that Katta Khan Törä, Kichik Khan Törä, Wali Khan Törä, Israil Khan Törä, Muḥammad Khan Törä, Ḥakim Khan Törä, Mirza Aḥmad Qushbegi, Muḥammad Naẓar Beg, Qadir Quli Beg, Khuday Quli Khan, ʿUmar Qul Bahadurbashi, Mir Baba Dadkhwah, Turdi Quli Dadkhwah, Baqi Beg Dadkhwah, Beg Muḥammad Qurchi, Tash Dadkhwah, Fayżullah Dadkhwah, Tashbay Dadkhwah, the Afghan Jamadar Dadkhwah,[4] and Khayr Muḥammad Topchidar had come to Kashgar as refugees with their children and some well-known and experienced warriors, over 7,000 ready warriors.

When Buzurg Khan and the Qushbegi heard this, they sent out the two *pansads* with cavalrymen to greet them. "If they have come to submit and follow our orders," they said, sending them off, "let us know, and lead them hither. If, however, they have some other purpose, then prevent them from passing beyond the guardpost—inform us, stop them, and fight them. We will follow after and come to your aid."

Those *pansads* met them on the banks of the Qizil River. Katta Khan Törä and Mirza Aḥmad Qushbegi said, "The Russians have taken our homeland.{167} We are trying to save our lives. Whatever else, we are countrymen. You have established Islam. If you would accept us into your service, we will serve you as much as we can," they promised. "If you will not, then we will find some way to make our livings. So we have come seeking refuge." Being so informed, the *pansads* brought this news and them to Buzurg Khan Törä for an audience. Afterward, and once they had separately renewed their vows, all were gifted robes of honor according to their stations and appointed to offices.

However, upon Wali Khan Törä's arrival, when he entered the city, they went unhindered, shouting through the streets and marketplaces, "The reign, the reign, the reign of Wali Khan Törä!" And they blew the trumpets and beat the drums, sounding out the *shadiyana*.[5]

When the Qushbegi learned of these happenings, he commanded the two *pansads* to go with a platoon and bring Wali Khan Törä to his throne room. Then he chastised him, "We here, still unable to conquer the Chinese city, have suffered such trials and afflictions and have been doing such deeds. Yet you have found a handful of rabble and rebels and hope to take the rule of this country for yourself. You came before and failed to capture Kashgar, but killed Muslims, built your towers of skulls, and spilled much blood in vain, wasting the blood of thousands of men before you fled. Now when we are fighting the Chinese and suffering such hardships, you, a man of no account, plan to make this city your own." His rage flared up, and he pulled out his sword, and just as he was about to assault him, Katta Khan Törä and some other courtiers intervened and pulled Wali Khan Törä away, asking the Qushbegi to forgive his crimes. Yet he had two drummers and three attendants killed by hanging. He sent Wali Khan Törä to Yengi Ḥissar. No one saw or knew of what had happened.

* * *

At the battle of Khan Eriq, the Kucha Khojas were defeated and fled. Yarkand too entered the Qushbegi's domain. The Khojas in Yarkand worried and grew fearful, and they gave Yarkand up as well. Observe the prosperity of that felicitous and fortunate one—mark: with one bullet, he killed two quarries and with one attack, conquered two cities.

When the Qushbegi learned that Yarkand had been left unattended, he took Buzurg Khan Törä and other high officials with him and went to Yarkand, where they seized control. The Dungans there{168} would not submit, but shut their city up tightly and refused to open the gates. While all of the units under the *törä* were encamped in siege of Yarkand city, Beg Muḥammad Qurchi joined together with several Qipchaqs and two-faced people, and as the union wavered, the door opened to Satanic quarrels and factiousness. Without Buzurg Khan Törä's knowledge or agreement, they led him astray from the road ahead. Without weapons they stole him away to Kashgar and took him into the New City, where they beat the drum of rebellion. When the Qushbegi learned of this treacherous news, he sent Katta Khan Törä and Jamadar Dadkhwah to Kashgar with some cavalrymen. When they came, they gathered information and tried to send an emissary in. No trace of accord could be found. Both sides made ready for war.

Meanwhile, less than ten days later, Kichik Khan Törä was established in Yarkand, while the Qushbegi came to Kashgar. There were battles every day, and many men perished. It was the season of Capricorn, and the harshness of the winter weather and the chill of the driving snow descended from the

Court of the Almighty upon friend and enemy soldier alike. Sixty days passed in this manner. In the end that farsighted and patient one, which is to say that rock of prosperity the Qushbegi Ghazi Ataliq, sent some of his grandees as emissaries to the traitorous *qurchi* to propose a truce, which was the source of their salvation.

Once those emissaries had explained their intent, the *qurchi* replied, "At last agreement has been brought about between us. There is no chance for further assistance or leniency. The best thing to do is this: if the Qushbegi should permit us and not do us harm, then every last one of us Qipchaqs will take our children and return to our homeland."

They took this response back and related it in detail. The Qushbegi agreed and responded as such. The Qipchaqs prepared themselves, and once nearly 200 of their leaders had exited the gates, they closed those gates tightly again and allowed no more to leave. Those who left, left; those who remained, remained. The wives and children of those whom the *qurchi* had led onto the road fell into the hands of the Qushbegi. Some of them were executed. Some of them were imprisoned. The traitors were dealt with, and the land enjoyed peace.{169} But Buzurg Khan Törä could not raise his head for his shame.

Then the Qushbegi opened the door of graciousness to his attendants, and he dressed them in robes and showered them with coins. All of the troops and the cavalry gathered around the Qushbegi. As it is said, CHARITY MAKES A SLAVE OF MEN—and they fell in line behind the Qushbegi. Buzurg Khan Törä had some 600 private cavalrymen. Seeing this graciousness, they went over to the Qushbegi's side, so that the *törä* was left with only some fifty cavalrymen. Ultimately the *törä* was sent to Yengi Ḥissar with five cavalrymen, and then he was separated from them as well, alone and isolated. The Qushbegi placed some of his own cavalrymen and attendants into the *törä*'s service, to guard him as their prisoner.

When that *qurchi* left for Khoqand, His Highness the Khan learned of it. "You Qipchaqs," he said, his rage overflowing, "disturbed these cities and handed them to the Russians. And you fled to Kashgar, and disturbed Kashgar as well!" So he ordered the *qurchi* and his Qipchaqs to be executed at once, sending them with haste after those caravans that travel on the road to annihilation and never return. Henceforth the Qipchaqs did not flee Kashgar. That *qurchi* was one of the grandsons of Köroghli Bahadur, whose family had for generations ruled with grandeur in the Dasht-i Qipchaq.[6] From that day forth, all of the Qipchaqs bowed their heads and submitted to the khan's commands. This is another reason for the Qushbegi's good fortune.

If a king has fortune,
Victory will meet this king.

2:3 Yaʿqub Beg's Rise to Power

How Muḥammad Yaʿqub Beg Qushbegi Ghazi, by the Grace of That Divine Creator and Master of Khans, Sat Upon the Throne of the Sultanate; His Settlement of Conflicts and His Regulation and Drilling of the Army; the Conquests of Maralbashi and Yarkand; and the Submission of Khoja Isḥaq Törä

MUḤAMMAD YAʿQUB BEG the Ataliq had, in accordance with his desire, brought peace and order to all the disturbed and disorderly. He placed his complete faith in Unsleeping God, the Almighty, the All-Powerful,{170} the Avenger, and so he became the independent lord and master of all the towns of Kashgar and Yengi Ḥissar. He appointed governors and fiefdoms, and by his fortune he displayed abundant grace and favor to the cavalrymen. He was free of worry and at repose. By the grace of the Magnificent Lord, his star arose into an auspicious constellation. Yet day and night no other intent crossed the mirror of his heart but to prepare cavalry and infantry and to have weapons forged.

In those days, however, ill news came to his sublime audition to the effect that Isḥaq Törä of the Kucha Khojas had ridden from the east with an army of apocalyptic mien and established himself in Yarkand. So he had the cavalry and infantry accounted for, and 12,000 mounted cavalrymen and 3,000 soldiers on foot were recorded. He made Jamadar Dadkhwah general over 3,000 infantry, granting him guns, standards, and drums, and appointed eight *pansads*, emboldening them all with his world-conquering command. He also made Mirza Aḥmad Qushbegi a general with eight *pansads*, and 3,000 cavalry appointed to him. He granted them flags and standards and pleased them with his sun-bright command. He made ʿUmar Qul Bahadurbashi a general, with eight *pansads* appointed and 3,000 cavalry. He kindly provided them with flags and standards, and he distinguished them with his sublime command. Then he made ʿAbdullah Pansad a general, giving him eight *pansads* and 3,000 cavalry, gifting them flags and standards, and he dignified them with his world-conquering command. Finally His Highness commanded eight *pansads* as his own personal guard and 3,000 cavalry as his retinue, under the largest standard.

In this auspicious moment, he made Mirza Aḥmad Qushbegi a *shighavul* and commanded him to march on Maralbashi and besiege it. He commanded the rest of his generals to mobilize troops and to follow one after the other, and he manifested kingly pomp and sultanic ceremony, as together with those high officials and ever-victorious soldiers he placed his feet into the stirrups of victory. They traveled until they came to Maralbashi, where they erected the tents. In Maralbashi there were 3,000 people, Dungans and Muslims. These were Dungans who had pledged allegiance to the Kucha Khojas, entered the fold of Islam,{171} and were living peacefully by their own farming. When they heard the news, they shut the doors of the city tightly, climbed to the tops of the walls, and prepared for battle. Armies approached from either side.

A week passed. They dug tunnels, placed gunpowder inside, and lit it on fire. This blew up one side of the wall and threw it into the air. Everyone rushed forward at once and took the city. Those whose predestined moment of death arrived, went; those who were to stay, stayed. They made one Ma Dalaoye the leader of the Dungans and the New Muslims, and placing those Dungans under his command, marched them to Kashgar. Maralbashi was granted to Ḥakim Khan Törä. Hamdam Baturbashi was made his *baturbashi*, and all were joyous beyond joy. It was the second day of Rabi al-Awwal in the year 1283 [July 15, 1866].

Oh, dear friends, observe this ruler's skill at chess: with a single jump of the knight, he checked and mated the king—that is, Isḥaq Khoja was now pinned down in Yarkand. No one could travel from Aqsu and Kucha to Yarkand, nor from Yarkand to Aqsu or Kucha. They could not pass, and no one knew what had happened. After this fortunate conquest, the Qushbegi Ghazi

[*Yaʿqub Beg—ES*] gathered his victorious soldiers and marched them upon Yarkand to war with Isḥaq Khoja. He brought Buzurg Khan Törä along with the army as a prisoner. They traveled until they came to Yarkand, where they displayed pomp and ceremony, and passing unrestrained past the Old City and the New, they went to the Holy Shrine of the Seven Muḥammads. There they pitched their tents on a patch of soft, broad, flat, and high ground.

The Dungans ruled separately in one city, while Isḥaq Khoja commanded the New City. Meanwhile, the Ataliq Ghazi was also enacting his rule. However, when the Dungans and Isḥaq Khoja came to Yarkand, they had taken Kichik Khan Törä into the New City. They locked the gates up tight and would not let him leave. Now the Khan Khoja heard that the Ataliq Ghazi had taken Maralbashi, and he placed Ḥamuddin Khoja in command of 1,000 soldiers and sent him marching to Maralbashi. Ḥakim Khan Törä became aware of this, and he went to Charbagh to fight them. More than ten days passed in this manner, and sometimes he was victorious and sometimes defeated. In the end, by the grace of the All-Powerful, the Clement, Ḥakim Khan Törä won the day and seized captives and booty. He sent the happy news of this victory to that lofty court along with gifts.{172} When they arrived at that auspicious hour, they were blessed with the Ataliq Ghazi's philosopher's-stone gaze. They made him boundlessly happy and grateful, and he gifted robes of honor, money, and weapons to his attendants. To the noble *törä* he dispatched royal robes of honor with a Kazakh horse and standards, banners, and weapons, displaying his kingly grace and favor.

Yet Yarkand was not conquered, and its siege dragged on. At no point had the Dungans shown any inclination to a truce, because they numbered over 25,000 and were well armed. Ultimately the Dungans and Isḥaq Khoja joined forces. One night, 7,000 Dungans and 2,000 Muslims armed themselves with guns, falconets, grenades, and *jezail*s and left the city in secret, ready to make a nighttime attack. Niyaz Beg passed information about this to the Badawlat, and that night, he divided his forces into four parts and sent them in four directions, leaving the tents empty and unattended. As they were praying to God, the Dungan party came slowly like ants and locusts, then all at once fired their wasps into the tents from all sides.[1] Nimbly they charged their horses in, but then they saw that it was like a place left to the *div*s and *ifrit*s. Just as it was dawning upon them that there was no trace of humankind within these tents, and as they stood in shock and surprise, all of a sudden, like the wrath of God, the soldiers came from all directions, loudly shouting "God is great!" and sending a great commotion across the loftiest of the spheres. They slaughtered the Dungans so that the bodies of the Dungan dead lay piled upon the ground like unthreshed wheat in farmers' fields. And the Dungans' blood and the surface of the black soil together became red and rosy like a tulip garden in the wilderness. For a day and a night until the midmorning, the fire of slaughter burned like this. Some few escaped with their lives from the arrows of destiny, from this storm of sudden danger, into the city of salvation. Some fell prisoner and died by the sword of execution and wrath.

And on this great victory, a royal command came: "Let two thousand bold soldiers strip themselves naked, run for the wall,{173} take the city, and massacre its people."

At that moment, the general and several officers intervened. "Oh, Compassionate King," they said to him, "should the bold soldiers go and take the city, the blood of many men might be spilled. Perhaps if it were first attempted to send an emissary, when they do not agree to terms, then perhaps one could send soldiers to the wall to seize the city." The Qushbegi agreed, and he sent ʿAbdulkhaliq Ishan as an emissary to the Khojas and the Dungans.

That day was a Friday. He sent an emissary into the city, who declared, "Today being Friday, we offer you the terms of a truce. Should our conquering armies enter your sublime presence, you, your property, and your lives will not be harmed. However, should you resist, young and old alike will perish under horses' hooves, all will be met with a disastrous looting, and you will be taken prisoner." Whether they liked it or not, they could not but accept the conditions of the truce. The Khojas and the Dungans with their families were obliged to take themselves to that heavenly throne room, where they received kingly grace and favor. There they turned over their guns, weapons, and all other accoutrements necessary for rule to the officials of the state treasury.

Yaʿqub Beg and Isḥaq Khoja then became intimates, and they made many speeches, binding together the chains and the foundations of friendship and affirming them with solemn oaths. They showed their veneration and respect, and Yaʿqub Beg granted Isḥaq Beg a charger that he rode himself, along with a fine saddle and full tack. He lifted him onto the horse himself to ride it and sent him in the direction of Kucha. And to the remaining soldiers he likewise presented robes, money, horses, and beasts of burden in proportion and sent them on their way. To the Dungans too he showed limitless benevolence, making them all obedient to him. Some of them he sent to Kashgar, to serve under Ma Dalaoye. He drew the pen of forgiveness across the infractions of the rest, pardoning them.

He granted Yarkand to Muḥammad Yunus Jan Shighavul, honoring him by entrusting to him all the affairs of state, of resolving disputes, and of dismissing from office. He made Niyaz Eshikagha Beg the *shighavul* to the Shighavul.{174} He made Kifak Labar his *bahadurbashi*, and Qażi Żiyauddin Damolla his chief judge. He honored them with this command, and the land was at peace.

They stayed for a few days, and then his presence alighted in Kashgar. It was the twenty-fifth day of Rabi al-Thani, (the month of Libra), 1283, a sheep year [September 6, 1866].

2:4 Khotan Campaign

How His Highness the Badawlat Determined to Go to War in Khotan; the Result of Its Conquest; the Ruination of the Ḥajji Padishah, and His End; How the Gazelle of His Goal Emerged from the Land of Khotan, and How That Desire Took Up Residence in His Bosom

THAT SUCCESSFUL AND experienced king, Muḥammad Yaʿqub Beg the Ataliq Ghazi, that pivot of the world, basked in the conquest of Yarkand and returned to Kashgar, the seat of the sultanate, where he opened the door of justice and closed the portal of tyranny, securing his charge to tend to the people. Through grace and favor he won over the hearts of the good and the grand of that country, of the noble and common alike, and transformed their opposition and enmity into stability and peace. He had the Holy Word recited for the victorious spirits of the holy shrines, and he offered prayers and *Fatihas*. He personally lit fires in their cauldrons and poured water into them,[1] and gave generous charity to the poor and the widows, bringing smiles and laughter to their faces. Before they knew it, they began to pray for his good fortune.

Yet his desire for conquest and inclination to annexation grew greater day by day. In particular, the prospect of subjugating lovely Khotan stirred and infatuated his heart. He knew, however, that the people of Khotan were boundlessly faithful to the Ḥajji Padishah, and that men from the ages of seven to seventy by their own free will sacrificed their lives for him in battle. "Never has it been written in any chronicle, nor seen at any time," he said, "that a stranger has stretched out the hand of conquest from the garden of his intent all the way to his goal when in such a city a ruler had such confidence in his people, and the people such unity and concord with their ruler. Where there is concord, there is prosperity; and where there is prosperity, naturally concord awaits.

"They say that some person was journeying somewhere. Another person came across him and said,{175} 'Where are you coming from? And where are you going to? And what is your name?' He answered, 'My name is prosperity. In whatever country concord is to be found, that is whither I go. And from whichever country concord and unity are lifted, it is thence that I take myself to another place.'

"Now in Khotan there is concord and unity. It would be impossible for us to subjugate it by strength, with guns and great cannons, knives and maces. Yet the Ḥajji Padishah is seventy years old, and a defect has entered into his thinking, as the sun of his life sinks into the west." In his perplexed rumination, he placed the head of thought upon the knee of imagination, and with a gaze of deep concentration, he went to make a reckoning (of his forces). He looked with the eye of examination, and he said, "If I should contrive some design, and that design is in accordance with my holy destiny, then there is a chance of conquering it." So he took steps toward his deceptive design, setting his clandestine trap and spreading his seeds of falsehood. He played at sleight of hand, and he plunged into long and distant worries and the sea of thought that has no shore. And in this sea of thought, amid the foam of imagination, there shimmered the flower of his intent.

Now he raised his head high, and gazing upon his forces, he commanded them, "Prepare yourselves. We are going on pilgrimage to a holy shrine." With great battalions,[2] and four generals, forty *pansads*, sergeants [*sarjāng*], *labars*,[3] and cannoneers, they rode with 15,000 bold soldiers, and taking Buzurg Khan along, they came to Yarkand. On the eighth day of Barat in 1283, a sheep year [December 16, 1866], they stayed in Yarkand for a week. He observed his soldiers, and he gave them robes, money, horses, and weapons, and all fell into place.

He wrote a letter to the Ḥajji Padishah in the name of Buzurg Khan Törä. "It has been some time since I came to the land of Kashgar," it said, "and I have restrained myself as much as I can endure from making pilgrimage to the great shrines in your honored country. Now my hope is this: I request that I might make pilgrimage to the tomb of my ancestor, Imam Jaʿfar al-Ṣadiq. Should my 'uncle' the Ḥajji Padishah grant me passage and give me license, I would wish to make this pilgrimage and meet with my 'uncle' the Ḥajji Padishah. I reveal this desire of mine to your honored audition, and so have written this hopeful letter in hopeful appeal." Buzurg Khan Törä sealed this deceptive letter with his noble seal. Yaʿqub Beg sent him on his way with those reliable servants while he followed behind, and where the domain of Yarkand ends{176} and that of Khotan begins, he pitched his tents.

When the Ḥajji Padishah heard about this, he sent his son, Niʿmatullah Khan, to greet them with bedding, shelter, and gifts. Yaʿqub Beg got news of his approach, and he sent men ahead to retrieve him with great honor, and they held a fine feast. Then he honored him with gifts of a golden turban cloth and a robe fringed with gold, all gold; weapons inlaid with gold; and a charger horse with a fine saddle and full tack, all of it emblazoned with gold and silver. And he granted robes and money to his soldiers too, saying, "Praise be to God, that I have come to this place! I have achieved my desire to see my prince, whose beauty illuminates the world.

"Now my desire is this, that I might be granted an audience with my 'grandfather,' the Ḥajji Padishah. Would that this hopeless nothing might be granted entrance into the tent of his presence, I would sweep the dust beneath his feet with my beard; and would that he might consider this foolish slave among the humblest order of his servants, and so bless me with his sublime regard; and should it be his kind and noble command, it would raise my debased and ill-esteemed head, abject in the filthy earth, to the heights of the Two Wild Sheep.[4] No other desire at all occurs to your humble servant's guileless heart. Should my 'grandfather,' the Ḥajji Padishah, begrudge his own blessed arrival, such that I may not go in person to grovel at his honored throne, nor declare my servitude with heart and soul, nor clip one strand of light from the sun of his fortune and see his world-illuminating beauty, then I shall be utterly confounded." In this manner, by the use of some comely and winning words and arousing requests, he won over the prince's heart and stirred the Ḥajji Padishah's to passion.

Now he sent General ʿAbdullah to accompany the prince (Niʿmatullah Khan), and he placed some incantations into his ears like royal pearls, one after another. And he had a piece of tile shaped like a little booklet carved into the image of the Holy Word, and had it adorned with several layers of gold-fringed silks and satins, and golden coins and wrappings. He gave it with great honor to the general, and told him, "Go into the presence of my 'grandfather' the Ḥajji Padishah on my behalf, and make my sincere devotion known to his great audition. If he should not believe, then take this Word of the Lord and present it to him on my behalf, and back it up with solemn oaths and pledges, making him guarantees.{177} Then you will surely get to enter my 'grandfather' the Ḥajji Padishah's presence, and the prince will pass the rest of this humble slave's sincere requests along." And he sent them on their way.

They entered the presence of the Ḥajji Padishah and held an audience with him. Once the formalities had concluded, the general made all that the Ataliq Ghazi had ordered, and perhaps more, known to the Ḥajji Padishah's audition. Placing the hand of manners upon the breast of humility and joining his hands together, he bowed his head to the Ḥajji Padishah's commands in the circle of his entourage and stood at the threshold. However, just as milk mixed with water cannot be separated again, it could not be distinguished which of his words were false and which true. So the Ḥajji Padishah was confused, and he asked his son to explain the matter. But he had never witnessed the deceitful heavens, nor learned from the experience of time, nor ever awakened from the stupor of negligence. For every time the general encouraged the Ḥajji Padishah to go and greet Yaʿqub Beg, this callow prince tempted him a thousand times with all sorts of praise for him. The Ḥajji Padishah's most illuminated estimation became resolute in its course.

When the Lord of the Worlds determines to open the door of fortune to His servants, then, for whatever reason or cause, fortune and honor will be granted them. The Qushbegi's scheme indeed happened to be in accordance with the divine plan. The traces of his incantations bore results: the door of prosperity slammed shut; the smaller passages of tyranny opened; and the eye of reason closed. The prince and the general, as though they were two lieutenants of fate, drove the poor Ḥajji Padishah toward a dark pit and place of ruin, though on his own two feet he came face to face with the hungry lion and the bloodthirsty tiger.

Yet the Ḥajji Padishah said, "I have had an ill-omened dream . . . What events might be revealing themselves from behind the veil of the unseen?" As a precaution, he summoned a thousand of his attendants, cavalrymen, and guards and went with them toward his destination.

Now his gaze fell upon the encampment. The Qushbegi too saw him from a distance and rushed out to greet him, and rubbed his face and eyes upon the Ḥajji Padishah's ring. He took the horse's reins in his hands, now placing them about his own neck, and with four *pansads* walking on all four sides, they brought him to the entrance to the throne room. There they lifted him from his horse, and holding him by his armpits, they brought him into the throne room and sat him down.

The Qushbegi said, "They say, WHOSOEVER EMBRACES A PILGRIM OR A GHAZI EMBRACES A THOUSAND PROPHETS. The meaning of this holy hadith is, 'Might one be blessed with an embrace?' " And he stood up, waiting.

{178} The Ḥajji Padishah stood up too and embraced him. And Yaʿqub Beg picked him up as he embraced him, and within the throne room there was another tent, and he carried him into it. There some men stood ready. They seized him. They knocked him over. They tied him up and stripped his clothes off. No one knew or saw what had taken place. ALAS, ALAS, witness humankind's deceit!

When a human opens their mouth to deceive,
They are helpless. Satan is a filthy devil!

Meanwhile, the Ḥajji Padishah's loyal cavalry had not dismounted from their horses but stood guard on his orders. Then a letter came in the Ḥajji Padishah's name that read, "This evening I will stay and converse with my 'little brother' the Qushbegi and will stay the night with him, and tomorrow he will accompany me into the city. Do not worry, but return to the city. All of you should go about your own business. Let Niʿmatullah Khan come and meet us in the morning." And on the letter were written the names of some twenty or thirty capable and responsible warriors of good repute. "Bring these with you tomorrow." The Ḥajji Padishah's seal was pressed upon it.

When the soldiers saw this letter, they said, "Surely all sorrow is now hidden in the mine of nonexistence, while joyous Jupiter has shown its face, and Venus and Jupiter are conjoined in one house!" And without even dismounting their horses, they turned and entered the city.

The next morning, the Ataliq Ghazi set out for the city. When he had come to a place two (one) *paotai* away, the prince Niʿmatullah Khan, accompanied by the twenty or thirty capable officers, met with His Everlasting Majesty.

They were well met, and Yaʿqub Beg said, "My 'grandfather' the Ḥajji Padishah will come along after me. Let us go together." And he sent them along.

They separated one man from another and brought them into the tent, where they (imprisoned or) eliminated them. Then (the Pansad) ʿAziz Beg the Executioner was deputized with some cavalrymen to finish off the Ḥajji Padishah's treasury. When they arrived, they sent the Ḥajji Padishah's children away and seized the treasury in his palace.

Then His Highness the Badawlat established his tents before the city and made his arrival with sultanic pomp. He ordered his generals, sergeants, *labars*, and personal guard to follow him in a column into the city, whence they retrieved the Ḥajji Padishah's attendants, some of whom they executed and others imprisoned.

The Ḥajji Padishah's wives and children, his soldiers and subjects,{179} said to each other, "Has our Ḥajji Padishah come? Where has he gone? And why doesn't he enter the city? These Qipchaq Andijanis have seized the city (and the palace)! What could have happened?" They could not fathom the reason for it but stood baffled and confused, looking about astonished, dumbfounded. So matters stood for two days and nights.

Yet, as the people of those villages each began to realize what had happened, 10,000 or 15,000 men came from the city's surrounding villages bearing weapons and cudgels. "Where is our Ḥajji Padishah?" they demanded, "Where is our Ḥajji Padishah?" as they chased those cavalry and soldiers they encountered in the bazaar through the streets, striking them down. They reproached and abused them with coarse words and foul phrases that come not readily to the pen. No matter what reprimand or admonishment they received, they would not listen but continued their reproaches, never appeased. It was impossible to withstand these ruffians' abuse, and the Andijanis were left without options. Some of them, wielding their cudgels, marched to the throne room.

Now came a royal command: "Fight them and kill them." And for every one that they killed, ten more came; and for every ten, thirty.

"That way the noise is!"[5] the ruffians said, as they marched onward, stepping over the bodies of their own, until they came to the throne room. The Ataliq Ghazi could not stand idle but mounted his horse and gave them the order for a massacre. All of the soldiers set themselves to the massacre, slaughtering until no living thing, not even a donkey, dog, or cat, was left alive.

The next day, more than 10,000 armed men from Qaraqash came, forming a militia, wielding their cudgels, with their rough provisions carried in sacks with their openings tied closed, hanging from their necks. These too they massacred, sending them to join those who had come before them. Next men from Chira mobilized,[6] and they too came with their cudgels and provisions. When they saw and realized what had happened, they threw themselves like moths into the still-burning flames. They took their places in the chamber of destruction. Khotan has six towns, and one after another, men came unawares from each, 5,000 or 10,000 of them. And they sent those men on their way without joining with men from any other place, or having one follow another.

When the Khotanese say, "That way the noise is!" and set their minds to something, they do not waver at all. Those who happen to stand up do not stop until the task is done. Those who did not arise{180} but stayed where they were, were safe. Those who chose to rise up and march to the city cried out, "Ḥajji Padishah, oh, my Padishah!" They cast themselves into their own destruction, saying, "Without our Padishah, dying is a thousand times better than living!" They would not waver from their course to save their lives, nor did they think it right to flee. Witness their actions, born out of sheer ignorance.

But the cavalry and soldiers grew weary from killing men, and their hands calloused. They reported this to the Ataliq Ghazi. So his conquering armies brought all of those butchers who had come to market, and those outsider butchers who were staying in Khotan, and ordered them to kill men. These stood at the edge of a trench, killing men and throwing them into the ditch and into deep pits. Both the ditch and the pits were filled to the brim.

At the gates he posted his generals, *pansads*, *labar*s, and soldiers, and those whom they apprehended were sentenced to death and handed over to the soldiers. Each separated one of them from the others and took them to the place where they would be killed. And as they went, they said, "If you have anything, give it to me, and I will not kill you, but set you free." Some of them refused, preferring death, and died. Others gave them a hundred *tangga*, or as little as one *tangga*, and freed themselves from death. They saved their own lives and returned to their homes. Some said, "I have no money on me right now." And even if they offered to get it for them or have it brought to them, they would still need to do something to be set free. The soldiers went to pillage in places three or five *tash* away, or even farther.

So five days and nights passed in this way.[7] The trade in death was brisk. The common people witnessed the destruction. At last, the Ataliq Ghazi issued an order putting an end to the massacre.

It is related in the history books that, "When ten thousand men perish, one of the dead will raise his hand up. And if twenty thousand men perish, two of the dead with raise their hands up. And if a hundred thousand men perish, then one of the dead will stand up straight." In Khotan, five [four] of the dead raised their hands. From this it may be known that 50,000 [40,000][8] men died there.

{181} Had that happy and fortunate one, Yaʿqub Beg[9] the Ataliq Ghazi, that pivot of the world, not contrived in such a way, then the conquest of Khotan would not have been achieved. The faith that the people had in the Ḥajji Padishah was beyond all bounds.

* * *

Once the massacre was over, they made an accounting of the contents of the Ḥajji Padishah's treasuries and submitted it to the court. The treasure and weapons were all present and accounted for. Apart from silver, gold, and copper coins, there were gold bars gathered into sixteen chests. Evidently the Ḥajji Padishah had not given his soldiers any fine thing, for fear it would go to waste, nor even did he spend any of the state's property on his own wives. He was a king for thirty months, and during that time he directed even the produce of his ancestral lands to the kitchens. Even his clothing went to their expenses. They tallied up everything that had been collected from the land in accordance with the Shariah, or that had fallen into their hands as booty from the Chinese and the begs, and placed in into the treasury, where it was not lost but treasured. When his Highness the Badawlat saw this, he smiled and cheered, and he said, "I called him 'my father'—and truly, he is my father indeed!"

The Ḥajji Padishah had adopted the customs of one of the sultans of bygone days, Caliph ʿUmar b. ʿAbdulʿaziz [r. 682–ca. 720] of the Umayyad house. He had 400 big one-humped camels specially outfitted with saddles and *numnah*s of broadcloth, bridles and girdles of raw silk with tassels tied upon them, and decorated with rows of camel bells—such that no camels had ever before been so outfitted in these parts, and the eyes of all who saw them were struck blind! All of these things came into the Ataliq Ghazi's possession. All of the Ḥajji Padishah's treasures, his weapons and instruments, were packed onto those camels and taken away to Kashgar, the seat of the sultanate.

If a king has fortune,
Victory will meet this king.

* * *

He granted gifts to his high commanders, *pansads*, and generals, and to his fierce cavalrymen and soldiers, AS IS RIGHT AND PROPER, delighting them and satisfying their every need. To the shrines of the martyred imams in Khotan he sent sheep, cows, rice, money, and robes, and he appointed trusted servants.{182} He donated generous offerings to them, which were distributed to the worthy poor, and the Holy Word was read aloud. He gave the merit to the victorious spirits of the holy shrines, but to the poor and the widows, and to the preachers, he gifted clothing and money, and received their thanks.

When this was over, he appointed Niyaz Eshikagha Beg of Yarkand as the independent governor and fiefholder of Khotan. He was granted plenipotentiary power in all matters of state and placed in charge of resolving disputes, management of affairs, and official appointments. To this he appended the six towns of Khotan, which spanned an area forty days' travel in size, and placed them under his royal command.

There were reasons for his bestowal of a province upon Niyaz Eshikagha Beg. The first was that His Highness the Ghazi had come to Yarkand at Niyaz Beg's invitation. There he had fought with Ḥamuddin Törä and, when he found himself unable to match him in battle and fled, Niyaz Beg followed behind. For a distance of two *tash*, they had ridden rein to rein and stirrup to stirrup, consoling each other and making apologies as they conversed at length, and something in the Qushbegi's scheming mind stirred, and he resolved to take Niyaz Beg back to Kashgar with him. Niyaz Beg realized this, so he turned his horse around as though to go and water it, but then he put the whip to it, fleeing back to Yarkand with haste and spiriting himself away. The Qushbegi praised him and thought, "What a sharp-witted man! To put our mind at ease, he accompanied us this far. Yet he was concerned for his children in Yarkand and returned. This is a capable man."

Another was this: in Yarkand, when Isḥaq Khoja and the Dungans had sent 9,000 soldiers out from the city to stage a nighttime attack, Niyaz Beg had secretly sent a man to inform the *qushbegi*, "Tonight many soldiers are marching out. Take this into consideration. I can do no more." The Qushbegi, that clever bird, being so informed, took precautions and thus achieved his goal. These events were related in the first epic.[10]

Another was this: Niyaz Beg was the Ataliq Ghazi's colleague in contrivance and schoolmate in the art of deception. Each was the other's companion and pillion rider, and their stars arose into the constellation of companionship, as their lucky stars took equal places in a single house. For this reason, the Ataliq Ghazi granted him such a province as Khotan, with six towns and a domain forty days' travel across. Not once did he utter, "What profit could come from Khotan?" Indeed it never crossed his mind.{183} Whatever he did, he was his own man. All of this notwithstanding, Niyaz Beg's intentions with regard to the Ataliq Ghazi were never correct. Ultimately that was the reason that deceiving Niyaz Beg came to his inescapable end. These events, God willing, will be related later on.[11]

So he gave Khotan to Niyaz Beg without any oversight. By royal mandate, Khalman Pansad was made his general and Ḥajji Tarab his military judge. Soon, however, he had the general arrested. He had the military judge arrested as well, and caused them to suffer terrible punishment and torment.

It was the twentieth day of Shawwal, in the year 1283 [February 25, 1867], when Yaʿqub Beg returned to the capital with his high officials.[12] When they had traveled four stages, he had ʿAziz Beg the Executioner seized and killed. The reason was that at Khotan he had been sent before anyone else into the Ḥajji Padishah's treasury and record room, and he treacherously took the opportunity to steal 200 *yambu* in accord with the "right of soldiers." He was held responsible for his crimes. Moreover, earlier on, he had soured on Yaʿqub Beg and flirted instead with Buzurg Khan Törä. These events have been written about. He was called "the Executioner" because, when Wali Khan Törä had earlier come to Kashgar (and made his tower of skulls), he had served him as executioner. He was originally from Yengi Ḥissar. Now he was unhappy with the salt given him, so he had committed treason. He received his punishment.

Whoever sows their seeds in this earthly field, whether of good or ill, will surely never see their fruits in this transitory world, not taste their sweetness. They will not follow him into the world to come. Oh, Lord—with Your beneficence, lead all of your servants upon the right road and save them from the crooked and uneven paths, but preserve the mean—which is equity and truth—in the shadow of Your justice. Amen.

2:5 Ḥabibullah's Virtue and His Reign

A Brief Account of the Ḥajji Padishah, Mullah Ḥabibullah Padishah, and His Reign

THE ḤAJJI PADISHAH was originally a mufti. For generations, his ancestors had been officials at the Shariah court in Khotan and made great efforts to promote the Shariah, enacting the orders of that court. He himself had led the life of a pious and abstemious mufti, never stepping foot in any unclean place, never skipping his nightly prayers whether at home or abroad, never letting his eye drift to sleep after midnight. He tended a parcel of land inherited from his ancestors,{184} where he worked his hoe, drove his cart, and gathered his harvest. "From the work of my hands and the sweat of my brow," he thought, "I will eat a righteous meal." He sustained himself on the fruits of his labors and satisfied his own needs thereby. Whenever he went to the home of an official beg or *akhund*, or to the home of any Muslim, he would never drink the tea or eat the bread. One of his men would bring tea in a teakettle, and he would drink his own tea, recite prayers and the *Fatiha*, and leave.

One time, he went to Aqsu for some affair, and there he went to the begs' and *akhunds*' houses to read the *Fatiha*. He brought tea in a teakettle, drank of his own tea, recited the prayers and *Fatiha*, and left. In those days in Aqsu, Hadi Khalifa of Aqsu was the leader of the Sufis as regent for Ishan Jan Ḥażrat

Khalifa. The mufti had gone to recite the *Fatiha*, but he did not drink Hadi Khalifa's tea, drinking his own instead.

Someone asked Mullah Ḥabibullah, "Hadi Khalifa is also a pious and abstemious man. Why did you not drink his tea?"

"Yes indeed, he is pious and abstemious," he answered. "Yet he does not sweat from his brow or eat by the labor of his own hand. Whatever one brings him as 'offerings,' 'tithes,' or 'alms' is consumed in his kitchens. Verily, one who has fixed his eyes upon the offerings of others is not devoid of covetousness. Moreover, he possesses the minimum wealth that necessitates that he should give alms. According to the Shariah, it is not permissible for one who possesses this minimum to partake of tithes or alms. For this reason I drank not his tea but my own." When he said this, everyone praised him. But he took without hesitation rice, tea, and bread from the homes of those farmers who, in accordance with the Shariah, paid their alms and tithes with money gained from hard labor and the sweat of their brows.

When he stepped down from office, he set off on a journey to the Holy Land, and he stayed in the Two Holy Cities for seven years. Around great Mecca and illustrious Medina he gained great fortune, and, having attained a certain amount, he returned to his homeland. That was at the time when the Khojas of Kucha established Islam and, having fought to a draw in the battle at Jam with the emperor's people, fled with their lives. Timur Ghazinachi Beg, the son of the late governor of Khotan, Alish Ḥakim Beg, was the governor of Bay. He fled and spent three or four days hiding near Aqsu. When he heard what had happened, he went to Khotan, where he inquired with the agent and so learned the heart of the matter.

{185} The people of Khotan too found out, and so were overtaken with the inclination to establish Islam and eliminate the Chinese. The people of that land asked each other, "Whom shall we make our leader?" In the end, after some deliberation, they decided upon Mullah Ḥabibullah Ḥajji Mufti. All of them together sat him upon the white felt and unanimously made him their king in accordance with the customs of bygone sultans. They laid hands on the infidels, established Islam, and whether they were Chinese or Dungans, massacred them all just the same. They killed them and did not even spare the little children, and he was then established upon the throne and issued his commands.

While the Ḥajji Padishah was working hard on behalf of the common people's contentment, Naẓiruddin, the Shaykh Khoja of Kucha, sent the man called Ḥajji Ghazinachi marching from Yarkand at the head of 3,000 Muslim and Dungan soldiers to attack him. Because he had sent a letter written in ill-mannered and inappropriate language, the Ḥajji Padishah had taken offense. He sent his son, ʿAbdurraḥman Khan Ṣudur, out at the head of some soldiers. There was a battle, and many were killed, and the army of Kucha fled in defeat. Many men perished. The Ṣudur Khan was struck by a bullet and passed away.[1]

"Nevertheless," the Ḥajji Padishah said, "they are the Khojas of Kucha, who are the reason for holy Islam and our magnificent fortune. If they had not established Islam, then we would have had no cause of our own. Yet they killed the Emperor of China's good men, before colluding with his bad men—that is, uniting with the Dungans—and ruling their land. It is on this account that I would not swear allegiance or submit to them." He wrote as much in a message, and their hearts softened. So he sent Aḥmad Mirab Beg at the head of fifty or so men with gifts as emissaries to the court of the Khan Khoja, and indeed to bow their heads in submission to his command. But the Khan Khoja would not receive them. These events were related in the first epic.

* * *

Before these events took place, he had already sent his son, ʿAbdurraḥman Khan, to the capital at Khoqand with gifts to request their aid, indeed even to pledge allegiance to them. He was granted an audience, and afterward he was detained there for several days of feasting and hospitality. ʿAbdurraḥman Khan was given the title of *ṣudur* and granted horses, weapons, and robes of honor. His men too were favored with the bestowal of robes, clothing, and money in proportion,{186} and to the Ḥajji Padishah were gifted robes, clothing, turbans, and weapons as appropriate to his station. Nar Muḥammad Parvanachi was made commander in chief with 200 cavalry, and Mirza Baba Beg Ḥissari chief secretary with fifty men, all to accompany the Ṣudur Khan.

When this party came to Kashgar, the Qushbegi had just then been in combat with Ḥamuddin Törä at Yarkand for many days. They encountered each other in Yarkand. The Qushbegi ended up taking Nar Muḥammad Parvanachi with his cavalrymen, and likewise those of Mirza Baba Beg. He sent Mirza Baba Beg and two others to accompany the Ṣudur Khan, gifted him some weapons, and sent them off to Khotan. The Ḥajji Padishah assigned Mirza Baba Beg to an appropriate station and a pension for his daily expenses, showing him grace and favor. He found him a wife from a fine place and married her to him.

He named the old Chinese city "the Citadel." He had a great palace built there, and commanded also the construction of a Friday mosque and lodge. They instructed all the people of Khotan in the Shariah—in city and country, young and old, men and women alike. One man was made *khalifa* to every ten men, to instruct everyone on such vital matters as the pillars of Islam, the proofs of the unity of the divine, the ninety-nine obligations, prayer, fasting, alms, tithes, the Ḥajj, and knowledge of menstruation and of childbirth. They would remind them and try to instruct them, and to show them restraint and circumspection. Everyone, man or woman, from the ages of seven to seventy, took lessons and did repetitions like a schoolchild.

Every Friday, he would have himself carried to the great mosque in a carriage.[2] And while he prayed, behind him and to his sides, six to twelve men stood erect with big swords bared, as if ready to slice a man up. But they would not bow or prostrate themselves. They must have read with nods and signs. And such was their circumspection that, should an enemy have approached during the prayers, they would not have permitted any harm to come to the Ḥajji Padishah. The ordained time for such harm to befall this circumspect king would come later when he walked, doomed, into the throne room of Yaʿqub Beg Ghazi, and met with some misfortune. These events were related earlier.

He proclaimed that Khotan would be called "the City." Twice he would read the Friday prayers. Out of caution, he would not have the midday prayer read, nor other traditional prayers. He had silver coins struck at Khotan as *mis̱qals* according to the Shariah. On one side they struck, THERE IS NO GOD BUT GOD, AND MUḤAMMAD IS THE PROPHET OF GOD, and on the other side, STRUCK IN LOVELY KHOTAN.[3] And the writing on his seal read, HE (THE PROPHET) IS THE BELOVED OF GOD, TO WHOM WE TURN FOR INTERCESSION.

Whenever a thief or gambler was discovered, they would be killed without a second thought or hesitation.{187} It is written that a man once stole a hoe from a farmer's field in the countryside. He confessed, and they buried a great cannon in the ground, pointed its mouth high into the air, and put powder into it. They bound that thief, set him upon the cannon's mouth, and set it alight. This thief was propelled upward by the powder, which split his four quarters into four parts, blowing them up into the air until they were out of sight, then came back down again. They did this that very day, after the Friday prayer. All the people around saw it happen, and their hearts leaped and shuddered. Another man had stolen six ears of unripe corn from the cornfields in the countryside. He was brought in and interrogated, and he confessed, whereupon he was hanged. For this slight infraction, the man's blood was spilled as an example to others. He took his power of punishment to an extreme. (He felt no hesitation at all when ordering someone killed.) The Ḥajji Padishah was old, with no teeth left in his mouth. Yet he only had to gum his lips, and no matter what sort of man it was who stood before him, the chaff of that man's existence would be scattered to the winds.

"All those who farm in the countryside districts," he declared, "are to cast aside their hoes and their bales, and all their implements, in the fields where they farm. They are to go to their homes and spend the night there, and the next morning, go again about their affairs. And they shall leave their gates, doors, and shops open as they sleep." Now the power of punishment was taken beyond its extreme. But were we to relate this in detail, it would fatigue our readers and our listeners.

* * *

Two months before misfortune befell the people of Khotan, the Ḥajji Padishah had a nightmare. He arose anxiously from his bed. After the morning audience, he summoned trusted scholars and learned interpreters of dreams, to whom he narrated his nightmare. "In my dream," he said, "the people of Khotan had bodies but no heads. What could the meaning of this dream be?" All were shocked. And as they stood there in thought, unable to say anything, the Ḥajji Padishah gave his own interpretation. "The meaning of this dream is this: have all of the trees in the lands around Khotan, both fruit-bearing and not, cut down to the height of a man and carved with heads." All of the scholars and wise men cheered him. On this account, all the trees in the vicinity of Khotan, fruit-bearing and otherwise, were cut down to the height of a man and carved with heads. This sort of dream interpretation was out of accord with the divine plan. In the end, by His ordination, such misfortunes as have been related fell upon the head of the Ḥajji Padishah and upon those of the common people.

{188} His forefathers had committed themselves to mendicancy and became known as dervishes and pious men, all of them religious leaders. Yet they were ignorant of matters of government and knowledge of warfare. Moreover, dervishhood and military leadership proved to be incommensurable. Would that he had once been in the service of some lofty king, and in a warrior profession, so that he might have gained a steady foundation and experience therein; surely then he would have discerned some means to ward these disasters off.

Thus it is related in the history books how people would find men whose families had been great leaders, established steady foundations, and ruled for generations, or their relations, and sit such men upon thrones, and swear allegiance to them. And in their blessed tracks the common people would find peace and the country, unity; and it would prolong the life of the state and cause its government to run well. Even if their descendants from time to time should happen to fall upon the road of poverty, when they ascended to government, they would not draw its affairs down into a state of excess and wanton but rather, in moderation, would establish the plan of government and the people's ease in their proper center. They would establish their own foundations, and all in accordance with the wisdom of the saying, THERE IS A SAYING FOR EVERY SITUATION AND A MAN FOR EVERY STATION. It is a well-known proverb that "Hunters have to hunt!" The one about the hunters must surely be a saying of the shaykhs. And when little children play, they ask, "What does your daddy do?" And when they reply, "My daddy is a blacksmith!" they say, "Go—be a blacksmith." And if they reply, "My daddy is a farmer," they say, "Then farm." Those are no idle words.

> You have to do what your father does;
> That is how the Lord bestows your daily bread.

Thus it is known that every man should count himself as worthy of taking up his father's profession, demonstrate his gratitude for the fine things that the Lord has granted, always ask to be sheltered from those matters that are beyond his station, and demonstrate careful circumspection and absolute prudence. And should he overstep the bounds of his station and forget his place, then what befell the Ḥajji Padishah shall befall that man.

> {189} Should the crow wish to learn the partridge's way,
> He cannot learn it, but will forget his own way.

The Ḥajji Padishah failed to value his ancestors' ways, as well as his own dervishhood, which were to him a boundless fortune and unending peace. He was no credit to his bygone life, and indeed he felt regret for losing it, but he could not recover it. He became enamored instead with his later kingship, which was wanting in piety, and came to believe himself deserving of his own elevation. He deceived himself into thinking that he had now acquired "that boundless fortune." And yet his kingship over men and women, old and young, family and friend, and indeed over the moneys and the lives of all the people of Khotan, its six towns and Qaraqash, became a great disaster, and his rule like unto a severe punishment, such that the lives and property of everyone met with the pit of elimination and were destroyed.

There is no permanence in swift fortune,
And no faith in horses and the striking of swords.

2:6 The Conquest of Aqsu and Kucha

How His Highness the Ataliq Ghazi Mobilized Mounted Men in Pursuit of the Conquest of Aqsu and Kucha; and in One Attack Several Cities Were Conquered; How He Plucked a Bloom from the Garden of His Intent, Seized His Goals, and Returned to the Light of His Throne; and How Factiousness Reared Its Head

WHEN HIS HIGHNESS the Ataliq Ghazi conquered Khotan, Yarkand, Maralbashi, and Yengi Ḥissar, along with their domains, he granted Khotan to Niyaz Eshikagha Beg; Yarkand to Muḥammad Yunus Jan Shighavul; Kashgar to Alash Bi; Yengi Ḥissar to Kamil Khan Törä; and Maralbashi to Ḥakim Khan Törä. He made each of them an independent governor and fiefholder. Now in repose they busied themselves with training cavalry and soldiers and preparing weapons of war.

At that happy hour, several men of Ushturfan rebelled against the rule of the Khojas of Kucha and sought allegiance instead to the Ataliq Ghazi. Now they rode for Aqsu, inciting others along the way. A letter came from ʿAbdurraḥman Dadkhwah and Magistrate ʿAbdullah of Aqsu, inviting Yaʿqub Beg. Tokhta Eshikagha Beg of Kucha now offered to seize that city for him. Meanwhile, the concord that held among the Khojas of Kucha now met its end in discord. As this fortunate news met the Ataliq Ghazi's royal audition, the desire to conquer Aqsu and Kucha excited the surface of his heart anew.

His Highness the Badawlat had 3,000 of his own brave and battle-hungry personal guards readied;{190} 3,000 bold cavalry and infantry under Jamadar Dadkhwah, all outfitted with drums, banners, and trumpets and guns, muskets, and cannons; 3,000 fully equipped cavalry under General ʿUmar Qul; 3,000 brave cavalry assigned to General ʿAbdullah; and 3,000 heroic cavalry under the command of Mirza Aḥmad Qushbegi. Now he summoned their commanders at the appointed hour. "The fortress at Maralbashi has stood idle since its siege was ended," he suggested. "What if we sent you there with all of your armies to repair it?" They all agreed that it was a fine idea, and they stood eagerly ready and waiting.

It was in the year 1284—which was the year of the monkey—on the fourth day of Muḥarram, in the month of Gemini [May 8, 1867], that they rode in pomp and ceremony to Maralbashi, where they set up the tent court and remained for four days, during which no command was forthcoming. On the fifth day, the generals said, "What do you say we go to Aqsu and Kucha and make pilgrimage to the (holy) shrines of the shaykhs?" And all replied together, "We are at your command! Let us demonstrate our obedience with heart and soul." Then General Mirza Aḥmad Qushbegi was sent ahead with his soldiers to reconnoiter, and Hamdam Baturbashi and Ghazi Pansad were placed at the vanguard. Eight *pansad*s were appointed to each general, to whom were granted banners and standards. Each general was favored with two camels or horses outfitted in gold and six in silver. Each *pansad* was gifted two camels or horses outfitted in silver. And those camels and horses in their gold and silver fittings were made to charge ferociously ahead of the generals and *pansads*. The magnificence of each general was like unto that of a lofty king, and the pomp of each *pansad* like that of a governor of some land. And all the Quran reciters and imams who had been appointed to those *pansad*s walked before them, wielding the Holy Word.

This great and furious host rode from Maralbashi in ferocity until they came to Chilan. There they seized a Dolan and asked him, "Do the Khojas have soldiers on this road?"[1] And he responded, "In Yaydi they have two hundred soldiers. And in Say Eriq they have fifty." Now that they knew the heart of the matter, they spent the night at the foot of Yaydi. In the morning,{191} as the soldiers passed from the place where they had laid over toward Aqsu, the Kucha soldiers were caught unawares, taken prisoner, and marched off to Maralbashi. Their leader was called Tokhta Khalifa. He was executed.

Some of those soldiers, however, had gone to water the horses. They found out what had happened and fled back to Aqsu to inform Jamaluddin Khoja. "They seized the soldiers at Say Eriq," they said, "and took them prisoner."

When Yaʿqub Beg's army came to the riverbank, at a distance of two *tash* from the city, Jamaluddin Khoja sent his son Yaḥya Khoja there, leading 3,000 soldiers. "Pull the boats in!" he ordered them. "Get ready, and when the battle begins, do not let them cross over to this side of the river." However, the soldiers of the Ataliq Ghazi had never planned on using the boats, but instead crossed the river wherever it was suitable. The boats were never used. In a single assault, they pushed the Kucha soldiers back and set them to flight. The soldiers scattered and ran in every direction to save themselves.

Hamdam Baturbashi and Ghazi Pansad pursued them until they entered the city of Aqsu and climbed to the top of its palace. Then rang out cries of "The reign, the reign, the reign of Muḥammad Yaʿqub Beg Ataliq!" and the drums beat out the *shadiyana*.

When Jamaluddin Khoja witnessed what was happening, he and his wife jumped off of the cliff behind the palace. Jamaluddin Khoja went and concealed himself in the Shrine of Fakhruddin.[2] His wife hurt her leg and fled to someone's house. Meanwhile, troop after troop, with the conquering armies blowing their trumpets and beating their drums, and the magnificence of those armies and the marching of those brave soldiers, the Ataliq Ghazi with his high officials arrived in the sultanic seat of Aqsu in sultanic glory and the splendor of victory. In the midst of all that, Jamaluddin and his cavalry were seized and brought to him. After some rebuke, his transgressions were struck out with the pen of forgiveness. He was given robes of honor in accord with his station and sent to Yarkand, where he was quartered in a chamber together with the Ḥajji Padishah. The city of Aqsu and all its surrounding pastures were brought to heel and pacified.

Now Khoja Naẓar Beg Ḥissari, along with Mumin Yüzbashi, was ordered to lead thirty-nine cavalrymen from Chilan to Ushturfan. "The people of Ushturfan have come to detest the Khojas, and the Khojas likewise the people of Ushturfan, and they grow weary," he said, as he sent them on their way. "But Burhanuddin Khoja supports us. Do not give that son of the Khojas any trouble, but go into the palace of that illustrious house and observe what happens in that country."{192} They came to Ushturfan, and there they collected the keys to the treasury and arsenal. They sent Burhanuddin Khoja and his son to Aqsu with Mumin Yüzbashi and three other men. These events were related in the first epic.[3]

*   *   *

The Ataliq Ghazi made Ḥakim Khan Törä the governor of Aqsu, granting him all of the places in Bay and Sayram as well, and making him an independent governor and fiefholder. Hamdam Baturbashi was granted the rank of "special *baturbashi.*" Mullah ʿAbdullah of Khotan was made his chief judge by royal decree.

Now Tash Khoja Pansad was sent with 250 of his cavalrymen as an advance party to Kucha, and they came to a place called Say Langar one and a half *tash* away from Bay. But then there came a force of 4,000 from Kucha, led by Ibrahim Törä, Baqi Törä, Yusuf Bahadur, Yaʿqub Bahadur, and Taliʿ Bahadur. They captured Tash Khoja Pansad at Qushtami and killed him along with 160 of his cavalrymen. (Two months later, Tash Khoja Ishan's skeleton was exhumed, along with that of another honored commander. They were cleaned in the river and placed in a bag, and taken to Kashgar, where they were buried in the Shrine of Afaq Khoja, for they were among the ranks of the greatest of men.)

So the soldiers of Kucha turned back the Badawlat's battle-hungry men and pursued them until they passed the place called Jogha. The Khotanese held their ground at Jogha, denying them water and blocking the road. Most of the soldiers made camp at Yaqa Eriq, and they placed men in every cave of the mountains to wait in ambush,[4] and so killed many men. They hanged those who fell into their hands alive upon poplars and lit fires under them, roasting them to death like kebabs.

When His Highness the Ataliq Ghazi heard what had happened, the fire of his rage flared up, and he ordered many brave soldiers to mobilize. And the Badawlat himself placed his feet into the stirrups of victory behind them. The generals and *pansads* feared the fire of His Highness's rage; in unison they spurred their horses and took Jogha. When they arrived at Yaqa Eriq, they beheld the disaster that had befallen their soldiers. Their patience was finished, their rage unrestrained, and on the edge of that plateau [*say*] they made such a fight that the corpses of the dead lay more numerous even than the black stones of the plateau.{193} In the end the conquering army won the day. Some of the Kucha soldiers fled, led by Ibrahim Törä. The rest died by the punishing sword and the fury of rage. Some of them were taken prisoner and hauled off to Aqsu. Nearly 3,000 of the Kucha soldiers perished. More than 800 of the Ataliq Ghazi's cavalry met their ends.

Then Ḥamuddin Törä came marching from Kucha at the head of 4,000 soldiers more. He saw the urgency of the moment, and finding it necessary to take the path of submission, he offered himself into the Ataliq Ghazi's service. Their meeting was blessed to occur at Yaqa Eriq. The Ataliq Ghazi was very pleased with Ḥamuddin Törä, and he gifted him robes of honor and moneys, saying, "Until we return from Kucha, you will go to Kashgar, and stay there as my guest. Whenever we should get a loaf of bread, then it shall be shared equally between us." He sent him on his way under guard with such promises. As the Quran says, FULFILL YOUR PACTS [5:1], and accordingly he was faithful to his promises, and he remained in the highest offices of the *töräs* and the foremost ranks of officials. Two years later, Yaʿqub Beg grew angry with the *törä* and exiled him to the Afaq Khoja shrine.

Next His Highness the Badawlat with great pomp and sultanic magnificence rode from Yaqa Eriq toward Kucha, until he came to Qizil, where he camped. He sent Khayr Muḥammad Topchidar Pansad and his cavalry to reconnoiter, and they found that the Khan Khoja had sent yet another force. They routed it with one more assault. Thereafter they passed into Kucha, of which they gained control, and made their camp at Shamal Bagh. They sent a communique to His Highness and waited for his response. That day His Highness the Ghazi Badawlat arrived in Kucha in his eternal magnificence, and his tent palace was erected in Bulaq Bashi, a place below Shamal Bagh. There he alighted.

The Khan Khoja was seized and brought out of the city, and made to pay a visit to the Ataliq Ghazi, who lambasted him with several rebukes but then scratched out his transgressions with the pen of forgiveness. He gave him robes of honor according to his station and sent him into the palace with some trusted servants. But as soon as the Khan Khoja entered that palace, he stabbed and killed one of those servants. Then he got hold of a rifle and some weapons, and he ascended to the top of the wall, shouting, "Where have my soldiers gone? Won't you fight these Andijani Qipchaqs, kill them, and drive them from the city?" While he made this great commotion, he ran about like a drunken lunatic.

At that point not one of his soldiers was left. All of them had fled for their lives. Now guards came from the Ataliq Ghazi,{194} who seized him, bound him, and carried him away. No one saw or knew what had happened to him, where he had gone, where he stayed, or in what place he was buried. He disappeared without a word, without a trace. The rest of his story was related in full in the first epic. We have refrained from repeating it here.[5]

* * *

The Ataliq Ghazi assigned trusted servants to account for all of his treasure, weapons, guns, and such things as were necessary to kingship, and had them remanded to the royal treasury. All of the treasures and arms of the Chinese, from Qumul to the Six Cities, had been gathered in this treasury. All of them were now transferred to the palace of His Highness the Badawlat and sent off to Kashgar, the seat of the sultanate.

Now that the affairs in Kucha were concluded, Isḥaq Khoja was brought from Korla. Royal decree granted him all the lands of Kucha, Shahyar, Bügür, and Korla, over which he was appointed as an independent governor. Tokhta Eshikagha Beg was made to serve as head of his personal guards.[6] Mullah Yusuf Akhund was appointed by royal decree as chief judge. Yaʿqub Beg stayed two months in Kucha, making pilgrimage to the holy shrines, giving alms to the vagabonds and the meritorious, and having the Quran recited, dedicating its benefit to the purified spirits.

At an auspicious hour he left for Kashgar, the seat of the sultanate, but when he arrived at Aqsu, he spent a month there. He had seventeen of Aqsu's leading men imprisoned and driven away to Yarkand with their families, including Mullah ʿAbdulbaqi Mufti Akhund, Muḥammad ʿAbdullah Eshikagha Bek, ʿAbdullah Qażi, and Qasim Beg. And he had the Word of the Bestower of Desires read for the holy shrines of Aqsu, gave generous alms to the vagabonds and the deserving, and ordered their great pots to boil. He paid these kindnesses, received visitors, and then placed his boots into the stirrups of victory and rode away to Ushturfan. He stayed there for twenty days, and made ʿIlawuddin Beg steward [*sarkār*] to Muḥammad Baba Toqsaba. He also made generous donations to the shaykhs of the shrines, and received their visits.

When this was over, he set out for Kashgar via Qaqshal and through the country of the Kyrgyz.[7] They traveled until they were two stages from Kashgar, [and approached Artush,] to the outpost at Saghun, where water flowed swiftly from a fissure. They declared that it was a grassy pasture and made camp there. But that night the weather broke. The crash of thunder and lightning resounded.{195} Then a little rain fell. In the middle of the night, they were caught unawares by a torrent of water that came rushing down from the cave, and it carried off the greater part of the treasure, weapons, camels, horses, chargers, soldiers, cannoneers, sutlers [*bazarchi*], and wranglers. And many of those perished, drowning in the water. However, they had set His Highness's tent palace up on higher ground, and the torrent had not touched it. The cavalrymen sought out the lost treasure and weapons and found some of them in places one or two days' distance away, but returned without most of them. These events were kept secret, while those who remained received gifts of robes of honor, horses, and weapons.

It was (early in) the month of Libra. Many [hundreds of] donkeys now came from Kashgar, laden with sweet melons, watermelons, peaches, grapes, figs, and such fruits. His Highness sliced the fruit himself, and from each fruit he took a slice, and the remainder he gifted to his soldiers of every rank, with kind words and a compassionate mood, and so swayed them greatly. Next he traveled on to Artush and made camp there, and next he alighted at Kashgar, the seat of the sultanate. It was the year 1284—the year of the monkey—on the twenty-second day of Jumada al-Akhira [October 21, 1867].[8]

When he was done making contributions to the holy shrines of Kashgar and visiting the poor, the widows, and the unfortunates, the sick, the weak, and the ones who pray, then he set about distributing offices and gifts of robes of honor, weapons, and moneys to the generals, *pansads*, and every single cavalryman and soldier in proportion. He was angry with General Mirza Aḥmad Qushbegi but hid it. He gifted 10,000 copper coins[9] to Buzurg Khan Törä and sent him off by the Badakhshan road on a pilgrimage to the Holy Land. In the span of ten months, Yarkand, Khotan, Ushturfan, Aqsu, Kucha, and Korla had all come into his domain. Indeed he was lord and master of all Moghulistan.

2:7 The Unification of the Seven Cities

How That Wise and Royal Sovereign, the Virtuous Yaʿqub Beg Ghazi, by the Grace of the Creator Achieved Mastery Over the Seven Cities, How He Spread His Cloth of Justice, and Other Sundry Events

{196} FOLLOWING THE conquests of Aqsu and Kucha, His Highness the Ataliq Ghazi returned to Kashgar, the seat of the sultanate, with his high officials and great commanders to rest, free of cares. All of the conflicts and enmities around Moghulistan had been concluded. As the Quran says, REFER IT TO GOD AND THE MESSENGER [4:59]—all bound the belt of submission tightly about their waists. They passed that winter in peace and repose. In time, the year turned, and then came the days of spring. And the sprouts of wildflowers lifted their heads from the black earth.

At this time, His Highness the Ataliq Ghazi commanded that workshops should be built in Kashgar, Khotan, Yarkand, and Aqsu. So goldsmiths began to manufacture purses, belts, quivers, bridles, saddle straps, blanket straps, and other such equipment, which they made with silver and gold. The blacksmiths were tasked with creating scimitars, knives, and stirrups to be inlaid with gold, as befitted a king. Meanwhile the coppersmiths were assigned to make great guns, shot, and bullets. The tailors sewed gold-fringed brocade of fine silk stuff[1] from Russia and Benares, and coats of cotton cloth, both fine and plain. The leatherworkers set to work on slippers of red leather,[2] and carapaces, sleeveless coats, and trousers of the fur of the lynx, fox, and lamb, and sheepskin hats with the fur on the inside or out.[3]

The cobblers and saddlers set to work making all kinds of boots, both fine and plain, purses, blanket straps, belts, quivers, stirrups, straps, and bridles. The carpenters, rifle makers, nail makers, metal casters, stitchers, embroiderers of gold thread, tentmakers, and other artisans all busied themselves with their own crafts. Some expert craftspeople were brought from Khoqand, the seat of the sultanate, to be chiefs over the other masters. They struck coins in the name of Malla Khan, as well as copper coins in the manner of those of the Emperor of China. Then directors were appointed to oversee the masters, and every artisan had a fixed monthly wage. No one was forced into it. Everyone came of their own free will to practice their own craft and received a wage in proportion to their service.

The gates of justice opened, and injustice was like the Simurgh taking refuge in the Mountain of Qaf. All the common people could not help but raise their voices in prayer on behalf of his good fortune, and in every mosque, after the Salawat[4] and the recitation of the Quran, they would pray for his fortune and longevity.

* * *

The Badawlat approached justice and good government with circumspection and ensured that the soldiers would not lay their hands upon the people's lives or treasure.{197} For example, once, when his conquering armies were on their way from Yarkand to Kashgar and had ended up at a settlement in the desert, there was an impoverished woman out walking on the road with several bowls of yogurt. A *yüzbashi* drank one of the yogurts without paying. That is when His Highness the Ataliq Ghazi arrived. The impoverished woman made a complaint to him that an officer had drunk one of her yogurts without paying.

He kindly asked her, "Would you recognize the soldier who drank your yogurt?"

"I would," she replied.

He took her among the soldiers, and she pointed one out, saying, "There—it was that soldier."

"Oh, mother!" he replied. "Let me slice open this soldier's stomach and have a look. But if no yogurt should come out, and I should kill you, wouldn't that be a bad end?"

"No, it would not," she replied. So he immediately had the soldier killed, and when he sliced open the stomach, that yogurt had not yet been digested. The impoverished woman received that soldier's clothing.

Another example: When His Highness the Ghazi first arrived in Aqsu, a cavalryman took two bundles of hay from a hay dealer without paying, forcing him to hand it over to give to his horse. The owner of the hay made a complaint. The Badawlat investigated, located the cavalryman who had taken the hay, charged him with the crime of "taking by force," and had him executed as an example. After that, never again did any soldier force someone to give them something, demand anything less than the market price, or use harsh words—all of that ended. When they bought or sold, they were polite and easy.

Another: When the Ataliq Ghazi was on his way to Aqsu and passed through Maralbashi, one of his sons shot at something. It turned out that a donkey had been grazing in that direction, and the bullet happened to lodge in that donkey, and it died. The owner of the donkey made a complaint, saying, "This cavalryman has shot one of our donkeys dead," and he showed him.

When the Ataliq Ghazi saw this, he brought his son and had him beaten with no forbearance. "Did you think that you could shoot a donkey because you are the Ataliq Ghazi's son? And shoot for no reason?" he said, his rage flaring, giving him a hard lesson. On that, he departed. A fear descended upon the hearts of the generals, *pansads*, commanders, cavalry, and infantry when they saw this happen, and all of them begged forgiveness anew.{198} Gripping their lapels, they pledged their obedience.

Of course, it is necessary for a king to take some measure of his officials' crimes, and not to ignore their transgressions but punish them. If he does not, then others charged with carrying out his orders will get ideas, and the bindings of his rule will grow loose and its measures hollowed out until the common people's livelihood and the discipline of the army both fall apart, and he will no longer be able to put them back together.

In those remarkable and fortunate days, the habit of senselessly, forcibly demanding things disappeared completely, both among the people and among the soldiers. Everyone acted as through His Highness the Ghazi was present, and whether he was near or far, hidden or present, night or day, no one attempted to do anything senseless or inappropriate, nor could they even think of doing so. Whether he was hidden or present, near or far, they acted as if he was right there watching. This is how they understood it, and it is what they believed. Reporters—that is, secret observers [*maraqchilar*]—were present at all times, in all places, ready and waiting, but people never knew that, or recognized who they were.

* * *

To return to our story: the soldiers now numbered over 50,000, and the number of salaried artisans in the atelier too grew near to 50,000. The treasuries were somewhat replenished. Now the Ataliq Ghazi's rule extended to Baghrash and Ushaq Tal in the east, Muztagh and Zavqi[5] in the north, Alay and Badakhshan [Irkeshtam] in the west, and Qarangghu Tagh, Lop, and Cherchen in the south. Now he mobilized servants to count all of the mountains, deserts, summer pastures, winter pastures, and all the wildernesses, cities, towns, and villages within the realm, as well as deserted and ownerless lands, especially those which had been taken as plunder, and the *khaniya* farms and lands.[6]

In one case, Muḥammad Naẓar Qushbegi, Mirza Qasim Mukhtar, and Mirza ʿAbdulʿaziz Bukhari were dispatched to Aqsu, with Magistrate ʿAbdullah of Aqsu to oversee them, to take control of the orchards, farms, nameless wildernesses, pastures, and *khaniya* left over from the Dungans and Chinese.[7] In the old days, when the Emperor of China's people took control of the Seven Cities, all forty-six begs in Aqsu, including the governor and the deputy governor, were rewarded for their service with land and people, in place of a salary or provisions from the treasury [*khaniya*]—more for the higher-ranking ones,{199} less for the lower-ranking. For example, the man serving as governor of Aqsu would be assigned 100 households, sixty for the deputy governor, and down the ranks to four households along with their land. They were rewarded with the prize of people ordered to farm and serve them. Until the time of Islam, whichever man was commanded to fill that position would receive that grant of land to plant, and people to set to work and to serve him. This ancient rule was enacted throughout all the Seven Cities. But they treated those people like property they had bought, like purchased slaves, indeed like slaves they had inherited from their fathers. They believed that they had the right to take money, firewood, or anything else from those people, or the produce from their fields. And these people could not even mix with the common people of this country, or take any office as [irrigation chief,] *onbashi*, muezzin, or custodian, not even for money.

They were popularly known as "seal-bottomed serfs,"[8] and they got no respect. [The land that the Emperor of China rewarded to the begs was also called "*khaniya* land."] (And when the country was conquered by the Chinese again, the land that Chinese officials irrigated and cultivated was also called "*khaniya*.") So the Ataliq Ghazi's officials took control of this land, sold it to nearby towns and villages, and took the money to the royal palace. The land in Aqsu from Aqyar and Kälpin to Qushtami and Onbash yielded 556,000 *pul*, and Bay and Sayram yielded a little under 400,000.[9] This was also the case—or more so—for the rest of the Six Cities.

Every year, some high-ranking officer would come with a few secretaries and tell us, "Some of the royal land has not been sold. We have come to inspect it." So they would inspect it, and on whatever pretext they would say, "We have recovered it." And they would take several thousand *tangga* to the royal palace. The Ataliq Ghazi himself would affix his personal seal to a document saying that he had sold this land and received the money, and then pass it on to the chief scholars to affix their seals. Ultimately they would say that the judge's fee had not been paid on the sold land, and they would levy a judge's fee of one *tangga* for every *daqian*,[10] and a fee of four *tangga* out of every 100 *tangga* on the person who purchased the land. And so they gathered hundreds of thousands of *pul* from the Seven Cities.

Around that time, at a meeting where the common people of Kashgar had gathered,{200} a man said wittily—or perhaps sarcastically—"What a wondrously fine and peaceful reign this has turned out to be! This is the time when the skylark makes its nest upon the sheep's back!"

There was a wise and witty mullah there among the scholars of Kashgar, Mullah Muḥammad Yar Khalifa. "His Highness has sold off all the land in the Seven Spheres," he joked in reply. "The skylark has nowhere left to nest. If it didn't nest on the back of a sheep, where else could it?"

* * *

It is written that, during the reign of the Kucha Khojas, the son of Muḥammad ʿAli Khan, Muẓaffar Khan, came from Kashmir to the country of Yarkand. Then he went to Kucha, and while he was journeying from Kucha to Korla, he heard that Yaʿqub Beg and his conquering armies were on their way to Kucha, so he moved on from Korla to Ürümchi. Muẓaffar Khan lived for a time in exile, and during that time, some of the merchants from Ferghana then passing through on their way from Ili happened to recognize him. The

Dungan leader, Daud Khalifa, noticed how much respect they were showing him, so he likewise decided to honor him with several chests of tea and silver. The other Dungans also brought him gifts, and as the money collected in his hands, people began to gather around.

Around that time, several of the higher- and lower-ranking officers who had been in the service of Muḥammad ʿAli Khan and then fled from Khoqand, such as Mirza Aḥmad Qushbegi, Nar Muḥammad Parvanachi, Mir Baba Dadkhwah, and Ghazi Pansad, wrote a series of letters to Muẓaffar Khan. "If it would by any means be possible for you to convey your august presence to Aqsu, or at least to Kucha," they wrote, "then we would elevate you as khan, Khan of the Seven Cities, and we would be in your service, for you are our leader, our prince, our lord and master!"

The profession of his ancestors, and his hopes of governing, becoming a leader, and being installed as sultan all upset his heart. So he gathered some deserter Dungans and Namanganis far from home and made of them an entourage, while some wealthy men who lusted for power lent him the funds in their possession, and they also took loans from others to give him that money. They prepared horses, arms, and banners and marched as one to Korla, and as they sounded the drums and trumpets, they conquered Korla and occupied it.

The governor of Korla, Ḥajji Beg, fled, and he sent a message detailing what had taken place there, sending a messenger to the capital at Kashgar at great speech, like a bolt of chattering.[11] When the Ataliq Ghazi[{201}] learned that Muẓaffar Khan had entered Korla, he grew worried about his officers there, for he was their leader and their prince.

Immediately a royal proclamation was issued to Isḥaq Khoja. "Take your cavalry to attack Muẓaffar Khan," it read, "and insofar as possible, capture him alive. If that is not possible, remove the body, so as to demonstrate your obedience." As soon as these orders arrived, Isḥaq Khoja and 2,000 of his cavalry went straight to Korla, where they did battle with Muẓaffar Khan. Muẓaffar Khan was left with only a few soldiers and could not match him, so he hid in his tent. A number of dastardly Qalmaqs had gathered together. When they saw the conquering armies approaching, they carried themselves far away. Now they surrounded that tent and from every side shot into it, bringing Muẓaffar Khan to his end. His tent palace, for all the holes, now resembled a sieve. This took place in the year 1285, a Chicken Year, in the month of Libra [late summer 1868].

The governor of Aqsu, Ḥakim Khan Törä, had taken position in Qizil by royal command and was garrisoning it. He did not allow those serving the foreigner, the *pansads* and cavalry, to enter Kucha. He was faithful to the royal commands because the Ataliq Ghazi was very cautious and worried about this, though he would not reveal that fact to the generals, *pansads*, and commanders in Kashgar until Muẓaffar Khan was disposed of. But they took a Namangani who had grown rich, Musa Kilal Bay, and three other Namanganis to Kashgar, where they were executed. Now they were triumphant over the "triumphant" [*muẓaffar*] khan, and peace was achieved.

* * *

Around that time, the Learned Sayyid Aḥrar Khan Törä and Sayyid Ardilani Damollam arrived in Kashgar from the country of Ferghana.

Two men named Shaykh Muḥammad and Shaykh Aḥmad also traveled from Iraq and stayed for a few days in Badakhshan. Thence they sent a letter to congratulate Yaʿqub Beg the Ataliq Ghazi and to share some of their own wisdom:

> We are sons of Holy Mecca and *sayyids* of authentic genealogy. We have received good news from the Gardens of the Great One, and fortune has brought us to these parts. For a while now, we have remained here by leave of the ruler of Badakhshan. May God bless Your Highness, a king who has shown such love for Shariah.
>
> {202} It has been deemed appropriate that we might offer some words to your royal self on the subjects of the worldly and the next-worldly. Information has been delivered to us from the invisible world beyond to the effect that, by the wrath of God, a great celestial disaster is now preparing to befall all the lands that you rule. A solution must be found before this takes place. So let all of your scholars, generals, and commoners, all creatures great and small, show their love for the great spirits, repent, plead, cry and weep, and gives alms and tithes, and pray for salvation from this great disaster. We too are busying ourselves with prayer both night and day.

The moment he received their letter, His Highness summoned all his great nobles and his wise and learned judges, along with all of his commanders and *pansads*, and explained the letter to them. He led them all in a special prayer of repentance, and then they made a proclamation to the regional governors and common people: "Every one of you must cease any forbidden or frivolous acts and begin instead to repent and give alms."

The people of all the cities understood, and they began to weep in sincere repentance. The court also wrote to the two shaykhs, asking them for protection and sending them gifts. When the two shaykhs heard this, they thought, "What we said affected all the people of the Seven Cities under Yaʿqub Beg's rule! Now let's go there ourselves and try to share a little more wisdom. What could go wrong?" Now they set the snare of deception, and they scattered their grains of falsehood and exhibited their knowledge of tricks and deceits as they fabricated a claim. Shaykh Muḥammad now claimed, "I am the Mahdi of the End Times!" while Shaykh Aḥmad played his vizier, and they arrived in the territory of Yarkand. "I have come," he announced after a few days had passed, "to bring you to repent and to pledge your allegiance, and call you to the righteous path!" And he made his claim to be the Mahdi.[12]

At that time, a judge well versed in jurisprudence, Żiyauddin Damolla, was the chief judge and officer charged with Shariah in Yarkand. He said to them, "Don't sully your snouts with these baseless claims and absurd ambitions." And though he preached to them with the hope of the Shariah, it made not a dent on those deviants' callous hearts.

So he wrote about this incident to His Highness. When he learned what had happened, he passed a sentence upon those false claimants in accordance with the Holy Shariah.{203} "Save the Muslims from these petty men's greed," he wrote to Żiyauddin.

When Żiyauddin Damolla read the contents of that letter to those liars and proclaimed the sentence upon them, they made an even greater, more impossible claim: "The Lord of the Worlds by His own will has made Himself incarnate in the living form of Yaʿqub Beg! Right now, the Lord of the whole world is Yaʿqub Beg. Know this. We have been sent by Yaʿqub Beg. He knows. If you should kill us, then for every drop of our blood, an army of thousands of armed soldiers will be summoned to lay the Seven Cities to waste—nay, the whole world! Do not underestimate us, or a great disaster will afflict you!" And they made such false claims that the graceful pen cannot compose. GOD FORBID. Now the Shariah-loving scholars came together, and with all the words of the *mujtahidin*, they ordered those liars to be stoned to death. All the nobles and commoners in the land showed up, and they brought the failed false claimants out onto a broad field and buried them up to their waists. First, the chief judge began and cast a stone. Next, everyone, young and old, threw a stone or brick until they died, and this pure land was cleansed of those lying infidels' greed.

* * *

Around that time, a number of merchants had received permission to travel to Hindustan. However, some Shighnani bandits snatched them from the road, taking them prisoner, and this news reached the royal ears. He was enraged and ordered 7,000 soldiers to be readied to go to Shighnan and attack Asghar ʿAli Khan, under the command of General ʿAbdullah and Chief Secretary Ḥajji, along with twenty *pansad*s and a number of battle-hardened commanders, and provisions and weapons loaded on the backs of 600 camels, as well as 10,000 sheep and other equipment. "Go and retrieve the merchants and all their money and property from the king of Shighnan," he commanded them. "If they submit to us, then draw up a treaty with them and return. But if they should refuse and you come to blows, then loot and pillage, put them to the sword, take captives." He sent them on their way. They crossed the desert and wilderness and traveled until they came to Shighnan, where they sent an emissary to Asghar ʿAli Khan with a letter of reprimand.

When Asghar ʿAli Khan realized what was happening, he lost his senses. He handed over the merchants with all of their money and property, which satisfied them.{204} Then he drew up a treaty of friendship, and even sent a message in which he bowed his head in submission. "I did not know," it read. "This deed was done by disobedient subjects. They have been punished severely, and I and all of us deeply regret these inappropriate actions. If you still wish to massacre and pillage us, then that decision rests with Yaʿqub Beg. If you would show mercy and find it acceptable to grant us a place in the circle of your servants, then my humble self will be your aged servant. I did not send an emissary to congratulate you earlier, though it would have been appropriate—that was my oversight. Let us nevertheless bind ourselves firmly together with the rules of friendship and a pact of peace. Indeed, I have within the veil of chastity a bud of early springtime, which has never felt the zephyr's breath, nor has any man reached out to pluck a pomegranate from her garden. If your refined mind should wish it, then I would send her to join your woman slaves." He added some pleasing words and requested that this petition be presented to Yaʿqub Beg's royal audition. When that letter arrived, it was sent to His Highness the Ghazi.

His Highness was pleased when he read it, and he wished to add Asghar ʿAli Khan's daughter to his harem, so he sent the Lady Pansad Tokhta Khan[13] with men and many gifts. A treaty of friendship was concluded with Asghar ʿAli Khan, and they bound themselves in a relationship of father and son, and drew up a plan for their alliance. On account of this magnificent attack, the ruler of Hunza, Safdar ʿAli Khan, also submitted. The ruler of Wakhan too signed a treaty of submission, and all of the rulers of Kohistan came under His Highness's rule, and thus established peace in their lands and safety on their roads.

* * *

Now the month of Capricorn [early winter] was approaching, and it was time for the Ninety. All of the officials who were under His Highness's command and within his domain revived the customs of the lofty khans and *qaghans* of bygone days, respected kings and great sultans, and set themselves to work on transporting the Ninety Gifts. Every one of them sincerely lent to him, interest free, all of the items that they had in their possession, and they made great efforts to present those gifts to him at Kashgar, the seat of the sultanate.

Among them, the governor of Khotan, Niyaz Ḥakim Beg, presented before his royal vision:{205} a mine's worth of gold, some eight *charak* in weight; 1,000 *yambu*; 400 horses, 200 of them fully outfitted with fine saddles and tack and 200 of them with bit and bridle, *numnah*s, and bedrolls; on 400 more horses, lynx, fox, and lamb skins; girdles, waistcoats, breeches, and caps; Rum-style sleeveless coats; golden brocade, satin, mixed silk, cotton,[14] and pure silk from Benares and Russia; lovely robes, shirts, and such necessities made of cotton fabric, both fine and plain, with red leather down to the laces and pockets;[15] fresh leather boots, both fine and plain, with everything, down to their footcloths; nine by nine beautifully engraved teapots; nine by nine copper cookpots, strainers, and ladles; nine by nine ewers, washbasins, and boxes, including cases; nine by nine precious Lahori korma pans; nine by nine extravagant silk carpets embroidered with calligraphy; and other such desirable things in numbers beyond counting.

They stayed for some days. Each day at breakfast time, they would bring in a nine of *yambu*, nine bundles of robes, and a nine of horses outfitted with fine saddles. Then they would pay their respects, make their prayers for his eternal fortune, and have breakfast together. All of the high officials would give their good wishes, and they would raise the finger of surprise to the teeth of thought and bite. The rest of the governors likewise brought their gifts before the royal vision, as they were able, one after the other. He was grateful to all of his chiefs, and he gave to each of them several robes of honor, turbans, weapons, and signs of particular kingly favor. And to their men too he gifted robes of honor and monies, and granted each of them permission to retire happily to his resting place.

God, make the sun of his glory eternal in this world and the next. Amen.

2:8 The Ottoman Empire

How Allegiance Was Pledged to the Protector of the Two Holy Cities, Commander of the Faithful, and Caliph Upon the Earth, ʿAbdulʿaziz Khan (MAY GOD MAKE HIS ABODE IN PARADISE!), and an Emissary Sent with a Letter of Allegiance and Gifts; How This Was Found Acceptable to the Enlightened Mind of the Caliph Upon the Earth, and He Sent a Decree with a Tablet[1] of Office and Crown; and How He Took the Seven Cities Under His Protection and Subordinated Them to Rum

WHEN THE ATALIQ Ghazi granted leave to his governors to return to their own domains, and the chill of winter likewise returned to its homeland, a new year began its transformations, and the days of spring came in. The plants began to rear their heads,{206} and the turtledoves began to sing, as the sweet-voiced nightingales brought joy with their calls to the mirrors of the hearts of the Knowers and the Lovers. The buds of fragrant flowers blossomed, illuminating the page of the Earth like the Sun itself with glistening flowers of every color. People's hearts were gladdened, and all enjoyed repose. In the midst of these spirit-raising pleasures, entertainments, and diversions, as people gave prayers of endless gratitude to the Eternal and made supplications, Yaʿqub Khan Qażi Törä of Tashkent returned from pilgrimage to the Two Holy Cities and arrived in Kashgar. In their conversations, which touched upon all manner of subjects, he encouraged His Highness the Badawlat to send an emissary to the Caliph Upon the Earth, Guardian of the

Two Holy Cities, and Commander of the Faithful, ʿAbdulʿaziz Khan b. Abdulmajid Khan (MAY GOD PERPETUATE HIS RULE!), and to submit to the rule of Rum.[2]

"Since he is the Commander of the Faithful and Caliph Upon the Earth," His Highness said, self-deprecatingly, in great humility, "then who am I to send an emissary to deliver my greetings?"

Now the Qażi Khan Törä replied, "After the Russians took Tashkent, the pious scholars of that land said, 'Now these lands are forbidden to us,' and they refused to submit to Russia, but chose instead to follow the traditions upon the paths of prayer and emigrate to the Holy Land. I was among them, and I too wished to emigrate. However, after completing the pilgrimage to the two Holy Cities, while on the journey back, I came to Rum. I stayed there for a few days. And there I was fortunate enough to spend time in the company of prominent and powerful men.

"The great caliph has heard that, while the Russians have taken Tashkent, a few Muslims in the emperor's country have rebelled, established Islam, and brought about their dominion. So he has decreed that, in the mosques, after the Salawat and recitation of the Quran, they should offer prayers for the success of the Muslims in the east who have established Islam. He himself has faced east to offer this prayer. However, when he asked the ḥajjis the name of that ruler who has achieved his aim in establishing Islam, some of them said, 'The Ḥajji Padishah of Khotan.' Others informed him that it was 'the Khojas of Kucha.' Still others told him it was 'the Sultan of Ili.' He did not know the proper name of the one who established Islam.

"Seeing as he is the Caliph of Rum of the Ottoman Dynasty, protector of all the Muslims of the world, whenever Muslims are successful in their rebellions, he is pleased, and he prays for their success.{207} When he hears that they have met with defeat, it pains him and saddens him, and he prays for their freedom. In every case, it is the duty of the caliph to learn when Muslims somewhere have risen up and mark it, and indeed to illuminate their fortunes and bring them fame. Now these lands of Moghulistan have come under Your Highness's command. It is surely necessary that you inform him."

The felicitous and fortunate, Yaʿqub Beg Ataliq Ghazi the Lucky, agreed. He had gifts prepared: all the fine and beloved things of the emperor's land, silks and satins, fragrant tea, lovely porcelain, silver and gold, Kazakh and Qalmaq horses, nine by nine comely Chinese virgin girls, and nine by nine young Chinese slave boys. At an auspicious hour, he sent them on their way with Qażi Khan Törä and some trusted servants. They traveled until, at a happy hour, they came to the sultan's city of Rum, and there they were granted an audience with the Commander of the Faithful and Caliph Upon the Earth of the Ottoman Dynasty. They presented him with the gifts and carried out the emissarial ceremonies.

The Commander of the Faithful and Guardian of the Two Holy Cities, ʿAbdulʿaziz Khan (MAY GOD BLESS HIS VICTORY!), was positively delighted with the gifts and grateful for them, and he showed the Qażi Khan Törä every honor and granted him gifts. He had them stay a while and feasted them, giving them leave to return home with his reply. He granted the Ataliq Ghazi the title of Master of the Royal Stables, appended the Seven Cities to Rum, brought them into his protection, and, regarding the Ataliq Ghazi as an important king, granted him a golden crown, bejeweled and gilded, encrusted with such jewels as diamonds and rubies[3]; a great and kingly fur hat and robe, which down to their edges had precious jewels, lightning-flash diamonds and pomegranate-red [Badakhshani] rubies, set in rows of golden rings; a fine Rum-style sleeveless robe; a scimitar, its handle and scabbard encrusted likewise with diamonds, rubies, and such limpid jewels as topaz and emeralds set in gold; and an ornamented sword and a rifle, both inlaid all over with silver and gold, so that even the ramrod was covered in silver and gold. Such precious and lovely things, which darkened the eyes of all who beheld them,{208} were sent by an earthshaking command and returned with those emissaries by royal grace and kingly favor.

They were received at a fine and felicitous hour, and His Highness the Ataliq Ghazi viewed them. He was so pleased that, like a bud, he could not contain himself but blossomed like a flower, and placed the kingly crown and royal fur hat upon his fortunate head. He clothed his body in the robe and all the other gifts. He buckled the royal sword about his blessed waist. He took that rare rifle into his hands, turned to face Rum, and gave many praises with his prayers. It was as though the world-illuminating sunlight and moonlight and all the stars of the seven spheres had alighted upon the form of Yaʿqub Beg the Ataliq Ghazi. The cheers of congratulation from all his courtiers great and petty rang across the dome of the sky. And several days of celebrations were arranged, during which all of the wise scholars, powerful leaders, and high-ranking commanders received robes of honor, and everyone was pleased. Then they struck gold, silver, and copper coins in the name of ʿAbdulʿaziz Khan, implemented his commands, and named the Seven

Cities a domain of the Caliph of Rum of the Ottoman Dynasty. It was the year 1286 [1869/70].[4]

* * *

It has been related that the genealogy of these sultans of the Ottoman dynasty, and the honored line of their ancestors, can be traced back to Turk b. Japheth b. Noah (PEACE BE UPON HIM!). The Turk peoples are more numerous than other tribes. They are peerless in bravery and fearlessness, and without equal in generosity and high-mindedness.

In some histories it is written that, when Islam had just recently been revealed, the Quran was sent to Hindustan, but they did not respect it and threw it upon the ground. It was sent to Turkestan. Their leader held it over his head and showed great humility. When the Arabs received this happy news, one of the friends of God who lived in those days uttered these words: "The Hindus will always be poor no-accounts. Never will their cities or villages have honor. The Turks will always be great friends and highly esteemed, and may they always be victorious. Only rarely will anyone defeat them." The words of the friends are the words of God. Always have the words of the friends come true.

Constantinople is a great city. It is a vast and expansive city, grand and remarkable in the extreme. Constantinople was constructed by a descendant of Sam b. Noah (GOD BLESS HIM!), a ruler named Constantine. On all the surface of the world there was no city like it. In olden times, it was the capital and seat of the caesars and of the Christians.{209} Today it is known as the capital of the Ottoman sultans and called by the name Istanbul.

The Ottoman dynasty descends from the line of Qay Khan b. Kün Khan b. Oghuz Khan. It has also been said in some histories that THIS IS ALL TALK. But Oghuz Khan was the son of Qara Khan, who was the son of Moghul Khan, and Moghul Khan was the descendant of Turk b. Japheth. Earlier, in the prolegomenon, we described how Oghuz Khan was born a Muslim to the infidel Qara Khan, and how perhaps he was an Uwaysi.[5] He was king over most of the inhabited world for 170 years. He had six sons. To each of those sons, God granted four sons, making twenty-four BRANCHES [*shuʿba*], that is twenty-four branches [*shakh*], in total. Each of those sons began one TRIBE [*qabīla*], that is, one tribe [*urugh*], each of which claimed to be the tribe of such-and-such, traced their descent to the name of some forefather and made it their sign.

In the year 622 [1225], when Chinggis Khan left for the west, the leader of the tribe of Qay was Sulayman Shah Qay. He moved his nation of 50,000 families away, fleeing to the other side of the Euphrates and Tigris toward Rum. At that time, he was a beg and a commander, and his station was in a place called Mahan in Turkestan. For this reason he lived out his life being spared these great disasters.

After him, his son, Ertugrul Beg, who was intelligent and perceptive, took his father's place as beg. When his age was approaching 100, he made his son, Osman Beg, his *kaymakam*.[6] This Osman Beg was in the service of the Seljuq Sultan ʿAlauddin. Because he fought with the Christians and prosecuted many holy wars, conquering and subduing many of their cities, Sultan ʿAlauddin was pleased with him and gave him the rank of sultan. Sultan ʿAlauddin decreed that, every time Osman ate food, mounted his horse, or dismounted his horse, drums would play. He sent him drums. At that moment, the sound of drums came from Osman Sultan's gate. "What is that sound?" he asked, and was informed that Sultan ʿAlauddin Seljuqi had sent him military drums, and that this was their sound. Out of respect for the drums, he rose from his place and took three steps, and with each step he bowed. This custom is still followed. Whenever they hear military drums, they walk three paces and bow three times.

{210} By this time, Osman Beg had become both a general and the leader of a people. During his reign as sultan, the state of the Seljuq Sultans came to an end. Because they feared that Islam might be weakened or fragmented, all the Muslims gave the reins of rule to Osman Sultan, and they together pledged their allegiance to him. Once he had ascended the throne and taken charge of all affairs of state, he gave himself the title of Osman Khan, and Osman Khan was the founder of the Ottoman dynasty.

Their first kingship was that of Osman [*ʿU͟sman*] Sultan, and this is the reason they are called the Ottoman [*ʿU͟smaniyya*] sultans, but the word *ʿU͟smaniyya* is also a chronogram for this event.[7] He had the Quran recited and coins struck in his name. Each day, his fortune and sultanate increased, and he carried out conquests, adding several countries to his domain. He followed his assembled wise men's advice and created new rules and countless laws for the management of the state and the care of the common people, which he established as regulations. Today his great descendants still follow his customs, rules, and laws, and they do not permit themselves to deviate in the slightest from the rules and laws that Osman Khan established.

This is why his magnificence increased daily, as did his independence. He was born in the year 655 [1257], ascended to the throne in 699 [1299/1300], and ruled for twenty-six years. In 726 [1326], at the age of seventy, he walked into that sublime world. After that, his son Orhan[8] sat upon the throne and ruled for thirty-five years. Then his son, Murad I Khan, took the throne. He was very brave and bold, and he was called “the Devotee of God.” He was martyred in the war with Rum. Then Sultan Bayezid Yildirim sat on the throne. He was a contemporary of Amir Timur, and there were many wars between them, which are recounted in histories. Then his son Mehmed I Khan sat on the throne. He ruled for six years. Then Murad II took the throne. He ruled for thirty years. The Sultan Mehmed II took the throne. He ruled for thirty-three years. He conquered Istanbul, so they called him Mehmed Khan the Conqueror, and he is very well known. Up until that point, it had been in the Christians’ domain. The conquest of Istanbul was encoded in the chronogram A GOOD LAND [34:15].[9{211}] Mehmed the Conqueror was the seventh ruler of the House of Osman.

To sum up: The first of the sultans of the Ottoman dynasty was Osman. From the first sultan to the present day, which is to say through the reign of Sultan ʿAbdulḥamid Khan b. ʿAbdulmajid Khan (MAY GOD PERPETUATE HIS RULE AND CAUSE IT TO SPREAD ACROSS THE WORLDS!), thirty-one caliphs have ruled for 641 years,[10] while many Muslim kings from among the Umayyads, ʿAbbasids, Seljuqs, Ghaznavids, Samanids, Khwarazm Shahs, Chagataids, and Timurids have come and gone. None of their dynasties lasted for 600 years. The reason is this: Because those sultans were unjust and negligent and delighted in sensual pleasures, their sultanic dynasties went extinct and came to their ends.

Because the great Ottoman sultans in their actions were righteous Sunnis, gave relief to God’s creatures, and permitted themselves no carelessness or inattention in their concern for the common people, their dynasty has been so longevous that they have taken on the role of kings of kings. God, may the shadow of this dynasty forever be cast over the people of Islam, and may their dynasty be over all other dynasties. OH GOD, HELP THE SOLDIERS OF THE SULTANS OF ISLAM WITH YOUR SUPPORT!

Rum is such a magnificent city that neither the power of thought nor the graceful pen is sufficient to describe it. It is said that Rum was built by Rum b. Ayz b. Isḥaq[11] (PEACE BE UPON HIM!). The name Rum does not specify a country but indicates a vast clime comprising a number of countries. The exterior of the city measures thirteen *tash*. Within the city are 600 hammams. The Chicken Bazaar and other bird markets measure one *tash*.[12] One can imagine the rest!

* * *

May it not be concealed from your wise lordships that my purpose in this little chronicle in describing the lands of Kashgar, and then detailing for a while Constantinople and Rum, describing their rulers, and narrating their genealogies, is this: those ancient sages who investigated the geometry of the Earth and divisions of the climes pronounced that Rum, Constantinople, and many other cities were among those of the sixth clime, and of the seven stars, connected them to Mercury. They judged that, in the sixth clime, the Pole Star was at forty-five and one quarter degrees. Constantinople and the cities of Moghulistan belong to one clime, and the appearance and character of their peoples and the lengths of the hours of their days and nights{212} are the same. Moreover, since Kashgar, of the cities of Moghulistan, entered the protection of and allegiance to the Great Khaqan and King of Kings, I therefore recorded a description of Rum on this page.

* * *

Around this time, an emissary came from the White King of Russia. He paid all due respects and spoke kindly. The purpose of this emissary's visit was to contract a treaty of friendship with the Ataliq Ghazi, and perhaps even to bring him under his command, so that the Seven Cities would produce income for his realm. Several of his emissaries came with such an intent. They would be well attended to, given a nice answer, and sent away. Another of their goals was that, just as they had entered the country of Ferghana by deception at Aq Masjid on the pretext of a fish, they were searching for some pretext to enter the Seven Cities.[13] The Ataliq Ghazi never gave up his secrets, but would refuse to meet with them in person and send them with great caution on their way.

An emissary from the Frankish queen named Forsyth Sa'ib[14] also came around this time. He signed a treaty of friendship with the Ataliq Ghazi and said, "We ask that you sign no treaty with another country but only ally with us. If you were to need any weapons or soldiers, then we would station a consul with ten or twenty thousand armed soldiers in Kashgar, and were they to be defeated by some enemy, we would send more to assist and protect you, and we would match your payments of the soldiers' salaries. Once sixty years passed in this way, then sixty years later, you would hand the Seven Cities over to us, and in that event, we would rule it, and we would not withhold our education and civilization from your descendants. In this regard let us strengthen our pact with sure guarantees." Once all of the emissarial ceremonies had been completed, they were hosted and feasted well for a few days. The Ataliq Ghazi disagreed with the queen's aims, so he sent them on their way with a letter full of pleasing and eloquent words establishing the treaty of friendship.

* * *

Another affair: Around that time, there came both an emissary from the White King, coveting the Seven Cities; and an emissary with a message from the queen asking to station a consul and soldiers to assist the Ataliq Ghazi. Yet most importantly, there came the news that the Emperor of China had sent soldiers to reclaim his old domain.

"Let me send an emissary," he decided, "into the presence of the King of Kings and Caliph Upon the Earth, the Commander of the Faithful of the Ottoman Dynasty.{213} Let my message say that there is no other desire in my heart but that he send a king with twenty or thirty thousand soldiers and append the Seven Cities to the domain of the Ottoman dynasty, and that I may join the ranks of the least of his liegemen, tutty my eyes with his sky-scraping capital and lofty court as if they were kohl, and be granted a pilgrimage to the Two Holy Cities. If he should find this to be an auspicious hour, then I would wish to fulfill this intent." When he said this, all the high officials and nobles praised him, saying this plan was very good.

But just then, his royal audition was receiving the news that those dark armies had come like ants from Beijing and arrived at Qumul, where they waited in dark array. And so, by the command of the Potent, he rode off for Turfan. There was no opportunity to send the emissary as he had intended. The desires of this strong man, master of destiny, were lacking in the eyes of the sublime Judge and so came to naught. THANKS BE TO GOD IN ALL THINGS.

2:9 Battles with the Ürümchi Dungans

How the Dungans of Ürümchi Displaced the People of Korla and Kucha; How His Highness the Badawlat Ghazi Ataliq and His Conquering Armies Spurred Their Horses to Ride Eastward and to War with the Dungans; How They Plucked the Blossom of Intent from the Garden of Desire, as They Had Wanted; and Other Events

AS THE WRITERS of the news of the world tell the story, the fortune of His Highness the Ataliq Ghazi daily found increase without limit. Indeed, his fortune and kingship were like that of a second Timur Kuragan. The year turned, and the days of spring arrived. At the end of the season of Taurus [*mid-spring—ES*], all at once there appeared from the direction of Turfan 20,000 Ürümchi Dungans, led by men named Uzi Yanshay and Lan Shing Yanshay.[1] They and their lackies appeared in the territory of Korla. It was the year 1287 [1870].

Previously, Mir Baba Dadkhwah and Chief Secretary Ḥajji had been ordered to Korla. Chief Secretary Ḥajji was commanded to establish a tax office at Korla, and Mir Baba Dadkhwah to construct a great guard post at Ushaq Tal. A chief guardsman and cavalrymen had been assigned to him, and now these were sent in hopes of heading off the Dungans and stopping their approach. However, because the cavalry were few, they could not match them, and the beg of Korla, Ḥajji Beg, led them in flight to Kucha. They sent this terrible news, and when the messenger arrived{214} (, who in his haste had summoned the swiftness of the path of the Moon in the first sphere and sent it traveling into the heavenly spheres), Ḥakim Khan Törä was ordered to take 2,000 cavalry and make war against the Dungans.

As soon as he saw this royal command, he handed Aqsu over to Mirza Baba Beg the tax collector and to Muḥammad Saʿid Qurbashi. He took cavalry, infantry, cannons, and guns, and in a place called Qara Yaghach one *paotai*'s distance from Kucha, they came to face the Dungans. A battle ensued, with mounted cavalry on one side and bold infantry on the other, and just as the flames of combat flared and rose, all of a sudden, the cavalry fled. Those bold infantry sought refuge in an orchard, and there, as they held the Dungans at bay, their ammunition ran out, and they were left helpless. The Dungans rushed upon them from every direction, boxing them in, and slaughtered them, seizing the city of Kucha. Nearly 2,000 cavalry and infantrymen were killed.

Ḥakim Khan Törä and Isḥaq Törä's cavalrymen fled, but they could not reach Aqsu so stayed in Bay instead. Most of the people of Kucha took their children and traveled to Aqsu via Yulduz Bagh and Muqur. But no infantry or cavalry remained in Aqsu. So the commanders brought the wealthy foreign merchants, the traders and their sons, and armed them, pressing them into service as cavalrymen. The tax collector kept close watch day and night and monitored the land. And when he learned of those useless and inconstant men who had fled from Kucha, he had some of them imprisoned. All of Aqsu was in suspense.

Then someone said, "We'd better gather information about the Dungans in Aqsu. We wouldn't want them to try anything." Now those cavalrymen were sent out with the command, "Wherever you find Dungans, capture them and bring them here." They set out and retrieved nineteen innocent Dungans, who were just going about their business and farming. These were locked up.

After a little investigation, they could see that these were peaceful Dungans. Having just locked them up, now they cautiously made to set them free. They felt regret and said, "We ought not have captured them. Now whatever the matter is, let us quietly send them off and just submit a report saying that they were peaceful Dungans." They found this agreeable and put the Dungans into two carts, and under two men as their guards, sent them off to Kashgar with the report. But at that time, His Highness the Ataliq Ghazi was riding from Kashgar and coming up the road. When he arrived at

Qaraqchin, the flames of his rage were flaring up, and it was just then that they greeted him.

"What Dungans are these?" he asked.

"The tax collector of Aqsu has sent your humble servants," said the guards, and they presented the report.

{215} "Line the ones in the first cart up on this side of the road," he ordered, "and the ones in the second cart on that side. Kill them." So he ordered their execution. The nineteen innocent Dungans were killed. He neither looked at the report nor even took it in his hand. The reason I discuss this is to illustrate the flames of the king's rage. Oh, dear friends, BEWARE, BEWARE! Prayer for refuge from the rage of kings TRULY, TRULY, is one of the most important things.

The governor of Maralbashi, Darwish Mirakhorbashi, and his cavalry had been sent after the *törä* to reinforce him. Those soldiers went to Kucha under the two *törä*s and the governor of Maralbashi, where they were made to bury the dead soldiers. They remained at Kucha.

At this time, His Highness the Ataliq Ghazi came with his victorious troops and graced the refuge of Aqsu with his blessed footsteps. Now he heard that the Dungans had turned and left, and the flames of his rage stilled somewhat. But he burned inside for the Muslims' lives and property, and it angered him greatly. He had Shamsuddin Aʿlam Akhund of Aqsu, his son Bahauddin Akhund, Hadi Khalifa, Muḥammad Khoja Khaṭib Akhund, and Mulla ʿIsa Akhund banished[2] and sent away to Kashgar. He granted Aqsu to Chief Secretary Jiyan and ordered him to build a great palace there. He stayed for ten days, then arranged his generals into a column to march behind him. He placed his boots into the stirrups of victory and went to Kucha.

He was angry with Ḥakim Khan Törä so took him along on the march to Turfan. He was angry too at Hamdam Baturbashi and Mir Baba Dadkhwah, and his rage came, but he kept it concealed. No one saw where they went, nor knew what had happened.[3]

His Highness had assigned one of the eight *pansad*s to each of his generals, and in each *pansad* were five *yüzbashi*s, and each of those had his own guards—and so they set out with what was recorded as 25,000 brave and ready cavalry and soldiers, not counting the store men, wranglers, and sutlers. Each general was like unto a great king, and their might was greater than that of a governor. The might of the others has been described in brief.

Then followed a *pansad*'s worth of guards, executioners, and furious sentries,[4{216}] and on a cart, the criminals, with chains around their necks. Some of them were bound to the cart with iron rings, some shackled soundly within it, while the cart itself was caged with iron wires, and all around it could be seen the watchmen and executioners with their hatchets and battleaxes bared.

And then came a *pansad*'s worth of hashish-addled mendicants, mad and fearless, all in a crowd. They raised their standards and followed on foot behind the glorious army, and wherever it made camp, they would make their own someplace off to the side. The next morning, they would pass among the army and beg for "SOMETHING FOR GOD." When they got alms, they took them back to their own habitations, where they were under their own *babas*' command. When His Highness had distributed robes of honor, to these men too he had gifted patchwork caps and monies, and they had accordingly shown him a loving disposition. He greeted them and was grateful to them. Indeed, they were exempt from the taxmen's reckonings. From all of this, one may guess the ferocity and glory of the rest of the soldiers.

Two days beforehand, in the place where they would make their camp, there would be a market, with meat, oil, rice, fodder, bread, rolls, hay, and firewood; grocers with all sorts of vegetables; halva, raisins, and sweetmeats; and all kinds of confections, jams, and exhilarating drugs. All these things that could not be found in the cities were ready to hand in the army market; whether in pond or farmland, in desert or mountain, there they were.

And whenever they rode out on campaign, there traveled as their companions fifty cartloads of gold and silver coins, and fifty cartloads of red and copper coins;[5] and on 200 lovely camels, all sorts of robes, mail, breeches, sheepskin hats, and boots, both fine and plain; and on 200 camels, the horses' tack and saddles; and of the 1,000 horses, 500 were fully outfitted, while 500 went unsaddled with numnahs. A horse would be granted to a cavalryman who led a slave or walked on foot, or whose horse had died. There could also be seen several carts of his own private fattened Kazakh and Ḥissar sheep, and several carts of chicken eggs; of mutton fat and oil; of earthenware ovens; of spades, axes, adzes, lamps, and candlesticks; and of brooms large and small.

And among the main detachment, with the *pansads* and the commander in chief, were over 500 water bearers who gathered water in waterskins and brought it around on horseback, whether at lake, desert, or river, so that whether they were on campaign or in camp, the water in their skins would never run low. And when they raised the tent camp, they would sprinkle{217} the excess water in front of it. Then there were 4,000 or 5,000 sheep and milk cows accompanying them with their calves. Every morning, starting with the leaders, they would bring out fresh milk tea to all the soldiers for their breakfasts; and hot bread, and sugared buns and rolls; and also delicious halva and meringue; and sweet foods like rice pudding and sweet biryanis; with fine and fragrant tea. Their kitchen servants were in two ranks, and on either day, one took its turn. Whenever they arrived somewhere, the cooks would be there making pilaf and soup in several great cookpots. As soon as they arrived, they would distribute the food to everyone in equal portions, to great and petty—to the commander in chief, the generals, the pansads, the personal guard, and the royal entourage.

Such was the generosity of His Highness's table, that wherever they went, on campaign or in camp, there was a nine of platters of rice reserved for the flying birds, for crow, dove, and sparrow, and walking beasts as well. There were several members of the royal entourage and guard assigned to this. Every day, when the rice was being distributed to the cavalrymen, they would spread this rice on their plates, place the meat atop it, and cut it into little pieces, which they would place on the grounds of the royal palace in His Highness's sight, or else in front of the camp. Those crows and doves who had become accustomed to it, and whom they had tamed, would feed, and they would fatten. They would in their own tongue give prayers of praise to the Creator and Provider (Exalted be His glory!) and fly away. Not one was captured or harmed. Even such creatures as these benefited from His Highness's beneficence—they were not excluded from it.

His own kitchens consumed sixty *charak* of rice each day, and likewise was the consumption of each of the generals' and the *pansads*' respective sculleries. Every day, the governors would send rice on no fewer than 200 or 300 donkeys, and flour and fodder on no fewer than 400 or 500 horse carts, never running short. So he traveled, that joyous and fortunate Yaʿqub Beg Ghazi, that famed warrior, with this sort of pomp and ceremony, until he raised his lofty tents in the palace at Kucha. From the time of the Prophet to the present day, surely no human being had seen or heard any Muslim king in the land of Moghulistan form such a furious, glorious host and march it along this road.

Now Isḥaq Khoja and his belongings were relocated from Kucha and taken away to Yarkand, where he was entrusted to the Shighavul Dadkhwah and a salaried position granted to him.{218} Tokhta Eshikagha Beg too was taken and placed into the ranks of his personal cavalry. He gifted Kucha to Nar Muḥammad Parwanachi. Then he rode from Kucha and took up his position at Korla, where he made Niyaz Muḥammad Toqsaba the governor.

At this happy hour, all those distressed and wandering merchants who had been plundered and robbed in Korla and Kucha and there parted from their money and their merchandise, and had fallen onto the road of poverty and hunger, now cried and threw themselves upon the ground to present their pleas. He was merciful and gifted robes to some and money to others. "I have heard how you have suffered," he said. "Now I shall give you your money from the treasury. Return often to pay your respects. I will dispatch a secretary, and you must record your expenses truthfully. I shall give you your money accordingly." He dispatched Chief Secretary Zaynulʿabidin Makhẕum. Some wrote down the truth. Others made a "one" appear as a "ten." His Highness the Ghazi Badawlat in the light of discernment realized that they had lied and deceived, and told them, "After Turfan has been conquered, we will give you your money. Return often to pay your respects." Eventually, when Turfan was conquered, he obtained a fatwa from the Islamic scholars, according to which he examined the amount of tax that had been collected by the government and distributed moneys accordingly.

* * *

His Highness the Badawlat marched from Ushaq Tal and came to Qaraqchin, where he ordered General ʿUmar Qul to march with his *pansads* via the Yilanliq road to Toqsun. General ʿAbdullah and his *pansads* and cavalry were ordered to Toqsun via the Aghir Bulaq road. These two commanders approached the Dungans in Toqsun simultaneously from either side. There they battled, and won, and took Toqsun. There were some 2,000 Dungans there, of whom about 200 fled with their lives to Turfan. The rest were put to the sword.

Now His Highness went to Turfan, and they erected his royal tents in a place called Dadong. Two days later, 6,000 Dungans marched out from the city of Turfan to a place called Yamshi, where they fought. It was a bitter battle. In the end they were defeated, though some of them fled to the city, while the rest were put to the sword, destroyed by fury and rage. Dadong, it seems, is the very source of wind, so they certainly could not stay there. The tents were erected again in a place called Yar.[6]

At that auspicious hour, 17,000 Dungans came marching from Daud Khalifa (the *Laorenjia*) in Ürümchi to the aid of the Dungans in Turfan.[7] They arrived four days later. The Dungans in Turfan were evidently aware that they were coming. Eight thousand Dungans{219} emerged from the city, and they attempted to enclose the conquering army from two sides. Now General ʿUmar Qul and General ʿAbdullah fought them on either side, while every one of the other generals and *pansads* showed bravery beyond that of the stories of Rustam and Sam Nariman.[8] Eventually the door of victory was opened for the conquering army. A few fled to their homes with their lives, while the rest fell prisoner. They were sent on the path from which there is no return.

Next they pitched their tents and made their camp at a place five stages' distance from the city of Turfan. And all around the perimeter, they readied trenches, walls, battlements, gates, and gun towers and set them firmly in place. All of the cavalry and infantry were brought inside the walls. Every night, a *pansad* and 500 men would take their turn making the rounds of the city, keeping watch and patrolling. Several sutlers were in the city, and some of them had made a place for themselves outside the walls for each to take shelter from snow and rain, wind and storm, cold and heat. The city of Turfan remained unconquered, and the siege dragged on. Every week or so, a large number of Dungans would leave the city, fight, and, unable to match them, return inside the city again.

Now the Lukchinese made common cause with the Dungans, rebelled, and prepared for war. General ʿUmar Qul and General ʿAbdullah were ordered to march on Lukchin with their men. When they arrived, battle broke out, and they were victorious and took possession of that place. Then, just as they were reaching out to eat their food, a royal message came that said, "Come immediately, without question," for it seemed that another 12,000 Dungans had come from Ürümchi. When the generals got there, they joined battle. Eventually they hemmed these Dungans in.

But one day, as the soldiers were giving prayers of thanks to God, General Khayr Muḥammad Topchidar the Afghan turned on His Highness, and he fled into the Dungan city. And he emboldened the Dungans and heartened them for war, building up their lust for battle, and showed them many tactics. One night, Khayr Muḥammad took a large group of Dungans with him and went out to the army's fortress. As some entered and others climbed to the top of the walls, Jamadar Dadkhwah realized what was happening. In a rush, he ordered the guns to be loaded with silver{220} and copper coins and fired, which killed some of them, while others were captured alive and executed. Khayr Muḥammad Topchidar was wounded and fled with his life back to the Dungans.

Once everything had calmed down, they reconnoitered and found that some twenty or thirty cavalrymen from the advance guard had been killed where they slept, and that is how the Dungans had been able to reach the great host.

Now His Highness asked Jamadar Dadkhwah, "What sort of cavalrymen were they, who found out about the attack and warned you about it?"

"Two Afghan cavalrymen warned me," he replied, and pointed them out.

His Highness asked those two Afghans how it was that they had found out, such that they could report it.

"If you would forgive us," they replied, "we would say . . ."

"I forgive you," he said.

So they replied, "We wanted to smoke weed, so we went to the camp looking for a light. But then we couldn't find any fire, and as we were going back, we saw some strange and hostile men. We hurried back to inform Jamadar Dadkhwah."

Before this time, when His Highness found out about someone smoking weed or hashish, he would have them severely punished or even executed. But from this day forward, he granted permission to smoke weed and hashish. These weed smokers had been wakeful in the drowsiness of weed. In gratitude, he made the two Afghans *yüzbashi*s of the artillery and honored them with fine horses outfitted with tack, robes of honor embroidered with gold, and their own tents.

The remarkable thing is that, on that night, when the soldiers of sleep had won a victory over His Highness the Ataliq Ghazi and all his armies and pillaged all movement and feeling, and those armies had nearly been surrounded and thrown into chaos, God kept them in His protection. So all of them gave charity in proportion, and thanks unto to the Lord. ʿAbdulqahhar Beg and Khoja ʿAbdullah Beg, prominent men of Turfan, had a generous amount of fine and coarse grains sent to the conquering armies from their own produce, doing them great service. They received audiences with His

Highness and, by his world-commanding order, were honored with allowances, which pleased and honored them.

* * *

The city of Turfan was under siege for nine whole months, with no sign of victory. The Dungans were locked up inside, and matters hung very much in the balance. All of them gathered in the great lodges, where they affirmed their oaths to each other anew and renewed their pledges. They were about to throw themselves like moths against the conquering army and were discussing strategy.

There was a great cannon that had been newly forged at Turfan, and just then, Jamadar Dadkhwah wanted to see if it would fire. So he lit the fuse and aimed it toward the Dungans' city. It was fired at dawn. And it was loaded with carcass shot, shaped like a cookpot,{221} and the carcass shot landed in the doorway of the lodge where the Dungans were conferring. There it burst open, and several more shot went off. Many Dungans were killed and some wounded.

Thus did fear from the unseen world and tremors of terror descend upon their hearts. "This *Lao* Padishah[9] is a powerful man," they worried. "He knew what we intended and that we were making our plans—that's why he fired on us. There's nothing else for it. Let's send a man to beg for peace." So they sent an emissary to pledge their fealty and declare their intention to submit. His Highness graciously accepted their requests. All the Xiao Yuanshuai's Dungans hung their weapons around their necks and went to throw themselves upon the mercy of that Heaven-like court. Servants brought good wishes, and they were granted the benefit of an audience. And he received the Xiao Yuanshuai and all the Dungans as guests, granting them robes of honor, placing them at ease as he honored them by bringing them into his service. In sum, Turfan was conquered according to his desire, and Ḥakim Khan Törä was honored by being made an independent governor. Ḥaydar Quli Pansad was made his general. Khoja ʿAbdullah Beg was honored with his position as his steward, and Qażi Surkh Abi with his as chief judge.

Now that he was free from the affairs in Turfan, he passed judgment upon Maʿṣum Khan Khoja of Sayram and on Wayid Khalifa—who had been the governor of Turfan, whose stories were told in the first epic, and who had done much service to the Dungans and killed many of his cavalry. He had Maʿṣum Khan Khoja executed in Korla.

Wayid Khalifa was sent to Aḥmad Beg, the governor of Bay, along with a royal command that read, "Kill Wayid Khalifa by your own hand immediately upon his arrival." By this lofty decree, Aḥmad Beg killed Wayid by his own hand. That night, he dreamed in terror that the dead Wayid was chasing him with a knife in his hand. Aḥmad Beg lay in bed seven days until he died. His sister, Niyaz Khan, ruled Bay and Sayram for six months. Then Bay and Sayram were granted to Muḥammad Amin Toqsaba.

2:10 Conquest of Ürümchi

How the Ataliq Ghazi Rode to Ürümchi and Seized the Opportunity of Conquest; How the Leader of the Nanshan Chinese, Xu Xuegong, Submitted; How He Battled the Dungans and Achieved a Great Victory; and How in Glory He Returned to His Throne Room

{222} THE STORY is told that, after the blessed Ataliq Ghazi completed the conquest of Turfan and Lukchin, he resided there for ten months.

At that time, the Laorenjia Daud Khalifa in Ürümchi was like unto a great king or true khan among the Dungans of Ürümchi and Turfan. Several times he sent his troops to make war, though sometimes he forged treaties of friendship, sending correspondence—that is, establishing relations. Now His Highness, the great Ataliq Ghazi, sent ʿAzim Qul Pansad and four other *pansads* with 1,500 cavalry to Daud Khalifa in Ürümchi. When Daud Khalifa heard, he sent some men out to meet them, show them the requisite honors, and bring them to camp in front of the city. He had prepared a broad camping ground for them and set them well at ease. Around the time of the evening prayer, he dispatched many Dungans, who took the cavalrymen by surprise and engaged them in battle, killing many of them. The *pansads* retreated with some 400 cavalry and fled back to the royal palace.

* * *

Between Ürümchi and Yulduz, in a place called Nanshan,[1] there were more than 10,000 households of Chinese who had managed to escape Isḥaq Khoja's massacres. Their leader was called Xu Xuegong.[2] They would battle with the Dungans, sometimes winning, sometimes losing. At that time, Xu Xuegong heard that His Highness the Badawlat had come to Turfan and killed the Dungans, and understood that he had wiped them out. So he took his younger brother, Ma Shaoye,[3] with him, along with 2,500 Chinese, who were fully outfitted with weapons, and went to throw himself upon the Ataliq Ghazi's mercy. He had come bearing gifts of 8,000 sheep, 800 horses, 800 cows, and several hundred sheep, and on several hundred camels he brought food, gold ingots, silver, porcelain, satin, and fine tea. They showed tremendous honor and beneficence to these Chinese. They stayed for a few days, after which Xu Xuegong left Ma Shaoye there with 1,500 Chinese to serve, while he himself returned to Nanshan with 1,000 men. These Chinese served the Dungans in Turfan well during many engagements.

Eventually His Highness rode to Ürümchi at great speed. Although His Highness had conquered Turfan, by the light of perspicacity he knew that it would count for nothing{223} until Ürümchi was conquered; so, on the fourteen day of Rajab in the year 1287, in the month of Sagittarius [October 10, 1870],[4] he rode for Ürümchi. He sent General ʿAbdullah ahead to scout. He himself followed after in glory with his feet in the stirrups of victory. The Dungans of Dabanchi came out to greet him with gifts, seeking forgiveness in obedience to him, and received the blessing of peace.

When they came to the boundaries of Ürümchi, they made their camp at the place called Decius,[5] at the head of the river that carries water from the mountaintops to Ürümchi. They constructed walls and trenches and laid up there. It was thirty stages from there to Ürümchi. Yet the bitter cold of midwinter[6] and the freezing snowstorms laid the soldiers to waste. Some of the sutlers and wranglers perished as well. Yet Xu Xuegong had coal brought to them on many carts and camels, doing them great service. Twenty-seven days passed in this way.

Now, by order of the Laorenjia, 60,000 Dungans had prepared to carry out a nighttime attack. Just at the moment of the evening prayer, they set out toward those conquering armies. The weather froze. Snow fell. The winds kicked up. The night too turned as black as the Dungans' hearts. Between the city of Ürümchi and their army lay half a *tash* of mountain road. Some of the Dungans climbed into a hole, while some climbed another hill, got turned around, and lost the road, becoming panicked. In short, they were divided into three parts—truly, in all four directions! They could not traverse thirty stages in one long night. Surely this was a blessing from the Almighty.

After His Highness the Ataliq Ghazi had performed his morning prayers, he looked out and saw that there were banners upon the mountains. All rode out together to meet them face to face, and as they battled, more banners appeared from another direction. And while the flames of their fighting rose and flared, some came carrying banners from yet another direction. Now as great battles were taking place, all at once they gained the advantage over the infantry and forced them to retreat. His Highness was in the company of 16,000 soldiers.{224} All of them had entered the fray. There were some 300 cavalry from his personal guard attending him.

Per His Highness's orders,[7] Nis̱ar Maʿṣum Ḥażrat had brought Mirza Aḥmad Qushbegi to pay his respects. He was granted an audience, and His Highness the Ataliq Ghazi honored him with a place in his personal cavalry. Now when he saw that the infantry were coming in retreat, he looked at Mirza Aḥmad Qushbegi and gave the order: "Take these soldiers who fled and beat them, kill them, cut them into pieces." When they arrived, the Qushbegi's soldiers cut down five or six infantrymen. The rest of the infantry saw this, and they turned around and assaulted the Dungans. The Qushbegi ordered his personal guards to advance behind them, while he climbed atop a hillock[8] to observe. It was such a bitter fight that it defies all description. Most of the Dungans were on foot. The bitter cold ruined them. Some of them even froze to death. There was a high mountain there. Some Dungans had gone up atop it and were firing from it, while the cavalry and infantry were struggling to fire on them from down below. The corpses of the Dungans were rolling down from on high, tumbling, falling. The cavalry and infantry took those Dungan corpses and made of them a shelter in which to take cover. In the end they were victorious and wiped them out.

Of all the victories won by His Highness the Ataliq Ghazi's officers, there had never been a battle such as this. By the might and compassion of the All-Powerful, they had achieved victory over such mighty enemies. Some few of the mounted warriors had fled from that place of sudden danger and encountered the Laorenjia. The rest had found themselves afflicted in the drowning waters of death and lay buried beneath the snow. This joyous victory was thanks to Mirza Aḥmad Qushbegi, and limitless gratitude was shown to him.

The Dungans had left Ürümchi with a half-baked plan to "Go there, capture them, kill them, and take their horses, pack animals, weapons, money, and equipment as booty." They had said to their children as they got on the road, "Tomorrow, let us tie up the captured horses. Come out with ropes to greet us." But the cavalry and infantry were victorious,[9][134v] and as they pursued the fleeing Dungans, they came upon nearly 10,000 of the Dungans' children, aged twelve to fifteen, and each of them with a rope in their hand. These were the children who had come out to tie the horses their fathers and elder brothers would take as booty, and ride them. All of them were killed, sent with haste to follow their fathers upon the road of no return.

* * *

When the Laorenjia heard[135r] what had happened to the fleeing Dungans, he thought that there must be some way to save himself, as well as the city. So he came up with a half-baked plan, whereby he sent about 10,000 school-aged children, young boys and girls, out in front of the battle-hungry army, each with a copy of the Quran in their hand and reciting some part of it. General ʿAbdullah and Fayż Yüzbashi were pursuing the Dungans with their cavalry and warriors, and as they approached, they did not notice the schoolchildren, nor pay them any concern, but trampled them to death beneath their horses as they went on their way. As they reached the gates and fired upon the city, an order was given that they should not enter, and so they did not, but reined in their horses. Eventually General ʿAbdullah went blind in one eye. His rudeness and unkindness surely caused his blindness. Fayż Yüzbashi too died shortly thereafter.

Several of the cavalry and infantry had taken the Dungans' little children as booty. When His Highness saw this, he asked, "Why did you take our enemies' children alive?" He had the soldiers who had taken prisoners executed. He had the captured children killed as well. Many Dungans died on this account—the guilty and the innocent, the mature and immature, boys and girls, young and old.

Now an emissary came from Daud Khalifa to say, "We ask that the armies of the *Da* Padishah not enter our city. Our women and children are greatly afraid. Let us submit to you, and whatever order you give, let us accept it with heart and soul."

His Sovereign Highness accepted. Daud Khalifa had gold and silver, fine tea[135v] and porcelain, and all such things brought as gifts into his heavenly presence. Although he did not go in person, he sent his apologies in a letter, in which he bound the belt of obedience tightly about his waist and said, "If you wish to have me executed, that is your right as king." His Compassionate and Felicitous Highness was satisfied with this and sent a kind response.

The Badawlat had brought with him the leader of the Turfan Dungans, the Xiao Yuanshuai. On account of his service, in spite of his past transgressions, he now made him the Da Yuanshuai of Ürümchi.[10] By royal decree he granted him a golden belt and robe, a fine double-barreled rifle, weapons, cannons, and banners, as well as Ürümchi. And all of the six towns subordinate to Ürümchi, such as Qutubi, Changji, and Manas, were also included in this grant, and presented to him by that world-shaking command. And in those six towns, that Da Yuanshuai selected whatever Dungans he found suitable, and these he appointed to each of the cities as a *xiao yuanshuai*. He gave them command, robes, and weapons, and they submitted themselves to the Da Yuanshuai.

Now this Da Yuanshuai wrote to His Highness, "I know not the rules and laws of Muslim kings, nor their customs. Likewise am I weak in the art of diplomacy. I request one of Your Majesty's servants, that he may educate me in these practices." His Highness agreed, and he selected Zaynulʿabidin Makhẕum from among his chief secretaries to be stationed at Ürümchi as [the Da Yuanshuai's] *salamagha*.[11]

Yet all the peoples of the human race know of Ürümchi's terrible cold.[136r] If not for the fact that Xu Xuegong brought them coal from Nanshan, it would have been difficult for them to survive. His younger brother too had done much welcome service. Now Xu Xuegong once again came for an audience bearing many gifts. His Highness was greatly pleased, and he gifted to Xu Xuegong a black fur coat trimmed in cloth of gold, a fine single-barreled rifle, a golden belt and clothing, a fine horse outfitted with gold, and a great big hat. And to his younger brother likewise[136r, 5] {225} did he visit such limitless beneficence. And to the remaining soldiers he gifted bedrolls, and girdles, cuirasses, and trousers, and hats with the fur either inside or out, all made of lynx and fox, as well as moneys, each according to their station. And he thanked them with 10,000 bags of grain ordered from the Da Yuanshuai.

* * *

So His Highness the Ataliq Ghazi remained in Ürümchi for three months, pacifying his domain. He set out with his conquering army for Turfan, where they stayed for two months. He displaced some Dungans and drove them off to Aqsu and Ushturfan. Next, with great contentment, he placed his boots into the stirrups of victory and traveled until he came to Qarashahr at the end of the month of Aries.[12] He intended to stay for a few days, and so ordered a fortress to be constructed on the banks of the Qarashahr River. He himself led the work, ramming earth and laying brick. When they saw this, neither the generals nor the *pansads*, great commanders, high ministers, or anyone else young or old could stand idly by, but set to work ramming the earthen walls and building the fortress until it was complete.

At that time, the khan of the Qalmaqs, named Khatun Khan, had come to a place near Korla called Qara Modun. With the intention to bring this people to submit, and to win them over, he sent a messenger to invite them for a visit. Khatun Khan declined to enter Qarashahr, but sent a group of officials—lamas, representatives, and princes—with gifts to have an audience. They came with some 500 Qalmaqs. They stayed there for a few days and were treated as guests. Every day, they were treated to hospitality with sugared meringue and halva, tasty dishes and sweet candies, almonds and pistachios, raisins and candies, jellies and milk, biryanis and rice pudding, and fragrant tea.

Meanwhile, Muḥammad Musa Toqsaba was sent with a few cavalrymen to retrieve Khatun Khan whether he wished it or not, without letting these Qalmaqs know or bringing him into Qarashahr, but taking him to Korla by another route. They set him up in the house of a man named Akhund Chaghan. After that, they had robes of honor prepared for the Qalmaqs in yellow linen and yellow *daba* cloth [in Qalmaq style].[13{226}] He gifted them with robes of honor, moneys, and supplies in return. Yet these Qalmaqs were unaware that their khan had come to Korla, so they contentedly returned to their own lands. A stipend and provisions were arranged for Khatun Khan, and he was remanded to the governor of Korla, Chief Secretary Ḥajji.

Now there came a letter from Ürümchi that said, "Xu Xuegong has come to Ürümchi with many soldiers, killed the Da Yuanshuai, and looted and pillaged." This unhappy news became known to his esteemed audition. And as that news arrived, Zaynulʿabidin Makhẕum brought gifts of gold, silver, tea, silks, and porcelain on thirty-some carts, along with fifty or so Dungans, and came to pay his respects and display these gifts to the sublime gaze. This chief secretary had previously been sent from the Da Yuanshuai to Xu Xuegong as an emissary, which he was not particularly willing to do. He had been on the way to Ürümchi, carrying the gifts, and then thought, "I ought to visit His Highness and pay my respects. Ürümchi's weather suits me little indeed." The incident had come to pass only two days after he had set out on the road. No other news about what happened had come to the chief secretary in the meantime.

His Highness, in a fine mood, explained to the chief secretary what had happened with Xu Xuegong in Ürümchi. "By the command of the Lord of the World," he said, "you, chief secretary, have somehow been delivered safely to our sublime court." And they gave prayers of thanks and praise.

For that chief secretary was a wise mullah and poet, skillful in every field, who had served as chief secretary to many khans and acquired a great reputation. He proved his worth again in the service of His Highness, being incomparable in the skills of the secretary and peerless in writing. Through the clarity of his intelligence and the power of his perspicacity, he had composed a *divan* of *ghazal*s and *naẓm*s in the style of the *Divan* of Fużuli.[14] His pen name was Mahjuri. He collected therein much advice, lessons, and learning, but did so through subtle nods and allusions, such that when wise men read it aloud at their gatherings, they would raise the thumb of surprise to the teeth of surprise and bite. The chief secretary's fine qualities, and the nimbleness of his rhymes, are immediately apparent to anyone who casts an equitable gaze upon his *divan*. This is a selection from it:

> Should the fate of this Forlorn One [*Mahjuri*] be to circle the Kaaba,
> I would strike my head and supplicate myself for past deeds.

His Highness the Ghazi with the beneficence of his jeweled tongue showed him his kingly grace and said,{227} "If Ürümchi rebels, one can send soldiers to bring them to heel. If the Da Yuanshuai is killed, we can ennoble another Dungan with the royal command, and he will be the Da Yuanshuai. But you, chief secretary—it would be impossible to find another you."

His Highness the Badawlat Ghazi stayed in Korla and Qarashahr for three months. Next with great splendor he moved his tent palace and came to rest with the nobles in Aqsu in his new royal palace, which had been built in the manner of the citadels and palaces of the khans of Ferghana. He was pleased by this, and he honored the foreman Niyaz Baqi and Master Baqimanda with royal gifts. It was the year 1288, the Year of the Bird [1871].

2:11 Ḥakim Khan's Campaign to Ürümchi

How by Order of His Majesty the Ataliq Ghazi, Ḥakim Khan Törä Marched Upon the Dungans in Ürümchi; How His Son Sayyid Beg Quli Beg Was Sent After to Render Aid; the Events That Came to Pass; How He Brought the Flower of His Intent per His Intention to His Palm of Intent; and How He Wiped His Face at the Sublime Court

THE FORTUNATE AND venerated *ghazi* joyfully took his place on the throne in Aqsu. Yet when he was two stages away from Aqsu, a communique came from the governor of Korla, Ḥajji Mirza. "Some two thousand traitorous Qalmaqs," it said, "joined forces, with arms and banners, and secretly entered Korla during the night. They murdered about two hundred men, taking their lives. They fled into Yulduz."

The story was that Ḥajji Mirza had learned about the Qalmaqs' rebellion. He had taken cavalry to block their route through the mountains at a place thirty stages from Korla called Khal Khaman,[1] and did so. Those Qalmaqs took another route into Korla, took Khatun Khan, and fled.

Another is this: News had been received by the sublime audition that Xu Xuegong of Nanshan and his soldiers had entered Ürümchi, killed the Da Yuanshuai, and plundered it. The story was that there had been an old enmity between Xu Xuegong and the [*former—ES*] Xiao Yuanshuai.{228} It was for this reason that he aided His Highness the Ghazi, presented him with gifts, and served him with his soldiers—he wanted to kill the Xiao Yuanshuai. He did not want the Xiao Yuanshuai to be made the Da Yuanshuai, and he felt tremendous jealousy and envy over his elevation.

Another story: "Ten thousand bags of grain had been ordered from the Da Yuanshuai for Xu Xuegong. Xu Xuegong had said, 'I want them now!' The Da Yuanshuai apologized: 'The people possess no grain at all. I will give you the grain at threshing time.' But he would not agree, and so these battles took place."

At this auspicious hour, the Ataliq Ghazi had made Nar Muḥammad Parvanachi from Kucha a general in command of Ürümchi with 2,000 cavalry. He was placed in command of all the forces and ordered to march on Ürümchi. Chief Secretary Ḥajji was ordered to march from Korla with 500 of his cavalry. Ḥajji Mirza "tossed" [*tashladi*] Tashlan Qażi Beg into his own position. Ḥakim Khan Törä was also ordered to march from Turfan. Now Ḥakim Khan Törä, Nar Muḥammad Parvanachi, Chief Secretary Ḥajji, General Ḥaydar Qul, and Maḥmud Beg Pansad Urgenchi marched separately for Ürümchi with 8,000 cavalry and infantry. After the death of the [*former—ES*] Xiao Yuanshuai, his son Ṭalib Akhund was recognized as his successor and made the Da Yuanshuai. He remained obedient. His Highness likewise became a "student" [*ṭalib*] to Ṭalib and honored him with a royal decree that made him Da Yuanshuai. Now Ḥakim Khan Törä, in alliance with the Dungans, sought revenge on Xu Xuegong, and they marched with their conquering armies upon the Chinese at Nanshan and fought with them. The nonbelievers could not match them, so they abandoned Little Nanshan and fled into Great Nanshan. All of the *törä*'s armies under the *törä* remained at Little Nanshan, and they reported what had happened.

A response came from His Highness. "If the Chinese have fled," it said, "then your task will not go well. So pass the winter at Ürümchi." It was a bird year. Once they came to Ürümchi, it turned out that the Da Yuanshuai Ṭalib Akhund had been deposed and locked in a house, and Daud Khalifa made their leader. He would not allow them into Ürümchi. So Ḥakim Khan Törä set his hand to battle. The Dungans were victorious. They reported this to His Highness.

Yet Fayż Yüzbashi, Arslan Qul Qipchaq, and Taghay Qirshaq there displayed such bravery as exceeded even the epics of Rustam, Sam, and Nariman.

Throughout, the Lord had granted them grace and help, and these warriors were the means for that help.

* * *

{229} The moment that this report reached His Highness's presence, he ordered General ʿUmar Qul and ʿAzim Qul Pansad to march from Aqsu with 1,500 soldiers to the aid of the *törä* and *parvanachi*. When they arrived, they made a bitter fight and took the Laorenjia's capital, which was called the Laocheng, entered it, and took power. The city of Hancheng too was taken. At this time, the Laorenjia had fled with some Dungans to Manas. Four *pansads* of soldiers now protected and served the *törä*. Sixteen *pansads* of loyal Dungans were ordered to protect the Laocheng and Hancheng, to collect news from the road toward Manas, and to serve as guards. So thirty-five days passed. But the Laorenjia had gone and allied with Xu Xuegong at Nanshan. His younger brother, Ma Shaoye, took 4,000 Chinese as his companions and joined with the Laorenjia. The Dungans prepared 16,000 soldiers, so that they made 20,000 in total, and they pursued those *pansads* down the road, took the Hancheng, and took power. The *törä* and all his cavalry were besieged in the Laocheng, and for four whole months the soldiers of Islam did not stick their heads out at all. (Ürümchi's old city was called Hancheng. When Daud Khalifa was elevated as khan, they built another city near this one, to be a capital for Daud Khalifa, and named it Laocheng.)[2]

And inside those two cities were limitless numbers of bullets, gunpowder, spears, swords, and other implements of war. And there were 8,000 cannons, great guns,[3] falconets, arrows, bows, and quivers lying ready. And there was much grain and oil in the granaries. During the peaceful times, the things that the traders brought from Beijing and stored in the *sarais* and way stations[4] were limitless: all sorts of fine and fragrant teas, porcelains, silks and satins, and all manner of excellent goods from Beijing. When the owners of those goods, the merchants, had been taught Islam and brought into the Islamic community, they had been allowed to maintain ownership of and responsibility for their own goods. Whenever something was needed, it would be taken and made use of. On the king's behalf, the *törä* had recorded the goods and money kept at some of the *sarais*. The remainder was granted to the cavalry. Even the lowest of the cavalrymen each received about 30,000 *tangga* in property and goods.

However, in those days when things were expensive, this was worth nothing, and it was quickly used up. Nevertheless the cavalrymen made shirts, loose trousers, and socks from the silks and satins, because there was nothing else to be found, no cotton cloth, printed cloth, or plain rough-spun.{230} And the quantity of every kind of tea was such that, when the cavalrymen needed to stable their horses, they would stack the brick tea high like unbaked bricks, and use horsehead-brick and lath tea in place of wood, and daub them with mud to build stalls.[5] And in the days when the horses in their great hunger could get no hay, they would smash those bricks into pieces to feed them. And that which they could not eat was trampled under the horses' hooves into nothing.

* * *

Another remarkable event: After the Dungans had built the Laorenjia a city, they had also built a Friday mosque at a spot a hundred paces outside the gate, and raised its minaret to a great height. Now, one night during the siege, a number of Dungans entered that Friday mosque and climbed up the minaret, whence they fired upon the city. No one stuck their heads out, but they were greatly worried.

Ultimately it was decided, "If we meet with these Dungans face to face and fight them, it will be impossible for us to take them. The best course of action is to send a few cavalry and infantry running out there to take them—there is no other way." So together they readied 300 men by selecting ten or fifteen bold warriors from each *pansad.* All of them were stripped to their trousers and their swords and scimitars strapped unsheathed to their bellies, while they held knives in their hands. They soaked some rugs in oil, set them aflame, and sent the men running toward the Friday mosque. It was the month of Aquarius, and the weather was cold, and Heaven and Earth alike were ice and snow. When they reached it, they set the gate on fire. And on every side, they broke down the walls, entered the Friday mosque, set fires, and seized it, winning the day. They took those 300 or so Dungans alive, but bound them together and made them lie on each other. Atop them they piled rugs and felts and such, and sprinkled a great deal of oil over them, setting them on fire and burning them alive.

They sorted out the Dungans, and of the guilty found 340 Dungans, who were made to take responsibility for their crimes, and each of them was tied to a pillar. Each *pansad* of cavalry was given twenty or thirty of those Dungans to use as target practice for an hour, and they shot as long as they could, for an hour. As the Dungans' skeletons reduced to mincemeat, they began to look like raw dough. The force of the bullets caused their flesh to fly away into the air.{231} After an hour, they ceased fire, and it was ordered that the Dungans' relations should come and retrieve the bodies to bury them. They came and looked, but found that they could not recognize them, not by their clothing or by their countenances. They took them all away and buried them. Some 1,500 Dungans had died. Over 300 of the cavalry and infantry had been killed.

* * *

During the siege, they managed by some contrivance to send a messenger to Kashgar. This was when the Ataliq Ghazi had stayed nine months in Aqsu and now returned to Kashgar. The moment the messenger arrived and he became aware of the situation, he placed his eldest son Beg Quli Beg in command of Muḥammad Karim Dadkhwah, ʿAli Beg Pansad, Muḥammad Saʿid Pansad, Nawruz Pansad, Khalman Pansad, Ish Muḥammad Pansad, Bukhcha Bardar, and Mir Karim Qurchi with 5,000 cavalry; and 2,000 infantry under Törä Qul Labar, Muḥammad Raḥim Pahlavan, and Khalil Efendi, with drums and banners; and four great cannons with scattershot and cannoneers under Umar Khoja Ishan; all were sent to aid the *törä.*

This "Boy Beg" [Beg Bachcha, *meaning Beg Quli Beg—ES*] too had readied himself with valor, kingliness, and a military discipline in the manner of the Ataliq Ghazi, and in great pomp he placed his boots into the stirrups of victory and traveled until, in thirty-six days, he came to Toqsun. The governor of Toqsun, Jahan Dadkhwah, served him as best as he was able. The Boy Beg, having been informed fully of the situation, rested there for five days before making a move toward his destination. The Dungans of Dabanchi mostly remained loyal to the Laorenjia, and they rudely displayed their disobedience, but without conquering Dabanchi, it would be impossible to go to Ürümchi. So he devoted efforts to besieging the city of Dabanchi, and after forty days victory was revealed, and the flower of the Boy Beg's intent came into his hand. Over 1,000 Dungans died. Some 250 cavalry were killed.

After the conquest of Dabanchi, they hurried to Ürümchi and to the aid of the *törä*. They maneuvered, the *törä* from within the city and the Boy Beg from without, and great and bitter battles took place. In the end they were victorious and brought the Dungans into the domain. It was the year 1289 [1872].{232} Nearly 15,000 Dungans and Chinese died. Xu Xuegong's younger brother, Ma Shaoye, had turned a somersault and tumbled likewise into the nethers of Hell.[6] Over 1,000 cavalry and infantry had perished. They wrote this joyous triumph up in a proclamation of victory, which they sent to the royal court. But during those days when the cavalrymen were trapped inside, they had been utterly helpless. Prices rose to an extreme. One could not get a *jin* of bread for a *sar* of silver. Their very costly horses too passed away. They broke down the walls [that they had made for the horses], diluted the plaster and adobe in water, and cleaned off the hay for them. Even this was no use. After the conquest of Ürümchi, the *törä* and his cavalrymen were granted leave to return to Turfan[, his homeland].

The Boy Beg and his cavalry stayed on in Ürümchi for two months, and then the general rode for Gumadi with [Khalman] Pansad and their cavalry and infantry. In Gumadi they found another 12,000 strong and capable Dungans. They were at siege in Gumadi for four months. Many bitter battles took place, but in the end the Dungans could not match them, and they bowed their heads in submission. They came out with gifts and were honored with the gift of peace. The Boy Beg granted them their own lands and stayed a few days before leaving. Khalman Pansad had drunk the nectar of martyrdom.

* * *

Meanwhile, His Highness the Badawlat had sent Yaḥya Yüzbashi of Marghinan as an emissary to the Laorenjia in Manas, bearing with him a letter, gifts, and sweet words like candy. When the Yüzbashi arrived at Manas and was conducting the emissarial ceremonies, the Laorenjia, Daud Khalifa, said, "I will not listen to the words of the Andijanis. Nor will I see his emissary." And in his rage and barbarism he had the emissary hanged to death, and killed three other men besides.

When His Highness the Ataliq Ghazi heard that the Laorenjia had taken such deplorable actions, the flames of his fury erupted, and he sent ten *pansads*, under Allah Beg Pansad, Ḥamuddin Pansad, and Akhund Pansad, with 12,000 battle-hungry soldiers. When these arrived, they encountered the Boy Beg, and in this auspicious hour rode until they arrived within the borders of Manas. They besieged the city and did battle. They were several times victorious and several times defeated.

Ultimately,{233} by the grace of the Most Merciful, they conquered Manas. Yet, during the conquest, the Laorenjia swallowed drugs and gifted his soul to the Collector of Souls and his property to his armies, and achieved peace. Over 300 cavalrymen had been killed. In excess of 3,000 Dungans had died. And the Dungans' city was brought into the Ataliq Ghazi's domain again.

* * *

They recorded all of the Dungans—young and old, rich and poor—who lived in the six towns of Ürümchi and wrote them up in a notebook, and they placed a tax on the rich of at least 10 *sar* on each 1,000 *sar*, then 800 *sar*, then 600 *sar* in proportion, which they collected into the treasury. After they had collected the plundered money, each fell into abject poverty, so they remembered their skills and busied themselves with their crafts. In Kashgar, there was a great and famed Dungan named Ganja Akhund, from Salar. He was made Da Yuanshuai over the Dungans in Ürümchi, while the Dungan Yusuf Beg Yasavul was made his head guard. They were granted weapons and banners and sent off to Ürümchi. Once they had arrived in Ürümchi, the Boy Beg turned the Dungan leaders of Ürümchi over to Ganja Akhund, then returned with his armies to Turfan. He had the Word of the Lord of the Worlds recited for the great shrine in Turfan, provided many charitable donations to be given to the mendicants, received their blessings, and rested.

* * *

The governor of Korla, Chief Secretary Ḥajji, had neglectfully let Khatun Khan go and killed several of the Qalmaqs. His crimes were hung around his neck, and he was removed from office and brought to Kashgar, where he was sentenced to three years of rectification and penitence. Korla was granted to Niyaz Muḥammad Toqsaba. When previously the Badawlat had considered Nar Muḥammad Parvanachi one of the old and great officers, and so commanded him to go to Ürümchi with the *törä*, he had raised him to the rank of general so that in battle, even the *törä* was made subject to the *parvanachi*'s commands, by royal and sublime decree. When he came to Ürümchi, he had secretly accepted some cash from Ṭalib Akhund, the son of the murdered Da Yuanshuai, and written to His Highness, "If you make Ṭalib Akhund the Da Yuanshuai, all of the Dungans will be 'students' [*ṭalib*] of Ṭalib Akhund." Consequently, His Highness too became a "student" of Ṭalib Akhund and by royal decree made him the Da Yuanshuai.

However, the Dungan leaders, and indeed nobles and commoners alike, were hesitant to accept Ṭalib Akhund's rule and so accepted the Laorenjia's leadership again. Xu Xuegong too held a long-standing grudge against the Xiao Yuanshuai. That story has been told.

All of the Dungans,{234} noble and common alike, evidently believed that he was

An exceptional master of supplication,
Manifest his miracles and inspiration!

If only Nar Muḥammad Parvanachi had again requested that Daud Khalifa be made leader of the Dungans, and by royal decree Daud Khalifa had been made their leader; then there would have been no conflict, and the blood of many Dungans, infantry, and cavalry would not have been spilled. It was according to this reasoning that Nar Muḥammad Parvanachi was removed from his post in Kucha, reprimanded, and taken to Kashgar, where he was locked up in an icy room to freeze to death. Kucha was granted to Amil Khan Törä.

In Ürümchi and Manas, Arslan Qul Qipchaq, who had suffered a warrior's hardships, was made *pansad*. Taghay Qirshaq was made *yüzbashi* in command of the personal guard. Fayż Yüzbashi had been impudent to his own *pansad*, Maḥmud Beg Urgenchi, so he was reprimanded and stationed at Muzart Pass. But he fled. When they caught him and were marching him off to Kashgar, he ran away again. They caught him, found him guilty of his crimes, and executed him.

There came a royal decree that 1,000 cavalry should be stationed in Ürümchi's Old City. Turdi Quli Dadkhwah was made a general, with four *pansad*s assigned to him, and stationed in Ürümchi. Each year, four *pansad*s would take turns garrisoning it.

In the year 1290 [1873], the Boy Beg returned in victory and glory to alight in Kashgar, the sultanic abode, where he proceeded to the royal court and was honored with an audience with the Ataliq Ghazi. All of the property that had been taken from the Dungans by way of plunder or confiscation—gold and silver, tea and porcelain, silks and satins, weapons of war—was recorded one by one and accounted for in the royal treasury. He related in detail to the royal audition all of those events that had come to pass in the Dungans' city. In gratitude, he was elevated to the rank of commander of the forces over a glorious army and of leader of the forces. And all the other generals and *pansads*, and down to the common cavalrymen, commanders, and infantry, were granted ranks and robes of honor in proportion, and so were honored by this royal gift.

A great festival was arranged as a show of thanks, where gifts of robes of honor and of money were bestowed upon the scholars and the learned, the great sayyids and generals, the commanders and common cavalry, the soldiers and farmers, indeed every person, including the poor widows and the vagabonds. Alms and prayer rugs were given to the dervishes, who recited prayers, and some Quran reciters of well-regulated speech [*murattib*] recited the Word roaringly and in full, in gratitude for the blessings of the pure spirits.

* * *

On the first occasion, His Highness the Ataliq Ghazi appended Ürümchi to the realm and turned back. On the second,{235} the Boy Beg went and conquered it on his own. In the interim, three whole years had passed and much treasure had been expended, so much indeed that the taxes from the Seven Cities were insufficient. The supply of charger horses in particular had been devastated. And because the cavalrymen and infantry, in the days when prices were high, had taken the horses' meat, when the weather was hot, they were afflicted with bellyaches and food poisoning, meeting with the arrows of judgment.

Over 2,000 of the Dungan people, by the sword of rage or of royal justice, or indeed by the command of the Almighty, faced the drowning water of ruin and populated the city of nonexistence. "And when a few Dungans die, there are still more Dungans." And yet the number of those who died in the days of war—young and old, grown-ups and children, boys and girls—could not be enumerated or reckoned by anyone other than the Knower of Mysteries. Muslims were killed as well.

* * *

From the beginning of [the time of Islam] to the present day, soldiers and merchants have plundered the children of the Chinese, Qalmaqs, Dungans, and Kazakhs. Some were sold for a little rice, fodder, or bread, or were given in gratitude into service that could fill their bellies. They would raise the girls to adulthood and take them as wives, or give them as wives to others in accord with the traditions of the Prophet. They would be married and have children. And when those children grew up, they would join the ranks of men and mix with the Muslims.

They would send those plundered children to school to study, educate them, and teach them to write, and others they made into artisans and set to work in a craft. Some of them were made Quran reciters of well-regulated speech, and they attained fine qualities. At that time, nearly every household had one or two "New Muslim" captured children. All of them joined the community of Islam. Beyond the Cities, they would take them away to the country of Ferghana and kingdom of Bukhara, Turkestan, or Badakhshan, or even to Rum or Hindustan. They remained firmly still within the Islamic community, took land and property, and made their livings.

God, in Your perfect power and by Your grace, forgive the sins both great and small of those New Muslims, and of all those Muslims who place the holy verse THERE IS NO GOD BUT GOD, AND MUḤAMMAD IS HIS PROPHET upon their tongues. And on the Day of Judgment, in the Fires of Reckoning—just as the holy hadith says, THOSE WHO SAY SINCERELY THAT THERE IS NO GOD BUT GOD, AND MUḤAMMAD IS HIS PROPHET, SHALL ENTER PARADISE[7]—{236}would that the divine gaze by its glorious alighting give us our share, and that You in Your clemency should open the doors of Paradise before the faces of Your servants. At Your magnificent gate, nothing is strange or wondrous.

BY YOUR GRACE AND GENEROSITY.

2:12 Second Expedition to Turfan

How the Royal Badawlat Muḥammad Yaʿqub Beg Went Again to Turfan; What Happened There; How His Administration of the State Shifted from Ascent to Descent, and Some Unexpected Events Came to Pass; and the Sun of His Fortune Declined Into the West

IN THE YEAR 1288 [1871], which was a bird year, at the end of the month of Gemini [late June], His Royal Highness the Ataliq Ghazi completed the conquests of Ürümchi and Turfan and returned to Aqsu, the seat of the sultanate. There he removed Chief Secretary Mullah Chopan from office and made ʿAbdurraḥman Dadkhwah of Kucha the governor of Aqsu, and Muḥammad Musa Toqsaba his *salamagha* and *kaymakam.* He stayed nine months in Aqsu, then returned to Kashgar, making his second son Ḥaqq Quli Beg a *pansad* and general in command of cavalry and infantry in Aqsu, as well as *kaymakam* in his own stead, while also honoring him with the office of *salamagha.*

In the year 1289 [1872], Beg Quli Beg was ordered to the aid of Ḥakim Khan Törä in the second conquest of Ürümchi. He pacified the marches of Ürümchi in fourteen months and returned in the year 1290 [1873], in the month of Cancer [early July], to be honored with an audience with His Royal Highness the Ghazi. This story has been told.

Peace came in the year 1291 [1874].

But in the year 1292 [1875], two famous Dungans named Dakhu and Shokhu, who were mentioned in the prolegomenon, came up from Lanzhou and Qumul and arrived in Turfan with over 30,000 Dungan warriors.[1] "We wish to offer ourselves," they claimed, "into the service of the king who established Islam, His Highness Muḥammad Yaʿqub Beg Ghazi, and place ourselves at his command, that we all may fight together against the idolaters of Beijing."

* * *

Many Chinese soldiers had come from the direction of Beijing, but the Dungans could not match them and fled hither. Ḥakim Khan Törä sent the soldiers much food and supplies but would not allow them to enter Turfan, instead sending them by an indirect route toward Ürümchi and Manas, where he indicated to them a broad parcel of land and pastures that, if they cared to cultivate it, would bear returns. So they busied themselves with the tasks of agriculture. These Dungans had plundered the people of Qumul,{237} and moved the great and petty men of the city and country, the towns and villages, with their wives and children, driving them before them on foot or horse, hungry and naked, in great distress. Ḥakim Khan Törä showed them compassion and sent food and supplies out to every city, countryside, town, and village, showing them great mercy.

Earlier on, before His Highness had made his arrival in Turfan, the Da Yuanshuai and Xiao Yuanshuai had gone with 30,000 of their Dungans to Qumul, where they murdered the Wang Khan and took prisoner his wife, Fujin Khanim; his son; and several of his men. They plundered, and brought those people to Turfan. These events were recounted earlier.

* * *

A year earlier, His Highness had sent an emissary to London and the Frankish queen, bearing gifts, along with his lieutenant ʿAbduṣṣamad, with a letter establishing the ties of friendship. This she looked upon very favorably, and she sent 20,000 factory-made percussion rifles, rare and fine. Once these arrived, all of them were distributed to the soldiers.

The second time, Aḥrar Khan Törä and Muḥammad Janbay were made emissaries, and they were sent with many presents and plenty of money with the goal of retrieving rifles and other such implements of war. At a fine hour, they had an audience with the Frankish queen and returned to the palace of His Highness with 40,000 fine Frankish double-barreled rifles and pistols, twelve master craftsmen to make rifles, and 200 packets of fine and fragrant tea—and each packet weighed over 100 *jin*. They cut open each of these 200 packets of tea and spilled their contents, making a threshing ground of the royal throne room—it resembled a great pile of chaff. From the generals to the commanders, the *pansads*, the cavalrymen, the soldiers, and indeed all of the stablemasters and footmen of high and low rank were gifted ten dishes, or five dishes, or at least one dish of tea. From this gift to all, not a single servant was left wanting. It was such fine and fragrant tea that all the palace, indeed all the city, was perfumed as with the finest musk, and it perfumed everyone's hearts.

* * *

However, in those days, the desire to carry out another campaign clouded the mirror of His Highness the Ghazi's heart. Then came an emissary from the country of Ferghana and the Qipchaq Aftabachi.[2] "Lend us 2,000 Dungans with cannons, guns, and weapons," the message read. "I am fighting a holy war against the Russian infidels, that I might tear Ferghana from Russia's hands."{238} The Aftabachi had won a number of Qipchaqs over to his cause, refused to submit to Russia, and was hiding out in some remote place. His Highness the Ataliq Ghazi responded immediately, as though divinely inspired, "A war has suddenly come up over in Ürümchi. I have been directing my armies with the intent to ride there in person. As soon as possible, once we have returned safely, I shall go myself with many soldiers to render you aid, for this great war will not be ended with 2,000 Dungans!" With these sweet words he made his excuses and sent an emissary on his way.

* * *

And so, as the rays of the sun of his fortune turned from ascent to descent, and the zenith of his state from the heights of exaltation to the deepest lows, the most noble and excellent man of the age, in the month of Libra, in the year 1292 [October 1875], which was a dragon year, set out in the direction of the great dragon's mouth. With anguished steps he came to Yengi Ḥissar. While he was riding, some of the high officials, led by Jamadar Dadkhwah and General ʿUmar Qul, sent him a letter of well-wishing. "Your Highness the Badawlat," it read, "we would that you would not move from your royal palace. Whatever service you may require, command it, and we, your humble slaves, will go and serve."

"Go and serve the Boy Beg in Kashgar," he replied, rejecting them. "I will go myself." The reason was that he had heard that Jamadar Dadkhwah and General ʿUmar Qul believed that if they did not go, there would be no end to the war. So he did not send them either, nor take them along with him, but instead they rode on their own. Or so it is written. THE RESPONSIBILITY IS UPON THE NARRATOR.

* * *

Then from the Chinese emperor came many grim soldiers, and likewise came the ugly news that they had arrived in Qumul.

His Highness the Ghazi alighted in Yarkand. He heard that the chief judge of Yarkand, Mullah Numan, had done many excessive things that transgressed his bounds, namely that he had constructed a great house and tower in the manner of a royal palace. One night he went in person to see it with his own eyes, and the next morning, he ordered some servants to do the chief judge ill and imprison him, and to remand his possessions to the royal treasury.{239} Then he ordered 200 soldiers to go and destroy the buildings, and in their place to build a latrine. It was destroyed in fifteen days and a bathroom constructed. He stayed in Yarkand for twenty days, and then with great fanfare rode until he came to settle in the palace at Aqsu. At that time, the governor of Khotan, Niyaz Beg, came to see him with ninety presents in hand. Yet he gave him no response, but had him turned away. And the winter weather broke, and the spring days came. Meanwhile, he had been mobilizing soldiers to march to Turfan and Ürümchi.

In the year 1293 [1876], he set out toward his destination and took Niyaz Ḥakim Beg with him as his companion, placing his boots into the stirrups of victory. Gradually they arrived at the palace at Kucha: 10,000 cavalry under the Dungan General Ma Dalaoye, Ḥaydar Qul Dadkhwah, Karim Bay Mirza Shighavul's son Isḥaq Jan Pansad, ʿAbdurraḥman Dadkhwah's son Ḥafiẓ Beg Pansad, Qadir Pansad, Mamur Pansad, Muḥammad ʿAli Pansad, and Pasar Pansad; and 3,000 soldiers under Törä Qul Labar, Kifak Labar, Muḥammad Efendi, Khalil Efendi, Muḥammad Raḥim Pahlavan, and ʿUmar Khoja Ishan; with drums and trumpets, guns and cannons, flags and banners, and such pomp as was mentioned earlier, perhaps even more. They stayed there for a few days, then moved on and camped at Korla.

Now Yusuf Beg Yasavulbashi came to pay his respects, with gifts and a message from the Dungan Ganja Akhund, the Da Yuanshuai in Ürümchi: "Some Chinese have come from Beijing and camped in Gucheng." When he read the message, he sent Taghay Yüzbashi all the way to Ürümchi and Gucheng to corroborate it. That *yüzbashi* went to Ürümchi, and when he returned, he reported, "Some have gathered there—a few lines of scattered Chinese. It is true that they have reached Gucheng as well." At that point, they had moved on from Korla, passed also through Qarashahr, and made their camp in Ushaq Tal. Thereafter they sped from place to place until they came to Toqsun.

While they were in Korla, he composed a command to his son Ḥaqq Quli Beg in Aqsu for him to come immediately, with the names of a series of commanders and *pansads*.{240} By the royal command, twenty-some *pansads*, *labars*, and sergeants under the command of Muḥammad Karim Dadkhwah, Bachcha Batur Pansad, ʿAlimbay Pansad, and ʿAli Beg Pansad rode with 10,000 soldiers. They came to Toqsun and paid their respects to His Highness. By then he had ordered a fortress to be built in Toqsun. He commanded the Boy Beg and his cavalry to be stationed in that city. It was (the beginning of) the month of Leo.

His Highness the Ghazi stayed in Toqsun, while General Ma Dalaoye was sent marching to Gumadi with 1,500 Dungan cavalry, along with ʿAzim Qul Pansad and four other *pansads*. They went to Ürümchi, and ʿAzim Qul Pansad rode from Ürümchi to Gumadi. Ma Dalaoye and the rest of the *pansads* stayed in Ürümchi. Now some Chinese came out from Gucheng and battled with ʿAzim Qul Pansad and shut him and his soldiers up in the city, besieging them. Ultimately the grim soldiers were victorious, and they took Gumadi. They martyred ʿAzim Qul Pansad and some of his cavalry. Ma Dalaoye followed with his soldiers and rode to Gumadi to render aid. Yet he could not reach it but encountered the Chinese at a fortress called Qidaowan, where there was a bitter battle.[3]

As victory was within their grasp, a royal command arrived: "Do not fight the Chinese. Ma Dalaoye is to come immediately with his soldiers."

Once Ma Dalaoye had returned, he was sent marching to Kashgar with some 100 soldiers, with the command: "Go to Kashgar. Take 5,000 cavalry and prepare them. When the time arrives, I will send you orders telling you to come."

Yet ʿAzim Qul Pansad and most of the cavalry who had gone to Ürümchi had been killed. The wounded among them came to His Highness. He did them no courtesy. Then seven *pansads*, including the governor of Korla, Niyaz Muḥammad Toqsaba, Ḥaydar Qul Pansad (Dadkhwah), and Ish Muḥammad Pansad, were ordered to Dabanchi to build a fortress there. As soon as the fortress was completed, all of the troops went in and garrisoned it.

At that time the Dungans called Dakhu and Shokhu came from Manas and Ürümchi and paid their respects to His Highness. They were hosted there for a few days, and feasted and presented with gifts, and when they were returned to Ürümchi, their hearts were gladdened with robes of honor and presents of money.

But His Highness addressed every general and *pansad* and emphasized to them, "Do not fight the Chinese."

{241} Although the cavalry did not fight but stood where they were, the Chinese came to do battle. The cavalry had no choice but to fight for their lives. So they protected themselves, but His Highness asked angrily, "Why did you fight?"

And so, His Highness's purpose suited the Emperor of China, who sent a message saying, "Let us bind the bonds of friendship fast, by your sure faith." Yet this wish of his did not come to be. Some high-ranking Chinese officers fell into [the cavalry's] hands alive. He did not harm them but had them remanded to the governors of Aqsu, Kucha, and Bay; provided them with excellent stipends; and for a time maintained them very well. But later the order came to kill them all.

Inʿam Khoja Ishan was sent as a spy to learn about the Chinese. When he went, he assessed the situation, returned, and reported, "The Chinese are innumerably, endlessly many. One cannot even see where their banners begin or where they end. These must be the soldiers whom the Emperor of China ordered hither." And Baqish Mirab of Aqsu, Ṣiddiq Beg, and Yusuf Beg of the *törä*'s cavalry, and some of the cavalry from the Six Cities, fled into China. And Maqbul Beg and Shahbaz Beg Yüzbashi of the Turfan Begs had sent a letter to the Chinese. This letter fell into His Highness's hands, and he grew suspicious. He had those begs' wives and children, and some other men who were sympathetic to the Chinese, banished and driven off to Yarkand, or even as far as Sarikol.

Another story is this: The Badawlat said, "If I were to fight the Chinese and win, LIGHT UPON LIGHT [24:35]; should the result be contrary, then in those days,

Where could I go?
The roads are long and sandy.

I must be a guarantor for Muslim blood, for their lives and property." So concerned, he ordered that none should say that they fight with the Chinese. They began to retreat from Turfan to Korla. They stayed in Toqsun for four months. In the month of Scorpio, they made for Korla.

At first, as he could not be forced out of Bay and Korla, it seemed like things would end well. Yet his strategizing was out of accord with what the Lord fated, and he walked on his own two feet into the mouth of destruction. He possessed such wisdom and ingenuity as no king in existence had ever possessed, and he ruled the Seven Cities for fourteen years. Everything he did,{242} he did according to his own wisdom. Never in his reign of conquest did he employ an honest minister, nor could anyone bring a justice-seeking word to the attention of his august audition, nor did he intervene on behalf of someone accused of a crime or argue their case. This is to say that, when his fortune advanced, it seemed as though every act simply worked out, whether it were wise or not. Then, when his fortune receded, it seemed that the Divine Plan would work out according to its own design, even if he had been a minister as wise as Bozorgmehr.[4]

Navai's[5] words are apt:

Should fortune recede from someone, all the gold they get is dirt;
If they get ash, it will be silver—should they possess fortune.

* * *

When His Highness was forced to turn back for Korla, he left his beloved son, Ḥaqq Quli Beg, to garrison Toqsun with 10,000 cavalry and infantry, with weapons and cannons, and emphatically told him not to fire upon the Chinese. One day after His Highness had marched for Korla, ʿAshur Maḥram from Yengi Ḥissar, who was his treasurer, removed the treasury, taking some cash for himself, and fled with several men to join the Chinese. Some cavalrymen pursued him, but as they drew near, ʿAshur Maḥram scattered coins upon the road. He left coins for the men pursuing him. ʿAshur Maḥram went, and he encountered the Chinese. All those who served His Highness the Badawlat bit their lips; they had no choice but to bow down. Thus was ʿAshur Maḥram made governor of Yarkand.

* * *

Meanwhile, the Chinese had arrived at Dabanchi. Niyaz Toqsaba held his fire and kept his patience for several days. In the end it was no use. There were some 2,000 cavalrymen and soldiers. About 400 of them formed a column [as though] on exercises, went out the gate, and fired on the infidels. In the briefest of moments, they killed about 1,000 infidels. Yet His Highness's orders to cease fire were coming in then, one after the other. The spirits of the generals and the cavalrymen alike were divided, and they entirely lost the heart for holy war. In the end the Chinese came in increasing numbers, fired their guns and cannons, and took Dabanchi. As for the men of the Six Cities, they were made to lay down their arms. There were some foreign *yüzbashi*s among Niyaz Toqsaba's seven *pansads*. All of these were imprisoned, and some time later, those *pansads* were martyred. The rest were evidently marched off to a Chinese city some three months' journey from Beijing. They stayed twenty years among the Chinese, and some of them passed away. Others returned and left for the country of Ferghana.[6]

{243} At that time, Ḥaqq Quli Beg was in Toqsun. He had all the important things that remained in the granaries set on fire, including the grain, and fled for Korla. The Chinese armies had camped at the place called Yamshi seven stages away. Ḥakim Khan Törä could not remain, either, but came to Toqsun. That day, the Chinese occupied the city of Turfan. Per their orders, the soldiers did not fire. If they had fired and fought them, there would have been collected in Turfan and Toqsun enough food, supplies, fodder, and firewood to last 30,000 cavalrymen for ten years. Instead, the grain in Toqsun was burned and reduced to ash, while the grain in Turfan fell into Chinese hands. The Chinese came to Toqsun five days after hearing that it had been abandoned.

* * *

Ḥakim Khan Törä, the Boy Beg, a general, and their cavalry and infantry came to Qarashahr. His Highness ordered them to come to Korla. They were afraid and would not go, but sent a communique that read, "Would that you ordered us, we would carry out holy war." Yet instead, the response came:

"There was a fortress built in Qarashahr on the far side of the river. Demolish that fortress and build one on the near side." This fortress was completed in short order. The *törä* and Ḥaqq Quli Beg had brought 30,000 cavalry with them, while over 3,000 of His Highness's personal guard of cavalry attended him. It was the beginning of spring. The *törä* and that party remained in Qarashahr for two months.

Meanwhile, His Highness's humors turned and the fire of his rage flared up, and moment by moment it intensified. One day he happened to be fiercely angry at Mullah Kamaluddin Mirza and had him beaten with a stick. The guards did not beat him enough to satisfy his rage, so he went and beat him himself, and kicked him.

Exhausted, he asked for cold tea. A servant brought him cold tea. He took it in his hands and drank. Yet it was not cold tea that he drank, but the nectar of fate. He fainted. He went stiff. He lay upon the ground. His color began to turn green. His body cracked and split. The Quran says, TRULY, WE ARE GOD'S, AND UNTO HIM WE RETURN [2:156]. When this momentous event came to pass, it was the year 1294, in the house of Cancer, on the fourteenth day of the month of Rabi al-Thani [April 28, 1877].

* * *

It is written that His Highness had no trust in Niyaz Ḥakim Beg, and Niyaz Ḥakim Beg even less in him. The two of them would plot to ambush each other but never found an opportune moment. Niyaz Ḥakim Beg was trying to save his own skin, on account of there being so many plots. Now he seized the moment. And he gave some of the servants money—as they say, MAN IS A SLAVE OF BENEVOLENCE—and won them over. One wicked servant{244} had for some time been in charge of bringing tribute from Niyaz Beg. Niyaz Beg had him brought in for an audience, and he taught him a way to kill the Badawlat. He gave him a great deal of money and made pledges to him, saying, "Take a poison that you know—or one that the Badawlat has tried successfully on others—and mix it into a cup of tea. When he enters a bitter rage, bring it in to him. In his anger, he will be unable to detect or distinguish it, and will drink it. Surely this method will do the trick!"

They say that it was this servant's evil temptation and deceitful design, a wicked whisper learned from that devilish master and vilest of teachers,[7] that, when the flames of Yaʿqub Beg's rage flared up, he politely brought him the poisoned tea. Yaʿqub Beg could not distinguish it and drank it. This stratagem was in accord with God's ordained plan, so he was finished.

Others say that, when he took the tea, in the light of his perspicacity he knew what it was. Yet he grasped it in his hand, recited three times, OH, MESSENGER OF GOD!, and drank it down all at once. Always, by tradition, are things done in threes, and so he proclaimed it three times.

Whichever way one does it, be they a lofty king around whom the world turns or a mean and lowly beggar, it is impossible not to drink the nectar of death or to taste the bitterness of life. When one's predestined death arrives, all living beings are equal and the same. As the verse says, FOR EVERY COMMUNITY THERE IS A TERM. WHEN THEIR TERM COMES, THEY SHALL NOT DELAY IT BY A SINGLE HOUR, NOR SHALL THEY ADVANCE IT [10:49], and it can be no earlier (nor later). Whenever that may be, by some cause one will depart from this unenduring world to that world to come. As it says, EVERYTHING RETURNS TO ITS ORIGIN, and this has always been the way of God. And all things belong to the True Agent. GOD DOES WHATSOEVER HE WILL [3:40] and DECREES WHATSOEVER HE DESIRES [5:1].

A king, the shadow of God's grace:
By his light, the Heavens found illumination;
But the light of his star met with decline.
He departed this ephemeral world—oh, oh!

EVERY SOUL SHALL TASTE DEATH [3:185]: none will be spared the nectar of fate, not the prophets, nor the saints, nor any human being. ALL THAT IS UPON IT PASSES AWAY [55:26]: in this inconstant world, dress yourself not in mourning clothes—a way out will never be found. It is clear as day to the minds of the scholars, to the nobles, and to all the children of men that the Ancient (MAY HE BE GLORIFIED AND EXALTED!) in His beneficence forever selects one man from among mankind and—THOU GIVEST SOVEREIGNTY TO WHOMSOEVER THOU WILT [3:26]—finds him worthy to hold the crown and bejeweled turban upon his blessed head, and places him upon the sultanic throne. THE SULTAN IS THE SHADOW OF GOD [UPON THE EARTH]: he is made the shepherd and sultan of humankind.

In the end the Self-Sufficient{245} by His perfect power removes His servants from this impermanent country—MAIDENS, SECLUDED IN PAVILIONS

[55:72]—and sends them to their lofty ends, and inclines them toward those restful GARDENS WITH RIVERS RUNNING BELOW [9:72].

From the *Mathnavi*:

To live a long life is an impossible task;
Life in this world is but a blink.
Kingship will not be forever;
There is no hope in worldly property.
For no one will life last forever;
There is no hope in worldly wealth.
This world is transitory—oh master, beware!
So imagine not eternity, oh friend!
He is the world's light, the Lord Eternal,
And when He directs it, you will disappear.

From the *Mathnavi*:

It is inconstant, this motley world;
No dulcimer to guide the melody.
As kings and glory hold no permanence,
So too do life and fortune hold no hope.
See: Every king who marched to rule the world—
Every one now lies in some dark place.
So, Keyumars and Hushang, where are they?[8]
Their crowns and their thrones, where are they?
What of Jamshid and Faridun, in the end?
Heaven left neither one alive, in the end.
Neither Kayanids nor Sasanids,
Neither Iskandar nor the Parthians.
What of Rustam, what of Sam?
Yazdegerd passed, same as Bahram.[9]
What of Chinggis, Khan of Khans;
Ogedei Khan, who was Qaghan;
What of Timur Shah, Protector of Islam,
Who conquered all the world, sending mighty armies,
Until the whole world knew their tyranny—
Which of them took not what was given?

Which of them was granted a seat at the sun's apogee?
Which of them lay not once more deep in the dirt?
Which of them was given a quaff of the spring of life?
Which of them raised not once more the poison cup?
When the point is made like this,
Which king is everlasting, which king a wretch?
Praise be to Him, Forgiving God,
Throughout this world and the next.

2:13 Merits and Demerits of Yaʿqub Beg's Rule

On the Praiseworthy Qualities of That Protector of the Faith and King of the Seven Cities, Muḥammad Yaʿqub Beg, Which Were the Reason for His Good Fortune; and His Reprehensible Qualities, Which Were the Cause of His Misfortune

THAT SPLENDID PROPAGATOR of the Shariah and friend to scholars, patron of the peasants and common man, subduer of the enemy and the tyrant, kind friend and father, Muḥammad Yaʿqub Beg the Ataliq Ghazi (MAY GOD PROTECT HIS TOMB AND RESTING PLACE!), by the Lord's perfect power was made with a lofty stature and rare nature, in that he was unmatched in understanding and intellect, unequaled in retentive powers, and unrivaled in the administration of government,{246} such as surely has never existed before among powerful kings. He would bestow the balance of his perspicacity upon beneficence to the people, and indeed, no deficiency would have prevented his potential authority from being realized as actual authority.

His domain extended to Gumadi in the east and Sarikol in the west—a journey of a hundred stages; and from Muzart Pass and Zavqi in the north to Qarangghu Tagh in the south—a journey of eighty days. He ruled within these boundaries as a sovereign sultan for fourteen years, and over thirty-four greater and lesser governors, who administered the territories of Ürümchi and the appurtenances of the Seven Cities. In his great modesty and judiciousness, he did not call himself a "sultan" or a "khan," and he had a seal, the size of which was like that of a watermelon seed, on which was engraved "Muḥammad Yaʿqub," together with "Badawlat Ghazi" in reference to his earlier title.[1] But he had beaten the drum of HE AND NO OTHER and had disdained all kings but himself. Five noble kings and khans did he subjugate, and gained their treasuries, weapons, soldiers, and subjects. His countenance was the color of wheat, kindly like a flower, with a round beard. He was of medium height, with a solid build.[2]

Early on he restrained himself within the Shariah's balance. His ways were like those of an upright Sufi or a mannerly scholar, while his clothes were like those of a fine merchant, and the horse on which he rode and his weapons were like those of an officer commanding a mere fifty men. And when he sat, he sat upon a white felt prayer rug or a reed mat, with turban and arms, kneeling as though in prayer. No one ever saw him remove his belt from his waist or sit cross-legged. He never sat in too high a place, nor upon a chest or throne.[3] He would never step into any impure place. Per the saying PEOPLE WILL FOLLOW THE RELIGION OF THEIR KINGS, officials of every rank always did ablutions. And when it came the time for prayers, and the muezzin at the mosque of the royal court read the call to prayer, every one of the muezzins would read it out together at the same time. (When His Highness went on a journey, a muezzin would recite it in one out of the roughly 700 tents that would be brought along.) Even the merchants in every shop would read it out as well, as all of the muezzins of the mosques across town and country called it out together at the same time, none of them too early or too late. From the start of the call{247} until people completed their prayers, they would find comfort as all of a city's muezzins gave the call. All the muezzins in their minarets would await the call of the muezzin in the royal mosque. They would get up in the night, before dawn, do their ablutions, and go to the mosque roof to pray. They stood ready in prayer, listening for the call. The inspector and his deputies[4] would go through the streets, calling, "Oh, muezzins! Be ready for the call to prayer! Be not late, nor early!" as they made their assessments and inquiries. Roughly 500 people would conduct each prayer together.

Among Niyaz Beg's gifts to Yaʿqub Beg was that he made for him a mosque. Its exterior was of coarse, pale yellow cloth and its interior of aquamarine cloth. It was supported by eight poles. From one pole to another it was bound by cloth-winding beams, tent ropes, and cords. Forty servants and forty sweepers were charged with tending to this mosque day and night. When it came time to set it up or pack it away, another 100 (120) guards would be its companions. And when they took it on a journey, the mosque would be loaded onto twenty horses and the prayer rugs on forty horses. Ten rows of men could pray inside it, and each row fit 550 men. The mosque in height was about four or five *gaz* higher than the tent palace. Atop four of the poles were four white domes, the size of a seated man, that shone like the sun and moon, so that they would shine in the sight of all who viewed them, even two or three *tash* away.

* * *

Neither the Badawlat's officials nor his subjects of any rank could go about the streets or markets without a turban. The inspector and his deputies made many inquiries and inspections. If they espied someone wearing a fur hat or cloth cap, they would cut that fur hat or cloth cap with scissors and rip it into pieces. There was no wine, hashish, *buza*, tobacco, singing, or dancing, no forbidden acts or frivolity, openly or in secret, and indeed they were expunged from among the people. The inspector's deputies were very attentive to anything that violated the Shariah. And the useless men—those in rebelliousness and wickedness, the ruffians, thieves, gamblers, carousers [*sögü*], and pigeon racers—all feared His Highness the Ataliq's vengeful judgment and the fury of his keen and wrathful sword, so they busied themselves praying for forgiveness.

If a man accused of brawling happened to be brought before him, he would remand him to his grim *yüzbashi*s and *pansad*s to be made an infantryman.{248} Twice each day he would rule on disputes. The cavalrymen and guards would call out in the markets, "Does anyone have any grievances?" If anyone did, they would be brought in, and if they did it correctly, they would have them testify, hear them, and then send them under guard to the judge. However many disputes or suits there might be, they would be resolved within an hour and in accordance with Shariah. So much did people fear His Highness's fury and punishment that they could bring no slander or animosity to their lips, and the defendants had no option but to tell the truth. Disputes that these days remain unresolved for a year, during the Reign of Islam would be resolved in a day at the Shariah court.

And the old grandees, the begs and aristocrats, were treated just the same as the serfs, miners, commoners, and farmers. One might say that, in that era, the wolf and sheep drank from the same pond, and the pigeon and the falcon hatched their chicks on the same branch.

In the history books they praise all the bygone sultans and long-past kings, such as Amir Timur Kuragan and Mirza Sultan Ḥusayn b. Mirza Bayqara (MAY GOD ILLUMINATE THEIR GRAVES!). Their lands and armies surely were numerous. Yet the Badawlat was never their inferior in magnificence or fortune, while those bygone sultans were not innocent of drinking or forbidden acts. Never did such forbidden acts take place, nor were they even heard of, neither in the Badawlat's government nor among the common people, nor indeed in his entire realm. Perhaps the Rightly Guided Caliphs—that is, the Abbasid Caliphs—were as painstaking in their censorship of drinking and forbidden acts. On this account, it would be no exaggeration to compare the Ataliq Ghazi favorably to the bygone sultans.

In sum, His Noble Highness made such efforts toward the strengthening and advancement of Shariah that not only the Shariah-loving scholars and the imams of foremost guidance but also the administrators and the commanders of the cavalry could never transgress the noble Shariah by even a hair's breadth. Should any slip or transgression among the scholars come to light, they would be afflicted with severe punishment and debilitating torture. When a man in any place became a mullah or a scholar of law, his ancestry and genealogy would not be considered or even regarded, but he would receive a proclamation appointing him as a judge, chief mufti, mufti, inspector, deputy inspector, professor, or imam, in accordance with the hadith, SCHOLARS ARE THE HEIRS OF THE PROPHETS.[5{249}] There were military judges and inspectors trained among the conquering army as well. They would rule on conflicts and disputes according to the commands of the pure Shariah.

When His Highness the Ataliq Ghazi subdued the people of the Seven Cities, per ISLAM DESTROYS WHAT CAME BEFORE IT,[6] he followed the example of the rightly guided imams (MAY GOD BE CONTENT WITH THEM ALL!) and completely eliminated those innovations and evil deeds that had become habits under many years of Chinese domination and per the hadith COMPANIONSHIP INFLUENCES had come to be viewed favorably in the hearts and minds of the people, and those detestable infringements that had come to be as commonly accepted as the Sunnah.

There had been no hammams in the Seven Cities. He had hammams constructed in Kashgar, Yarkand, and Aqsu. And he sent Ẕakir Jan Qari to Mecca, where he was charged with having a lodge constructed in the name of the Seven Cities. He began its construction but did not live to see it completed. He expanded the foundations of the holy shrines in the Seven Cities and commanded the officials in each of the cities to rebuild and renovate their structures. He appointed master craftsmen to ornament them with lodges, mosques, grand and lofty porticos, balconies, fired tiles, and carpeting, and to make them glimmer with plastered walls. He had little forts constructed at the way stations along the roads, with well-proportioned and pleasant buildings there.

One of his acts was to have the lodge and portico at the shrine of Afaq Khoja in Kashgar rebuilt. He specifically ordered its great dome destroyed and had a grand, enlarged dome built out of fired tiles, such a tall and well-proportioned dome as surely had never been built in the Seven Cities, nor even in all the land of Moghulistan. All those mosques, lodges, and grand and lofty porticos are still there now, and they shall persist down the generations. While His Highness's splendor and magnificence have vanished, his buildings and renovations remain as their traces.

* * *

Whenever His Highness was approaching a city, when he was one stage away, he would send a trusted servant to the mullahs who ran the schools and bring them gifts of clothing and copper coins. They would pay their respects and let the schoolchildren out, so that the mullahs and the students would all pay their respects. The mullahs who ran the schools would take their students out of the city to pay their respects. His Highness would dismount from his horse{250} and look upon them kindly like a mother hen.[7] And he would give them five or ten *tangga*, or at least one or two *tangga*, and to those studying the Quran, he gave a Quran, and to those learning the *haft-i yak*, he gave a *haft-i yak*.[8] Upon completing this act of charity, he would mount his horse and continue toward that city, or to his palace.

* * *

Whenever he placed his boots into the stirrups of victory, he would travel with at least 10,000 cavalry and infantry. (And every time he was to ride, trumpets would play, and then he would ride. Whether day or night, this was his rule.) And yet from so many soldiers, no huge crash or clamor, no noise loud or quiet, would arise. His order and discipline were such that no soldier could raise his voice to speak, and even the horses would not neigh. His cavalrymen were not even the tiniest bit lax. They did not allow themselves to rest or relax.

> If you are inclined, go ahead, relax;
> But the people in your country, they will get no rest.

This verse well suits the Ataliq Ghazi.

*   *   *

Of particular note were his proclamations, which were as thoroughly sound advice as a word of guidance from one of the shaykhs upon their prayer mats or a holy command from one of the *mujtahidin* scholars; and his documents and letters, which made one desirous for the advancement of the holy Shariah. I am blessed to record in full upon this page two of his edicts in Persian and one in Turki, and I have copied them from the originals, in hopes that they may motivate to prayer those faithful individuals who may scrutinize them in latter days.

A perfumed letter in Persian:

To the sincere preacher and military judge,

Following the reception of a message from he whose speech seeks justice, who chastises by his tyranny-penetrating scrutiny, and by the pen of the zenith and the nadir; who is the most learned in Shariah in the region of Guma, Muḥammad ʿAzim Beg, which arrived by way of Ṣaḥib ʿAziz Mergan,[9] I have taken stock of its contents, and it was cause for great happiness.

The Lord is the master of this world—the annihilation of which is manifest, and which is a world of the instruments of tyranny. In every moment He is manifest. You did not cast this far from your mind but truly demonstrated, with a heart filled with God's redemption, that it is the true grave.[10] We will never let a request for intercession against injustice go unanswered. One must speak truth, love truth, and walk in truth, which brings joy to the Merciful and happiness to the *mujtahidin* scholars. With regard to the redress of unjust acts, you displayed perfect diligence.{251} These true words are confirmed. 1289 [1872].

Another letter in Persian:

To the jurisprudence-sheltering military judge [Ibrahim],

Following the reception of a joyous message, concerning the arrival of the blessed mullah in the company of Luṭfullah Yasavul, which arrived by the hand of the messenger Muḥammad Mergan, respects were paid.

"The common people of Guma and Zanguya, and Duwa and Piyalma, and all those places, being notified of the royal proclamation, sent their greetings. Your unworthy servant, [myself] the judge, carried out an inquiry in the area of Guma and its territories. The duties of the common people are entrusted to the magistrates, together with the *aqsaqals*.[11] We went, and restitution and duties were decided by mutual consent. The lawsuits, disputes, and bygone conflicts between them were settled and decided, all of which we reported."

Muḥammad Karim Mirza together with Luṭfullah Yasavul of the fortified city of Yarkand submitted a deceptive report concerning the inspection of the area between the region's two rivers,[12] and concerning Muḥammad ʿAzim. On account of this deception and injustice, Aḥmad Yar Sarkar in the region of Quray, per the law, received a royal command, and in accordance with the ruling of the Shariah, he ascertained the truth: it was falsely reported.

You sent a supplicatory report, some humble pages. It arrived at a fine hour and met with grace, and when I found that its contents were clearly and exactingly expressed, this was occasion for great happiness. The elimination of conflicts and expulsion of injustice are more important than all else. It was done in the manner desired.

The second matter concerns the command of the Shariah and its advancement, for which, if a man should die, his reward is martyrdom. You know that you have shown great effort in this regard. Show nothing but high-mindedness, and if a genuine commitment is not displayed, then we will not be satisfied with the salt we have given you throughout. Refrain from tending to yourself—attain to tending to the Shariah.

Now I favor you with clothing and moneys, carried via the messenger Muḥammad Mergan. 1289 [1872].

A royal letter in Turki:

To that shelter of jurisprudence, Chief Judge ʿAbdullah,

After kind greetings, be informed: in these happy and auspicious days, by the grace of God and the fortune of Islam, you presented a petition, in hope that your prayers might find blessed agreement, that comprehensive supplications and perpetual prayers shall be made to the court of the great Lord of Glory in all the territories by night and by day, that the community of constant fortune and soldierly obedience shall be protected in the lamplight of restraint from sin from every disaster of the superficial and crisis of the spiritual, that by the five prayers that ask protection through the granting of victory the needs of the distressed, poor, and helpless common people shall be satisfied through the implementation of the Shariah's commandments, and that this splendor of fortune shall never be lifted from the people of Islam.

{252} You sent your younger brother, Mullah ʿAbdulkarim, with a satchel and a horse. The joyous meeting and blessed arrival took place on the twenty-fifth day of Muḥarram, after the Friday prayer [February 9, 1877]. The contents of the letter underwent thorough examination, and they were reason for gladness and cheer.

It is the favor of the all-encompassing Lord of the Peoples that the radiant light of the sun of Shariah of the great Prince of Men and of the Living, the Messenger of the Merciful, shines upon the people of the Seven Cities. Those equitable in virtue and the jurisconsults of the community gave prayers for this fortune of Shariah and fulfilled their obligations assiduously. Should this humblest creature have any goal or intent apart from the holy Shariah's passage and the common people's ease, by all means should it be a goal for which you set your intent upon the banner and splendor of the Shariah of the Best of Mankind, and you must expend constant and assiduous effort toward the promotion and splendor of the commands of the holy law of the Prophet (PRAYERS BE UPON ITS MASTER!) and the rulings of the licensed jurisprudents (MAY GOD BE PLEASED WITH THEM ALL!). Seek this noble quality, and take it upon yourself to ensure that this quality and its fulfillment be cause for the tranquility of the common people. This transitory world shall pass; the Day of Retribution is the reward for countless hardships. Yet by the sublime compact they are entrusted to you, and to you they hold out hope. Be both behind them and before them. This is our hope, that you will give increase to their sincere prayers and supplications to the Court of the Incomparable, and to their great fortune.

SUCH BEING THE CASE are robes of honor and expenses granted to Mullah ʿAbdulkarim, and to you we have ordered clothing, turbans, caps, and headscarves. 1294

* * *

One more reason for His Highness's ascent to fortune and sultanship was this, which has been thusly written by one of the trustworthy and reliable men:

> We were from Marghinan. My father was a merchant. My father moved my mother and us off to Tashkent, and he boarded us in the house of a feeble old woman while he went off to trade among the Kazakhs. We lived in that feeble old woman's house for a long time. But whenever this old woman stood up or sat down, when she was still or when she was walking, whether it was day or night, rather than reciting PRAISE BE TO GOD! or THERE IS NO GOD BUT GOD! she would say, "Please grant fortune to Yaʿqub Beg! Please bring him honor and respect, and grant him peace!" She uttered nothing else but this.
>
> At that time, I was only eight or ten years old. I was wondering about this, so I asked my mother, "What is this feeble old person saying?" And she said, "This feeble old person has a son named Yaʿqub Beg. She is praying for her son."

{253} In those days, Yaʿqub Beg was sometimes serving as an official governing some land and sometimes as an officer in command of some cavalry. Not long after his mother wished him good fortune, he ascended to the sultanic throne in Kashgar. "He brought great honor and respect upon his mother, as well," it is said. And that is the truth.

This person had asked someone else: "Sheep bear two lambs every year at most. Why are they numerous? While dogs bear seven or eight puppies every year. Why are they few?" And he had received such a good answer: "A dog's puppy does not honor its mother but stands as it suckles. A sheep's lamb honors its mother and kneels as though genuflecting as it suckles. This is why sheep are many and dogs few. Another reason is this: sheep are gentle and polite; dogs are rude and cruel. 'All those creatures that are cruel will see suffering—they give no blessing to their children. All those creatures that are gentle, fortune will be their friend—their blessings too will be many.' " How happy and blessed is that fortunate man for whom his mother and father have prayed! Those for whom their mothers and fathers have prayed will find honor and repute in this world, and in the end truly will find a place in perfumed Heaven. O God, in Your generosity, grant that all people should be blessed with their mother and father's prayers. Amen. THANKS BE TO HIM AND HIS GENEROSITY.

* * *

The morals and laudable qualities of His Highness the Ataliq Ghazi have now been related in more or less every word and deed. Here is the appropriate place to end this little bit of a brief discussion. Were we to relate every single thing in detail, it might fatigue our readers and listeners, and so we have restrained ourselves, contenting ourselves with this much.

And yet, where one possesses praiseworthy qualities, reprehensible qualities await; and where one possesses advantages, disadvantages will accompany them. There is no rose without thorns, no honey without a bee. Every living thing possesses good qualities; naturally, they will be balanced by bad and disgraceful acts. The beautiful and the ugly are a pair, never separated. God's way has always been so—rage's thunderbolt appears with the coming of compassion's rain. This being the case, were we to explain his base qualities in brief, then it would be no surprise if our words should bind a flavor, bitter like an oxymel and sour like the juice of unripe fruit, to the readers' mouth and the listeners' ears, and thus impart pleasure, so that they come to find it appetizing and hunger for more.

* * *

In the history books, in their recollection of bygone sultans, the old writers would enumerate their positive characteristics and negative qualities.{254} Their intent surely was that kings, rulers, and officials in later times would realize that, if they similarly carried out good deeds, their fortune would be long-lasting, their life span would increase, and their fortune would remain until their children and their grandchildren's time, and on the page of the Earth they would leave a good name and a fine impression among the world's people, so that their name would never disappear but be a cause for prayer. And if they should cause evil and bring injustice and oppression, then their life span would be short and their fortune lessened, and their evil impression would be known upon the face of the Earth, and the people would curse such leaders through the generations, and their children would meet with evil days and fall into ruin. So perhaps they would force themselves to incline to the good path and come to land among the ranks of the beneficent. Therefore it appears necessary and fitting for His Highness the Ataliq Ghazi's reprehensible qualities and improper actions to be described in brief.

He became a great king in the manner I have told. Yet he never found any capable, upright, and vigilant man to make his vizier. He handled all the affairs of government himself. Indeed, he trusted no one. If only he had conducted affairs according to the counsel in the words of the Lord God who is without speech and without intent, the Lord of the Signs, AND CONSULT THEM IN AFFAIRS [3:159]! But he acted contrarily to this holy command. He bestowed upon the lordly Katta Khan Törä and Kichik Khan Törä some of the nectar that was meant for him at the end of his own life. The moment they drank it, its effects became manifest, and they traveled from this dusty world to those eternal gardens. He had Wali Khan Törä killed by pressing against a wall. He made Buzurg Khan Törä his own companion, claiming that he came on the *törä*'s orders, though he transported him as a prisoner. After he had conquered the Seven Cities and pacified them, he ordered the *törä* to go on ḥajj and expelled him from the country.

Early on, if anyone committed some crime, he could be convinced to forgive them. If someone did him only a little service, he would still reward them greatly. Later on, even if one paid him great service, he would reward them little, or even on some pretext subject them to brutal punishments. Before, for a bale of alfalfa and a bowl of yogurt, he executed one of his own men. By the end, even in cases where several men's houses were destroyed and the masters of those houses left as refugees, it was not enough to stir him to justice. He ever gave increase to officials' injustices and oppressions. Especially on his later campaigns, and the second time he rode for Turfan,{255} he would not allow a single petition to reach him, nor did he show any concern.

* * *

If a traveler or merchant should come from someplace, their goods would be opened up, inspected, and recorded, and then all of them would be taken to the royal palace. The wealthy owner of the goods would leave carrying the loading ropes and tattered wrapping rugs. But behind them came the tax collectors with their servants, saying, "One must pay the holy alms!" If the wealthy man said, "They took our goods to the royal palace!" then they would reply, "When the money is released from the royal palace, you will get your money. For now, pay the alms in part." And they would collect the alms. They would carry the money to the treasury and take out loans to pay the alms and for their own expenses. When the money was released from the palace, they would get it. However, if the money happened not to be released but disappeared, then they would end up living in the streets in poverty as tramps. And those who divided their inheritances were in the same situation, or even worse.

About officialdom: They sent servants out to the countryside, towns, and pastures to collect money from the harvest tax, and the tithe and alms, in accordance with the land tax. For 10,000 or 20,000 *tangga*, they would go from evening through daylight, and daylight through evening, never letting up, with great haste and business, allowing no delay or relief but collecting immediately. This was an indication of the speed of rule.

To be specific, Niyaz Ḥakim Beg put Khotan to ruin; ʿAbdurraḥman Dadkhwah, Aqsu; and Muḥammad Amin Toqsaba, Bay and Sayram. There is a well-known saying: "Every board has its own peg." Now these governors took the money from the common people. They took all of it to the palace, and they kept it for their own treasuries too. But they placed the blame on the Badawlat. The Badawlat's fault was that he never paid attention to the provinces' expenses and incomes, nor inquired about them. Each governor had about 500 or 600 magistrates, or at minimum, 70 or 80. Every year, they would go out to each town, seize a wealthy man from that town, and, whether he was willing or not, make him a magistrate. As soon as he received his license, he would be made to go out in the company of some attendants to start collecting money. And for an entire year they would collect the alms, tithe, harvest tax, and land tax from the common people, all of those taxes that were allowed by Shariah. Once these were submitted, the villainous attendants and cruel-natured secretaries would go to inspect those unfortunate magistrates. They would record "one" as "10" and "10" as "100," and the magistrate would be liable for 10,000 or 20,000 more *tangga* than was really owed.{256} He would sell off his land and livestock, his rugs and mats, even his cookpots and spoons, for money to give to the officials. If it should happen that these things of his were insufficient, then he would have to provide a document stating, "I am Magistrate So-and-So. I owe so many thousands of *tangga* to the royal palace." The money that the magistrates had first taken from the common people was called "by Shariah"; the money that was later taken, after the inspection, was called "by Truth."[13] And if anyone sought redress, their complaint would go to these same governors. They would use the balance of the money as they wished, enacting whatever tyranny they could.

When those old begs and lordlings who had kept their ornamental plumes and caps and held out hope for the return of the Chinese, or those begs whose hearts were endowed with vengeance and hypocrisy, happened to meet their end, then His Highness would perspicaciously take note, and he would send malignant and tyrannical officials and shame-faced secretaries to the partitions of their estates. Once he sent the secretaries Mirza Qasim Mukhtar and ʿAbdulʿaziz Bukhari to the partition of the estate of Magistrate ʿAbdullah of Aqsu. Those secretaries assessed the price of a single one-eyed peacock feather at 10,000 *tangga*, and that of one Chinese cap at 5,000 *tangga*,[14] meaning that a feather and a cap were assessed together at 15,000 *tangga*, and they collected the inheritance tax accordingly. They likewise assessed the remaining property, calculated one-fortieth of that as inheritance tax and "military fees," and so apportioned 46,000 *tangga* in inheritance tax and military fees. All of the property and livestock was sold for money, and it made 26,000 *tangga*. The rest they begged from relatives and attendants. Even the deceased man's daughter soon found herself among the imperial wives of the royal palace.

On that topic: Stories tell that the young Muslim, Dungan, Chinese, Shighnani, Qalmaq, and Kazakh youths and young women taken prisoner by his command and conquest, and ladies and wives of great leaders, numbered more than 600. Among his wives he also had a "*pansad* wife" named Lady Tokhta Khan. She was in command of the other wives, taught them lessons and etiquette, and prepared them to be suitable for His Highness's companionship. In every city a great house was built and many chambers assigned within it,[{257}15] and in each chamber several women were locked, with some trustworthy young boys assigned to serve them, but also to report on them.

Even as he had made use of them at least once, those women could not control their own carnal desires but pestered those prepubescent boys, and as things came to pass that were contrary to the law, the blood of many women and young boys was let through several cruel punishments, and the houses where they lived were burned down. No other man could have a wife that he had taken, and if he did, he could have no hope of living. When he wanted to, he would gift one to one of his generals, *pansads*, or cavalrymen. And when he went on campaign, they would build chambers of wood atop ten or fifteen carts and lock the ladies inside, taking them along but revealing them to no one. Whenever his heart desired, he would keep their company. Evidently, he entered into matrimony with many of those women by some means that was in accordance with the law.

* * *

It is the tendency of the men of Ferghana to be fond of stallions, and seldom to ride upon geldings. One time, Niyaz Ḥakim Beg made him a gift of tall and fine Qalmaq and Kazakh horses, which were sent to the stables. Soon the Badawlat went to the stables and had several of the horses brought before him, at which point he saw that all of them had been castrated. His mood was spoiled, and he asked the master of horse, "What kind of man would castrate these horses?"

He responded, "There is a man from Kucha named Yusuf Beg who fixes horses. I hear that he went to Khotan and castrated Niyaz Ḥakim Beg's horses. He's back now."

So he summoned the young man and asked him, "I hear that you fix horses. Are you very expert at it?"

"In all the Six Cities," he responded, "there is no one more expert than I at fixing horses."

"How many horses have you fixed?" he asked.

"I have castrated at least twenty thousand horses," he said.

"And how do you castrate them?" the Badawlat asked, getting down to the essentials. He observed the method carefully and sent him away. He turned to his master of horses and asked, "Did you see his method of fixing horses? Can you also do it?"

"If you order it, I will," replied the master of horses.

"In that case," he ordered, "use the method that Yusuf Beg showed us to castrate him with his own tools." And he left the stables.

Yusuf was seized for "the crime of castrating horses."{258} And as they squeezed his two stones with his very own tools, they sliced them open and twisted his two stones off, and threw them away. He died two days later.

* * *

Whenever his fortunes began to turn, the great king's mood would shift, and so would affect the common people as well as the army and servants. The generals and officers or the cavalry would don their robes, mount their horses, spend their money, take their wives, and prepare the foods that their hearts desired. As they chewed on those foods, they could not raise a single doubt or complaint about their ruler to their lips. And they did not respect the "right of salt," but lived in ease and ingratitude. They received their punishments in the end, and suffered the consequences of their actions.

* * *

It is written that, in the town of Fayżabad in Kashgar, as a man was driving birds away and scattering seed, another man came and asked him, "Hey, brother—what have you planted here?"

"Doesn't matter what I wanted to plant," he replied, "I've ended up planting Chinese."

The questioner smiled and laughed. Not six months later, the Chinese camped on that plot and set up a barracks. They say that the Chinese even built a city and settled there.

Wherever two commoners met, they entertained themselves by spinning yarns from truth and fact about the news that the Chinese were coming.

In Kashgar, several men were in a meeting place, and another entered to join them, saying, "Oh, oh!"

"What happened, that you say 'Oh?' " they asked him.

"It's only been 'Islam' for a year and a half," he replied. "Will Islam last for fourteen years? I am exhausted from it going on so long."

Mentioning this brings a story to mind. Once upon a time, three devout worshipers who had answered God's call were heading out on a journey. And on the road their gaze fell upon some discarded old skeletons. "What creatures could these old skeletons belong to?" they wondered. "Let us investigate the situation." One of them prayed, and upon the skeletons appeared flesh, sinew, and blood vessels. Another of them prayed, and they came to life. Up jumped a great and mighty ravenous lion and a bloodthirsty tiger. They had died of starvation. They saw the three devoted men,{259} tore them into pieces, and ate them up. Today these Chinese for whom people prayed are just like that hungry tiger come to life.

* * *

Oh, dear friends! They tell in the history books how the kings of old have always been lauded for their kindness and wrath, their elegance and awesomeness, their aspects of clemency and punishment. Later on, these aspects must be present in kings and governors as well, because kings and governors cannot dispense with kindness and benevolence, and neither can they do without displaying wrath and punishment. A king who is kind and clement but does not believe punishment to be necessary will not achieve peace for the common people, but his country will fall into division and ruin. And if one is cruel and wrathful and does not find justice necessary, neither will the common people find peace, nor even will he, but one by one, the cries of the victims of tyranny—their hearts awake in the early morning—will rise to the Court of the Peerless. When He accepts them, He will make the tears shed from the sighs of contrition into a roiling, bloodthirsty sea, and then such a king, and likewise his servants and family, his standards and flags, drums, and trumpets, will be dashed upon this dirt of contempt and drowned in the inundation of the waters of annihilation, and destroyed. It is a matter of drawing lessons and deriving morals from the happenings of this motley world. SO TAKE HEED, O YOU WHO ARE POSSESSED OF SIGHT [59:2]!

Recline not, honored friends, in fleeting fortune
From you shall it be taken soon, good fortune
Laying your fine body down upon this dark ground
Destroying ostentation, ending the trumpets

When the Lord in His mysterious wisdom fates any ruler or benefactor to possess their rule or benefit, first He takes their excellent qualities and praiseworthy actions, and installs in their place improper deeds and reprehensible morals, turning gratitude for their benefit to ingratitude therefor. He then darkens the sun of their fortune, dims the light of their good fortune, or extinguishes them altogether. He too places the crown of sultanate upon the heads of those high-flying men worthy of fortune and causes the parading trumpets to blow. Be they an exalted king or a poor beggar of no note, Lord grant they that shall accomplish good deeds in this transitory world and exceed the ranks of the well reputed. Amen!

Build in this world a fine construction,
That renown and permanence may remain.
Among the pages remain the good names
{260} Of those who were kings like Chosroës.

2:14 Ḥakim Khan's Enthronement

How the Ranking Generals and Their Troops of Certain Fate Together Seated Ḥakim Khan Törä Upon the Seat of Khanship and Throne of Sultanate, but the Spheres Did Not Concord Therewith, and So, as LOVE OF HOMELAND IS WITHIN THE FAITH, He Departed for His Own Homeland

WHEN HIS HIGHNESS the Ataliq Ghazi Badawlat cast off his transitory fortune and delighted instead in his eternal end, remanding his life to the Harvester of Souls and his kingly possessions to his sons and to the Qipchaqs—or perhaps to the Chinese and the Qalmaqs—then it was that Niyaz Ḥakim Beg and Aḥrar Khan Törä brought his royal corpse inside to lay it out, and they sent a letter detailing the dreadful situation speedily to Ḥakim Khan Törä and Ḥaqq Quli Beg, who were in Qarashahr.[1]

Three days later, the Boy Beg arrived [from Qarashahr]. Up until that point, Niyaz Ḥakim Beg had been worried for himself. So whenever there was a petition, he would take it in "to present to the Badawlat" as usual, and then emerge again to tell them, "His Highness's royal humors are a tiny bit upset. He will be out in a while." They had let no one know and no one enter, and kept this up for three days. That is when the *törä* arrived, with generals, cavalry, and infantry.

Niyaz Ḥakim Beg, Aḥrar Khan Törä, Karim Bay Mirza, Muḥammad Musa Toqsaba, Tashbay Dadkhwah, Atabay Pansad, and all of the commanders and soldiers together agreed to sit Ḥakim Khan Törä upon a white felt and elevate him in the tradition of the sultans of yore, thus making him their khan and ruler. They opened the doors to the treasury and the lids of the chests, and they began to distribute robes of honor, money, weapons, and horses outfitted with fine saddles to all of the soldiers great and small under the Dadkhwah's leadership. Seven days passed in this manner.

One night, the Boy Beg departed with His Highness's corpse and bier. The Dadkhwah and the other ranking men reasoned, "The Boy Beg has taken the Badawlat's body and headed for Aqsu at great speed. What if he goes to Aqsu and secures the treasures there, and then goes to Kashgar and collects those treasures, and then he and his brother take possession of the treasures? Then what if they pay no heed to us but leave for Andijan? Without any treasures, how will we fight the Chinese?"

The Dungan Dakhu and his party had also left for Korla. Now Korla was granted to Dakhu, and the son of the Wang of Kucha, Akhund [Aq] Niyaz Beg, was made his translator and head of his personal guard. This Akhund Niyaz Beg{261} had gained a reputation among the Chinese and Dungans in the Badawlat's service as a translator and head of his personal guard. Bay Muḥammad Charchi Bash was ordered to garrison Korla with 500 men to head Dakhu off, and now all of the armies under the *törä*'s command made for Aqsu. They arrived in Aqsu in short order.

The Boy Beg had come to Aqsu ahead of them, and as he was securing some of the treasures, all the armies arrived, including the Kyrgyz and Qipchaqs. Two days had passed. The Boy Beg took His Highness's corpse and marched for Kashgar. "I am taking my father's body to Kashgar," he had explained in a letter, affirming his good intentions, "to bury it at the Shrine of Afaq Khoja. I will speak with my older brother, and then either my brother will come to you, or I will. We will make holy war against the Chinese." Then he had set out on the road.

Now Niyaz Ḥakim Beg and some wicked, rebellious, malevolent, and ill-intentioned men blew upon the flame of corruption with their wicked breath, and it caught fire. They wrote a letter to Kashgar for the elder Beg, which read, "The Young Beg has gone. His behavior is suspicious. Be vigilant."

The elder Beg read the letter, and he understood its meaning. Yet in his heart he was terrified of the younger Beg. He collected himself, found his strength, and sent Muḥammad Żiya Pansad out with some of his personal guard to greet his younger brother. He had sworn those guards to kill Ḥaqq Quli Beg on sight, and to loot his possessions for themselves. They left

Kashgar and met him at a place called Longkou. They all dismounted their horses, had a pleasant meeting, drank some cups of tea, and then mounted again and reported.

As Ḥaqq Quli Beg was leaving unawares, all at once, a guard named Qajar fired an arrow. It went flying past him.

"What's this bullshit?" Ḥaqq Quli Beg said, and pulled his sword from its sheath. But as he charged them, the guard fired another arrow. He tumbled from his horse and met his end.

They disposed of his possessions and fled. Some of the men of Kashgar learned what had happened, and they buried him in a ravine, leaving a sign there to find it again. It is still known as Ḥaqq Quli Beg Ravine. It was the twenty-second day of the month of Jumada al-Awwal in 1294, in the season of Libra [June 4, 1877].

* * *

His Highness the Törä established himself in Aqsu, the seat of the sultanate, and he alighted upon the throne of khanship. The Qipchaqs and Kyrgyz looted the treasury. They called this looting "The Khan's Pillage." In those days of interregnum, Niyaz Ḥakim Beg fled toward Khotan with his guards. Ḥakim Khan Törä by his first sublime command made ʿAbdurraḥman Dadkhwah the governor of Aqsu. He removed Amil Khan Törä from Kucha and bestowed it upon Muḥammad Raḥim Khan Törä. He favored Ḥakim Bay Pansad{262} with Ushturfan. He gifted Bay and Sayram to Musa Mis Begi.[2] Muḥammad Musa Toqsaba and Atabay Pansad were made *hudaychi*, and he granted them gold. He appointed Batur Bachcha Pansad as general over all the armies. Karim Bay [Qul] Dadkhwah and Mullah ʿAlimqul's son Sher Muḥammad Mirza were made generals. The *pansad*s tallied up the cavalry and submitted a written report. Kifak Labar, Muḥammad Raḥim Pahlavan, and Muḥammad Efendi were made generals, and all of the cannons, falconets, drums, weapons, and standards were assigned to them. There were eight generals, and 3,000 cavalry were given to each, along with their *pansad*s, and they received weapons, horses, and beasts of burden by royal favor, which pleased them.

Now the news began to arrive that Beg Quli Beg was coming from Kashgar on the way to Aqsu, along with his innumerable soldiers under the command of Jamadar Dadkhwah, General ʿUmar Qul, and Alash Bi Dadkhwah. Ḥakim Khan Törä likewise led a number of brave leaders of the forces, and the remaining generals and commanders followed in a column one after the other. He rode with 25,000 cavalry and infantry and traveled until he arrived at the place called Yaydi four stages away from Aqsu.

The Boy Beg's advance guard[3] was led by Alash Bi Dadkhwah. He had established his camp at Chöl Quduq. However, Muḥammad Saʿid Pansad and Ḥafiẓ Beg Pansad were the advance guard for His Highness Ḥakim Khan Törä, and when they arrived, battle ensued. They turned Alash Bi Dadkhwah and his cavalry back and seized some of the cavalrymen as prisoners, whom they took back with them when they paid their respects to the *törä*. Akhund Pansad of Kashgar and his cavalry fled and joined the *törä*'s side, and they went to pay their respects. Joy and happiness came over everyone.

That day they rested, but the next day, as two bloodthirsty rivers and vast armies came face to face, they arranged the ranks and prepared for battle. The fire of slaughter flared up, and it began to rage as both sides suffered losses. The *törä*'s braves turned back the Boy Beg's cavalry, and just as it seemed that they were about to take them, Atabay Hudaychi broke ranks, and with his cavalry he turned away from the *törä* and fled over to the Boy Beg's side. Now the Boy Beg's side gained strength, while the *törä*'s side weakened. Just then, an arrow struck one of the *törä*'s closest companions, Ḥusayn Maḥram, in the head, killing him. The *törä* turned back. Generals Karim Qul Dadkhwah, Karim Bay Mirza, and ʿAli Beg Pansad likewise{263} turned back. Muḥammad Musa Toqsaba, Muḥammad Raḥim Pahlavan, and Kifak Labar passed through Kälpin with 1,500 cavalry and infantry, setting their sights on getting to Andijan via Qaqshal [and Qara Bulaq].

They fought for six hours. About 1,500 cavalrymen and infantry were killed on both sides.

Atabay Hudaychi went over to the Boy Beg's side, paid his respects, and donned the robes of honor. "There were many treasures at Yaydi," he told the Boy Beg. "I fear they may be lost."

"In that case," the Boy Beg commanded, "you march ahead and guard the treasuries."

So Atabay arrived there with speed, and as he was taking those treasures for himself, Ḥakim Khan Törä arrived. Atabay fled. Ḥakim Khan Törä had him captured, stripped, bound, and brought before him.

"What ill have you suffered on my part?" he demanded. "I honored you with the rank of *hudaychi*. But you were ungrateful for it." He summoned a feral, unbroken horse—an untamed, wild horse—and had him tied to its tail, making it drag him, and set it loose. He was torn into pieces until he was no more.

Ḥakim Khan Törä gave the order to pillage the treasures, and they stole them away.

> Complain not about others—by your own work be vexed;
> For you planted the seeds of loss, and loss you harvested.

> The candle burned the moth;
> Indeed it was burned of its own accord.

Ḥakim Khan Törä came to Ay Köl and then to Aral, through which he crossed as he passed over to Ushturfan. Then he went up the Bedel Pass to Issiq Köl, but he did not remain there either, and instead went to the country of Ferghana and took up residence in a place called Asaka [in Marghinan], which was the neighborhood of his ancestors. Nearly 10,000 cavalry and infantry had fled along with the *törä* and Muḥammad Musa Toqsaba.

* * *

Some cavalrymen under the command of Bachcha Batur remained, and they stopped to pay their respects to the Boy Beg, who received them. Several officers, officials, and soldiers who had no confidence in the Boy Beg fled and scattered in all directions, such as Khotan. Some of them went into the desert but could not find their way out, and died.

* * *

His Highness the Ataliq Ghazi was gone. The splendor and currency of Islam went with him. His Highness the Ataliq was known by the epithet "The Fortunate One" [*Badawlat*], so he was named.

God, let the light and love of holy Islam not be forgotten in the hearts of Muslims, but let it be resurrected among the Muslim community. Amen.

Oh God, gather us among the community of the Muslims and of the poor. In honor of the Master of the Prophets and of the Messengers. Amen.

2:15 The Rise and Fall of Beg Quli Beg

The Reign of His Highness Beg Quli Beg b. Muḥammad Yaʿqub Beg Ataliq; the Conquests of Aqsu and Khotan;{264} His Fortunes; and Events That Came to Pass

THE BODY OF His Highness the Ataliq Ghazi was taken by Beg Quli Beg's younger brother, Ḥaqq Quli Beg, who made for Kashgar. On account of the efforts of certain seditious and ill-motivated men, or perhaps indeed by the will of the Almighty, he first sullied himself with his brother's innocent blood, marking himself for chastisement in this world and the next. Thereafter he determined to march upon His Highness Sayyid Ḥakim Khan Törä and kill this enemy.

With over 15,000 soldiers under General ʿUmar Qul Dadkhwah, Jamadar Dadkhwah, and Alash Bi, in the year 1294, on the fourteenth day of Jumada al-Akhira [June 26, 1877], with great pomp and mounted on horse, they did battle with the *törä* at the places called Chöl Quduq and Yaydi. Muḥammad Qabil Yasavulbashi and Pasar Pansad were shot to death. Jamadar Dadkhwah was wounded and relieved of duty when a bullet shot off his thumb. Just as defeat seemed imminent, they achieved victory. Ḥakim Khan Törä turned and fled. (These events have been narrated.)

His Highness the Boy Beg and his high officials traveled until they arrived in Aqsu, the seat of the sultanate, and he was installed upon the throne inherited from his father. Consequently, Aqsu, Kucha, and Ushturfan all came under the Boy Beg's rule. All of the commanders and *pansads* who had been loyal to the *törä* were chastised, and some of them imprisoned, while others were expelled to Kashgar and Yarkand. Now that the affairs of Aqsu were set in order, he appointed ʿAbdurraḥman Dadkhwah as its governor. He removed Muḥammad Raḥim Khan Törä from Kucha and granted it instead to Amil Khan Törä. Muḥammad Baba Toqsaba in Ushturfan had previously been removed from office, taken to Kucha, and imprisoned. Now he was brought back from Kucha, and his domain returned to him.

Amil Khan Törä went to Kucha, but he was idle and inattentive. Amil Khan Törä had placed five *pansads* as a garrison at Bügür, under the command of Qadir Beg Pansad of Kucha, Mamur Pansad of Shahyar, and Alash Dadkhwah's younger brother, Yoldash Bi Pansad. These *pansads* considered the situation unfolding around them, and they formed an evil intention. They conspired together and decided,{265} "It was we who led the rebellion in Kucha in the first place—we who killed the Chinese and became the masters of their domains. Now the Chinese have emerged again and come to Turfan. Today or tomorrow, they might come to Kucha. Dakhu and Shokhu seem to be great and powerful enemies of the Emperor of China. So let us wrest Kucha from the Andijanis and rule it ourselves, and if we should capture Dakhu and Shokhu, and make of them a gift to the Chinese, it should be no surprise if that were reason enough for them to scratch out our former crimes with the pen of forgiveness." That night, they broke camp at Bügür and set out on the road for Kucha. They came to an inn in a place called Toqnay one stage away from Kucha, where they gathered 2,000 irregulars from the mountain villages. They marched from there through the night and surrounded Kucha on all sides.

When Amil Khan Törä was told, he said, "Would Qadir Pansad dare? Don't talk nonsense." He ignored it and went back to sleep.

There were a thousand Dungans and soldiers in Kucha, as well as guns and cannons. Qadir Pansad sent someone in secret and won them over to his side. Then dawn broke. When the *törä* awoke and opened his eyes, the tables had already turned. He was shocked but prepared for battle. Both sides fired shots. Some 180 of the *törä*'s men perished, including ʿAbdullah Beg. The *törä* could not match them, so fled for his life to Aqsu. Qadir Pansad seized Kucha for himself.

Not a month had passed before Qadir Pansad learned that Dakhu and Shokhu had shifted their men from Korla and were coming toward Kucha.

He readied 5,000 men and went to battle them at Qara Yaghach and Öchqara. Some 300 men lost their lives, and the Dungans won. The soldiers of Kucha could not match them but scattered and fled. Qadir Pansad, to save his own life, hid away. The Dungans seized Kucha for themselves. Witness the power of the Potent: within the space of one month, it passed from Amil Khan Törä to Qadir Pansad, and the Dungans took it from Qadir Pansad, but then it fell at last to the Chinese.

This is all to say that this world is a decrepit, white-haired old woman, and yet it sees itself as young and fair, so every day it reaches its hand out to another husband and embraces him. This is its way, that every night it gives its heart to the love and kindness of another man,{266} while all that time it is beating the *shadiyana* to announce the sultanate in some other place, while the sermon is read every Friday in some other sultan's name. Since the days of old, this disordered world has presented such an ephemeral turn to every honored leader.

* * *

As Niyaz Ḥakim Beg fled Aqsu, he went to Khotan, where he sounded the drum of rebellion and beat the rhythm of I AND NO OTHER.

The Boy Beg heard about this, so he brought affairs in Kashgar to an end and prepared to go and rebuke Niyaz Beg in Khotan. He rode with 24,000 soldiers in total, outfitting all his cavalry with guns and cannons, drums, standards, weapons, and fine horses, and under the leadership of General ʿUmar Qul Dadkhwah, Mirza Aḥmad Qushbegi, Jamadar Dadkhwah,[1] Alash Bi Dadkhwah, the Dungan General Ma Dalaoye, Sher Muḥammad Pansad, ʿAlimbay Pansad, Akhund Pansad, and Abulqasim Pansad. They traveled magnificently in accord with His Highness the Ataliq Badawlat's sultanic rules until they came to Yarkand. At Yarkand they were joined by the Shighavul Dadkhwah and 1,000 men, and then they marched to the place called Ziba at the border of Khotan.

Niyaz Ḥakim Beg too heard what was happening, and he placed his younger brother, Muḥammad Amin Lashkarbashi, and his son in command of 10,000 cavalry and infantry and 20,000 fanatical irregulars, to march as 30,000 men to battle against the Boy Beg. Both sides drew up in formation, and a battle ensued. Most of the disorganized club wielders raised from Khotan perished, and in the end the Boy Beg's cavalry were victorious. Muḥammad Amin Beg fled in alarm with his panicking men. Niyaz Ḥakim

Beg was ready. When he learned what had happened, he fled toward Keriyä and gave the order for his cavalry, infantry, and irregulars to loot the palace's treasuries.

The Boy Beg won the day, but when he learned that Niyaz Ḥakim Beg had fled, he ordered Abulqasim Pansad and Mirza ʿAli Pansad to go ahead with 800 cavalry and seize him, while the rest marched from Ziba. Once they had won in Khotan, he sought advice from his commanders, Mirza Aḥmad Qushbegi, ʿUmar Qul Dadkhwah, Jamadar Dadkhwah, and the Shighavul Dadkhwah. "Now that we have taken Khotan," he said, "let us carry out holy war against the Chinese. Shall we go to Aqsu through the towns [of Khotan]? Or shall we go first to Kashgar [or Yarkand], and then proceed from there? What do you say?" He opened it up to discussion.

As they all lowered their heads in thought, saying nothing, the Shighavul Dadkhwah spoke up. "The clime of the emperor is larger and greater than any other," he said. "Your father knew this,{267} so he did not fight with them. Some good warriors came back from the battle at Yaydi, and they left for their own homelands. Some others lost their lives. Now the best course of action is this: that we choose not to fight with the Chinese and not to spill Muslim blood. Let us retrieve our wives from Kashgar, make our way up the mountains from Yarkand, and go into the service of the Caliph of Rum, or else make pilgrimage to the Two Holy Cities."

The Boy Beg looked at the others. "What do you say?"

"Our brother the Dadkhwah's plan is a good one," they said. "We agree."

The Boy Beg found it agreeable as well. "In that case," he said, "as we return from Khotan, let our wives come to Yarkand," and he sent ʿAshur Muḥammad Sarkar to retrieve their wives. He himself entered the city of Khotan and made a spectacle of his arrival. Then he granted Khotan to Saʿid Beg of Kucha, with full command of all affairs of state, and set the affairs of Khotan in order. On the eighteenth of Shawwal [October 26, 1877] he departed, and he arrived at Yarkand. Their wives had likewise come from Kashgar.

However, as soon as their wives had left Kashgar, the general in Kashgar, He Dalaoye, broke the bonds of submission, and now he was preparing for rebellion. When Abulqasim Pansad had been sent in pursuit of Niyaz Ḥakim Beg, those *pansad*s had decamped, made a sixteen-day journey in only four days and nights, and came to a city called Niya. There Niyaz Beg's younger brother, Muḥammad Amin Lashkarbashi, and his cavalry finally stopped and did battle. Some 200 men from either side perished. Mirza ʿAli Pansad was hit by a bullet, and he drank the nectar of martyrdom. Now, as they marched four days' journey in only one, many of the cavalrymen's horses grew tired in the desert and halted there. In the end those *pansads* had to turn back, while Niyaz Beg traveled toward the Chinese.

When Abulqasim Pansad and his party returned to Khotan, Saʿid Ḥakim Beg hatched an evil plan with the intention to capture and imprison them. In the end, however, the *pansad* joined his cavalry, and they remained together, so that they passed unmolested to Yarkand, where they greeted the Boy Beg. And they reported the actions of the unfortunate Saʿid Beg. The Boy Beg sent men and labeled Saʿid Beg a villain, proclaiming his crimes and removing him from office. The former governor of Bay, Muḥammad Amin Toqsaba, had been made governor of Qaraqash, and now Khotan was granted to him.

* * *

Meanwhile, his Highness the Boy Beg had made General Bachcha Batur commander over all of the generals in Aqsu. Ḥajji Artuq Mirza was made general of all the infantry,{268} and guns and cannons, drums, and weapons were given him. In total, there were 5,000 cavalry and infantry in Aqsu. This was when Qadir Pansad in Kucha had rebelled and taken Kucha for himself. Amil Khan Törä came fleeing toward Aqsu.

Also around this time, as he planned to bring the governor of Ushturfan, Muḥammad Baba Toqsaba, to Aqsu, seize Qadir Pansad, and take control of Kucha, he sent ʿIsamuddin Pansad at the head of four other *pansads* to Qara Yulghun. His plan was that they would enter Kucha via Tajik.[2] He sent five other *pansads* with an army to Yaqa Eriq, intending that they would take the highway into Kucha, seize Qadir Pansad, and conquer Kucha.

While they were making these plans, the news came that the Chinese had invaded and occupied Kucha, while the Dungans had fled into Sayram. The foreign *pansads* in Kucha had arrived at Yaqa Eriq ahead of the Dungans, and when they encountered each other there, they all joined forces to fight against the Chinese. But the Chinese were victorious, and they began to march along the highway. Those *pansads* fled along the road through Qizil Bulaq and came to Aqsu, where they reported what had happened to General Muḥammad Baba Toqsaba. Everyone was in shock, and they became suspicious of ʿAbdurraḥman Dadkhwah in Aqsu, whom they imprisoned. They seized the head of his personal guard as well, labeled him a criminal, and sent him to Kashgar.

Ultimately, everything that they had planned was turned on its head, and they were thrown into confusion. At the bedtime prayer, Muqim Jan Ishbashi was made the governor of Aqsu. Through the night, they recorded everything in the Dadkhwah's treasury. Dawn broke. Their cavalry scattered. The general and *pansads* said, "We will fight with the Dungans," and they set out on the road. One after another, bits of news came, and they heard that the Dungans had fled toward them, and now they had arrived; and that the Chinese came in tumultuous pursuit, marching nearer. The general and his party could not remain but set out on the highway, and as they did so, they could neither go and face the enemy nor go back into the city, so they had no choice but to set out for Kashgar. By now it was nearly noon. The Dungans came like ants, but neither did they enter the city, but passed it by to head for Ushturfan. They marched for thirty stages before they made camp. That night, the whole Dungan people passed them by.

When the dark of night was lifted and the morning appeared, then like a false dawn the dark army came into view. In the year 1294, the Year of the Horse, on Wednesday, the seventeenth of Shawwal, in the month of Cancer [October 25, 1877],{269} the dark hooves of the dark horses of the Emperor of China's dark armies fell upon Aqsu's ground.

* * *

That general and his cavalrymen, who had lost all hope for Aqsu and Kucha, bowed their heads in submission to the command of that Lord of Lords, the Beneficent. Some of them fled for their lives through Ushturfan toward Issiq Köl. Others went to Kashgar and Yarkand. Now as the Boy Beg was receiving news of these events, dissension broke out among the cavalry, and some fled to Kashgar and others to Yengi Ḥissar. The Boy Beg's rage was inflamed, and he went to Yengi Ḥissar. There he killed Akhund Pansad, who was one of those who had fled, and had many of his personal cavalry hanged, while he had others imprisoned. The remaining cavalrymen, thus controlled, fell in line again.

Now he decided that he would take care of the New Muslim He Dalaoye in Kashgar and then carry out holy war against the Chinese, so he rode to attack He Dalaoye. At this point, Alash Dadkhwah was besieging him. The

Boy Beg and all his generals, cavalry, and infantry were battling them with all their might, because all of the treasure, and all of those men's wives, families, and property, were in Kashgar's New City. All of them were now held by He Dalaoye and his Chinese.

They bound together branches to make tall ladders, built mantlets, and worked as much and as hard as was possible. Twenty-eight days passed in this way, but they could not achieve victory. On the ninth day of Dhu'l-Hijjah [December 15, 1877], they dug holes beneath the walls and towers, placed gunpowder inside, and though they pledged that the next morning they would light it on fire and take the city, that next morning the Chinese arrived. There was no time to see to the wall or to any other matter. They were forced to set out on the road to Andijan.

Mirza Aḥmad Qushbegi stood at the Sand Gate with over 1,000 cavalry. He permitted the cavalry and the foreign merchants to leave in peace, showing them great mercy. After the Chinese soldiers entered the city, Mirza Aḥmad Qushbegi and his soldiers left it and stole away to Andijan. The Chinese became masters once more of their ancestors' domain.

Of such a great and glorious king no legacy or trace remained, none save for stories. One may derive a lesson or moral from how these strange events came to pass.{270} The Quran says: SO TAKE HEED, O YOU WHO ARE POSSESSED OF SIGHT! [59:2]

The Lord, who is the MASTER OF SOVEREIGNTY, [3:26]
To whomsoever He gives THOU GIVEST SOVEREIGNTY,
What right does a man have, to take SOVEREIGNTY?
King of Kings that He is—THOU WRESTEST SOVEREIGNTY.

Whatever the Creator desires, so it is.
That which His creations desire, where is it?

* * *

Unsleeping God's (BLESSED BE HIS KINGSHIP!) breath of fortune suddenly blew, and the lamp of Islam's light was extinguished from over the people of the Seven Cities. From the east, the dark army kicked up the dust of tyranny, and it was as though a black sackcloth covered the people of the Seven Cities' heads. Suffering came upon the pious Muslims like a great catastrophe. But those who only looked like Muslims—the hypocrites—were joyous and laughing as though at a great celebration, and they gained a happiness without end. Now that, by the will of the Creator (BLESSED BE HIS KINGSHIP!), this was how things were fated to be, it was clear as day to one and all that there was no choice but to submit to their command. And so, reluctantly, the great and pious scholars and the high-ranking officials grudgingly bound their belts and prepared themselves to serve.

(Never fall content with what the Lord has given—
The Lord Himself gifted it.)

The kings have left, gone is the rule of all guardian kings;
Long now, all government has been in rotten men's hands.
I asked why this was. Men of wisdom said to me:
"If you knew this world—and all its shameful people!"
Wounded they are, the wise men's hearts, by this grief,
All of this world's vice and wanton, all of those with laughing mouths;
The wise men's heads would never fit in easily anywhere,
Their property, all their instruments, in disarray.
The common people are a flock of sheep, and their shepherd to watch over them, Chinese;
The wolves now have their way—ravening beasts among all the flock.
They hid themselves (like the phoenix), the wise men, thinking themselves so clever;
Their debasement became so clear—all their words are drunkenness.
Fear—if the beauties of Paradise are what you need, oh, slave;
Lament—high Paradise is for all fearing men.

2:16 Niyaz Ḥakim Beg

A Brief Account of Niyaz Ḥakim Beg's Treachery, His Unworthy Deeds, and Their Consequences

{271} NIYAZ ESHIKAGHA Beg came from a family of well-heeled farmers in Yarkand. From the time of his youth, Niyaz was a servant to Chinese officials. As it is said, YOU ARE THE COMPANY YOU KEEP, and as Niyaz Beg climbed the ladder of officialdom, he acquired the disposition of the Chinese. When he was the deputy governor of Yarkand, the uprising broke out across the Seven Cities. In Yarkand he served ʿAbdurraḥman, and then the Dungans in kind. When the Khojas of Kucha came to power, he served at their pleasure. When Yaʿqub Qushbegi rose to power, Niyaz served him in turn.

Because of Niyaz's close friendships with boys and his secret comings and goings, the headman Yaʿqub of Kucha was alarmed. He objected to Niyaz, "You're happy to consort with everyone indiscriminately. You don't serve a single master. This is no good."

"I have no way of knowing who will gain control of this country," Niyaz countered him. "For this reason, I serve all of them alike. If you should happen to ascertain the victor and inform me of your determination, then I'll no longer need to go from door to door."

From this brief introduction, it ought to be clear to the reader that, when the Creator of the World in His ancient wisdom created Niyaz Beg, He endowed his nature with covetousness, so that the reward of covetousness in this transient world would be apparent to all. This will be discussed shortly. God willing—He is the Patient!

* * *

Yarkand fell to the Ataliq Ghazi. He granted it to his head guard, Muḥammad Yunus Jan. Niyaz Beg was made head guard to him in turn. This was supposedly so that Niyaz Beg would learn the ways of Islam. Then the Ataliq Ghazi subjugated Khotan. He made Niyaz Eshikagha Beg the governor of Khotan in his own right, and made his younger brother Muḥammad Amin Beg the commander of the forces stationed in Khotan, with eight battalions of 500 men each. Niyaz Beg was the governor of Khotan for twelve years.

From early on in his time as governor, and throughout his twelve years there, every Friday after prayers, one of his messengers would come and present him with twenty *yambu* of gold dust. It was never less and never late. Twice a year,{272} there was a great gift-giving ceremony. This has been enumerated. We will refrain from repeating it.

One time, on some pretext, His Highness sent a letter of appreciation to Governor Niyaz Beg. It turned out to be a particularly kind letter, which read, "As soon as you read this letter, find a driver and a guard, and come to my court in secret by night. Do not tell anyone. You will be received at such-and-such time. We will talk."

Niyaz Beg immediately located a driver and a guard. When he arrived at the appointed time at the gate of the New City of Kashgar, two guards were waiting with lanterns in anticipation of his imminent arrival. He dismounted and entered to meet with His Highness, while they took the horses into the stable. They spoke for about four hours, and then he left. Niyaz had with him two little chests filled with 3,000 or 6,000 *sar* of pure gold bars, just about a whole gold mine's worth. That night he carried them inside, held an audience with His Highness, and received his royal favor. Niyaz stayed for two nights and returned to Khotan.

Per His Highness's command, it was ordered than an atelier be constructed in Khotan. Niyaz Beg directed the construction himself. Its craft and its management were exceptional. Its weavers specialized in producing silk rugs, the like of which had probably never been made before. This atelier produced gifts even finer than those made by His Highness's craftsmen. They made four nines of silk rugs decorated with prayer niches and gifted them to Mecca. They prepared another four nines of such rugs, which they sent to

Medina. The weight of each rug was no less than 100 *jin*. They made another nine of silk rugs and a nine of wool rugs, and gave them to the Shrine of the Companions of the Cave. They demolished all of the shrines, mosques, and lodges in Khotan, and then rebuilt and expanded them. The city's Friday, festival, and neighborhood mosques were plastered and decorated with fired tiles. They dug cisterns and wells at every station along all of the roads leading to Khotan, and they built a bunch of domes, chambers, mosques, stables, kitchens, and inns. They settled people here and there to reclaim land.

His Highness singled Niyaz Beg out of all of the officials in his realm, esteeming and respecting him above all others.{273} This is because, between Muḥammad Yaʿqub Beg Ataliq from the land of Ferghana and Niyaz Ḥakim Beg from the country of Moghulistan, neither was the superior or inferior of the other in counsel nor in etiquette. "As they say, EVERYONE SEEKS OUT THEIR OWN KIND." This means, "They suit and equal each other in rank." When they saw each other, it was as though they blended together like honey and butter, each annihilated into nothing. Yet each was obsessed with assassinating, ambushing, or plotting to eliminate the other, although they could never find the opportunity. His Highness the Badawlat put so much toil and struggle into his conquest of the Seven Cities, and into his control of them, that the two-tongued pen struggles to describe it. He enjoyed entertainment and debauchery beyond description with Governor Niyaz Beg and his children. It was as if Yaʿqub Beg had come from Ferghana just for Niyaz Beg.

In twelve places, they prepared grand buildings with fired tiles, great gardens, and large pools. They lined the cisterns and the channels, through which water ran into the gardens, completely with tiles and daubed them with plaster to decorate them. Every day they would go out with the children in boats onto the pools, and they would revel in entertainment, music, and song.

He had one special garden made, which he called the "Speckled Palace." They dug out a plot of land[1] to the depth of a spear's length, threw away the soil, and had high walls of fired tiles built around it. He had a cloth made of silk in the same size as this garden and had tall pillars set up. From pillar to pillar he had silk threads strung, and then covered the opening at the top with silk and enclosed within it pairs of birds and wild and domestic animals. In that garden, they raised all sorts of trees and plants never encountered in the countryside: every kind of tree, fruiting or not, from orchard and wilderness; roses and eglantines; and everything down to the desert grass and the thornbush. Every day they would feed a few bags of grain to the herbivores, and they would slaughter a few dogs or donkeys{274} and toss them to the carnivores—the tigers,[2] wolves, foxes, and the like. They would go and entertain themselves there whenever they wished.

Whatever Niyaz Beg desired to do, it was reason enough to do it. He governed Khotan in such a way that no man was free to question him. None of the people of Khotan, man or woman, from ages seven to seventy, could ever be free from their service to Governor Niyaz Beg and the monarchy. Their tyranny grew so great that it was impossible for it to grow greater. If we were to describe it in full, then the story would go on and on, and we would derive nothing from it but sadness. The very description of it was beyond the comprehension of the intelligent and the contemplation of the wise. Though farsighted masters would place the head of scrutiny to the knee of cognition, plunge themselves into the river of recollection, and there bob up and down, nevertheless they did not summon into view the shores of their desires or the banks of their goals. And when the gracefully moving pen dove into the inkpot sea, it could not raise its head again.

All the cunning at the top of Niyaz Beg's head amounted only to the barest thread, the slightest trace of the rays of the Badawlat's sun of fortune. Let the Ataliq Ghazi's greatness be evident from this. Nevertheless, Governor Niyaz Beg's scheming won the day, and in the end he vanquished the great Badawlat. To put it simply, however much benevolence and faith His Highness the great Badawlat possessed, Niyaz Beg's treachery was a hundred times greater.

Once, Governor Niyaz Beg sent an uncle of his from Khotan to Lanzhou through the dunes of Lop to send his regards to the Chinese officials and to invite one of them back. For months, through the desert dunes, through many tribulations along the trackless road, at last he brought a letter bearing news. Niyaz read the letter, heard the report, and debriefed his uncle so as to get a good understanding of the situation. Then he had a hole dug in a house, closed up its mouth with debris, and tossed felt cushions over it. Without letting on,{275} he brought that uncle to the house and invited him to stand by the hole. The uncle lost his footing and immediately fell to the bottom of the hole. Right away, they brought in dirt and sand on sledges, filled up the hole, and buried him. A guard found out, and he reported the matter to His Highness the Badawlat. When the Badawlat read the report, he favored

Governor Niyaz Beg with a letter. "A certain guard has betrayed you," it read, "and sent a report. I did not believe a word of it. You shall punish this guard." As soon as he received this letter, Niyaz Beg had the guard killed.

Later on, His Highness the Ataliq Ghazi passed on to the eternal world, and Niyaz Beg went to Khotan. There he illuminated the hidden sedition in his nature and openly pounded his drum of rebellion. When the Boy Beg came to Khotan, Niyaz Beg sent his younger brother Amin Beg and his son out to battle them at the head of 30,000 men. At the city called Ziba, fighting and killing broke out, and blood was shed unjustly. The soldiers of Khotan could not stand their ground, so they fled. Back in Khotan, Niyaz Beg had gathered his men, who were waiting and preparing their cannons.

When Niyaz Beg received the news that his army had fled the field, he plotted to light the cannons' fuses and massacre Khotan's people and soldiers. When Niyaz Beg's officers and attendants found out about this plan, they wept. Niyaz Beg ceased his unworthy scheme and instead issued an order for pillage: "Whether you are a soldier or a civilian, go get what is in the palace and the treasury. Divide it up and take it." With his trusted men and nobles, he packed up his valuables and ran for the hills. He took the Keriyä road toward China, hoping they would treat him favorably, and then made his way straight to Korla. At every stage along the road, there would be horses stabled. So at each stage Niyaz Beg would ride a fresh horse, but when they were exhausted, he would cut their tendons and put them out of commission. This is how he managed a sixteen-day journey in four days. While they fled, they would kill every Andijani traveling the road right where they were, whether they were cavalrymen or merchants. There were thirty foreign cavalry on guard with Tash Bachcha. First Niyaz Beg's party plucked out their eyes. Then they killed them all.

Abulqasim Pansad pursued them across the desert with 800 cavalry. Most of them stopped to rest their horses, so about 400{276} cavalrymen arrived in the city of Niya. It was a bloodbath. Some 200 men were lost from either side. Because of their small forces, they were unable to seize victory. We have told this story already.

In short, Niyaz Beg fled in such a way and with such intentions, and eventually arrived at Korla, where he joined with the Chinese. At that time, per the orders of the Qazi Islam Chief Justice Mullah ʿU̱sman (MAY GOD HAVE MERCY ON HIM AND FORGIVE HIM!) and all of the imams, together with the scholars of Khotan, a decree was issued concerning the infidelity of Niyaz

Beg on account of his rebelliousness and hypocrisy. WHEREFROM WE SEEK REFUGE IN GOD.

* * *

Around that time, the Chinese commander Lushi Daren was in Bay and Zongtong Daren in Aqsu.[3] Niyaz Beg brought some of his silver and gold to the Chinese. He sent a petition to Lushi Daren and Zongtong Daren. They commanded him to come to them, so that pariah Niyaz Beg appeared before Lushi Daren, then went to Kashgar. At this time, Lushi Daren was in Aqsu and Zongtong Daren in Kashgar, while Dong Daren[4] was in Yarkand.

After they met and Niyaz Beg got some rest, he told the officials, "I have been the governor of Khotan for twelve years. During that time, I have gathered twelve years' worth of taxes for the Great Khan from the people of Khotan and hidden it away. If you would command it, I would take what I have hidden, which rightfully belongs in the Great Khan's treasury, and hand it over to the army. Nevertheless, I appeased the '*Lao* Padishah' by giving him even more than this."

When Zongtong Daren heard this, he asked, "What was it you used to do?"

"I was a deputy governor of the fourth rank in Yarkand," he answered.

"You are a terrible person!" said Zongtong, disapproving. "He had faith in you and raised you up. He made you the governor of a great city, and yet you betrayed the lord who gave you 'salt.' You are not such a good person after all."

Finally Niyaz Beg brought the officials to Khotan, where he revealed the hidden treasure hordes one by one. He presented each as "the soldiers' reward."

One such hidden treasure was this: in the city of Khotan, on one side of the palace gardens, there was a place where the ground was uneven. All around that spot, they raised tall walls and claimed that a martyr was buried there. Within those walls he had built a room for recitation, a hermitage, a guest house, a kitchen, a stable, a mosque, and a pilgrimage site. He also built two tombs.{277} Within them he hid over 1,500 *yambu* and several gold bars. Over them they placed tall banners and flags, and so made them into shrines of high standing and courtly pilgrimage sites. They took the land and the shops, made them into an endowment for the shrine, and granted the proceeds to the readers and the dervishes. Every Monday and Thursday, they would slaughter a cow and several sheep, vowing to give the meat to the poor. They distributed the meat to deserving parties and received their blessings in kind.

Whether they came from Hindustan or Turkestan, from Ferghana or Badakhshan, honored guests and masters would stop at that shrine for at least three days, perhaps a week, to pray in seclusion. When they encountered each other, they would inquire, "So, have there been any miracles at this shrine? Has anyone received visions?"

The covetous prayer reciters from the shrine would reply, "This is a very great and honored shrine. No other shrine has given us such grace as we have received from this shrine." They would smile and say, "This is a *secret* shrine. It was revealed through the might of His Highness's prosperity! The wishes of many men came true, and they achieved their desires."

Instead of sparing a single one of the corvée laborers who had carried the silver and gold, who had dug into the ground and buried it, they buried those workers in some place along with the treasure, and likewise the guards and cavalrymen. Indeed, Niyaz Beg sent everyone who got wind of these secrets to join them, and that is why no one learned the truth about the treasure or heard anything about it at all.

In the end Niyaz Beg brought the Chinese to Khotan. He had all of the banners and such atop the shrine pulled up and thrown away, then opened the tomb. They removed the silver and gold and handed it over as "the soldiers' reward." The whole time, they had been hiding silver and gold, making fools of the masters and pilgrims by calling it a "great shrine," and deceiving Muslims.

> Anyone who opens their mouth to deceive
> Will be ruined. Satan (CURSED BE HE!) is unclean.

This saying suits the beg's character well.

In another garden, Niyaz Beg hid 1,000 *yambu*, and over it he planted an orchard of pomegranates, grapes, apricots, and all sorts of saplings. Now they pulled up all of the trees and threw them away, removed the *yambu*, and handed them over. In another garden there was a pond, at the bottom of which were hidden many{278} precious stones of jade, which so attract the eyes of the people of Beijing. They took these out and presented them as well. Elsewhere, they removed 700 *yambu* and some gold, which they handed over as "the soldiers' reward." Thus had Niyaz Beg hidden a great amount of silver, gold, and stones of jade. They unsealed each one and presented them to the officials. All of the Chinese, great and petty alike, praised Niyaz Beg. They granted him the governorship of Yarkand for faithfully keeping his oath.

Yet Niyaz Beg had set his sights on another goal: to extract from the officials a truly great appointment—a hereditary position. He had no interest in being the governor of Yarkand.

"The Chinese to whom I swore my oath, for whom I wished and hoped—these are not those Chinese!" thought Niyaz Beg, disappointed. He slipped back into his old habits and harbored ill intentions toward the Chinese. He built secret workshops in Yarkand and set about preparing armaments. One by one, he called together all of his old cronies from the city and countryside and plied them with promises. He gained their friendship and their hopes with sure assurances and firm oaths. Niyaz Beg set a time to act. As the miraculous hadith says, HE WHO DIGS A PIT FOR ANOTHER WILL FALL INTO IT HIMSELF, and it came back to him.

An artillery officer had a grievance against Niyaz Beg. He informed Dong Daren of what was going on. Dong Daren sent someone to investigate in secret, and when he found these things were true, sent twenty soldiers with an execution order. They daubed this "royal arrow"[5] on the house where Niyaz Beg was living. He became a prisoner in his own home. Yarkand was given to Qadir Eshikagha Beg of Kucha. Twenty days passed. A company of soldiers was sent from Kashgar with their officer, and they put him in a bare wagon. They bound him, paraded him in humiliation through the bazaar in broad daylight, and carried him off to Kashgar.

Niyaz Beg's natural spite for Muslims and enmity to Islam were such that, before his tyrannical existence even came into this bright world, an author (now deceased) had already bestowed a poem that captures this beg's life:

> If in the Beginning one's rug was woven with black,
> Even Zamzam waters will never whiten it, no matter how often it is washed.

In the first instance, Niyaz Beg had been the reason the lamp of the fortune of the Khojas of Kucha was extinguished. Later, His Highness the Ataliq Badawlat, who possessed a domain of six provinces like Khotan,{279} ordered another to be added to them, an independent province with 700 magistrates and a realm that took forty days to traverse. He granted this province to Niyaz Beg with authority over life and death and entrusted him to wield the reins of government as he wished. Niyaz Beg was not satisfied with such station and power, nor was he aware of his fortune in spending his life in the lands of Islam, so in place of gratitude he substituted ingratitude. As once again he coveted an office from the Chinese infidels and placed his faith and hope in it, the signs of his fall from Islam into apostasy and of his utter foolishness and misfortune became manifest.

> Grace will be extended to you, if you give gratitude;
> It will slip right from your hands, if you give ingratitude.

What is even more shocking was that Niyaz Beg plotted such treachery against that very crown of fortune who had been the cause of his prosperity, and even made efforts to eliminate him. He expended effort to take the life of the younger Beg while he intrigued to spill the blood of the elder Beg, and so set his sights on the arrow of reproach. This was recounted above.

Niyaz Beg feared the wrath of the Chinese. He had hidden some of the poison that he had given to Yaʿqub Beg in the setting of his diamond ring. He took the poison from the fitting and placed it in his own mouth. The bright world grew dark before his eyes, and he said good-bye to this life. Such ignominious deeds, such repugnant acts received their punishment in this world of retribution.

The officials did not move Niyaz Beg from the place he had died, nor did they say funeral prayers, but after forty days bathed his corpse in alcohol to putrefy it, and only when they had made malodorous carrion of it did they carry out its burial.

> Doing evil will create evil, and good acts, good in kind;
> Barley grows from barley, wheat from wheat.

When he was in power, he senselessly spilled the people's blood. In the end, after his government came to an end, by his own hand he spilled his own blood.

* * *

Let it be heard that the chief guard Muḥammad Yunus Jan Dadkhwah was the autonomous governor of Yarkand for twelve years. Yet his fortune was greater than that of Governor Niyaz Beg. He was a mullah, clerk, and secretary, and a person who was superior in his piety and expressive of his religion.[6] And he never came into conflict with the Shariah over taxation. In every case, he continuously and scrupulously maintained the law of the Prophet. He never permitted himself to oppress anyone.

However, when the people of Khaqan began to advance, he grew afraid and fled toward Sarikol with many generals, cavalry, and soldiers. Since it had snowed in the mountain passes,{280} and because of the bitter cold, they could not cross over, so returned to Yarkand. They ran into the Chinese officers. Some of them they martyred. Others they imprisoned. However, they heaped honors upon Muḥammad Yunus Jan. Zongtong Daren said to him, "I have heard that you are a very fine man. Your only defect is that you are *yiren*[7]—a person from another land. If you were to stay, I would appoint you to a position. Should you choose to return, I would send you on your way with an escort and money to travel." Muḥammad Yunus Jan replied that he wished to leave. Zongtong Daren, despite the fact that he was obviously his enemy, gave him a horse, guards, and 500 pieces of silver and sent him off to Ferghana.[8] He received his reward for the good deeds he had done for God's creations.

If a man does good, no one will forget him;
If a man does ill, no one will wonder where he's gone.

* * *

The point of this verbose and detailed discussion is that it is necessary for later officials to know that Muḥammad Yunus Jan Dadkhwah and Governor Niyaz Beg lived under one king and at one time, and that both of them were likewise made governors of two great cities. Each received the royal command in kind. Yet, if one examines their deeds and their fates with the gaze of concentration, one will discern that, for one of them, former enemies became sincere friends. He aided them, gave them respect, and worked to realize their goals as though they were his own. He ensured the safety of their lives and property, resolved all enmity between them, made them his kith and kin, and so unified them. As for the other, whoever was a good friend and eternal brother to him, it was as if he made mortal enemies of them. He would not protect them, but withheld his respect and cast them into a lowly station. He would deprive them of their livelihoods and leave them joyless and hopeless. He separated them from their relatives, clans, children, and friends. He spared not their livelihoods, gave no rest to their lives, and deposited them in the ground.

In sum, those who regard the welfare of the people as their greatest duty and hold themselves to the path of justice will{281} see their reward clearly in this material world. Those who devalue the livelihoods of the people, who oppress them and pay no heed to their tears, will likewise see their reward in this undoing world. On the Day of Judgment, for those who have done good, it will be as in the Quran: TRULY THE PIOUS SHALL BE IN BLISS. [82:13] That is to say, truly they will find their place in the eternal sublime paradise called "bliss." As for those who cling to their evil ways, TRULY THE PROFLIGATE SHALL BE IN HELLFIRE. [82:14] That is, they will be stricken with eternal suffering in Hell, the "fiery furnace." Verily that will be their final place.

OH GOD, GUIDE US TO THE STRAIGHT PATH AND DELIVER US MUSLIMS AND THE NEEDY FROM WRONGDOERS. AMEN.

2:17 Notables During Yaʿqub Beg's Era

A Brief Account of the Jupiter-Countenanced Scholars and Pious Men During the Era of His Saturn-Ranked Highness the Ataliq Badawlat; of His Secretaries, as Cultured as ʿAṭṭar[1]; and of His Battle-Hungry Soldiers, as Furious as Bahram

WITH THE ASSISTANCE of the purified spirits of the lofty shrines in the domain of the Seven Cities, and by the blessings of the exalted answers to those efficacious prayers of "those whose prayers are answered," the learned *ṣaḥib duʿa*s, His Highness the Badawlat ruled over the people of the Seven Cities for fourteen years. Without the assistance of the purified spirits of those exalted souls, and of the Pole and of the Forty, it would have been impossible for him to achieve such great fortune.

In *The Breaths of Fellowship*,[2] it is related that "The falling of rain from the sky, and the greening of the plants of the earth, are all by the blessings of the great saints; and the victory of Muslims over the nonbelievers, by the grace and assistance of those miraculous saints. And there are 2,000 of them. It is they who are the lords and masters of the world. And they do not know each other. Nor do they know their own greatness. They are hidden from ordinary people in every respect. Those who are masters of THE UNTYING OF THE KNOTS, and are the exalted ones at God's court, number 300. These are called the GOOD. And forty of them are called the SUBSTITUTES (or 'the Forty'). And seven of them are called the HOLY. And four of them are called the STAKES. And three of them are called the PRINCES. And one of them is called the POLE or SAINT. No member of these ranks knows the others, yet in every action they require the license of the others."

{282} The purpose of this preamble is this: during the era of His Highness the Ataliq Ghazi, there were many great and eminent *sayyids* and scholars of lofty rank. Among his conquering armies, which numbered over 80,000, and his especially accomplished soldiers were several who overflowed with piety, so that the shaykhs and saints of the age could not match one-tenth of their faith and devotion. But they were not without impudent and impure men either. In short, the multitudes of the lofty scholars, the ranks of the victorious soldiers, and the masses of the common people are of course not without members of the GOOD and the HOLY. Those people are of course hidden and concealed. THE UNSLEEPING LORD raises whomsoever He wishes to these ranks; and to whom He wishes to show this great fortune, He shows it. THAT IS THE BOUNTY OF GOD, WHICH HE GIVES TO WHOMSOEVER HE WILL. AND GOD IS POSSESSED OF TREMENDOUS BOUNTY. [62:4]

* * *

Sayyids of the refuge of lordship, accomplished *ṣaḥib duʿas*, and scholars wise in Shariah and learned in jurisprudence, who were among the best of the era of the rule of the Ataliq Badawlat, some of whom have cast off the borrowed clothes of life and taken their leave for Eternity, and others of whom are still in the realm of the living:

One of this rank was **Buzurg Khan Törä b. Jahangir Khan Töra.** He stayed for some years, then returned to his own homeland. His story was told earlier. His Highness **Sayyid Katta Khan Törä**: By the command AND GOD CALLS UNTO THE ABODE OF PEACE [10:25], he made passage to the gardens of the Eternal. He was buried in Kashgar. Also his younger brother **Kichik Khan Törä**, who was buried in Aqsu. **Israil Khan Törä** passed away in Old Turfan. **Muḥammad Raḥim Khan Törä** returned safely to his own land. **Ḥakim Khan Törä b. Katta Khan Törä**: His story was told earlier. He returned to his own homeland, and the news has been heard that, in this very year, the year 1321 [1903/4], he made passage from this fallen world to the gardens of Eternity. **Aḥrar Khan Törä**: Returned in health to his own homeland. The virtues of these sayyids are to the peoples of humanity LIKE UNTO THE SUN IN THE MIDDLE OF THE SKY.

Among the Sufi paths:

Maḥmud Khoja Ḥażrat was unmatched in his perfected virtues. He was one of His Highness the Ataliq Badawlat's masters and guides. He died in Kashgar and was buried there (during Yaʿqub Beg's rule). **Aḥmad Khoja Shaykhulislam**[3]: His virtues and fine qualities were beyond description. He went on pilgrimage to the Two Holy Cities. **Sayyid Ardilani Mullah**: A scholar and deeply read theologian.{283} Expended his efforts on teaching at the Afaq shrine, from which many students benefited. **Ishan Taji Khoja Ṣudur**, a grandson of Shaykh Khawand-i Tahur[4]: an honored and esteemed individual who had gone as the emissary of His Highness Malla Khan to the Frankish queen and did his duty appropriately. He returned to his country.

A man from Hindustan called "**Crazy Father**" [*Divana Ata*], with the aspect of a mendicant but the fury of a king. An aged man, impoverished in and painfully devoted to the Qadiriyya path, and endowed with strange habits. One of His Highness the Ataliq Ghazi's faithful masters and guides. This year he has reached the age of 118.[5] He brought the cauldrons of the Ghawṣiyya to the boil, gave food to the honored and the worthy, was a refuge to the poor and downtrodden, and has made his home in Ushturfan.

The learned *qaris*, well regulated in speech, who gathered in that era, such that surely there has never been such a gathering in any other time or place:

Qari Mullah Ṣaliḥ was an accomplished imam and one who could tunefully recite the Quran from memory. A pious [*ṣaliḥ*] believer and Muslim, and thus aptly named.

The Kashgari masters and scholars: **Mullah Muḥammad Sharif Khalifa:** He taught for fifty or sixty years, bringing great benefit to students, and lived out his life displaying total effort. Many students benefited. He possessed BENEFICIAL KNOWLEDGE. They say that some 300 students of his were honored with licenses indicating their recitation of the entire Quran and efforts in learning. He lived to the age of eighty-five. He passed away on the seventeenth of Ramadan in 1310 [April 4, 1893]. **Chief Judge Mullah Mir Muḥammadi Akhund**: A pious man deeply versed in theology and Shariah. **Mullah ʿAbdurrashid Akhund Aʿlam**: A religious mullah deeply versed in the Shariah. **Mullah Muḥammadi Akhund Aʿlam**: A good-tempered and well-spoken teacher, unmatched in poems and riddles, unequaled in interpreting difficult texts. **ʿAbdulkhaliq Ishan**, the younger brother of the aforementioned chief judge: Advanced in the ways of the Qadiriyya and Chushtiyya, humble but possessing great power. One of His Highness the Ataliq's masters and guides. (His Highness had great faith in him.)

In Yarkand: **Żiyauddin Damolla**, judge of the region, master of scholars and great men, who was chief judge.[6] His commands were made in accordance with fatwas from scholars of Islam, as it says: SO JUDGE AMONG THE PEOPLE WITH TRUTH [38:26].{284} He returned safely to his own country. **Mullah Qasim Akhund** was chief mufti, and **Mullah Numan Akhund** the *inspecting judge*, and there were the Sufis **Kabir Ṣaḥib Ḥażrat**, **Miskin Ṣaḥib Ḥażrat**, and **ʿAbdurraḥman Ḥażrat**. Every one of these was praised more highly than if they were kings of the age and rulers of the era.

In Khotan: **Chief Judge Mullah Ibrahim**. He was learned in religion, truth-speaking and truth-seeking. In issuing his judgments in the Shariah, he was the most advanced of all the judges; in enacting the pillars of the Shariah, he was superior to all the jurisprudents.

In Aqsu: **Mullah ʿAbdullah Akhund** of Khotan, who was chief judge: A pious believer, unmatched in his knowledge of religion and unequaled in that of law and justice, who was firm in his issuing of judgments of Shariah in accordance with the words of the *mujtahid* imams. In finding justice between two disputants and bringing an end to their conflict, judgeship suited this man's nature perfectly. He passed away in 1307 [1889/90].[7] **Mullah Muḥammad Ḥasan Akhund** was the *aʿlam akhund*. He was a knowledgeable scholar worthy of his office. He was proficient in every science, and his mind was sharp and his disposition refined. He passed away on Thursday the twenty-seventh of Ramadan, 1310 [April 14, 1891]. **Mullah Ismail Akhund** was the mufti. A theologian, good natured and well spoken, of polite speech. Approved of by all kinds. **Mullah ʿUs̱man Ḥajji** of Bay, whose story was told in the first epic: In his time, he was before all others, firm in the faith, self-disciplined beyond all others, better versed than all others in law and letters. Yet he had little to commend him in terms of knowing the intricacies. He was the present author's teacher. **Mullah ʿAbdullaṭif Ḥajji Akhund**, who had studied in Bukhara, was the most learned of his age in the sciences, in texts, and in fundamentals. He was a teacher, a God seeker, a lover of the poor, and mindful of the hereafter. **Shamsuddin**, of those of Aqsu who had been *akhunds* and masters of Shariah since the old days, was the *aʿlam akhund*. A faithful and pious man, of simple appearance, possessing divine favor, whose prayers were answered, unequaled in his power of Quran memorization and without parallel in his complete recitation. Passed away in 1295 [1878]. **Hadi Khalifa:** He passed his life prostrated in prayer. The successor of Mir Ghiyas̱uddin's grandson Ishan Jan Ḥażrat. Passed away in Kashgar during His Highness's reign. **Mullah ʿAbdulbaqi Ḥajji** was the mufti. He was unequaled in intelligence and unparalleled in wisdom and knowledge of the law and of poetry.{285} In his own time, he was like a great king. He spent his whole life in song and feasting. Yet he was a man of fine character and fine conversation, generous and kind to travelers. He passed away in 1301 [1883/4].

Of the Sufi orders: **Nis̱ar Maʿṣum Ḥażrat**: A grandson of the godly imam, renewer of the second millennium, and eternal Pole and Saint, Aḥmad al-Faruqi Sirhindi.[8] Lived in Aqsu. A *ḥafiẓ*[9] of the divine Word, abstemious, a lover of ascetic devotion, and equitable in his judgment of proofs of the divine. He passed away in 1292 [1875] and was buried in Aqsu. Another of this great family was **Muḥammad Miyan Fażl Ṣadiq Ḥażrat**, the son of Ḥażrat Kalan. A *ḥafiẓ* of the holy Word who passed his nights awake in asceticism. Generous to the destitute, with a poor mendicant's aspect but the qualities of a king. He went off to Ferghana (Almaty), where he died and was buried. The military judge **Mullah Ibrahim Akhund**, from Ferghana: A pious, Shariah-loving, and abstemious scholar. **Qipchaq Mullah Nar Quli Akhund**, the military mufti, was discerning of the good and the wicked. **Mullah Saʿadat Akhund** was fond of accounting. He served as judge in Bay and Sayram. **Judge Mullah Akram Shah Akhund** lived off his land, by his labor and the sweat of his brow. He was a pious theologian. When the Dungans under Dakhu first arrived, he was tragically and senselessly killed by a Dungan bullet. He attained the rank of martyrdom. It was the year 1294 [1877].

In Kucha: **Mullah Yusuf Akhund** was appointed to the office of chief judge. A legal specialist skilled in the Shariah, and possessed of eloquent speech. Yet a delicacy was evident in his holy disposition and an excessive cheerfulness in his nature. He was removed from office a year [two years] later. But he was favored again with the position of absolute judge in Aqsu. **Mullah Allahyar Akhund** was made chief judge of Kucha. He was a zealous man, pious and plain, a theologian of the age who possessed religious habits, and sedate, whose judgments accorded with the Shariah of the Prophet and whose orders were appropriate to the words of the Rightly Guided Imams. He was one of your humble author's teachers. When he was going on pilgrimage to the Two Holy Cities, he passed away in Amritsar. It was the year 1304 [1886/7]. His younger brother **Mullah ʿAli Ḥajji Akhund** was the temporary chief mufti. He was a polite, well-spoken, and well-mannered mullah of few words. **Mullah ʿAbdulqadir Akhund** was the mufti.{286} He is a mullah well versed in the law, of good temper and good company, and inclined to the study of poetry. And he is a man capable of enjoying a feast. Today he is ensconced in the office of chief judge and in the fortune of life.[10]

In Korla: **Mullah Aḥmad Akhund** was chief judge. He was a man of lesser learning but of greater religiosity.

In Turfan: **Qażi Surkh Abi** was appointed to the position of chief judge. He was a pious mullah and theologian. Yet he was a man whose honored disposition was possessed of a sensitivity and highmindedness, and a quickness of speech. He was presently dismissed from his position.

Mullah Timur Akhund of Turfan was made chief judge. He was a pious theologian, well versed in Shariah, and abstemious. His abstemiousness was such that, when Ḥakim Khan Törä was governor of Turfan and the revolution was clearly nigh, he was entrusted with 1,500 gold coins. Before he had an opportunity to return them, things fell apart. Later, after twelve years had passed, this judge said, "All this time, no one has come looking for what was entrusted to me. So as to return it while I am still alive, I shall take a pilgrimage to the Two Holy Cities." He left Turfan and came to the country of Ferghana, where he received an audience with Ḥakim Khan Törä, and he placed before him the entrusted coins, just as they had been given to him.

And when he did so, the *törä* said, "What is this? Entrusted when?" He had no idea. He had forgotten about it. Once the judge had related the story and explained himself, the *törä* recognized him. He praised him and said, "In such a time as this, there is still such an honest man! I must have forgotten." The *törä* happily greeted him and made him his guest for several days, entertaining him before sending him on his way.

From Turfan to the country of Ferghana is about a sixty-day journey. When he came to Samarqand, he fell gravely ill and passed away. His son was traveling with him. He commanded his son, "If I should 'bow my head to God,' and you were to go on the ḥajj from here, there would be nothing left. Go to Turfan and see your younger brother, and divide the money in accordance with the Shariah. You take your own part of it and perform the ḥajj yourself." And then he passed away. The son, per his father's command, went to Turfan, then completed the ḥajj on his own.

There was a scholar named **Mullah S̱abit Akhund**. He was proficient and deeply read in every field. Students would say, "This man surely is gifted." He made his living as a teacher. There was also **Mullah Polad Shaykh**, one of the shaykhs of the Shrine of the Companions of the Cave, who was highly esteemed and wealthy. He was banished and made to stay in Aqsu.

While there were many other exemplary scholars and great men of their age in the Seven Cities during this time,{287} we have limited ourselves to these scholars just described.

* * *

Those who in that era governed the Seven Cities and served as its governors were: in Kashgar, **Alash Bi Dadkhwah**; in Yarkand, **Muḥammad Yunus Jan Shighavul Dadkhwah**; and in Khotan, **Niyaz Ḥakim Beg**. Each of their stories was told in its own place.

At first, **Ḥakim Khan Törä** was made the governor of Aqsu. Two years later, Chief Secretary **Mullah Jiyan** was made governor. He governed for eighteen months. Then **ʿAbdurraḥman Dadkhwah** of Kucha was made governor. **Muḥammad Baba Toqsaba** was made governor of Ushturfan. **Muḥammad Amin Toqsaba** was made governor of Bay and Sayram. **Isḥaq Khoja** was made governor of Kucha. Two years later, **Nar Muḥammad Parvanachi** was made governor. Then it was granted to **Amil Khan Törä**, while Turfan was granted to **Ḥakim Khan Törä**. Ürümchi was given to the Dungan **Ganja Akhund**.

* * *

His Highness the Ataliq Ghazi (MAY GOD ILLUMINATE HIS GRAVE!) would handle all the affairs of government himself. He appointed no fine or wise man to be his minister. In the place of such a minister, he had pious and prudent secretaries and scribes of exceptional experience to give him counsel, who were entirely dedicated to the state, good government, and the welfare of the people, and he would handle all settlements of disputes, and appointments and dismissals, according to their illuminated thoughts. The income and expenses of each area, the number of commanders and soldiers and the accounting of their horses and armaments, and the expenses of the treasury, the atelier, and kitchens[11] were all entrusted to his chief secretaries. Indeed, the chief secretaries would set all of the affairs of government in order, then report what they had done. All of the problems with petitioners and emissaries were solved by the chief secretaries. After the power of His Highness himself, the power of the chief secretaries was greatest, and the chief secretaries were afforded great honor and respect. Yet they were not entirely free from his wrathful punishment.

When Buzurg Khan Törä and His Highness first arrived, they came with Chief Secretary **Yaʿqub**. He was unequaled in intelligence and skill and unparalleled in the scribe's art. He served three years in the position of chief secretary. Eventually he fell ill and died. Then **Mirza Barat** was made chief secretary. He was unable to keep good records. Then **Mullah ʿIsa** was made chief secretary. But he was not successful.

Eventually **Muhiyyuddin Makhdum**, the son of Ḥajji Aʿlam Akhund of Kashgar, was appointed chief secretary. He is known as "Secretary League" [*Mirza Farsakh*], because he measured the road from Kashgar to Turfan in leagues and marked them with stones. He was very prudent, exceptionally experienced, clever, and smart,{288} quick with a pen, capable as a secretary, and wise in every field, and he got along with everyone. And he knew seven languages, and could read and write in six scripts.

Mullah Kamal Mirza of Bukhara, **Kamaluddin Mirza** of Tus, **Mullah Barat Mirza**, **Awliya Mirza**, **Katta Khoja Mirza**, **Shadi Mirza**, and **Kashif Khan Törä Mirza** all served at the chief secretary's side.

After that, Chief Secretary **Zaynulʿabidin Makhẕum** of Marghinan came to Kashgar. The assessment of this man was related earlier. The Boy Beg, near the end of his reign, sent this chief secretary (to Aqsu) with forty mounted cavalry to meet the Chinese officers and go as an emissary to Zongtong Daren. He came armed, and when he passed through Maralbashi, he encountered Zongtong Daren's cruel-hearted soldiers. As neither side knew the other's intentions or even their language, all those soldiers saw was a mass of armed men. The soldiers fired, killing all the cavalry. A bullet struck the Makhẕum in the mouth and lodged in his cheek. As he lay there unconscious, Zongtong Daren arrived.

His Highness's treasurer ʿAshur Maḥram and Ṣiddiq Beg of Aqsu had come as translators. They recognized him and said to Zongtong Daren, "This was the '*Lao* Padishah's' man. He was a very good and peaceful man."

"If that is the case," Zongtong Daren ordered, "bring him safely to where I have made camp."

Once they had brought him in, the Chinese surgeons were summoned, and they removed the bullet. But when Zongtong Daren asked him to speak, he could make no reply, but indicated by signs and gestures, "Bring me an inkwell, pen, and paper." When they had brought it to him, he wrote his intentions out.

In response to the text the Makhẕum wrote, Zongtong Daren asked, "When you learned that the Great Khan's armies were coming, why did you come to meet us armed?"

"I had no idea," he wrote. "The Boy Beg feared for his life and ordered me to go forth as an emissary."

Then he asked, "So he gave you this order hoping for your death?"

"The Boy Beg is young," he wrote, "and in his youth, he gave me this order contrary to counsel. I could not refuse to go."

"You have told the truth," Zongtong Daren said, praising him. "Take this man under escort to Kashgar." And he granted the Makhẕum money for travel expenses.

When they arrived in Kashgar, a fine place was appointed for him, along with a stipend, as for four or five days they continued to question him, reverently.{289} Eventually, though the winter was cold, he wished to return to his own land. The spring days came, and the turtledoves raised their voices. The Chief Secretary Makhẕum too began to speak, and he asked, at last, to return home.

"The soldiers did not know you, so they shot you," came the kindly reply. "Please do not take it to heart, but be happy, and forgive us." So they apologized and gave him 200 silver coins and a horse, with leave to go to the country of Ferghana. He received the reward for goodness in this life and went safely to Marghinan, where he saw his family.[12] He went on pilgrimage to the Two Holy Cities and, having achieved his goal, returned to Marghinan, where he passed away.

There were many great secretaries, including **Najmuddin Mirza**, **Ḥajji Artuq Mirza**, **Mullah ʿIsa Mirza**, **Mullah Qasim Mirza**, and **Mullah Karim Mirza.**

And then there was **Mirza Baba Beg Ḥissari**, of the Begs of Ḥissar, who had been chief secretary to Qanaʿat Shah Ghazi Ataliq in Tashkent and governor of Marghinan, whom General Mullah ʿAlimqul had sent to be chief secretary to the Ḥajji Padishah, and who was also the governor of Qarghaliq, who by order of His Highness the Ataliq was appointed tax collector of Aqsu.[13] From Ushturfan to Korla, all offices of tax collection, taxes in accord with the Shariah, guardposts, and passports were under this tax collector's jurisdiction. He was a pious and just man. Every week he would recite the entirety of the Holy Word by sections, and the entirety of the *Waymarks of Benefits* as well.[14]

Your humble author, Mullah Musa b. Mullah ʿIsa Khoja Sayrami, passed seven years of his life in service to that tax collector. I never saw him step into any impure place. Winter and summer, he would perform his ablutions with cold water. He made not even a hair's transgression of the fine Shariah. He reserved a chamber for prayer. There was nothing at all in that chamber save for two unfired bricks, two prayer rugs, a Quran, one *Waymarks of Benefits*, and a bookrest. No one but me had permission to enter that chamber.

One day, when the weather was cold, I entered it for some important matter, and he had just finished his ablutions. The ablution water had frozen in his moustache and beard, and even in his eyebrows and "little beard" [*maqal*]. Immediately I exited and placed a generous amount of coal into a brazier, lighting it on fire, and as it began to smoke, I carried it in and placed it before him. He hurriedly warmed his hands and face and thanked me. Then he sent me out, saying, "Oh, kid,[15] take that flame away, and warm yourself up. Don't let me get accustomed to such comforts." He would never light a fire in the room where he prayed.

And he would say,{290} "I am sixty years old. What was white, I have made black, and what was black, made white. I have lived my life carelessly. When I go to the divine court, with which face and which eye shall I go, and how shall I look upon my beautiful God? Would that at the end of my life I could stain my white beard in red blood, and take it as a gift to Him; would that I might die in holy war!" And he would weep and weep, as tears flowed in droplets from his eyes like spring rain.

And I would say in my heart, "And should the Chinese come, in defense of your own life, through which mountain pass will you flee, and which guardpost?"

In the end, in Yarkand, in the hands of the nonbelievers, he drank the nectar of martyrdom. He got what he desired. Most evenings he would stay awake all night and pass the time in prayer. Apart from prayer, he had little other occupation.

An anecdote: seventeen great begs, including Qadir Quli Beg, Amil Khan Törä, Muḥammad Amin Toqsaba, and Qari Mukhtar, were all martyred at Yarkand in one day. When this tax collector's head was separated from his body, it bounced several times, and it laughed a cackling laugh. When the people who had gone out to see the show heard it, they raised the finger of astonishment to their teeth of imagination and praised him. The contemptible nonbelievers were left staring in shock as well. After this happened, some trustworthy merchants came from Yarkand and told your humble author about it. "That tax collector," they asked me, "what good deeds had he done, and what fine qualities did he have, that it could have happened this way?" I told them what I knew, and they praised and thanked me.

In those auspicious and fortunate days, there were secretaries whose elegance and inventiveness in composition and the arrangement of words—whose perfumed pens—were like the style of the letters and anecdotes of Mirza ʿAbdulqadir Bedil (MAY GOD HAVE MERCY ON HIM!)[16]—of which every letter is a rosy-cheeked beloved and every dot a limpid pearl, so that the spectacle of a world-encompassing garden becomes clearly visible to the reader's eyes, and an increase of mirth is granted them; and secretaries, masters of volumes and true in their skill, whose eloquence of the pen and gracefulness of language meant that every letter was a cause for the common people's comfort, and every dot a consolation to their troubled hearts, and a reason for ease; and ingenious secretaries, who had no worry or fear of giving voice to the tyrannical and the treacherous, and whose pens were like a scorpion's sting or a surgeon's{291} biting lancet; we were not without such men.

* * *

Among the ranks of that good and just ruler's eminent generals and victorious soldiers were **Muḥammad Naẓar Beg** and **Qadir Quli Beg**, who traced their descent back to the Baburian khans of the country of Ferghana; and **Khuday Quli Khan**, a descendant of the khans who for a time sat upon the khanal throne (in Khoqand) and was known as "the Beltmaker Khan" [*Balbaqchi Khan*].

There were many great and noble begs and lordlings who had served the old khans of Khoqand in their day, gained their imperial favor, governed lands, and established their nobility: **Mirza Aḥmad Qushbegi**, **Nar Muḥammad Parwanachi**, **Baqi Beg Dadkhwah**, **Mir Baba Dadkhwah**, **Fayżullah Dadkhwah**, **Qosh Dadkhwah**, **Hamdam Baturbashi**, **Mirza Qasim Mukhtar**, **ʿAbdulghaffar Beg** of Bukhara, **Muḥammad Amin Beg** of Ḥissar, **Khoja Naẓar Beg**, and **Bukhcha Bardar Hudaychi**. They reposed in the shade of His Highness's imperial reign as generals brimming with glory, carrying out his orders. And besides them there were many other noble and accomplished generals who had lost their positions.

Yet the general who counted the days of war and battle among the categories of entertainment and feasting, or perhaps even above them, and who was the most glorious was His Highness the Ataliq Ghazi's eldest son, General **Beg Quli Beg**, commander in chief and leader of the forces. His second son, **Ḥaqq Quli Beg**, was also a general. And **Mirza Aḥmad Qushbegi** was a general. And there was none greater than he, who had in the days of the old khans governed Tashkent for several years and then come from the country of Ferghana. His Highness made him a general, but out of anxiety developed a secret grudge against him. Later he softened again and favored him. This story was told earlier. There was also **Qipchaq ʿUmar Quli Dadkhwah**, who was made a general. He was powerful in the country of Ferghana and the presence of the khans. He served as a general for fourteen years, and then in fortune returned to his own land. **ʿAbdullah Pansad** was made a general. For several years he battled, greater even than the tales of Rustam, or of Sam or Nariman. In the end the light drained from his eyes. A short while later, his body was sent under guard to Mazar-i Sharif in Balkh with a donation of 200 *yambu*. Several warriors and *pansad*s whom he had trained himself served as generals in his place. And **Qipchaq Turdi Quli** was made a general. Later, after he retired, he lived in Kucha. He was a pious Muslim who applied himself little to anything but prayer.{292} Returned safely to his own land. And **Qipchaq Muḥammad Musa Toqsaba** was a general. He was stationed in Aqsu as His Highness's *salamagha* and *kaymakam*. And the Afghan **Jamadar Dadkhwah** was made a general and placed in command of the cannons, guns, and infantry. He was a very severe man, brave and bold. He left in safety, went on pilgrimage to the Two Holy Cities, and, having achieved his desires, passed away. And **Kifak Labar**, **ʿAbdurraḥim Pahlawan**, **ʿUmar Khoja Ishan**, **Törä Qul Labar**, **Muḥammad Efendi**, and **Khalil Efendi** too held the rank of general.[17] Then there was the greatest of all the guards, who took the rank of general, **Tarab Khoja Yasavulbashi**. Later, when he retired, **Muḥammad "Qabil" Beg Yüzbashi** was made chief of the royal guard in his place.[18] He was called this because he was a very able [*qabil*] person. He died from a bullet in the Battle of Yaydi. The governor of Korla, **Niyaz Muḥammad Toqsaba**, was also made a general and stationed at Dabanchi, with six *pansad*s under the command of **Ḥaydar Quli Pansad** and **Ish Muḥammad Pansad**. He fell into Chinese hands and was martyred. One of the famed *pansad*s was **ʿAzim Qul Pansad**.

He fought with the Chinese at Gumadi and was martyred along with some of his cavalry. **Karim Bay Dadkhwah**, **Karim Bay Mirza**, and **Sher Muḥammad Pansad** all eventually became generals. They returned safely to their own lands. Chief Secretary **Ḥajji Artuq** was also a *pansad*, and he held the position of general.

Mullah Faẓil was a *qari* of well-regulated speech and a secretary. **Maḥmud Beg Urgenchi**, of the Urgench begs, was a great *pansad*, pious, and of undoubted bravery. **ʿAli Beg Pansad** and **Allah Beg Pansad**, of the Uratepe begs, were great and fine men. And there were over 200 *pansads* and generals girded with the golden belt and robes, such as **Abulqasim Pansad**, **ʿIsamuddin Pansad**, [**Atabay Pansad**,] **ʿAlimbay Pansad**, **ʿId Muḥammad Pansad**, **Baqi Beg Pansad**, **Mir Karim Qurchi**, **Bay Muḥammad Parashbashi**, **Akhund Pansad** of Kashgar, **Nawruz Pansad**,[19] and other *pansads*, *labars*, and sergeants.

Of the men from the Six Cities: Niyaz Ḥakim Beg's younger brother **Muḥammad Amin Beg** was a general. The Dungan **Ma Dalaoye** and the New Muslim **He Dalaoye** too were generals. There were *pansads*, generals, and *yüzbashis* among the Dungans and New Muslims.

Ḥafiẓ Beg, the son of (Governor) ʿAbdurraḥman Dadkhwah of Aqsu, was a *pansad*. By the standard of the mullahs and scholars of the time, he had no deficiencies, nor was he lacking in fine qualities. He began in his father's service and then performed the ḥajj. This year he has once again returned from pilgrimage to the Two Holy Cities.{293} As the "motion of the spheres" did not suit Ḥafiẓ Beg's mind and the men of the times did not accord with his humor, he abandoned the city and favored the country. Some time later, the city leaders came and retrieved him, and appointed him in the office of judge. He is still in the position of judge.

There was also **Qadir Pansad** of Kucha. When the Chinese came, for a short time he took an official position. Then he went on a pilgrimage to the Two Holy Cities but died along the way. His story was told earlier.

There was also **Mamur Pansad** of Shahyar. When the Emperor of China's armies came to the Cities, he refused to submit to them, but, following the tradition of the Sunnah and the appropriate path, he desired to emigrate to the Holy Land. So he migrated with a number of people, with the goal of making pilgrimage to the Two Holy Cities, and departed from Shahyar. When they came to the place called Abad in Aqsu, Zongtong Daren and his soldiers went one night and captured his people. The *pansad* fled with some of his men, but when they arrived at Yarkand, they were apprehended. Some officers came in to meet him, and they asked him many things.

They asked him, "Now what is your intention?"

"I would that you would return the horse and arms that the Ataliq Ghazi gave to me," he replied, "and go out with your soldiers onto a broad battlefield, where I will fight with you and your soldiers and die in battle. That is my wish. I have no other intention than this."

This angered the officers greatly, and as a lesson to all, they killed him, cut off his head, and sent it around to Aqsu and Kucha (Yarkand) to be displayed.

And there was the singer **Aḥmad Akhund b. Mullah Rustam** of Aqsu, who was a servant and boon companion to His Highness the Badawlat at home and abroad, and was trusted for seven years during the campaigns in Turfan and Ürümchi to aid in the writing of tales, news, and stories. Your humble author asked this singer—orally and in person—for news of Ürümchi and tales of Turfan, then verified them with other trusted men to confirm them. For the fact that it is impossible for one man to be present in every place is evident to the minds of all wise men.

2:18 The Biography of the Author

The Name and Genealogy of the Author of This Book; and a Narrative of His Experiences

{294} YOUR SERVANT, Mullah Musa b. Mullah ʿIsa Khoja Sayrami, who is of less account than a speck of dust, offers this, that in the beginning, when I was at the start of my education, my late father took me to Kucha in the hope that I might become a scholar. There he placed me into the service of Mullah ʿU̱sman Akhund (GOD BLESS HIM!). After a few years as the dirt of the madrasa and the ruin of the students, when I had gained some slight ability to distinguish the licit and the illicit, the Dungans in Kucha rose up against the Great Khan and established Islam.

At the time, your humble author was in Sayram. Then Burhanuddin the Khaṭib Khoja came from Kucha with his son, Maḥmudin Khoja, and Mullah ʿU̱sman Akhund, all riding for Aqsu with the glorious intention of establishing Islam and swinging the sword of Shariah, as it says: PARADISE IS UNDER THE SHADES OF SWORDS.[1] And they passed through Sayram. Your servant also met with them and, against my inclination, found myself in their company until we came to Qara Yulghun. The governor of Aqsu, Saʿid Beg, came leading a host of Chinese soldiers, and we did battle. We could not match them, so we fled. Your servant and a few others took the road toward Muqur, and we traveled up across desert wastes to the town of Yulduz Bagh in Kucha.

There I was stripped of my clothing and my horse, and they wished to make of me a gift to the Chinese.

A week later, news came that the Kucha Khojas had again readied men and marched for Aqsu, and I was set free. I walked from Yulduz Bagh on foot and alone to Kucha. There it was as though the actions of the people of Kucha had manifested a glimpse of Judgment Day, and no refuge was to be found anywhere. In the end I went to the shrine of ʿArshuddin. Mullah Allahyar Akhund and Mullah Yusuf Akhund were in the shrine's garden and at their ancestor's feet, in seclusion and busy with constant prayer. They received me, and I told them all that had taken place. I stayed there with them for twenty days.

Now Maḥmudin Khoja brought to Kucha the happy news of the conquest of Aqsu. We saw each other and stayed there for four or five days, until he was to return to Aqsu. I went with him. I came to Sayram, and when I looked upon it, I saw how suddenly that country had changed. The situation made it impossible to stay there. So I went with him to Aqsu, and then I went to Ushturfan, and I lived there until these lands submitted to the Ataliq Ghazi Badawlat. That story was told in the first epic.

Then I spent eleven years in the service{295} of the tax collector whom the Ataliq Ghazi assigned to Aqsu, acting as his secretary, ever in his closest and most intimate companionship. The ordinary lives to which God had fated us passed well, with our hearts at peace, without worry. Now this totally incapable one—who is full of shortcomings from head to toe, and is of no account and weak beyond words—found himself a place in a corner and was living his life in prayer as a good subject, unburdened and innocent of everything, staying alive. THANK GOD FOR THAT.

* * *

As I said, I am from Sayram, and if this ignorant, incapable wretch did not provide at least a brief explanation of Sayram and the events surrounding it, then his heart would feel uneasy. What has been passed down from our ancestors and other white-haired old men across the generations, in writing and without doubt, is this: two hundred years ago in Ili, a treacherous Qalmaq named Khung-Taiji from the line of Churas came to rule over Moghulistan as khan and *törä*. He ruled from the eastern border in Qumul and Barköl to the northern border at the Great Sea, the western border up to

Tashkent, Chimkent, and Sayram, and the southern border down to Qaranghu Tagh. One time, he led his armies to conquer Tashkent and Sayram and append them to his realm. Khung-Taiji left another Qalmaq to rule in his place, along with a number of Qalmaqs as his companions. When he left and was approaching the borders of Ili, the people of Sayram rejected his rule. They killed those Qalmaqs and rebelled. However, a few Qalmaqs fled with their lives, and once they encountered Khung-Taiji and explained to him what had come to pass, Khung-Taiji did not return to Ili. Instead, according to his own customs, he uttered a few oaths and turned back to Sayram, which he conquered for a second time, pillaging it and putting some people to the sword.

The people of Sayram are composed of three houses, or three "lines": the Khoja Line, the Shah Line, and the Amir Line. Khung-Taiji chose the noblest and greatest of these three lines—twenty households of men from each, making sixty households—took them prisoner with their women and children, and removed them to his own country of Ili. They were kept in Ili for a year, more or less, and then sent to Old Turfan. They lived in Turfan for two years. During that time, Khung-Taiji "made his home in the Chamber of Nothingness." Then they heard the news that the Emperor of China's armies had entered Ili and the Six Cities, and they thought, "At last, we may return to our own homeland!" As it says, LOVING ONE'S COUNTRY IS WITHIN THE FAITH—in hopes of returning to their homeland, and of seeing{296} their families once again, they departed from Turfan. But when they came to Muzart Pass they encountered the leader of the Chinese soldiers, who asked them, "What people are you?" When they had explained their situation, he told them with feigned compassion, "Many of the emperor's soldiers have come here, and the roads are in chaos. Until these lands are pacified, perhaps you could stay here and farm." So on that pretext he offered them no leave, but instead had them taken to Yaqa Eriq and settled there.

They stayed there for a few years as well, but eventually moved to Bay and settled there. They stayed for some time too but could not remain. "That notch in the mountains seems like it has plenty of space," they said, and so they came to this land of Sayram and settled down here. Because they were originally from Sayram near Tashkent, they named this place Sayram as well. Ultimately, these lands ended up under the Chinese.

That was the time when there were few people in the Seven Cities, and they were not well cultivated. The Chinese officials wished to make the people of Sayram their subjects and to secure their loyalty. One man from the Amir Line was particularly devoted to government and official duties. The Chinese officials asked him, "How shall we go about getting these people to submit to the Great Khan and serve him?"

"These people only obey my orders," he answered. "I can get them to submit to the Great Khan as his subjects, if you would grant me an official rank." They agreed and passed it up to the Great Khan, who gave him an office equivalent to that of the third-rank governors of Aqsu and Kucha. This is why in the old days the governor of Sayram was of equal rank to those of Aqsu and Kucha, even though it had fewer people and less land.

The people of these three lines over the generations mixed all together, but among themselves they can still distinguish one from the other. They say that the Shah Line can be traced back to the ancient Kayanid kings and Tajik shahs. The Amir Line goes back to the viziers and generals who once governed the country. The Khoja Line consider themselves "Alavis"—that is, they say that they are directly descended from ʿAli (MAY GOD ILLUMINATE HIS FACE WITH NOBILITY!). "We are his descendants," they say with pride. Your servant comes from this line. A blessed genealogy passed down from our ancestors still exists. Blessedly, fortunately, it exists.

The point of this introduction is this:{299}2 in every religion, among the aristocracy, in Arabia and Persia and among the Turk, Tajik, and Mongol tribes, they protect their genealogies. Every group of people has traced itself back to some tribe and maintained that direct genealogy. They respect the bones and skeletons of their ancestors and take pride in them. Even the Chinese, Qalmaqs, Kyrgyz, and Qipchaqs, in preserving their ancestors' genealogies, teach them to their children and emphasize to them how each tribe is proud of its own line, and they are proud to say that "We come from such-and-such a line." Even those who are strangers to religion please themselves by narrating their ancestors' genealogies!

This being the case, it is likewise deemed necessary that your servant also reveal the relation and genealogy of his ancestors: Mullah Musa b. Mullah ʿIsa Khoja b. ʿAziz Khan Khoja b. Niyaz Khan Khoja b. Ishan Sultan Khoja b. Ishan Padishah Khoja b. Ishan Shah Jahan Khoja b. Ishan Gharib Shah Khoja b. Ishan Sayyid Jalaluddin Bab b. Ishan Sayyid Jamaluddin Bab b. Ishan Sayyid Kamaluddin Bab b. Sayyid Ibrahim Bab b. Sayyid ʿAbduljabbar Bab b. Sayyid ʿAbdulkarim Bab b. Sayyid ʿAbdulmajid Bab b. Sayyid ʿAbdulwadud Bab b. Sayyid ʿAbdulʿaziz Bab b. Sayyid Arslan Bab b. Sayyid Ilyas Bab b. Sayyid

Maḥmud Bab b. Iftikhar Bab b. ʿUs̱man Bab b. ʿUmar Bab b. Ismail Bab b. Isḥaq Bab b. ʿAbdulkarim Bab b. ʿAbduljalil Bab b. ʿAbdulrahim Bab b. ʿAbdulrahman Bab b. ʿAbduljabbar Bab b. ʿAbdulfattaḥ Bab b. Imam Muḥammad Ḥanifa b. ʿAli (MAY GOD BLESS HIS FACE!), MAY GOD BE PLEASED WITH THEM ALL!

This blessed genealogy was specially prepared in the country of Samarqand, in the year 945 [1538/9], during the reign of ʿUbaydullah Khan Ghazi, when the aforementioned Sayyid Kamaluddin Bab was presented with a khanal decree impressed with the seals of all the great scholars of that age and adorned also with the seal of that khan. It still exists. And I am blessed to copy this decree in full, from the original, into this little chronicle.

A royal decree:

> The Words of the Abulghazi, ʿUbaydullah Khan: Let it be known to our dear and fortunate friends, our young and joyous children; to the worthy begs, pious officials, esteemed ministers, and trusted deputies; and specifically{300} to the governors and imams of Sayram; and its holy men, judges, and wise schoolmasters; and *yüzbegis*, *onbegis*, lords, chieftains, khojas, and fellows; and all the elders of the Turks and Tajiks settled in every village and town:
>
> By our Shariah-adorned mind and felicitous intent, on account of his dedication and attention to the flourishing of holy Islam—to the strengthening and furthering of the religion of the Shariah of the Lord of the Humans and Jinn (UPON WHOM THE BEST OF PRAYERS AND MOST PERFECT PEACE!)—we have bestowed upon the imam of the Tümän of Sayram, that excellent man of exalted lineage, that master of interpretation, the noblest of all holy men, Sayyid Kamaluddin Bab, the office of *shaykhulislam*.
>
> Those who see this decree shall recognize the aforementioned gentleman as *shaykhulislam* and leader; and those who note the privileges afforded to this great office shall recognize the necessity of answering to them, and paying him his due respect. May no one recognize any partner in this office; may no man intrude upon his affairs. May the Shariah-loving Judge Faridun and other judges recognize the aforementioned gentleman as their leader. Let all documents pertaining to the Shariah receive his signature and seal. May no one act contrarily to his commands. And let the *ḥafiẓ*, imams, and muezzins, and the residents and leaders of holy shrines, deviate not from this gentleman's words, which are in accord with the Shariah and with the resplendent faith. They shall be his helpers, venerate him, and never disobey him. Nor let them ask for a new decree or

request any indulgence.[3] And may they enjoy that gentleman's concern to its greatest extent. Let there be no occasion for error.

A sealed decree made in a dog year, in the month of Ṣafar, in the year 945 [July 1538], in the region of Samarqand.

I record the names of these dead old men and a decrepit old decree upon this page so that, by the honor of these bygone people and of the marks on an ancient khan's decree, this solitary page may acquire some of that honor and perhaps join their ranks. Another is that it may be cause for those who read and listen to it to pray for those honored ancient khans. How could any other intention find its way into your servant's spiteless heart?

* * *

In the history books, it has been related how, when one became khan, *qaghan*, king, or sultan, extreme attention was paid to genealogy. In every reign, the genealogies of one's ancestors would be scrutinized,[4P299] and one would be raised up by some people as their ruler, and they would submit to his command. Their great fortune and honor came by the grace of that King of Kings and Judge of Judges (EXALTED BE HIS POWER!). When a humble subject of such a king (both outward and inward) did him worthy service and happened to attract his attention, he would pay them royal kindness and appoint to them a monthly stipend, and they would receive a decree favoring them with the great fortune of an official rank and a *tarkhan* to be passed down from generation to generation. Later kings and khans would seek out the progeny of those who had done such service, and they would be happily rewarded with the receipt of their ancestor's rank and stipend. In certain years, they would go to the palace and receive an audience, and they would be freed from want or need.

Oh, King of Kings! Oh, Judge of Judges! Oh, Noble of Nobles! True kingship is that which belongs to You (EXALTED BE HIS SULTANATE!). So, may You, by Your ancient command, choose some from among Your creations and Your servants to grant them in Your kindness great fortune and generosity, and exalt them, to make them intimates of the lofty Court, and May You likewise separate their descendants from the parasites among Your servants, and by Your perfect power place them in this world on the path of righteousness with the right guidance of God, down the generations until the End of the World, and at the end forgive their transgressions both large and small.

May You grant them the fortune and nobility of the beauty of Your perfected world. And may You also allow your humble author to enter into their ranks, and draw the pen of absolution across his sins both old and new, cutting out the dots of his sins with the penknife of pardon and exchanging for his sins the worthiness of the lofty Court. At your Gate, nothing is strange or impossible. OH, JUDGE OF JUDGES! OH, NOBLE OF NOBLES! OH, YOU ARE THE BEST OF HELPERS, FOR HE ANSWERS THOSE WHO PRAY. BY THE MASTER OF THE MESSENGERS AND SEAL OF THE PROPHETS. AMEN.

2:19 Reconquest of the Chinese Emperor

How by the Emperor of China's Royal Command His Great Officials Again Found Dominion Over the Seven Cities—That Is, the Domain of Moghulistan—and How He Became King Once More Over His Ancestral Domain

IT IS WRITTEN that, during the reign of Daoguang Khan,[P300] the Khan of the Clime of Khaqan-i Chin,[1] the Clime of Khaqan and its territories were prospering, and its borders were very peaceful and tranquil. When he had reigned for thirty-two years[, he passed away]. Then Xianfeng Khan reigned as khan for twelve years. At that time, the people called "Long-Hairs"[2] challenged him for the khanship, and many great battles and slaughters ensued. Then Tongzhi Khan took the throne. During the seventh year of this khan's reign, the Dungan people in the Seven Cities also rose up and rebelled against him. This story was narrated earlier, at the end of the prolegomenon.

They say that, during the reign of Tongzhi Khan, the land of Khaqan-i Chin and its surrounds fell into great chaos. The fortune tellers and astrologers cast the lots, studied the khan's star of fortune, and reported to him, saying, "Until the Great Khan gives up the khanship and goes down under the ground, this ill omen will never be lifted from the Great Khan's lands. This is known from the movement of the spheres." There is a cemetery for the imperial ancestors one *paotai*'s distance from the capital at Beijing. The khan, in accordance with this prediction, left his capital for that cemetery, where he had a tunnel built under the ground, with a path running through.

He remanded the khanship to his son, or perhaps one of the other princes, whose name was Guangxu. He lowered his head and, joining the ranks of the Brahmins, he went underground, believing, "Now I shall be forbidden from walking upon the surface of the Earth!" The stories say that he may have left that cemetery but hid himself. They say that that tunnel might have been there since the khans of old, and this was the rule whenever something like this happened.

That prince, Guangxu, was only three years old. So the grand secretaries and governors-general, in accordance with their own bizarre traditions and beliefs, begged Heaven for one year, which they gave to the khan.[3] He was now four years old. They begged the Earth for one year, which they gave him. He was now five years old. His mother gave him one year. He was now six years old. The grand secretaries and governors-general together gifted a year to him. He was now seven years old. They believed that their khan had ascended to the throne at the age of seven and showed him the proper respect. But his mother took him in her arms, and she sat on the throne, proclaiming the khanal commands. THE RESPONSIBILITY IS ON THE NARRATOR.

{301} At this auspicious hour, the fortune tellers and astrologers were summoned again to cast the lots, study the khan's star of fortune, observe the Milky Way, the Dipper, and the sightings of the planets, and scrutinize their degrees and minutes. And when they had done so, they reported to him, "The rising, falling, degree, and position of the new Great Khan's stars are all in a high place, while the stars of his enemies are declining. The lands are at peace. As evidenced by the spheres and their stars, your ancestral lands are coming under your control once again. Wheresoever you order your armies, they will be victorious."

Now Grand Secretary Li and all the other grand secretaries, which is to say the high ministers, together said to the Great Khan: "The Dungans have conquered Lanzhou and many other cities to our west, and laid the common people to waste. Ili has been conquered by the Russians. The Chantous of the Nan Lu Ba Cheng are now ruled by a man who came from the west and became king.[4] In the Great Khan's good fortune, he no longer has any enemies here. We request that we send armies to collect the common people who in bygone days were under the Great Khan's rule in those western regions."

The Great Khan responded generously, "Understood. In that case, let the armies go and reclaim those cities. If they face resistance, let them fight, and occupy the territory. If they face no resistance, then let them settle those who submit. May they fight to reclaim every last inch[5] of my father and grandfather's land until a thousand soldiers have died. I am the Great Khan. I have forgiven my subjects' crimes." General Jing[6] was ordered to Ili with 40,000 soldiers. Lushi Daren[7] was ordered to Nan Lu Ba Cheng with 25,000 soldiers. When these officers and their armies arrived at Lanzhou, Lushi Daren was joined by the governor-general of Lanzhou, Zongtong Daren.

* * *

The Dungans rebelled against the Emperor of China and elevated one of their own scholars, Ma Hualong, as their khan, and he enacted his commands. These events were briefly discussed in the prolegomenon.{302} After Ma Hualong died, two famed warriors from among his braves, Dakhu and Shokhu, became the Dungans' leaders. They fought with the Chinese, sometimes winning, sometimes losing and fleeing. They lived for eleven or twelve years in the cities and countryside around Lanzhou, raiding the Chinese. Now they heard that those armies had come by the Great Khan's command and occupied Lanzhou, and they fled to Qumul, where they stayed for two months. Then, out of fear, they likewise terrorized the people of Qumul and forced nearly 10,000 of them to march to Turfan with them. These events have been narrated.

At that time, the Great Khan's armies came to Qumul.[8] The Jangjung and his army made camp in Xihu. Lushi Daren set up headquarters in Qumul. Zongtong Daren took up position in Gucheng. While they were riding toward Turfan, they heard that the Ataliq Ghazi Badawlat had come and camped there with 30,000 troops and artillery. This concerned them, so they sent a message to the governor-general of Lanzhou, writing something like, "This king has personally led 30,000 troops to Turfan. His strength is great and his armaments are many. His men are brave. This is ill news. Would you, Gong, grant us the aid of a few more soldiers?"

The governor-general, Governor-General Gong Zong,[9] read the message. "I am riding personally to your aid with 60,000 soldiers," came his reply. "Worry not—proceed toward the objective." This strengthened the officers' and soldiers' resolve, and they went on their way.

They stayed in Qumul for about ten months. Then Lushi Daren arrived in Turfan by the highway. Zongtong Daren entered Turfan via Ürümchi and Manas. They stayed in Turfan for about nine months. Then they rode over to Korla. As they departed from Korla, they pursued Dakhu and Shokhu. Those Dungans had the fine idea that their soldiers would not pillage the Muslims' goods or destroy them, nor would they stop in any place to seize the common people's belongings or lives, so they managed to march a twenty-day road in twelve days and make it from Korla to Aqsu. And yet a new terror surely descended from the invisible world upon Dakhu and Shokhu's hearts, for nowhere could they find rest or repose, and as they fled, they could enter no city. Then they divided up those things that they had taken possession of,[10] P304 and Dakhu went toward Kashgar through Ushturfan and via Qaqshal, while Shokhu and his men took the highway into Kashgar.

* * *

Zongtong Daren entered Aqsu in the year 1294, the Year of the Horse, on Wednesday, the seventeenth day of Shawwal, in the season of Sagittarius [October 25, 1877].[11] They stayed for forty days in Aqsu, and then Zongtong Daren rode to Kashgar along the highway. Luying Uchu[12] went to Ushturfan and marched to Kashgar through Qaqshal. Luying Uchu and Zongtong Daren entered Kashgar together, while Dong Daren and his army set out for Yarkand. When these dark soldiers entered Kashgar, Mirza Aḥmad Qushbegi [and the Boy Beg] fled with their lives to Ferghana. Dong Daren then went and conquered Yarkand and likewise brought Khotan to submission. The people of the Seven Cities, of all Moghulistan, now came under the rule of the Emperor of China's officials. The rays of Islam's light were blotted out by a cloud of tyranny. Verily the holy hadith became manifest: ISLAM BEGAN AS SOMETHING STRANGE, AND IT WILL RETURN TO HOW IT WAS.[13]

The host of troops had arrived just as the Dungans led by Dakhu and Shokhu had gone to Kashgar to the aid of the Boy Beg and were fighting He Dalaoye. Dakhu and Shokhu fled to Russia through the guardpost at Chaqmaq. Shokhu and a number of Dungan soldiers fell into the hands of the emperor's army, and they died. Dakhu submitted himself to Russia along with [his children and] some 40,000 Dungans. The White Emperor[14] accepted their submission and made them his subjects, granting them land. All of them became his wealthy benefactors, happy and carefree.

* * *

From the time the Great Khan's soldiers left Turfan until they conquered Kashgar, not a single living man shot at them or blocked their way. Rather, the leaders of every city went out to greet them, paid their respects, and did them as much service as they were able. Yet the officers entered each city and issued a proclamation of punishment: "Bring the bad men out to us. We will put them to the sword as an example to all."

"The bad men were frightened for their lives," the local leaders would reply, "so they fled. The peaceful, good people did not leave their own lands." The Chinese officers accepted that. But if the leaders told them, "These were bad men—please give them their punishment," then they would kill them.

However, the officers would not decide for themselves whether a man was good or bad. "Whether you are foreign or local," they ordered, "or soldier or civilian,[P304] bother no one, but be at peace and act as good subjects. Be good. Do not upset yourselves. The Great Khan has issued a decree forgiving all of your past crimes." This they announced in every town and village by pasting up *gongshi* notices. Everyone felt relieved when they read them.

* * *

Now Mirza Aḥmad Wang Beg's son Mirza Ḥamid Taji Beg was made the governor of Kashgar; Yusuf Shang ʿAli Beg, that of Kucha; Qasim Qażi Beg, that of Aqsu; Muḥammad Tokhta Beg, that of Bay and Sayram; ʿAlauddin Beg, that of Ushturfan; and Aḥmad Mirab Beg, that of Khotan.

Tokhta Niyaz Yüzbashi was appointed governor of Yarkand, and this is why: when the Boy Beg returned from pacifying Khotan, he said, "I will fight the emperor's armies." He ordered the Shighavul Dadkhwah, "Send a great supply of straw, fodder, flour, and rice to Maralbashi." Accordingly, they sent foodstuffs such as flour, rice, and fodder to Maralbashi, with Tokhta Niyaz Yüzbashi in charge. While he was waiting there with the supplies, Zongtong Daren and Dong Daren arrived at Maralbashi. So he gifted those foodstuffs to the emperor's armies, and he said to them, "When I heard that the Great Khan's many armies had marched such a long way to collect his old subjects, and that you had already gotten to Aqsu, I gathered food from my very own farming upon my very own beasts' backs and waited here to greet the army." When they heard that, they were very happy and praised him, saying, "You are a good and kindly man!" They made him the governor of Yarkand on this account.

They tallied up all the grain in the granaries of every city and added it to the treasury. Then they drafted a list of all sorts of necessities—grain and firewood, alfalfa, straw—that were in the people's possession. Then they wrote to the country's leading merchants: "Let them set for us the daily market prices on all goods such as these. We will give the common people's copper and silver money from the Great Khan's treasury according to the prices that have been set. We will use nothing that has not been paid for." They warned the merchants, "You will not dishonor us by raising or lowering the prices and bringing disaster upon the common people."

The begs and local leaders weighed the grain,{303} and they set prices for the thornbush, the desert grass,[15] and the willow catkins, which they submitted in a list. The officials looked at it and said to them, "If we pay money according to this list, won't it turn out badly?"

And they replied, "No, it will not."

"In that case," the officials ordered them, "guarantee to us that it will not come to a bad result, and give us a promissory note."[16]

They made their guarantee with a promissory note, which is to say a document, which read, "If the money is paid at this price, it will not bring a bad result, and in case it does, then we are its guarantors, in this world and the next." Afterward, all sorts of necessities were collected from the common people: fine grains, coarse grains, straw, firewood, alfalfa, hay, carrying poles, wood, etc. And they did not keep the silver that they got but submitted it to the begs with nothing short. So five years passed peacefully in this temperate manner.

* * *

When His Highness the Badawlat conquered Aqsu and Kucha, he took the Khaṭib Khoja of Kucha and his sons away to Kashgar. Later, when the Great Khan's armies came, there was nowhere they could flee, so they stayed in Kashgar and concealed themselves in various places for a while. Eventually it got out to Zongtong Daren, who had the Khaṭib Khoja brought in and asked him many questions.

"Why did you throw the Cities into rebellion," he asked, "and kill the imperial agents, the *dalaoyes*, and the soldiers?"

"We were in a place outside of the city of Kucha called Mazar Baghi," he replied. "One night, some Dungan and Chantou gamblers and carousers set fire to the city, and they killed the imperial agent, the soldiers, and the merchants. When they tried to make Aḥmad Wang Beg their leader, he told them, 'I have received the favor of the Great Khan. I will not be your leader.' And so the crowd beat him to death with their clubs. They killed the governor of Kucha and seven other begs and looted their possessions. Three days later, a number of Dungan gamblers came up to Mazar Baghi, and it is true that they made us their leaders against our will. We were afraid, so we led them. But it was not our choice. Soon the '*Lao* Padishah' took possession of these lands. He removed us to Kashgar to keep us here."

"At that time, how old were you?"

"I was sixty-two. Now I am eighty-one."[17]

Zongtong Daren sent the Khaṭib Khoja away, handing him into the custody of Ḥamid Taji Ḥakim Beg, the governor of Kashgar. "I will send a report to the Great Khan," he said. "Then you will follow his command."

Nine months later,{304} a decree came from the Great Khan: "He is an old man. I have forgiven his crimes. If he will return to his own land, then pay his travel expenses and send him on his way." And in accordance with this command, he was brought out again and received the Great Khan's generosity.

"Go back to your own land," he was told, and given a hundred silver coins for his travel expenses. He was sent back to Kucha, and a special travel permit was placed in his hand. After that, his sons, Maḥmudin Khoja and Ḥamuddin Khoja, likewise received travel permits, went to Kucha, and rejoined their relatives. Not a single person could open their mouths to speak against them. They did whatever they pleased.

* * *

Dong Daren was very steadfast in his heretical religion, and he felt great spite and enmity toward the Muslims. In zealotry and bravery he exceeded all the other officers, and in daring and fury he was, when compared to the other commanders, like a great storm. For a slight offense he beat Alp Beg, the governor of Sarikol, to death. He coerced the people of Kashgar, shouting,

"Show me the corpse of the '*Da* Padishah!"[18] and left them no choice but to show him. He took his soldiers to open up the Ataliq Ghazi's tomb. Then they mounded up firewood, set it aflame, and burned it down. There was no choice.

This was a delight to those lax in their faith, to the ignoble and the hypocritical, but a cause for suffering to good Muslims, the pious and the prudent, and their eyes dampened, and they busied themselves with prayers for forgiveness from the court of the Holy One who lacks nothing.

*　　*　　*

With regard to these strange events, the great scholars say that the dead have earned ranks among the martyrs, but those who lived are deserving of humiliation and disgrace. These strange events, which happened in relation to the Ataliq Ghazi, also occurred in relation to earlier kings and true caliphs. In the *Garden of Purity*, Muḥammad b. Khwandshah related how the first of the ʿAbbasid Caliphs to sit upon the throne, al-Saffah, or ʿAbdullah b. Muḥammad b. ʿAli b. ʿAbdullah b. ʿAbbas (MAY GOD BE PLEASED WITH HIM!), commanded that the Banu Umayya, which is to say the descendants of Muawiya, should open their tombs, though they should not damage the tomb of ʿUmar ʿAbdulʿaziz. So the Muawiya opened the tombs, but within them they found nothing but dirt. Then they opened the tomb of Yazid b. Muawiya, but there was nothing within but ash. In ʿAbdulmalik b. Marwan's tomb, there was only his head. The torso and limbs of Hisham b. ʿAbdulmalik were all present, but dismembered. They took these out and{305} gave them a powerful whipping. After that, they hanged his corpse high, then set it on fire and burned it, and scattered its ashes.

Sulayman b. ʿAli b. ʿAbdullah b. ʿAbbas (MAY GOD BE PLEASED WITH HIM!) was the governor of Basra. He commanded that the leaders of the Banu Umayya be put to the sword, so all of them were killed, and their corpses were thrown into the streets. For several days the wild beasts and dogs of that city had their way with the flesh of the Umayyad leaders.

Muḥammad b. ʿAbdulmalik, ʿUmar b. Yazid, and ʿAbdulwaḥid b. Sulayman, of the sons of the Umayyad Caliphs, were very wealthy and possessed property beyond reckoning. All of them were killed. Sulayman b. ʿAli b. ʿAbdullah b. ʿAbbas seized all of their property. Those of the Banu Umayya who did not meet their end instead entered the road of poverty and took themselves away to the ends of the Earth to live in seclusion.

Oh, dear friends! Know this, that it was the year 132 [749/50], near the time of the Prophet. If during the age of the early followers, the Muslim kings and caliphs saw it fit to do such terrible things to other Muslim caliphs, what in this age are the infidels willing to do out of contempt for pious Muslims and Muslim kings?

About that time when the Chinese burned the corpse of the Ataliq Ghazi: these people were of the belief that, when a person dies, if their good deeds outweigh their bad, then such a person's soul will appear in another person's belly, and they will stand right up and appear as another person upon the Earth. But if their good deeds should be few and their bad deeds many, such people will become dogs, donkeys, or some such thing, and they will stand up again upon the Earth to do their service before they die again, appear in another woman's stomach, and live again. If someone has only a little debt, then they will at least be a chicken and lay an egg, and so pay their dues before becoming a person again. If someone does not pay their debts, then they are out of luck. A wealthy man's debt is never paid. They are very firm in these corrupt beliefs. This, they say, is why they are very afraid of becoming indebted to anyone.

To return to the story: their belief when they burned the corpse of the Ataliq Ghazi was that the *Lao* Padishah's soul would not{306} appear in another woman's belly to live again, and so would not cause another disturbance. Another of their beliefs is in the transmigration of the soul. AND GOD KNOWS THE TRUTH.

* * *

The emperor's officials governed in the manner previously described for five years. After that, they wished for all of the expenses of government to be supported by the land. They took everyone's land, whether much land or little, and they measured it in feet,[19] and they measured it in jots.[20] They measured it out and surveyed it. To those who had much they gave much grain, both fine and coarse, water, and straw; and to those who had less, less; and they recorded this in a register. They recorded the expenditures and revenues of each city and reported these to the Great Khan. There came a decree from the Great Khan: "Understood." The officials in every city collected grain according to the specified quota and took it into the treasury. The officials took it like this for ten or twelve years. As they did so, they took in more and more.

Now the Emperor of China's officials have been in power for more than thirty years. It is the year 1326 [1908].[21] And it has come to the point that people have abandoned the lands inherited from their ancestors and fled in every direction. Their farms, houses, orchards, and property have fallen into ruin, and now they are nests for owls, empty ground for *divs* and *paris*.

This is surely the intention that the Chinese officials hold in their hearts: "May the common Chantou people love their own Lord's compassion, and hold no hope in any other living thing, but only in their Lord. May they hope and wish for us, and never suffer needlessly, nor waste their lives away. Second, may they never feel license to be ungrateful to us or to any other people or king. Whosoever the Lord of the Heaven and Earth makes their ruler, may they never disobey him, but endure him patiently." If it were their intention truly to govern this country, then they never would have deemed such injustices permissible. Rather, they would have kept watch both on the Muslim tyrants and on the Chinese officials and punished them. But it would be no surprise if God the Merciful were in His kindness to grant His justice to these miserly tyrants.

Oh, you abjectly ignorant man, sinful without measure! Oh, you unsteady guide![22] What right do you have,{307} that you should make some design and waggle your tongue about the affairs of powerful kings, the esteemed holders of the reins? And what qualifies you, that you would even dare? Oh, you no-account busybody, don't waste your time, but offer up your words, idle as ape speech, and hurry toward their end.

* * *

Earthly kings and governors are proud to believe that they took the Cities by their own power and courage, but in truth, the True Mover and Lord is God Himself (BLESSED BE HIS KINGSHIP!). This being the case, whether it be a pious Muslim king or a wicked, impious infidel, that is the one whom the Lord of the Worlds in His ancient knowledge has found fit to place over His creations, and that is that. It follows that one must pray for every king and governor in every time and place, for them to be patient and to receive right guidance and to be just. If he should be a Muslim king, then praying for him is as obvious as the sun. But if he is an impious, wicked king, then it is indeed necessary to pray and ask for his right guidance, patience, and justice, for such kings as these are also among those favored by God.

Regardless of what happens, one must give thanks,
For what ill should come from it?

Oh, you witties! Know that the thornbushes that the gardeners plant around their boundary walls and the dogs that shepherds keep are also among those favored by God. If the shepherd had no dog, it would be impossible to protect his sheep from the wolves; and if the gardeners planted no thornbushes along their walls, it would be difficult to protect the fruit from thieves. From this it may be understood that it is necessary for the whole human race and all the common people to know that among the most important duties for people from all walks of life, and for all the human race, is to give thanks and praise to those whom the Lord has found fitting, in His perfect power, to place over us, His creations, and to pray for them. God, grant patience and justice to the rulers, and right guidance to the common people! Amen. IN HONOR OF THE LEADER OF THE MESSENGERS AND OF THE PROPHETS.

2:20 Virtues of the Chinese Emperor

A Brief Account of the Chinese Emperor's Justice and Love for His People, the Increase of His Praise and Dominion, and the Explication of His Greatness and Generosity

IN THE LATTER part of the prolegomenon to this little chronicle, it was related how every month officials in the Cities placed a yoke about the people's necks.{308} They called this the "head tax," and it was a tax on salt. Here is a detailed account of it. A bright and rational secretary named Mullah Akhund from Aqsu personally related the following account to your humble author:

* * *

Around about the year 1260 [1844], during the reign of Xianfeng Khan, the "Long-Hair" people, the English Christians, and the Dungans rebelled against the Great Khan. At that time he sent armies against them, but consequently lost the means to send funds to the Nan Lu Ba Cheng as he had done before.

The officials of these Seven Cities hatched a plan: "What if we opened some mines in the Cities to send silver to the Great Khan's treasury? And if we raised a tax, and took our chance to place a yoke about the common people's necks, we could collect it and tell the Great Khan about it, and then he would take us into his service, and we would gain positions and power . . ."

The assistant imperial agent at Aqsu, Man Daren, summoned the governor of Aqsu and all his officials.[1] They wrote down the number of people in every household in Aqsu, and they levied a tax of two silver *tangga* from each person in a household. They called this the "head tax." They collected 14,000 *tangga* of this "head tax" from the common people. The Great Khan did not know the truth of this, nor was there any inquiry, so it "disappeared."

So they placed a tax of two *pul* on the salt consumed every month by each person registered in a household. After three months, they were collecting six *daqian*, which is six *pul*. When they did the figures, they realized that this would add up to over 15,000 *tangga* every year from the whole region of Aqsu. They ordered this money to be collected. After three months, when those local officials had taken it from the common people, they brought it to the governor's offices. I, Mullah Akhund, was appointed to count the salt tax and look after it.

When they were collecting the tax, some of the family of the old khans of Ferghana got hold of some land in Aqsu. They settled there, plowed the soil, and farmed, and they totaled over 1,500 households of commoners producing food for the Great Khan's granary. In those days, they had an *aqsaqal* named Mirza Bay. The governor of Aqsu sent a sealed order to Mirza Bay Aqsaqal: "Collect one *daqian* of salt tax from each of the commoners under you every month. Send it to the treasury."

The *aqsaqal* reasoned that he should inform his superior in Kashgar before collecting any salt tax, and so he sent the letter to the head *aqsaqal* in Kashgar.

When the head *aqsaqal* found out,{309} he sent a petition to the khan's agent in Yarkand along with the order. The khan's agent read it. He thought, "I should get to the bottom of this," and sent an agent in secret to Aqsu. The agent assessed the truth of the matter, returned to Yarkand, and informed the khan's agent.

Also around that time, the governor of Bay, Qasim Beg, traveled to Yarkand on official business. The khan's agent there verified the matter with him in a memorial. The agent sent a memorial to the Great Khan that said, "A high official in Aqsu named Man Daren is taking advantage of the Great Khan's good name and collecting a tax on the salt that women use. Should this be heard of in some land, near or far, it will be a bad end. I respectfully submit a memorial to this effect, and I request someone to investigate this matter."

When the Great Khan received the memorial, he was angry. He ordered an agent called Kui Daren to investigate and find out the truth. When the Aqsu agent, Man Daren, heard that that agent was coming to Aqsu, he began to worry. He got seventy-two Chinese and local officials of varying ranks, all led by the governor of Aqsu, to write a memorial that read, "We did not collect a tax on salt. This is a lie." I, Mullah Akhund, likewise produced a false report. It read, "I did not collect money."

About that time, the agent assigned to the investigation arrived in Aqsu. The common people told him what the matter was with the salt tax. The agent took me in too, and asked me to tell him the truth. It felt so difficult for me to come up with lies instead of the truth. They say the truth will set you free, so I told them the truth: "They collected one *daqian* of tax every month on the salt that each person registered in a household used, and they gave it to me. Once they had collected 1,600 *tangga*, someone realized that the Great Khan was angry. No more money was collected."

They asked me, "At this time, do you possess any of this money?"

I replied, "Some is still there, but the magistrate above me demanded the rest. What they lost, they replaced by taking even more. It's all in my notebook."

They wrote a memorial confirming the truth of what I had said. When the agent at Aqsu heard about it, he said to them, "I said there should be no investigation! Why did you do an investigation?" He ordered them beaten with eighty strokes of the two-*jin* rod, and he locked them up tight in jail. Eighty days passed in the meantime.

Then a proclamation came from the Great Khan: "Take the mullah who collected the salt tax; the governor of Aqsu, ʿAshur; the governor of Bay, Qasim; and the magistrate, Mullah ʿAshur, to Ili.{310} The general and the khan's agents are to interrogate them carefully and uncover the truth." Per the proclamation, the four of us were taken to Ili. Around that time, the governor of Aqsu, Ḥamid Taji Beg, had vacated his governorship, and a man named ʿAshur Beg was holding the office, wielding the seal temporarily.

Twelve officials sat in a row, including the general and the khan's agents, and interrogated us very carefully and slowly, one by one. Every month they brought us in for questioning four or five times. On some days they would question us three or four times. They interrogated us like this for eight months. Much of what they asked for they found difficult to believe. In the end they took it down and wrote a memorial to the Great Khan.

The Great Khan sent a proclamation back to the assistant agent that read, "Take them back to their native places. Inquire among the common people and report back to me." He permitted them 5,000 silver for expenses, as well as 50 silver from each station for daily expenses. The khan's agent galloped away on the Ürümchi-Turfan road to Aqsu. The Aqsu agent questioned the Taji Ḥakim Beg, ʿAshur Ḥakim Beg, and the other Chinese and local officials, took down what they said, and wrote another memorial.

They asked me about the missing 1,006 *tangga* and six *pul.* I scrambled through the depths of my brain for the names of anyone I could recall. But they were short four *pul.*

"What did you do?" they asked me.

"Can I think about it and answer you then?"

"Answer," they said.

Eventually they took me in for formal questioning seven more times over two *daqian*, which is four *pul.* In the end I told them, "I wrote out a receipt for these four *pul*, and I handed a copy with my thumbprint to the men who brought me the taxes."

They wrote that down in the record and brought in the Taji Ḥakim Beg. They asked him, "Did this mullah who received the tax money give you a receipt?"

"He didn't give me a receipt," he said.

"All right," they said, "write down 'He didn't give me a receipt' in a letter, and stamp your seal."

With that, they ceased the interrogation and sent the Great Khan a report on the situation.

The Great Khan sent a proclamation: "Understood. I am afraid my people have been abused by their officials. I, the Great Khan, had no news of it.{311} So I have stripped seventy-two Chinese and local officials of their offices, including the assistant imperial agent Man Daren, the governor of Aqsu, and the governor of Bay and Sayram. No more may they be involved in official matters. I have sent them to the Lifan Yuan, and when I check the statutes, I find a statute that says these officials are to be bound and exiled 5,000 *li.* As I, the Great Khan, am a mighty mountain, and my people a tiny river, I have forgiven their crimes. Each of them shall proceed to their native places and be good subjects. Another proclamation: I have recently ascended to the throne. I have forgiven their crimes."

In the tenth year of Xianfeng Khan's reign [1860], the Great Khan learned of the tax incident, and the interrogations were conducted. By the time the interrogations were over, the khan had passed away, Tongzhi Khan had become khan in his place, and three whole years had gone by. The peaceful khan took pity on me, and he wrote, "Much wrong has been done to you, mullah. But you did the right thing. I am pleased with you and grant you thirty silver. Be a good subject."

* * *

This was the story he told me. At the time, your humble author was a bachelor. I was also registered as a "household" and paying three *daqian* every three months.

Oh, worthies of our time! Oh, brilliant minds of this age! This is how great the Great Khan's justice and love for the people was: these 1,000 *tangga* and six *pul* in Seven Cities reckoning were only about{312} sixty-two and a half silver in Chinese reckoning, and 160 *som* in Russian reckoning. For this little money, the Great Khan ordered his agent to come from Ili. Not only did he spend thousands of silver from the treasury on his travel expenses, he gave out several thousand more for petty expenses.

The Great Khan said, "I am the Great Khan. Without royal permission, my officials oppressed my people by taking a *daqian* from them every month." He sent people to assess the truth of the matter, then stripped seventy-two officials of the third and fourth ranks of their offices, including the assistant imperial agent. He even had the *yüzbegi*s, imams, muezzins, and *aqsaqal*s who had collected the salt tax interrogated for days and their testimonies recorded, then stripped them of their offices as well. One must be surprised at this, and when one looks upon it with the eye of discernment, must notice his great justice. If the Great Khan hears of even a mere *daqian*, he will take thousands of silver from his treasury and investigate thoroughly. Today officials use the budget as an excuse to take a thousand *tangga* from a common person for no reason and bring themselves to a princely station. Their cries for justice cannot be heard by the Great Khan. The Great Khan exalts his officials but hears no news of the deeds{313} and tyranny they do.

Mentioning this brings something to mind. It is recorded in books of history that, a long time ago, Anushirvan the Just went on the hunt and came to stay the night in a village. It turned out that his cooks had not brought the salt and black pepper they needed. They thought about it and appropriated the salt they needed from the village instead. When Anushirvan heard about this, he sentenced the head cook and all of the other cooks to death and hanged them.

Anushirvan said, "The kitchen salt is a small thing. One mustn't spend much on it. Without permission, they took it as they saw fit. Now, if I had turned a blind eye to the matter and not executed them, then bit by bit, it would have grown all out of control. This habit would have become a matter of practice and a plague upon the people. The root of tyranny is a tiny thing, but it can grow all at once. It is easy to nip in the bud, but if it happens to grow large and become a habit, then it will be a tyranny upon the people. If it expands into the system of government, then there will be no easy way to put it back in its place. One needs to put a stop to things when they are still small."{314} This is why they called Anushirvan "the Just"—although there are many reasons they called him "the Just." This is just one of them.

Regardless, this is what I mean by bringing this up: it appears that the truth of the tyrannies exacted by those officials sent to take office in these remote parts is not known to the Great Khan. Should he happen to learn the truth, he will have it investigated well and with care. He will display to the utmost his love for the people, bring the sun of his justice to everyone in equal measure, and protect them. The extent and qualities of his justice have been evident for six or seven thousand years, since the time of Noah to ours. Generation after generation, the descendants of Chin and Machin became khan. The successes and flaws of their khanships and the details of their succession are not recorded in books of history.

It is recorded that, although Alexander of Rum seized the world from the Peshdadi kings, he nevertheless negotiated with the Chinese emperor, achieved a truce, and left. Later on, whereas Chinggis Khan seized several territories from those kings who lived in the time of the Seal of the Prophets, at the same time the Great Khan of China was inclined to sign a truce, so he gave his daughter to Chinggis Khan and made him his son-in-law. Chinggis Khan took the Great Khan's daughter as his own{315} and returned to his own lands. He was unable to establish himself as ruler.

Later still, Amir Timur Kuragan (MAY GOD ILLUMINATE HIS TOMB!) decided to conduct a holy war against the emperor of China. For three years he summoned soldiers from across his realm until there were 366,000 men ready and supplied. They rode for Beijing. When they arrived at the old city of Otrar, north of Tashkent, winter came, and the weather turned cold. He planned to winter there and ride out in spring, but many of the soldiers and officers froze to death in the bitter cold. The generals consulted with each other, then sent a report to the amir: "It's getting too cold. Let's winter in Tashkent, Chimkent, or Sayram, then leave in the spring."

Timur was enraged. "How could I turn tail and run, for a little cold?" He walked out in front of his throne room in barely a shirt and called up his barber to cut his hair. The air was frigid in the month of Aquarius. The barber was cutting away his hair; Azrael was cutting away his life. They say that his body froze and stiffened in the bitter cold. This is why, when he went to Beijing, he could not achieve his objective but passed instead on to the next world. This must have been nothing but the favor of God, that God protected the emperor of China and the people of his land, on account of his justice. This is how, across the ages, they raised the banners of those kingdoms that surrounded them and never honored any kingship but their own. Russia, Germany, Italy—Christian or otherwise, when they attacked the emperor of China,{316} their schemes were broken.

Truly, the Great Khan is like a tall mountain. Although he moves like one who has grown fat, in his capital, he is a pillar of the state. Other kings and lords are like a river before him. A river is something that, no matter how many mountains it may lash itself against, it cannot win against the mountain—instead it flows on to other places. All of the awesomeness and strength of the emperor of China's government must derive from the depth and quality of his justice and mercy, from the generosity of his country's people, and from the greatness of his beneficence and righteousness, the breadth and gravity of his character.

One of the reasons for his country's size and breadth is that, as it is written, "For every city with a population of 100,000 households, or at least 50–60,000 households, he stations a *chinchi*. One imperial agent oversees eight *chinchi*. One general oversees four imperial agents. Finally, one governor-general oversees two generals. This way, there are twenty-one governor-general territories and their people in the Great Khan's domain." Each territory overseen by a governor-general is called a province. Today, each territory overseen by an imperial agent has two circuit intendants to monitor it.[2] By this estimate, there are 236 imperial agent-level territories, with their people, within the

Great Khan's domain. In this little chronicle, we have described the reign of the king Yaʿqub{317} Beg Ataliq. By this estimate, he was king and ruler of a territory equal to just one of these imperial agent-level territories. Take this estimate and consider the greatness of the Great Khan's government, the expanse of his land and people.

The nobility of his intention is such that he does not give the land and people passed down to him from his ancestors to other kings. Nor does he covet the lands and people of other kings, nor the property, money, wives, or children of another domain's people. Nor does he ever trick, deceive, or lie to his high officials, or to merchants or petty traders. He keeps his word. His generosity and gravity of spirit are such that, when a neighboring king sends an emissary bearing coarse and impetuous words, he will be dignified and serious and never take it to heart. Instead, he will generously reply with polite, gentle, sweet words and hold to the path of compromise. When an official commits a crime, whether he be high or low, and is stripped of office, the Great Khan never takes his money for some penalty or other. No matter what, if some money has been collected, it remains with him. Stripping someone of office is seen as stripping someone of life.

If his little people do not violate the rule of *li* and go about whatever craft or business to make their living, then they never have any issues. He never takes their money for the treasury. If someone who does not know the rule of *li* should commit a crime, and they say, "I do not know the rule of *li*," then he forgives them. He does not force them to "Study our rule of *li*,{318} or enter into our customs." He likes it when each people remains within its own sect and holds fast to its community.[3]

If officials do not send him memorials, then no matter how much may happen, he does not involve himself. If they should happen to send a memorial, then he will question it delicately and carefully, inspect the root problem, discern, and find the truth and essence of the matter for them.

To sum up what we have said, the Great Khan's justice is such that, by reason of his justice, of the qualities and depth of the just government he gives his people, for the whole of this long era, no other splendid ruler could realize their ill intention to send armies to attack him and reduce his kingship. If there is any khan or king who holds fast to justice and benevolent government, and who manifests his love for his people, the True King (Great is His dignity!) by means of His perfect power will shelter that khan in His protection. He will forever defeat that khan's enemies. Moreover, the people's prosperity and capability, the cultivation of the land, the height and splendor of the gardens and buildings, and the largeness of the harvest and plenty of their livelihoods result from the king's surfeit of justice and good government. The army owes its wealth, capability, and strength{319} to the common people's wealth and capability.

The sages of old said, THERE IS NO KING WITHOUT KINGDOM, AND NO KINGDOM WITHOUT THE PEOPLE, AND NO PEOPLE WITHOUT JUSTICE AND GOOD GOVERNMENT. This means: there is no country unless it has common people; and there are no common people unless they have property; and property does not thrive unless the common people thrive; and the common people do not thrive unless justice and good government thrive.

There is a hadith that says, JUSTICE AND GOOD GOVERNMENT ARE BETTER THAN THE WORSHIP OF THE TWO RACES. That is, an hour of justice done is better than the faith of humans and jinn alike. At dawn on the Day of Judgment, when all are assembled for their accounting, they will ask each king and khan in turn about justice. If they have done it, then answering the rest of the questions will be easy. The time of ascetics and age of the faithful will last for seventy years of trial and tribulation, and then when they believe, in one hour things that had not been possible before will be granted to just kings. This is the lot and duty of the kings and khans of great states, generals, governors, and judges of the Shariah alike. Of course, the *yüzbashi*s and *mingbashi*s, imams and muezzins of the villages, even all those who head households—they too, according to their stature and power, require patience, justice, and good governance. If each of them is just to the people, children, servants, and all others in their care, then they will surely receive their reward. A just country will be destroyed and put to ruin by bad government and tyranny. When one does not do justice in a place that needs it but instead gives it carelessness and inattention, this is tyranny.{320} And when, in a case meriting execution, one does not execute but shepherds and forgives, this too is tyranny. When one does justice, regardless of the recompense or the outcome, and in the proper moment does not diminish good government but practices it, the outcome will be in proportion. A king is hopeless without justice, forever rudderless without good government. When the *mujtahid*s (GOD BLESS THEM ALL!) decided to permit something that was important for the general welfare, they would issue a judgment on its permissibility. This is why kings, even in cases where the penalty of death was not ordinarily licit, could take the general welfare and needs of the nobility into consideration, and thus pursue capital punishment as appropriate to the well-being of the commoners. The common people's tranquility and the country's prosperity derive from the kindness and good government of a powerful king.

Oh God, the Perfect! With your perfect power, grant justice and guidance in peace to all of the *qaghans* of the world, kings of the age, and grim earthly rulers, be they faithful Muslims or apostate infidels. Day by day, grant them justice and love of the common people without measure. Amen.

God forbid that a king should forget justice and good government, and that infidelity should emerge among the common people and rulers alike, for it is clear as the sun itself to every race of people that, GOD FORBID!, if that were to happen, then those unfortunates would fall trampled into nothingness beneath horses' hooves. Every king, every ruler, must surely know that it is their duty—yes, their duty!—{321}to know that justice and compassion are indeed their duty, and to pray to God that He will grant patience, justice, and right guidance to all the common people, and to the rulers.

Here concludes the sermon.

* * *

Dear friends and brothers true, may this be a summary of the discourse for your lofty intellects: the common people, who were debilitated beyond description, could not cast off the cruel oppressions and coercive exactions of the infidels and the tyrants, so they cried out from the depths of their hearts and importuned the holy throne of the Eternal. They were blessed with a response, as the Khojas of Kucha gained ascendancy over the tyrants. It was as though the common people had been liberated from the cruel punishments of the Abyss and ascended unto the heights of Paradise. They rejoiced, and cries of joy rang out across the indigo sky. But these Khojas in turn opened the door of tyranny, and forgot their prior lives. The common people turned their faces to the court of the Peerless, and they were weeping. The supreme and Peerless Almighty (EXALTED BE HIS POWER!) in His grace placed their prayers into the place of response, and he brought Yaʿqub Beg the Ataliq Ghazi to rule over them. The people gave prayers of thanks for their liberation from the dominion of the Khojas of Kucha and the burdens of the war tax,[4] and every one of them was joyful. And for a time, their tablecloths were rolled out.[5] Eventually, however, the Ataliq Badawlat's character changed, and{322} his evil deeds became more and more apparent.

Once again the common people lost their patience, and they would no longer stand for the government's exactions. Now they rubbed their faces upon the threshold of the Creator's holy court and filled their eyes with tears, as they hoped and begged for the emperor of China, and they wept, and in their weeping, they supplicated as never before.

In the end, by the grace of God the All-Powerful, the Ever-Forgiving, the Magnificent, the emperor's officers made their arrival in the Seven Cities, which he appended to his domain and birthright—indeed, he became lord and master over the inheritance of his forefathers' throne once more. The common people—and of course the old begs and officials—were rejoicing, as though their own uncles and parents had been resurrected, and in their surfeit of love they bloomed like blossoms, no longer able to hold their joy within. Each of these events has been related in turn.

The argument that follows from these premises is that the cries, prayers, and supplications of the common people—indeed, of any living thing—in the holy court of the eternal Creator, the All-Powerful who says BE! AND IT IS [36:82], will never go unnoticed. The verse says, I SHALL RESPOND TO YOU [40:60]: Whenever one of His creations prays sincerely, truly the Lord, the Bestower of Desires, will make manifest his response. A hadith reads, HIS RECEPTION OF THE SUPPLICATION OF THE OPPRESSED BRINGS AN ANSWER, THOUGH THEY MAY BE AN INFIDEL. That is to say that one ought to fear the prayers of the oppressed, for,{323} even should they be infidels, the response is near. No matter which of God's creations, or which of the nations, or what sort of person, their prayers will be received in God's court, although the response may not be apparent to His servants' minds or seen by their eyes. So, that being the case, let them absolutely, a thousand times absolutely, fear the cries of the common people, indeed of all God's creatures.

* * *

Today, the emperor's officials have placed those precious goods of equity and justice into the niche of forgetting, and they increase their tyranny moment by moment. The eyes of the suffering and the oppressed have begun again to fill with tears.

Oh God, in Your perfect power, grant justice to kings and right guidance to the common people. In latter days, the wise—indeed, all faithful Muslims—must know and believe that ALL DESTINY, GOOD OR BAD, COMES FROM GOD: nothing, good or bad, is beyond the will of God. May they righteously correct and deepen their faith, and not be deceived by the grace and compassion of created beings. It is clear to every race of people that, should any created being forget the clemency of the true Creator and hope instead for the clemency of some creation, then that creation will become an enemy to them, and in place of fidelity they will have torment, and in place of grace, wrath.

How happy the man,{324} how blessed, who commits himself always to the Creator of All Things (EXALTED BE HIS GLORY!) and hopes for His compassion. He has held the sun-bright Book of God tightly in one hand, and in the other, that candle of guidance, the Sunnah of the Prophet, and he has read both these lights.[6] In the midst of error, when they show him the way, the True King (EXALTED BE HIS KINGSHIP!) will preserve him by the beacon of His own guardianship, and protect him from the tyranny and wrath of untrue kings—nay, from all misfortunes in this world and the next—and place him among the noblest ranks, making him to prosper in His unending sight, and granting him a place among the sublime.

BY HIS GRACE AND GENEROSITY, PRAISE BE TO GOD, WHO MADE SUCCESS OUR COMPANION, AND THE STRAIGHT PATH OUR WAY. AMEN.

Description of Moghulistan

3:0 Introduction

Epilogue: A Brief Description of the Borders and Situation of the Realm of Moghulistan, the Enumeration of the Seven Cities, the Dispositions and Habits of Their People, and the Shrines of Holy Personages

IN THE HISTORY books, namely the *Tarikh-i Rashidi* by Mirza Ḥaydar Kuragan (MAY GOD ILLUMINATE HIS RESTING PLACE!), who was a ruler of the Seven Cities, the borders of Moghulia were copied from the documents of bygone kings. The *Tarikh-i Rashidi* relates: "The eastern boundary of Moghulistan is at Barköl and Qumul. Its northern boundary is at the Great Sea.[1] Its western boundary is at Chaqsaman in Tashkent, Samghir in Andijan, and La'l Kani[2] in Badakhshan. The southern boundary is at Tibet and the Uyghur country.{325} Its length and breadth span three months' journey. In the documents, the land within these boundaries is called 'Moghulistan.' "[3] Ürümchi, Tarbaghatai [*Chung*], and Ili are also included within these borders. Within Moghulistan, the cities are called the "Seven Cities." The "Seven Cities" refers to Kashgar, Yarkand, Khotan, Aqsu, Ushturfan, Kucha, and Old Turfan. The people of Khaqan call the Seven Cities *Nan Lu Ba Cheng*, which apparently means "the eight cities on the southern side." In this case, the eighth ought to be Korla. The ancient capitals of Moghulistan during the era of the Muslim khans were Yarkand and Turfan.

In the lands of the Seven Cities are many lofty tomb-shrines of holy men and tombs of great saints where people make pilgrimage. Nevertheless, the majority of their names, genealogies, and stories are unknown. Even if we have their names and hagiographies, most of those hagiographies do not accord with the old history books. It seems as though some men in every age have ignored the history books and instead written hagiographies as they pleased, with the result that some shrines are called things like "Ram Father," "Cock Father," "Shrine of the Poplar," "Silver-Eyed Father," "Beard Father," "Bull Camel Father," etc. As people do not know their names, they have become known by these names. Their hagiographies likewise seem to have been compiled in the same manner. Although their [holy] names are surely different, each of their stories is narrated at the place where they alighted. GOD WILLING, HE IS FORGIVING!

* * *

The wise and noble geometers of bygone and latter days alike, when describing the surface of the Earth as well as its wildernesses and inhabited places, made great endeavors to determine their locations in degrees and minutes.{326} And the quarters of the world from the beginning of the eastern boundaries to the end of the western, the surface of the world, are divided by the motion of the seven planets into seven parts, and each of these parts is called a "clime." And each clime is connected to one of the seven stars, so that the first clime is bound to Saturn, the second to Jupiter, the third to Mars, etc., according to this scheme. The wise old authors who compiled those chronicles recorded the manners, appearances, and humors of the people belonging to each clime, as well as the cities, seas, wildernesses, and settled places, and enumerated them in detail in their useful books, and gave them embellishment. Your humble author, who is ignorant and without merit, full of defects from head to toe, and unequal to such a weighty task, makes so bold as to record upon this page, in their seven stations, the Seven Cities and some of the manners of their people. GOD IS MY GUIDE AND HELP.

3:1 Kashgar

THE FIRST AND greatest of the Seven Cities is Kashgar.

Kashgar is an ancient and famous city. The people of Kashgar are customarily friendly to scholars and the *ṣaḥib duʿa*. The alms and offerings that its merchants and wealthy farmers pay, and the efforts of its craftsmen, are superior to those of other cities. Particularly with regard to the currency of the scholars and the trade of the merchants, it would not be incorrect to describe it as a "second Bukhara."{327} It has little land in proportion to its people, and the city's own produce and foodstuffs are insufficient to feed it. Every week, no fewer than 2,000 donkey loads of grain arrive in Kashgar from Yarkand. It has little pastureland, and it is deficient in livestock.

The tomb-shrines of holy men in the land of Kashgar include:

That of Afaq Khoja. His name was Khoja Hidayatullah Khoja b. Yusuf Khoja b. Muḥammad Amin Khoja b. Makhdum-i Aʿẓam (MAY GOD SANCTIFY HIM!). He is rich in praise and commendation.

There is also Sultan Sutuq Bughra Khan Ghazi, who is said to have been a descendant of Afrasiyab, and who in the year 330 [941/2] converted to Islam through the efforts of Abu Naṣr Samani. The people of the Seven Cities likewise accepted Islam in the blessed footsteps of this holy personage and joined the community of Muslims. In 370 [980/1], the people of Khotan converted to Islam. The hadith FIRST MUSLIM AMONG THE TURKS, SUTUQ refers to this personage. His shrine is in Artush, and it is well known.

Also: Sayyid Jalaluddin Baghdadi, Quṭbullah Khoja, Ḥasan Fażlullah [Fayżullah] Khoja, and Ordam Padishah, which is also called Qizil Arslan Khan. Their hagiographies have not been consulted. There are also many other holy shrines and honored pilgrimage places, but this much is sufficient.

3:2 Yarkand

YARKAND IS AN ancient city. Its people have a helpless manner about them. They are masterful and disciplined in their work.{328} They give great currency and support to Sufi masters and have much faith in them. There are many Hindu, Kashmiri, Afghan, and Badakhshani travelers among them, although they seldom go traveling themselves. All of their people are fine farmers. Their land is broad and pure, and their produce and foodstuffs are sufficient for the city, or more. Their pastures are beyond measure and very plentiful with every kind of livestock and yak. Their dried fruit is abundant, their produce readily available and inexpensive, and their lands without limit.

Famous shrines: That of Khoja Muḥammad Sharif Pir-i Buzurgwar.

And also the Shrine of the Seven Muḥammads. It is called the "Seven Muḥammads" because it is where seven holy men named Muḥammad lie. They say that they came from the Forty [*Chihil-Tan*].

The Golden Shrine is where the bodies of the Muslim khans are, who ruled the Seven Cities for over two hundred years, from the reign of Sultan Saʿid Khan Bahadur to those of Ismail Khan b. ʿAbdurraḥim Khan and Muḥammad Amin Khan, and who made their capital in Yarkand. The Mongols honored and respected the bodies of the khans and would refer to them as "gold," so that every command upon which the khan's eye fell or that the khan's hand had pressed with a seal would be called a "golden command" or "golden document." This is probably the reason it is known as the Golden Shrine.

There is also the Sayyidzada Shrine, for the several children and grandchildren of Khoja Isḥaq b. Makhdum-i Aʿẓam[329] who were under the leadership of Khoja Shuʿayb and Khoja Shadi, themselves descendants of Makhdum-i Aʿẓam. There are other shrines as well—they are numerous.

3:3 Khotan

KHOTAN IS A very ancient and famous city. The character of its people is such that they are peerless in being true to their word, unrivaled in their unity and firmness, and incomparable in their forbearance. There are many pious abstainers among them, although the impure and evil are even more numerous. All of their people are skilled craftsmen of great natural talent, with an ingenuity beyond calculation. They are able to master every craft, display it to a customer, make a trade, and bring in cash. They produce many rolls of silk. There are gold mines, as well as quarries for jade. No matter how much cash the great merchants bring from all around to trade, they will hand it all over and still have custom to do. Khotan's wares go to other cities, but the cash never leaves, except for the gold.

Relative to the number of people, Khotan's land is insufficient, and most of it is desert. Its produce and foodstuffs are also deficient. Its fruits are juicy and plentiful, and its pastures and wildernesses boundless. Their livestock are also numerous.

In the land of Khotan is located the tomb of the famed Imam Jaʿfar Ṣadiq (MAY GOD BE PLEASED WITH HIM!). It is a major shrine. All of the common people believe that the blessed body of Imam Jaʿfar Ṣadiq (MAY GOD BE PLEASED WITH HIM!) is in the land of Khotan. In the history books, however, and specifically the *Garden of Purity*, it is related: "Imam Jaʿfar Ṣadiq b. Imam Muḥammad Baqir b. ʿAli (known by the epithet 'Ornament of Worshippers') b. Imam Hussein (MAY GOD BE PLEASED WITH HIM!){330} passed away in the year 148 [765] during the reign of the ʿAbbasid Caliph Abu Jaʿfar al-Manṣur al-Duwaniqi. He was buried at the feet of his father, Muḥammad Baqir, and his grandfather, the Ornament of Worshipers.[1] His blessed body is in the Cemetery al-Baqiʿ."[2]

From this it can be surmised that certainly some great holy man by the name of Jaʿfar fully mastered the innate tradition and attained the rank of an imam and a leader, and at that time, his disciples said something to the effect of, "He is like a second Imam Jaʿfar." The word "second" [*s̱ani*] through common error became twisted into "Ṣadiq," because the word "second" and the word "Ṣadiq" have the same syllabic weight and are quite close. Seeing as how he had perfectly mastered the ascetic practice and the innate tradition, there was nothing to constrain the Provider of Needs from granting him the generosity and erudition of Imam Jaʿfar Ṣadiq (MAY GOD BE PLEASED WITH HIM!). THAT IS THE BOUNTY OF GOD; WHICH HE GIVES TO WHOMSOEVER HE WILL, AND GOD IS POSSESSED OF TREMENDOUS BOUNTY [57:21].

In this manner one finds in Khotan many important and exalted shrines, such as those of Imam Jaʿfar Ṭayaran, the Sacrificed Imams [*Imam Ẕabiḥullah*], Imam Qasim, and Imam Hashim. There too is a place where the tyrant Küchlüg Khan murdered several men of faith, which is known as the Desert Martyrs [*Qum Shahidan*]. This is why they call the city "Khotan, the City of Martyrs." Those imams' miraculous acts were apparent and well known.

Whichever human being serves a spiritual guide and manifests the tradition as it truly is, there is no doubt that the Merciful Lord in His grace will exalt them.[3P333] Within every human being is a potential saint. But attaining the rank of a saint in actuality happens through one's profession and labor.

Another thing: to the great and lofty saints has the Unsleeping God in His grace distributed high ranks, so that at any moment there will be seen one in Syria, another in Mecca, and another in another country. No one ever knows whether those personages go from their own place to some other, or if they disappear for a day or half a day. Such things as this are made easy by God's mysterious power. Or perhaps these imams already come from that class of the exalted.

It is related in that reliable book, the *Garden of Purity*: a long time ago, in the year 614 [1217/8], a Nayman leader called Tayang Khan battled with Chinggis Khan but could not match him, and it may be that Tayang Khan died at that time. His son, Küchlüg Khan, could not remain in his own country and nation, so he took several men with him to Kashgar, which he conquered. He committed such injustice there that the crops were destroyed beneath the feet of the livestock, and he had them set aflame, annihilating them. This nonbelieving, infidelish tyrant's officers entered the houses of great and mean men alike as they pleased, and they sat at their leisure in front of their wives and children. They had no regard for the heads of the households. This Küchlüg was a fire worshiper, and his wife a Christian.[P334] He called all of the people to his own religion and forced them to it. Whoever chose Küchlüg's religion was left in peace. If they should refuse, they would be subjected to cruel punishments and debilitating torture, and then killed.

Next, Küchlüg went to Khotan, and he called the people of Khotan to his religion. "Whoever is a person of the faith," he commanded them, "or a person of the knowledge, or a wearer of the turban, come forth." They came out onto a broad place. More than 3,000 people of the knowledge and wearers of the turban presented themselves. Küchlüg said, "Who among you will not conceal their true words, and will not fear, but in honesty dispute and debate about religion?"

An erudite Khotanese mullah and scholar named Mawlana ʿAlauddin Muḥammad (MAY GOD ILLUMINATE HIS RESTING PLACE!) bound the belt of truth about his waist, went before Küchlüg, and presented evidence and proofs in favor of the revelation of Muḥammad. And that filthy infidel treated him with utter disregard. Truth was victorious over falsehood, and knowledge over ignorance. Yet Küchlüg was now compelled to speak his piece. It was shameful. In his shock and embarrassment, ragefully he brought absurd words to his lips with respect to Muḥammad Muṣṭafa (BLESSINGS OF GOD BE UPON HIM AS WELL AS PEACE!), and he dared to speak rudely.

At that moment, that fine-dispositioned and deeply pious man, unable to bear the weight of his zealousness and scorn, reproached him: "Oh, Küchlüg! May your mouth be filled with black dirt from accursed enemies!" When Küchlüg heard these words, he had that pious imam seized and imprisoned, so that he would be forced to turn away from Islam and accept the religion of the fire worshipers. In the end, they found that{331} he would not turn from the revelation of Muḥammad. Ultimately, that truth-speaking imam was "four-nailed" to the madrasa that he himself had built, which is to say nailed with four nails to the madrasa wall, and tortured for several days and nights. That imam, worthy of approbation, raised the Shahada to his lips. He spoke words of wisdom to the common people: "Fear not the tortures of this world, that you would give up the revelation of Muḥammad. Do not allow the rewards of the next world to go to waste for the sake of this transitory one. THIS LIFE OF THIS WORLD IS NAUGHT BUT DIVERSION AND PLAY. AND SURELY THE ABODE OF THE HEREAFTER IS LIFE INDEED, IF THEY BUT KNEW [29:64]." They martyred that teacher of truth, ʿAlauddin Muḥammad Khotani, and they killed many people of the turban. But then, across these lands, the call to prayer, the *takbir* and Salawat, and the Friday prayers and communal prayers rang out as one. The gates of the unjust and the villainous were opened. The downtrodden and the abstemious raised their voices in prayer, and their prayers hit the mark of agreement.

At that time, Chinggis Khan had conquered the cities of China and returned to his capital in repose. Now he was informed, "Küchlüg has gone to Kashgar and Khotan, and there visited injustices upon the people, ruining and annihilating many [thousands of lives and homes]." Soon after, Chinggis Khan sent one of his *noyans*, Jatta Noyan, with several 10,000-units [*tümän*] of soldiers to attack Küchlüg.[4] When Jatta Noyan came, Küchlüg could not match him but fled into Badakhshan, where in those wastelands he met his end. Someone cut off his head and sent it to Chinggis Khan. He had ruled the Seven Cities for over four years. It is said that Jatta Noyan commanded that all people should hold to the customs of their ancestors{332} and to the religion that they wished. And the people rejoiced, for it seemed as though, when compared to the previous era, now this would be an era of holy Islam, though the *noyan* were a stranger to revelation.

* * *

Such events occurred to the people of the Seven Cities in eras past. My purpose in recording them here on this page is that you shall know this: such occurrences were visited upon our ancestors in olden days. Although they experienced such injustice, they did not abandon the commandments of the Lord and His Messenger. Nor did they turn away from the revelation of Muḥammad. With regard to the events of our times, raise many prayers of thanks and praise, and pray.

Another purpose of mine is this: that truth-speaking scholar, ʿAlauddin Muḥammad Khotani (MAY GOD ILLUMINATE HIS GRAVE!), led the Muslims in debating with the impure nonbelievers, and he would not give the revelation of Muḥammad up. And so he lost his sweet life. His martyrdom gives great reason for the people of Khotan, and indeed all of the Seven Cities, to be proud. This story is enough to demonstrate this to the Seven Cities.

3:4 Aqsu

THE PEOPLE OF Aqsu are candid, gentle, simple, well mannered, humble, and anxious. They lack a sense of mutual familiarity and unity, and are scattered; they lack mutual affection or ability to come to an agreement, and are in discord. And they do not store their produce but have great faith in God. The people of this city mostly purchase their bread daily from the market. For this reason, the cooks' and bakers' trade is very developed and brisk. Artisans are few,{333} farmers many. Their fruits and harvests are sufficient for the city. The rice is excellent, and it is transported to other cities. Its pastures are broad, and its livestock numerous, enough to sustain it, or more.

In the land of Aqsu there is a shrine from an illustrious house, that of Mawlana Jalaluddin Kataki. It is in Ay Köl. He was one of the grandsons of Khoja Abu Ḥafiẓ Kabir Bukhari. His story was related in the first epic.

There is another important shrine called Imam Baṭṭal Ghazi. They say that his name was Imam ʿAbdurraḥman Alavi, and he was the fourth son of Imam Muḥammad Ḥanifa, who was one of the sons of ʿAli (MAY GOD BLESS HIS FACE!). The Lord of the Worlds knows.

There is also an honored shrine called Sultan Maḥmud Ghaznavi. It is famous. However, the tomb of Sultan Maḥmud Ghaznavi is in the city of Ghazna. This one must have had the same name as that holy figure, or perhaps his name was Sultan Maḥmud, and through common error, the epithet "*ghazi*" became "Ghaznavi."

And there are the two shrines of Shaykh Junaid Baghdadi[1] and Sirri Saqti[2] (May God sanctify them!). The *Breaths of Fellowship* says that they were buried in Baghdad at the al-Shuniziyya Mosque. Also, the one called Sirri Saqti is apparently Saqi Ata. Surely through common error Saqi Ata came to be called Sirri Saqti. In each case, they are shrines that bestow grace and pilgrimage places that bestow one's desires.

To the north of Aqsu, at the base of a mountain six *tash* in height, is an exalted shrine, the holy name of which is Qirmish Sayyid al-Muslimin. It has a hagiography.{334} In its hagiography, it is written that in the thirty-third year of the Hijra [653/4], the Prophet sent Qirmish Sayyid al-Muslimin with 33,000 great companions to attack the community of fire worshipers at Qahqa Jadu in the city of Barbar.[3] But the infidels won the day, and these 33,000 great companions were martyred in some of the towns of Ushturfan and Aqsu. Their blessed bodies were buried in this land.

In reliable books, however, it is related that those great companions were buried in such places as al-Baqiʿ, Syria, Kufa, or Egypt. In the year 33 [653/4], the third caliph, ʿUs̱man b. ʿAffan (May God be pleased with him!) was on the throne, and the Prophet had departed this transitory world for the gardens of the eternal. Moreover, it was only during the reign of the Umayyad Caliph al-Walid b. ʿAbdulmalik, through the efforts of the Commander in Chief Qutaiba b. Muslim, that Bukhara, Samarqand, Ferghana, Turkestan, and Kabul were conquered and converted to Islam, and that was in the ninety-first year of the Hijra [709/10]. When Qirmish Sayyid al-Muslimin came, if those cities had not yet converted to Islam, then through which lands could those hosts of great companions have passed? Certainly this is something for the wise and the intelligent to consider. Another thing is that, according to reliable books, those great companions could not have crossed to the other side of the Amu River.[4P339[202v, 4]] This is because at that time, the lands on this side of the Amu had not yet accepted Islam. According to this reasoning, one may not place any value on this hagiography. Although there may in some other country or land be a city called the city of Barbar, and perhaps a nation of fire worshipers, and a leader named Qahqa Jadu, and although those great companions may have been sent unto that city, to say that Ushturfan was anciently called the city of Barbar is simply erroneous, suspicious, or a lie. Nevertheless, this is an exalted shrine. Its miracles are clearly manifest and well known. In any case, [those entombed within] are holy warriors who undertook holy war against the infidel and were martyred. Perhaps they simply had different names or lived in a different time. Some ignorant man, who had not derived the least clue from historians or biographers such as your humble author and had no idea of the original words, labored in vain by his own sort of invention and called the result a "hagiography." When one inspects this hagiography and compares it with accounts in reliable books, the truth of it becomes clear.

There are many other shrines, but because their names or when those people passed away are unknown, I do not dare discuss them.

* * *

Another thing: Abulḥasan Ḥażrat came from the Country [of Ferghana] to the Seven Cities and stayed for a while in Aqsu, where he awakened the Muslims' dulled hearts with warnings, prohibitions, and proofs. He brought them out of error and the pit of mortal peril into salvation and onto the edge of the righteous path.[P340] He inlaid the precious pearls of generosity and victory upon the mirrors of his sincere disciples' hearts, exalted them step by step, and then chose to go on his way.

When His Highness the Ataliq Ghazi first made his appearance, this holy personage likewise placed his blessed steps upon the ground of Aqsu and took up residence there. Every one of the prominent scholars, whose hearts were not inclined to Sufis, submitted to him with heart and soul and joined the ranks of his faithful disciples, so they became his personal followers. He was part of the Khafiyya order of the Naqshbandiyya. And he performed miracles.

One of his miracles was this: one of his faithful disciples was absolutely enamored with epic tales such as the *Book of Kings* and the *Adventures of Amir Ḥamza*.[5] The Ḥażrat noticed this and forbade it. Another day, when the Master was passing by, he noticed again that he was sitting in the place where he had been reading the epics. That disciple was thinking, "Afrasiyab and Kaykavus, what kings they were! They fought such wondrous battles!" and he drifted off to sleep. In his dream, he saw two enormous and awesome kings, one chasing after the other. And as they passed, the people said, "Look, it's Afrasiyab and Kaykavus!" He was frightened by the press of the crowd and awoke. In the morning, when he went to the circle of remembrance and sat within it during the *tawajjuh*,{335} the Master began to preach.[6] "Have you seen Afrasiyab and Kaykavus?" he asked. "They are nothing but a pair of infidels." That disciple of his repented anew, and never again did he go to the place where he read the epics.

Another thing: one of his young disciples, a man named ʿAbdulkarim, had a donkey. Every morning it would escape and run off somewhere. He would send someone to look for it while he attended the circle of remembrance. But in his heart, he worried, "Where has that donkey gone? And when might it be found?" As he worried, it came time to attend *tawajjuh*. The Master gave the *tawajjuh*, and he raised his head and reproached him, "Oh, you whelp! Are you this upset about your donkey disappearing? Collect your thoughts. You will find that donkey, and you will find a horse, as well." He repented anew and apologized. Today, the Chief Judge Mullah ʿAbdulkarim is incomparably rich in property and in horses and donkeys. I heard about this by word of mouth and wrote it on this page.

If I were to describe in detail this holy personage's name and his praiseworthy qualities, it would make a whole hagiography of its own. I only dared to provide a brief discussion so that his name and works may never be forgotten among the people. He passed away on the eighteenth day of Ṣafar in the year 1285 [June 10, 1868]. According to his will, he was buried on his own plot of land [in Aqsu]. In the Sufi books, it is said that he was a "perfected master," and that "his conversation could be compared to the philosopher's stone." That is, this personage's conversation was indeed like the philosopher's stone. And the "perfected master"{336} was this man. But the gracefully moving pen dares not offer any further praise or description.

Your humble author, Mullah Musa b. Mullah ʿIsa Khoja Sayrami, was working for a tax collector at the time. I was young and proud then, and several times I found myself in his company, although I never had the opportunity to kiss his hand. Now all of thirty-six years have passed.[7] Until the end of my life, that holy personage's company and love will be a turmoil in my heart. I have never seen or encountered any holy master such as he.

> When the meeting of friends came about, ah, I knew not its worth!
> I knew not that we would never meet again, that eternal separation awaited.

3:5 Ushturfan

USHTURFAN IS AN ancient city. Its former name was Uch, or perhaps the city of Barbar. During the reign of Manṣur Khan, its people acted improperly and rebelled. Consequently, he grew angry and sent his general, Amir Jabbar Barhi Beg Dukhtui, with an army to put the people of Uch to the sword and scatter the survivors across the lands. Then he had people relocated from Turfan and settled there. They cultivated it. For this reason, their towns and villages are named Turfan town and Turfan village. They attached the name Uch to the name Turfan and called it Uchturfan, and perhaps by common error it came to be called Ushturfan.

Ten years after the emperor of China's rule was established, when the people of Ushturfan were in rebellion, countless soldiers came and conquered it for the second time. And they put the people to the sword, but{337} relocated people from across the Six Cities and settled them there. They cultivated it. To this day, they are called migrants. This story was told in the first epic.

This is why the people of Ushturfan are divided into several factions. There are few artisans or craftsmen. Its people are farmers. The soil is good. Its produce is plentiful and inexpensive.

In the land of Ushturfan is located a prominent shrine called The Honored Imam [*Imāmlarim*]. The name [of the saint] was Imam Muḥammad Ghazali. There is also a shrine in Qazghan. Its name is Imam Aḥmad Ghazali. However, the *Breaths of Fellowship* relates: "Imam Aḥmad Ghazali was buried in Qazrin." The names "Qazrin" and "Qazghan" are quite close to each other. AND GOD KNOWS THE TRUTH OF MATTERS.

There is also the Cooling Shrine [*savutqi*]. It is called the Cooling Shrine because, they say, in the year 33 [653/4], after Qirmish Sayyid al-Muslimin was martyred, the Prophet and Messenger ordered ʿAli, the Lion of God (MAY GOD EXALT HIS FACE!), to go to Qahqa Jadu and the city of the fire worshipers. So the two honored princes, ʿAli Sher-i Yazdani and ʿAli Sher-i Khuda, were sent as merchants in the company of several of the Companions' young children. Miraculously, through mystical translocation, in one day and one night they arrived at the city of Barbar. They alighted by a spring, where they tied up Duldul (ʿAli's mule) at a willow by the head of the spring and let her cool off. That copse of willows sprouted, then stood upright, then sank again, then stiffened, turned green, and kept doing so until there was a bag's worth of food, sometimes sinking onto the ground, sometimes standing upright and sprouting.{338} No one ever cuts its branches, whether moist or dry, or upsets it, but they care for it very much.

Below the willow is a spring, which they call THE SPRING OF THE SERPENT, because the serpents gathered there by the command of the prophet Sulayman. When the blessed steps of ʿAli (MAY GOD EXALT HIS FACE!) arrived, he said, "Oh, serpents! Get yourself out of the spring. For here we will pitch the Prophet's grand tent palace!" And the serpents moved out of the spring. Nevertheless, the waters of that spring were bitter like the serpent's venom. Those princes spat into the spring's waters, and the waters became sweet. This is why they call it the Cooling Shrine. People visit, and they take the waters to drink, which they call a "blessing," and, so blessed, they take it in every direction. In the shrine's hagiography, it is called "The Arrival Place[1] of ʿAli (MAY GOD EXALT HIS FACE!)." Some chronicles state that ʿAli (MAY GOD EXALT HIS FACE!) never traveled hither from Iraq. The Lord of the Worlds knows the truth. But it is not a worthless place. Its miracles continue to be manifest.

There are many other shrines and pilgrimage places. Most of them are called by the names of great Companions. The truth of it is unknown, and there are no records. For this reason I did not dare to write about them. It is in any case widely known that Ushturfan is a place where many battles{339} have occurred.

3:6 Kucha

THE ANCIENT NAME of Kucha was Kusan. The character of the people of Kucha is that they are very strong in their mutual familiarity and unity. All of its people are warlike, good-tempered, and witty, and the ambition and bravery of its women and its invalids are greater than that of the men. They possess no shortcomings in their knowledge of management or in their crafts. But they have no love of outsiders. These days, outsiders are collecting in Kucha from all directions, and day by day there are more settlements and communities, while the houses of commerce are flourishing. Relative to the number of people, the land is plentiful and of good quality. Every week, at least 500 donkeys and other beasts of burden come from Bay and Sayram bearing grain and oil. Every variety of fruit and food is more plentiful than in other cities, and juicier, and traders take dried and fresh fruits to every other city. The livestock are numerous and sufficient for the city, or more.

The resting place of Mawlana ʿArshuddin Waliullah is in the land of Kucha. Thanks to the blessings of this holy personage, Tughluq Timur Khan and his people converted to Islam, and the lamp of Islam was lit in the land of Ili. That khan called him the Great Mullah. His story was told in the first epic.

There is also a shrine called Shaykh Niẓamuddin Dehlavi. Some people say the name Dehlavi as Dehbudi. It is a shrine that is in every respect magnificent and conferring of blessings.

There is also an important shrine named Balkh Ata. The origins of its name and the time when the saint lived are unknown.

There is also a pilgrimage place called Grandchild Khoja [*Nabira Khwajam*].[340] They say that he was one of the grandchildren of Bahauddin Naqshband (MAY GOD BLESS HIM!).

There is also Baba Qambar Waliullah, who is famous, as he was Ali's (MAY GOD BLESS HIS FACE!) stablemaster. This shrine shares its name with others: there are also shrines called Baba Qambar Waliullah in Ushturfan and Khotan.

There is another important shrine, which they call by the name Ibrahim Adham (MAY GOD BLESS HIM!). This famous chief of the saints is buried in Mecca. This must share a name, or else its name is Ibrahim Atam, and by common error the name Atam came to be said as Adham. AND GOD KNOWS.

3:7 Turfan

TURFAN IS AN ancient city. Its people are true to their word, steady and mature. While they lack all cunning and gall, they possess great faith and belief. It is lacking in water, and for the most part people use *karez* to irrigate. The land is excellent. Its produce is sufficient for the city. Its cotton bolls and coarse cotton cloth are also excellent. Manna[1] is also peculiar to Turfan, and its grapes and raisins are plentiful and juicy. They are taken to every city. It has much land.

This land is home to the Shrine of the Companions of the Cave. However, commentaries on the Quran state that the Companions of the Cave were "in a city called Tarsus in Rum."[2] When the exegetes and historians write "in Rum," it indicates Rumchä, because the name Rumchä indicates the seat of great kings and *töräs* in days of yore. "God in His mysterious wisdom obscured the Companions of the Cave from the common people," they each relate,{341} "such that their names and number are also obscured. Their shrines are located in several places across the Earth."

One is "in a city called Tarsus in Rum." This is what has been related in commentaries and chronicles. A second is "on Banan Mountain in the country of Palestine." The third is "in Aden, in the quarter of Fariqa." Fourth is "in the mountains of the Maghreb." Fifth is "in Hindustan." Sixth is "in Isfahan." The seventh is "in Armenia."

This is the eighth, which said to be "in the empire of China." It appears that the original name of Ürümchi was Rumchä, and that, through common error, an extra letter *alif* was appended to the beginning of the name Rumchä, and to the end, perhaps, was joined a letter *ya'*. And so it was named Ürümchi.

Another thing is that, in the Turki tongue, there is a thing called *chä*. When the Turks wish to make some large thing diminutive, they do so with the word *chä*—that is, they make things small with the word *chä*. For example, "little garden" [*baghchä*], "little plot" [*ḥavelichä*], "little rooster" [*dekchä*]. An orchard, which is large and formal, is called an "orchard" [*bagh*]. If it is smaller, however, it is called by the name "garden" [*baghchä*]. "Little plot" and "little rooster" follow the same rule. Accordingly, Rumchä ought to mean Little Rum. What the commentaries say about how "The Companions of the Cave were in a city called Tarsus in Rum" would be correct, as Tarsus طرسوس has also by common error turned into Turfan طرفان. Perhaps it is also no longer called Tarsus but instead Turfan because the word fell clumsily on Chinese, Mongol, Kyrgyz, Qipchaq, Tatar, Uyghur, and Qalmaq tongues.

The time of the Companions of the Cave was earlier than that of the Prophet ʿIsa (MAY GOD SANCTIFY HIS PROPHET, AND HONOR HIM!). Therefore, it has been over two thousand years. Over the course of such a long period of time, the Tatar people ruled on several occasions, the Mongol tribes for several generations,{342} the Uyghur peoples several times, the Muslim kings for several periods, and the Chinese nation for several eras, and each of them has called the Cities by different names. For example, Ürümchi in Chinese used to be called Hongmiaozi.[3] Now it is called Xinjiang Province.[4] This being the case, it would not be too distant from the intellects of the intelligent to think that the names Little Rome and Tarsus have changed.

* * *

The Word of the Lord has also touched upon the Companions of the Cave. Because they believe that the Quran has described the cave, people from all over Moghulistan, and even Ferghana, Turkestan, and Hindustan, take a five-month-long journey to bring offerings and make pilgrimage. The shaykhs act as guides to the pilgrims and play various tricks and scams on them, saying, "Here is where to dismount your horse. Here is where{343} to pray. Here is where to make a circumambulation." They offer information as though they were the guides in the Holy Land, but they get something by their scams. Some people believe that "If one is unable to make the ḥajj, then making one pilgrimage to the Shrine of the Companions of the Cave is the same as making half of a ḥajj."

The mountain on which the Shrine of the Companions of the Cave is located is very tall. One ascends via a number of ladder-like staircases. At the top, there are a number of chambers, porticos, and little porches; mosques, prayer niches, and pulpits; and places to pray, comprising a number of buildings all around the shrine. The shrine's servants dwell there and live by the produce of the pious endowment. Its shaykhs also number over 300 households. Past Muslim khans and governors out of generosity made them part of the pious endowment. They believe that "Decius's city and palace were here in the realm of Turfan, and the Companions of the Cave slept in this cave."[5]

Sometime after the year 1000 [1592], Afaq Khoja went to Turfan. He saw how the people of Turfan came to this place and greatly venerated it, and at first he disbelieved, and forbade it. Later, however, he meditated and did *tawajjuh*, and he realized that revelations were received in this cave.{344} Now he addressed the people, saying, "Previously I had suspected that this shrine was a place of idols. Upon meditating, however, it has become evident to me that my suspicions were incorrect, and that your beliefs are correct. There is no doubt that this is the place of the Companions of the Cave. Make pilgrimage to this place, and treasure it." This is documented.

Another thing: it seems that, until the year 1000 of the Hijri, no one knew that the Companions of the Cave had been inside this cave. Indeed, the infidels had made of it an idol temple, and it was long a place where they had lodged lamas, *lodos*,[6] and Brahmins, and venerated them. This continued until the year 1070 [1659/60], when Sultan Saʿid Baba Khan Bahadur [d. 1680], who was a descendant of Tughluq Timur Khan, was king of Turfan and Qumul. At that time, it was common for people to come from all directions to make pilgrimage and circumambulate. He observed the people's beliefs, found them acceptable, and so appointed shaykhs, custodians, and lamplighters; installed imams and muezzins; granted it (land for) a pious endowment; assigned trustees; and remanded the shrine to a custodian. By the giving of this royal command, this cave came to be regarded as that of the Companions of the Cave, and it gained fame.

I have copied this proclamation{345} in full and from the original onto this page:[7]

A royal proclamation:

The words of Sultan Saʿid Baba Khan Bahadur the Victorious, who is the trace of the aura of rule and auspiciousness, and of faith and justice daily increasing; the magnificent Lord of the Fortunate Conjunction; the cream of the sultans of Arabia and Persia; the chain that binds the country's security; intermediary of mankind's tranquility; intrepid and munificent, of burgeoning fortune and long life;

To the brothers who are valiant and generous, youthful and fortunate,[8]

And to the sons who are companions in dignity, of enormous power, peers of the Sun, like unto the Moon;

To the exalted commanders who glorify the kingdom, and you prudent and capable viziers, you chief judges of lofty rank, and scholars whose duty it is to act; and judges, you people of the Shariah; and leaders, you noble princes above the peoples; may it be evident to all, noble and commoner alike:

These family men, Khoja Ayyub, Mullah Qumush Habib's son Kuchak, and Mullah Malik, on account of their having been in service to the shrines of Ḥażrat Sultan and of the Companions of the Cave (MAY GOD BLESS THEM!), by royal favor have been made, respectfully, lamplighter, custodian, and superintendent of the kitchen, and they have been granted *tarkhans*. They shall enjoy this *tarkhan* from son to son, from daughter to daughter. May their flowing water—for ablutions—never be cut off. They shall be dedicated, undisturbed and with minds at ease, to the work of prayer. Seeing clearly this grant of a *tarkhan*, no one, nor any patrol, under the leadership of the governor or overseers of Turfan, and especially those who come and go to the *sahib takbirs*[9] and judges in Yangkhay and Tuyuq, such as laborers and listeners,[10] couriers,[11] or messengers,[12] or the various officials,{346} may under any circumstances contest with or oppose them. They may not be asked to pay tax or tribute, or any other tax, such as quartering, corvée, labor, *oqush*, *tir*, providing mounts to post riders, the field tax, the artisan tax, or the provisioning of couriers,[13] nor may such be imposed upon them or levied from them.

Whosoever acts contrarily to this command, may they be bereft of the mercy of the Lord, the intercession of the Prophet Muḥammad, and the forgiveness of the angels. They shall be unworthy of the Companions of the Cave, and they shall be afflicted with the curse of all other humans and jinn. On the Day of Judgment, they will be assembled among the unjust. And they will suffer eternal torment.

Commanded in the royal country of Turfan, in the month of ʿAshur, on a Wednesday, in the year 1078 [June–July 1667], the Year of the Mouse.[14]

(There are two stamps affixed to it. They were read, but they were not recognized.)

Those people who come from far and near to make pilgrimage make a display of their own virtue. Indeed, with their own reputations in view, and according to the fashion of the day, they seek to please the shaykhs and custodians and gain their favor. Instead of regarding the commentaries and chronicles that say, "It has been known that this cave is the place of the Companions of the Cave," taking pleasure in their own imaginings, they say, "This place truly is the cave of the Companions of the Cave."

{347} And others have gone to great inconvenience and suffered in vain to create hagiographies and manufacture important shrines and pilgrimage places, saying that "Ürümchi's original name was Rumchä," and " 'Tarsus,' through common error, was also changed into the name 'Turfan.' " They have taken some unknown ancient town of no account and caused it to be known as "Decius's city." These are the stories that old and aged people tell. Apart from that, there is no clear evidence for the Companions of the Cave having been in Turfan, nor are there any earlier documents to demonstrate the shrine's existence.

Great scholars who have partaken of a pilgrimage to the Cave of the Companions have attempted to corroborate this cave's characteristics with the Quranic verse, and they say that it is different from the cave described in the Lord's own words. Having come to this realization, they have explained the evidence for why the cave in Tuyuq is not the Cave of the Companions. However, some scholars have determined the contrary, that the Cave of the Companions is certainly in Tuyuq, and they have brought evidence. One scholar makes judgments in a manner contrary to another. For this reason, your humble author, Mullah Musa b. Mullah ʿIsa Khoja Sayrami, had been overcome by skepticism and contrariness, and in meditation on this skepticism and doubt had drowned in the deep waters of discernment and reflection.

{348} I was thinking in bewilderment upon the weak and strong points of these scholars' armies of opposing statements when there came to Moghulistan for the second time the First Among Sayyids and Mawlanas, the Example to the Licensed Scholars, the Cream of the Exacting

Jurisprudents, the Expert Scholar and Celebrated Writer, ʿAsalizada al-Shaykh Saʿid al-Shaykh Muḥammad b. al-Shaykh ʿAbdulwaḥid b. al-Shaykh ʿAli al-ʿAsali al-Shami al-Tarabulsi.[15] Your humble author enjoyed his company, and as for five months we kept each other's company at home and abroad, day and night, I sought his guidance on the Companions of the Cave.

"I have journeyed twice to the shrine of the Companions of the Cave in Turfan," he said. "In my investigations of the cave, I have relied on clear *ayah*s in the Word sent by the Lord Himself in the great Quran and on the words of past exegetes as definitive proofs. Several proofs argue that the Cave of the Companions is in a city called Tarsus in Rum, and not in Turfan. So, with an eye to the general benefit of faithful Muslims, and indeed all people, noble and commoner alike, I have clarified those proofs and collected them into a tract," which he gave to me. I read it, and once I had informed myself, I translated it into Turki.{349} He kindly had a look and checked it, and I included it in the epilogue of this chronicle. May it come under the scrutiny of the well spoken, and of nobles and commoners, and as they shake their heads in concession, may they be congregated among the faithful. And if they should reject it, and twist their necks on account of its castigations, then may the truth and ardor of the Word of God, and of the great *ayah*s sent down that concern the characteristics of the cave, grant proper guidance to such people. Amen.

* * *

From {349, 7} to {381, 3} of the Beijing manuscript, Sayrami provides a translation of al-ʿAsali's arguments against the authenticity of the Shrine of the Companions of the Cave in Tuyuq, Turfan. This discussion takes up roughly 8 percent of the total length of the manuscript. I have chosen not to include it in this translation, not only because of the need to conserve space but also because this section stands outside the flow and structure of the rest of the book. As Sayrami would say, to discuss it at length would surely exhaust the reader. A brief summary:

1. *There is no proof of any tomb of the faithful having existed in Tuyuq before the time of the Prophet.*
2. *Arab and Persian chroniclers and exegetes long ago wrote that the cave was in Tarsus. The embassy to China from the Timurid court of Shahrukh made no note of this shrine during their journey through Turfan in 822 [1419].*[16]

3. *Turfan did not convert to Islam until around the year 800 [1397/8], long after its neighbors. The first evidence of the cave is the aforementioned document endowing the shrine, which suggests that Sufis deceived Turfan's rulers.*
4. *Ürümchi is attested as a Mongol name. Moreover, Rum is a great empire, and its location is extremely well known. There is no evidence that its territories ever extended this far. Those who suggest that the Turks' and Mongols' conquests might have brought some Romans to Moghulistan, where they settled with their religion, have no evidence.*
5. *Historians write that the Companions of the Cave were very large, so that they could not possibly fit inside this cave—indeed, even a sheep cannot fit through the doorway.*
6. *The description of the passage of the sun over the cave's entrance is contrary to what takes place at Tuyuq.*
7. *The Quran relates that the Companions, while they slept, moved about and continued to grow their beards and fingernails, such that their appearance was terribly frightening, while a dog kept guard at the door. If this were the case, then how could anyone go and look at them? It is written that the shaykh went to the cave to light the lamps whenever they burned out. It is also written that during Yaʿqub Beg's time, an Arab went to see the cave, and within he saw that the Companions were wrapped in fine cloth, while their dog had turned to stone. All of these are lies that contradict the Quran. Humans carve idols out of stone—that is probably what he saw.*
8. *The Companions' story is well established in the literature on wondrous things, and much has been written in several different languages that contradicts the local story. Moreover, making pilgrimage to any place except for Mecca and Medina is heresy.*
9. *There is nothing special about caves—they are found all over the world. Moreover, those who believe that a pilgrimage to the cave (or any other such shrine) is equivalent to half of a ḥajj are infidels. This shrine is probably a fake, much like the one that Niyaz Ḥakim Beg built to fill with gold and silver during the reign of Yaʿqub Beg.*
10. *If God had not described the cave, then people would suspect every cave from east to west. If the cave had been here, there would be a record of it. Instead, Sufis, shaykhs, and kings have done infidelish things, which became customs, such as bringing animals to sacrifice at shrines while praying for children, etc. A number of hadiths clearly specify that this is wrong.*

3:8 Lop

A STORY: THERE is a strange and wondrous thing to tell, that in the realm of Moghulistan, at the southeastern tip of the Six Cities, is a large and famous land called Lop. The author of the *Tarikh-i Rashidi*, Mirza Ḥaydar Kuragan (MAY GOD ILLUMINATE HIS GRAVE!), wrote on the basis of ancient chronicles, and in his own book he included an account and enumeration of the seventeen great cities of Lop, name by name, explaining how its people were numerous, and the places where it was cultivated.[1] This includes the city of Katak, the city of Tarkan, the city of Chan, and the city of Lop. Today, the cities of Katak and Lop remain known, while the rest have been buried under the sands of wrath. They say that sometimes, after a windstorm, one of them will be exposed, and then it will disappear again. The story goes that one night, the wrath of God descended, and instead of a storm, sand rained from the sky, burying the city and all its people. (It is written that the grave of Afrasiyab was also in this place.)

These days, people who have seen this place write that Lop is bounded on the east by the territory of a Chinese city called Lanzhou Province.{382} To its north are Qumul, Turfan, and Korla. To its west it goes to Shahyar, Cherchen, Khotan, Lhasa, and Chaba.[2] It is a very broad land, some four or five months' journey across. The Khotan, Yarkand, Aqsu, and Korla Rivers all pass through this land. Sometimes these rivers flow as one, and sometimes they flow separately, and they flow into Beijing. It is known that over 12,000 households of people once settled around the rivers and on their banks and lived on their branches and islets.

Yet they know nothing of agriculture or how to plant. Nor do they have buildings, orchards, farms, or houses, or even fruits, nor perhaps have they ever seen or learned about such things. They hunt fish from the rivers and make their meals of them. They even dry them, making them into jerky, or even into a kind of powder[3] to eat. They build reed huts to live in. They have many livestock, which they do not quarter in one place. Rather, they drive their livestock wherever they wish. Wherever they go, they build a hut of reeds and live in it. However large a river might be, they place little skiffs and rafts on it and thereby cross it without fear or distress. Everyone from the age of seven to seventy{383} possesses the knowledge of natation, that is, how to swim. When a sizable catastrophe takes place, they cross the river and take their livestock to some place a month or forty days' journey away. They have no fixed stopping places. The whole land is a reedy wilderness, a boundless desert waste. And there are many great but changeable ponds and water-bearing springs.

It is written that now many Russian and French doctors of science are journeying there. They have explored the land of Lop and there found a goldmine. A Chinese official, a Frank, and a Russian have constructed buildings over it. THE RESPONSIBILITY IS UPON THE NARRATOR.

Most of the land of Lop is sandy. On winter days, they pile up plenty of firewood, light it on fire, and heat up the sand, so that they and their wives and children can lie in the hot sand. Both men and women spin wool and make clothing from it. They have never submitted to any king or khan, and perhaps they have never even been invited into the rule of any king or khan.{384} The land of Lop is within the domain of the Great Khan, and yet, to this day, he has shown greatness and generosity in never bringing these people under his rule, nor has he had any affair with them. This is how their ancestors have lived since olden days. They are a wild tribe of the children of Adam. If they are Muslims, they have no mosques; if they are infidels, they have no idol temples. Perhaps they are people who have never been called to the faith. Those of their people who live near the Cities know our language, while those in remote places know it not, but speak among themselves in their own language. They hardly ever leave, or never.[4]

When the people of the Cities go there, they are afraid and do not draw near, nor do they mix with people or associate with them. One of their reasons, it is said, is that if they care to go to the cities, mix with people, and associate with them, they will be infected with smallpox and die. So they mix only cautiously, and they keep their distance. And because these people have never eaten food made of wheat, they never break out in pustules. During the reign of the Ataliq Ghazi, he conquered the people of{385} Lop who lived close to Korla and brought five or six of their leaders to Aqsu. All of them were white-haired old men in their sixties or seventies. Some of them caught smallpox. They rested for several days, and once they had recovered, they returned to their land. If any person among them catches smallpox, young or old, they hastily pour some water into a bowl with fish meat and move somewhere far away. In a week or ten days, someone will come and ask from a distance how they are doing. If they say that they have smallpox, then they never go near.

Nearly ten years ago, some of the Dungans in and around Chengdu Province rose in armed rebellion against the Great Khan.[5] Many armies were sent, and they did battle, but the Dungans could not match them, so more than 80,000 households of Dungans fled. When they appeared at the borders of Lop, a group of Qalmaqs called frost and rain down, and snow, rain, and ice fell from the sky. Many Dungans perished, but 40,000 households of them arrived at Lop. Now that they were in the Seven Cities, many soldiers came from Ürümchi and Korla to block their path.{386} They fought, and many were killed, but then both sides were satisfied by the swearing of oaths, and they were allowed to stay in Lop. They were allowed to settle there and farm. This was the reason the Great Khan decided to recall the people of Lop, add them to his domain, have a city built, station officials and soldiers there, and cultivate the land.

However, it became apparent that because the sands of wrath had once been sent down upon Lop, it does not yield much of a harvest. Still today, men and merchants from every city carry foodstuffs, goods, and all sorts of clothing there. And the people of Lop too have begun to make their clothing from such things as chintz, printed calico, fine cotton cloth, roughspun, coarse cotton cloth, and printed coarse cotton cloth. Yet they say that most of them have taken their wives and children and driven their livestock back over the river, and disappeared into the wilds. They would not submit.

It is written that it has now been a generation or more since Sufis, mullahs, and *ṣaḥib duʿa* from the Cities went there to instruct them in the Islamic faith, the Pillars of Islam, and the unity of the Sublime Deity. Most of them entered into the Muslim community, and they began to build mosques and lodges out of reeds, and to pray.

{387} God, grant these people Your guidance, correct motivations, and true belief. Amen. OH, LORD OF THE WORLDS!

3:9 Postface

I KNEW NOT the worth of precious life, nor did I value it, but passed it in vain, and now I am over seventy years old, and I approach my place in nothingness. I sighed in regret, for not a single memorial remained upon the world's page or in the people's mouths to remember your ignorant, meddling, foolish servant. Hoping for forgiveness from the Potent, the Veiler, the Generous, the Pardoner, I offered up my words as I have done, and as I reflected upon this, my afflicted heart recalled a poem:

> I lived my life in injustice and negligence—pardon me, O Patient one!
> Chase me not from among the good men on the Resurrection Day.
> Hoping for goodness, I wrote a history as a monument.
> Might they give the good news?: "Be pardoned!" Might I receive clemency?[1]

In the Year of the Hijra of the Prophet 1326,[2] on the tenth day of the honored month of Shawwal, this work was completed [November 5, 1908].

PRAISE BE TO GOD, that every word that begins and ends with GOD SAID or THE MESSENGER OF GOD SAID shall be accepted in the lofty court and in the presence of the Creator,{388} and that they will be cause for others to pray.

Yet the musky pen composed these epics, stories, and confused, scattered words in a very brief period of time. It is my hope that those who are attentive to the details and nuances of the words, and those wise people who are familiar with new and old stories and epics, might cover up these accounts' deficiencies and amend them.

I composed this little chronicle when over seventy was I;
Sharp of mind, but weak of body, coughing and wheezing was I.
If you should see deficiencies in these, my confused words,
Be kind and emend them, please, for in such a state am I!

This ignorant, destitute, incapable[3] pauper [exercised] his abilities as best he could; and in accordance with the words THAT WHICH IS NOT FULFILLED IN FULL, SHOULD NOT BE ABANDONED IN THE DETAILS,[4] I refused to allow myself to be negligent or careless. What I desire from the Generous and the Munificent, from the Court of the Blessed, is this: grant that it may be accepted in the sagacious sight of the courageous and the noble. Amen.

God, by Your power, illuminate the black heart of your weak and hapless servant with the light of Your unity and the lamp of knowledge, and at that weary hour,{389} when it is time for your sinful servant to make his journey, in Your munificence, deprive him not of Your endless kindness and boundless grace. Amen. PRAISE BE TO GOD, THE LORD OF THE WORLDS!

Completed, with the help of the omniscient Lord, in the year 1329, on the 10th of Rajab [July 7, 1911].[5]

Notes

Introduction

1. Mary Louise Pratt, "Arts of the Contact Zone" *Profession* (1991): 33–40. For a similar author in a different late-Qing context, see Matthew W. King, *Ocean of Milk, Ocean of Blood: A Mongolian Monk in the Ruins of the Qing Empire* (New York: Columbia University Press, 2019).
2. John E. Woods, "The Rise of Tīmūrid Historiography," *Journal of Near Eastern Studies* 46, no. 2 (April 1987): 81–108.
3. Ondřej Klimeš, *Struggle by the Pen: The Uyghur Discourse of Nation and National Interest, c. 1900–1949* (Leiden: Brill, 2015), 39–59.
4. James A. Millward, *Beyond the Pass: Economy, Ethnicity, and Empire in Qing Central Asia, 1759–1864* (Stanford, CA: Stanford University Press, 1998), 197–203, 232–52.
5. For an introduction to this period, see Susan Mann Jones and Philip A. Kuhn, "Dynastic Decline and the Roots of Rural Rebellion," *The Cambridge History of China, Volume 10: Late Ch'ing 1800–1911, Part 1*, ed. John K. Fairbank (Cambridge: Cambridge University Press, 1978), 107–62. For the Taiping specifically, see Stephen R. Platt, *Autumn in the Heavenly Kingdom: China, the West, and the Epic Story of the Taiping Civil War* (New York: Knopf, 2012).
6. For histories of the Muslim uprisings, see Wen-djang Chu, *The Moslem Rebellion in Northwest China 1862–1878: A Study of Government Minority Policy* (The Hague: Mouton, 1966); Jonathan Lipman, *Familiar Strangers: A History of Muslims in Northwest China* (Seattle: University of Washington Press, 1997), 150–38; and Hannah Theaker, "Moving Muslims: The Great Northwestern Rebellion and the Transformation of Chinese Islam, 1860–1896" (PhD diss., University of Oxford, 2018).
7. Eric Schluessel, *Land of Strangers: The Civilizing Project in Qing Central Asia* (New York: Columbia University Press, 2020), chapter 6.
8. On post-Mongol Perso-Islamic models of power and their incorporation of astrology and justice, see Afzar A. Moin, *The Millennial Sovereign: Sacred Kingship and Sainthood in*

Islam (New York: Columbia University Press, 2012), 1–55; Roy Mottahedeh, *Loyalty and Leadership in an Early Islamic Society* (London: I. B. Tauris, 1980).

9. On history, memory, and loss in the Taiping and post-Taiping, see Huan Jin, "Stitching Words to Suture Wounds: A Manuscript Diary from the Taiping-Qing Civil War (1851–64)," *Late Imperial China* 40, no. 2 (2019): 141–82; Tobie Meyer-Fong, *What Remains: Coming to Terms with Civil War in 19th Century China* (Stanford, CA: Stanford University Press, 2013); Zhang Daye, *The World of a Tiny Insect: A Memoir of the Taiping Rebellion and Its Aftermath*, trans. Xiaofei Tian (Seattle: University of Washington Press, 2013).
10. See Hodong Kim's assessments of the sources in *Holy War in China: The Muslim Rebellion and State in Chinese Central Asia, 1864–1877* (Stanford, CA: Stanford University Press, 2004).
11. Rian Thum, *Sacred Routes of Uyghur History* (Cambridge, MA: Harvard University Press, 2014), 5–6.
12. For more information on this individual's adventures in Xinjiang, including his encounter with Sayrami, see David Brophy, "'He Causes a Ruckus Wherever He Goes': Saʿid Muḥammad al-ʿAsali as a Missionary of Modernism in North-West China," *Modern Asian Studies* 54, no. 4 (2020): 1,192–24.
13. Änwär Baytur has fortunately published them in modern Uyghur transliteration (Änwär Baytur, ed., "Mulla Musa Sayrami sheirliridin tallanma," *Bulaq* 15 [1985]).
14. Mullā Mūsá b. Mullā ʿĪsá Khoja Sayrāmī, *Tārīkh-i Amniyya* (Qazān: Ṭabʿkhāna-ye madrasa-ye ʿulūm, 1323/1904). Although the Arabic-script front matter gives 1904 as the publication date, the Russian-script cover gives 1905. 1322 AH spanned March 18, 1904–March 7, 1905, and the book was approved by imperial censors on October 13, 1904. The book's actual printing probably took place in early 1905.
15. Lund University Library, Jarring Prov. 478, "An Historical Account of the Reign of Yakub Bek Ataliq Ghazi," 208b.
16. Paul Pelliot, *Carnets de route 1906–1908* (Paris: Indes Savantes, 2008), 114–15.
17. S. F. Oldenburg, "Dnevnik Turkestanskoi ekspeditsii, snariajennoi po Vysochaishemu poveleniiu Russkim komitetom po izucheniiu Sredniei i Vostochnoi Azii," in *Istoriia izucheniia v kontse XIX—pervoi treti XX veka*, ed. M. D. Bukharina (Moskva: Pamiatniki istoricheskoi mysli, 2018), 526, 541, 555–56. A chronogram (*tārīkh*) in TA/StP, meant to encode the date of composition, switches *yakhshi at* "good name" for *yakhshi aṭ* "good horse," which produces the wrong date. Possibly the scribe did not check the sums.
18. Nos. 8/69 and 11/70, Yusuf Beg Mukhlisov, *Uyghur klassik ädibiyati qol yazmiliri katalogi* (Ürümchi: Shinjang yärlik museygha täyyarliq körüsh bashqarmisi, 1957), 45–46. Mukhlisov (46) lists another "*Tarikh-i Amniyya*" that, judging by its description, is actually a copy of Ṭalib Akhund's *Ṣaḥibnama*. Weirdly, Mukhlisov also renders *Tarikh-i Ḥamidi* as "*Tārīkh-i Ḥumaydiya*" (45).
19. I have made the determination of the copyist and his patron through an extensive examination of this and other manuscripts, as well as Swedish mission sources. Limitations of space preclude a full discussion.
20. See my translation of this text: Eric Schluessel, *The World as Seen from Yarkand: Ghulām Muḥammad Khān's 1920s Chronicle* Mā Tīṭayniŋ wāqiʿasi (Tokyo: NIHU Program Islamic Area Studies, 2014.
21. Reproduced in Miao Pusheng, ed., *Xibei shaoshu minzu wenzi wenxian* (Beijing: Xianzhuang shuju, 2006), 2–415.
22. Abduraop Polat, "Musa Sayrami Tarih-i Hamidi III: inceleme-metin-dizin" (PhD diss., Ankara Üniversitesi, 2002).

23. Polat, "Musa Sayrami Tarih-i Hamidi III."
24. Molla Musa Sayrami, *Tarikhi Hämidi*, trans. Änwär Baytur; Musa Sayramiy, *Tarikhi Hämidi*, trans. Abduraop Täklimakani (Istanbul: Täklimakan Uyghur näshriyati, 2019).
25. Maolamusa Sailami, *Yimide shi*, trans. Aili Wufuer, in Miao Pusheng, ed., *Qingdai Chahetai wen wenxian yizhu* (Wulumuqi: Xinjiang renmin chubanshe, 2013), 315–538.
26. Muḥammad Ṣadiq Kashghari, *In Remembrance of the Saints: The Rise and Fall of an Inner Asian Sufi Dynasty*, trans. David Brophy (New York: Columbia University Press, 2020).
27. Seyyed Hossein Nasr, Caner K. Dagli, Maria Massi Dakake, Joseph E. B. Lumbard, and Mohammed Rustom, eds., *The Study Quran: A New Translation and Commentary* (New York: HarperCollins, 2015).

Terminology

1. On the concept of "Kazakh," see Joo-yup Lee, *Qazaqlïq, of Ambitious Brigandage, and the Formation of the Qazaqs: State and Identity in Post-Mongol Central Eurasia* (Leiden: Brill, 2015), especially 21–36. In 2:11, where "Kazakh" is used alone to describe people, I believe this is because it rhymes with "Qipchaq," and the euphony of the phrase takes precedence over ethnographic precision. The same may be true of the usage in 2:13.
2. Waleed Ziad, "From Yarkand to Sindh via Kabul: The Rise of Naqshbandi-Mujaddidi Sufi Networks in the Eighteenth and Nineteenth Centuries," in *The Persianate World: Rethinking a Shared Sphere*, ed. Abbas Amanat and Assef Ashraf (Leiden: Brill, 2019), 125–68.
3. Muḥammad Ṣadiq Kashgari, *In Remembrance of the Saints: The Rise and Fall of an Inner Asian Sufi Dynasty*, trans. David Brophy (New York: Columbia University Press, 2020), 237n66.
4. Timur K. Beisembiev, *Annotated Indices to the Kokand Chronicles* (Tokyo: Research Institute for Languages and Cultures of Asia and Africa, 2008), 742.

0:0 Preface

1. *qushbegi*: contraction of *qoshun-begi* "head of the army" (Timur K. Beisembiev, ed. and trans., *The Life of ʿAlimqul: A Native Chronicle of Nineteenth Century Central Asia* [London: Routledge, 2003], 20–21n24–25; *Annotated Indices to the Kokand Chronicles* [Tokyo: Research Institute for Languages and Cultures of Asia and Africa, 2008], 805).
2. A hadith recorded in Shah Waliullah Dehlawi's *Forty Ḥadith*, no. 5 (https://sunnah.com/shahwaliullah40:5, accessed September 10, 2022).
3. *qaghan:* "great khan."
4. TA/Kazan at ˂6,8˃ reads: "The reason for this writing is the Dadkhwah Muḥammad Amin Bay Aqsaqal." This is the only indication of a named patron of his work, and it does not appear in other versions of the text.

   TA/Pelliot [3v, 6] and TA/Lund 8v, 19 read instead: "The reason for this writing is those beneficent friends and benevolent brothers, whose minds are comprehending and hearts faithful and free of doubt or anger."

   All examples of TA then read: "Another is that, at this time, when all of the lands around it are in contention and enmity, this country of Moghulistan is in a state of peace and stability. For these two reasons, I have named this work the *Tarikh-i Amniyya*."

5. *Mishkat al-Maṣabiḥ*, book 2, Hadith 25 (https://sunnah.com/mishkat:223, accessed September 10, 2022).
6. This hadith, called *Man Mat* ("If a man dies"), is particularly important in Imami Shiism, in which it emphasizes the importance of following a spiritual leader (Me'ir M. Bar-Asher, *Scripture and Exegesis in Early Imāmi Shiism* [Leiden: Brill, 1999], 190–92).

0:1 History After Noah

1. Sayrami presents here the story of humanity's origins as most people in his society knew it, through the history of revelation, with his own interventions and innovations that alter or challenge that narrative. On the politics of these stories in the Seven Cities, see Eric Schluessel, *Land of Strangers: The Civilizing Project in Qing Central Asia* (New York: Columbia University Press, 2020), chapter 6.

   The *Garden of Purity* (*Rawżat uṣ-Ṣafā'*) is a universal history written in Persian by the Timurid court historian Muḥammad b. Khwandshah, a.k.a. Mirkhwand (1433/4–1498), and completed by his grandson Khwandamir (1475/6–1535/6) after 1502. This comprehensive work synthesized accounts from a range of different Arabic and Persian sources and so became an exceedingly influential history, which was also translated into Chaghatay. It is expected that Sayrami would consult this work, and not surprising that parts of the prolegomenon follow its narrative very closely (Philip Bockholt, "Mīrkhvānd," in *Encyclopaedia of Islam, THREE*, ed. Kate Fleet, Gudrun Krämer, Denis Matringe, John Nawas, and Everett Rowson, accessed July 20, 2022, http://dx.doi.org/10.1163/1573-3912_ei3_COM_40284).

   The *Selection of Chronicles* (*Muntakhab at-Tawarikh*) by Muḥammad Ḥakim Khan (b. 1802/3), written in 1843, is "a voluminous history" and personal record of pilgrimage recounting in Persian the history of Ferghana and the world through the eyes of an independent scholar without a court patron (Timur K. Beisembiev, *Annotated Indices to the Kokand Chronicles* [Tokyo: Research Institute for Languages and Cultures of Asia and Africa, 2008], 167; Muḥammad Ḥakīm Khān, *Muntakhab al-tawārīkh*, ed. Yayoi Kawahara and Koichi Haneda, vol. 2 [Tokyo: Research Institute for Language and Cultures of Asia and Africa ILCAA, 2006], xxii–xxix, 31–44). The author is not the same person as the Ḥakim Khan Törä who appears frequently in the *Tarikh-i Ḥamidi*.

   The *Tarikh-i Rashidi* of Mirza Ḥaydar Dughlat was an influential Persian-language chronicle of Moghulistan during the Yarkand Khanate by an aristocrat who was intimately familiar with its politics. Sayrami evidently considered it the best history of the region, and the only one worth speaking of in the centuries since its completion in 1546 (Wheeler M. Thackston, trans., *Tarikh-i-Rashidi* [New York: I. B. Tauris, 2012], vii). Sayrami may have been reading an expanded version of this work in Chaghatay, such as the one held at the Institute of Oriental Studies of the Academy of Sciences of Uzbekistan (Manuscript No. r.10191), part of which has been edited and published (Amanbek Jalilov, Yayoi Kawahara, Sawada Minoru, Shinmen Yasushi, and Hori Sunao, eds., *Addendum to Tarikh-i Rashidi: Translation and Annotation with Introduction and Indexes* [Tokyo: NIHU Program Islamic Area Studies TIAS, 2008]). This "addendum" to the *Tarikh-i Rashidi* was completed in 1837/8, nearly three centuries after Ḥaydar's death, by Khoja Muḥammad Sharif under the patronage of Ẓuhuruddin Ḥakim Beg of Kashgar (r. 1830–1848). It brings the history up to the early nineteenth century.

TH/Jarring lists two more works. The first is the *Shahrukhiya*, or *Tarikh-i Shahrukhi*, of Niyaz Muḥammad b. Mullah ʿAshur Muḥammad Khoqandi (fl. 19 c.), which dates to 1871/2. This is a history of Ferghana up to that year, a lithograph of which was published in Kazan in 1885 (*Tā'rīkh-i Shāhrukhī* [Qazan: Maṭbaʿkhāna-i Madrasa-i al-Kubrā, 1885]; H. F. Hofman, *Turkish Literature: A Bio-Bibliographical Survey, Section III: Moslim Central Asian Turkish Literature* [Leiden: Brill, 1969], vol. 4, 275–77). It is less likely a work that Beisembiev indicates as the *Tarikh-i Shahrukhiyya*, a "lost chronicle composed by the [khoja] of Chadak?" mentioned once in the *Chronicles of Khoqand* (*Indices*, 877). This *Shahrukhiya* is also mentioned in 1:11 in the TA/Pelliot manuscript, as well as in the St. Petersburg manuscript (Timur K. Beisembiev, *"Tā'rīkh-i Shākhrukhī" kak istoricheskii istochnik* [Alma-Ata: Izd-vo "Nauka" Kazakhskoi SSR, 1987], 59), so it clearly influenced Sayrami earlier in the research and writing process. The second is an unidentified *Zubdat al-akhbār*, the title of which could indicate a number of different works.

2. A "rainmaking stone" *yada tash* is used in Central Asian rainmaking rituals, usually by immersing it in a bowl of water. Sayrami here notes the pronunciation as it was among settled Turks (*yada*) and Kyrgyz (*jada*).
3. Throughout the *Tarikh-i Ḥamidi*, Sayrami follows a common practice of his day and refers to the entire Qing empire or China as "Beijing."
4. Sayrami's text indicates "wings" (*qanat*), while his source, the *Garden of Purity*, specifies that Machin took feathers from a wondrous bird (Muhammad bin Khâvendshâh bin Mahmûd, *The Rauzat-us-safa; or, Garden of Purity*, trans. E. Rehatsek, ed. F. F. Arbuthnot [London: Royal Asiatic Society, 1891], part 1, vol. 1, 96). Sayrami refers to Qing officials' wearing peacock feathers as a sign of rank and distinction.
5. *tongchi:* "translator, interpreter" < Ch. *tōngshì* 通事. This older word for a "go-between," later "interpreter," indicated in Xinjiang a Turkic-speaking Muslim who spoke Chinese and made a living by shifting text between languages. See Schluessel, *Land of Strangers*, chapter 3.
6. *Dāchīng:* "Great Qing (empire)" < Ch. *dà Qīng* 大清.
7. Sayrami has identified Alanqoa's homeland—and thus that of the Chinggisids—not as Mongolia, but as Qarashahr in the northern part of southern Xinjiang. This area, between his hometown of Sayram near Kucha and the Muslim land of Turfan, was under the domination of Buddhist Torghut Mongol princes.

0:2 Chinggis Khan and His Descendants

1. Rum: Indicating "Rome," or rather the former Byzantine, later Ottoman, territories of Anatolia and Constantinople.
2. Muhammad Muhsin Khan, trans., *The Translation of the Meanings of Sahih al-Bukhari*, 9 vols. (Lahore: Kazi, 1979), 4: 114–15.
3. Hadith recorded in *Sunan Abi Dawud*, Book 39, no. 16, accessed September 10, 2022, https://sunnah.com/abudawud:4306.
4. The *Mishkat al-maṣābīḥ* is one of the earliest and most popular collections of hadith (J. Robson, "Ḥadīth," in *Encyclopaedia of Islam, Second Edition*, ed. P. Bearman, Th. Bianquis, C. E. Bosworth, E. van Donzel, and W. P. Heinrichs, accessed July 7, 2022, http://dx.doi.org/10.1163/1573-3912_islam_SIM_5444). I have been unable to locate this particular hadith in the *Mishkat*, but it is fairly well known and can otherwise be found in the *Ṣaḥīḥ*

of al-Bukhārī (Muhsin Khan, trans., *The Translation of the Meanings of Sahih al-Bukhari*, 9: 234).

5. *ṣaḥib duʿa:* Literally "master (or possessor) of prayer."
6. The *yasa* or *yasaq* was thought of as the Mongol legal code, and *yosun* as Mongol custom. The *yarghu* was a more independent system of jurisprudence, carried out by *yarghuchi~jarghuchi*, while *qanun* indicates sultanic law.
7. *Gāngjāng* refers to the *Gāngjiàn yìzhī lù* 綱鑒易知錄, a simplified version of the *Comprehensive Mirror of Governance* (*Zīzhì tōngjiàn* 資治通鑒) that presents the history of the emperors of China in abbreviated form. The following paragraphs are sourced from the first few pages of this book, via Qurbān-ʿAlī Khalidi, *Tawarikh-i khamsa-i sharqi* (Qazan: 1910), 718–20. Compare: Wu Chucai, comp., *Gangjian yizhu lu, juan* 1 [*Wǔ dì jì*] (Taipei: Chengwen chubanshe, 1964; reproduction of Shanghai Hongwen'ge edition, *wùxū* [1898]), 2b–3b. Thank you to Devin Fitzgerald.
8. *Ṭaykhawfūs* < Ch. Tàihào Fúxī 太昊伏羲, one of the ancient culture heroes credited with inventing civilization.
9. "Lu Wang" indicates the pseudo-historical figure Jiǎng Zǐyǎ 姜子牙 (fl. 11 c. BCE), known as Lǚ Wàng 呂望, who was instrumental in the downfall of the Shang dynasty and establishing the Zhou, which Confucians considered the golden age of learning and good government, as well as the foundation of the Chinese political order. Sayrami summarizes Khalidi, *Tawarikh-i Khamsa-ye Sharqi*, 710–11.
10. The account of Chinese dynastic history is based on Qurban ʿAli Khalidi's *Tawarikh-i Khamsa-ye Sharqi*, 745–49, with some deviations, for example: where Khalidi has *Ṣūng*, Sayrami has *Ẓūng*. The Song (960–1279) is the twenty-second dynasty in the *Gangjian*'s reckoning, and the third to be called Song. The first Song emperor, Taizu (r. 960–976), ruled for seventeen years—while the *Gangjian* gives sixteen, Qurban ʿAli Khalidi converted the dates to Hijri years and so gives seventeen (735). The title *shindī khwāngdī* in Khalidi and Sayrami possibly comes from his posthumous name *shéndé* 神德, plus *huángdì* 皇帝 "emperor." He was not exactly a contemporary of al-Qadir (r. 991–1031). As for "Zhao Di," the Song surname was Zhao, and the last emperor's given name was Dibing. Khalidi renders this name in full as *jūwāwdī bīng*, where Sayrami swaps the final syllable for *shingdī*.
11. Zhū Yuánzhāng 朱元璋 (r. as Hōngwǔ 洪武 1368–1398), known as Míng Tàizǔ 明太祖 "grand progenitor of the Ming" for his founding of the Ming state (1368–1644).
12. This calculation, using Chinese rather than Hijri years, dates the age of the Qing 清 (1636–1912) to 1644, the year of the Manchu conquest. As Sayrami himself indicates, however, the Qing began its conquest of the Ming and captured Beijing during the reign of the child emperor Aisin Gioro Fulin, who reigned as Shùnzhì 順治 and was the son of Hong Taiji, called Qīng Tàizōng 清太宗 (r. 1636–1643), who founded the empire.
13. Śākyamuni: the historical Buddha.
14. Ḥasan Buzurg, a Chinggisid, was the founder of the Jalayirid dynasty (1340–1410), also known as the Ilkanids or Ilganids, after his ancestor Ilga Noyan. Michael Hope, "Jalāyirids," in *Encyclopaedia of Islam, THREE*, ed. Kate Fleet, Gudrun Krämer, Denis Matringe, John Nawas, and Everett Rowson, accessed August 30, 2022, http://dx.doi.org/10.1163/1573-3912_ei3_COM_46054.
15. The numerical values of the letters of *alam* total 71 years of age. TH/Jarring has "world" (*ʿālam*), but the values of these letters add up to 141.
16. The "Six Books" refer to six reliable hadith collections. See n. 2, this chapter, above.

17. Ibn al-Jazari (1350–1429), the leading scholar of readings of the Quran in the fifteenth century, known for this manual of Prophetic traditions. Shady H. Nasser, "Ibn al-Jazarī," in *Encyclopaedia of Islam, THREE*, ed. Kate Fleet, Gudrun Krämer, Denis Matringe, John Nawas, Everett Rowson, accessed August 30, 2022, http://dx.doi.org/10.1163/1573-3912_ei3_COM_30840.
18. The letters in *ʿAbbās kusht* add up to 853 [1449].
19. The values of the letters in *Khorasan* add up to 912 [1506/7].
20. Kuchkunji Khan (r. 1512–1531), ruler of the Khanate of Bukhara.
21. See 1:7 and 2:7.
22. "Manglai Suya" is properly "Manglai Sübe."

0:3 The Dughlat Tribe and Its Amirs

1. The *Tarikh-i Rashidi* has "Inchü-Malik" (Thackston, trans., *Tarikh-i Rashidi*, 7).
2. TA/Lund "fourteen"; TA/Pelliot, TH/Jarring "fifteen."
3. TH/Jarring clarifies that he was sent away for fear that Amir Timur would have him killed.
4. TA/Pelliot: 19 Dhu 'l-Hijja [December 17, 1419].
5. In the *Tarikh-i Rashidi*, "Saniz" or "Sanistir" (Thackston, trans., *Tarikh-i Rashidi*, 46n1).
6. levirate marriage: A practice once common in Inner Asia, whereby a man marries his sister-in-law upon his brother's death, or marries his stepmother upon his father's death.
7. Bolor was a name for "the land of the infidels between Badakhshan and Kashmir" (Thackston, trans., *Tarikh-i Rashidi*, 76).
8. Mirza Aḥmad Wang Beg b. Mirza Isḥaq Wang Beg b. Mirza ʿU̱sman Beise Beg b. Mirza Hadi Beg (d. 1864), Ch. *Aimate* 愛瑪特. According to Hodong Kim, who worked from the Qing *Veritable Records*, Aḥmad Wang Beg was governor of Yarkand until 1852, then dismissed on false charges of corruption, then made governor of Kashgar before being dismissed from this position again on false charges. He was assigned again to duties in Yarkand but dismissed a third time (Kim, *Holy War in China: The Muslim Rebellion and State in Chinese Central Asia, 1864–1877* [Stanford, CA: Stanford University Press, 2004], 37–39). For a genealogy, brief biography, and narrative of his death, see Wang et al., comps., *Xinjiang tuzhi*, ed. Zhu Yuqi et al. (Shanghai: Shanghai guji chubanshe, 2017), 444–45, 1880, 2055. He will return in 0:6 and 1:1.
9. TH/Jarring also gives 1326; but TA/Pelliot, 1320; and TA/Lund, 1321.
10. The Manchu title *beise*, Chinese *bèizǐ* 貝子, indicated a prince of the fourth-highest rank. H. S. Brunnert and V. V. Hagelstrom, *Present Day Political Organization of China* (Shanghai: Kelly and Walsh, Limited, 1912), 5.
11. The *Zubdat al-Masaʾil* "Compilation of Examples" is a handbook of jurisprudence used at the Kashgar Islamic court. See Eric Schluessel, "Islamic Law in Xinjiang," in *Routledge Handbook of Islam in Asia*, ed. Chiara Formichi (New York: Routledge, 2021), 128; Paolo Sartori, "Between Kazan and Kashghar: On the Vernacularization of Islamic Jurisprudence in Central Eurasia," *Die Welt des Islams* 61, no. 2 (2020): 1–31.
12. Possibly the same ʿAbdulkarim Bukhari (d. after 1830/1) who in 1818 wrote an untitled treatise documenting his travels in Central Asia (M. Zand, "'Abd-Al-Karīm Boḵārī" in *Encyclopædia Iranica* [London: Routledge, 1982–], vol. 1, fasc. 2, 121–23. The *ʿAqaid* is

probably the same text attested in a pre-1875 copy in the Lund University Library, Jarring Prov. 63. This manuscript describes itself as a translation from Arabic to Chaghatay of a text called the *ʿAqaid-i Islam* by "Muḥammad Karim b. Ḥakim Bukhari." See also Muḥammad Ṣadiq Kashghari, *In Remembrance of the Saints: The Rise and Fall of an Inner Asian Sufi Dynasty*, trans. David Brophy (New York: Columbia University Press, 2020), 243n138.

13. The *ʿAjayib al-Makhluqat* by Zakariyya al-Qazwini (ca. 1203–1283), or something claiming to be that work, is known in Turkic translation (H. F. Hofman, *Turkish Literature: A Bio-Bibliographical Survey, Section III: Moslim Central Asian Turkish Literature* [Leiden: Brill, 1969], vol. 5, 67–69). Examples include Lund University Library, Jarring Prov. 361, and Uppsala University Library, O Nov. 588, but these do not include information on the translator, patrons, or occasion for translation. They may reflect an earlier translation also found in nineteenth-century East Turkestan represented by a manuscript in the Russian Academy of Sciences, Institute for Oriental Manuscripts, B 798 (Dmitrieva, *Katalog Tiurkskikh rukopisiei Instituta Vostokovedeniia Rossiiskoi akademii nauk* [Moscow: Vostochnaia literatura, 2002], 72–73).
14. "imperial agent" *amban:* A Manchu term for "high official."
15. *shāngtāng wä shāng yāmūnigha. shāngtāng wä shāng* possibly < Ch. *cānzàn (dàchén)* 參贊(大臣) "assistant imperial agent" and Ch. *cānjiàng* 參將 "lieutenant colonel." There was a *cānjiàng* stationed at Yarkand from Daoguang 8 (1828) onward, corresponding with Aḥmad Wang's tenure there from 1852 to 1860 (Wang et al., *Xinjiang tuzhi*, 490). That office was subordinate to the Yarkand *cānzàn* established in 1831. These would have been Aḥmad Wang's superiors.
16. *jongsi*: Metathesis of *jīngsū* < Mo. *ǰingse* < Ch. *dǐngzi* 頂子 "button of rank" (David Brophy and Onuma Takahiro, *The Origins of Qing Xinjiang: A Set of Historical Sources on Turfan* [Tokyo: TIAS Department of Islamic Area Studies, 2016], 227). Musa Sayramiy, *Tarikhi Hämidi*, trans. Abduraop Täklimakani (Istanbul: Täklimakan Uyghur näshriyati, 2019), 105, and Molla Musa Sayrami, *Tarikhi Hämidi,* trans. Änwär Baytur (Beyjing: Millätlär näshriyati, 2007), 103, both give *jongyi* or *jongye*. However, TA/Pelliot, TH/Jarring, and TH/Beijing all clearly read *jūngsī.*
17. *yambu:* < Ch. *yuánbǎo* 元寶, a silver ingot used as currency.
18. They probably traveled directly north from Yarkand to Aqsu, passing through present-day Maralbashi and Fayżabad. Sarigh Qomush and Kelin Zali Köl would be along that route. Tadam may have been along the difficult desert road from Kucha to Khotan.

0:4 Tughluq Timur Khan

1. *Tarikh-i Rashidi*: Sher Muḥammad Khan (Mirza Ḥaydar Dughlat, *Tarikh-i Rashidi*, trans. Wheeler M. Thackston [New York: I. B. Tauris, 2012], 32).
2. "*divs* and *paris*": Two supernatural creatures in the Perso-Islamic tradition, similar but not equal to "devils and fairies," though they are locked in eternal opposition.

   In TH/Beijing, this passage is found following "and so he was buried in Aqsu." TA/Pelliot instead places it here, where it arguably makes more sense. I follow TA/Pelliot.
3. Compare the description of the plunder in *Tarikh-i Rashidi* (147).
4. For more on the problem of the animal calendar in East Turkestan, see Masami Hamada, "Rupture ou continuité: Le calendrier des douze animaux chez les Musulmans

Turcophones du Turkestan oriental," in *Mélanges offerts à Louis Bazin* (Paris: L'Harmattan, 1992), 285–91. Hodong Kim offers further comment in "Eastern Turki Royal Decrees of the 17th Century in the Jarring Collection," in *Studies on Xinjiang Historical Sources in 17th–20th Centuries*, ed. James A. Millward, Shinmen Yasushi, and Jun Sugawara (Tokyo: Toyo Bunko, 2010), 75.

There is even variation between manuscripts of the TA/TH in their presentation of animal years, perhaps on the basis of their places of copying. For example, TH/Beijing {227, 236} twice identifies 1288 AH as the Year of the Bird, while TH/Jarring (92v, 96v) in both instances calls it a Year of the Mouse. In either case, however, the manuscript identifies both 1078 AH and 1288 AH as the Year of the Bird/Mouse, so they are consistent. Had the cycle proceeded as normal from 1078, 1282, not 1288, ought to have been a Bird/Mouse year. Clearly, in Sayrami's presentation of the facts, the animal year cycle applies to the Islamic lunar calendar, and this reckoning skipped six years of a twelve-year cycle.

5. *muqam:* < Ar. *maqām* "mode," in the East Turkestani context indicating a musical "suite consisting of sung poetry and stories, dance turns and instrumental sections" (Rachel Harris, *The Making of a Musical Canon in Chinese Central Asia: The Uyghur Twelve Muqam* [New York: Routledge, 2016], 1).
6. The dates that Sayrami gives for the reigns of the Dughlats throughout this section seem to disagree with previous sources, namely Maḥmud Churas's untitled chronicle, as well as with the *Tarikh-i Rashidi*, which gives different dates for Saʿid Khan. Space precludes a full discussion, but compare Shāh Maḥmūd Churas, *Khronika: Kriticheskii tekst, perevod, kommentarii, issledovanie i ukaziteli O. F. Akimushkin* (Moscow: Nauka, 1976).
7. Compare Kashghari, *In Remembrance of the Saints*, 32.
8. The Junghar title Khung-Taiji here refers to Galdan Khan (1644–1697). For details, see Kashghari, *In Remembrance of the Saints*, 240n96.
9. This account is somewhat garbled. Khoja ʿAbdullah should properly be Khoja ʿUbaydullah. The MSS all read *Sayr-* or *Siyar-i Sharīf* "The Noble Journey" or "The Noble Biography," indicating another name for the *Maʿārij al-nubuwwa fī madārij al-futuwwa*, a lengthy and popular biography of the Prophet, which Muʿīnī (d. 1501/2) completed in 1486 (E. Berthels, "Muʿīn al-Miskīn," in *Encyclopedia of Islam, Second Edition*, ed. P. Bearman, Th. Bianquis, C. E. Bosworth, E. van Donzel, and W. P. Heinrichs, http://dx.doi.org/10.1163/1573-3912_islam_SIM_5444). The Lund University Library holds several manuscript volumes of this work's Turkic translation, the earliest of which dates to the beginning of the nineteenth century: Jarring Prov. 86, 145, 190, 243, 252, 266, 388, 428, 434, 442, and 444. Hofman notes several MSS of a translation "in the language of Kashghar" by Muḥammad Raḥim Miskin dating to 1170 [1756/7] (H. F. Hofman, *Turkish Literature: A Bio-Bibliographical Survey, Section III: Moslim Central Asian Turkish Literature* [Leiden: Brill, 1969], vol. 4, 193).
10. TA/Pelliot and TH/Jarring read "Khwajas" for "Muslims." *Qara Khan* literally means "Black Khan," and *Aq Khan*, "White Khan." Brophy explains that the term *Qara Khan* actually referred to the Junghar garrisons (Kashghari, *In Remembrance of the Saints*, 239n90).
11. *jūngtāng:* < Ch. *zhōngtáng* 中堂 "grand secretary."
12. Lǐfānyuàn 理藩院: The special Qing institution for the management of the "outer" peoples of the empire.
13. Sayrami refers to Chinese "statutes" *lǜ* 律. See 1:1, n. 3, and 1:4, n. 1, below.

14. The distinction between "White Mountaineers" (*Aq Taghliqlar*) and "Black Mountaineers" (*Qara Taghliqlar*) plays an important role in East Turkestan's political history. Sayrami, like most people in his time, understands these terms as mapping onto two competing branches of the descendants of Makhdum-i Aʿẓam, those descended from Isḥaq Khoja and those from Afaq Khoja. However, they previously indicated a different factional conflict. See Kashghari, *In Remembrance of the Saints*, xxi–xxiv.
15. TH/Beijing: "1252 [1836]," which is surely a slip. This date comes from TH/Jarring.
16. On the Qing genocide of the Junghar Mongols, see Benjamin Samuel Levey, "Jungar Refugees and the Making of Empire on Qing China's Kazakh Frontier, 1759–1773" (PhD diss., Harvard University, 2013).
17. Taranchi: A distinct population of Turkic-speaking Muslims and their descendants who were relocated to the Ili Valley to act as *taranchi*, literally "cultivators," to support the Junghars and later the Qing garrisons there. See David Brophy, *Uyghur Nation: Reform and Revolution on the Russia-China Frontier* (Cambridge, MA: Harvard University Press, 2016), 30–35.
18. See 1:9 "The Rise of Maḥmudin," where this "blessed tea" is part of Sufi rituals.
19. *ʿushshāq*: Sayrami points out an irony here, that these Sufis, meant to be the "friends of God" or "lovers" in the sense of drawing nearer to God, were anything but holy.
20. Sayrami refers to the Qing system of official titles: *wang* < Ch. *wáng* 王 "prince"; *gōng* < Ch. *gong* 公 "duke"; *beise* < Manchu *beise*, Chinese *bèizǐ* 貝子 (fourth rank); *beile* < Manchu *beile*, Chinese *bèilè* 貝勒 (third rank) (H. S. Brunnert and V. V. Hagelstrom, *Present Day Political Organization of China* [Shanghai: Kelly and Walsh, Limited, 1912], 5–6 [the titles in general], 440 [in Turfan and Qumul]).
21. TH/Jarring tells us that it is Muḥammad Musa Beise Beg's *sons* who are in Aqyar. TA/Pelliot indicates that *he* was in Aqyar.
22. Sayrami apparently describes a temple for tutelary gods, suggesting that these *begs* were made into minor deities who protected Xinjiang. A similar temple built in honor of Cangling (or another Qing military leader), also in Ushaq Tal, is noted in 1:11, n. 1, below.
23. *tarkhan:* A tax-exempt, hereditary fief.

0:5 The Holy War of Jahangir

1. The events described in this chapter correspond to those of 1826–1828, when Jahangir occupied Kashgar and requested Khoqand's assistance, including the details of Jahangir's refusal to meet Muḥammad ʿAli Khan unless both remained mounted atop their horses, and of the Khoqandi forces' breaching of the Kashgar citadel (L. J. Newby, *The Empire and the Khanate: A Political History of Qing Relations with Khoqand, c. 1760–1860* [Leiden: Brill, 2005], 95–104, 117–19).
2. The old Qing garrison's fortress was incorporated into Kashgar's city walls.
3. *qara cherik:* Lit. "dark army." This phrase is difficult to translate well. The word *qara* indicates "black, dark," but also "large, great," as in the name Qara-Khitay for the Khitan empire. In the *Tarikh-i Ḥamidi*, the term refers exclusively to the army of the Qing, so implies both that "great army" (Manchu *amba cooha*, Ch. *dàjūn* 大軍) and its dark, threatening, looming quality. Yet, as a reviewer points out, *qara* can also indicate

"commoner," as in the "militias" (*qara kaltäk*) that so many local powers raised, so *qara cherik* may indicate soldiers from outside the Qing's elite banner armies. This may be the case, given that the Qing did rally Green Standard forces to the fight again Jahangir (Newby, *The Empire and the Khanate*, 101). In certain places, Sayrami emphasizes the "darkness" of this army, as in 2:15. Consequently, I have chosen to render the phrase as "dark army" to preserve consistency and express its connotations as succinctly as possible.

4. < Ch. "(Jahangir) *dòngtan, dì dòngtan* 動彈，地動彈."
5. *Āy Jāngjūng*: < Ch. "general" *jiāngjūn* 將軍. The identity of "General Ai" is mysterious, as I can find no Qing military leader from this conflict with such a name. However, given the timing and this figure's actions, General Ai should be Cangling (Ch. Chánglíng 長齡, 1758–1838) of the Mongolian Plain White Banner, who served as Ili General in 1825–1826. The name Ai may derive from confusion with I Šan (Ch. *Yìshān* 奕山, 1794–1878), who held the same office in 1837–1840 and in 1845–1854 during the incursion of Wali Khan.
6. "Nazugum" is an epic about a young woman of the same name. She participates in a revolt against the Qing and is exiled to Ili, where she is forced to marry a Qing soldier. Instead, she resists, kills him, flees, and eventually dies as a martyr. For the many meanings of Nazugum, see Kara Abramson, "Gender, Uyghur Identity, and the Story of Nuzugum," *The Journal of Asian Studies* 71, no. 4 (2012): 1069–91.
7. Wali Khan Töra, a descendant of Afaq Khoja, made multiple incursions into Xinjiang in the 1850s, most notably in 1857, where he briefly imposed a bloody reign of terror in Kashgar before the Qing armies expelled him. He is legendary for building towers of skulls.
8. *gaz:* A unit of length roughly equivalent to an ell or cubit.
9. *īmān* is translated here as "blessing," but the more literal translation is "faith." The soldier, perhaps unwittingly, informs the woman that the Andijanis have no faith.

0:6 Muslims Under Chinese Rule

1. *wayshāng:* "suburban market" < Ch. *wài* 外 "outer" and *xiāng* 廂, a term indicating a settled area near a city. Chinese-language reports from eyewitnesses record that *xiāng* just south of Kucha's city were some of the first to be burned. National Palace Museum, Taipei, *guji* 098967, memorial dated TZ 3.5.14.
2. Chinese Táng Wáng 唐王 "King of Tang," referring to a ruler of the Tang dynasty (618–904). Here refers to Tang Gaozong 唐高宗 (r. 649–683), to whom the caliph ʿUs̱man (r. 644–656) sent a diplomatic mission led by Saʿd b. Waqqas, uncle of the Prophet, in 651.

   This story closely resembles origin stories that the Hui told about themselves. See Svetlana Rimsky-Korsakoff Dyer, "T'ang T'ai-tsung's Dream: A Soviet Dungan Version of a Legend on the Origin of the Chinese Muslims," *Monumenta Serica* 35, no. 1 (1981): 545–70; Haiyun Ma, "The Mythology of the Prophet's Ambassadors in China: Histories of Sa'd Waqqas and Gess in Chinese Sources," *Journal of Muslim Minority Affairs* 26, no. 3 (2006): 445–52; Zvi Ben Dor Benite, "From 'Literati' to 'Ulama': The Origins of Chinese Muslim Nationalist Historiography," *Nationalism and Ethnic Politics* 9, no. 4 (2004):

83–109; Eric Schluessel, *Land of Strangers: The Civilizing Project in Qing Central Asia* (New York: Columbia University Press, 2020), 181–85.

3. *changshila* "drama" < Ch. *chàngxì* 唱戲. Gunnar Jarring, ed., *Culture Clash in Central Asia: Islamic Views on Chinese Theatre—Eastern Turki Texts Edited with Translation, Notes and Vocabulary* (Stockholm: Almqvist & Wiksell International, 1991), 35.
4. Mǎ Huàlóng 馬化龍 (d. 1871) became the leader of the Sufi Jahriyya order in Xining around 1849.
5. The second Opium War or Arrow War (1856–1860).
6. Wú Sānguì 吳三桂 (1612–1678) was a military leader who helped the Qing conquer China, then led the Rebellion of the Three Feudatories (1673–1681) in hopes of seizing power for himself. Sayrami probably means to indicate the Red Turban Rebellion and Dacheng state (1852–1864) in Guangdong and Guangxi. Many people in Xinjiang referred to the Taiping (1850–1864) as the "Long-Hairs," using the word *changmoza* < Ch. *cháng máozi* 長毛子 "long hair." The "other" Dungan uprising is probably the Panthay (1856–1873), which was centered in the southern province of Yunnan.
7. The general at Ili was the highest Qing official in Xinjiang from 1759 to 1864.
8. Suǒ Huànzhāng 索煥章 was a lieutenant colonel (*cānjiàng* 參將) in the Qing army, and son of Suǒ Wén 索文, the former marshal (*tídū* 提督) of Ganzhou. He was known as a *dàlǎoyè* 大老爺, a respectful term for Chinese officials (Hodong Kim, *Holy War in China: The Muslim Rebellion and State in Chinese Central Asia, 1864–1877* [Stanford, CA: Stanford University Press, 2004], 41–42). See 1:12, n. 7, below.
9. *kawlan* < Ch. *kǒuliáng* 口糧 (Kim, *Holy War in China*, 223).
10. A *kökbashi* was a local irrigation manager responsible for building and maintaining irrigation infrastructure and ensuring an equitable distribution of water.
11. MS d.w.l.y: A mysterious pair of syllables, likely < Ch. *dàolǐ* 道理 "sense; ways; reason; principles." TH/Jarring (32v) includes an annotation by the scribe indicating that *d.w.l.y* means "Shariah."
12. *kūbay* < Ch. *kǒuwài* 口外 "beyond the Pass (at Jiayuguan)."
13. That is, it became unreachable, like this mythical phoenix in its lofty nest.
14. *yan say* < Ch. *yáncài* 鹽菜, literally "salt and vegetables," but referring to an allowance for purchasing food.
15. *gosi khaṭ* (TH/Jarring: *gongsi khaṭ*) < Ch. *gōngshì* 公示 "public notice."
16. *janla* < Ch. *juānnà* 捐納 "office purchase."
17. *chanto* < Ch. *Chántóu* 纏頭, literally "wrapped head." A Chinese term for Turkic-speaking Muslims with a pejorative connotation.
18. Reynold A. Nicholson, trans., *The Mathnawí of Jalálu'ddin* Rúmí, 4 vols. (London: Luzac, 1926), book II, 383.
19. I cannot locate this hadith, but it appears to be a rephrase of the Quran [8:28].
20. The term *dādkhwāh* has a range of meanings. Its literal meaning is "petitioner for justice." Hodong Kim regards *dādkhwāh* as a "synonym" of *ḥākim beg* "governor" (Kim, *Holy War in China*, 103). Certainly, Yaʿqūb Beg appointed many *dādkhwāhs* to rule "provinces" (*wilāyat*) in Moghulistan, but also *ḥākim*, and several *dādkhwāhs* were not *ḥākims*. In the Khoqandi context from which Yaʿqūb Beg came, which would have influenced the terminology of the Khoja state as well, a *dādkhwāh* was not necessarily a governor, but an "honorary title of middle rank with tax immunity" (Timur K. Beisembiev, *Annotated Indices to the Kokand Chronicles* [Tokyo: Research Institute for Languages and Cultures of Asia and Africa, 2008], 769).

1:1 The Holy War of Rashuddin Khoja

1. TH/Jarring: "130 or 140"; TA/Pelliot: "140 or 150." Sayrami's final revision offers a precise year. He dates the uprisings to 1281 [1864] (see 0:6), which, minus 118 Hijri years, yields 1163 [1749].
2. "Salt" stands for all that a ruler gives their servants, and those servants' obligations to that ruler. For a complete discussion of this metaphor and its origins, see Hamada Masami, "Jihâd, Hijra, et 'devoir du sel' dans l'histoire du Turkestan oriental," *Turcica* 33 (2001): 35–61.
3. The *lū* referred to here is probably again Chinese *lǜ* 律 "law," indicating codified law or statute. See 0:4, n. 13, above, and 1:4, n. 1, below. Sayrami reprises the question of *lǜ* much later in the text.
4. Muhammad Muhsin Khan, trans., *The Translation of the Meanings of Sahih al-Bukhari*, 9 vols. (Lahore: Kazi, 1979), vol. 4, 63.

1:3 The Failure of the Aqsu Campaign

1. Probably at Qarabagh.
2. *yinfan:* "barracks" < Ch. *yíngfáng* 營房.
3. *Paotai* is a unit of distance about two miles in length < Ch. *pàotái* 炮台 "fort; cannon platform," as it indicates the notional distance between small fortresses along a road (Gunnar Jarring, *Central Asian Turkic Place-Names—Lop Nor and Tarim Area: An Attempt at Classification and Explanation Based on Sven Hedin's Diaries and Published Works* [Stockholm: The Sven Hedin Foundation, 1997], 334).
4. *Li* would seem to indicate here—as elsewhere—the Chinese *lǐ* 禮 "rites," which to Sayrami and others stood for the whole of Chinese law and morality (Eric Schluessel, *Land of Strangers: The Civilizing Project in Qing Central Asia* [New York: Columbia University Press, 2020], 25–31). It is used here to give the line a Chinese flavor. TH/Jarring reads instead *jā'iz* "permitted," invoking a similar concept in Islam. Sayrami, at least in his later revisions, would have been aware of Qurban ʿAli Khalidi's interpretation of *lǐ* as "religion" (*dīn*) and "rites, customs" (*āyīn*) (*Tawarikh-i khamsa-i sharqi*, 747). Contrast with *lū* < Chinese *lǜ* 律 "law, statute" above. Baytur agrees and notates it as *qa'idä* (< Ar. *qāʿida*) "rule" (177). Alternatively, this could be read as *lǐ* 理 "sense," as in *dàolǐ* 道理, a word that Sayrami invoked above (see 0:6, n. 11). I am grateful to Jun Sugawara for thoughts on interpreting this sentence.

1:4 The Success of the Aqsu Campaign

1. *Khaniya*: Sayrami's lengthy discussion of *khaniya* (kh.n.y.h) in 2:17 indicates that the term is more or less synonymous with "state property" or "treasury"—something can be sent to the *khaniya*—while land that Chinese officials open through reclamation or grant to local aristocrats is also *khaniya*. *Khaniya* appears in the same form in the *Lī kitābi*, a clumsy translation into Chaghatay of a late Qing primer (Nikolai Katanov, "Man'chursko-Kitaiskii 'li' na narechii Tiurkov Kitaiskogo Turkestana," *Zapiski vostochnogo otdeleniia imperatorskogo Russkogo arkheologicheskogo obshchestva* 14 [1901]: 31–75, 37;

see Eric Schluessel, *Land of Strangers: The Civilizing Project in Qing Central Asia* [New York: Columbia University Press, 2020], 28; compare Xin Xia, *Shengyu shiliutiao fu lü yijie*, reproduced in Zhang Yifan, ed., *Zhongguo lüxue wenxian, di si ji* [Beijing: Shehui kexue wenxian chubanshe, 2007]). Katanov, the editor, glosses it as خانيه = خنيه казенный, государственный "official, state" (52n49). The word is found in a passage translated from the Qing Code, part of which reads: *Atap qoyghan yī tän yärni oghrilap satqan kishi khaniya yärni oghrilap satqan kishigä okhshash lūy lūy bilän bänläydur* "One who has stolen and sold granted 'righteous land' [*yī tän* < Ch. *yì tián* 義田] is to be punished according to the statute [*lūy lūy* < Ch. *lǜ* 律 "statute," doubled] for one who has stolen *khaniya* land." (On *lǜ/lūy*, see 0:4, n. 13, and 1:1, n. 3, above.) The parallel passage in the Qing Code reads, "When one steals and sells 'righteous land,' the crime must be punished according to the statute for stealing and selling official fields" 盜賣義田，應照盜賣官田律治罪 (*Duli cunyi*, statute 93, "stealing and selling fields and dwellings" 盜賣田宅, substatute 4, "Legalizing Space in China," https://lsc.chineselegalculture.org/eC/DQLL_DC_1905/3.3.10.93.4). The word *khaniya* was thus used to translate "official fields" (*guāntián* 官田), precisely indicating land held by the state. Albert von le Coq also published a version of this text based on how it was read aloud. His work confirms that the word was pronounced, in his transcription, *χā̆'nī*, or *khanī* ("Das Lî-Kitâbi," *Kőrösi Csoma Archivum* 1, no. 6 [1925]: 450). It therefore seems most likely that *kh.n.y.a* was shorthand for *khāniya*.

shang: Sayrami plays with the alienness of the term *shang* and its multiple meanings. First of all, Sayrami appears to be incorrect about its etymology. Although the word does derive from Chinese *cāng* 倉 "granary," it came into Turkic via Mongolian as *šang/sang*. This *šang* was a regular tribute duty that the Junghars imposed upon the Muslims in exchange for their protection, a transfer of goods from inferiors to superiors. Indeed, *šang* was what the Junghar khans called their treasury (Hosung Shim, "The State Formation of the Zunghar Principality: A Political History of the Last Centralized State of the Eurasian Steppe" [PhD diss., Indiana University–Bloomington, 2021], 576–78). However, Sayrami is proposing an etymology from Chinese that was later suggested by Chinese observers themselves. This etymology assumed that the *shang* duty derived its name from the verb *shǎng* 賞 "to bestow upon inferiors," which indicates here gifts from the emperor to his subjects (Saguchi Tōru, *Jūhachi-jūkyū seiki Higashi Torukisutan shakai shi kenkyū* [Tōkyō: Yoshikawa Kōbunkan, 1963], 111–12). As Joseph Fletcher points out, this is the opposite meaning of *shang* from that used in the context of the Junghar-Turkic relationship ("The Biography of Khwush Kipäk Beg [d. 1781] in the *Wai-fan Meng-ku Hui-pu wang kung biao chuan*," *Acta Orientalia Academiae Scientiarum Hungaricae* 36, no. 1/3 [1982]: 171n14). Sayrami then plays on this "Chinese" meaning of *shang* by saying that the Khwajas *shang*'ed (*shǎng* "gave to inferiors") the cloth (*shang* < *cāng*) to their soldiers. The word *shang* < *shǎng* 賞 is also attested in Eastern Turkic in this period, as well as a verb *shangla-* "to bestow," so the reason for the confusion is evident.

2. *ṭayṭay* "woman" < Chinese *tàitai* 太太.

1:5 Expedition to Ushturfan

1. Mölchär Mountain in Chinese texts is named *Wūchì shān* 烏赤山 "Ush Mountain" (Ma Dazheng et al., eds., *Xinjiang xiangtuzhi gao* [Wulumuqi: Xinjiang renmin chubanshe,

2010], 332, 335). It is today called *Yanzi shan* 燕子山. On the meanings of *mölchär/bölchär*, see 1:7, n. 5, below.
2. There are parallels between this legend and that of the "Fragrant Concubine," a member of the Makhdumzada Khoja lineage who was married to the Qianlong emperor and sent to live in distant Beijing (James A. Millward, "A Uyghur Muslim in Qianlong's Court: The Meanings of the Fragrant Concubine," *The Journal of Asian Studies* 53, no. 2 [1994]: 427–58).
3. Sayrami recounts the Ush Uprising of 1765. Compare James A. Millward, *Eurasian Crossroads: A History of Xinjiang* (New York: Columbia University Press, 2007), 108–9.
4. TH/Jarring: "Ush." TH/Beijing, however, is specific about spelling: elsewhere, the city is called Ushturfan, with *sh*, while here Sayrami specifies Uch, with *ch*. There is no obvious reason to connect migration with the name Uch, but Sayrami may be suggesting a folk etymology from *öch* "revenge; hatred," or from *köch* "migration." Chinese sources hold that its name derives from the Uch Mountain inside the city, what is called Mölchär Mountain in this text. *Uch* means "tip" or "point," which is the definition given in many Chinese sources.
5. Muhammad Muhsin Khan, trans., *The Translation of the Meanings of Sahih al-Bukhari*, 9 vols. (Lahore: Kazi, 1979), vol. 3, 340.

1:6 Kashgar Campaign

1. TA: "Jumada al-Awwal" [October 13, 1864]. Sayrami updated his narrative, so we may infer that he corrected himself.
2. TA/Pelliot, TH/Jarring: "1,000."
3. *kūtwāl* "seneschal."

1:7 Yarkand Campaign

1. TH/Jarring: "4,000."
2. Täklimakani (Musa Sayramiy, *Tarikhi Hämidi*, trans. Abduraop Täklimakani [Istanbul: Täklimakan Uyghur näshriyati, 2019]) corrects Sayrami's arithmetic to "6,000" (210).
3. *khūyjā*: "settler." TH/Beijing (129) clarifies: *khūyjā, yaʿnī dehqān*, while TH/Jarring (54v) provides the same gloss in a marginal note. Täklimakani agrees: *dehqanchiliq qilidighanlar* "those engaged in farming" (210). Aili Wufuer's Chinese translation does not include this word, suggesting that it is not a transparent term, as does the fact that TA/Pelliot miswrites it as *khoja* [69v]. This term is elsewhere paired with "(Chinese) trader" *mäymäychi*, so its meaning of "(Chinese) farmer" seems obvious. A modern dictionary of Ürümchi dialect gives: *hùérjiā* 戶兒家 "country person (derogatory)" (Li Rong and Zhou Lei, eds., *Wulumuqi fangyan cidian* [Nanjing: Jiangsu jiaoyu chubanshe, 1995], 67). Abdurishid Yakup's lexicon of the Turfan dialect agrees—*χuřǯa* "farmer"—and provides a possible etymology from Mongolian *xurŋa* "to harvest" (Ferdinand D. Lessing, ed., *Mongolian-English Dictionary* [Berkeley: University of California Press, 1960], 989; Yakup, *The Turfan Dialect of Uyghur* [Berkeley: University of California Press, 1960], 451). I agree with Yakup's assessment, as the term *khūrjā* bears a similar meaning in a document from Turfan dating to 1908 (*Qingdai Xinjiang dang'an xuanji* [Guilin: Guangxi shifan daxue chubanshe, 2012], vol. 70, 53–54). We find it again in 1937 on a document surveying

villagers' occupations in Turfan: the term *khūrjā* appears, but not *dehqān* "farmer" ("Tulufan xian minzhong fandi lianhe choubei weiyuanhui Kalahujia xiang gongmin mingdan," Xinjiang Uyghur Autonomous Region Archive, M16.021.YJ.6025). In the present text, however, both *dehqān* and *khūyjā* appear, the latter only when referring to Chinese farmers. Sayrami even offers a gloss in 1:12: "There were many Chinese merchants and *khūyjā*—that is, farmers [*dehqān*]." Hence "settler," capturing the meaning of "someone who has come from outside to farm." Interestingly, an earlier document from 1886 indicates a contrast between *dehqān* as "landowner" and *khurja* as "one who works the land," or possibly a *dehqān*'s "tenant" (*Qingdai Xinjiang dang'an xuanji*, vol. 79, 218). (Thanks very much to Kevin Kind for pointing this document out.) It may be that the term *khurja~khuyja* gradually fell out of use during this time period, or that it had local meanings in places like Turfan that did not translate to other oases.

4. TA/Pelliot, TH/Beijing: *qoqtada*; TH/Jarring: *choqchada*. Baytur: *qoqtida* (197) (Molla Musa Sayrami, *Tarikhi Hämidi*, trans. Änwär Baytur [Beyjing: Millätlär näshriyati, 2007]); Täklimakani "somewhere" *bir yär* (212). My interpretation via "Dis. ĞBĞ" (Gerard Clauson, *An Etymological Dictionary of Pre-Thirteenth-Century Turkish* [Oxford: Clarendon Press, 1972], 582–83); Tobol *kökty* "hollow; the holes in trees where birds make their nests" (W. Radloff, *Versuch eines Wörterbuches der Türk-Dialecte*, 4 vols. [St. Petersburg, 1893], vol. 2, 514).
5. *mölchär:* "mantlet." TH/Beijing, TH/Jarring: *m.l.j.r* < Mo. *moljar* "battle station." Baytur: *potäy* < Chinese 炮台 *pàotái* "fort," literally "cannon platform" (197). Täklimakani: *egiz härikätchan munarä, potäy* "tall, movable towers, *paotai*" (212). Aili Wufuer: *mù pàotái* 木砲台 "wooden cannon tower" (Maolamusa Sailami, *Yimide shi*, trans. Aili Wufuer, in *Qingdai Chahetai wen wenxian yizhu*, ed. Miao Pusheng [Wulumuqi: Xinjiang renmin chubanshe, 2013], 410). However, the word *potäy* is not mentioned here in the manuscripts, while it is found frequently elsewhere in this very text to indicate postal stations, defensive towers, and distances, and it appears again only a few lines below. It is useful to look to earlier texts: Eiji Mano, *Bābūr-nāma (Vaqāyiʿ)*, 2 vols. (Kyoto: Syokado, 1995–96), notes that two manuscripts of that work alternate between the forms *boljar~moljar* (536.4). Thackston translates this word variously in his *Baburnama*, ex. "the posts of the right and left flanks of the center and of the royal tabin" (Wheeler M. Thackston, trans., *The Baburnama: Memoirs of Babur, Prince and Emperor* [New York: Modern Library, 2002], 398 [335]). Elsewhere, they are "batteries" from which artillery were fired, which supports the translation of *paotai* (Mano, ed., *Bābūr-nāma*, 539.8; Thackston, trans., *Baburnama*, 400 [336]). But it is clear from one description of a siege that "The left wing and center advanced [from their *moljar*] with their [one-handed] shields in place" before setting up their ladders and clambering up them to storm a fortress (Mano, ed., *Bābūr-nāma*, 341.21; Thackston, trans., *Baburnama*, 270 [217b]). Doerfer offers a primary definition of "meeting-place," with a secondary and later definition, "section of a siege ring around a fortress" (*Sektion eines Belagerungsringes um eine Festung*), that confirms the sense of surrounding an enemy and closing in on them (Gerhard Doerfer, *Türkische und mongolische Elemente im Neupersischen*, 4 vols. [Wiesbaden: Franz Steiner Verlag, 1963] vol. 1, 229–32). I think Täklimakani is right that it was a movable siege tower, but not one for firing cannons. Rather, I think it was more of a movable shield, like the mantlet familiar from medieval European siege warfare.
6. The phrase indicates the Chinese calculation of population by the number of *dīng* 丁 "able-bodied men."

7. Mir Ghiyaṣuddin was the teacher of a famed shaykh of the Mujaddidi order, Shah Awliya, who reportedly died in 1837 and in life brought the teachings of Aḥmad Sirhindi to Yarkand. He and his disciples then spread out across East Turkestan and northwest China, (re)discovering shrines and gradually establishing their teachings. Modern sources establish a connection between the Yarkand Mujaddidi community and the Qirmish Ata shrine outside of Ushturfan (see 1:9, n. 7, below), so it would make sense for such a key figure as Mirza Jan Ḥażrat to be sent there for safety (Rian Thum, "The Naqshbandiyya Mujaddidiyya in China," *The Journal of the Royal Asiatic Society*, forthcoming; Waleed Ziad, "From Yarkand to Sindh via Kabul: The Rise of Naqshbandi-Mujaddidi Sufi Networks in the Eighteenth and Nineteenth Centuries," in *The Persianate World: Rethinking a Shared Sphere*, ed. Abbas Amanat and Assef Ashraf [Leiden: Brill, 2019], 125–68). Mirza Jan Ḥażrat will play a key role in the events of 1:9, and he is also discussed in 2:5.
8. See 2:7 for more about Muẓaffar Khan, and 0:2 for a preview of his fate.

1:8 Campaign to Kashgar and Yarkand

1. TA agree that his name was "Ṣiddiq," while TH/Jarring, probably erroneously, indicates that he was the "son of Ṣiddiq." He may be the same as Ṣiddiq Dadkhwah, who commanded Kuchanese forces.
2. *shadiyana:* A "celebration" rhythm, played at festivals, but also to celebrate the accession of a new ruler (Rachel Harris, *The Making of the Musical Canon in Chinese Central Asia: The Uyghur Twelve Muqam* [New York: Routledge, 2016], 53).
3. *segah:* One of the modes of the *muqam* (Harris, *The Making of a Musical Canon*, 96–97).
4. *dū* "a roll of the dice" < Chinese *dǔ* 賭 "gamble;" *bāy* < Chinese *bài* 敗 "lose."

1:9 The Rise of Maḥmudin

1. *Mishkat al-maṣabiḥ*, Book 1, Hadith 26 (Sunnah.com, accessed September 10, 2022, https://sunnah.com/mishkat:28).
2. Muhammad Muhsin Khan, *The Translation of the Meanings of Sahih al-Bukhari*, 9 vols. (Lahore: Kazi, 1979), vol. 4, 63.
3. The Iftar feast places the events of this anecdote in Ramadan 1283 [January 7–February 5, 1867].
4. Mullah Shakir's (b. 1805) *Ẓafarnama* confirms Sayrami's role in local administration (Molla Shakir, "Zäfär-nama dastanidin," in *Äsirlär sadasi: kona Uyghur ädäbiyatining nämuniliri*, ed. M. K. Hemraev [Almuta: Qazaqstan dölät güzäl ädäbiyat näshriyati, 1963], 314–15).
5. *sāng* < Ch. *cāng* 倉 "granary."
6. *jīng* < Ch. *jīn* 斤, a unit of weight.
7. "The Shrine of the Poplar" *Mazār-i Tārāk:* The Shrine of Qirmish Ata, which Sayrami includes among those of Aqsu (3:4), and which is intimately tied to the sacred landscape of Ushturfan. Qirmish Ata was an important Islamizer whose legend was intertwined with that of ʿAli, and whose companions' tombs are pilgrimage sites near Ushturfan. The shaykhs of the Shrine of Qirmish Ata would have been powerful local figures

capable of mounting a challenge to the Kucha Khojas' rule (Rahilä Dawut, *Uyghur mazarliri* [Shinjang khälq näshriyati, 2001] 163–65; N. N. Pantusov, "Les mazâr musulmans de la ville d'Uch-Turfan et de ses environs [en territoires chinois]," trans. P. Garrone, *Journal of the History of Sufism* 3 [2001]: 185–86; Ömärjan Häsän, "Qirmish Atam: Insap Qilinglar . . .," *Miras* 5 [2001]: 57–63; Agnieszka Joniak-Lüthi, "Xinjiang's Geographies in Motion," *Asian Ethnicity* 16, no. 4 [2015]: 428–45, 437–39). Sayrami is very skeptical of the veracity of Qirmish Ata's legend (3:4) and, while he admits the shrine's power, dismisses the legitimacy of its attribution. This skepticism may be associated with his rejection of the Ushturfan sectarians as described in this chapter. We may speculate that the *khojas* who later welcomed Yaʿqub Beg to Ushturfan and Aqsu included some of these Ushturfan Khojas (1:16). Meanwhile, the "Ḥażrats" of Yarkand and the "Ḥażrats" of Ushturfan were probably part of the same network of Mujaddidi Sufis (Hodong Kim, *Holy War in China: The Muslim Rebellion and State in Chinese Central Asia, 1864–1877* [Stanford, CA: Stanford University Press, 2004], 45, 64; Waleed Ziad, "From Yarkand to Sindh via Kabul: The Rise of Naqshbandi-Mujaddidi Sufi Networks in the Eighteenth and Nineteenth Centuries," in *The Persianate World: Rethinking a Shared Sphere*, ed. Abbas Amanat and Assef Ashraf [Leiden: Brill, 2019], 168).

8. *shānglaw* "headman" < Chinese *xiānglǎo* 鄉老.
9. *shūfāng*: probably < Ch. *chúfáng* 廚房 "kitchen."
10. "The Shrine of the Valley" *Qoltuq Mazar*: The shrine of Qadir Khurasan (Pantusov, "Les mazâr Musulmans," 185–86, 196). This was a major site, and the shrine of Qirmish Ata's most significant companion.
11. Kim, *Holy War in China*, 91, 240fn98.
12. See 0:4 "Tughluq Timur Khan" for the story of how this "blessed tea" came to Ushturfan.
13. *khalifa:* Here, this term indicates the head of a branch of a Sufi order. Elsewhere, it seems to mean instead a "lieutenant" who commands soldiers.
14. TH/Beijing has *almaghandurmiz* "We have not *taken* their holy names," but all other versions have *anglamaghandurmiz*, "We have not *heard* their holy names." TH/Beijing's variation is probably a scribal error.
15. Sufi Allahyar Samarqandi (1644–1724) was an important Chaghatay poet, and his *Ṣabat al-ʿajizin* "The Persistence of the Weak" an influential work. This passage corresponds to lines found in Lund University Library, Jarring Prov. 79 (which is a manuscript of the same work, erroneously labeled *Ṣabat al-ʿazizin*), 39r and 39v, although they are in a different sequence.
16. *durud:* Or *taṣliya*, the invocation of God's blessing upon the Prophet Muḥammad (A. Rippen, "Taṣliya," in *Encyclopaedia of Islam, Second Edition*, ed. P. Bearman, Th. Bianquis, C. E. Bosworth, E. van Donzel, and W. P. Heinrichs, accessed September 5, 2022, http://dx.doi.org.proxygw.wrlc.org/10.1163/1573-3912_islam_SIM_7436).

1:10 Khotan and Ili

1. *ṣudūr:* An honorary title, but also "minister" (Timur K. Beisembiev, *Annotated Indices to the Kokand Chronicles* [Tokyo: Research Institute for Languages and Cultures of Asia and Africa, 2008], 789; Francis Joseph Steingass, *A Comprehensive Persian-English Dictionary: Including the Arabic Words and Phrases to be Met with in Persian Literature, Being, Johnson and*

Richardson's Persian, Arabic, and English Dictionary, Revised, Enlarged, and Entirely Reconstructed [London: Routledge, 1977]). Compare 2:5, n. 1, where the Ḥajji Padishah's son and *ṣudur* is named ʿAbdurraḥman Khan.

1:11 The Conquest of Qarashahr

1. A thorough search of the sources turns up no concrete information about any temples in Ushaq Tal prior to 1864, or about any shrines to Cangling, who was probably this "General Ai" (see 0:5, n. 5, above), outside of Ili. However, what Sayrami describes here is a temple to a tutelary deity. See a similar temple in 0:4, n. 22, above.
2. *ṭaypaw* "wall guns" < Ch. *táipào* 台炮.
3. *khodän* "grenades" < Ch. *huǒdàn* 火彈.
4. Aẕar Bigdeli's (1722–1781) 1760 *Ateshkada* ("The Fire Temple"), "the most important Persian anthology of the twelfth/eighteenth century" (J. T. P. de Bruijn, "Ādhar, Ḥājjī Luṭf ʿAlī Beg," in *Encyclopaedia of Islam, THREE*, ed. Kate Fleet, Gudrun Krämer, Denis Matringe, John Nawas, Everett Rowson, accessed August 1, 2022. http://dx.doi.org/10.1163/1573-3912_ei3_COM_24761).
5. The material of these bags is here called *Lop*. Probably a variety of *Apocynum*, a kind of plant used widely by the people of Lop for its fibers, which can be used to weave clothing and containers (Sabira Ståhlberg and Ingvar Svanberg, "Ecological Adaptation in the Taklamakan Desert," *Anthropos* 105, no. 2 [2010]: 423–39). Katanov's informant, Mejit Akhund, described the Lopluqs' gathering and preparation of a special kind of hemp (N. Th. Katanov, *Volkskundliche Texte aus Ost-Türkistan: aud dem Nachlass von N. Th. Katanov*, ed. Karl Heinrich Menges [Leipzig: Zentralantiquariat der Deutschen Demokratischen Republik, 1976], 52–61).
6. Sayrami here means the Qalmaqs, who afterward appear as part of the Khojas' army.
7. *qara say*. A *say* indicates an elevated area of land with eroded edges. Stein, who used the word extensively on his physical maps, calls it a "Turkī term for a gravel plateau, plain, or slope" (Aurel Stein, *Innermost Asia: Detailed Report of Explorations in Central Asia, Kan-su and Eastern Īrān*, 4 vols. [Oxford: Clarendon, 1928], 275). Stein describes one such *say* south of Qarashahr in detail (771).
8. This refers to the romance of Farhad and Shirin, wherein the sculptor Farhad was commanded to win Shirin as his wife by carving a staircase into Mount Behistun. When Farhad finished his task, Shirin's betrothed lied to him that Shirin had died, and so Farhad took his own life with his spade, his blood flowing into the nearby canal. When Shirin found his body, she decided to join him in death, and wherever the drops of their blood mingled, a tulip grew.
9. *tājī* "prince," as Ḥamid is the son of a *wang* "king."
10. *kāh* < Manchu *hiya*, meaning "guard, page, chamberlain" (Jerry Norman, *A Comprehensive Manchu-English Dictionary* [Cambridge: Harvard University Asia Center, 2013], 175) or "officer of the bodyguard," "senior bodyguard" (David Brophy and Onuma Takahiro, *The Origins of Qing Xinjiang: A Set of Historical Sources on Turfan* [Tokyo: TIAS Department of Islamic Area Studies, 2016], 227, 268, 269).
11. This paragraph blends TA/Pelliot, which names his companions, with TH/Beijing, which specifies their method of execution.

12. "Lushi Daren" indicates Zhang Yao, the commander who was then garrisoning Kashgar. See 2:19, n. 7, below.
13. *dīngẕā* "prison." Baytur does not include or translate the word (Molla Musa Sayrami, *Tarikhi Hämidi*, trans. Änwär Baytur [Beyjing: Millätlär näshriyati, 2007]). Täklimakani expands the whole word to *döngdingzidä* (246), which might be meant to indicate Döng Dangza, the town near Ushaq Tal mentioned in 1:12 (Musa Sayramiy, *Tarikhi Hämidi*, trans. Abduraop Täklimakani [Istanbul: Täklimakan Uyghur näshriyati, 2019]). The term *döng yamun* indicates a section of the yamen used for imprisonment in Bilal Nazim's version of "Nazugum" (Bilal Nazim, "Nuzugum," in *Obraztsy taranchinskoi narodnoi literatury sobrannye i perevedennye N.N. Pantusovym*, *Proceedings of the Society of Archaeology, History and Ethnography at the Imperial University of Kazan* 25 [1909 (1882)]: 34–42, 39). The most likely etymology is to *diànzi* 店子 "inn," also the root of modern Uyghur *dingja*.
14. "punish": *bänläymiz* بَنلايمز, with the shortness of the vowel in the first syllable suggested with *fatha*. Baytur: "we will punish" (*jaza berimiz*), presumably < Ch. *biān* 鞭 "a whip; to flog" (247). Täklimakani: "we will handle it" (*bir täräp qilimiz*), presumably < Ch. *bàn* 辦 "to handle" (267). I have not seen the interpretation *pänläymiz* < Ch. *pàn* 判 "to judge." TH/Jarring: *bandläymiz* "we will confine you" < P. *band* "shackle," although the insertion of <d> may be an overcorrection. However, Jarring does indicate a verb *bɛnlɛ-* "to tie, to fasten" < P. *band* (Gunnar Jarring, ed., *The Thiefless City and the Contest Between Food and Throat: Four Eastern Turki Texts* [Stockholm: Almqvist and Wiksell, 1989], 74). I believe that Baytur is correct because of the frequent occurrence of *biān* 鞭 in legal documents and the use of the same term to mean "to punish" in contemporary Chaghatay-language documents, for example the communique from the Khanate of Khoqand to the Ili General dated 22 Rabi al-Awwal 1245 [September 21, 1849] (National Palace Museum, Taipei, *guji*, 081955).
15. *bīyūjīng*. Täklimakani: *sürüshtürmäymiz* "we will not investigate them" (267). Baytur: *keräk yoq* "there is no need" (247). Baytur's transliteration is *buyujing*, presumably < Ch. *bù yǒu qíng* 不有情 "they are not of interest." I would offer *bie wu qing* 別無情, which appears in Qing documents in two forms: 1. In *bié wú qíngbì* 別無情弊 "there are no other circumstances of the crime," used in official documents to indicate that investigations have only identified certain infractions to be prosecuted. This phrase appears in the substatute of the Qing Code concerning official corruption. 2. As simply *bié wú qíng* "there are no other matters," as in *cǐ wài bié wú qíng* 此外別無情 "apart from this, there is nothing else to consider."
16. TH/Beijing: *gūsī khaṭ* < Ch. *gàoshì* 告示 "proclamation." TH/Jarring: *kūngsī khaṭ* < Ch. *gōngshì* 公示 "public notice." Both are attested elsewhere. The language reflects the awkward text of official documents translated from Chinese, which often sought word-for-word equivalence for each Chinese character in Turkic.
17. That is, Ḥamid Taji Beg's original goal was to retrieve his daughter from Isḥaq Khoja and end her marriage with him. The notice was not in fact directed at him specifically. Rather, the Xiang Army authorities who then occupied the region were attempting to end a growing problem of human trafficking and wife-selling (Eric Schluessel, *Land of Strangers: The Civilizing Project in Qing Central Asia* [New York: Columbia University Press, 2020], 128–37).
18. Found in several hadith compilations, among them: Mohammed Muhsin Khan, *The Translation of the Meanings of Sahih al-Bukhari*, 9 vols. (Lahore: Kazi, 1979), vol. 8, 82–83.

1:12 The Conquest of Turfan

1. *Aghir Bulaq*: Arghai Bulaq, on the road from Kucha to Turfan, past Qarashahr.
2. Stories and heroes from the *Shahnama*.
3. See Sayrami's description of "The Presence" in 1:9.
4. Muḥammad Yunus Jan (ca. 1829–1900s) of Tashkent appears several times in the story. Sayrami evidently respected him greatly. He came to Kashgar as a "refugee" and later returned to Ferghana, where he penned several works of historical importance, including the *Life of ʿAlimqul* text referenced several times in these notes (Timur K. Beisembiev, *Annotated Indices to the Kokand Chronicles* [Tokyo: Research Institute for Languages and Cultures of Asia and Africa, 2008], 415; *The Life of Alimqul: A Native Chronicle of Nineteenth Century Central Asia* [London: Routledge, 2003]).
5. A *charak* was a unit of weight used to measure grain. Its valued varied greatly, but in Kashgar in the early twentieth century, it was roughly 6.72–9.027 kg. For one set of equivalences, see Gustav Raquette, *Eastern Turki Grammar: Practical and Theoretical with Vocabulary*, 3 vols. (Berlin: Reichsdruckerei, 1912), vol. 1, 35–36.
6. Täklimakani interprets this term as "Changga," a nickname meaning "the unkempt" (Musa Sayramiy, *Tarikhi Hämidi*, trans. Abduraop Täklimakani [Istanbul: Täklimakan Uyghur näshriyati, 2019], 274). I find it more likely to be *janggi(n)* "lieutenant," a Mongol-Manchu term used at the court of the Turfan Wang (David Brophy and Onuma Takahiro, *The Origins of Qing Xinjiang: A Set of Historical Sources on Turfan* [Tokyo: TIAS Department of Islamic Area Studies, 2016]).
7. The Dungan leaders in Ürümchi are discussed at length in 2:10. However, they are meanwhile mentioned several times in passing. "Daud Khalifa" was one name of Tuǒ Míng 妥明 or Tuǒ Délín 妥得璘 (d. 1872), a respected Dungan religious leader, probably a member of the Jahriyya. He plotted the uprising in Ürümchi with Suo Huanzhang. Suo Huanzhang, a.k.a. Suo Dalaoye, was probably also a member of the Jahriyya and disciple of Ma Hualong (Hodong Kim, *Holy War in China: The Muslim Rebellion and State in Chinese Central Asia, 1864–1877* [Stanford, CA: Stanford University Press, 2004], 41–44). (See 0:6, n. 8, above.)
8. TH/Jarring: "16,000."
9. Sayrami offers a folk etymology for the name "Gǔchéngzi" 古城子 as "dog worms" *gǒuchōngzi* 狗蟲子.
10. TH/Beijing: "two hundred." Täklimakani: "two hundred households" (275). TH/Jarring: "200,000."
11. *Santan*. Although there was a town in this area called Sāntún, the army clearly marched westward toward Fukang, and a town called Sāntái 三台 would have been on its route.
12. Jirma Depot: MSS: j.b.h.k.w. Baytur: Jibärku (Molla Musa Sayrami, *Tarikhi Hämidi*, trans. Änwär Baytur [Beyjing: Millätlär näshriyati, 2007], 256); Täklimakani: Jibako (276); Wufuer: Jíbākù 吉巴庫 (Maolamusa Sailami, *Yimide shi*, trans. Aili Wufuer, in Miao Pusheng, ed., *Qingdai Chahetai wen wenxian yizhu* [Wulumuqi: Xinjiang renmin chubanshe, 2013], 315–538, 427). Ch. Jíbākù 集巴庫, later Jíbākù 吉巴庫 or Jíbùkù 吉布庫. A garrison post west of Murkhu and along the Jirmatai River (Wang Shu'nan et al., comps., *Xinjiang tuzhi*, ed. Zhu Yuqi et al. [Shanghai: Shanghai guji chubanshe, 2017], 21, 586, 1306). The earliest form of this toponym that I can locate, recorded on the 1720 Kangxi map, is Jirmatai, meaning "[river or stream] with young fish" in Oirat Mongolian. (Thanks to Ling-wei Kung for help with this identification.) In the Qianlong

era, when the name Jibaku was first recorded, it was used as a depot (*kù* 庫) for the army or merchants, so that the name Jirma was shortened and slightly mutated to Jiba. This Mongol toponym, blended with a Chinese term, which found its way into Chaghatay, is therefore difficult to translate, but I favor "Jirma Depot" as a way to capture the alienness of *ku* and the obscurity of the name "Jirmatai."

13. "Qara Basun" is probably Jiādé chéng 嘉德城, constructed at the base of Qara Balghasun Mountain (Ch. Kālǎbāěrgāxùn 喀喇巴爾噶遜) in 1782, later called Dábǎnchéng 達坂城 (Songyun, *Xinjiang shilüe*, reproduced in *Xu xiu siku quanshu*, vol. 732 [Shanghai: Shanghai guji chubanshe, 1995–99], *juan* 2, 2b, 36b, 44a, 45b; Li Delong, ed., *Xinjiang si dao zhi* [Beijing: Zhongyang minzu daxue chubanshe, 2010], 14). A second commander and battalion (*shǒubèi* 守備) were stationed there, and it was a site of settlement and land reclamation. This is well southeast of Ürümchi, suggesting that these forces were not traveling in a straight line, but rather made some forays near Ürümchi to clear the area immediately around the Dungans' seat of power.
14. Sayrami uses two versions of the name of this place: the Kazakh name Mori, > Ch. Mùlěi 木壘; and Murkhu < Ch. Mùlěi hé 木壘河 "Mori River" (Kim, *Holy War in China*, 231n128).
15. Sāngāh Chanza < Ch. Sān ge quánzi 三個泉子 "Three Springs"; Yīban Chanza < Ch. Yīwǎn quánzi 一碗泉子 "One-Bowl Spring." Both settlements east of Ürümchi.
16. I cannot identify a word between "old" and "young:" *b.y q.r.*?
17. Here is inserted: *Ba-ḥurmata ṭah wīs.*

1:13 The Campaign to Murkhu

1. Dolan: A name for a group of people whom most Muslims considered inferior. Popular wisdom held that Dolans, although Muslims, were descendants of some ethnically different group (L. J. Newby, *The Empire and the Khanate: A Political History of Qing Relations with Khoqand, c. 1760–1860* [Leiden: Brill, 2005], 98–99).

1:14 The Submission of Qumul

1. TA/Pelliot: 18 Dhul-Hijja 1282 [May 4, 1866].
2. The titles *Dā-yan-shay* < Ch. *Dà Yuánshuài* 大元帥 "great marshal" and *Saw-yan-shay* < Ch. *Xiǎo Yuánshuài* 小元帥 "lesser marshal" are ranks. They refer to leaders of the Ürümchi Dungans, and although it is not entirely clear which of several military commanders might be meant here, Kim suggests that Daud Khalifa was effectively a powerless figurehead under their influence (Hodong Kim, *Holy War in China: The Muslim Rebellion and State in Chinese Central Asia, 1864–1877* [Stanford, CA: Stanford University Press, 2004], 43–44). I suspect that this *Da Yuanshuai* was Niè Bùchōng 聶布沖, an early Ürümchi Dungan leader. We will return to some of these *yuánshuài*s in 2:10.
3. Mongol *jüldü* "prize." Doerfer: "reward for a meritorious deed" (*Belohnung für eine verdienstvolle Tat*) (Gerhard Doerfer, *Türkische und mongolische Elemente im Neupersischen*, 4 vols. [Wiesbaden: Franz Steiner Verlag, 1963], vol. 1, 294). *Jasaq* refers to the banner system used in Qing Mongolia, as well as to a deeper tradition of Mongol law. Here it is a hereditary land grant for a Qing Turco-Mongol aristocrat.
4. Possibly "jade" < Ch. *bìlǜ* 碧綠 "jade green"?

5. *Fūjīn* < Ch. *fújìn* 福晉 "princess consort" (H. S. Brunnert and V. V. Hagelstrom, *Present Day Political Organization of China* [Shanghai: Kelly and Walsh, Limited, 1912], 8); *khanim* "lady."
6. The Turki language in this period could mark the relative status of speaker and listener. The Qumul Wang's announcers evidently edited statements to ensure the proper levels of humility and respect.
7. "Turk" in an older sense of "illiterate people."
8. *yingfan* < Ch. *yíngfáng* "barracks." See 1:3, n. 2, above.
9. It is unclear who the Xiao Yuanshuai in Turfan was.
10. "fiefholder:" *soyurghal* < Mo. *soyurqal*, a hereditary, tax-immune fiefdom granted in return for military service (Maria Eva Subtelny, "Socioeconomic Bases of Cultural Patronage Under the Later Timurids," *International Journal of Middle East Studies* 20, no. 4 [1988]: 480–81).

1:15 Isḥaq Khoja's Western Campaign

1. Yarkand's New City was just west of its Old City.

1:16 Dissension and Demise of the Kucha Khojas

1. "overseer:" *darugha*, an old Mongol term for "governor" (Gerhard Doerfer, *Türkische und mongolische Elemente im Neupersischen*, 4 vols. [Wiesbaden: Franz Steiner Verlag, 1963], vol. 1, 319–23). The term's meaning varied across time and space in post-Mongol Eurasia. In this context, it indicated a petty official charged with duties such as tax collection.
2. Mazar Baghi: Literally "The Shrine Garden," the town that grew around the ʿArshuddin Shrine.
3. *maʿjūn:* A mixture of spices, sometimes sugar, often hashish.
4. *khoshang* "pasties" < Ch. *héshāng (bāozi)* 和尚(包子), lit. "monk buns," today indicating flat, pan-fried buns. *tang boṗa* "sugar dumplings" < *tang boba* < Ch. *tángbāo (bāo)* 糖包 (包) "sugar buns." Both are described in Gunnar Jarring, *Materials to the Knowledge of Eastern Turki: Tales, Poetry, Proverbs, Riddles, Ethnological and Historical Texts from the Southern Parts of Eastern Turkestan* (Lund: C.W.K. Gleerup, 1946–1951), vol. 4, 158. *yutaza* "fried dough" < Ch. *yóutiáozi* 油條子 "sticks of fried dough."
5. *Lisān al-ghayb* "voice from the hidden world" was Shirazi's sobriquet. The stich is taken from Ḥafiẓ, translation by Clarke (Henry Wilberforce Clarke, trans., *The Dīvān, Written in the Fourteenth Century by Khwāja Shamsu-d-Dīn Muḥammad-i-Ḥāfiẓ-i-Shīrāzī, otherwise known as Lisānu-l-Ghaib and Tarjumānu-l-Asrār* [Calcutta: Government of India Central Printing Office, 1891], 32).
6. *toqsāba*: "(probably, contraction of "Tōq ṣāḥibi") (commander of detachment which had a banner [tūġ]; he was close by rank to pansadbashi and corresponded to Russian lieutenant colonel)" (Timur K. Beisembiev, *Annotated Indices to the Kokand Chronicles* [Tokyo: Research Institute for Languages and Cultures of Asia and Africa, 2008], 415; *The Life of ʿAlimqul: A Native Chronicle of Nineteenth Century Central Asia* [London: Routledge, 2003], 750).

7. Mohammed Muhsin Khan, trans., *The Translation of the Meanings of Sahih al-Bukhari*, 9 vols. (Lahore: Kazi, 1979), vol. 4, 63.
8. Based on O YE WHO BELIEVE! OBEY GOD AND OBEY THE MESSENGER AND THOSE IN AUTHORITY AMONG YOU . . . [4:59] But the passage here is abbreviated and slightly misspelled.
9. *baturbashi* "military head (of a place)" (Timur K. Beisembiev, *The Life of ʿAlimqul: A Native Chronicle of Nineteenth Century Central Asia* [London: Routledge, 2003], 24n36), but also, in Khoqand, a "military chief in vilayat [province], also managing affairs with nomads" (Beisembiev, *Annotated Indices*, 733).
10. This comment on Rashuddin Khoja's outward appearance is meant to reveal something of his inner dispositions through the study of physiognomy (*ʿilm-i firāsat*). See Emin Lelić, "Physiognomy (*ʿilm-i firāsat*) and Ottoman Statecraft: Discerning Morality and Justice," *Arabica* 64, no. 3–4 (2017): 609–46.
11. *mujtahid:* referring to a someone capable of formulating opinions on the basis of sound judgment, personal effort, and the fundamental principles of the Shariah.
12. Naẓiruddin Khoja. TH/Jarring clarifies, "The elder brother of Jamaluddin Khoja."

2:1 The Arrival of Yaʿqub Beg and Buzurg Khan

1. Nar Muḥammad was later one of the Khoqandi refugees in Kashgar. He is called "Nar Muḥammad Parvanachi" below (Timur K. Beisembiev, *Annotated Indices to the Kokand Chronicles* [Tokyo: Research Institute for Languages and Cultures of Asia and Africa, 2008], 492).
2. That is, Khudayar Khan fell from power, while Malla Khan became the Khan of Khoqand.
3. TH/Beijing: *Māchīnī*, indicating South China; TH/Jarring: *Bäjīnī*, indicating Beijing; TA neither.
4. Probably not a crown in the European sense, but a bejeweled turban with an aigrette, or jeweled ornament. See 2:8, n. 3, below.
5. Thank you to Nicholas Walmsley for this translation.
6. The title *shighavul* indicates the individual charged with managing ceremonies at a court and with escorting ambassadors. Beisembiev renders it "Senior Master of Ceremonies," while Doerfer gives "guest attendant" (*Gastbegleiter*) (Timur K. Beisembiev, ed. and trans., *The Life of ʿAlimqul: A Native Chronicle of Nineteenth Century Central Asia* [London: Routledge, 2003], 2; Gerhard Doerfer, *Türkische und mongolische Elemente im Neupersischen*, 4 vols. [Wiesbaden: Franz Steiner Verlag, 1963], vol. 1, 355–57; Ghiyathuddin Naqqash, "Report to Mirza Baysunghur on the Timurid Legation to the Court at Peking," Wheeler M. Thackston, trans., in *A Century of Princes: Sources on Timurid History and Art* [Cambridge, MA: Aga Khan Program for Islamic Architecture, 1989, 290.)
7. *hudaychi*: "ordinary master of ceremonies, middle courtier rank inferior to shighavul; . . . could command detachment of 100 men" (Beisembiev, *Annotated Indices*, 830); *ṗarwānachi*: "one of the highest court ranks in Kokand after qushbegi" (742); *eshikaghasi*: "1. Main gatekeeper in ruler's palace. 2. Middle [in Mawarannahr] or high [in Chinese Turkistan] administrative rank" (731).

2:2 Refugees from Khoqand

1. A place very near Kashgar, now a neighborhood of the city.
2. See the description of the Battle of Khan Eriq in 1:8.
3. He Dalaoye's name was Hé Bùyún 何步雲 (Hodong Kim, *Holy War in China: The Muslim Rebellion and State in Chinese Central Asia, 1864–1877* [Stanford, CA: Stanford University Press, 2004], 87). Official reports from the reconquest describe him as a garrison relief soldier (Ch. *huànfǎng guānjūn* 換防官軍) (National Palace Museum, Taipei, *gugong* 142347, memorial dated GX 3.12.18).
4. Sayrami refers to Jamadar Dadkhwah and his soldiers as *Oghan* = *Afghan*, indicating "Muslims from Northern India" (Timur K. Beisembiev, *Annotated Indices to the Kokand Chronicles* [Tokyo: Research Institute for Languages and Cultures of Asia and Africa, 2008], 837, 840). Jamadar Dadkhwah came from Sialkot, Punjab, served in the Sikh army under the British, and then joined the Khoqandi army (Kim, *Holy War in China*, 245n63). His name as given in the text, *Jāmaʿdār*, is indeed not a name but a rank, *jāmadār*. Gordon describes him as an "Afghan of gigantic stature" and gives a short biography (T. E. Gordon, *The Roof of the World* [Edinburgh: Edmonston and Douglas, 1876], 90–92).
5. Wali Khan Törä: see 0:5, n. 7, above.
6. Beisembiev identifies Köroghli Bahadur as Muḥammad Naẓar Biy Kuroghli Parvanachi Qipchaq (d. 1852), who was the "head of the Qipchaq clan of Yetti Qashqa, father of Khal Muḥammad Dādkhwah and grandfather of Bek Muḥammad Qipchaq, governor of Shahrikhan, 1840s–1852" (*Indices*, 409–10).

2:3 Yaʿqub Beg's Rise to Power

1. The word for a falconet, *zamburak*, literally means "wasp."

2:4 Khotan Campaign

1. That is, he helped cooked cauldrons of pilaf as an act of charity.
2. *katta tugh*: *tugh* "Middle [500–1000 men] military unit" (Timur K. Beisembiev, *Annotated Indices to the Kokand Chronicles* [Tokyo: Research Institute for Languages and Cultures of Asia and Africa, 2008], 750).
3. MS *lāwar* < *lābar* "title of an officer commanding a corps of infantry (500 men)" (Robert Shaw, *A Sketch of the Turki Language as Spoken in Eastern Turkistan [Kàshghar and Yarkand]* [Calcutta: Baptist Mission Press, 1878], 178).
4. *farqadān*: Two stars in Ursa Minor. These are the lowest of Ursa Minor and therefore turn just below the pole star—so, Yaʿqub Beg would achieve great heights, but not as great as Ḥabibullah Ḥajji, the "pole" around whom he would "revolve."
5. *Gholi nemä däytu bu*. This is Sayrami's rendering of an idiomatic phrase in Khotan dialect. Mirsultan Osmanov glosses the word *gholi* as "really" (MU *zadi*) (Osmanov, *Hazirqi zaman Uyghur tilining Khotän diyalekti* [Ürümchi: Shinjang khälq näshriyati, 2004], 33–34, 319). Täklimakani (Musa Sayramiy, *Tarikhi Hämidi*, trans. Abduraop Täklimakani [Istanbul: Täklimakan Uyghur näshriyati, 2019], 367) and Baytur (Molla Musa Sayrami,

Tarikhi Hämidi, trans. Änwär Baytur [Beyjing: Millätlär näshriyati, 2007], 341) translate this literally as "What do you call these?" There are phrases in varieties of English that might suit as (unsatisfying) translations. Rather than make any false equivalence or potentially offensive comparison between Khotanese speech as depicted by an outsider and the language of any particular group in the present, and instead to emphasize how the author is indexing the speaker's rustic character as he understands it, I offer Shakespeare: specifically, how that English playwright voices the Scottish thane Macduff, when he arrives to overthrow the tyrant Macbeth and detects the sound of battle (*Macbeth*, 232, line 5.7.15). I am grateful to Mutallip Anwar for help interpreting this phrase.

6. *qil quyruq bolup:* Total mobilization, in which each household sends a warrior (Beisembiev, *Annotated Indices*, 807).
7. TA/Kazan: "three days and nights, maybe more."
8. TH/Jarring renders this not as *ällik ming* "five thousands" but as *bäsh tümän* "five ten-thousands," making the same number in a different way.
9. TH/Beijing: A carat is inserted at this point, indicating a marginal note reading (at least in part), "Muḥammad Yaʿqub Beg, the king(?) who killed Muslims."
10. See 1:15 "Isḥaq Khwaja's Western Campaign."
11. See 2:16 "Niyaz Ḥakim Beg."
12. TA/Kazan: 18 Shawwal 1283 [February 23, 1867] in "the Year of the Sheep."

2:5 Ḥabibullah's Virtue and His Reign

1. Compare 1:10, n. 1, where the Ḥajji Padishah's son is named Ibrahim Khan.
2. *cho* < probably Ch. *chē* 車 "carriage," where *e* has often been perceived as a rounded vowel *o*.
3. This description matches the silver *tangga*, in the shape and weight of a *misqal*, described in Vladimir Nastich and Wolfgang Schuster, *Catalog of Pre-Modern Central Asian Coins 1680–1923: Janid (Later Period), Bukhara, Tashkand, Shahrisabz, Khoqand, Khiva, Khorezm Republic, Dzungar (Later Period), Islamic East Turkestan* (Bremen: Bremer Numismatische Gesellschaft, 2017), 239–40.

2:6 The Conquest of Aqsu and Kucha

1. Dolans were forced to work farms to maintain postal relay stations in remote places such as Yaydi, and so would have more knowledge of comings and goings on the road (L. J. Newby, *The Empire and the Khanate: A Political History of Qing Relations with Khoqand, c. 1760–1860* [Leiden: Brill, 2005], 98–99).
2. To be clear, this was not his brother Fakhruddin, but the shrine of a saint named Fakhruddin.
3. See 1:16 "Dissension and Demise."
4. *buluqturma* = *boqturmä* "ambush" (W. Radloff, *Versuch eines Wörterbuches der Türk-Dialecte*, 4 vols. [St. Petersburg, 1893], vol. 4, 1804).
5. TH/Jarring (82v) includes a longer passage, which contradicts TH/Beijing:

The Ataliq Ghazi learned what had happened and sent guards to seize him, who removed him from the palace and killed him. Jamaluddin Khoja had evidently taken a woman in marriage who was married to another man, or was in the waiting period after divorce. Fakhruddin Khoja would not submit to the strictures of Shariah but mocked the judges and muftis. In accordance with the wise imams (MAY GOD BE PLEASED WITH THEM ALL!), an opinion was obtained from the muftis, and this opinion made known to the Khojas. They were made to answer for their crimes and were executed as a lesson to all. Ibrahim Khoja too was killed."

6. Tokhta Eshikagha Beg was the chief minister of Kucha, whose secret letter invited Yaʿqub Beg to come and conquer it. (See 1:16 "Dissension and Demise.")
7. Yaʿqub Beg took the faster but more perilous mountain road through Qaqshal Yol Pass. His treasure and captives most likely took the slower but flat and easy route across the lowlands.
8. TA/Pelliot: "2 Jumada al-Akhira 1284 [October 1, 1867]."
9. *surkh ṗul*: An odd way of rendering the usual *qizil ṗul* "red coin," meaning "copper coinage" < Ch. *hóngqián* 紅錢 lit. "red coins." See 2:9, n. 5, below.

2:7 The Unification of the Seven Cities

1. *kim-khwāb* "gold-brocade, a kind of cloth with flower-pattern, an embroidered cloth" (Gunnar Jarring, *Garments from Top to Toe: Eastern Turki Texts Relating to Articles of Clothing* [Stockholm: Almqvist and Wiksell, 1992], 83); *tavar* "cloth; silk-stuff" (88); *shāhī* "silk, silk-stuff" (87).
2. *kisht-i būlghār*, where *būlghār* indicates "a kind of red leather" (Jarring, *Garments*, 79). TA/Kazan: *bulghan-kisht*; TA/Pelliot, TH/Jarring: *bawulghan-kisht*.
3. *tälpäk, tumaq*. A *tälpäk* has its sheepskin on the inside and wool outside, while a *tumaq* is the opposite.
4. Salawat: Prayer in honor of the Prophet Muḥammad.
5. Zavqi: Probably the same place as the Joqi or Javqi mentioned in the Turkic expansion of the *Tarikh-i Rashidi* (104), and the Jauqu mentioned in Ḥaydar's original (Mirza Ḥaydar Dughlat, *Tarikh-i Rashidi*, trans. Wheeler M. Thackston [New York: I. B. Tauris, 2012], 220). On that basis, I take it to be a mountainous area near both Kashgar and Ushturfan, on the road to Issiq Köl, where Kyrgyz dwelt.
6. On *khaniya*, see 1:4, n. 1, above.
7. Here begins a page-long parenthetical about *khaniya* in the middle of a sentence. In the Turkic text, we will not see the verb for some time. I have taken some structural liberties in order to make it work in English.
8. *qongi tamghaliq yanchi: tamghaliq*, meaning something that has had a seal or stamp applied to it, like a document, indicating here that the serfs were "owned" by a master; *qong* meaning "bottom" or "ass." The term *yanchi* does not exactly mean "serf," and it derives from Mongol *enjü*, indicating a household servant. Nevertheless, by the Qing period, among the Mongol estates, the term became roughly equivalent to a personal serf (*khamjilga*) (Christopher P. Atwood, *Encyclopedia of Mongolia and the Mongol Empire* [New York: Facts on File, 2004], 508).

9. *pul:* A copper coin worth one-fiftieth of a *tangga* (Robert Shaw, *A Sketch of the Turki Language as Spoken in Eastern Turkistan [Kàshghar and Yarkand]* [Calcutta: Baptist Mission Press, 1878], vol. 2, 59; Vladimir Nastich and Wolfgang Schuster, *Catalog of Pre-Modern Central Asian Coins 1680–1923: Janid [Later Period], Bukhara, Tashkand, Shahrisabz, Khoqand, Khiva, Khorezm Republic, Dzungar [Later Period], Islamic East Turkestan* [Bremen: Bremer Numismatische Gesellschaft, 2017], 241–43).
10. *dāchän* < Ch. *dàqián* 大錢. A Chinese-style copper coin with a hole in the middle.
11. *sarī' as-samīrda barq-i khāṭibdek.* Sayrami appears to be making a joke here. We might expect "like a bolt of lightning" (*barq-i khāṭif*). Sayrami has changed one letter—*khāṭif* to *khāṭib*—to replace "lightning" with "preacher," where the latter word is more broadly connected through the root *kh.ṭ.b* to acts of speech, particularly acts of addressing others. We could easily take this to be a scribal error, or a corruption via the pronunciation in Eastern Turki of *f* as [p]. Unfortunately, it is only present in TH/Beijing, so there is no external corroborating evidence of that point. However, the other half of the phrase, *sarīʾ as-samīrda*, more clearly contains the element *samīr* "conversation partner." This is slightly different from the more obvious *sarīʾ as-sayr* "at great speed." Hence my attempt to translate an evident pun.
12. Mahdi: An Islamic messianic figure.
13. On this "Lady Pansad" Tokhta Khan, Yaʿqub Beg's wife who managed his other wives, see 2:13.
14. *bī-qaṣab*: "A Panjab mixed silk and cotton, called by the Yarkandis Bikassab" (J. E. T. Aitchison, *Hand-Book of the Trade Products of Leh with the Statistics of Trade from 1867 to 1872 Inclusive* [Calcutta: Wyman & Co., 1874], 255).
15. *qirīm*: "Turki term for the Panjab leather *Lakhí* . . . Leather of goat's skins dyed red" (Aitchison, *Hand-Book*, 140–41).

2:8 The Ottoman Empire

1. *pāyza* < Mo. *paiza* < Ch. *páizi* 牌子 "tablet."
2. Rum: The Ottoman Empire, or "Rome," indicating the former Byzantine lands.
3. A *tāj* here indicates not a crown in the European sense but a bejeweled turban with an aigrette (*sorghuch*), a turban ornament in the shape of a plume. Compare examples from the Ottoman treasury in J. M. Rogers, ed., *The Topkapı Saray Museum: The Treasury* (Boston: Little, Brown, 1987), items 18–20, notes on 191. Thanks to Gwendolyn Collaço for advice on Ottoman material culture.
4. The remainder of this chapter is included only in TH/Beijing.
5. Uwaysi: One who has become a Sufi through a nontraditional path, particularly without initiation from a living master, and instead through contact with a spirit.
6. *kaymakam:* A "deputy governor" in Ottoman usage, indicating someone with plenipotentiary power.
7. The letters in *ʿUsmaniyya* add up to the year 676 [1277/8].
8. MS *Özkhan*.
9. *baladatun ṭayyabatun*. The numbers add up to 857 [1453], the year of the Ottoman conquest of Constantinople.
10. Sayrami's counting is confusing. 641 years after the stated date of Osman's ascent to the throne (699 AH) gives far too late a date (1340 AH [1921 CE]). The date of Osman's

birth (655 AH) is too early, yielding 1296 [1878]. 676 is the value of the chronogram for the founding of the Ottoman house above, but it also seems to be several years too early for Sayrami's composition of this part of the TH, as 676 + 641 = 1317 [1899]. Sayrami could have been working from another source.

11. Rum, son of Esau, son of Isaac.
12. The Chicken Market (Tavuk Pazarı) may seem like an odd thing to mention, but it was just outside Istanbul's Grand Bazaar (Kapalıçarşı). It would have made quite an impression on a traveler.
13. See the beginning of 2:1, which recounts how Yaʿqub Beg agreed to sell some Russians "the fish in the river" at Aq Masjid, which became a pretext for the conquest of Ferghana.
14. This passage refers to Thomas Douglas Forsyth (1827–1886), a British administrator in India who in 1873 was sent on a diplomatic mission to Yaʿqub Beg with the object of gathering information about his state and the country, as well as establishing trade and, evidently, a British-aligned buffer state between the Qing, Britain, and Russia in Kashgaria. For his account, see T. D. Forsyth, *Report of a Mission to Yarkund in 1873* (Calcutta: Foreign Department Press, 1875). Forsyth's name is written *furṣat*, meaning "opportunity," which may be a pun. His title is given as *ṣāʾib*, which may also indicate faint mockery of his status as "master" (*ṣāḥib*), as his Hindustani servants would have called him.

2:9 Battles with the Ürümchi Dungans

1. It is unclear who Uzi Yanshay or Lan Shing Yanshay were, although other documents confirm a Dungan incursion in 1870 (Hodong Kim, *Holy War in China: The Muslim Rebellion and State in Chinese Central Asia, 1864–1877* [Stanford, CA: Stanford University Press, 2004], 95, 231n113). "Yanshay," here as elsewhere, < Ch. *yuánshuài* "martial." See 1:14, n. 2, above.
2. *aq öylük qilip:* Literally "to make them white tents," referring to the yurts used by nomads. In every instance in the *Tarikh-i Ḥamidi*, the phrase is used when someone is forcibly removed from their home and sent elsewhere, hence "banished" (for individuals) or "displaced" (for groups of people).
3. Hamdam Baturbashi and Mir Baba never appear again in the narrative. Sayrami implies that Yaʿqub Beg secretly killed them. Beisembiev offers no information about Mir Baba subsequent to his departure from Khoqand and offers little on Hamdam (Timur K. Beisembiev, *Annotated Indices to the Kokand Chronicles* [Tokyo: Research Institute for Languages and Cultures of Asia and Africa, 2008], 472, 507).
4. "guards": *qurbashi*; "sentries": *mīrshab.* These words' definitions are closer to "commandant" and "night guard," but both meanings seem awkward here (Beisembiev, *Annotated Indices*, 803).
5. *qizil ṗul wä chaqa ṗul*, literally "red coins and copper coins." This is an odd distinction to make, since copper coins were generally known as "red coins" (*qizil ṗul*) anyway. See also *surkh pul*, 2:6, n. 9, above.
6. Yar: The Yar neighborhood just north of Turfan.
7. Ch. *lǎorénjiā* 老人家, a polite term for an older and respected person.
8. Rustam and Sam Nariman: Heroes from the *Shahnama.*

9. "*Lao* Padishah" indicates Yaʿqub Beg, whom Niyaz Beg calls in conversation with the Chinese commanders the "old king": *law* < Chinese *lǎo* 老 "old." This usage of *law* is also attested in documents from Turfan (ex. *Qingdai Xinjiang dang'an xuanji*, vol. 40, 331).

2:10 Conquest of Ürümchi

1. Nansan < Ch. *Nánshān* 南山 "South Mountain," the mountainous area south of Ürümchi.
2. Xù Xuégōng 徐學功 (*Shī Shī Gūng*, 1842–1912): According to Xu's official biography, he was a Han Chinese man from Ürümchi and son of a garrison soldier, who grew up in poverty but took delight in martial arts and eventually became a local strongman. His escape with twenty or so companions into the mountains of Nanshan was a natural extension of his activities, and as other Han refugees gathered with him, he became an unlikely hero. National Palace Museum, *guzhuan*, 007181.
3. Xu's younger brother was actually named Xù Xuédì 徐學第, according to Qing accounts (Hodong Kim, *Holy War in China: The Muslim Rebellion and State in Chinese Central Asia, 1864-1877* [Stanford, CA: Stanford University Press, 2004], 241n118; National Palace Museum, *guzhuan*, 007181).
4. *Qush faṡli* "bird season" is a misspelling of *qaws faṡli* "the month of Sagittarius." Täklimakani agrees (Musa Sayramiy, *Tarikhi Hämidi*, trans. Abduraop Täklimakani [Istanbul: Täklimakan Uyghur näshriyati, 2019], 453).
5. About Decius, the place and the person, see 3:8 "Turfan."
6. *bahman wä day*: The tenth and eleventh months of the Islamic solar year; the first and second months of winter.
7. TH/Beijing here includes a word I cannot decipher: *yengi dākāyiqchiliqdin nijāt taṗip* "when he was newly liberated from *dākāyiqchiliq*." Täklimakani offers no translation (455). Baytur takes it to describe Mirza Aḥmad Qushbegi, "who was newly released from imprisonment" (Molla Musa Sayrami, *Tarikhi Hämidi*, trans. Änwär Baytur [Beyjing: Millätlär näshriyati, 2007], 415).
8. *lāhim?* Meaning unclear. This is the beginning of the line—part of the word could be missing. Täklimakani: "the battlefield" (*jäng mäydani*) (455); Baytur simply gives "he went ahead" (415). TA/Pelliot: *özlari ham tofagha barip* "he went up a hillock."
9. There are two pages missing from TH/Beijing text between {224} and {225}. The following passage is translated from the intervening text as presented in TA/Pelliot [134v–136v].
10. According to Kim, this Xiao Yuanshuai, made Da Yuanshuai, was Suo Huanzhang ("Suo Dalaoye") (Kim, *Holy War in China*, 96). See 0:6, n. 8, and 1:12, n. 7, above.
11. The term *salamagha* is somewhat obscure, though its literal meaning suggests a "greeting servant." Beisembiev notes only one instance of it in one manuscript and provides no definition (Timur K. Beisembiev, *Annotated Indices to the Kokand Chronicles* [Tokyo: Research Institute for Languages and Cultures of Asia and Africa, 2008], 779). It appears again at the beginning of 2:12, where another trusted man is made *salamagha* and *kaymakam* (plenipotentiary "deputy governor") to a new and untrusted ally: ʿAbdurraḥman Dadkhwah of Kucha, formerly in service of the Kucha Khojas, is made governor of Aqsu, and Muḥammad Musa Toqsaba from Khoqand is his *salamagha* and *kaymakam*. This

seems to indicate that Zaynulʿabidin Makhẕum will similarly be the real power in Ürümchi. *Salamagha* must then be a high-ranking title with significant power, probably the equivalent and synonym of a *shighavul* "master of ceremonies" (see 2:1, n. 6, above).

12. *Ḥamal:* The first month of spring in the solar calendar (Gustav Raquette, *Eastern Turki Grammar: Practical and Theoretical with Vocabulary,* 3 vols. [Berlin: Reichsdruckerei, 1912], vol. 1, 69–73).
13. *lankah:* "Lanka: A linen fabric that was formerly imported in large quantities from Russia to Leh" (J. E. T. Aitchison, *Hand-Book of the Trade Products of Leh with the Statistics of Trade from 1867 to 1872 Inclusive* [Calcutta: Wyman & Co., 1874], 150). *Daba:* yellow dye derived from the tamarisk (Gunnar Jarring, *An Eastern Turki-English Dialect Dictionary* [Lund: CWK Gleerup, 1964], 79).
14. Muḥammad b. Sulayman Fużuli (ca. 1494–1556).

2:11 Ḥakim Khan's Campaign to Ürümchi

1. TA/Kazan: Qalqi; TA/Pelliot: Qal Qaman; TH/Jarring: Qalqi Man.
2. *Hànchéng* 漢城, lit. "Han (Chinese) city"; *Lǎochéng* 老城 "old city." This may be confusing to the reader, as the *Laocheng* was newer than the *Hancheng*. In fact, the first Qing settlement at Ürümchi was the walled Manchu garrison, called Gōngníng 鞏寧. Then the Chinese city, or *Hancheng*, of Díhuà 迪化 was built north of Gongning. Gongning was destroyed in the uprisings, but this *Laocheng* "old city" was built on its ruins (Ma Dazheng et al., eds., *Xinjiang xiangtuzhi gao* [Wulumuqi: Xinjiang renmin chubanshe, 2010], 4). So, the new Muslim city was actually a continuation of the "old" Manchu settlement.
3. "great guns" *tayṗaw* < Ch. *dàpào~tàipào* 大炮 "great gun."
4. "way station" *däng* < Ch. *diàn* 店 "inn."
5. Sayrami plays on the names of different shapes of compressed tea. "Brick tea" [*takht chay*], or literally "plank tea," is followed by "horsehead and lath tea" [*aṭbash chezä chay*]. A "horsehead" [*aṭbash*] of tea was not in the shape of a brick, but a cylinder (Robert Shaw, *A Sketch of the Turki Language as Spoken in Eastern Turkistan [Kàshghar and Yarkand]* [Calcutta: Baptist Mission Press, 1878], vol. 2, 2). Sayrami's "lath tea" [*chezä chay*] does not appear to be attested as a term for compressed tea, but is perhaps a joke, suggesting that tea had even been compressed into the unlikely shape of long, thin strips of wood to be nailed to horsehead cylinders (in place of upright studs) to form walls, which could then be covered in plaster. So we have a building made of tea instead of wood: bricks, studs, and lath!
6. Xu's official biography states that, in the spring of 1872, Ürümchi Lieutenant-General Jǐnglián 景廉 marched his soldiers to Gucheng, whence he dispatched an emissary to Xu, who agreed to organize his guerilla forces into a series of regular military units. He went on to enjoy a long career as a military officer in post-reconquest Xinjiang (National Palace Museum, *guzhuan*, 007181).
7. *Mishkat al-maṣabiḥ*, Book 5, Hadith 97 (Sunnah.com, https://sunnah.com/mishkat:1621, accessed September 10, 2022), citing *Sunan Abu Dawud*, Book 21, no. 28 (Sunnah.com, https://sunnah.com/abudawud:3116, accessed September 10, 2022).

2:12 Second Expedition to Turfan

1. "Dakhu and Shokhu" are not mentioned by name in the prolegomenon, although 0:6 does mention that Dungan leaders fled before the Qing reconquest and came beyond the Jiayu Pass into Qumul. "Dakhu" refers to the "Big Tiger" (Chinese *dà hǔ* 大虎), the *nom de guerre* that the Hui leader Bái Yànhǔ 白彥虎 (1830–1882), a.k.a. Bái Sù 白素 or Muḥammad Ayūb, took in 1873. "Shokhu" is the "Little Tiger" (*xiǎo hǔ* 小虎), Bai's ally Yú Xiǎohǔ 于小虎 (n.d.) (Hodong Kim, *Holy War in China: The Muslim Rebellion and State in Chinese Central Asia, 1864–1877* [Stanford, CA: Stanford University Press, 2004], 160–61, 165).
2. ʿAbdurraḥman Aftabachi, leader of an 1875 uprising in Ferghana, and afterward an officer in the Russian military (Timur K. Beisembiev, *Annotated Indices to the Kokand Chronicles* [Tokyo: Research Institute for Languages and Cultures of Asia and Africa, 2008], 296).
3. *Jīdābānī:* I infer from location that the place referred to is Qīdàowān 七道灣, a settlement east of Ürümchi on the road from Turfan to Gumadi. Baytur: *Chidawan* (Molla Musa Sayrami, *Tarikhi Hämidi*, trans. Änwär Baytur [Beyjing: Millätlär näshriyati, 2007], 446). Täklimakani omits this passage (Musa Sayramiy, *Tarikhi Hämidi*, trans. Abduraop Täklimakani [Istanbul: Täklimakan Uyghur näshriyati, 2019], 490).
4. Bozorgmehr: A wise minister in the *Shahnama*.
5. ʿAli-Sher Nava'i (1441–1501) was one of the most famous and beloved writers of early modern Central Asia.
6. Many members of the Khoqandi regime were imprisoned in Lanzhou.
7. Thank you to Jun Sugawara for helping me untangle this phrase.
8. Keyumars, Hushang, Jamshid, Faridun: Heroes from the *Shahnama*.
9. Bahram: A legendary warrior from the *Shahnama*.

2:13 Merits and Demerits of Yaʿqub Beg's Rule

1. Yaʿqub Beg's seal can be seen on a letter to the emperor of China dated after Tongzhi 9 [1870] in the National Palace Museum, Taipei, NPM *guji* 107866. It is indeed a small oval seal reading simply "Muḥammad Yaʿqub," dated 1284 [1867/8]. See the analysis by Shinmen Yasushi and Onuma Takahiro, "First Contact Between Ya'qub Beg and the Qing: The Diplomatic Correspondence of 1871," *Journal of Asian and African Studies* 84 (2012): 5–37.
2. *chārsū murabbaʿ*. Täklimakani: *soqa sändäldek* "like a mortar or anvil" (Musa Sayramiy, *Tarikhi Hämidi*, trans. Abduraop Täklimakani [Istanbul: Täklimakan Uyghur näshriyati, 2019], 505); Baytur: *dughilaq* "plump, squat, pudgy" (Molla Musa Sayrami, *Tarikhi Hämidi*, trans. Änwär Baytur [Beyjing: Millätlär näshriyati, 2007], 458).
3. *kāt [kārt] takht. kat* "bin, chest" (Gunnar Jarring, *An Eastern Turki-English Dialect Dictionary* [Lund: CWK Gleerup, 1964], 165). Täklimakani: *kat, karwat üstidä* "upon a *kat* or bed" (505).
4. *ra'īs muḥtasib:* Both *ra'īs* and *muḥtasib* indicated an officer in Khoqand and under Yaʿqub Beg whose duty was to patrol the streets, inspect and regulate market prices, and detect and punish moral deviance (Timur K. Beisembiev, *Annotated Indices to the Kokand Chronicles* [Tokyo: Research Institute for Languages and Cultures of Asia and Africa, 2008], 775, 816). The two terms were not exactly synonymous, and Sayrami also uses each of them separately here. Rather, as a British travel account confirms, the *ra'īs* oversaw a team of *muḥtasib* (T. D. Forsyth, *Report of a Mission to Yarkund in 1873* [Calcutta:

Foreign Department Press, 1875], 36). *Iḥtisābchi*, the term used two paragraphs later, appears to be a synonym of *muḥtasib*, and it is derived from the same Arabic root *ḥ.s.b.*

5. *Mishkat al-maṣabiḥ*, Book 2, Hadith 15 (Sunnah.com, https://sunnah.com/mishkat:212, accessed September 10, 2022).
6. *Mishkat al-maṣabiḥ*, Book 1, Hadith 26 (Sunnah.com, https://sunnah.com/mishkat:28, accessed September 10, 2022).
7. *khulq-i mulāyim birlä kürük körüp*. Modern Uyghur *kürük:* "a broody (nesting) hen." Täklimakani: "received them" *qobul qildi* (511).
8. *haft-i yak:* Seven *surahs* of the Quran used as a primer.
9. MS is vocalized to indicate *mergan*. < Mo. *margan* "fine archer" (Gerhard Doerfer, *Türkische und mongolische Elemente im Neupersischen*, 4 vols. [Wiesbaden: Franz Steiner Verlag, 1963], vol. 1, 496–98).
10. *Gūr-i ḥaqq ast*. Refers to humans' final resting place until the Day of Resurrection.
11. *qamtū numūda: qamtū* "(<Mongolian?) (confrontation [of suspects])" (Beisembiev, *Annotated Indices*, 803), but "together, in company" (Martti Räsänen, *Versuch eines etymologischen Wörterbuchs der Türksprachen* [Helsinki: Suomalaid-Ugrilainen seura, 1969], 229).
12. This report would have concerned the Beshkent tract, which was positioned between the Yarkand (or Zarafshan) River and the Tiznaf River.
13. There is a Sufi joke in this. Here, "Shariah" *sharīʿat* indicates the Shariah as not only a guide to legal tax collection but also the first step on the Sufi path to enlightenment. "Truth" *ḥaqīqat* means not only "reality," in the sense of the truth that has undergone "inspection" (*taḥqīq*, from the same Arabic root *ḥ.q.q*), or what is "really" owed, but also transcendent Truth, the third step on the path.
14. Sayrami gives the numbers here in Persian: *deh hazār tangga, panj hazār tangga*.
15. TH/Beijing {257} corresponds with the beginning of the facsimile and transliteration provided in Abduraop Polat's dissertation (160).

2:14 Ḥakim Khan's Enthronement

1. The events of this chapter are helpfully summarized in Hodong Kim, *Holy War in China: The Muslim Rebellion and State in Chinese Central Asia, 1864–1877* [Stanford, CA: Stanford University Press, 2004], 173–74.
2. *mis begi:* Literally "copper beg." Refers to someone in charge of mining operations, in this case at the copper mines in the mountains near Bay.
3. *chap̣avul:* "cavalry or nomadic raid" (Timur K. Beisembiev, *Annotated Indices to the Kokand Chronicles* [Tokyo: Research Institute for Languages and Cultures of Asia and Africa, 2008], 758; Robert Shaw, *A Sketch of the Turki Language as Spoken in Eastern Turkistan [Kàshghar and Yarkand]* [Calcutta: Baptist Mission Press, 1878], vol. 2, 91).

2:15 The Rise and Fall of Beg Quli Beg

1. At this spot, Täklimakani's translation (Musa Sayramiy, *Tarikhi Hämidi*, trans. Abduraop Täklimakani [Istanbul: Täklimakan Uyghur näshriyati, 2019], 543) makes a sudden jump from {266, 5} to {276, 1}, which is partway through 2:16 "Niyaz Ḥakim Beg." The text then interpellates the remainder of 2:16 from {276, 1} to {280, 5}, up to the end of its

"Second Epic, Chapter Fifteen" (554). Täklimakani's translation then begins its "Second Epic, Chapter Sixteen" with the text starting from {270, 17} and reproduces the text from {276, 1} to {280, 5}. The result is that the second half of Täklimakani's "Chapter Sixteen" is duplicated as the second half of "Chapter Fifteen." It is missing the original second half of 2:15, which I present here. The reason for the confusion appears to be the retelling of this same incident in similar terms, such that Täklimakani probably mixed up the second half of {266} with the second half of {275}, both of which describe the battle with the Boy Beg at "a city called Ziba" (*Zibā degän shahar*) and mention "both sides" (*ikki ṭaraf*) (563). Baytur (Molla Musa Sayrami, *Tarikhi Hämidi*, trans. Änwär Baytur [Beyjing: Millätlär näshriyati, 2007], from 495) has the correct text, as does Polat's dissertation (Abduraop Polat, "Musa Sayrami Tarih-i Hamidi III: inceleme-metin-dizin" [PhD diss., Ankara Üniversitesi, 2002], 169).

2. Tajik: Not an ethnonym but a place name, indicating an area west of Kucha, at a less-traveled pass between Kucha and Bay. (Baytur has *Tijik* [498]. Polat's dissertation gives *Tici* [171].) So the army was divided into two columns, one entering Kucha along a northern route via Tajik, and one entering Kucha along a southern route via Yaqa Eriq.

2:16 Niyaz Ḥakim Beg

1. The text states that the area of this plot was two *taghar*, literally two "bagfuls." A *taghar* was a unit of weight, while the area of the plot of land excavated was of the size that could have been seeded with two "bagfuls" of grain (Gustav Raquette, *Eastern Turki Grammar: Practical and Theoretical with Vocabulary*, 3 vols. [Berlin: Reichsdruckerei, 1912], vol. 1, 33–36).
2. *Yolbars* is generally translated as "tiger." If Niyaz Beg indeed kept big cats in a menagerie, they might have been now-extinct Caspian tigers (*Panthera tigris virgata*), which were found in the Tarim Basin until the mid-twentieth century.
3. "Zongtong Daren" is Liú Jìntáng 劉錦堂 (1844–1894), one of the top commanders of the reconquest and later Xinjiang's governor. The name given here refers to a pair of titles: Chinese *zǒngtǒng guān* 總統官 "corps commander" and *dàrén* 大人, a respectful term of address for an official. Zongtong Daren's movements correspond with those of Liu Jintang as recorded in official Qing sources. In 2:19, Zongtong Daren is referred to as the "governor-general of Lanzhou," but I suspect that Sayrami has confused him for Zuo Zongtang, whose name is quite close to *zǒngtǒng* but who did not command forces in Xinjiang in person. Ṭalib Akhund in the *Ṣaḥibnama* notes that Zongtong became the governor (*shūngfū* < Ch. *xúnfǔ* 巡撫 "governor") (Jarring Prov. 117, 128r).
4. Dong Daren indicates Dǒng Fúxiáng 董福祥 (1839–1908), a former rebel commander and Han from Gansu who commanded a large force of mainly Hui soldiers and later chose to serve under Zuo Zongtang's command.
5. *khan oqi*: A sign daubed on someone's house to indicate that they were marked for execution.
6. Muḥammad Yunus Jan possessed a reputation as "a scholar and a gentleman." T. D. Forsyth notes that he "has risen to distinction by the use of his pen, rather than by the use of the sword" (*Report of a Mission to Yarkand in 1873* [Calcutta: Foreign Department Press, 1875], 21).

7. *yiren* < Ch. *yìrén* 夷人 "outsider." We must be cautious with the translation of *yì*, which English speakers came to translate as "barbarian." Sayrami provides a more neutral gloss.
8. Reports from British agents in Yarkand assert that Muḥammad Yunus Jan was apprehended by Alif Beg of Sarikol and delivered to the Qing forces, who imprisoned him. They then offered him passage back to Khoqand, but he refused and instead offered his services. On Alif Beg's death, the army freed him and placed him under surveillance (India Office Records, L/P&S/7/20).

2:17 Notables During Yaʿqub Beg's Era

1. Fariduddin ʿAṭṭar (ca. 1145–ca. 1221): An important Sufi poet and mystic.
2. *Nafaḥāt al-uns*, literally "Breaths of Fellowship," often rendered less literally as "Lives of the Saints": An important Sufi hagiographical work composed by Nuruddin ʿAbdurraḥman Jāmī (1414–1492).
3. A *shaykh al-Islām*, here *shaykhulislam*, referred to the chief Islamic scholar in a region, whose legal opinions were particularly influential. In many states, including under the Timurids and Ottomans, the *shaykhulislam* was appointed by the ruler.
4. Beisembiev describes the latter figure thus: "Šaykhāvand-i Ṭahūr/Šaykhāntāvīr/Šaykh Khāvand-i Ṭahūr (son of Šaykh ʿUmar Bāġistānī; saint and protector of a part of Tashkent; ancestor of Yunus Khᵛāja" (Timur K. Beisembiev, *Annotated Indices to the Kokand Chronicles* [Tokyo: Research Institute for Languages and Cultures of Asia and Africa, 2008], 272). Täklimakani understandably misreads it as *Khudāwand*, which is after all a more common name (Musa Sayramiy, *Tarikhi Hämidi*, trans. Abduraop Täklimakani [Istanbul: Täklimakan Uyghur näshriyati, 2019], 577).
5. TA/Pelliot (176v), TH/Jarring (114r): "114 years old," indicating the earlier composition of those texts. TA/Kazan does not give an age but confirms that "He is living in Ushturfan" (272).
6. Son of Qażi Mirza Raḥim Jan Tashkandi, Bukharan envoy to Malla Khan in 1861, who left for Kashgar in 1865 after the death of ʿĀlimqul (Beisembiev, *Annotated Indices*, 286).
7. TH/Jarring: 1300 [1882/3]. TA/Pelliot: 1307.
8. Aḥmad al-Faruqi al-Sirhindi (1564–1624): An important figure in the Naqshbandi Sufi order and the progenitor of the Mujaddidi networks that have played a role in this story. See 1:7, n. 7, and 1:9, n. 7, above.
9. *ḥafiẓ*: One who has memorized the Qur'an.
10. TA/Kazan: "judge" (276); TA/Pelliot: "chief judge" (178v). Perhaps he ascended the ranks between 1903 and 1907.
11. This spot, at TH/Beijing {287, 12}, corresponds to TH/Jarring at (115v, 13). TH/Jarring's text was evidently copied from a manuscript in which the pages were out of order, so the text skips to (117v, 11).
12. At about this point, the passage of text that is out of order in TH/Jarring ends at (118r, 19) and then jumps back to (116r, 20).
13. In TH/Jarring, a copying error has interpellated the biography of Mirza Baba Beg Ḥissari into the autobiography of Sayrami in the following chapter.
14. The *Dalā'il al-Khayrat* (Waymarks of Benefits) is a collection of prayers for the Prophet Muḥammad written by Muḥammad Sulayman al-Jazuli al-Shadhili (d. 1465).

15. *botam*: Literally "my little camel," used as a term of endearment.
16. Bedil (1642–1720): a Sufi saint and poet who was the foremost representative of the literary style known as *sabk-i Hindī*.
17. In TH/Jarring, this list is found below after the mention of Ḥajji Artuq Mirza. TH/Jarring clarifies that "Törä Qul Labar" is one person.
18. At TH/Beijing {292, 6}, TH/Jarring diverges again: the text skips from (117v, 11) to (115v, 13).
19. TH/Jarring: "Nawruz Pansad, Ishan Qul Pansad, Muḥammad Efendi and Khalil Efendi of Rum, Bay Muḥammad Charchibashi, Bukhcha Bardar, Mir Karim Qurchi, Nar Muḥammad Parashbashi . . ." TA/Pelliot: "Abulqasim Pansad, Ḥisamuddin Pansad, Muḥammad Efendi and Khalil Efendi of Rum, Bay Muḥammad Charchibashi, Bukhcha Bardar, Karim Bay Qurchi, Nar Muḥammad Parashbashi, Khalman Pansad, ʿId Muḥammad Pansad, Baqi Pansad, Nawruz Pansad, Akhund Pansad . . ."

2:18 The Biography of the Author

1. Muhammad Muhsin Khan, trans., *The Translation of the Meanings of Sahih al-Bukhari*, 9 vols. (Lahore: Kazi, 1979), vol. 4, 63.
2. In TH/Beijing, pp. 295–96 are duplicated as pp. 297–98. Hence this translation appears to skip from p. 296 to p. 299. TH/Beijing also falls out of sequence with Polat's dissertation (Abduraop Polat, "Musa Sayrami Tarih-i Hamidi III: inceleme-metin-dizin" [PhD diss., Ankara Üniversitesi, 2002], 200): {299} is Polat's manuscript page 297, {300} is Polat's 298, etc.
3. *farvānachä tilämäsunlar*, reading *farvānachä* as "order; indulgence (diminutive)." Täklimakani gives "ask for another person" (Musa Sayramiy, *Tarikhi Hämidi*, trans. Abduraop Täklimakani [Istanbul: Täklimakan Uyghur näshriyati, 2019], 606), which reads *farvānachä* as *parvānachi* or *farmānchi*. Baytur similarly reads this as *pärwanichi:* "ask for another *parvānachi*" (Molla Musa Sayrami, *Tarikhi Hämidi*, trans. Änwär Baytur [Beyjing: Millätlär näshriyati, 2007], 550).
4. Here TH/Beijing is missing two pages between {300} and {301}. They can be found in Polat's dissertation as manuscript pages 299 and 300.

2:19 Reconquest of the Chinese Emperor

1. Sayrami occasionally refers to the land of China as *Khāqān-i Chīn*, literally "Great Khan of China," which term indicates the legendary ruler of China in Persian literature. Sometimes he refers to it simply as *Khāqān* "Great Khan," indicating the country by that ruler's title. Others during his time did the same.
2. On "Long-Hairs" *Changmoza* as a term for the Taiping, see 0:6, n. 6.
3. "grand secretary": See 0:4, n. 11. "governor-general": *z̤ūngdū* < Ch. *zǒngdū* 總督.
4. *Nan Lū Bā Cheng*, from Chinese *Nánlù bāchéng* 南路八城, "eight cities of the Southern Route," where the Southern Route indicates the Muslim-majority area stretching from the Turfan Depression across the Tarim to Kashgar. Sayrami discusses the term further at the beginning of the epilogue.
5. *fūng* < Ch. *fēn* 分, a very small unit of length.

6. "General Jing" *Jīng Jāngjūng* refers to Jinshun 金順 (1830–1886), where *jāngjūng* < Ch. *jiāngjūn* 將軍 "general." Jinshun, a Manchu of the Irgen Gioro clan, was one of the chief commanders of the reconquest force and from 1876 served as the new Ili General.
7. *Lūshī Dārīn* indicates Zhang Yao 張曜 (1832–1891), the provincial commander in chief of Guangdong and key reconquest commander, who entered Turfan from the east and Qumul while Liu Jintang entered from Ürümchi and the west. He later garrisoned Kashgar, leading to the post-reconquest episode described in 1:11. The term *lūshī* remains obscure. Regardless, this character's movements follow those of Zhang Yao as recorded in official documents. Another account of the uprisings, the 1899 *Ṣaḥibnama* of Ṭalib Akhund b. Mullah Niʿmat Mingbegi of Khotan, confirms the identification of Lushi Daren with Zhang Yao by placing him at key events in the Gansu and Xinjiang campaigns (Jarring Prov. 117, 2r–4r, 128r).
8. The events of the reconquest are outlined in Hodong Kim, *Holy War in China: The Muslim Rebellion and State in Chinese Central Asia, 1864–1877* (Stanford, CA: Stanford University Press, 2004), 165–77. Its details are recorded in Wang Dingan's (1833–1898) 1889 chronicle of the Xiang Army's achievements, *Xiangjunji* (Taipei: Chengwen chubanshe, 1968), j. 19. I find Wang's account to be rather selective, however, so have consulted original documentary sources that recorded troop movements, particularly National Palace Museum, Taipei, *gugong* 142347, memorial dated GX 3.12.18.
9. *Zūndū Kūng Zūng* "Governor-General Gong Zong" indicates Zuǒ Zōngtáng 左宗棠 (1812–1885), the architect of Xinjiang's reconquest and reconstruction. The "governor-general of Lanzhou" must be that of Shaanxi and Gansu, whose seat was in Lanzhou, and which was Zuo's office during the reconquest. He was referred to respectfully as Zuǒ *gōng* 左公 "Duke Zuo."
10. There is another gap here in TH/Beijing, between {302} and {303}. The missing two pages are Polat's manuscript pages 303 and 304.
11. TA/Kazan: "early in the season."
12. The movements of "Luying Uchu" correspond with those of Xiang Army commander Huáng Wànpéng 黃萬鵬 (1832–1898), who was sent to approach Kashgar through the mountains and attack it from the west (*Xiangjun ji*, j. 19, 23b–25a). The name Luying Uchu remains mysterious.
13. *Mishkat al-maṣabiḥ*, Book 1, Hadith 152 (Sunnah.com, https://sunnah.com/mishkat:159, accessed September 10, 2022).
14. *aq pādishāh:* "White Emperor," the tsar of Russia.
15. *tikän* and *chigh*.
16. *chī khaṭ:* From Chinese *qī piào* 期票 "promissory note" (R. H. Mathews, ed., *Mathews' Chinese-English Dictionary* [Cambridge, MA: Harvard University Press, 1963], 69), with Arabic *khaṭ* "letter." Baytur (Molla Musa Sayrami, *Tarikhi Hämidi*, trans. Änwär Baytur [Beyjing: Millätlär näshriyati, 2007], 561) also glosses it as "promissory note" *til khät*, and Täklimakani (Musa Sayramiy, *Tarikhi Hämidi*, trans. Abduraop Täklimakani [Istanbul: Täklimakan Uyghur näshriyati, 2019], 617) translates it as "note of guarantee" *kapalät kheti*.
17. If the Khaṭib Khoja were sixty-two in 1281 [1864], he would only be eighty-one in 1300 [1882]. Either the account is inaccurate or he was held prisoner for several years after the reconquest. This is entirely possible, given that many of the Khoqandis were imprisoned at Lanzhou for several years.

18. *Dā pādishāh:* Like *Lao padishah* (2:9, n. 9, above), a blend of a Chinese word (*dà* 大 "big, great") and *pādishāh* "king."
19. *chizäläp* < Ch. *chǐzi* 尺子 "ruler" < Ch. *chǐ* 尺 "foot (measurement)" + denominal suffix -*lA*.
20. *funglap* < Ch. *fēn* 分, a very small unit of length, + denominal suffix -*lA*.
21. The Hijri year 1326 spanned February 1908 through January 1909. Täklimakani (624) renders the date as "1909 CE." Baytur (566), in what must be a typographical error, gives the Hijri year as 1320 but the Gregorian date as 1909. Thirty years earlier yields 1296 [1878/9], so "more than thirty years" is accurate. TA/Kazan gives 1321 [1903], the date of the *Tarikh-i Amniyya*'s composition, and notes that the Chinese have governed for "twenty-seven years," yielding 1294 [1877]. TH/Jarring appears once again to have peculiar defects that point to its possible origins as a blend of the *Tarikh-i Amniyya* and *Tarikh-i Ḥamidi*: it also says that the present year is 1326 (like TH/Beijing), but that the Chinese have governed for "twenty-seven years" (like TA/Kazan).
22. Implying "the blind leading the blind." Baytur (567) and Täklimakani (625) do not offer translations.

2:20 Virtues of the Chinese Emperor

1. The details of this incident are garbled, and it is difficult to match them to a specific historical event. I cannot locate an "assistant imperial agent Man Daren" (*chīng-chī ambani Man Dārīn*) in historical documents. However, the story about officials near Aqsu collecting an unfair tax during the Taiping period seems to correspond to the incident in 1853–1857 described in James A. Millward, *Beyond the Pass: Economy, Ethnicity, and Empire in Qing Central Asia, 1759–1864* (Stanford, CA: Stanford University Press, 1998), 210–11, in which officials in Kucha exacted a series of additional taxes on the populace in order to pay off loans to Chinese merchants, resulting in widespread discontent and a violent uprising. The superintendent of Kucha, Wūěrqīng'ā 烏爾清阿, was removed from office for his mishandling of the situation.
2. *chīngchī* or *chīnchī* possibly < Ch. *qīnchāi (dàchén)* 欽差(大臣) "imperial (commissioner)." Zuo Zongtang, and then Liu Jintang, held the rank of imperial commissioner in their capacity of coordinating Xinjiang military affairs. *zūndū* "governor-general" (see 2:19, n. 9, above). *dāṭayy* "circuit intendant" < Ch. *dàotái* 道台. *sīng* "province": We have elsewhere referred to the "provinces" [*ölkü, ölküchä*] within Moghulistan. Here, the word *sīng* < Ch. *shěng* 省 indicates one of the administrative units of China proper.

   Sayrami's description of the Qing official hierarchy blends the military administration that governed some of the empire's territory with the provincial system that governed the rest. As of 1907, the reorganization of Manchuria indeed brought the number of Qing provinces to twenty-two, including Xinjiang. However, the nine governors-general typically oversaw not one, but two or three provinces, which had their own governors; perhaps this is where Sayrami gets the idea that each governor-general commanded two "generals." If Sayrami's "generals" are provincial governors, then the "imperial agents" are actually equivalent to their subordinate circuit intendants. Indeed, Xinjiang had four such intendants. Below them were Sayrami's *chingchi*, indicating the magistrates and prefects of the provincial system who governed the lowest-level administrative units. Sayrami's confusion is understandable: the term *amban*, which before 1864 indicated an imperial agent in Xinjiang under the Ili General, was now applied often to magistrates and other Qing civil officials. The Ili General's administration persisted after the reconquest of 1877, and even after the establishment of Xinjiang province in 1884, and just as the relationship between the old military government and the new civil one confused the people who ran either one, likewise was it obscure to the people they ruled.

3. *li*: See 1:3, n. 4.
4. *tüshkünchi*: *tüškün* "tax, esp. war tax" (Gunnar Jarring, *Materials to the Knowledge of Eastern Turki: Tales, Poetry, Proverbs, Riddles, Ethnological and Historical Texts from the Southern Parts of Eastern Turkestan*, 4 vols. [Lund: C.W.K. Gleerup, 1946–1951], vol. 4, 185n8). I take Sayrami to mean that the Khojas' wars were a specific reason for the people's destitution. Baytur (Molla Musa Sayrami, *Tarikhi Hämidi*, trans. Änwär Baytur [Beyjing: Millätlär näshriyati, 2007], 583) preserves the word *tüshkünchi*. Täklimakani (Musa Sayramiy, *Tarikhi Hämidi*, trans. Abduraop Täklimakani [Istanbul: Täklimakan Uyghur näshriyati, 2019], 645) changes the wording significantly, writing that the common people were liberated "from the condition of a life of destitution" *namrat yasham muhitidin*, presumably through the meaning of *tüshkün* as "wretched," although his dissertation takes it instead to indicate the Khojas' "insatiability" (*düşkünçü, doymaz*) (Abduraop Polat, "Musa Sayrami Tarih-i Hamidi III: inceleme-metin-dizin" [PhD diss., Ankara Üniversitesi, 2002], 396).
5. *ʿadd-basāṭlarini yayghan boldi:* Täklimakani (644) omits this phrase. Baytur (583) renders it "For a while they spread their hands and feet out wide" *put-qolini bir qanchä waqit käng yayghan boldi*. I think that Baytur captures the underlying metaphor of generosity and sense of plenty.
6. *Bu ikki nūrni pütürdilär.* The final verb, *ṗütür-*, seems oddly used here. It ought to be the causative of *ṗütü-* "to write," but the causative of *ṗit-* "to finish" may be closer to the mark, or perhaps taking the meaning *ṗit-* "to believe." I suspect that the meaning "to finish (reading)" is correct. Täklimakani (648) renders this phrase as "by means of the miraculousness of these two remarkable lights" [*bu ikki khasiyätlik nurning kiramäti arqiliq*]. His dissertation transliterates the key word incorrectly as *futūr ve belā ve* (224). Baytur (585) omits the phrase.

3:0 Introduction

1. MS *Katta Tengiz*, Lake Balkhash. Rendered in Mirza Ḥaydar Dughlat, *Tarikh-i Rashidi*, trans. Wheeler M. Thackston (New York: I. B. Tauris, 2012), 227, as "Kökcha Tengiz."
2. Kuh-i-Lal ("Ruby Mountain") in modern Afghanistan.
3. Compare Thackston, trans., *Tarikh-i Rashidi* (225–27), which presents rather different boundaries. Sayrami was probably working from a later version of the *Rashidi*, possibly the Turkic translation (Amanbek Jalilov, Yayoi Kawahara, Sawada Minoru, Shinmen Yasushi, and Hori Sunao, eds., *Addendum to Tarikh-i Rashidi: Translation and Annotation with Introduction and Indexes* [Tokyo: NIHU Program Islamic Area Studies TIAS, 2008]).

3:3 Khotan

1. Meaning ʿAli b. al-Ḥusayn Zaynulʿabidin (ca. 659–ca. 713).
2. An ancient and famed cemetery in Medina.
3. Here TH/Beijing at the bottom of {330} is missing two pages, which are reproduced in Polat's dissertation as manuscript pages 333–34 (228–29). Abduraop Polat, "Musa Sayrami Tarih-i Hamidi III: inceleme-metin-dizin" (PhD diss., Ankara Üniversitesi, 2002).
4. "Jatta Noyan" is properly "Jebe Noyan."

3:4 Aqsu

1. 830–910, an important early Sufi figure. TH/Beijing: "Jandi."
2. Abū al-Ḥasan Sarī (al-Sirrī) b. al-Mughallis al-Saqaṭī (d. ca. 867). TH/Beijing *Sirsaqṭī*; TA/Pelliot *Sirrī Saqṭī*.
3. According to the hagiography, Qahqa Jadu (literally "chuckling sorcerer") is a mountain near Ushturfan, while the city of Barbar was in Aqsu. Qirmish Sayyid al-Muslimin was the name that the Prophet Muḥammad gave to a Muslim from Aqsu who had been forced to flee to Mecca, and whom the Prophet then commanded to return home with an army (Ömerjan Häsän, "Qirmish Atam: Insap Qilinglar . . ." *Miras* 5 (2001): 58).
4. Two pages are missing between TH/Beijing {334} and {335}, which are reproduced in as manuscript pages 339–40 in Abduraop Polat, "Musa Sayrami Tarih-i Hamidi III: inceleme-metin-dizin" (PhD diss., Ankara Üniversitesi, 2002). This passage also corresponds to TA/Pelliot [202v, 4–203r, 12].
5. The *Dastan-i Amir Ḥamza* is a collection of fantastic adventure stories starring the Prophet's uncle. There is a copy of its Chaghatay translation, probably made in Kashgar in the early twentieth century, in the Lund University Library, Jarring Prov. 384.
6. *tawajjuh:* A Sufi practice in which a master focuses upon their disciples in order to transmit their spiritual "light" into the disciples' hearts.
7. Thirty-six years after 1285 AH is 1321 AH, or 1903 CE.

3:5 Ushturfan

1. *qadam-jāy*. An "arrival place" is somewhat different from a typical shrine, which is conceived of as a mausoleum (*mazār*). On the meaning of *qadam-jāy*, see Thierry Zarcone, "Atypical Mausoleum: The Case of the Salomon Throne (Kyrgyzstan), *Qadam-Jāy*, Jinns-Cult and Itinerary-Pilgrimage," in *Muslim Saints and Mausoleums in Central Asia and Xinjiang*, ed. Shinmen Yasushi, Sawada Minoru, and Edmund Waite (Paris: Librairie d'Amérique et d'Orient, 2013), 203–10.

3:7 Turfan

1. *taranjabīn:* "Manna collected from *Alhagi maurorum*, Tourn. Imported from Turfan in small quantities via Yarkand to Leh for Kashmir" (J. E. T. Aitchison, *Hand-Book of the*

Trade Products of Leh with the Statistics of Trade from 1867 to 1872 Inclusive [Calcutta: Wyman & Co., 1874], 261).

2. Sayrami's description of Turfan in TH/Beijing is influenced by Qurban ʿAli Khalidi's description in *Tarikh-i jarida-i jadida* (Qazan: Qazan Universitetining ṭabiʿkhanasi, 1889).
3. Hongmyawzi < Ch. *Hóngmiáozi* 紅廟子 "red temple." This was a common way to refer to Ürümchi synecdochally by the red-colored temple and pagoda atop Red Mountain (*Hóngshān* 紅山).
4. Shinshangsen < Ch. *Xīnjiāng shěng* 新疆省, "provincial seat of Xinjiang." At this point, TH/Beijing departs significantly from earlier manuscripts. It is worth reproducing the text that follows in TA/Pelliot:

   > [205v, 2] With regard to the matter of the Cave of the Companions being in Turfan, there is a verse in the Quran: AND THOU MIGHTEST HAVE SEEN THE SUN WHEN IT ROSE MOVE AWAY FROM THEIR CAVE TO THE RIGHT, AND WHEN IT SET GO PAST THEM ON THE LEFT. [18:17] They say that this describes the mouth of the cave. In any case, it is apparently known that the Companions of the Cave were in this land of Turfan. And God knows the truth of things.
   >
   > There is also an important shrine called the al-Fatta'. Its original name was Alp Ata. "Alp" means hero. The leading imams and shaykhs of Turkestan named it with the word "Ata" (father). The great Alp Ata was the sixteenth-generation descendant of Imam Muḥammad Hanifa (MAY GOD BE PLEASED WITH HIM!). It is said that, FOR THE LOVE OF GOD, he carried out holy war against the infidels and was martyred. Perhaps his name was Abdulfattah. AND GOD KNOWS.
   >
   > *   *   *
   >
   > The number of great and holy shrines in the cities, villages, mountains, and wildernesses of the Seven Cities, where holy saints and shaykhs dwelled or were buried, is known only to the Lord, the Wise and Munificent. No human being can learn it from anyone.[205v, 12]

5. MS *Daqyānus*, evidently indicating the Roman emperor Decius (r. 249–251). On the identity of the Cave of the Companions and its connection to the imagination of antiquity, see Emine Gürsoy-Naskali, *Ashabu 'l-Kähf: A Treatise in Eastern Turki* (Helsinki: Suomalais-Ugrilaisen Seuran toimituksia, 1985), and Sidney Griffith, "Christian Lore and the Arabic Qur'ān: The 'Companions of the Cave' in *Sūrat al-Kahf* and in Syriac Christian Tradition," in *The Qur'ān in Its Historical Context*, ed. Gabriel Saʿid Reynolds (London: Routledge, 2009), 109–37.
6. Possibly < Tibetan *lodrö* "wisdom, intellect," sometimes used in the titles of Tibetan Buddhist clerics. Polat offers "*lodo* < Chinese 'idol' " (Abduraop Polat, "Musa Sayrami Tarih-i Hamidi III: inceleme-metin-dizin" [PhD diss., Ankara Üniversitesi, 2002], 349). There is another instance of this word on {354}, where it appears in the same set of "*lodos*, lamas, and Brahmins."
7. The same document is reproduced in full in Khalidi, *Tarikh-i jarida-i jadida*, 20–21; and in the manuscript of same at the Institute for Oriental Manuscripts of the Russian Academy of Sciences, C578. The latter is unfoliated, and in the microfilm copy held by the Sinor Research Institute for Inner Asian Studies at Indiana University, the pages have been rearranged, but the edict can be found around f. 22. Thanks to David Brophy for pointing me in the right direction.

8. The phrasing corresponds to a formula used elsewhere in edicts from the Khanate of Yarkand (Hodong Kim, "Eastern Turki Royal Decrees of the 17th Century in the Jarring Collection," in *Studies on Xinjiang Historical Sources in 17th–20th Centuries*, ed. James A. Millward, Shinmen Yasushi, and Jun Sugawara [Tokyo: Toyo Bunko, 2010], 78, 82, 85, 95).
9. *ṣāḥib takbir:* A master of recitative formulae who often played a key role in the organization of labor around piety (Jeanine Elif Dağyeli, "A Community of Order, Morale, Internal Discipline and Punishment in the Craft Milieu of Turkestan," in *Community Still Matters: Uyghur Culture and Society in Central Asian Context*, ed. Aysima Mirsultan, Eric Schluessel, and Eset Sulaiman [Copenhagen: NIAS Press, 2022], 234–49).
10. *ishchi wa gushchi:* "lower functionaries who performed miscellaneous duties and listened to rumors and complaints from people" (Kim, "Eastern Turki Royal Decrees," 68–69).
11. *suchi*, "courier," as an attested contraction of *shusunchi* (Gerhard Doerfer, *Türkische und mongolische Elemente im Neupersischen*, 4 vols. [Wiesbaden: Franz Steiner Verlag, 1963], vol. 1, 363). For *shusun*, see n. 13 below.
12. *tawachi* "inferior court rank . . . whose duty was to make public announcement or delivery of messages and orders; messenger, courier" (Timur K. Beisembiev, *Annotated Indices to the Kokand Chronicles* [Tokyo: Research Institute for Languages and Cultures of Asia and Africa, 2008], 748). Polat ("Musa Sayrami Tarih-i Hamidi III," 240) concurs.
13. A list of impositions: *alban, yasaq, özgä qonalghu, ḥashār, mardikār, oqush, tir, chap̣ar ulagh, qan, chaqār, shusun. ḥashār*: "communal labor" organized privately or by government (Kim, "Eastern Turki Royal Decrees," 72). *mardikār*: "conscription of people for repairing irrigation canals, roads, bridges, and town walls" (Kim, "Eastern Turki Royal Decrees," 72). *oqush*: MS *a.w.q.w.sh.* Obscure. Täklimakani's and Baytur's rendering of *oqush-pitir* (Polat, "Musa Sayrami Tarih-i Hamidi III," 370; Musa Sayramiy, *Tarikhi Hämidi*, trans. Abduraop Täklimakani [Istanbul: Täklimakan Uyghur näshriyati, 2019], 681) < Baytur (Molla Musa Sayrami, *Tarikhi Hämidi*, trans. Änwär Baytur [Beyjing: Millätlär näshriyati, 2007], 615) must be discounted, as must Täklimakani's later rendering as *oqush yetär*, on the basis of the next word, which is actually *tir*. Nevertheless, *oqush* as "reading" may be correct, but so might a connection to Old Uyghur *oqush* "lineage, family, retinue; space, field, area," or perhaps even *qosh*, as in "a pair of oxen," referring to a later tax on farms after sowing (Alexander Morrison, "Amlākdārs, Khwājas and Mulk Land in the Zarafshan Valley after the Russian Conquest," in *Explorations in the Social History of Modern Central Asia (19th–Early 20th Century)*, ed. Paolo Sartori (Leiden: Brill, 2013), 12n57). Hodong Kim notes the same term in a list of duties in an edict dating to 1088 [1677], Lund University Library, Jarring Prov. 277, line 21 ("Eastern Turki Royal Decrees," 101, 103). However, he was unable to translate it, as the context is similarly lacking. It seems best not to translate it here without further research. Thanks to Nicholas Kontovas for thinking through this with me. *tir*: MS *y.t.r.* Obscure. Sayrami evidently miscopied this document from Khalidi, who has *t.y.r. Tir* is perhaps < P. "arrow," implying the duty to supply arrows. However, the word also probably relates to the *tiravul* (spelt t.y.r.a.w.u.l) that Kim notes in another document, Jarring Prov. 223, dated to 1600 ("Eastern Turki Royal Decrees," 74, 81), the meaning of which remains obscure. *chap̣ar*: post riders (*chap̣ār*, < Turkic *chap-* "to gallop") (Doerfer, *Die türkischen Elemente*, vol. 3, 12–13). Compare *chapghunchi/chapuqchi* "raider; courier" (Beisembiev, *Indices*, 756). The *Tarikh-i jarida-i jadida* actually has *chiqar* both here and below, but I think that *chap̣ar* is likely, both because it fits with the list of duties paid to agents of the government

and because it would not necessarily make sense to repeat the term. *ulagh*: "postal relay mounts," or rather, the duty to provide them (Francis Woodman Cleaves, "The Mongolian Documents in the Musée de Téhéran," *Harvard Journal of Asiatic Studies* 16, no. 1/2 (June 1953): 91n3; Doerfer, *Die türkischen Elemente*, vol. 2, 102–7; Kim, "Eastern Turki Royal Decrees," 71–72, 74, 101). *qan:* < *qalān*, "obligations to the ruler" (Doerfer, *Die türkischen Elemente*, vol. 3, 488–90; H. F. Schurmann, "Mongolian Tributary Practices of the Thirteenth Century," *Harvard Journal of Asiatic Studies* 19, no. 3/4 [December 1956]: 334, 378, 385; John Masson Smith Jr., "Mongol and Nomadic Taxation," *Harvard Journal of Asiatic Studies* 30 (1970): 50–51). *chaqār*: artisan, or a place outside the citadel where artisans live (Doerfer, *Die türkischen Elemente*, vol. 1, 307–8). *shusun*: "travel provisions, especially for state couriers" (Doerfer, *Die türkischen Elemente*, vol. 1, 362–64). See *suchi*, n. 11, above.

14. ʿAshur: the month of Muḥarram. Assuming that the calendar used in Turfan during this period did not vary in its reckoning of days of the week from the current Hijri calendar generally in use, the proclamation's dating to a Wednesday limits the possible date to 7 Muḥarram [June 29], 14 Muḥarram [July 6], 21 Muḥarram [July 13], or 28 Muḥarram [July 20], 1667. For similar proclamations from Turfan during this period, see Hodong Kim, "The Cult of Saints in Eastern Turkestan—the Case of Alp Ata in Turfan," in *Proceedings of the 35th Permanent International Altaistic Conference*, ed. Chieh-hsien Ch'en (Taipei: 1992), 199–226.
15. Also known as "Shami Damulla" (d. 1932). On his visit to the Uyghur homeland and his interactions with Sayrami, see David Brophy, "'He Causes a Ruckus Wherever He Goes': Saʿid Muḥammad al-ʿAsali as a Missionary of Modernism in North-West China," *Modern Asian Studies* 54, no. 4 (2020): 1,192–24, especially 1,209–12.
16. Compare translations of this account by Ghiyathuddin Naqqash, "Report to Mirza Baysunghur on the Timurid Legation to the Court at Peking," trans. Wheeler M. Thackston, in *A Century of Princes: Sources on Timurid History and Art* (Cambridge, MA: Aga Khan Program for Islamic Architecture, 1989), 279–97; and Bellér-Hann, trans. *A History of Cathay.*

3:8 Lop

1. Cf. Mirza Ḥaydar Dughlat, *Tarikh-i Rashidi*, trans. Wheeler M. Thackston (New York: I. B. Tauris, 2012), 188, which otherwise presents a very similar account. In the manuscripts that Thackston consulted, only Lop and Katak are mentioned, but not Tarkan or Chan. These might have been included in a later version that Sayrami consulted.
2. Sayrami appears to locate "Chaba" in eastern Tibet. The term "Chaba" is obscure, although it may refer to the Changpa people living in western Tibet. Overall, the boundaries that Sayrami gives for Lop are confusing and give an exaggerated notion of its already massive size.
3. *talqan:* "parched grain ground into flour" (Gunnar Jarring, *An Eastern Turki-English Dialect Dictionary* [Lund: CWK Gleerup, 1964], 292).
4. Sayrami invoked tropes of the primitivity of the people of Lop. It is true that the Lopluqs speak a distinct variety of Uyghur, and that the material conditions of their way of life struck outsiders as unstable and "primitive." I find it interesting that Sayrami's depiction, which is included only in TH/Beijing, seems to reflect the same ideas espoused by European travelers. Indeed, it almost seems like a summary of Nikolai Przhevalsky's

(1839–1888) comments on the Lop people's language, dress, way of life, dwellings, and food (N. Prejevalsky, *From Kulja, Across the Tian Shan to Lob-Nor*, trans. E. Delmar Morgan [London: Sampson Low, Marston, Searle, & Rivington, 1879], 105–11).

5. Sayrami must be referring to the Hehuang Uprising of 1895.

3:9 Postface

1. TA/Lund and TA/Pelliot include here a chronogram encoding the date of the text's composition through letters given numerical values according to the *abjad* system: "Good name" (*yakhshi āt*). The letters' numerical values total 1321 AH, or 1903 CE, which was the date of the *Tarikh-i Amniyya*'s composition. (TA/St Petersburg also includes the chronogram, but it mistakenly swaps *tāʾ* for *ṭāʾ*, which provides an incorrect number, and consequently the chronogram "good horse.") A poem then follows:

    We have come to the end of my life—but I never made a good name.
    I lived in injustice and negligence—so I might have a good name.
    Hoping for goodness, I wrote a history as a monument.
    If you want to know its year, just say: "Good name."

2. TA/Kazan, TA/Pelliot, and TA/Lund read "1321" and note that it was a "Year of the Chicken."
3. TH/Beijing: *ʿadīm-i istiqāmat*; TA/Kazan, TA/Pelliot, TA/Lund: *ʿadīm-i istiṭāʾat*, which altogether fits the context better. TH/Beijing may represent a copyist's error.
4. Thank you to Mohammad al-Sudairi for helping me make sense of this phrase.
5. This date indicates the copying of TH/Beijing. In the photoreproduction in TH/Beijing, a note in Persian in a different hand below reads: *equivalent to the Christian year 1909, by the author's brilliant pen*. That date does not accord with the Hijri date as given, however. Curiously, in the manuscript as presented in Abduraop Polat, "Musa Sayrami Tarih-i Hamidi III: inceleme-metin-dizin" (PhD diss., Ankara Üniversitesi, 2002), 395, that passage seems to have been scratched out, and there seems to be other text appended to it that is not in the photoreproduction. Handwriting in Uyghur and Chinese presents the standard formula for converting Hijri to Gregorian dates and concludes that the manuscript was indeed copied in 1911. Whether or not the manuscript really was a holograph by Sayrami remains a matter of debate.

Bibliography

Abramson, Kara. "Gender, Uyghur Identity, and the Story of Nuzugum." *The Journal of Asian Studies* 71, no. 4 (2012): 1069–91.

Aitchison, J. E. T. *Hand-Book of the Trade Products of Leh with the Statistics of Trade from 1867 to 1872 Inclusive*. Calcutta: Wyman & Co., 1874.

Atwood, Christopher P. *Encyclopedia of Mongolia and the Mongol Empire*. New York: Facts on File, 2004.

Bar-Asher, Me'ir M. *Scripture and Exegesis in Early Imāmī Shiism*. Leiden: Brill, 1999.

Baytur, Änwär. "Mulla Musa Sayrami sheirliridin tallanma." *Bulaq* 15 (1985): 196–227.

Beisembiev, Timur K. *"Ta'rikh-i Shakhrukhi" kak istoricheskii istochnik*. Alma-Ata: Izd-vo "Nauka" Kazakhskoi SSR, 1987.

——, ed. and trans. *The Life of ʿAlimqul: A Native Chronicle of Nineteenth Century Central Asia*. London: Routledge, 2003.

——. *Annotated Indices to the Kokand Chronicles*. Tokyo: Research Institute for Languages and Cultures of Asia and Africa, 2008.

Bellér-Hann, Ildikó, trans. *A History of Cathay: A Translation and Linguistic Analysis of a Fifteenth-Century Turkic Manuscript*. Bloomington, IN: Research Institute for Inner Asian Studies, 1995.

Ben Dor Benite, Zvi. "From 'Literati' to 'Ulama': The Origins of Chinese Muslim Nationalist Historiography." *Nationalism and Ethnic Politics* 9, no. 4 (2004): 83–109.

Berthels, E. "Muʿīn al-Miskīn." In *Encyclopedia of Islam, Second Edition*, ed. P. Bearman, Th. Bianquis, C. E. Bosworth, E. van Donzel, and W. P. Heinrichs. http://dx.doi.org/10.1163/1573-3912_islam_SIM_5444.

Bilal Nazim. "Nuzugum." In *Obraztsy taranchinskoi narodnoi literatury sobrannye i perevedennye N.N. Pantusovym, Proceedings of the Society of Archaeology, History and Ethnography at the Imperial University of Kazan* 25 ([1882] 1909): 34–42.

Bockholt, Philip. "Mīrkhvānd." In *Encyclopaedia of Islam, THREE*, ed. Kate Fleet, Gudrun Krämer, Denis Matringe, John Nawas, and Everett Rowson. Accessed July 20, 2022. http://dx.doi.org/10.1163/1573-3912_ei3_COM_40284.

Brophy, David. *Uyghur Nation: Reform and Revolution on the Russia-China Frontier.* Cambridge, MA: Harvard University Press, 2016.

——. " 'He Causes a Ruckus Wherever He Goes': Saʿid Muḥammad al-ʿAsali as a Missionary of Modernism in North-West China." *Modern Asian Studies* 54, no. 4 (2020): 1,192–1,124.

Brophy, David, and Onuma Takahiro. *The Origins of Qing Xinjiang: A Set of Historical Sources on Turfan.* Tokyo: TIAS Department of Islamic Area Studies, 2016.

Brunnert, H. S., and V. V. Hagelstrom. *Present Day Political Organization of China.* Shanghai: Kelly and Walsh, Limited, 1912.

Chu, Wen-djang. *The Moslem Rebellion in Northwest China 1862–1878: A Study of Government Minority Policy.* The Hague: Mouton, 1966.

Churas, Shāh Maḥmūd. *Khronika: Kriticheskii tekst, perevod, kommentarii, issledovanie i ukaziteli O. F. Akimushkin.* Moscow: Nauka, 1976.

Clarke, Henry Wilberforce, trans. *The Dīvān, Written in the Fourteenth Century by Khwāja Shamsu-d-Dīn Muḥammad-i-Ḥāfiẓ-i-Shīrāzī, otherwise known as Lisānu-l-Ghaib and Tarjumānu-l-Asrār.* Calcutta: Government of India Central Printing Office, 1891.

Clauson, Gerard. *An Etymological Dictionary of Pre-Thirteenth-Century Turkish.* Oxford: Clarendon Press, 1972.

Cleaves, Francis Woodman. "The Mongolian Documents in the Musée de Téhéran." *Harvard Journal of Asiatic Studies* 16, no. 1/2 (June 1953): 1–107.

Dağyeli, Jeanine Elif. "A Community of Order, Morale, Internal Discipline and Punishment in the Craft Milieu of Turkestan." In *Community Still Matters: Uyghur Culture and Society in Central Asian Context*, ed. Aysima Mirsultan, Eric Schluessel, and Eset Sulaiman, 234–49. Copenhagen: NIAS Press, 2022.

Dawut, Rahilä. *Uyghur mazarliri.* Shinjang khälq näshriyati, 2001.

de Bruijn, J. T. P. "Ādhar, Ḥājjī Luṭf ʿAlī Beg." In *Encyclopaedia of Islam, THREE*, ed. Kate Fleet, Gudrun Krämer, Denis Matringe, John Nawas, Everett Rowson. Accessed August 1, 2022. http://dx.doi.org/10.1163/1573-3912_ei3_COM_24761.

Doerfer, Gerhard. *Türkische und mongolische Elemente im Neupersischen.* 4 vols. Wiesbaden: Franz Steiner Verlag, 1963.

Dughlat, Mirza Ḥaydar. *Tarikh-i Rashidi.* Trans. Wheeler M. Thackston. New York: I. B. Tauris, 2012.

Dyer, Svetlana Rimsky-Korsakoff. "T'ang T'ai-tsung's Dream: A Soviet Dungan Version of a Legend on the Origin of the Chinese Muslims." *Monumenta Serica* 35, no. 1 (1981): 545–70.

Fletcher, Joseph. "The Biography of Khwush Kipäk Beg (d. 1781) in the *Wai-fan Meng-ku Hui-pu wang kung biao chuan.*" *Acta Orientalia Academiae Scientiarum Hungaricae* 36, no. 1/3 (1982).

Forsyth, Thomas Douglas. *Report of a Mission to Yarkund in 1873.* Calcutta: Foreign Department Press, 1875.

Ghiyathuddin Naqqash. "Report to Mirza Baysunghur on the Timurid Legation to the Court at Peking." Trans. Wheeler M. Thackston. In *A Century of Princes: Sources on Timurid History and Art*, 279–97. Cambridge, MA: Aga Khan Program for Islamic Architecture, 1989.

Gordon, T. E. *The Roof of the World.* Edinburgh: Edmonston and Douglas, 1876.

Griffith, Sidney. "Christian Lore and the Arabic Qur'ān: The 'Companions of the Cave' in *Sūrat al-Kahf* and in Syriac Christian Tradition." In *The Qur'ān in Its Historical Context*, ed. Gabriel Saʿid Reynolds, 109–37. London: Routledge, 2009.

Gürsoy-Naskali, Emine. *Ashabu 'l-Kähf: A Treatise in Eastern Turki.* Helsinki: Suomalais-Ugrilaisen Seuran toimituksia, 1985.

Hamada Masami. "Rupture ou continuité: Le calendrier des douze animaux chez les Musulmans Turcophones du Turkestan oriental." In *Mélanges offerts à Louis Bazin*, 285–91. Paris: L'Harmattan, 1992.

Harris, Rachel. *The Making of a Musical Canon in Chinese Central Asia: The Uyghur Twelve Muqam*. New York: Routledge, 2016.

Hope, Michael. "Jalāyirids." In *Encyclopaedia of Islam, THREE*, ed. Kate Fleet, Gudrun Krämer, Denis Matringe, John Nawas, and Everett Rowson. Accessed August 30, 2022. http://dx.doi.org/10.1163/1573-3912_ei3_COM_46054.

Jalilov, Amanbek, Yayoi Kawahara, Sawada Minoru, Shinmen Yasushi, and Hori Sunao, eds. *Addendum to Tarikh-i Rashidi: Translation and Annotation with Introduction and Indexes*. Tokyo: NIHU Program Islamic Area Studies TIAS, 2008.

Jarring, Gunnar. *Materials to the Knowledge of Eastern Turki: Tales, Poetry, Proverbs, Riddles, Ethnological and Historical Texts from the Southern Parts of Eastern Turkestan*. 4 vols. Lund: C.W.K. Gleerup, 1946–1951.

——. *An Eastern Turki-English Dialect Dictionary*. Lund: CWK Gleerup, 1964.

——, ed. *The Thiefless City and the Contest Between Food and Throat: Four Eastern Turki Texts*. Stockholm: Almqvist and Wiksell, 1989.

——. *Culture Clash in Central Asia: Islamic Views on Chinese Theatre—Eastern Turki Texts Edited with Translation, Notes and Vocabulary*. Stockholm: Almqvist & Wiksell International, 1991.

——. *Garments from Top to Toe: Eastern Turki Texts Relating to Articles of Clothing*. Stockholm: Almqvist and Wiksell, 1992.

——. *Central Asian Turkic Place-Names—Lop Nor and Tarim Area: An Attempt at Classification and Explanation Based on Sven Hedin's Diaries and Published Works*. Stockholm: The Sven Hedin Foundation, 1997.

Jin, Huan. "Stitching Words to Suture Wounds: A Manuscript Diary from the Taiping-Qing Civil War (1851–64)." *Late Imperial China* 40, no. 2 (2019): 141–82.

Jones, Susan Mann, and Philip A. Kuhn. "Dynastic Decline and the Roots of Rural Rebellion." In *The Cambridge History of China, Volume 10: Late Ch'ing 1800–1911, Part 1*, ed. John K. Fairbank, 107–62. Cambridge: Cambridge University Press, 1978.

Kashghari, Muḥammad Ṣadiq. *In Remembrance of the Saints: The Rise and Fall of an Inner Asian Sufi Dynasty*. Trans. David Brophy. New York: Columbia University Press, 2020.

Katanov, N. Th. *Volkskundliche Texte aus Ost-Türkistan: aud dem Nachlass von N. Th. Katanov*. Ed. Karl Heinrich Menges. Leipzig: Zentralantiquariat der Deutschen Demokratischen Republik, 1976.

Khālidī, Qurbān-ʿAlī. *Tarikh-i jarida-i jadida*. Qazan: Qazan Universitetining ṭabiʿkhanasi, 1889.

——. *Tawarikh-i khamsa-i sharqi*. Qazan: 1910.

——. *An Islamic Biographical Dictionary of the Eastern Kazakh Steppe*. Ed. Allen J. Frank and Mirkasyim A. Usmanov. Leiden: Brill, 2005.

Khoqandi, Niyaz Muḥammad b. Mullah ʿAshur Muḥammad. *Tā'rīkh-i Shāhrukhī*. Qazan: Maṭbaʿkhāna-i Madrasa-i al-Kubrā, 1885.

Kim, Hodong. "The Cult of Saints in Eastern Turkestan—the Case of Alp Ata in Turfan." In *Proceedings of the 35th Permanent International Altaistic Conference*, ed. Chieh-hsien Ch'en (Taipei: 1992), 199–226.

——. *Holy War in China: The Muslim Rebellion and State in Chinese Central Asia, 1864–1877*. Stanford, CA: Stanford University Press, 2004.

——. "Eastern Turki Royal Decrees of the 17th Century in the Jarring Collection." In *Studies on Xinjiang Historical Sources in 17th–20th Centuries*, ed. James A. Millward, Shinmen Yasushi, and Jun Sugawara, 59–119. Tokyo: Toyo Bunko, 2010.

King, Matthew W. *Ocean of Milk, Ocean of Blood: A Mongolian Monk in the Ruins of the Qing Empire*. New York: Columbia University Press, 2019.

Klimeš, Ondřej. *Struggle by the Pen: The Uyghur Discourse of Nation and National Interest, c. 1900–1949*. Leiden: Brill, 2015.

Lansdell, Henry. *Chinese Central Asia: A Ride to Little Tibet*. 2 vols. London: Low, Marston, 1893.

Lee, Joo-yup. *Qazaqlïq, of Ambitious Brigandage, and the Formation of the Qazaqs: State and Identity in Post-Mongol Central Eurasia*. Leiden: Brill, 2015.

Lelić, Emin. "Physiognomy (*ʿilm-i firāsat*) and Ottoman Statecraft: Discerning Morality and Justice." *Arabica* 64, no. 3–4 (2017): 609–46.

Lessing, Ferdinand D., ed. *Mongolian-English Dictionary*. Berkeley: University of California Press, 1960.

Levey, Benjamin Samuel. "Jungar Refugees and the Making of Empire on Qing China's Kazakh Frontier, 1759–1773." PhD diss., Harvard University, 2013.

Li Delong, ed. *Xinjiang si dao zhi*. Beijing: Zhongyang minzu daxue chubanshe, 2010.

Li Rong and Zhou Lei, eds. *Wulumuqi fangyan cidian*. Nanjing: Jiangsu jiaoyu chubanshe, 1995.

Lipman, Jonathan. *Familiar Strangers: A History of Muslims in Northwest China*. Seattle: University of Washington Press, 1997.

Ma Dazheng et al., eds. *Xinjiang xiangtuzhi gao*. Wulumuqi: Xinjiang renmin chubanshe, 2010.

Ma, Haiyun. "The Mythology of the Prophet's Ambassadors in China: Histories of Sa'd Waqqas and Gess in Chinese Sources." *Journal of Muslim Minority Affairs* 26, no. 3 (2006): 445–52.

Mano Eiji, ed. *Bābūr-nāma (Vaqāyiʿ)*. 2 vols. Kyoto: Syokado, 1995–96.

Maolamusa Sailami. *Yimide shi*. Trans. Aili Wufuer. In *Qingdai Chahetai wen wenxian yizhu*, ed. Miao Pusheng, 315–538. Wulumuqi: Xinjiang renmin chubanshe, 2013.

Mathews, R. H., ed. *Mathews' Chinese-English Dictionary*. Cambridge, MA: Harvard University Press, 1963.

Meyer-Fong, Tobie. *What Remains: Coming to Terms with Civil War in 19th Century China*. Stanford, CA: Stanford University Press, 2013.

Miao Pusheng, ed. *Xibei shaoshu minzu wenzi wenxian*. Beijing: Xianzhuang shuju, 2006.

Millward, James A. "A Uyghur Muslim in Qianlong's Court: The Meanings of the Fragrant Concubine." *The Journal of Asian Studies* 53, no. 2 (1994): 427–58.

——. *Beyond the Pass: Economy, Ethnicity, and Empire in Qing Central Asia, 1759–1864*. Stanford, CA: Stanford University Press, 1998.

——. *Eurasian Crossroads: A History of Xinjiang*. New York: Columbia University Press, 2007.

Moin, Afzar A. *The Millennial Sovereign: Sacred Kingship and Sainthood in Islam*. New York: Columbia University Press, 2012.

Molla Shakir. " 'Zäfär-nama dastanidin." In *Äsirlär sadasi: kona Uyghur ädäbiyatining nämuniliri*, ed. M. K. Hemraev, 312–32. Almuta: Qazaqstan dölät güzäl ädäbiyat näshriyati, 1963.

Morrison, Alexander. "Amlākdārs, Khwājas and Mulk Land in the Zarafshan Valley after the Russian Conquest." In *Explorations in the Social History of Modern Central Asia (19th–Early 20th Century)*, ed. Paolo Sartori, 23–64. Leiden: Brill, 2013.

Mottahedeh, Roy. *Loyalty and Leadership in an Early Islamic Society*. London: I. B. Tauris, 1980.

Muhammad bin Khâvendshâh bin Mahmûd. *The Rauzat-us-safa; or, Garden of Purity*. Trans. E. Rehatsek. Ed. F. F. Arbuthnot. London: Royal Asiatic Society, 1891.

Muḥammad Ḥakīm Khān. *Muntakhab al-tawārīkh*. Ed. Yayoi Kawahara and Koichi Haneda. Vol. 2. Tokyo: Research Institute for Language and Cultures of Asia and Africa ILCAA, 2006.

Muhsin Khan, Muhammad, trans. *The Translation of the Meanings of Sahih al-Bukhari*. 9 vols. Lahore: Kazi, 1979.

Mukhlisov, Yusuf Beg. *Uyghur klassik edibiyati qol yazmiliri katalogi*. Ürümchi: Shinjang yälik museygha täyarliq körüsh bashqarmisi, 1957.

Nasr, Seyyed Hossein, Caner K. Dagli, Maria Massi Dakake, Joseph E. B. Lumbard, and Mohammed Rustom, eds. *The Study Quran: A New Translation and Commentary*. New York: HarperCollins, 2015.

Nasser, Shady H. "Ibn al-Jazarī." In *Encyclopaedia of Islam, THREE*, ed. Kate Fleet, Gudrun Krämer, Denis Matringe, John Nawas, Everett Rowson. Accessed August 30, 2022. http://dx.doi.org/10.1163/1573-3912_ei3_COM_30840.

Nastich, Vladimir and Wolfgang Schuster. *Catalog of Pre-Modern Central Asian Coins 1680–1923: Janid (Later Period), Bukhara, Tashkand, Shahrisabz, Khoqand, Khiva, Khorezm Republic, Dzungar (Later Period), Islamic East Turkestan*. Bremen: Bremer Numismatische Gesellschaft, 2017.

Newby, L. J. *The Empire and the Khanate: A Political History of Qing Relations with Khoqand, c. 1760–1860*. Leiden: Brill, 2005.

Nicholson, Reynold A., trans. *The Mathnawí of Jalálu'ddin Rúmí*. 4 vols. London: Luzac, 1926.

Oldenburg, S. F. "Dnevnik Turkestanskoi ekspeditsii, snariajennoi po Vysochaishemu poveleniiu Russkim komitetom po izucheniiu Sredniei i Vostochnoi Azii." In *Istoriia izucheniia v kontse XIX—pervoi treti XX veka*, ed. M. D. Bukharina, 479–572. Moskva: Pamiatniki istoricheskoi mysli, 2018.

Ömärjan Häsän. "Qirmish Atam: Insap Qilinglar . . ." *Miras* 5 (2001): 57–63.

Osmanov, Mirsultan. *Hazirqi zaman Uyghur tilining Khotän diyalekti*. Ürümchi: Shinjang khälq näshriyati, 2004.

Pantusov, N. N. *Materialy k izucheniiu narechiiya Taranchei Iliiskago okruga*. 9 vols. Kazan: Tipolitografiia universiteta, 1897–1907.

. "Les mazâr musulmans de la ville d'Uch-Turfan et de ses environs (en territoires chinois)." Trans. P. Garrone. *Journal of the History of Sufism* 3 (2001), 183–98.

Pelliot, Paul. *Carnets de route 1906–1908*. Paris: Indes Savantes, 2008.

Pickthall, Marmaduke William. *The Meaning of the Glorious Koran: An Explanatory Translation*. New York: New American Library, 1953.

Platt, Stephen R. *Autumn in the Heavenly Kingdom: China, the West, and the Epic Story of the Taiping Civil War*. New York: Knopf, 2012.

Polat, Abduraop. "Musa Sayrami Tarih-i Hamidi III: inceleme-metin-dizin." PhD diss., Ankara Üniversitesi, 2002.

Pratt, Mary Louise. "Arts of the Contact Zone." *Profession* (1991): 33–40.

Prejevalsky, N. *From Kulja, Across the Tian Shan to Lob-Nor*. Trans. E. Delmar Morgan. London: Sampson Low, Marston, Searle, & Rivington, 1879.

Qingdai Xinjiang dang'an xuanji. Guilin: Guangxi shifan daxue chubanshe, 2012.

Radloff, W. *Versuch eines Wörterbuches der Türk-Dialecte*. 4 vols. St. Petersburg, 1893.

Raquette, Gustav. *Eastern Turki Grammar: Practical and Theoretical with Vocabulary*. 3 vols. Berlin: Reichsdruckerei, 1912.

Räsänen, Martti. *Versuch eines etymologischen Wörterbuchs der Türksprachen*. Helsinki: Suomalaid-Ugrilainen seura, 1969.

Rippin, A. "Taṣliya." In *Encyclopaedia of Islam, Second Edition*, ed. P. Bearman, Th. Bianquis, C. E. Bosworth, E. van Donzel, and W. P. Heinrichs. Accessed September 5, 2022. http://dx.doi.org.proxygw.wrlc.org/10.1163/1573-3912_islam_SIM_7436.

Roerich, Nicholas. *Altai-Himalaya: A Travel Diary*. New York: Frederick A. Stokes, 1930.

Rogers, J. M., ed. *The Topkapı Saray Museum: The Treasury*. Boston: Little, Brown, 1987.

Saguchi Toru. *Jūhachi-jūkyū seiki Higashi Torukisutan shakai shi kenkyū*. Tōkyō: Yoshikawa Kōbunkan, 1963.

Sartori, Paolo. "Between Kazan and Kashghar: On the Vernacularization of Islamic Jurisprudence in Central Eurasia." *Die Welt des Islams* 61, no. 2 (2020): 1–31.

Sayrami, Molla Musa. *Tarikhi Hämidi*. Trans. Änwär Baytur. Beyjing: Millätlär näshriyati, 2007.

Sayrāmī, Mullā Mūsá b. Mullā ʿĪsá Khoja. *Tārīkh-i Amniyya*. Qazān: Ṭabʿkhāna-ye madrasa-ye ʿulūm, 1323/1904.

Sayramiy, Musa. *Tarikhi Hämidi*. Trans. Abduraop Täklimakani. Istanbul: Täklimakan Uyghur näshriyati, 2019.

Schluessel, Eric. *The World as Seen from Yarkand: Ghulām Muḥammad Khān's 1920s Chronicle* Mā Tīṭayniŋ wāqiʿasi. Tokyo: NIHU Program Islamic Area Studies, 2014.

——. *Land of Strangers: The Civilizing Project in Qing Central Asia*. New York: Columbia University Press, 2020.

——. "Islamic Law in Xinjiang." In *Routledge Handbook of Islam in Asia*, ed. Chiara Formichi, 125–37. New York: Routledge, 2021.

Schurmann, H. F. "Mongolian Tributary Practices of the Thirteenth Century." *Harvard Journal of Asiatic Studies* 19, no. 3/4 (December 1956): 304–89.

Shakespeare, William. *Macbeth*. Ed. A. R. Braunmuller. The Cambridge New Shakespeare. Cambridge: Cambridge University Press, 1997.

Shaw, Robert. *A Sketch of the Turki Language as Spoken in Eastern Turkistan (Kàshghar and Yarkand)*. Calcutta: Baptist Mission Press, 1878.

Shim, Hosung. "The State Formation of the Zunghar Principality: A Political History of the Last Centralized State of the Eurasian Steppe." PhD diss., Indiana University–Bloomington, 2021.

Shinmen Yasushi and Onuma Takahiro. "First Contact Between Yaʿqub Beg and the Qing: The Diplomatic Correspondence of 1871." *Journal of Asian and African Studies* 84 (2012): 5–37.

Smith, John Masson, Jr. "Mongol and Nomadic Taxation." *Harvard Journal of Asiatic Studies* 30 (1970): 46–85.

Songyun. *Xinjiang shilüe*. Reproduced in *Xu xiu siku quanshu*, vol. 732. Shanghai: Shanghai guji chubanshe, 1995–99.

Ståhlberg, Sabira, and Ingvar Svanberg. "Ecological Adaptation in the Taklamakan Desert." *Anthropos* 105, no. 2 (2010): 423–39.

Stein, Aurel. *Innermost Asia: Detailed Report of Explorations in Central Asia, Kan-su and Eastern Īrān*. 4 vols. Oxford: Clarendon, 1928.

Steingass, Francis Joseph. *A Comprehensive Persian-English Dictionary: Including the Arabic Words and Phrases to be Met with in Persian Literature, Being, Johnson and Richardson's Persian, Arabic, and English Dictionary, Revised, Enlarged, and Entirely Reconstructed*. London: Routledge, 1977.

Subtelny, Maria Eva. "Socioeconomic Bases of Cultural Patronage Under the Later Timurids." *International Journal of Middle East Studies* 20, no. 4 (1988): 479–505.

Sunnah.com. Accessed September 10, 2022. https://sunnah.com/.

Thackston, Wheeler M., trans. "Ghiyathuddin Naqqash: Report to Mirza Baysunghur on the Timurid Legation to the Ming Court at Peking." In *A Century of Princes: Sources on Timurid History and Art*, ed. Wheeler M. Thackston, 279–97. Cambridge: Aga Khan Program for Islamic Architecture, 1989.

—, trans. *The Baburnama: Memoirs of Babur, Prince and Emperor.* New York: Modern Library, 2002.

Theaker, Hannah. "Moving Muslims: The Great Northwestern Rebellion and the Transformation of Chinese Islam, 1860–1896." PhD diss., University of Oxford, 2018.

al-Tibrizi, Muḥammad. *Mishkat-ul-masabeeh.* Trans. A. N. Matthews. Ed. F. K. Khan Durrani. Part One. Lahore: Tabligh Literature Company, n.d.

Wang Shu'nan et al., comps. *Xinjiang tuzhi.* Ed. Zhu Yuqi et al. Shanghai: Shanghai guji chubanshe, 2017.

Woods, John E. "The Rise of Tīmūrid Historiography." *Journal of Near Eastern Studies* 46, no. 2 (April 1987): 81–108.

Wu Chucai, comp. *Gangjian yizhu lu.* Taipei: Chengwen chubanshe, 1964. Reproduction of Shanghai Hongwen'ge edition, *wùxū* [1898].

Yakup, Abdurishid. *The Turfan Dialect of Uyghur.* Wiesbaden: Otto Harrassowitz Verlag, 2005.

Zand, M. "'Abd-Al-Karīm Boḵārī." In *Encyclopædia Iranica*, [London: Routledge, 1982–], vol. 1, fasc. 2, I/2, 121–23.

Zarcone, Thierry. "Atypical Mausoleum: The Case of the Salomon Throne (Kyrgyzstan), *Qadam-Jāy*, Jinns-Cult and Itinerary-Pilgrimage." In *Muslim Saints and Mausoleums in Central Asia and Xinjiang*, ed. Shinmen Yasushi, Sawada Minoru, and Edmund Waite, 73–89, 203–10. Paris: Librairie d'Amérique et d'Orient, 2013.

Zhang Daye. *The World of a Tiny Insect: A Memoir of the Taiping Rebellion and Its Aftermath.* Trans. Xiaofei Tian. Seattle: University of Washington Press, 2013.

Ziad, Waleed. "From Yarkand to Sindh via Kabul: The Rise of Naqshbandi-Mujaddidi Sufi Networks in the Eighteenth and Nineteenth Centuries." In *The Persianate World: Rethinking a Shared Sphere*, ed. Abbas Amanat and Assef Ashraf, 125–68. Leiden: Brill, 2019.

Index of People

Index of Places